JUSTICE
LEWIS F. POWELL, JR.

Also by John C. Jeffries, Jr.

Federal Courts and the Law of Federal-State Relations

Civil Rights Actions: Section 1983 and Related Statutes

JUSTICE
LEWIS F. POWELL, JR.

✥

JOHN C. JEFFRIES, JR.

CHARLES SCRIBNER'S SONS
NEW YORK

MAXWELL MACMILLAN CANADA
TORONTO

MAXWELL MACMILLAN INTERNATIONAL
NEW YORK   OXFORD   SINGAPORE   SYDNEY

Charles Scribner's Sons	Maxwell Macmillan Canada, Inc.
Macmillan Publishing Company	1200 Eglinton Avenue East
866 Third Avenue	Suite 200
New York, New York 10022	Don Mills, Ontario M3C 3N1

Macmillan Publishing Company is part of the Maxwell Communication Group of Companies.

Library of Congress Cataloging-in-Publication Data
Jeffries, John Calvin, date.
   Justice Lewis F. Powell, Jr., and the Era of Judicial Balance/John C. Jeffries, Jr.
      p.   cm.
   Includes bibliographical references.
   ISBN 0-684-19450-3
   1. Powell, Lewis F. 1907–   .   2. Judges—United States—Biography.—I. Title.
KF8745.P69J44   1994   93-24360   CIP
347.73´2634—dc20
[B]
[347.3073534]
[B]

Macmillan Books are available at special discounts for bulk purchases for sales promotions, premiums, fund-raising, or educational use. For details, contact:

Special Sales Director
Macmillan Publishing Company
866 Third Avenue
New York, New York 10022

10   9   8   7   6   5   4   3   2   1

Printed in the United States of America

CONTENTS

CONTENTS

CONTENTS

ACKNOWLEDGMENTS

Many people helped make this book possible. The greatest debt is owed to Lewis F. Powell, Jr., who generously gave me access to his files and his memories without attempting to control what I wrote. He did not ask to see any part of the manuscript, nor was he invited to do so. The responsibility for errors or misjudgments is therefore entirely my own.

Thanks go as well to members of the Powell family. Josephine Rucker Powell answered many questions and allowed me to read her wartime correspondence with her husband. Eleanor Powell Dewey answered many questions about her brother's early life and made available to me her private files on the history of the Powells and the Gwathmeys. I also benefited from interviews with the Powell children and with a wide variety of relatives, friends, law partners, and former clerks.

Special mention should be made of the Justices of the Supreme Court. Other than Justices William O. Douglas and Potter Stewart, both of whom died before this project began, I have spoken with all of Powell's colleagues on the Supreme Court. They include Chief Justices William H. Rehnquist and Warren E. Burger and Associate Justices William J. Brennan, Byron White, Thurgood Marshall, Harry Blackmun, John Paul Stevens, Sandra Day O'Connor, and Antonin Scalia.

More than thirty friends read and criticized chapters in draft. I am especially grateful to my colleagues Michael J. Klarman and William J. Stuntz, each of whom reviewed more than half the manuscript. Additionally, I had the able assistance of Charles Kromkowski, a University of Virginia graduate student who researched Powell's service on the Richmond School Board; of Rebecca Lilly, who indexed portions of Powell's correspondence; and of a succession of University of Virginia law students who tracked down whatever I asked them to find. They include Brian Freeman, David Higley, Robert E. Lee, Michael Lincoln, Matthew Mason, Catherine Morgan, Eric Moss, Dennis O'Brien, and P. Hutchinson Perry.

Thanks go also to the administration and staff of the University of Virginia School of Law—to Madeline Branch and Glenn Taylor for computer services, to librarian Larry Wenger and archivist Marsha Trimble for allowing me to fill their rare book room with Powell's papers, and to Leslie Yowell for secretarial assistance. I am especially grateful to Dean Robert E. Scott, who arranged for me to have a semester's leave to complete this project.

Finally, several persons helped me in ways so far beyond the bounds of obligation or courtesy that they require special mention:

Anne Hobson Freeman wrote *The Style of a Law Firm*, a collective biography of the eight lawyers whose names have appeared in the title of Powell's firm. She made available to me the transcripts of her interviews with firm members. I am especially grateful for the chance to eavesdrop on her conversations with Powell's longtime colleague, George Gibson, who died in 1988.

Gail Galloway is the Curator of the Supreme Court and a particular friend of the Powell family. She answered numerous requests for information, helped assemble and select the photographs reproduced in this volume, and did everything within her power to make this project a success.

Patricia Hass brought this project to Scribners. Although she left the firm before the book was finished, she did not abandon her role as chief counselor and cheerleader. Her advice and encouragement are appreciated.

Peter W. Low, my colleague at the University of Virginia School of Law, devoted more hours than he or I expected to the task of devising a computer format for recording and retrieving statistical data about Powell's decisions. Some of this information is summarized in the appendix to this book.

Finally, Huston Paschal, a longtime friend, edited the entire manuscript and saved me from many infelicities. She brought to every line and paragraph a discerning eye, generous judgment, and exquisite taste.

JCJjr
Charlottesville, Virginia
August 1993

PREFACE

Shortly before Lewis Powell retired from the Supreme Court, a civil liberties leader called him "the most powerful man in America." The statement referred to Powell's position at the ideological center of a divided Court, and revealed the remarkable degree to which liberals had come to depend on the conservative from Virginia. Powell's role as occasional liberal savior had not been anticipated sixteen years earlier when President Nixon nominated him to the Supreme Court. At that time, most observers expected him to move in lockstep with the other Nixon appointees. Instead, Powell proved to be highly independent, open to argument, and unusually willing to reconsider his own preconceptions. The conclusions he reached surprised his admirers, confounded his critics, and set the course of American constitutional law for the better part of a generation.

This book tells the story of that man and his impact on the Supreme Court and on the nation. It is not a judicial biography in the narrow sense, as it covers Powell's life as well as his judicial service. It is also not a book aimed at lawyers. On the contrary, these pages are intended for the general reader. Legal jargon is avoided, and the discussion of cases is highly selective. No attempt is made to survey the nearly three thousand decisions rendered by the Supreme Court while Powell was a member.* Instead, this book focuses on six areas of commanding interest: desegregation, abortion, Watergate, the death penalty, affirmative action, and sexual equality.

These topics share two crucial characteristics. First, they aroused intense passion and debate. Indeed, most of them still do. Only the Supreme Court's resolution of the Watergate controversy in the Nixon tapes case can fairly be said to command anything approaching consensus approval. Second, the decisions in these areas are especially revealing of the individual beneath the judicial robes. Here the link

---

*For more comprehensive coverage, see George C. Freeman, Jr., "Justice Powell's Constitutional Opinions," *Washington and Lee Law Review*, volume 435, pages 411–65, and Jacob W. Landynski, "Justice Lewis F. Powell, Jr.: Balance Wheel of the Court," in Charles M. Lamb and Stephen C. Halpern, eds., *The Burger Court: Political and Judicial Profiles.*

between private man and public figure can be clearly seen, and the surprising impact of one Supreme Court Justice on the nation's history can be correctly gauged.

JUSTICE
LEWIS F. POWELL, JR.

THE RELUCTANT
JUSTICE

At nine o'clock in the morning on January 7, 1972, Lewis and Josephine Powell and their family arrived at the Supreme Court. They were met by the marshal and escorted first to Powell's chambers and then to a waiting room for coffee with Bill and Nan Rehnquist. A few minutes before ten, the marshal led them to the courtroom for the investiture ceremony. As the two families walked down the corridor, Nan Rehnquist asked Jo Powell, "Isn't this the most exciting day of your life?" "No, this is the *worst* day of my life," Jo blurted out. "I am about to cry."

Her husband was scarcely more enthusiastic. Only minutes before, he told his sister Eleanor that had he been able to consider the matter for another twenty-four hours, he would not have accepted the appointment. Even now, as he prepared to take a place second in power and prestige only to the presidency of the United States, Powell wondered whether he had made a mistake. Forty years earlier he had confided to his college sweetheart his ambition to sit on the Supreme Court; but when he finally had the chance, he was anything but eager. Of the ninety-eight men who preceded him in that position, few had approached the honor so reluctantly.

POWELL TRIED MORE THAN ONCE to say no. In 1969, when the Senate rejected the nomination of Clement Haynsworth of South Carolina, speculation turned to Powell. President Richard Nixon wanted to name a southerner to the Supreme Court, and Powell seemed a natural choice. A named partner in the Richmond, Virginia, firm of Hunton, Williams, Gay, Powell & Gibson, Powell was a southern lawyer with a national reputation. He had been president of the American Bar Association and of the American College of Trial Lawyers, a member of President Lyndon Johnson's Crime Commission and of President

Nixon's Blue Ribbon Defense Panel, a familiar presence in corporate boardrooms and a leader in the drive to provide legal services to the poor. Virginia Senator Harry F. Byrd, Jr.—"Little Harry" to those who remembered his powerful father—called to say that Powell was on a short list for the vacancy at the Supreme Court. Did Powell want Byrd to call the President?

Powell said no. He not only discouraged Senator Byrd but also wrote Attorney General John Mitchell asking that his name be withdrawn from consideration. Having seen his friend Clement Haynsworth defeated by civil rights and labor opposition, Powell feared the same fate. He had been chairman of the Richmond School Board and later of the Virginia State Board of Education in an era when, as he so delicately put it, the pace of desegregation had been "necessarily . . . more measured than civil rights leaders would have liked." He had spent a career representing corporations, banks, and business interests. It was likely, Powell told Mitchell, "that the nomination of another southern lawyer with a business-oriented background would invite—if not assure—organized and perhaps prolonged opposition."

Moreover, at age sixty-two Powell thought himself too old to go on the Supreme Court. It would be better for the President to appoint "a relatively young man, who will have the prospect of at least two decades of service." He therefore wrote Mitchell: "I am deeply grateful to the President and to you for such consideration as may have been given to me for the highest honor that can come to a lawyer. But I wanted you to know of my considered judgment that the nomination of a younger man less subject to controversy would best serve the public interest."

When Powell wrote those words, he had no way of knowing how seriously he was being considered; but Richard Nixon later said Powell was his first choice, and those who worked most closely with the Attorney General on Supreme Court nominations recall that Mitchell was keenly disappointed on receiving Powell's letter. In fact, Powell had turned down the likely prospect of appointment to the Supreme Court.

With Powell out of the running, the administration turned to the unfortunate G. Harrold Carswell, a Florida appeals court judge of no distinction. When he, too, was rejected, Nixon denounced the Senate as antisouthern and nominated Harry A. Blackmun of Minnesota, a longtime friend of Chief Justice Warren Burger and a politically safe choice. Confirmed without controversy by the Senate, Blackmun was sworn in on June 9, 1970, as the ninety-eighth Justice of the Supreme Court. Powell's time had apparently come and gone.

But only a year later, the administration found itself with two new vacancies to fill when Justices Hugo Black and John Marshall Harlan finally gave in to the ravages of age. In his letter to Mitchell, Powell had suggested Virginia Congressman Richard H. Poff, who now became a leading candidate. Poff, however, had signed the 1956 Southern Manifesto, in which southern Congressmen declared themselves unalterably opposed to racial integration. Faced with a fight over confirmation, Poff withdrew.

Still smarting over the rejection of Haynsworth and Carswell and the intimidation of Poff, Nixon turned to West Virginia Senator Robert Byrd. Nixon counted on Senate Democrats to confirm one of their own, even though Byrd had never practiced law, had never even passed a bar exam, and had made his Senate reputation chiefly as a master of pork-barrel politics. The legal community was aghast at the prospect. Even John Mitchell thought the President was going too far.

Facing growing dismay both inside and outside the administration, Nixon backed off. He still wanted a southerner and now decided that he also wished to appoint the first woman to the Supreme Court. Both nominees had to be "strict constructionists," Nixon's term for judicial conservatives who would not invent new rights for criminals. Mitchell came up with two names: Herschel H. Friday, a municipal bond lawyer from Little Rock, Arkansas, and Mildred L. Lillie, a state appeals court judge from Los Angeles, California.

Their names—along with those of Robert Byrd and three other possibilities—were sent in early October to the American Bar Association for evaluation of their professional qualifications. When the list leaked, Friday and Lillie fell from obscurity into derision. *Time* magazine ran an article on "Nixon's Not So Supreme Court," with photographs of the candidates captioned "No scarcity of betters" and "No approach to distinction." Conservative columnists Evans and Novak pronounced the administration's names "uniform in both mediocrity and acceptability to the segregationist South." Even Justice Harlan, sick in the hospital bed from which he would not rise, considered writing a letter of protest.

Chief Justice Warren Burger now intervened. Early in his tenure, the White House had asked Burger whether it would be inappropriate for the President to consult him on Supreme Court vacancies. On the contrary, replied the Chief, it would be "entirely appropriate" to seek his advice. He had been asked about Haynsworth and Carswell and had played a crucial role in promoting Harry Blackmun. Now the Court had lost two of its most distinguished members, and the administration proposed to replace them with nominees of modest reputation and uncertain confirmation. The prospect troubled Burger. The 1971–72 term of the Court had begun, as always, on the first Monday in October. If Friday and Lillie were rejected, or even if there were a long delay before they were approved, the Court might go a whole year with only seven Justices. A seven-Justice Court created a naturally unstable situation where close questions could not be authoritatively resolved. Burger decided to have one more try at dissuading the administration from pressing the potentially disastrous nominations it had in mind.

In a "personal and confidential" letter to Mitchell, Burger repeated a recommendation he had made once before. The administration should appoint Lewis Powell to the Supreme Court. Other possibilities mentioned by Burger included Alabama District Judge Frank M. Johnson and several northern judges who also seemed assured of quick confirmation.

Mitchell also heard Powell's name from Erwin Griswold, former dean of the Harvard Law School, who had been brought to Washington by Lyndon Johnson to be Solicitor General of the United States and had remained in that post in the new administration. Griswold touted Powell so persistently that one day Mitchell said sharply that Powell "has been sounded out, and he says he is not interested." Griswold countered with sage advice: "The only way you will ever know whether Lewis Powell will take the post is to have the President talk to him in person, and say he wants to nominate him and ask him if he is willing to have that done. . . . And if he is hesitant, the President should tell him it is his duty to accept the appointment."

And that is exactly what happened. On October 18, 1971, Mitchell learned that the ABA committee would endorse neither Friday nor Lillie. (The committee decided by a vote of six to six that it was "not opposed" to Friday and by a vote of eleven to one that Lillie was "unqualified" for the Supreme Court.) One or both candidates might have been confirmed despite the ABA but not without a fight. It looked like Haynsworth and Carswell all over again.

That evening Mitchell consulted the President and the next morning tracked down Lewis Powell. The call found him in New York, having breakfast in his room at the Waldorf-Astoria Towers. The day ahead included meetings with executives of Richmond's largest employer, the Philip Morris tobacco company (on whose board Powell sat), and with trustees of the Rockefeller-funded Colonial Williamsburg Foundation. Powell was preparing for these events when John Mitchell offered him an appointment to the Supreme Court.

Powell said no. His reasons for withdrawing from consideration in 1969 still applied. He was still too southern, too closely linked to business, and too old. Besides, he added, he had a "problem" with his eyes and might not have many years of vision left. Powell had long worried about what he described as a "weakness" in his eyes and had been led to believe that his vision might deteriorate with age, but in fact he was experiencing no particular difficulty with his sight at the time of this conversation. Invoking his eyes may have been a dodge. If so, the tactic failed, for Mitchell remained undeterred. The President wanted Powell, and unless there was a serious health problem, Powell should accept the appointment.

Despite his misgivings, Powell said nothing Shermanesque. He agreed to remain in his room that morning in case the President wished to speak to him directly. Either the President or Mitchell would call back by ten thirty. Powell cancelled his meeting at Philip Morris and waited for the call.

He telephoned his wife Josephine, who did not like the idea, then called their eldest daughter, Jo Smith, who was then living in New York. She had much the same reaction. "I felt that Daddy was being imposed upon and was having his arm twisted to do something to get the President out of an awkward position."* Powell also called his ophthalmologist, who reported that Powell had bothersome vitreous opacities or "floaters" in his eyes but that the retinas were stable and not deteriorating. He also had early-stage cataracts that might require surgery in eight to ten years. (After a full examination a week later, he concluded that Powell would "maintain useful vision for many years to come.")

Shortly after ten thirty, Mitchell called to say that the President still wished to make the appointment. Again Powell declined, this time proposing a number of alternatives.† Mitchell's reception of these suggestions was characteristically cryptic. When Powell hung up the phone, he had no idea who might be chosen, but thought that as for him the matter was closed.

---

* Three days later, when Jo Smith arrived at the River Club to play tennis, a woman who worked in the locker room said to her, "As I was coming off the subway I thought I saw your picture on the front page of the *Daily News*, but then I found out it was just some man from Virginia who had been named to the Supreme Court."

† Among Powell's candidates were several members of the Cabinet, including Mitchell himself (a suggestion that may have owed more to courtesy than conviction), Secretary of State William Rogers, Secretary of the Treasury John Connolly, and Secretary of Health, Education, and Welfare Elliott Richardson. Powell also suggested a handful of private practitioners (E. Smythe Gambrell, Leon Jaworski, David Peck, Charles S. Rhyne, and Whitney North Seymour, Jr.), law professors (Phil Neal and Dallin Oaks), and judges (Robert Ainsworth, Jr., John D. Butzner, Jr., Walter Early Craig, and Donald S. Russell).

That afternoon Powell attended the meeting of the Colonial Williamsburg Foundation, where he said nothing of the events of the morning. On arriving home in Richmond that evening, he found that the White House had been trying to reach him. Powell returned the call and was put through to the President, who brushed aside Powell's objections and pressed him to take the post. When Powell still hesitated, Nixon followed Griswold's advice. He told Powell of his responsibility to the South, to the Supreme Court, and to the country. It was, said the President, not a question of ambition or opportunity; it was Powell's *duty* to accept appointment to the Supreme Court.

"Duty" was the magic word. If there was one constant in Powell's life, it was his sense of duty. For Powell, obligation always came first. And when invoked by the President, Powell's instinct for service was powerfully reinforced by his intense personal feelings of devotion to his country. The combination of duty and patriotism proved irresistible.

Still, Powell did not give in. Acting more from innate caution and habitual methodicalness than from any thought that he might actually refuse the President, Powell agreed only to reconsider. He would call John Mitchell with his answer by five o'clock the next afternoon.

Shortly after Powell spoke to the President, Chief Justice Burger called to support Nixon's invitation. They discussed what could be done about Powell's investments, the necessity of disqualifying himself in cases involving former clients, the availability of life and disability insurance for Supreme Court Justices, and other details. On all these points, Burger was reassuring.

At nine the next morning, Powell had a complete physical, and the physician found no reason that he should not go on the Court. Two hours later, Powell met with the inner circle of senior lawyers who sat on the executive committee of his firm. They had been summoned mysteriously for a special meeting and had been asked not to leave the building until they had seen him. Powell told them of the President's offer and asked for their advice.

To Powell's surprise, everyone urged him to accept the appointment. Powell was surprised by their reaction. From the outset, he had focused on the negatives of the situation—the risks involved in confirmation, the challenge to his health, the necessity of leaving Richmond, even the reduction in income. The exhilaration that his partners felt caught him off guard. It even crossed his mind that some of them might welcome the opportunity to divide his share of the firm's profits. Perhaps they did. Perhaps Powell was a bit hurt that they were not upset by the thought of his departure. But more than anything else, Powell's state of mind reflected his sense of impending loss. He took enormous satisfaction in the practice of law, in the success of the law firm he had helped build, and in his controlling role in its affairs. That the natural joy and enthusiasm of his partners took him by surprise shows just how keenly he felt what Powell would giving up.

But accept he did. Powell spoke to his children and to his ninety-two-year-old father, and at precisely five o'clock the next afternoon he called John Mitchell. In his meticulous way, Powell had made a list of the political liabilities Mitchell should consider: his chairmanship of the Richmond School Board and later the Virginia State Board of Education during an era of standstill in desegregation, an article on civil disobedience in which he criticized Dr. Martin Luther King, Jr., his links to large corporations, his membership in the all-white Country Club of Virginia. None of that mattered, said Mitchell. The President still wanted Powell, and Powell finally agreed.

Mitchell then said that the President would wish to make the announcement, probably in a nationally televised broadcast the following evening. In the meantime, Powell should say nothing.

IN LATER YEARS Powell took a certain rueful pleasure in recounting that he had turned down a seat on the Supreme Court—as earlier in his career he had turned down the Supreme Court of Virginia, the Fourth Circuit Court of Appeals, the chairmanship of the Securities and Exchange Commission, and a variety of local posts. What he did not publicize was that almost immediately after agreeing to accept appointment to the Supreme Court, he tried to change his mind.

After Powell spoke to Mitchell on October 20, he and Jo spent a nearly sleepless night in the colonial mansion that had belonged to Jo's parents. The Powells had moved there after the Second World War, while they looked for a home of their own, and had never left. The house now belonged to Jo and to her mother, who still lived there. It symbolized the Powells' life in Richmond—the right house in the right neighborhood, imposing, enduring, and elegant. The prospect of leaving that home and her aging mother and the city where she had always lived dismayed Jo and disturbed Powell. Both were exhausted by the events of the last two days and nervous about what lay ahead. After several hours awake in bed, then went downstairs, drank a cup of tea, and decided they had made a dreadful mistake.

Early the next morning, when Powell called Mitchell to say that he was having second thoughts, the Attorney General's shocked reaction brought Powell to his senses. The President, said Mitchell, was count-ing on Powell. He had scheduled a national television broadcast to announce the nomination that very evening. There was no way they could cancel the broadcast without embarrassment, nor could they hope to find a suitable replacement in just one day. "You just can't do that to the President of the United States," Mitchell insisted. Powell agreed. As he later put it, "Mitchell made me focus on what an ass I was being, so I told him I would stay with my decision."

The evening that Nixon announced the nomination, Bruce Morton and a CBS camera crew arrived at the Powell home at midnight to interview the nominee. Lewis and Jo sat on a couch while Powell made appropriate noises about the honor of the nomination, but when Morton asked Jo how she felt, she burst into tears. Morton stopped the cameras, gave her a few minutes, and repeated the interview. This time she responded gracefully, giving Powell a gentle pat on the knee as she answered.

Powell's last-minute vacillation, which he later found embarrassing, reflected something more than indecision, something more than unease at the risks of confirmation or regret at leaving law practice. It exposed genuine self-doubt. Could he do the job? Would he be able, at age sixty-four, to rise to the challenge of a responsibility vastly greater than any he had known before? And would he be able to per-form with the distinction that he had always, in every sort of undertak-ing, demanded of himself?

Few knew Powell well enough to detect the anxiety beneath his self-control, but it was always there. His long string of achievements were not the fruits of easy confidence, but of ceaseless struggle against self-doubt. Fiercely ambitious, yet ineradicably unsure, Powell always had to prove himself. From childhood, he had followed a simple strategy. He would work longer, harder, and better than anyone else. He would master challenge by diligence, by never leaving undone anything that could be done to assure success. And it worked. The doctrine of salva-tion by effort had put Powell at the pinnacle of his profession, with wealth, influence, and the respect of the nation's lawyers. Others applauded the honor of a nomination to the Supreme Court, but Powell saw risk. At an age when he might have been expected to slow down, he would have to find the strength and energy to face a new challenge. Perhaps the Supreme Court would be more than he could handle. Perhaps it would defeat his strategy of work and more work. Perhaps it would expose him as the rather ordinary person he secretly supposed himself to be.

Rarely did such doubts break the surface of Powell's ordered life. They arose in the dead of that October night as he and Jo sat and pondered what they had done, but the crisis passed. John Mitchell's rebuke helped Powell regain his customary objectivity and self-control. Yes, of course, Mitchell was right. Powell would accept the nomination as agreed.

A meeting of the firm convened that afternoon so that Powell's many partners could learn the news. Although there seemed to have been no leaks from the executive committee, everyone knew that something was afoot, and attendance was unusually large. Three hours later, President Nixon addressed the nation. "Everything that Lewis Powell has undertaken," said the President, "he has accomplished with distinction and honor, both as a lawyer and as a citizen." Afterward, Nixon told reporters, "Some said he was too old. But ten years of him is worth thirty years of most."

When Powell called John Mitchell on October 20 to accept the nomination, he asked who was being considered for the other seat. Mitchell mentioned four names: Senator Howard Baker of Tennessee, Los Angeles lawyer (and future Attorney General) William French Smith, Judge William H. Mulligan of the Second Circuit Court of Appeals, and Assistant Attorney General William H. Rehnquist. Powell had never heard of Rehnquist. He was an Arizona lawyer who had worked in Barry Goldwater's 1964 presidential campaign before coming to Washington to head the Office of Legal Counsel in Mitchell's Department of Justice.

Like Powell, Rehnquist was a last-minute replacement for the names shot down by the ABA. In fact, he was preparing for a meeting on those candidates when Mitchell's deputy Richard Kleindienst told him not to come, because "[w]e're going to be talking about you." Only forty-seven years old, Rehnquist was neither a sitting judge nor a lawyer of national reputation. He was, however, extremely smart. He graduated first in his class from the Stanford Law School and won a prestigious Supreme Court clerkship with Justice Robert Jackson. At the Justice Department, Rehnquist impressed his colleagues by his quickness and his abilities as a lawyer. And there was the additional attraction that Rehnquist was firmly conservative. He came from that wing of the Republican Party that had cheered Barry Goldwater and would later produce Ronald Reagan. He could be counted on to cast the law-and-order votes that Nixon desired.

Powell's decision to accept the appointment had made Rehnquist's nomination more likely, as the two made a good package. Rehnquist's youth was balanced against Powell's age, so that the longevity the administration gave up in one appointment, it won back in the other. Rehnquist's obscurity was matched by Powell's prominence; his reputation for brilliance by Powell's capacity for judgment; his easygoing familiarity by Powell's grave reserve. One came from the West and the other from the South—both areas of Republican electoral ambition. The two even looked like opposites. Rehnquist favored long sideburns and loud clothes, while Powell projected an ascetic conventionality in dress and appearance. In every respect in which Rehnquist might be thought lacking, Powell provided reassurance. In all likelihood Rehnquist would never have been nominated had there been only one vacancy, but he became much more plausible when matched with Powell. As Kleindienst later recalled, they "thought it would be easier to get Rehnquist through if he were paired with Powell, whom everyone thought an ideal appointment."

But the Powell-Rehnquist confirmation partnership was not one-sided. If the pairing lent Rehnquist prestige, it helped Powell by diverting the opposition. As the younger, more conservative, and more vulnerable of the two nominees, Rehnquist drew the hostile fire. Labor, liberals, and civil rights leaders who tried to defeat Rehnquist were willing to accept Powell, if only to emphasize the contrast between the two. And both nominees benefited from comparison to those whose names had not gone to the Senate. Many wondered whether Herschel Friday, Mildred Lillie, and the others had been a mere smoke screen, designed to distract Nixon's opponents and soften them up for the eventual nominees. In the words of one columnist, Powell and Rehnquist "looked like legal Gullivers in contrast to the Lilliputians on the original list." Whatever Nixon's intention, public dalliance with lesser possibilities produced what *Newsweek* called a "stunned and for the most part happy reflex" of applause for the superiority of the ultimate nominees.

There were in fact controversies on the road to confirmation, but eventually both Powell and Rehnquist were approved by the Senate and so found themselves on January 7, 1972, preparing to take the oath of office as Associate Justices of the Supreme Court.

THE COURT CONVENED, as always, precisely at ten o'clock. The Justices emerged through the red velvet curtains that hung down behind the bench and took their places, the Chief Justice in the center and the Associate Justices alternating to his right and left in order of seniority.

The last chair on either end of the massive mahogany bench stood vacant.

As the older man, Powell went first. He sat in the well of the court in John Marshall's old chair wearing the great Chief Justice's watch, which had been lent to him by a fellow Virginian. The Attorney General presented the presidential commission of appointment, which the Clerk read aloud: "Know Ye: That reposing special trust and confidence in the Wisdom, Uprightness, and Learning of Lewis F. Powell, Jr., of Virginia, I have nominated and, by and with the advice and consent of the Senate, do appoint him an Associate Justice of the Supreme Court of the United States. . . ." Powell stepped up beside Chief Justice Burger, who administered the oath.

For an institution steeped in tradition, it is odd that Supreme Court investitures do not always feature the same oath. Every Justice swears to two different oaths. The first is the constitutional oath, which is administered to the President at his inauguration and to all other federal officers, including judges. They swear to "support and defend the Constitution of the United States against all enemies, foreign and domestic" and to "bear true faith and allegiance to the same." Powell had taken the constitutional oath three days earlier with only the other Justices present. The public ceremony involved a second oath, the judicial oath, administered only to federal judges: "I, Lewis F. Powell, Jr., do solemnly swear that I will administer justice without respect to persons, and do equal right to the poor and to the rich, and that I will faithfully and impartially discharge all the duties incumbent upon me. . . ."

Burger read the judicial oath phrase by phrase so that Powell could repeat it, but when it was done, Burger unexpectedly continued into the constitutional oath, which Powell now said a second time. Caught by surprise, Powell left out a few words toward the end, but was told by the Chief Justice that it did not matter and that he was now duly sworn in as the ninety-ninth Justice of the Supreme Court.

For the next fifteen and a half years, Powell labored to "support and defend the Constitution of the United States" as a Justice of the Supreme Court. During that time, the Justices rewrote constitutional law, altered the course of domestic politics, and reshaped American society. They recognized a constitutional right to abortion, revolutionized the law of capital punishment, and forced the resignation of a President. They wrestled with the intractable problems of race and grudgingly opened the door to the widespread use of racial preferences to benefit minorities. And for every step the Justices took, another was unsuccessfully urged on them, so that the full weight of their decisions lies not only in what they did, but also in what they refused to do.

These decisions did not move in one direction. The Supreme Court in Powell's time was neither consistently liberal nor dependably conservative, neither predictably activist nor reliably restrained. It was an era of judicial balance. The periods before and after were of a distinctly different character. In the liberal heyday of Chief Justice Earl Warren, the Justices commanded an end to segregation, greatly expanded the rights of criminal defendants, and zealously sought to reform many other aspects of American society and law. After Powell retired, the Supreme Court entered the conservative ascendancy associated with the Chief Justiceship of William Rehnquist.

In between lay a period—lasting for the better part of a generation—in which neither liberals nor conservatives dominated the Supreme Court. These were years of ideological stalemate and political pragmatism, of conflict and compromise, of decisions that owed less to dogmas of the left or the right than to a flexible search for justice, order, and decency in a changing world. And this Court's most characteristic voice, the one that proved most often decisive, was that of its most reluctant member, Justice Lewis F. Powell, Jr., of Virginia.

CHAPTER I

EARLY LIFE

LOUIS AND MARY LEWIS

Powell's father was born Lewis Franklin Powell in 1881, but for most of his life spelled his name Louis. His seventeenth-century relation, Captain Nathaniel Powell, arrived in Virginia with the original Jamestown settlers and served as the colony's acting governor. Though Nathaniel died without issue, the line was continued by his brother and heir Thomas Powell, who came over from England in 1635 and settled on the south side of the James River a few miles upriver from Norfolk in Isle of Wight County. From Thomas's two sons sprang the succeeding generations of Powells that populated the farms and villages of southeastern Virginia. In 1749, part of Isle of Wight County broke off and became Southampton County, where Louis's family still lived 150 years later.

Louis was the child of Joshua and Adelaid Grizzard Powell. He grew up hearing tales of his mother as an infant, rescued by a Confederate soldier who heard crying in the midst of a skirmish with Northern forces and removed the baby and her nurse to the safety of the Confederate lines. Orphaned at an early age, Adelaid Gizzard went to live with her Aunt Lucy and eventually married Joshua, one of nine sons of Littleton Greene Powell, who lived only a few miles away. Louis was the first of their ten children.

Raising cotton and peanuts in a land impoverished by war and Reconstruction was a hard life. Young Louis took over the chores of home and farmyard as he was able and found his education confined by the calendar of the harvest. He began classes in a log cabin, then moved to a one-room county school three miles from home. When the Powell children became sufficiently numerous, Joshua and his brother built a private schoolhouse between their adjoining farms, calling it "Midway." Louis and his siblings and cousins were taught there by young women of good family and "impressive Christian character."

For Louis, schooling stopped at age fourteen. Unable to persuade his father to let him work in a sawmill, he became a full-time farm hand. Two years of plowing and hoeing proved more than enough, and at age sixteen Louis was apprenticed for a hundred dollars a year to his uncle, Eugene Grizzard, who ran a general mercantile store in the village of Boykins. Louis liked shopkeeping no better than farming and after two years decided to move on. Realizing the defects in his education, he borrowed enough money from his father to pay for a six-month course at a business college and on January 1, 1899, caught the Atlantic Coast Line in Emporia, Virginia, for a new life in the city of Richmond.

The young man who arrived in Richmond that evening was physically strong, socially insecure, devout, and extraordinarily hard-working. Weekdays he studied; Saturdays he wrapped bundles at the Globe Clothing Company for a dollar a day; Sundays he devoted to church. He left one boardinghouse because the lodgers stayed up Saturday nights and slept late Sunday mornings, making it difficult for Powell to get breakfast in time for Sunday school. Powell looked to the church for social support, but in this respect he was disappointed. Tongue-tied and shy, he found that the other worshippers "gave me the glad-hand Sundays at the Church services and then left me to wander back to my boarding house where there was not a single person interested in me." It was two years before anyone invited him home for a meal.

As a boy, Powell had been fascinated by logging. Though he tried other jobs, he stayed on the lookout for a chance to get into the lumber business. Finally, in 1901, he started with the Alleghany Box Company at a salary of thirty-five dollars a month. Hired to work from 8:30 a.m. until 6:00 p.m., Powell asked to come in early so that he could learn the operations of the factory as well as the office. He soon found himself going back after supper to finish the clerical work he did not complete during the day. By this means, Powell mastered both the production and financial sides of the business. After six years his salary plus bonus had risen to the respectable figure of $125 a month.

POWELL'S EMPLOYER at the Alleghany Box Company, Basil Gwathmey, often mentioned a pretty young cousin, Mary Lewis Gwathmey, whom Powell would eventually marry. She came from Bear Island, a plantation at the junction of the North Anna and Little Rivers, twenty-four miles north of Richmond in Hanover County. Bear Island took its name from an escaped circus animal that was run to ground on a nearby island in the North Anna. Mary Lewis's father, Lewis Temple Gwathmey, was born there in 1847. After studying at Richmond College and in Leipzig, Berlin, and Paris, he accepted a position as professor of mathematics and modern languages at Howard College (now Sanford University) in Marion, Alabama. There he met and married Annie Kelly, who on April 19, 1881, gave birth to their daughter Mary Lewis.

Five months later Lewis Gwathmey was dead of typhoid fever. When his wife also died, their daughter was sent to Bear Island to live with a bachelor uncle, Edward Garlick Gwathmey, and his sister Eleanor.

Uncle Ned, as the family called Edward Gwathmey, had left the University of Virginia in 1861 to join the Confederate Army. Except for the winter of 1862, which he spent at home recovering from wounds suffered at Fredericksburg, he stayed with Lee till the end. Though he rarely talked of the war, Mary Lewis remembered hearing his vivid description of the grandeur of General Lee at the surrender and "the kindness of General Grant when he told his men not to cheer."

From Appomattox, Uncle Ned walked more than a hundred miles home to Bear Island. He took over management of the family farm and for fifty years ran a School for Small Boys on the property. A scholar by talent and inclination, Ned read Latin, Greek, French, and Italian. An announcement from 1894 states that the "pupils, few in number, are treated as members of the family, and are under the constant supervision of their instructor." When little Mary Lewis came to Bear Island, the household consisted of Uncle Ned and Aunt Ellie, various black servants, and, for nine months of the year, a collection of young boys with whom she played and studied.

The guiding spirit of this establishment was saintly Uncle Ned. He was devout, modest, and tenderhearted. His great-nephew, Lewis F. Powell, Jr., recalled the time when an old mule broke his hip and had to be shot. Uncle Ned, then over eighty, was so upset that he twice missed the mule's head from a distance of two feet. By this time, the owner was in "almost as bad shape" as the mule. Finally, young Lewis persuaded the old man to hold the lantern while he did the shooting, and the mule was put out of its misery, leaving Uncle Ned "as deeply distressed as if he had lost a very close friend."

Whether from nature or nurture, many of Ned's qualities showed up in his niece Mary Lewis. She too had an abiding religious faith and a kindly disposition. Throughout her life she was known as a warm, gentle, caring person. In the words of her husband, she was "beloved by all who knew her."

One spring day in 1904, Mary Lewis came to the Alleghany Box Company to pay a bill for her Aunt Eleanor, who used the company's products to ship pickles to northern customers, among them J. P. Morgan. Learning that the young lady would be in town for the weekend, Louis Powell arranged to see her that Sunday and subsequently to visit her at Bear Island. Many years later Powell wrote a book of recollections describing, among other things, his courtship of Mary Lewis. It sounds almost grim.

Socially and educationally, the Gwathmeys were Powell's betters. Burdened, as he said, by an "inferiority complex," Powell arrived at the nearby Taylorsville station wearing his Sunday suit and patent leather shoes, only to find himself loading ice and groceries into the one-horse wagon that would carry them to Bear Island. On his second visit, the Gwathmey cousins took him for a ride in their boat and dumped him in the river. Although "Mary Lewis took it as a big joke," Powell did not share her enjoyment. Soaked again when a thunderstorm caught him on the hike back to the Taylorsville station, he returned to Richmond "looking like a wet tramp." Still more trying was a treacherous walk to and from the Taylorsville Baptist Church on ground too icy for a carriage, with Powell supporting Aunt Eleanor, "then in her sixties and not very agile on her feet." The experience taxed Powell's patience "to the limit," but, as he guessed, "impressed Mary Lewis more favorably than many of my endeavors to win her love and admiration."

As Powell recounts it, the entire courtship was a tale of obstacles surmounted and battles won. Finally, in his "greatest triumph," he won her agreement to marry—but not before her twenty-fifth birthday. Thus it was on that date, April 19, 1906, that Louis and Mary Lewis became husband and wife.

THEIR FIRST CHILD, Lewis Franklin Powell, Jr., was born fifteen months later, on September 19, 1907. By this time the elder Powell had changed the spelling to "Louis" when he met a "Lewis" he disliked, but as the original spelling was now on both sides of the family, the parents restored it for the son.

Though Lewis Jr. would come to be known as a paragon of establishment Richmond, he did not come from a prominent family nor was he born in that city. Four months before the birth of their child, the Powells moved to Suffolk, Virginia, to help Louis's father in the ham business. Like many other Virginia farmers, Joshua raised hogs to sell as Smithfield hams. Marketed through jobbers in Norfolk, the hams brought very low prices; but in 1901 Louis went to New York City and struck a deal with the Waldorf-Astoria, which took all the hams that Joshua and his brother could produce, about six hundred a year. Intoxicated by a taste of success, Joshua decided to sell his farm and go into the business of curing and marketing hams on a large scale.

Fearing his father's lack of experience and limited capital, Powell moved to Suffolk to help. It was there, in the house at 206 North Broad Street, that Lewis Jr. was born. Doubts about Joshua's lack of capital proved all too well founded, and the ham business collapsed before it really got started, wiping out most of the family's savings.

Powell advertised for a job as a box plant manager and was hired to run a mill deep in the forests south of Petersburg. Owing chiefly to the difficulty of attracting experienced workers to this remote location, the venture did not flourish, and in the fall of 1908, Powell returned to the Alleghany Box Company in Richmond. After a few months he left to begin the business venture that was to occupy the rest of his working life and bring financial security to his family.

David M. Lea and Company of Richmond was a small and rather antiquated manufacturer of tobacco boxes, cigar boxes, and shipping cases, owned by the estate of Charles Whitlock. As Whitlock's son, Charles Jr., had neither the experience nor the inclination to run the business, a manager had to be found. Powell agreed to do the job for the modest salary of $125 per month plus a small percentage of the (then nonexistent) profits, but demanded $25,000 in new equipment. Young Mr. Whitlock's advisers were so reluctant to provide that sum that Powell thought it best to put the deal in writing. The document he had a lawyer draft specified his control over the operation of the business and the requirement for new capital but said nothing at all about his salary or job security. "[I]f I succeeded," Powell reasoned, "they would want me, and if I failed, even with a contract, we would both be unhappy."

He did not fail. By the fourth year of Powell's stewardship, sales had more than tripled, and David M. Lea was making a reasonable profit on higher revenue. Powell's income rose accordingly. In 1916 Charles Whitlock, Jr., died, and three years later Powell bought the business from his estate.

Powell made a go of David M. Lea despite a general decline in the wooden-box industry. He discontinued unprofitable lines and concentrated on making wooden shipping cases for tobacco and other products. He opened a shook mill to produce the slats for packaging and moved the main plant from Richmond to a better site south of town. When wooden boxes began to be replaced by other materials, Powell went into the production of corrugated boxes. He later added a line of low-priced furniture. There was, however, one rough period. In the early 1930s the business came so close to failure that Lewis Jr., by then a young lawyer, kept bankruptcy papers in his drawer ready for filing, but they were never used. Eventually, the company was sold to Sperry & Hutchinson on terms that left the Powells and their children, each of whom had been given shares, comfortably well off.

In all these developments the constant was hard work. During the early years especially, Powell worked twelve to fourteen hours a day, six days a week. Later he found more time for leisure, but never lost the capacity for sustained effort so clearly inherited by his eldest child.

FOREST HILL

When Powell returned to Richmond in 1908, the city was a lively hub of transportation and commerce with a population well over 100,000 (counting the residents of Manchester, which merged into Richmond in 1910). Politically, the business community was firmly in control. Blacks in Richmond, as elsewhere in Virginia, had been largely excluded from political power by the Constitution of 1902, which used poll taxes and literacy tests to reduce the black electorate by more than 70 percent. In a Richmond ward where there had been nearly three thousand black voters in 1896, only thirty-three managed to register under the new requirements. Public morality was strictly Victorian. The city's mayor campaigned, albeit unsuccessfully, to require that even manikins in store windows not appear without stockings. Despite such sentiments, Richmond was then (more than subsequently) a musical and theatrical center, featuring vaudeville, concerts, plays, and other entertainments.

Powell's association with the David M. Lea Company brought him into the Richmond business community, but into the social and cultural life of the city he did not venture. Instead, he settled his wife and baby outside Richmond proper in the suburb of Forest Hill.

Richmond lies at the falls of the James River. The James rises in the foothills of the Blue Ridge Mountains and flows generally eastward toward the falls. There it bends sharply to the south and flows in that direction for some distance before resuming its easterly progress toward Chesapeake Bay. Today Richmond straddles both sides of the James, but in 1908 the city lay only north of the river. On the southern bank, which was part of Chesterfield County, was the area known as Forest Hill.

The Powells moved there because it was the only "good neighborhood" they could afford, though the cottage they rented had no bath or running water. They purchased a lot at 4103 Forest Hill Avenue and built a small frame house, which was completed just in time for the birth of their second child, Eleanor Gwathmey Powell, on July 31, 1909. This house, which was enlarged and remodeled in 1921, was Lewis Jr.'s home until he married.

In the early years of the Powell's residency, Forest Hill was more rural than urban. Its chief thoroughfare was Forest Hill Avenue, a long dirt road running parallel to the James River, where Lewis would sometimes sneak off to go skinny-dipping. The Powells' lot accommodated the house and garage, a pack of hounds, two horses, a cow, and a flock of chickens. With no public schools nearby, Lewis began his education with Miss Kate Morton, an elderly lady who taught children in her home. With few other playmates nearby, Eleanor missed "Brother" so much that she was allowed to join him in school a year early, and every day the two of them walked hand in hand down the street to Miss Morton's.

Soon after Lewis and Eleanor started school, their family was enlarged by the birth of twins, Angus and Zoe, on March 20, 1914. Snow covered the ground that night, and the cab company that Louis called to bring a doctor and nurse refused to come. Frantic calls located another doctor who used a horse-drawn carriage but he arrived after the twins were born. In this way the Powells met Dr. M. Pierce Rucker, whose daughter young Lewis would eventually marry.

After Lewis spent three years at Miss Morton's, trolley lines opened from downtown Richmond to Forest Hill Park, only one block from the Powell home. Since Lewis could now conveniently cross the river, he started fourth grade in Powhatan Elementary School in south Richmond. At recess the first day, the other boys demanded Lewis's lunch and gave him "a hell of a beating" when he refused. For the next two days he stayed in the classroom with the teacher but soon realized that "if I didn't go out and brave the other boys, I would be a sissy." Lewis faced his tormentors and was accepted at his new school, but he never fit in with the rowdy working-class style of south Richmond.

Lewis Jr. was not the rough-and-tumble sort. He was a thin child, of above average height, with a head almost too large for his body and ears that stuck out so sharply that for a time he tried taping them flat while he slept. Well-mannered and quiet, he excelled at his studies. Even as a young boy, he had a modesty and fastidiousness that endured throughout his life. Seventy years later he still recalled with distaste the privy and open pissoir at Powhatan school. Yet he was an avid sportsman and athlete. During summers at Bear Island, he hunted rabbits, raccoons, and other small game, and birds of all sorts. In and after school, he was a dedicated player of games, especially baseball, and though not extraordinarily gifted, he easily made the team—and his way with the other boys.

Everyone said Lewis took after his mother; like her he was quiet, serious, and sensitive. Yet beneath that tender, almost feminine, exterior lay a fierce ambition. Like his father, Lewis had an iron determination to achieve, to be recognized, to establish himself as a person of consequence. Having clawed his way up from a hardscrabble past, Louis Sr. aimed chiefly at success in business. Lewis Jr., with the security of his father's income, yearned for a different sort of distinction. He dreamed about war and fighting. In the World War I series *Boy Allies* and the historical novels of G. A. Henty, Lewis read stories of teenage heroism and adventure. And like every southern boy, he imagined himself in the Civil War—at Chancellorsville, saving Stonewall Jackson from the fire of his own sentries, or at Gettysburg, hurrying Longstreet into the line before it was too late. Lewis used to put himself to sleep at night fantasizing that, as a soldier, he could win on the battlefield the recognition and acclaim he craved.

After three years at Powhatan and two at Bainbridge Junior High, Lewis entered McGuire's University School, a private boys school overlooking Richmond's William Byrd Park. This location gave the McGuire's boys ready access to the park's athletic facilities, which included a track (used for walking off demerits), a football field, and four baseball diamonds, but for young Lewis Powell it required commuting. Every day he caught a streetcar (segregated by law since 1906) at Forest Hill Park and rode to Seventh and Main streets in Richmond, where he switched to the Main Street line and rode to its end near the Boulevard, then walked the last few blocks to the school. The trip roughly outlined three sides of a square and took at least an hour. As the crow flies, the distance was not so far, and Lewis sometimes walked home across the Richmond, Fredericksburg & Potomac Railroad bridge, which was strictly forbidden to pedestrians, and occasionally used the cubbyhole in every third supporting column that enabled workmen and trespassers to escape passing trains.

The distance aside, Lewis liked McGuire's School. Started shortly after the Civil War by John Peyton McGuire and continued by his son of the same name, McGuire's was more elitist in precept than in admissions. Talented boys of modest means were accepted there, even if their families did not always pay. The school was founded on the

"the principle that nothing counted so much as character, and that honorable conduct was the sine qua non of a gentleman." Its motto was *Fides intacta*, with the additional admonition, in English, to "Be earnest, work hard, speak the truth."

Instruction at McGuire's school was geared to the individual student. There were three full-time teachers, plus two law students from the University of Richmond. The school gave no diplomas but sent each boy off to college when Mr. McGuire thought he was ready. Theoretically, a boy might choose any college, but McGuire's University School aimed squarely at *the* University, meaning the University of Virginia. Alternative possibilities were dismissed with the assurance that "boys prepared for the University of Virginia are, of course, ready to enter any other institution."

Lewis did well in English and history, which he thought easy, and less well in Latin and mathematics, in which he sometimes received help from Uncle Ned during the summers at Bear Island. His first love was sports. By the time he entered McGuire's School at age fourteen, he had reached a height of six feet, tall enough by the standards of the day to "jump center," as it was called when a jump ball followed every basket. He later captained the basketball team and also played baseball. His long reach made him a good defensive first baseman—always showing a large gap between the bottom of his trousers and the top of his stocking as he stretched for the ball—but he was not strong enough to be a power hitter.

Whatever his difficulties with the ablative absolute or a curve ball, Lewis did well at both studies and sports and won McGuire's highest prize, the Jack Gordon medal. According to Powell, Jack Gordon was a McGuire's boy who died young and whose family created the award in his honor. Another story says that John Peyton McGuire once returned to a class he had told to be silent and found the boys in an uproar. He asked who started it, but no one volunteered. Late that night, Jack Gordon and his father rang the bell at McGuire's house. "Mr. McGuire," said the father, "Jack did not report to you today that he was the one who started the conversation. And he came to say it, and to tell you before the next sun was up." In this version, the medal commemorates a punctilious personal integrity.

Perhaps both stories are true. In any event, Lewis left McGuire's with the Jack Gordon medal as the first official recognition of his superior qualities. The award gave Powell a public reassurance that he was not (as he secretly feared) ordinary, not a mediocrity, but in reality, as well as in his dreams, someone special. It was an experience he would constantly strive to replicate.

*   *   *

THE MORAL PRECEPTS of McGuire's School reinforced what Lewis learned at home. The Powells were devout Baptists. They believed in Sunday school, church services, Bible reading, and family prayer. In these matters, as in everything else, they were serious. Even as a young man living on his own in Richmond, Louis Sr. shunned frivolity and temptation. He would later write of that time that neither "Wednesday night's work nor social functions kept me from prayer service. When other boys in the boardinghouse were frequenting saloons and houses of ill fame, I was in my room studying my Sunday School lesson or reading a biography of some successful businessman." The same attitudes governed the household at 4103 Forest Hill Avenue. There was no drinking, no smoking, no dancing, no card playing, and on Sunday no games of any sort. Sometimes, religious scruple drew rather fine lines. Lewis Jr. and brother Angus were allowed to play catch on Sundays but not to use a bat or keep score.

Mary Lewis matched her husband's piety but sometimes took her children's part against his strict regime. When Lewis was sixteen and Eleanor fourteen, they were invited to a neighborhood dance and wanted so badly to go that Mary Lewis persuaded her husband not to forbid it. The children enthusiastically taught themselves to dance and turned out to be good dancers. A few years later, Eleanor was invited to a bridge party in Richmond. Again Mary Lewis intervened to allow her to go. Lewis brought a couple of friends home for intensive bridge lessons, after which Eleanor felt she "really did rather well."

If Lewis's father was the dominating figure in the household, his mother was the emotional center. Lewis Jr. was her firstborn and her favorite. She completed her errands in the mornings so that she would be home when Lewis returned from school. "I am always here when Lewis comes in," she later told Eleanor, "because I know he wants to know I am here." A friend of Zoe's recalled more than one occasion when she, Zoe, and Angus were engaged in animated conversation at the dinner table, only to be shushed by Mrs. Powell with the admonition that, "Lewis Jr. has something to say." She was, to say the least of it, "very impressed with her son," favoring him not only over the other children but even over their father. And Lewis basked in his mother's devotion. Zoe later said that at dinner Lewis never failed to ask for something different from the food on the table and that their mother happily obliged his special requests.

When Lewis Jr. grew up and went away to college, his relationship with his mother was inevitably diluted, but its character did not change. Hundreds of hours of interviews with Powell and with family members revealed no hint of distance between mother and son, no undercurrent of anxiety or trace of recrimination. He was always first in her affections, and she remained until her death in 1964 a source of unconditional love.

Lewis Jr.'s relations with his father were more complex. As an adult, Lewis was comfortable with his father, and by the time he had children, the old man so mellowed that he seemed to a granddaughter "sometimes gruff on the outside but gentle and merry within." Growing up, however, young Lewis rarely got beyond his father's gruff exterior. Louis Sr. was apparently without humor. His autobiography, published privately in 1958, reveals a man of enormous drive but no merriment. His only attempt at a light touch is a gruesome little story from his days as an apprentice clerk in his uncle's store. Every day the uncle brought table scraps for the family cat, which would inevitably leave a mess for Louis to clean up. Hating this chore, Louis put the cat in a sack and deposited it on a southbound train, so that he could truthfully tell the distraught family that he did not know where their pet was. "That," he concluded, "was one cat *that never came back.*"

Those who knew Louis Sr. at that time describe him as strong-minded, tart-tongued man of vehement opinions. His relations with his son suffered in consequence. Eleanor described the gap between them: "For a good many years of Lewis's growing up, he didn't seem to understand Daddy and his quick temper or sharp dictatorial manner of speaking, and Daddy did not understand this sensitive, sometimes quiet and shy boy."

Lewis Jr. believed his father was "very prejudiced" in favor of Eleanor, who was in truth their father's favorite. Later, when Angus came along, Lewis Jr. thought that he too "was closer to my father than I was." Lewis was forever trying to establish himself in his father's eyes and forever failing to win from him the praise and recognition that his mother so freely gave. Perhaps, as Eleanor thought, young Lewis's intense ambition to excel sprang from a desire to impress his father. Once when he was about fifteen, Lewis put the thought in words. "I am going to prove to Daddy," he told Eleanor, "that some day I will amount to something!"

Nearly fifty years later, when he became Mr. Justice Powell, Lewis Jr. had incontrovertible proof that he had amounted to something. His father was by then a very old man, living in comfortable retirement with his second wife, and on good terms with his famous son. Yet even at that distance, some echoes of the early tension remained. Lewis Jr.

recalled his father saying "rather more often than I thought necessary" that he could not believe his son was on the Supreme Court.

Yet young Lewis did not rebel. On Lewis's twenty-first birthday, his father wrote, "never in your life have you given me one moment's worry or concern." And it was perfectly true. Lewis Jr. stayed out of trouble and avoided any breach in relations. For the most part, he accepted his father's heavy hand while at the same time trying to establish his independence. This compliance was partly a product of the times. It was, as one of Powell's friends recalled, the "tail end of the Victorian era," when "children had profound respect for their parents" and "what the parents laid down was the order of the day." It also grew from the character of the man. Lewis Powell was by instinct a team player. As a boy and as a man, he worked to position himself within the conventions of the system. Whether it was his family or McGuire's School or the practice of law, he first adapted himself to the environment, then tried to adapt the environment to suit him.

Resentment was deflected from Louis Sr. toward safer outlets. Young Lewis "hated"—an unaccustomed word—mowing the grass, which his father made him do. He "hated" getting up early on winter mornings to start the furnace before the rest of the family came downstairs. Most of all, he "hated" Mollie the cow.

Louis Sr. believed in hard work, not only for himself but also for his son. As a boy spending the summers at Bear Island, Lewis Jr. had to work two hours in the morning and two hours in the evening as a farm hand. When he was older, he had summer jobs in a tobacco factory, in his father's plant, and as a surveyor for the city of Richmond. (He did miss one summer's work when he was seventeen and spent the time recuperating from an appendectomy.) As part of this program of work and responsibility, Louis Sr. bought a cow. The purpose was not only to provide milk but also to give Lewis Jr. the "wonderful discipline" of caring for the animal. The burden increased when he began to commute to McGuire's. Every morning and every evening, he had to feed and milk Mollie. No matter how late he arrived—after-school sports and the long trip home often got him there after dark—Mollie was waiting. "One of the happiest days of my life," he said later, "was when I went out there and found the damn cow dead." Since by this time Lewis was almost ready for college and the lessons of discipline were apparently well learned, the cow was not replaced.

In various small ways, Lewis differentiated himself from his father. He disdained fox hunting, which became his father's principal avocation, and virtually refused to mount a horse. Eleanor galloped around with her father chasing a pack of hounds, but Lewis Jr. stuck to hunting small game and birds, which his mother taught him to stalk with a small-gauge shotgun. Louis Sr. loved trains and automobiles and things mechanical. Lewis Jr. was completely uninterested and so unhandy that his daughters would say he did not know how to use a can opener. He liked team sports, which his father had never had the opportunity to play, and dancing, which his father thought immoral. While Louis Sr. "shot from the hip," Lewis Jr. cultivated an habitual judiciousness. He heard all sides of every issue before expressing an opinion, then stated his views with sometimes maddening moderation and balance. Even his quiet speaking voice, which became even softer when he was angry, contrasted sharply with his father's style.

Was Lewis Jr. reacting against the example of his father, or merely following his own natural instincts? It would be oversimplification to attribute every divergence between the two men to a repressed antipathy, but it would be missing something not to see that young Lewis Powell defined himself, at least in part, in opposition to his father.

Despite their different relations with their father, Lewis and Eleanor were always close. The isolation of Forest Hill and the lack of playmates drew them together. Being two years older than Eleanor encouraged Lewis to indulge his lifelong penchant for giving advice. Once, he proposed that she translate his Latin assignments and in return he would make himself available to her for advice on absolutely any subject. Later he offered her, free of charge, his views on her choice of college classes, her sorority, her clothes, even her deportment. At parties he sometimes whispered, "Eleanor, you are not smiling enough." Eleanor took all this in stride, though she later recalled "several very important decisions I wisely made contrary to his advice."

When Angus and Zoe were old enough to benefit from his experience, he tried the same approach on them, but with mixed results. According to Eleanor, Angus was "calm and equable, the sort of person who adapted to anyone of any age. He always got along superbly with Lewis"—and indeed with everyone else. He was the peacemaker in the family. The brothers remained close until Angus's premature death from cancer in 1979.

Zoe was another story. Lewis lamented to Eleanor that, "I just don't understand why I don't have any input in guiding Zoe or having her do what I tell her." But if Powell could not control his younger sister, neither could anyone else. She seemed to have sprung from different stock than the rest of the family. By Powell standards, she was a flamboyant party girl, who wore spike heels and dyed her hair. She was, in the words of family friends, "a law unto herself, always charging around in a very un-Powell-like manner," the only member of the entire family "who was not dead serious about her work and life in general."

As THE ELDEST of these children, Lewis was the first to leave home for college. He has said that his choice of college hinged on baseball. He was playing on the McGuire's team when it traveled to Lexington, Virginia, to play the freshmen of Washington and Lee. Powell stayed in the home of the baseball coach and athletic director, "Captain" Dick Smith, whom Powell remembered as an "attractive and persuasive person" who "held out the likelihood" that Powell could make the baseball team at W&L. Powell went to school there, but when he did not make the team, baseball faded from the scene.

There may well be more to the story. Having sent his son to McGuire's University School, Louis Sr. expected him to go to *the* University. So of course did John Peyton McGuire, another strong and domineering man, who was "shocked" at Lewis's decision to go elsewhere. Lewis became the first McGuire's boy ever to attend Washington and Lee and one of only three Richmond residents in the entire student body. A contemporary recalled that Lewis wanted "to strike out on my own."

The decision to attend Washington and Lee rather than the University of Virginia contained an element of defiance. Characteristically, Lewis chose his ground carefully and made a decision that, although disapproved by his parents and Mr. McGuire, involved no real danger. It was the low-risk rebellion of a cautious man.

WASHINGTON AND LEE

In September 1925, a few weeks before Powell's eighteenth birthday, a bus deposited him on the main street of Lexington, Virginia. He had taken the Chesapeake & Ohio Railroad westward from Richmond, through the Blue Ridge Mountains at Rockfish Gap, and into the Shenandoah Valley. He left the train at Staunton (pronounced "Stanton") and traveled by bus the last thirty miles up the valley to Lexington.

If a young man from Richmond had sought a community as drenched in the hagiography of the Old South as the capital of the Confederacy, he could not have done better than Lexington. This small town was the home of two distinctively southern colleges and the final resting place of the most revered of Confederate heroes, Robert E. Lee and Stonewall Jackson.

In the last years of the Civil War, Washington College—founded in 1749 as the Augusta Academy and renamed in 1798 in appreciation of a gift from the nation's first President—almost ceased to function. In 1865 it awarded only one college degree. Four months after Appomattox, the trustees of the looted and impoverished institution invited Robert E. Lee to become its president. His acceptance bought Washington College fame and honor throughout the South. When the great man died five years later (to be succeeded as president by his son, George Washington Custis Lee), the name was changed to Washington and Lee University.

Washington and Lee sits atop a long ridge overlooking the town of Lexington. The buildings, most of which date from the 1840s, are aligned on the crest of that ridge and feature a succession of neoclassical porches and white columns known as the Colonnade. In 1925, the Colonnade ended abruptly at Tucker Hall, a gray limestone building housing the law school. Tucker Hall was so ugly that the sight of it reportedly prompted a man who had killed a New York architect to proclaim, "My God, I shot the wrong architect." Halfway up the slope, facing the center of the Colonnade, is a simple brick chapel begun in 1867 at the request of General Lee. The configuration makes a graceful and impressive setting for genteel college life.

To the northeast, as the ridge broadens into a wide bluff, the mood abruptly changes. The warm red brick of Washington and Lee gives way to the austere gray masonry of the Virginia Military Institute. Like its civilian neighbor, the "West Point of the South" has its own particular hero: Lieutenant General Thomas Jonathan Jackson had been a professor of military science at VMI before the war, and his body had been returned to Lexington for burial. When Powell arrived in Lexington, the traditions and rituals of Stonewall Jackson's day were very much alive at VMI. The cadets lived, studied, drilled, and comported themselves according to regulations that had remained virtually unchanged since the founding of the Institute in 1839. Every afternoon the cadets marched out in full uniform of gray coats, black hats, white crossbelts, and long red sashes for Dress Parade. As a band played, the cadets wheeled and marched in perfect order and saluted the Stars and Stripes with the national anthem. Every aspect of student life was characterized by austerity, insularity, military discipline, and a violent pride in the honor of VMI. To the well-dressed, well-mannered, and comparatively cosmopolitan young gentlemen from Washington and Lee, VMI seemed like another planet.

Only mutual reverence for their respective heroes softened the ani-

mosity between the schools. They collaborated on January 19 in celebrating the birthdays of Lee and Jackson (though Jackson was actually born
on January 21) and on June 3, when the South observed Memorial Day.
Otherwise, rivalry prevailed. Tensions were exacerbated by college pranks.
Once two W&L boys stole "Matthew," one of Stonewall Jackson's four
apostolic cannons that guarded the gate to VMI, and parked it in front of
the Beta house. The next morning, VMI cadets swarmed over Washington
and Lee in a full-scale riot, retrieved Matthew, kidnapped two Beta boys,
and generally tore up the place. The bad blood engendered by generations
of such disputes was so serious that it was not until the 1970s that the two
schools begin to play each other in college sports.

When Powell arrived in this southern citadel in 1925, he was
"frightened to death" of his first extended stay away from home. His
parents had arranged for him to live with Dr. Glasgow, the widower
uncle of a Gwathmey cousin who, like almost everyone else in
Lexington, rented rooms to college students. Before he could find Dr.
Glasgow's, Powell was met by fraternity men who said he had been
recommended by people in Richmond and invited him to meet their
brothers. The dazed freshman agreed and did not reach his lodging
until late that night. Although fraternities could pledge a student
from the moment he first set foot on campus, Powell was not the sort
to make snap decisions. After a few days, he pledged a rival group with
a beautiful new house—Phi Kappa Sigma.

Powell and the other 356 members of the class of 1929 were quickly
introduced to peculiar local customs. Freshman were required to wear
green bow ties to all dances and were allowed to remain only one hour,
unless they brought dates or played freshman football. They were also
indoctrinated into the Washington and Lee "speaking custom."
Freshman had to speak first to all upperclassmen and members of the
faculty wherever they might be encountered, by name if known or otherwise by saying, "Hi, gentlemen."

After two years with Dr. Glasgow, Powell moved into the Phi Kappa
Sigma house, where the principal activities were drinking, carousing,
and sneaking young ladies past the housemother. As Powell's grades
suffered in this environment, he moved after one year to a basement
apartment in the home of Miss Annie Jo White.

The atmosphere there was entirely different. Annie Jo White was a
fiery, outspoken, white-haired "maiden lady," locally famous as the
originator of Fancy Dress Ball, an annual costume extravaganza that
had become the South's premier collegiate social event. She lived at
the foot of College Hill in one of a row of houses facing upward

toward the Colonnade. Columnist Charles McDowell, who grew up three doors away, says, "It was a Confederate world down in that hollow." Two doors to the left of Annie Jo White's was the Old Blue Hotel, which now housed students but had once been a stopping place for the stream of visitors who came to gaze on the tomb of General Lee and the skeletal remains of his famous warhorse Traveller. In Powell's day, the animal, since buried, was displayed in the basement of the Lee Chapel, where the reverence of the tourists sometimes outran their reason. During renovation of the biology department, the skeleton of a small prehistoric horse was placed alongside that of Lee's horse. "And this," the student guides would tell their worshipful listeners, "is Traveller as a colt."

Next door to Annie Jo lived Lelia Nance Moffatt, local grande dame of the United Daughters of the Confederacy and victor in a fierce campaign to prevent enlargement of the Lee Chapel. The original structure, described by supporters as a "dear, modest honest little chapel," housed a recumbent marble statute of the Hero of the South and below it the crypt where Lee and his family are interred. The president of Washington and Lee, Dr. Henry Louis Smith, had his heart set on a grander structure, which, incidentally, would have provided the university with a much-needed auditorium. The national UDC pledged $100,000 toward completion of the project, but the local Mary Custis Lee chapter denounced the renovation and campaigned against it with such tireless ferocity that Dr. Smith and his colleagues eventually gave up. Powell saw the redoubtable Mrs. Moffatt and heard the neighborhood boys sing:

> Lelia Nance Moffatt
> Sat on a toffet
> Under the UDC.
> So busy thinkin'
> How stinkin' was Lincoln,
> She forgot about Robert E. Lee.

Farther down the hollow lived Professor Gleason Bean, specialist on Stonewall Jackson and the world's greatest authority on the Battle of New Market, where 247 VMI cadets marched out to do battle (along with about 5,000 others) against northern forces aiming to capture the railhead at Staunton. On May 15, 1864, they sustained more than fifty casualties but helped inflict a decisive defeat on larger Union forces to achieve one of the few remaining Confederate victories of the war.

From Annie Jo White's front porch, Lewis could see the back of the Lee Chapel. When the VMI cadets approached the chapel, they stopped talking, saluted, and held the salute for ten paces as they passed the sacred spot. Every cadet did it, every time.

And in the front parlor was a photograph of Annie Jo as a small child, held by Robert E. Lee while seated on Traveller. Standing there with Annie Jo White, looking at her photograph with General Lee, Powell almost felt he knew the great man personally. In that parlor, said Charles McDowell (paraphrasing Faulkner), "The past wasn't over. It wasn't even past."

BY THE TIME he moved to Annie Jo White's, Powell was studying law. His undergraduate major was commerce, a practical curriculum that he mastered without undue effort. There is no sign of a grand intellectual awakening in the undergraduate, nor did Powell aim at any academic experience beyond good grades. His goal was law school, and by counting some law classes toward his undergraduate degree, he could complete both programs in six years. Consequently, in June 1929, when he was awarded a B.S. magna cum laude from the School of Commerce and Administration, he had already completed one year of law school.

Powell had always planned to study law. "I was interested in history," he recalled, "and it seemed clear to me that soldiers and lawyers made most of the history." Despite his youthful dreams, Powell "entertained no ambition for a military career, and so for me the only choice was the law." The choice seemed almost inevitable. Powell was a lawyerly young man—remembered by contemporaries as "bespectacled, sedate, professorial," with an air of quiet authority. At fraternity meetings, he would wait until everyone else had spoken, then summarize the discussion, and propose a decision. He spoke so softly that his fraternity brothers had to strain to hear and so slowly that they sometimes "had the urge to grab him and try to shake the words out of his mouth." Already he had developed a technique for controlling a meeting: Wait until everyone else has spoken, incorporate their views, then propose a decision. No one felt insulted or overridden when Powell got his way.

Powell became president of his fraternity and a leader in almost every aspect of college life. He was managing editor of the student newspaper, *The Ring-tum Phi*, and worked on the staff of the yearbook. He was one of fourteen members of his class elected to Phi Beta Kappa, and was also chosen for "the Circle," officially known as Omicron Delta Kappa, a national leadership fraternity begun at W&L.

He helped produce Washington and Lee's lavish balls. He received the Algernon Sidney Sullivan Medallion for the student "who excels in high ideals of living, and in spiritual qualities, and in generous and disinterested service to others." And along the way, he was "tapped" for a succession of exclusive clubs—the White Friars, the Thirteen Club, and the Sigma society for seniors.

Even in athletics, Powell managed to make a contribution, though not of the sort he intended. His baseball ambitions collapsed when a left-hander from Washington, D.C., beat him out for first base. He tried freshman football, but spent three days in the hospital after his first tackle and was told he had better quit. Powell's forte was not playing but recruiting. Captain Dick Smith twice sent him to Norfolk to see Lee Williams, then the best high-school athlete in Virginia. Lee's father had died, and his mother was reluctant to see him go so far away. Powell, who in his own words "always had a nice way with older women," worked on Mrs. Williams. He pledged to look out for her son, guaranteed that Lee would be asked to join Phi Kappa Sigma, and even agreed to room with him so that the new recruit could be assured of wholesome influences and social acceptance. Eventually, the prestige of the rooming situation ran the other way, as Williams lettered in all four sports and became a local legend.

With or without Lee Williams, Powell was the proverbial "big man on campus." Some years earlier a slightly disaffected student described the formula for social success at Washington and Lee. A "B.M.O.C." must "have a natural gift for conformity . . . combine in the proper proportion deference and pride, and—this was sometimes the hard part—have brains enough to pass his work with a minimum of study." Powell did much better than pass, but otherwise the description seems apt. He had the natural gift for conformity and was able to combine deference to authority and pride in his own performance in proportions so finely balanced that everyone liked and admired him. His status was backhandedly recognized by the inclusion in a campus newspaper spoof of a poem entitled "Great God Louie."

In his fifth year, Powell was president of the student body. He was urged to run as a senior but stepped aside in favor of George Lanier, a close friend who was leaving after four years and would not have another chance. The next year, Powell ran unopposed, polled the highest number of votes then on record, and served his term while taking courses as a second-year law student.

As president of the student body, Powell was responsible for Washington and Lee's honor system and for a variety of other duties.

His chief success, however, was entirely unofficial. Although Prohibition had been in force in Virginia since 1916 and was now the law of the land, Washington and Lee was anything but dry. Every Thursday night about ten o'clock, the local bootlegger pulled up behind the Phi Kap house to transact his business. Powell never partook. He had promised Louis Sr. that so long as he remained in school, he would not drink. Since his father was paying the bills, the demand seemed to the son "eminently reasonable." And there was the additional incentive of a $1,000 reward if he kept the faith. Powell did so, making him, after his sophomore year, the only member of his fraternity who did not imbibe.

One night the watchman at Sweet Briar College caught two W&L boys with white lightning in the rumble seat of their roadster. Although their cargo had been requested by Sweet Briar students, they were gentlemen enough not to implicate the young ladies. In consequence, they were accused of corrupting the innocent, and Sweet Briar president Meta Glass (sister of U.S. Senator Carter Glass) decreed Washington and Lee off-limits to Sweet Briar women for the remainder of the year. The ban included Fancy Dress Ball. Answering the distress of his constituents (and their Sweet Briar girlfriends), Powell corralled two other students for moral support and went to see Sweet Briar's Dean Dutton, who in due course ushered them into the presence of President Glass. Though he could later recall no more sophisticated strategy than simply begging for mercy, the awful edict was lifted after a face-saving vote by the Sweet Briar students to "take the responsibility for the conduct of their dates while on the Sweet Briar campus." Powell became a campus hero.

POWELL'S POSITION as president of the student body led to an interesting opportunity. In December 1929, he boarded a train in Richmond to attend, at Washington and Lee's expense, the fifth annual convention of the National Student Federation of the United States, to be held on the campus of Stanford University in Palo Alto, California. Joining him there would be his college sweetheart, Eleanor Wilson.

"Siddy," as she was called, did not go to Palo Alto as Powell's date but as student body president of Hollins College, located fifty-five miles southwest of Lexington in Roanoke, Virginia. Her presence may nevertheless have been an inducement for him to attend, as they had been seeing one another for some time. Striking, vivacious, and outspoken, Siddy Wilson came from a Philadelphia suburb. Neither she nor Powell remembers exactly when they met, but it was likely one of the dances that Washington and Lee hosted for women from Hollins, Sweet Briar, Randolph Macon, and Mary Baldwin. By Powell's senior year, he was her steady beau, though by modern standards, the relationship was not intimate. For one thing, there was not much opportunity. Dating at Hollins was strictly supervised. The ladies could be escorted around campus until early evening, when a curfew forced them inside. With others sharing the same sitting room, the young couples turned their backs on each other and faced the wall for a measure of privacy.

Wilson later recalled that "everyone was very well behaved." Powell was "circumspect, extremely proper, immaculate, and always a gentleman." Powell may indeed have been the young gentleman every father wishes his daughter to date, but there was also an element of romance. Though not conventionally handsome, Powell was slender, graceful, and an excellent dancer, whose appeal was enhanced by his standing with the other students. He was, recalls Wilson, "the pick of the lot! Any girl would have wanted to be with him."

Wilson and Powell dated off and on for years. That their relationship faltered may have had something to do with Powell's preference for a stay-at-home wife and Wilson's ambition to become an actress. She later had a long stage career, including appearances with José Ferrer in *The Silver Whistle*, with Tallulah Bankhead in *The Eagle Has Two Heads*, and in many other productions.

For the December 1929 trip to California, Powell and other student representatives from their region rode the Chesapeake & Ohio to Chicago, then changed to the Atchison, Topeka & Santa Fe. Including a day's layover to see the Grand Canyon, the trip took four days, and they arrived just in time for the opening session of the National Student Federation's fifth annual congress on January 1, 1930.

The National Student Federation of America grew out of a Princeton conference on United States participation in the world court. It has been described as "a moderate and middle-class student organization, politically lightweight and following a scattershot agenda." Federation members opposed Prohibition, supported international travel, and criticized athletic scholarships. They sponsored a magazine and arranged college screenings of *All Quiet on the Western Front*. Mostly, they wanted to get together "in a spirit of cooperation" to "foster understanding among the students of the world in furtherance of an enduring peace."

Powell shared this vague idealism. During his years in Lexington, he had been insulated from national politics. His mind was on campus affairs—fraternities and dances, student government, and recruiting athletes, as well as studying law. At the Palo Alto convention, he chaired a session on the honor system, which concluded that it generally worked better in small institutions. He also participated in testing by the Stanford psychology department, which found that Powell (and most of the other student leaders present) were neither extroverts nor introverts but "ambroverts," a neologism said to describe persons combining characteristics well suited to executive positions.

Aside from earnest speeches, the main business of the convention was election of the next year's officers. Siddy Wilson made an impression at the outset when someone proposed a pin that the delegates could wear to record their participation. This idea collapsed when Wilson rose and announced, "I did not come three thousand miles to award myself a medal." In the jockeying for electoral advantage, she and Powell allied themselves with an elegant, dark-haired young man named Edward R. Murrow.

As representative of the Pacific Coast Student Association (he was president of the student body at Washington State), Murrow made a stirring speech. Charging that American college students were too preoccupied with "fraternities, football, and fun," he called on the delegates to rouse their generation to the serious issues of world peace. Powell was enthralled. "Ed made the handsomest presence of anybody I'd seen," he later recalled. "And the speech, it had such a polished quality, not a bit theatrical, but he was so poised . . . so confident and mature. I was just enormously impressed." So were the other delegates. They elected Murrow president of the organization, Wilson vice-president, and Powell one of seven regional representatives to the NSF executive committee for the coming year.

It was in this capacity that Powell, in the company of Murrow, Siddy Wilson, and at least one other NSF representative, boarded the S.S. *Rotterdam* on July 26, 1930, to attend a convention of the Confederation Internationale des Etudiants in Brussels. Powell and Murrow shared a third-class stateroom and stopped for two weeks in England (Powell liked the British, but Murrow did not), before crossing the Channel to Ostend. Murrow, who had a habit of awarding private nicknames, called Powell "Judge."

The Brussels conference was not a success. The first item of business was a complaint by the German delegation that the program was printed only in English and French. Soon the Flemish-speaking Belgians joined the demand for linguistic parity. More serious was the question of whether the Germans would be admitted to full membership in the

Confederation Internationale des Etudiants or would continue to be relegated to observer status. Murrow, who was being touted for president of the organization, expounded the prevailing American campus view that the Treaty of Versailles was unjust, that the Germans should no longer be held accountable for the Great War, and that they should be given equal status in the CIE. The Europeans loved Murrow but not the Germans. He turned down the presidency of the CIE when the delegates refused to accept German membership.

Murrow biographer Joseph Persico has described the shock that confronted the Americans in Brussels. At home the NSF agenda "called for banning freshman hazing, protesting faculty interference in student government, and debating whether college credit should be given for the French club." The Europeans were older, politically active, and uninterested in campus controversies. Their efforts to end the "ancient, blood-soaked conflicts among their countries" soon bogged down in bitterness. The Serbs and Croats fought over who should represent their new collective nation of Yugoslavia; the Germans and the Poles feuded over Danzig; the Flemish students complained at being lumped in with other Belgians; and so it went. Frustrated and annoyed by these intransigent animosities, the Americans left feeling that nothing had been accomplished.

Socially, however, the trip paid off. Powell and Wilson enjoyed their time together in Brussels. She still has a photograph of Powell leaning on a railing in Brussels, hat in one hand and cane in the other, looking like a privileged young American on the grand tour, apparently unaffected by the Great Depression. After the conference, Powell and Murrow did make a tour, though not on a grand budget. They took a boat trip up the Rhine, with stops in Heidelberg and Basel, then visited Paris before returning to England for the voyage home. Powell arrived in Lexington just in time for the beginning of his last year of law school.

The European traveling companions became fast friends. Murrow later dated Powell's sister Eleanor when she was living in New York, came to Virginia to shoot quail at Bear Island, and invited Powell, then a lonely Air Corps captain, to use his luxurious apartment in wartime London. Their was, however, an unfortunate asymmetry in their relationship. While Powell witnessed Murrow's many triumphs, Murrow died before he could know the prescience of the nickname "Judge."

POWELL'S LEGAL EDUCATION at Washington and Lee differed hugely from its modern counterparts. Until the early decades of this century,

American law schools did not require applicants to have a college degree and were actually easier to get into than other undergraduate programs. In 1908, Washington and Lee raised its law department admission standards to equal those for other parts of the university and in 1923 required two years of college as a prerequisite to admission. The law school became not only harder to get into, but also harder to get out of. After years of permitting law students to graduate after two years, in 1920 Washington and Lee began to insist on three years of study for the LL.B.

These more demanding requirements depressed enrollment. In 1911–12, the Washington and Lee Law School had more than two hundred students. By Powell's first year, it enrolled barely half that number. As the dean, "Boss" Moreland, explained to the board of trustees, "the larger attendance in years past was caused in part by the standards prevailing in this school which were lower than those of some of our competitors." This advantage, he added, had been surrendered "[n]ow that we have built up our standards until they are as high as those enforced in any Southern law school."

Instruction was formal in style and in substance. In Clayton Williams's property class, a student had to stand to recite the facts of a case, then submit to a long interrogation on how the legal rule applied in other situations. Close analysis was taught by a varying the facts until the rule no longer made sense. "Uncle Skinny," as Williams was called, "would lead you clear out to the end of the branch and then saw it off, leaving you in midair." This was the "case method," a style of instruction that required the student to discern legal principles through the study of decided cases. The case method treated law as an inductive science. At its core lay the "assumption that the cases, once they were sorted out and properly classified, would themselves fall into patterns suggesting the true underlying principles."

By 1928, when Powell started law school, some version of this style of instruction was used in all classes at Washington and Lee. With a master teacher, the case method could be a powerful instructional technique, but in less accomplished hands, it could be merely an exceedingly roundabout way to learn the law. At least in upper-class courses, many Washington and Lee instructors lapsed into straight lecture. Nevertheless, reading assignments consisted mostly of reported decisions, and classroom instruction featured at least some Socratic interrogation.

Whatever the style of the individual professor, the focus was narrowly doctrinal. The now familiar notion of law as instrumental, as the means to some political or social end, was still very much in the background at Washington and Lee. The foreground was dominated by the idea of law as a science, an autonomous system of rules held together by its own internal logic. The doctrinal certainty that modern law students simultaneously crave and despise was transmitted and received without question. The approach was essentially formalist: It focused more on the logical application of formal rules and concepts than on the political or social context in which they might be applied.

Five professors covered the entire curriculum. Powell's favorite was Charles Rice McDowell, a former college coach and flight instructor affectionately known as Mr. Mac. McDowell talked like Will Rogers but was better looking. He was exceedingly popular and, perhaps not coincidentally, very easy. He said he believed in "putting the hay down to where the calves can reach it." Echoes of his abilities as a raconteur are caught in the stories of his son, columnist Charles R. McDowell, Jr., who grew up in the house at the foot of College Hill where "everyone gathered on Saturday nights to drink bourbon, tell stories, and sing songs."

According to his son, Mr. Mac found Powell "a little stiff and perhaps a little Richmond grand" but easily the "sharpest" student in the school. By that, McDowell would not have meant that Powell was intellectually creative, but that he had analytical ability, quick apprehension, and a good memory. McDowell's examinations in bills and notes consisted of a hundred yes-or-no questions. Powell dropped by his office one day to say that this format was thought bush-league and that he wished Mr. Mac would give essay questions instead. McDowell shot back that nothing in the entire subject was worth writing an essay on, and, besides, Powell would find the short-answer questions quite difficult enough to test his knowledge. As it happened, Powell missed only one question, and his "unheard-of" score of ninety-nine persuaded McDowell to include essay questions on his next exam.

Not all the teachers were so well liked. Raymon T. Johnson was called Patrick Henry by the dean because of his ability as an orator and Red-eye by the students because of his proclivity for the bottle. Powell's last law school exam was in Johnson's bankruptcy course. The papers had to be graded in time for graduation, and Red-eye was in no shape to do it. He asked Powell to mark the exams and swore on the Bible that he would tell no one of Powell's involvement. Powell agreed to grade all the papers except his own, to which Red-eye, without reading the paper, gave a grade one point higher than the best score in the rest of the class.

Powell also rescued Uncle Skinny Williams. In December 1934 a fire destroyed the law school building. Powell wrote Dean Moreland that his regret at the demise of old Tucker Hall was "purely sentimental, as I have never thought it either ornamental or adequate," but that he was "distressed at the loss of its contents." Among those contents were Williams's lectures. Apparently unable to remember them, Williams asked Powell for his class notes, which he used to reconstruct his own lectures. (Tucker Hall was rebuilt in the style of the surrounding buildings, thus extending the Colonnade.)

Williams's choice was not surprising, for Powell had a reputation for taking superb notes. Most of them survive in bound volumes that provide a highly detailed record of Powell's law study. Of greatest interest are his notes from the constitutional law class of Charles Porterfield Light, Jr.,* then just beginning a Washington and Lee teaching career that would span half a century. In later years, Light's constitutional law class reportedly evolved into "an exhilarating encounter with philosophy, sociology, and literature," but in the early years he apparently stuck to the cases. Powell's notes are crammed with judicial decisions and the rules they stood for. They are not much concerned with the social or political context in which the rules might be applied nor with what good or harm they might do.

Little of what Powell studied in his constitutional law class in 1929–30 would be familiar to today's law student. Professor Light's course concentrated on many constitutional doctrines that are today defunct or moribund. Powell's notes dealt at length with government regulation of the economy—a subject that is now rarely thought to raise a constitutional issue—but said almost nothing about race. The guarantees of due process and equal protection were considered chiefly in a lengthy review of the constitutional restrictions on taxation—another dead issue. Abortion, affirmative action, and the death penalty were of course not mentioned.

Equally striking is the formalist approach. Powell's notes focused almost exclusively on rules. They reflected a dogged attention to the results in particular cases and a pervasive indifference to the reasoning behind those results. There was no attention to theory and virtually no discussion of what a modern law student would call the "policy"

---

* Light's father had been manager of the Willard Hotel in Washington, D.C., and in an effort to drum up banquet business had founded the Alfalfa Club. Many years later, Powell became a member of the Alfalfa Club, chiefly known for sponsoring an annual no-women, no-reporters, boys-night-out extravaganza attended by virtually every politically powerful man in Washington.

behind the law. There was, in short, no sense of critical distance from the subject. Even judicial dissents were ignored. At least insofar as the course can be reconstructed from Powell's notes, the goal of instruction in constitutional law was detailed knowledge of the controlling decisions. That other judges (or scholars or students) disagreed with those decisions seems to have been thought irrelevant to the obsessive cataloguing of legal rules.

IN JUNE 1931 Powell graduated first in his law school class and left to spend an extra year at Harvard Law School. Louis Sr.'s disappointment at his son's choice of Washington and Lee doubled when he stayed there for law school. Having almost no formal education himself, the elder Powell wanted the best for his son, and that meant Harvard. As Powell recalled, the postgraduate year at Harvard was more than a suggestion. "He just told me I had to go."

Although Powell was technically a candidate for a master's degree in law, which he received in June 1932, his course work was essentially the same as any other Harvard law student's. As was then fairly common, an extra year at a prestigious national law school was used to enhance a degree from a more provincial institution.

Socially, the experience was drear. Powell lived comfortably in the third floor of a private home only a few yards from Langdell Hall, but he had few friends. The B.M.O.C. from Lexington, Virginia, was unknown and unnoticed in Cambridge, Massachusetts. A society of southerners held a dinner-dance in downtown Boston once a month, but otherwise his social life was "close to zero." He did become friendly with Frank Dewey, a third-year student from Des Moines who waited tables at a restaurant where Powell often ate. Dewey later married Powell's sister Eleanor.

Most of the time, Powell studied. At Washington and Lee, he had done exceptionally well on little effort. At Harvard, he knew that could not happen. The students were so much smarter, the professors so much more demanding, and the whole atmosphere so much more intellectual. Consequently, Powell recalled, "I worked my tail feathers off."

Powell enrolled in three classes and two seminars. The large classes were in public utilities law, corporate reorganizations, and equity; the seminars, in administrative law and jurisprudence. He also sat in on other classes, including that of the intimidating Bull Warren, who furnished the model for Professor Kingsfield in *The Paper Chase*.

Nothing so well illustrated the gap between Harvard and Washington and Lee—indeed, between Harvard and almost every other law school in the country—as the seminar in administrative law. Today, a course in that subject would examine the administrative agencies that dot the legal landscape. Before the New Deal, however, independent agencies were uncommon. In those days, administrative law was largely constitutional law, focusing chiefly on the division of government into the legislative, executive, and judicial branches and the allocation of powers among them.

Teaching this subject was Felix Frankfurter, leading critic of the prosecution of Sacco and Vanzetti, legal mastermind of the New Deal, and inspiration to generations of young lawyers. At the session of February 2, 1932, Frankfurter pronounced himself pleased by President Hoover's nomination of Benjamin Cardozo to the Supreme Court. Eight years later when Cardozo died, President Roosevelt chose Frankfurter to take his place.

If the students in Frankfurter's administrative law seminar of 1931–32 had been told of his appointment to the nation's highest court, they would not have been surprised. His brilliance was everywhere recognized, if not uniformly appreciated. Some of the students might also have been thought plausible long-term prospects for that honor. Harold M. Stephens, an older man who had returned to Harvard for a doctorate in law, would soon be appointed to the D.C. Circuit Court of Appeals and was later seriously considered for the Supreme Court seat that went to Frankfurter. Louis Jaffee would become a specialist in administrative law (in the modern sense) and have a brilliant career on the Harvard law faculty. Powell's closest friend in the seminar was Paul Freund. "He was so brilliant," Powell would later say, "that I always felt like a dummy in his presence." Freund, who also became a Harvard professor, was twice seriously considered by President Kennedy for appointment to the Supreme Court, but each time the nod went to someone else. Nonetheless Freund left a rich legacy. As Powell said in a tribute to his old friend, Freund affected "the way generations of students, scores of scholars, and at least one Supreme Court Justice think about the Constitution."

Amid all these stars, it is unlikely that anyone in the seminar would have identified as a candidate for the nation's highest court the quiet graduate student from Virginia. "Terrified" by Frankfurter's rapid-fire volubility, Powell sat at the far end of the table, taking voluminous notes and saying as little as possible. Certainly Frankfurter himself did not single Powell out, as he did so many other gifted young lawyers, for his special attention and flattery.

What Powell received from Frankfurter was not personal interest but an approach to law vastly different from anything he had learned at Washington and Lee. Frankfurter did not just read the cases; he fought with them. He was skeptical, probing, and opinionated. Powell's class notes reflect the change in direction. They are full of argument and counterargument, comment and criticism, and attention to dissents. And Frankfurter was an avowed enemy of the rule-bound formalism that dominated the classrooms of Washington and Lee. In reviewing a question of separation of powers (specifically, whether Congress could provide for jury trial in contempt proceedings), Frankfurter let fly. According to Powell's notes, Frankfurter insisted that "we get 'nowhere' by analytical dialectics—or by figures of speech—instead find out what *actually* has been the relation bet[ween] Congress and courts—what has Congress actually done?" Frankfurter was "very vehement" in opposing "any resort to *formalism* and analytical theories to settle problems of practical importance." "Logic," said Frankfurter (quoting Learned Hand), "shall not be allowed to stifle understanding."

Powell heard much the same thing from Frankfurter's intramural adversary, the longtime dean of the law school, Roscoe Pound. To Powell, Pound seemed an authoritarian personality with wretched eyesight and a gruff manner. He presided at the end of a long table with a button that he used to summon help from the library. (Powell was impressed when Pound rang and asked for a book, then sent it back because it was an English translation. He had wanted the original Latin.) Powell sat at the opposite end of the table with Dick Keeton, who bedeviled the old man by eating hard-boiled eggs in class. Pound could hear the eggshells crack on the table but could not see who or what was making the odd noise.

Pound's subject was jurisprudence. Defined by Webster's as the science of law, jurisprudence was part philosophy and part intellectual history, featuring (at least in Pound's version) elaborate classifications of various approaches to law. Powell learned of neo-Kantians, neo-Hegelians, neo-realists, neo-idealists, and many others. Pound himself favored "sociological jurisprudence." This approach focused on "the workings of law rather than its abstract contents" and stressed the social purposes to be served by law rather than its formal organization and concepts. Law, said Pound, was "a social institution which may be improved by intelligent human effort." Although Pound was increasingly at odds with Frankfurter (and many others of the younger generation), his aspiration for law was not inconsistent with Frankfurter's disdain for the formalist tradition of law as an autonomous body of objective rules.

*   *   *

IT IS TEMPTING, in light of Powell's later career, to try to find in his decisions as a Justice the influence of his training as a student; but much had changed. Forty years elapsed between Powell's last law school class and his first experience as a judge, and the great events of the Depression, the New Deal, World War II, and the civil rights movement had transformed constitutional law, as they had American society. The precedents that Powell studied so meticulously in 1928–32 had little bearing four decades later. Nor did Powell's studies fix in his mind any particular theoretical perspective on the law. He was by temperament unreceptive to the influence of abstractions; and his law training was, at least at the conscious level, overwhelmingly nonideological.

The most that can be confidently said is that Powell's education strengthened two attitudes already well established in his character. First, law training at Washington and Lee encouraged respect for authority. Never a rebel, Powell came to law school predisposed toward the status quo. Studying cases reinforced that inclination. The decisions of appellate courts were important because they were the decisions of appellate courts. They were authoritative pronouncements by official institutions. And those institutions professed to be guided—and in large part were guided—by their own prior pronouncements. The entire academic experience was an exercise in reasoning from authority, with a bias toward accepting the past as blueprint for the future. At this exercise, Powell excelled.

The second part of Powell's legal education, the year at Harvard, developed the idea that legal rules and decisions could be looked at practically, as they were applied, according to the effects they produced in society. He was not told of any overarching theory by which to evaluate outcomes. He was not taught any ideological imperative to which the law should be made to conform. Instead, he learned that the test of law was experience, that the only external standard for evaluating legal rules was to look at results, and that results should be judged pragmatically. The emphasis was not on concept and categorization but on observation and fact. Intellectual consistency took a backseat to common sense.

These two impulses often diverged. The formalist tradition was inward-looking and backward-leaning. Legal decisions were judged by consistency with other legal decisions. The results captured in legal doctrine were past results, and the reliance on precedent retarded change. The implications of this approach were, in the literal sense, conservative—tending to preserve from ruin or injury the accomplish-

ments of the past. By contrast, the concern for the social consequences of legal doctrine was outward-looking and potentially progressive. "Sociological jurisprudence" stressed flexibility and innovation to
avoid undesirable results.

Powell's judicial career played out the tension between respect for
authority and the need for change. He never lost his regard for precedent
or his reverence for the law as an institution. For Powell, constitutional
law was always something different from—and better than—ordinary
politics. It was more objective, more rational, and more high-minded. For
him, the decisions of the United States Supreme Court were intrinsically
deserving of respect. Psychologically disposed toward acceptance and
conformity, he embraced law chiefly as a tradition rather than as an
instrument of change.

But Powell did not think precedent was sacrosanct or that law could
be isolated from social concerns. On the contrary, he thought it necessary that law should change, that it should fit the facts and respond to
the lessons of experience. He was too practical to think otherwise.
Never much interested in ideological abstractions, Powell readily
accepted the idea that the ultimate test of law was how it worked.
Although he did not share Frankfurter's impulse for reform or his rest-
less curiosity, Powell did agree with the focus on results. If the law did
not work, if it failed of its objectives and imposed unintended costs,
then it should change.

Forty years later, the balance between conservatism and flexibility
was to be the essence of Powell's work as a judge. Both principles were
grounded in his personality and powerfully reinforced by his training in
law.

CHAPTER II

YOUNG
PROFESSIONAL

RETURN TO RICHMOND

Powell left Harvard at the depth of the Great Depression and immediately turned down one of the best job offers imaginable. John W. Davis was perhaps the nation's leading lawyer. He had been the Democratic nominee for President in 1924 and, having lost to Calvin Coolidge, returned to Davis, Polk & Wardwell, the Wall Street firm that still bears his name. At the time of his death, he had argued more cases before the Supreme Court than any lawyer in this century, including (perhaps unfortunately for his later reputation) the losing side in *Brown v. Board of Education.*

Davis was a graduate of Washington and Lee and a member of the board of trustees. Powell met him as president of the student body. Now Davis invited the young man to New York and offered him an associate's position at $150 a month, but Powell decided to return to Richmond. At first, this looked like a mistake. Powell assumed that he could get a job with McGuire, Riely, Eggleston & Bocock, the firm of his father's lawyer, Henry C. Riely, for whom Powell had clerked one summer. In the grip of the Depression, however, the McGuire firm was not hiring. Powell offered to work for nothing, but was told that the firm could not afford to provide an office. After being turned down by almost every firm in town, Powell landed a job at fifty dollars a month with Christian, Barton & Parker.

To make his way in the straightened economy of the 1930s, a young lawyer needed ability, drive, and luck. Powell had all three. The job with Christian, Barton & Parker turned out to be a blessing in disguise. At that time, the firm had the three named partners and, with Powell, three associates. Powell worked directly for Andrew Christian, an overriding, bellicose man who "was disliked by more people than liked him." Christian believed that, in order to be viewed as good fellows by their colleagues at the bar, most lawyers represented their clients with less than all-out vigor. Christian himself did not make that mistake. He was "very rough" on other lawyers, both in and out of court. Powell recalled that, "I was embarrassed with him on more than one occasion."

But Christian was never rough on Powell. He had lost a son to a football accident in 1909 and seems to have taken Powell under his wing. No doubt it was difficult to be hard on a young man who was so hard on himself. With Andrew Christian, Powell proved himself his father's son. He resolved to be the first to arrive every morning and the last to leave every night. "I needed some leeway in the morning, so I would get there half an hour before anyone else. I could tell when everybody else had left. If Andrew Christian, for whom I was working, would stay downtown and work after dinner, he would have wanted me to stay. In any event, I did."

Christian rewarded Powell with a rare opportunity. The most important litigation in Richmond at that time arose out of the receivership of the American Bank and Trust Company, which never reopened after the bank holiday of March 1933. Receivership is a state proceeding analogous to bankruptcy. The receivers try to maximize the assets of the insolvent institution and pay off the claims of creditors. For this purpose the receivers had engaged Andrew Christian as their lawyer.

One of his responsibilities was to hear claims by people who said the bank owed them money. After a few hearings, Christian turned this duty over to Powell, who in the course of two or three dozen such proceedings met virtually the entire Richmond bar. Far more controversial was a suit by the receivers of the failed bank against the former directors on the ground that they had negligently allowed mismanagement of its assets. The directors included some of Richmond's most prominent citizens, including several friends of Louis Sr. The litigation came to a head in a hearing on the defendants' motion to dismiss the suit. To Powell's astonishment, Christian asked him to make the argument.

In a courtroom crowded with senior lawyers, Powell spoke for more than an hour. He later thought he had made a "stupid" argument—by relying too much on cases and not enough on reasons—but at least three persons were favorably impressed. One was Christian, who sat at a table by Powell's side and never said a word. Another was the judge, who ruled in favor of the receivers. The third was T. Justin Moore, general counsel of the Virginia Electric and Power Company, named partner in Richmond's largest law firm, and one of three court-appointed receivers for the American Bank and Trust Company.

T. Justin Moore was a hard-driving, red-haired man of forty-two, so aggressive that some thought him downright mean. As a young man, he had taken a part-time job with the power company and, by dint of an extraordinary capacity for work and unequaled knowledge of the company's affairs, rose to the post of general counsel. Even in the midst of the Depression, Moore could attract clients. One associate compared it to "the aroma of a bitch in heat." When Moore walked into the room, every businessman present wanted him for his lawyer. Eventually a law firm with a long connection to the power company (and the desire to keep it) persuaded Moore to come in as a named partner. Accordingly, on April 1, 1932, the firm became Hunton, Williams, Anderson, Gay & Moore.

Powell had been turned down by Hunton, Williams immediately after law school, but Moore now offered him an associate's position. Powell consulted Christian, who advised him as he might have advised his own son. Even though Powell had practiced law for only two years, Christian offered to make him a partner and to add his name to the firm's title. Yet despite this generous invitation, Christian urged Powell to take the other job. Hunton, Williams, said Christian, was "the best law firm between Washington and Houston." With bigger clients and the most sophisticated business practice of any Virginia firm, Hunton, Williams would provide a more secure foundation for the young lawyer's ambitions. Perhaps Christian sensed that Powell lacked the tooth-and-nail aggressiveness to be a great litigator, that his abilities and instincts inclined more toward corporate law. In any event, Christian advised that Powell would have "a better future" at Hunton, Williams—provided, of course, that he could put up with the large-firm bureaucracy.

Powell took Christian's advice. On January 1, 1935, he braved the bureaucracy and became an associate of Hunton, Williams, Anderson, Gay & Moore. He was their fourteenth lawyer.

THE HUNTON OF HUNTON, Williams was Eppa Hunton, Jr., a founding partner of the firm who died in 1932. His son, Eppa IV (because both Eppa Jr.'s father and his grandfather carried the name), had just been admitted to the partnership. The recognized leader of the firm and one of two surviving founders was Edmund Randolph Williams.

Randolph Williams entered law practice with the inestimable

advantage of already having clients. His father owned John L. Williams & Sons, Richmond's leading investment banking firm, and one of his brothers, John Skelton Williams, became a prominent financier, organizer of the Seaboard Air Line railroad, and Comptroller of the Currency under Woodrow Wilson. By the time Powell came to the firm, most of the lawyering associated with these connections had been turned over to someone else. At age sixty-one, Williams devoted his time to charity.

Inside the firm, Williams was a father figure, revered by the younger lawyers for his modesty, humanity, and good sense. In the words of Anne Freeman, the firm's historian, Williams had a "special gift for identifying and then nourishing the finest qualities in each man's personality." Powell described him as a "counsellor," a man who "sought solutions rather than conflict," the "sort of person you'd like to go to, just as you would like to have a family physician in whom you had total confidence." Williams was a peacemaker. In a firm overfull of combative egos, he got along with everyone. Indeed, it was said that there were only two people in the world whom Randolph Williams disliked, and since neither Franklin Roosevelt nor Harold Ickes was in the firm, his feelings for them did not impair his effectiveness as head of the Hunton, Williams family.

Of all the egos that Williams had to tame, the most towering belonged to his fellow founding partner, Henry W. Anderson. By 1935 Anderson had become a legendary figure. Like some god from Greek mythology, Anderson had flaws and foibles so extravagant that he would have seemed ludicrous were it not for an equally outsized talent and reputation. As it was, he constantly hovered on the edge of self-parody.

Henry Watkins Anderson was born on a farm in Dinwiddie County, Virginia, in 1870. Like Louis Powell, Sr., he could not afford college and so went to a business school, where he learned typing and shorthand. For years he supported himself as a clerk and managed to get a law degree while working as the secretary to the president of Washington and Lee. He began practice with Beverley Munford, a Richmond lawyer who represented railroads. When Munford joined in founding Munford, Hunton, Williams & Anderson, he took Anderson along as a junior partner; and a few years later when Munford withdrew from the firm as a result of tuberculosis (his name was later dropped), Anderson took over his clients.

In 1904 Anderson began an association with Frank J. Gould, son of railroad magnate Jay Gould, and (with Frank's sister Helen) financial backer of electric street railways and the emerging electric power

industry in Viriginia. Anderson's connection to the Goulds "would catapult [him] into a world of high finance, corporate management, and
lucrative law suits" involving electric utilities in Virginia and railroads
across the nation. The beginning was the five-year receivership of the
Virginia Passenger and Power Company, which eventually emerged as
the state's largest utility, controlled by the Goulds. In 1908 Gould
hired Anderson to represent him in the first of a string of railroad reorganizations, an arcane and complicated field of practice in which
Anderson soon won a national reputation. He became, in Powell's
view, "the leading railroad reorganization lawyer in the United States."

In the midst of this ascent, Anderson left Richmond on a Red Cross
mission to Rumania. That unfortunate country entered World War I
in 1916 on the side of Britain and France and within three months was
largely overrun by the Germans. Two hundred thousand refugees died
in the unoccupied remnant. As head of the relief mission, Anderson
was awarded the rank of lieutenant colonel, which accounted for his
style from that day forward as Colonel Henry Anderson. (When Powell
returned from active service in World War II with the rank of full
colonel but did not adopt the title, another partner commented that,
"Real colonels don't.")

During his year in Rumania, Anderson fell in love with Queen
Marie, a woman as self-dramatizing and grandiose as her American
admirer. Disappointed in her marriage, Marie "placed herself in staged
medieval settings and instituted a kind of court of love and cult of
chivalry. She surrounded herself with knights-errant who would place
her on a pedestal, worship her from afar, and do great deeds in her
name."

Anderson worshipped Marie from near and far, and when he
returned to Richmond aglitter with decorations from the Balkan countries (he was reportedly offered the crown of Albania), his continuing
infatuation with Marie alienated the fiancée he had left at home. It
was Anderson's poor luck that the affronted woman was future
Pulitzer Prize–winning novelist Ellen Glasgow, who left behind an
indelible portrait of the man she had once loved. "[L]ong before I
knew him," Glasgow wrote, "he had reached the top of his ladder and
the ground below was liberally strewn—or so malice remarked—with
the rungs he had kicked aside. If there is any social top in Richmond,
he was standing upon it. People might laugh at him. . . . They might
ridicule his English accent. . . . They might ridicule his slightly
pompous manner and his too punctilious way of living. They might
ridicule his English clothes, his valet, his footmen in plum-colored liv-

ery; but it was his accurate boast that only death kept them away from his dinners."

Popular reaction to this personality was predictably mixed. Crusty old Archibald Robertson, who came to the firm with Justin Moore in the early 1930s, was tolerant of Anderson's extravagance: "If you *like* to put on dog, and got the *money* to put on dog, and know *how* to put on dog, I think you ought to be able to put on dog without being ridiculed." Others thought Anderson a "pluperfect snob"—and worse. Certainly he was a man of vaunting arrogance. When young George Gibson interviewed at the firm, he was ushered into the august presence and was asked whether he could "look up law." "I think so," said Gibson; "I can certainly try." "Well, that is a good thing," Anderson responded, "for to put *me* to that task would be like putting a thoroughbred to the plow."

Anderson's politics were as unusual as his personality. He was a Republican in Virginia at a time when such creatures were rarely found east of the Blue Ridge Mountains. He was a friend and golfing partner of William Howard Taft and aspired to the United States Supreme Court. In 1921 Anderson became the Republican nominee for governor. He called for better roads and schools, attacked the one-party system, and, in an era when Virginia Democrats still ran against Reconstruction, tried to speak sense on the issue of race. "[I]t must be recognized by any fair-minded person," Anderson argued, that whites "are morally charged with . . . the duty to see that there is but one standard of justice in Virginia which shall be applied to rich and poor, white and colored, without discrimination. No free government can be founded on two standards of justice."

This position did not prevail. The handicap of being a Republican was in any event insurmountable—even Anderson's mother could not bring herself to vote for one—but his decidedly undemocratic campaign did not help. Anderson would arrive for a campaign appearance in a long touring car, wait for his English chauffeur to open the rear door, deliver an intelligent and well-phrased speech, and then reenter his car and leave for the next town. Glasgow said of him (as Bagehot had said of Gibbon), "he was the sort of person a populace kills."

Although George Gibson was Anderson's principal lieutenant, Powell did one case with him—the disastrous (for the railroad, not the law firm) reorganization of the New York, New Haven & Hartford Railroad. At the time, Anderson was a receiver of the Seaboard Air Line and commuted to New York in a private railroad car. He and Powell were met at Penn Station by a black limousine and taken to the

Ritz-Carlton at 46th and Madison, where Anderson would go directly to his suite. He never bothered to check in or pay a bill. After their first meal, Powell asked whether Anderson had forgotten to pay. "No," said Anderson, "I don't sign anything here." What about the tip, Powell queried. "I don't tip anyone either." Only later did Powell learn that the great man's custom was to send at Christmas a freight car of hams and produce to be divided among the hotel employees.

When Powell prepared to bill the client for the firm's services, he discovered that Colonel Anderson did not keep records of his time. "I'm not a plumber," Anderson announced, "or a bricklayer. I don't charge by the hour." He simply assigned a figure to his services, which were rarely undervalued. "I can be of more help to a railroad client thinking about its problems while I shave in the morning," he told Powell, "than most of you could be in a month." Unfortunately, it fell to Powell to give this explanation to the Interstate Commerce Commission when the firm applied for its fee, but the commissioners knew Colonel Anderson and accepted his valuation.

POWELL WENT TO HUNTON, Williams expecting to work for Justin Moore, but before he had walked in the door his time was preempted by Thomas Benjamin Gay. When Moore joined the firm as a named partner in 1932, Gay had been there nearly twenty-four years. He came as an unpaid associate in 1908, worked his way onto the payroll, and in 1916 became the first addition to the original partnership. Eleven years later his name was added to the firm's title.

Over time the rivalry between Gay and Moore settled into an accommodation. Moore was the business-getter. He surpassed Henry Anderson in attracting clients and became the dominant partner of his generation. Gay remained the firm's chief administrator. He looked after the management side of the firm, including the hiring of new lawyers.

The carving out of a separate sphere for each man would eventually lessen the friction between them, but in 1935 the contest was still raw. When Powell arrived, Gay pulled rank. As Moore had come to the firm with two associates, Gay said Moore was "hogging the staff" and insisted that the new associate be assigned to him. And so it happened that Powell left Andrew Christian, who treated him as a son, to work for a man who found generosity of any sort an unaccustomed impulse.

The rivalry between Gay and Moore was sharpened by personality. Moore was an aggressive, earthy man who "would ride roughshod over people without batting an eye," but who inspired from his family and friends an abiding affection. Gay was a fastidious little "bantam roost-er" of a man, dapper in dress, formal in manner, and perfectionist in approach. It was impossible not to admire what Gay had accomplished in his life, but the man himself was not easy to like.

Orphaned at age fourteen, Gay went to work as a runner at John L. Williams & Sons and was taken under the wing of the Williams fami-ly. Eventually he made his way through the law courses at the University of Virginia (supporting himself by selling typed copies of his class notes for ten cents a class) and took a job with Randolph Williams's law firm. Gay made himself indispensable to the senior partners and in time became a surprisingly effective trial lawyer. He embarrassed his colleagues by wavering back and forth between a broad "a" and the flatter accent of his youth, but he was intimidating to judges and impressive to juries. Confident, direct, and forceful, Gay would stand right in front of the jurors, look them straight in the eye, and challenge them to disagree. There was nothing folksy or familiar in his approach, only energy, intensity, and determination.

Inside the firm, Gay had much the same style. He was a man who could send a messenger to sharpen a box of pencils, make him do it again because the pencils were not sharp enough, then methodically break every point because they were now too sharp. Nor was he forgiv-ing of errors by a young lawyer. Powell once drafted an opinion letter for Gay's signature. The letter went to a Wall Street law firm, which returned it with a courteous note saying, "in light of this recent deci-sion by the Virginia Supreme Court"—which Powell had missed— "you may wish to reconsider your opinion." Gay never let Powell forget the mistake. (Powell may have had this incident in mind forty years later when his fellow Justices relied on misinformation given Powell by a law clerk. When the clerk discovered the error, Powell wrote the Justices taking the blame for the mistake in his research—and never mentioned the matter again.)

The same clerk was present in 1974, when Gay, now nearly ninety years old, visited his former associate at the Supreme Court. Finding Powell closeted with Justice Stewart, Gay chatted amiably with the clerk for a few minutes until Powell emerged to greet him. "Hello, Lewis," he said. And Powell responded, "Hello, Mr. Gay." Why, the clerk later asked, did Powell call his longtime partner Mr. Gay? "Because," Powell answered, "he has never invited me to call him any-thing else."

Personalities aside, working for Gay was a good introduction to law practice. Gay had a disciplined mind and high standards. He was a trial lawyer and therefore a generalist, so Powell did not get bogged down in some narrow specialty. He worked on a wide variety of matters, including accident claims against the firm's railroad clients and business disputes of all sorts.

Under Gay's leadership, Powell also filed the first registration statement from Virginia under the Securities Act of 1933. When a local insurance company brought Gay a relatively small issue of preferred stock, he turned the matter over to Powell. Registration of such an offering required elaborate disclosure to the Securities Exchange Commission of the operations and finances of the issuing company. Powell filed the necessary documents, only to discover that the SEC staff scheduled a hearing to investigate an alleged misstatement on the balance sheet. The problem was that the company's office building was carried at its appraised value rather than at the lower figure of its original cost. After two days of inconclusive hearings on what the building was really worth and whether the representation had been honestly made, Powell asked to see the head of the registration division, Baldwin Bain. The old-boy network now took over. When Powell entered the office, Bain rose, gave him a fraternity handshake, and announced, "Lewis, I am a Phi Kappa Sigma from Washington and Lee. What in hell do you want?" Bain diagnosed the problem as "the young lawyers up here [who] like to do everything they can to hold protracted hearings." He ordered the registration approved, and Powell gained a hometown reputation as Virginia's leading securities lawyer.

He also became known locally as co-counsel in an annexation proceeding. In Virginia, unlike most states, cities and counties are mutually exclusive. For a city to expand into an adjacent county requires a judicial annexation proceeding, with compensation to the county for the land and capital improvements lost to it. In 1939, Richmond filed suit to annex portions of Henrico and Chesterfield counties, including the Forest Hill area where Powell had grown up. Henrico hired Gay to contest the annexation. He, Powell, and a third lawyer named Irvin Craig found themselves in high-stakes litigation lasting several months. The effort was so intense that it broke Craig's health, but Powell seems to have flourished. The *Times-Dispatch* reporter covering the dispute later remembered Powell as "a very nice, very pleasant, soft-voiced, self-effacing young lawyer who was helping Gay and who knew the answer to just about every question I could think of." As to the outcome, "we lost it," said Powell, "as we should have."

The annexation suit aside, most of Powell's cases went quickly. Trials rarely lasted longer than a few days, and even if the outcome was appealed, the case would ordinarily be resolved within a year to eighteen months. Powell was often in court and often on his own. In this respect, his early experience differed from that of today's young lawyer. The focus of modern litigation has shifted from the trial itself to the pretrial exchange of information known as discovery, a process that often drags on for months or years. A junior associate in the litigation section of a large firm may rarely see the inside of a courtroom. For Powell, by contrast, it quickly became familiar territory. Although he later shifted from trial work to corporate practice, he always had a litigator's background. In truth, Powell was temperamentally more suited to consultation than to controversy—he said he gave up jury trials because they kept him awake at night—but unlike many office lawyers he was never intimidated by the prospect of litigation and indeed occasionally returned to it when his regular clients had important trials. Trial experience and the confidence that went with it were valuable legacies of the early years with Gay.

On January 1, 1938, Powell was admitted to the partnership. Most new partners had to wait seven years or longer, but Powell made partner after only three years at the firm. Only the dazzlingly brilliant George Gibson had been promoted as quickly. Powell became the firm's tenth partner.

Powell now had job security and increased income, but the change in status did not free him from Gay. Powell was still Gay's subordinate, working on cases for Gay's clients, and was still far away from enjoying either the reputation or the independence that he craved.

RELATIONSHIPS

On returning from Harvard in 1932, Powell moved back into his old bedroom in the house on Forest Hill Avenue. "It would never have occurred to me to leave home until I got married," he said later. Lack of money reinforced that expectation, as even in the Depression fifty dollars a month did not go far. Eleanor had graduated from Randolph Macon and was also living at home. It was her job to drive Powell to and from work, and given his determination to be the first to arrive and the last to leave, his hours were irregular. When he called to say he was ready to go, Eleanor would drive downtown, hoping to find him on the street but invariably having to wait. "It's just outrageous," she complained. "Why aren't you ready when I get here?" "Well," Powell replied, "someone has to wait, and I just want to make sure it's not me."

Shortly after returning to Richmond, Powell renewed a friendship with a man he had known as a boy. J. Harvie Wilkinson, Jr., was a year ahead of Powell at McGuire's School, where he too had won the Jack Gordon medal. Wilkinson went from McGuire's to the University of Virginia and then to New York for two years before returning to Richmond to a job at the State-Planters Bank. He was a dapper fellow, of slightly less than average height, with an ebullient personality and a keen sense of humor. Despite differences in personal style, he and Powell had much in common. Both were intelligent, purposive, and public-spirited. Both had turned down careers in New York to return to Richmond, and both had strong feelings for their city and state and for their institutions of higher learning. Though both were intensely ambitious, their ambitions ran less to personal fortune than to influence and standing in the community.

Powell and Wilkinson became best friends. The intimacy between them was unequaled outside family, and it became more distinctive as the years went by. Half a century later, Harvie Wilkinson would be the only person alive who could address the Supreme Court Justice as "Lord High Poo-bah" and be received in good spirit.

In the 1930s, however, Powell and Wilkinson were not merely friends. They were also allies and co-conspirators in a plan to take over Richmond. Wilkinson would become president of State-Planters and name Powell as the general counsel. To this alliance of bank and law firm, they would need to add a link to government. Neither of them could foresee running for office; Powell had no taste for it, and Wilkinson's position "almost forbade it, since bankers were not the most popular people." So they aimed at unofficial influence. In 1940, Powell organized Democrats for Willkie, the first of many such groups supporting national Republican candidates. On the state level, both Powell and Wilkinson supported the political organization of Virginia's junior Senator, Harry Flood Byrd.

And were all these future developments really thought out so far in advance? Yes, said Wilkinson, "we planned and planned, in countless areas of life, business and social." They met at the Occidental Restaurant, where lunch, soup to nuts, was twenty-five cents. As Wilkinson later recalled, "we were both driving for the top and to each other we never pretended anything else, [though] I hope we kept it sufficiently under cover so as not to be obnoxious."

The most important collaborations between Powell and Wilkinson came after World War II, when both men were more prominent, but already in the 1930s, their scheme was underway. Wilkinson arranged for Powell to represent State-Planters in the bankruptcy of the Hartsfield Print & Die Company in Spartanburg, South Carolina. Thinking that he needed the prestige of an older lawyer, Powell associated Randolph Williams, and the three of them went down to Spartanburg for the opening proceeding. Powell and Wilkinson shared a hotel room, and when Powell awoke early the next morning, he slipped on his topcoat and began to review some papers while Harvie slept. Williams came in from the next room and announced, "Lewis, it is ever thus. The lawyer works from dawn to dusk, while the client lies in bed asleeping."

In the Hartsfield Print & Die case, Powell learned to distrust experts. He had hired an engineering firm in Atlanta to make an appraisal of the value of certain property. The engineers promised to arrive early on the morning of the hearing, and by eleven o'clock, when they finally showed up, Powell was frantic. Out in the corridor during recess, he asked for their appraisal. "Well," said the engineers, "we have three. Would you like our high estimate, our low estimate, or our medium estimate?" Powell was shocked. "This is a court of law," he told the experts. "Which estimate can you swear to?" "Oh well," they replied, "it's just a matter of judgment. We could swear to any of the three."

The same case produced the only known instance when Powell completely lost his self-control. Perhaps owing to the number of lawyers or some oddity of architecture, the counsel tables in the Spartanburg courtroom were arranged two deep. One day Powell was speaking from behind the rear table when a lawyer seated in front of him turned around and called him a "goddamned liar." Powell climbed across the table and took a swing at the man, for which he was promptly held in contempt of court. Fortunately, the provocation had been overheard by an influential local lawyer who told the judge what was said and persuaded him to withdraw the contempt citation. "Ever since then," Powell later recalled, "I've been quiet in courtrooms. I've been no trouble."

At about the same time, Wilkinson and Powell took the first steps in their plan to make Powell the bank's general counsel. Wilkinson persuaded his boss, Harry Augustine, that it was unwise for the bank and its trust department to rely exclusively on the same lawyers. Acting as the trustee or executor of private clients, the trust department would sometimes deal on their behalf with the bank of which it was a part. In such cases, there was a potential conflict of interest. Wilkinson argued that someone on the bank's board of directors should come from a different law firm, so as to provide an independent perspective on such problems. At age thirty-three, Powell was too young for such responsibility; so in 1940, the bank elected Thomas Benjamin Gay to the board of directors. Five years later he became general counsel. As the two young plotters expected, when Gay retired, he relinquished both his seat and his client to Powell.

POWELL AND WILKINSON were also active socially. In 1932 they joined the Lonely Hearts, fourteen young men and women of intellectual pretension and matrimonial intention, who met once a month for "serious discussion" of a topic that one of them would prepare. Powell's first talk was on the Supreme Court. The Lonely Hearts scandalized Richmond when they all took the same Pullman to New York and stayed on the same floor of the St. Regis Hotel. It was all "on the up- and-up," said Powell, but there was enough partying that a house detective had to dissuade Harvie Wilkinson and two girls from singing in the halls. However informative such occasions may have been, they failed in their essential purpose, as there was no match made between members of the Lonely Hearts.

By this time Powell had fallen out of touch with Eleanor Wilson, who had gone to New York to launch her acting career. He came close to an offer of marriage to Henry Riely's daughter Emma, but the moment passed. (Emma's brother John had a spectacular record at Harvard Law School but was excluded from his father's firm by a strict rule against hiring offspring. He therefore went to Hunton, Williams, where he became a dominant figure in the firm after Powell's departure.)

In 1934, Powell had his first date with Josephine Pierce Rucker. Actually, it was their second first date. A few years earlier, when Powell was home on vacation from Washington and Lee, he was persuaded by his mother to call Jo Rucker, then still at the Collegiate girls' school in Richmond. Her father, M. Pierce Rucker, had been Mrs. Powell's physician ever since he had come out to Forest Hill on that snowy evening in 1914 to deliver the twins. Mrs. Powell idolized Dr. Rucker and hoped for a match between her son and his daughter, but the young people found themselves "bored to death" and did not soon repeat the experience.

After returning from Harvard, Powell heard at a cocktail party that Jo Rucker had set the Sweet Briar school record by broad-jumping twenty-two feet—information that left him rightly incredulous. A few days later he saw her picture in the newspaper. With the kind of figure that used to be called statuesque, Jo had taken a temporary job as a model at Miller & Rhoads, a local department store. When Powell saw the photograph, he decided to try again. Fortunately he came well advertised. Jo had attended Sweet Briar with his first cousin, Frances Powell, who "really thought he hung the moon." So when Powell called to ask about her broad jump, Jo "really thought I had it made."

The young woman Powell met for the second time in 1934 was very beautiful. (More than a decade later she was still listed first on a newspaper's roster of Richmond's ten best-looking women.) She moved with the grace and assurance of a natural athlete. At Sweet Briar, she excelled not only in the broad jump and the high jump—her record was in the latter event and it was four feet, eleven and three-quarter inches—but also in swimming, diving, basketball, and field hockey. She was quick to laugh, with a warm smile and a buoyant personality. If there was anything not to like about Josephine Rucker, Powell did not find it.

This time the date went well. Even so, Powell was not the sort to rush into things, and it not until late 1935 that he asked her to marry him. Jo agreed, and they were married in a huge ceremony (all of his fellow Lonely Hearts were groomsmen) at St. Mary's Methodist Church on May 2, 1936. She was twenty-five; he was twenty-eight.

The couple took a first-floor apartment at 1210 Park Street, which, for Jo, meant a decline in circumstances. She had spent most of her childhood in a large stone-fronted house at 2020 Monument Avenue, Richmond's most prestigious residential address. Monument Avenue was (and is) a 140-foot-wide thoroughfare with a large grassy median. It runs east and west from a huge equestrian statue inscribed with the word LEE. Other intersections have statues of J. E. B. Stuart (who, like Lee, faces south because he returned from battle) and Stonewall Jackson (who faces north because he did not) and Jefferson Davis (who faces east, perhaps because he did not go). When Jo grew older, her father opened a maternity hospital on Stuart Circle, and the family moved to that address. The Ruckers did not aspire to high society, but they were prominent, respected, and moderately well-to-do.

Jo now had to manage the household, including maintenance and small repairs, which her unmechanical husband never attempted. Owing to the ravages of the Depression, the $1,000 that Louis Sr. had promised his son for not using alcohol had not been paid. Now he gave them a wedding present of a new Oldsmobile. The car stayed at home with Jo, while Powell commuted on foot or by streetcar to the Hunton, Williams offices in the Electric Building at Seventh and Franklin streets.

At the time of his marriage, Powell earned $300 a month from law practice and supplemented his income by teaching economics in the evenings at the University of Richmond. Jo managed the family finances and gave her husband a daily allowance for the streetcar, lunch, and incidental expenses. When the Occidental raised the price of its complete lunch from twenty-five to thirty-five cents, Harvie Wilkinson wrote Jo asking that the stipend be increased to a dollar a day. By that time, the Powells could afford that sum, but money was still relatively tight. But then so was Jo. Long after they had become wealthy, she still had a deserved reputation for thrift.

In 1938 the Powell's moved to a larger apartment at 311 West Franklin; and on July 1 of that year, Jo gave birth to the couple's first child, whom they named for Jo's mother. Little Josephine McRae Powell was variously called Jo-Jo, Sunny, and (by her father) Jody. Two years later on Powell's birthday, Ann Pendleton Powell was born. She was called Penny.

WHEN POWELL WAS considering marriage to Jo, George Gibson advised against the match on the ground that "she is not intellectual enough for you." Later Gibson thought "it turned out to be the best marriage he had ever seen."

In 1936 Josephine Powell was beautiful, vivacious, and obviously in love. Half a century later, she was still all three. She embraced Powell's ambitions, tolerated his long hours, and deferred to his wishes. He was always the center of her life. The primacy that he had learned from his mother to think was his by right, he also assumed with Jo, and she willingly put his interests first. On all important questions, Powell set family policy. Many years later, their children would laugh only half facetiously at the idea of Jo contradicting her husband: "Did she have a different point of view from him? Are you kidding?" She was supportive in every way.

She was also—and to a degree that Powell did not fully appreciate—immensely valuable. In later years Powell's habitual reserve would come to seem severe and to younger lawyers sometimes intimidating. Her warmth and charm smoothed the way. As the wife of one of his partners wrote, obviously from personal experience, "Jo Powell has the knack of making everybody, from the youngest associate's wife to the most senior executive or judge, feel completely at ease, thereby compensating on occasions for a certain austerity in her husband."

With his legendary devotion to work, Powell placed enormous demands on himself and on his wife. To an outside observer, their relationship may have seemed one-sided. Years later a younger family member commented that "she does most of the giving and he does most of the taking." But however old-fashioned the Powells' relationship may seem to a different generation, it was completely successful. They lived happily ever after.

CHAPTER III

WARTIME

IN UNIFORM

On the afternoon of December 7, 1941, Lewis and Josephine Powell returned to the house at Bear Island from a long walk in the winter sunshine. Waiting for them was the news of Pearl Harbor. Powell said later that he had long been impatient for the United States to come to England's aid, but while that may have been his view by the winter of 1941, it was not his position the year before. In August 1940, Powell helped the Junior Bar Conference draft a public information campaign supporting defense preparedness, but a private letter revealed his doubts about active belligerence. "I am now deeply concerned," Powell wrote the chairman of the Junior Bar Conference, "with the course of events in this country which I think are leading us almost inevitably into the war. The sale of the fifty destroyers [to the British] yesterday is only the latest bit of evidence that this Administration is intertwining the interests of the United States with those of Britain so inextricably that we will soon find ourselves an active belligerent." "If we are drawn into the war now," Powell continued, "and gradually expend the few resources which we have in a gamble on a British victory, I feel that we then would be in a desperate situation."

By 1941 Powell himself was chairman of the Junior Bar Conference, and the public information campaign was up and running. Its purpose was to "inculcate a deeper understanding of, and devotion to, the democratic way of life" and to stress "the imperative necessity for immediate action" to protect it. The program provided speeches, radio scripts, and research on such topics as the history of the Constitution, labor and the national defense, the fifth column in America (advising against suspicion of "our neighbors of German and Italian stock"), and civil rights in the German totalitarian state (virtually none) and in German-occupied Belgium and France (even fewer). It was clear where the lawyers' sympathies lay.

But now that Pearl Harbor had decided the question of the nation's involvement, what would Powell do personally? Randolph Williams, Ben Gay, and Justin Moore said he would be crazy to go. "You might get killed and leave a wife and two children with no way to support themselves," he was told. Only Colonel Anderson said what Powell wanted to hear. "Lewis," Anderson said, "this war will in all probability be the greatest event in the history of the United States during your lifetime. If you sit it out in Richmond, Virginia, practicing law, you'll regret it." Powell agreed. As he wrote Jo, "I could never have looked my children in the face if I had ducked this responsibility."

Thinking it the place for educated gentlemen, Powell chose the Navy, only to find that he could not pass the eye test. After several weeks of trying to "educate" his eyes by memorizing eye charts, Powell wrote the Undersecretary of the Navy, whom he had met at dinner, but received in return "the letter I deserved," saying "there was nothing he could do about me—or my eyes."

Powell eventually gave up on the Navy and volunteered for the Army Air Forces, which, for nonfliers, allowed poorer vision. He went to Washington, where he was told that his age and education justified the rank of captain and that he would be given thirty-days notice before being ordered to active duty. Powell returned to Hunton, Williams to wait for that warning, but a telegram of April 29 ordered *First Lieutenant* Powell to proceed on *May 1* to Miami Beach, Florida, and to report not later than the next day to officer's training school. Powell dragooned a secretary and an associate and worked all night getting his files ready to hand over to other lawyers. On May 1 he boarded a train for Miami Beach, arrived there on the morning of May 2, was bawled out for being late and told to report immediately for drill. He took off his suit coat and marched about in shirtsleeves and lawyer's shoes, feeling like an idiot. Only after blistering his feet did he have a chance to buy a uniform—blouse, trousers, shirt, undershirt and wings from Saks Fifth Avenue for $65.90.

After six weeks of physical training and military indoctrination in the unlikely environs of Miami Beach, Powell went to the Air Force Intelligence School at Harrisburg, Pennsylvania, for a course in combat intelligence. Each day began with exercise, followed by map reading, combat operations, briefing, and interrogation. The demanding schedule exactly suited Powell. He was one of ten honor graduates and repeated his usual explanation for success: "I worked hard, and some others didn't."

Before leaving Harrisburg, Powell spoke to the authorities about the possibility of remaining there on the faculty. Though he felt he had to enlist, he had no wish to be a hero, and Jo was very anxious that he remain in the country. He tried, but when the request was denied, he concluded that "probably it is best that I be with a combat unit."

DESPITE HIS TRAINING HONORS, Powell's first operational assignment was a disappointment. He asked for a unit with America's top-of-the-line heavy bomber, the four-engine B-17. Instead, he was sent to the 319th Bombardment Group, training in Louisiana with the two-engine B-26. The B-26 was designed for low-level bombing and high-speed getaway. It was called the "Marauder," but airmen gave it other names—the "flying coffin" or (in Powell's sanitized version) the "flying prostitute." When fully loaded, the plane was not fast enough to escape the murderous antiaircraft fire that could be brought to bear at low altitudes. Inside quarters were cramped and uncomfortable. Powell flew his first simulated mission with pilot Bill Dover, who was killed a few days later when two planes had a "very unattractive" collision in midair.

The airmen needed time for training, but time was one thing they did not have. In late August, only two months after the unit was organized, the 319th was ordered to Europe. Three of the group's four squadrons ferried their planes across the North Atlantic, flying in stages from Maine to Labrador to Greenland to Iceland to Scotland. It was not a good trip. Hampered by inexperience and Arctic storms and by the Army's habit of reporting bad weather *after* it arrived, the 319th straggled across, leaving disabled planes and equipment strewn along the route. (The lesson learned, the fourth squadron later made its way safely across the South Atlantic.)

Powell and the advance ground echelon reached Britain by a different route. They crowded onto a troop train in Baton Rouge and spent two days and nights en route to Fort Dix. They did not know their ultimate destination but were forbidden to say even that they were going to New Jersey. The extravagant secrecy moved Powell to a rare breach of the rules. He called Jo from Baton Rouge and told her cryptically to go see her friends Dr. and Mrs. Kennedy, adding: "I don't mean stay with them, but just stay in the biggest hotel where they are." This strange request translated as a direction that Jo go to the Bellevue-Stratford in Philadelphia, which she did. Powell's mother and little Jo soon joined her there, and the reconstituted family had several evenings together in nearby Trenton, New Jersey, just outside the base.

On September 3, Powell bade them good-bye: "I shall never forget my depression that night," he confided to his wartime diary. "Leaving

Mother and Jo was difficult enough, but what really tore the roots of my heart was leaving baby Jo—this because she was old enough to *wonder* why I was going but too young to *understand* why, and also because I hated to miss any part of her beautiful 'little girlhood.'"

He also wrote Jo:

My glasses are so cloudy with suppressed tears that I can scarcely see to write—and if I could see there are no words which express my love and admiration for you, and my appreciation for all that you have been to me.

Don't be too sad about my little trip—I will be back and we will have a home of our own and live happily ever after.

The next night fifteen hundred men of the 319th Bombardment Group marched to the railhead, from which they were taken by train to Jersey City and from there by ferry to the New York side of the Hudson River, where, at about five o'clock on the morning of September 5, they boarded the *Queen Mary*. Later that day, Jo visited her sister-in-law Eleanor in New York, watched the big ship slip out of the harbor, and wondered if her husband were on board.

Because his superiors went with the planes, First Lieutenant Powell became the senior officer in the detachment, but this small dignity brought him no comfort. Powell's men shared the *Queen Mary* with seventeen thousand men of the First Infantry Division, most of whom had already spent two or three days on board. Powell was assigned to a stateroom so crowded that he thought there had been some mistake. He asked for another room, only to be told that he was merely the last of sixteen persons crammed into a double berth.* The bunks were stacked four deep. Powell's top berth was almost impossible to get into, and once there, he could not bend his knees. Even so, he lived in luxury compared to the enlisted personnel, who rotated sleeping on deck and below, with two meals a day, no bath or change of clothes, and scarcely room to turn around.

This floating mass of manpower would have been a spectacular kill for German U-boats, yet the *Queen Mary* sailed without convoy or escort. As the great ship could easily outrun submarines, she was safe from anything except ambush. Word of U-boat packs on the route ahead prompted evasive action. Several times the ship changed course

---

* After the war, the Powells crossed on the *Queen Mary* in an identical stateroom, which accommodated two persons in twin beds.

and once made a huge turn north of Iceland to avoid a U-boat trap. For the last two days, there were violent shifts in direction every few minutes, a sensible precaution that proved hard on queasy stomachs. Finally, on September 11—a day late due to the evasive maneuvers— the ship entered the Irish Sea from the north and picked up British air and naval escort to the Firth of Clyde. From there, Powell and his men went by train to a rudimentary airfield at Shipdham, England, seventeen miles due west of the city of Norwich.

POWELL'S ARMY CAREER seemed to move in six-week segments. The stints in Miami Beach and Harrisburg passed easily enough, but during the six weeks in England, he was frustrated, anxious, and cold. Frustration came with the territory. The 319th arrived in England without planes or flight crews, and the advance echelon left before most of the planes caught up. They could not train, although experience was desperately needed, nor was it clear exactly what they should train for. The B-26 could not be used for long-range bombing of Germany, so the men were left to wonder when and where their unit might be put into action. Powell correctly guessed North Africa, but there was no official word and no special preparation. Instead, the airplane mechanics and support personnel of the 319th spent their time drilling with small arms. There was no real intelligence work. Powell attended some not very useful classes, but mostly, he and his men marked time.

The lack of a clear objective exacerbated Powell's anxiety. He was not afraid of German bombing, which by this time was greeted with insouciance. ("Air raid alert during tea was ignored by all," his diary reports.) But he worried about his next assignment. On October 18 he was attending the Aircraft Recognition School on the Isle of Man when a telephone call ordered him back to his unit. Powell was anything but eager: "I hate to leave England," he confided to his diary. Wherever he might go would be unpleasant and "infinitely more hazardous." "I don't think I am a coward, but I do so want to live through this thing to see my beloved family again. It would be different, in degree at least, if I didn't have such a lovely wife and babies."

When he returned to his unit, he found that gas impervious clothing had been issued in his absence—to everyone but him. The complaints mounted. "I dread going into this battle so vulnerable to gas," he wrote in his diary. "Every man for himself and God help the absent, the weak or the sick—this is the Army creed: apparently it is difficult for a gentleman to remain such in the Army."

Powell's most persistent concern in England was the weather. In

September in his hut at Shipdham, he slept in long underwear and pajamas under as many as five blankets and wondered what he would do when winter really came. Coal was not yet available, so he had his men scrounge for wood, but what they found was green and slow to burn. He spent nearly half of his six-month supply of ration coupons (required "to buy anything you really want") on an officer's greatcoat. On the Isle of Man he got the Central Hotel's choice room—"the one with hot water pipes running through it"—but the rest of the place was like an icebox. The problem was a policy designed to conserve fuel: "It is not 'officially' cold over here until Nov. 1st—regardless of what the thermometer says."

So Powell called for reinforcements. Two weeks after arriving in England, he asked his wife and mother to send two sweaters, one light and one heavy, plus gloves, socks, helmet liner, and *very heavy wool underwear*," all by the fastest means. A few weeks later, he decided that what he really needed was a sleeping bag, an innovation of which he seems to have been previously unaware, and again wrote home.

These demands proved frustrating for all concerned. The mails were slow and irregular, especially early in the war, and miscommunication prevailed. Six weeks after Powell asked for the sleeping bag, Jo wrote with the helpful news that Zoe thought that men were issued sleeping bags in cold climates and anyway it looked like Powell was headed for a warmer place. Worse, on December 14, Powell got a cable from his father saying that he should "buy a sleeping bag over there." Powell exploded. "This is like wiring me to come home immediately for Christmas. It would be just about as easy to do. If I could have bought a sleeping bag in England *of course* I would have done so—then I would have gotten it immediately. . . . I am afraid you have no conception of how difficult it is to get anything in these countries that have been in the war for three years." By this time, Powell was in North Africa, but he still wanted a sleeping bag—*and* an air mattress. He closed on a conciliatory note ("Don't worry about this letter . . . I'll just continue sleeping in all my clothes, and this will save time both in the morning and at night"), but he was sorely disappointed. The bedroll finally arrived in North Africa in February of the next year.

Powell's best time in England was a long weekend spent in London en route to the Isle of Man. He stayed the night of Saturday, October 3, in the officers club and celebrated his return to civilization—"clean sheets, pillow, hot water, bath, shampoo, American coffee, etc." The next day he got in touch with Ed Murrow, who took him to lunch at Claridge's and put him up in Murrow's luxurious apartment. That night Powell watched

Murrow make a "This . . . is London" broadcast from a small room in the basement of the BBC's Broadcasting House and "was thrilled to hear the cross-Atlantic conversation between the staff in London and New York. When Ed was talking I wanted to speak also, thinking that Jo or Mother might be listening in." Afterward, Powell, Murrow, and Charles Collingwood sat up until two in the morning speculating on the future of the second front. On Monday, Ed Murrow rejoined his wife in the country, but Powell stayed on for two days in their apartment, with a housekeeper who somehow produced oranges for his breakfast and served a five-course dinner for Powell and his friend Paul Rockwell. It was a style of living he would not soon see again.

The October 18 telephone call to the Isle of Man alerted Powell to the impending departure. A week later he boarded the *Moultan*, an ancient passenger liner that formerly ran between England and India, but that now was anchored at Goorick in the Firth of Clyde, where the *Queen Mary* had arrived six weeks earlier. As Powell's diary noted, "we are back exactly where we started."

NORTH AFRICA

Shortly before midnight on October 26, 1942, more than thirty ships carrying American troops left the Firth of Clyde under escort by the Royal Navy. They sailed north along the Irish coast and then turned southwestward into the Atlantic, confirming North Africa as the destination. Ten days later, they passed the Strait of Gibraltar and steamed east across the Mediterranean. Under cover of darkness, the convoy reversed course, slipped back westward, and stood offshore near the port of Oran in western Algeria.* Other Allied forces were poised for landings at Casablanca and Algiers. Operation Torch was about to begin.

In the predawn blackness of November 8, Powell watched, or rather listened, from the deck of the *Moultan* as men from the First Infantry Division attacked Arzeu, twenty-five miles east of Oran. By first light, the beach was secure, and the fighting moved inland. A similar landing to the west was designed to capture Oran in a quick pincer movement, but here, unlike in Europe, the French defense was heavy and

---

*   The feint worked. After the war, Powell asked the head of the German Air Force intelligence for the Mediterranean why the convoys had not been attacked. He replied that they thought the ships were headed for Sicily or Malta or perhaps to reinforce the British Eighth Army in the eastern desert.

effective. On the third day, the men of the 319th landed, then marched seven miles to the air force staging area at St. Leu and spent the night trying to hide from the rain in open foxholes. By the next day, Powell had found better accommodations, eventually working his way up to a well-appointed bedroom overlooking the Mediterranean from a house with modern plumbing.

On November 18 Powell and his men were trucked thirty miles to the airport at Tafaraoui. With two hard-surfaced runways, Tafaraoui was a military prize; as a billet it was anything but. Powell moved into a bare barracks with little water and no toilet—to which he had the usual American reaction: "These stupid French will spend money and effort on everything in life except the fundamental things like sanitation and personal hygiene." (He had the same complaint at Telergma a few weeks later: "The wash room is typically French—utterly inefficient and stupid. Our latrines are either open French ones or just slit trenches in full view of all. There is no such thing as privacy, and I no longer care.") At Tafaraoui, Powell slept on the floor and walked a mile and a half between the barracks and a partially wrecked hanger where the intelligence room had been set up. When the rains came—and they came with a vengeance in December 1942—everything except the runways turned to sticky mud. This was bad enough to slog through, but much worse for men sleeping on the ground. Tafaraoui, they said, where the mud was "deep and gooey."

Powell wrote Jo that he spent "an appalling amount of time just trying to live—eat, sleep, shave, bathe, and wash clothes." To cheer up the folks at home, he penned a lighthearted panegyric to the Army helmet: "Really, it is the most useful and versatile hat in the world. It has an outer steel cover and a detachable inner lining of fibre. The steel cover is used regularly by all of us for the following: as a helmet for protection (rarely); as a wash basin (every morning); as a tub for washing socks, underwear, etc.; as a seat (remarkably comfortable); as a bucket or basket to carry ration tins and other commodities; as a stewpan or pot for cooking, etc., etc. The fibre lining was designed for and is used as a sun helmet. In the winter a woolen skull cap makes the whole ensemble the most satisfactory kind of headgear—being fully waterproof—and I hope—bulletproof."

Powell's diary and letters show a constant attention to the circumstances of living. Despite his worry that he might not see his "lovely wife and babies" again, he seemed to fear death less than degradation. His diary is filled not with intimations of mortality (he personally was not in combat), but with the details of his struggle to maintain order and dignity in his daily life. Surprisingly, the discomforts did not depress him. In fact, he took a sneaking pleasure in the discovery "that it is possible to live and be happy like this." But he was by no means eager for deprivation. He peppered his family with requests—for clothes, candy, medicines, airmail stamps, magazines, etc., etc. Frustrated by the lack of news, he asked for the "News of the Week" section of the Sunday *New York Times* to be sent by airmail every Monday morning. Inevitably, he was disappointed. For example, he asked for prescription dark glasses. When Jo wrote back that the local authorities said he should get them from his "nearest medical center," he shot back: "These people are utterly stupid. Do they think we are fighting this war near Walter Reed hospital?" Jo got the glasses, plus a pair of clip-ons with "side wind and sand protectors," but by this time the rules had changed and the post office would not accept the packages without an authorization from Powell's commanding officer. Only when this was forwarded did Powell finally get his sunglasses.

AT TAFARAOUI the 319th's ground personnel caught up with some of their air crews but heard bad news of the rest. Four planes and one crew had been lost before they ever got out of England. The journey to North Africa had cost two more planes, including that of the group commander, who had been shot down over Cherbourg.

By the time the 319th's depleted forces reached Tafaraoui, the plan that brought them there had been abandoned. Oran had been intended as headquarters for the Twelfth Air Force, commanded by Major General James H. Doolittle of the famous raid on Tokyo. Its location allowed operations in western North Africa, but the fighting quickly moved east. Medium-range bombers had to follow, so a few days after the ground personnel of the 319th arrived at Tafaraoui, their planes departed eastward—first to an airport outside Algiers, then to points farther east, settling finally at Telergma, an unpaved but unsoggy airfield south of Constantine. At the same time, two groups of B-17s, which had been based at Maison Blanche, were found vulnerable to attack by Axis aircraft from Sardinia. They were moved west to Tafaraoui, from which place, with their much longer range, they could still be effective.

These confusing reassignments were the circumstances of Powell's first combat. He eventually caught up with his own planes at Telergma, but for several weeks he was miles away from the pilots he was supposed to serve. Instead, he worked for whatever units happened to be where he was, including the B-17s at Tafaraoui. The result was a haphazard, episodic experience.

Early raids were aimed chiefly at Tunisian airfields, from which the Luftwaffe covered Erwin Rommel's retreat westward from Alamein. Railroads, bridges, harbors, and shipping were also Allied targets. Powell's chief job was to interrogate returning flight crews, a task he approached with the painstaking preparation of a litigator. "Some intelligence officers," he wrote later, "in their anxiety to let the crews go, will tend to hurry through an interrogation. I am convinced that *thoroughness* is the prime attribute of worthwhile interrogation, and all crew members and interrogators must be instilled with this idea." On one occasion he had an unpleasant argument with a major who led a B-25 mission and wanted to "claim the earth," but who had to accept Powell's more modest valuation. On days when the planes did not fly, Powell conducted classes. As always, he was happy when working. During a week in mid-December, missions were flown nearly every day, and Powell was busy from dawn to dark with briefing, interrogation, report writing, and lectures. His diary records his satisfaction: "I really feel that I am now making a contribution to the war."

Occasionally, there were diversions. From Tafaraoui, Powell and a friend hitched into Oran, where they managed a bath at a public bathhouse and a dinner of Army food in the town's best hotel. There they were joined by three Army nurses, who were welcomed, though "homely as mud hens." An attempt at Christmas shopping produced only a few handkerchiefs for Jo, and he sent them along with the assurance that he intended "to deliver a more suitable present in person" next Christmas. It seemed a long way off.

THOUGH POWELL THRIVED on this activity, his unit did not. From the start, the 319th was dogged by failure and bad luck. Pressed into service without adequate training and equipped with a difficult aircraft, the group lost several planes and one commander before ever seeing the enemy. A new commander arrived on November 27, 1942, and the next day the group flew its first combat mission against the harbor at Sfax, Tunisia. This raid was concluded safely, but four aircraft were lost in the next week, including that of the new commander, who was shot down and captured. Owing to a lack of delayed action fuses, the planes had flown at four thousand feet, a suicide altitude where even light antiaircraft fire could kill. On December 14 the 319th tried an even lower altitude, racing in to bomb Sousse harbor at barely one thousand feet. This trick surprised the antiaircraft gunners, and the planes got away after damaging the docks and some ships in the harbor. But when the tactic was repeated the next day, a squadron commander was shot down. A few days later, two more B-26s were lost in the same way, and low-level bombing of defended land targets was virtually abandoned.

The 319th then stood down for ten days, while the crews practiced "skip bombing"—a dangerous tactic designed to make up for the lack of dive bombers and the difficulty of hitting ships with conventional techniques. In skip bombing, a handful of medium bombers, with high-altitude cover from a squadron of fighters, would fly directly at an enemy ship at an altitude of less than two hundred feet. When close to the target, they would launch five-hundred-pound bombs that were supposed to skip across the ocean like stones on a pond. If the target was unprotected, this kind of attack was murderous; but if the target was adequately defended by antiaircraft fire, skip bombing was suicidal.

For a few weeks in early 1943, the 319th did great work with skip bombing. The group first tested the technique against Axis shipping from Sicily on January 15. A week later, the 319th sank at least one freighter and damaged several others in three consecutive days of sea sweeps, but lost two planes in the process. The next day still another B-26 went down. Unsuccessful shipping attacks were made on January 27 and 28. On the 29th, planes from the 319th performed brilliantly, attacking an enemy convoy, setting fire to one ship and damaging another, but losing two more aircraft.

By this time, morale was shot. Losses continued to mount, and the Axis powers had begun to beef up the air and naval escort for their convoys. The young crews kept flying, but a few had to be threatened with court-martial. Even the bravest airmen could not be indifferent to the fate of their comrades or to their own grim prospects. As neither equipment nor men were speedily replaced, combat capability dwindled to a fraction of authorized strength, and the few crews still flying felt even more exposed. Strangely, there is no mention of these problems in the surviving portions of Powell's diary. Almost certainly, they were the topic of entries that, as a later entry comments, "may have said too much" and therefore were cut out and burned. This surmise is consistent with the few words that remain at the end of the excision: ". . . blame them. Several have talked to me about it." In any event, the facts are clear: even the official Air Force history acknowledges that the 319th suffered "a serious lowering of morale."

Matters came to a head on February 13, as Rommel and the Afrika Corps were cutting their way through green American troops to the Kasserine Pass. As Allied commander Dwight David Eisenhower cast around for the means to resist this advance, General Doolittle ordered a raid against the Axis airbase at El Auoina. Doolittle came to watch as the attack turned into disaster. Of the eighteen planes scheduled for the mission, only sixteen were ready to attempt it. Seven did not get off the ground, and four more turned back. Only five reached the target, and of these, two were shot down. (The crew of one plane were killed. The other landed behind enemy lines and miraculously escaped capture; they returned to the 319th to find their clothes and personal effects already distributed among their comrades.)

Disgusted by what he had seen, Doolittle immediately pulled the group from combat. On February 27, the 319th turned over some of their few operational planes to another understrength group and retired to French Morocco for rest and refitting.

ON THE DAY of the 319th's disastrous last raid, Powell left the unit. Major Harry Bowers, head of operational intelligence for the Twelfth Air Force, had spent the night with Powell's squadron and invited the young lawyer to join the headquarters staff in Algiers. At first Powell was reluctant to leave the young flyboys whom he so much admired, but Doolittle's decision to withdraw the 319th from combat quickly changed his mind. Whatever a headquarters job had to offer was "far better than going back to Oran to do nothing for two months."

The unit that Powell now joined had just been constituted the Northwest African Air Forces, under the command of the senior American airman in Europe, Major General Carl "Tooey" Spaatz. The Northwest African Air Forces, or NWAAF, was a truly integrated command; it combined the U.S. Twelfth Air Force and various elements of the RAF into the largest concentration of air power in the Mediterranean.* NWAAF headquarters was very small. Most personnel were assigned to one of five subordinate commands: a strategic air force under Jimmy Doolittle, a tactical air force brilliantly led by Air Vice Marshal Sir Arthur Coningham, a coastal unit, a training command, and a photographic reconnaissance wing commanded by Lieutenant Colonel Elliott Roosevelt. In this structure, the overall headquarters functioned as an elite command and planning

* The units, personnel, and equipment of the Twelfth Air Force were transferred to the Northwest African Air Forces on February 18, 1943, but the empty shell of the Twelfth Air Force was kept alive as the administrative headquarters for the U.S. elements in the combined command. That Powell later misdescribed his assignment as Twelfth Air Force headquarters is not surprising, for, as the official history recounts, "the half-existence of the Twelfth served mainly to mystify all but a few headquarters experts." Technically, Powell transferred directly from the 319th Bombardment Group to NWAAF headquarters and served there until he returned home in August 1943.

group. Its staff members were removed from the front line of battle but brought close to the nerve center of decision.

For Captain Powell, as he had recently become, the move to NWAAF meant a swift translation "from fox hole to feather mattress." His last diary entry in Telergma ended with an envious dig at friends in Algiers, "living in the utmost luxury, with proverbial wine, women, and song." When Powell next sat down with his diary, he himself was in Algiers, sitting in a comfortable twelfth-floor apartment overlooking the harbor. His room-mate, Major Charles L. Marlburg from Maryland, had the only bed-room, but Powell had the living room with a balcony and a marvelous view.

Powell must have been the ideal roommate, for his schedule kept him out of the house. He worked chiefly on preparing the daily intelli-gence report. This work began at the end of the day, when the latest intelligence could be collected and digested for use the next morning, and lasted until just before dawn, when Powell walked back to his apartment through the blacked-out streets of Algiers. Evenings off he spent with Marlburg and others. Paul Rockwell knew all the good eat-ing places, and another friend, Jim McKeldin, arranged dinners in a seaside villa that he ran for an American general. This agreeable rou-tine ended in late March, when, with the increasing constriction of the Axis bridgehead in Tunisia, NWAAF moved an advance headquarters to Constantine. Powell spent his last Sunday in Algiers investigating the Roman ruins at Tipasa and concluding with a steak dinner in the Hôtel du Rivage. On March 25, after two days of trying to wrangle a place on a flight to Constantine, Powell reluctantly left Algiers.

While Powell was in Algiers, there occurred an unpleasant event that he later deleted from his memory. He was recruited to serve as prosecutor as a special court-martial and won convictions against six men from an M.P. company. His diary provides no details but vividly records his reaction: "The capt. and first sergeant of this co. were brutes! I never imagined anything like them in our Army." Their crimes may have been something Powell did not wish to remember, as forty years later, he had no recollection of their nature.*

Powell remained at Constantine for seven weeks, with much the same duties as before. NWAAF's first order of business was to support Allied ground forces in driving the Germans from North Africa. This

---

* From this point, the record of Powell's service in North Africa becomes more sketchy. Entries in his diary, which had lately grown less frequent, now ceased alto-gether. A later notation explains that he was "working increasingly with high level intel-ligence" and thought it best not to say more than was reported in his letters home.

required the interdiction of Axis shipping, and the intelligence background for selecting shipping targets became Powell's particular responsibility. He worked chiefly with photographic reconnaissance and reports from combat crews and the intelligence information received from higher authorities.

On May 13 Powell was sent as a special courier to carry top-secret appreciations to Eisenhower, then at field headquarters near the collapsing German lines. Powell delivered the papers to Eisenhower's aide, Lieutenant Commander Harry Butcher, met General Sir Harold Alexander, and took a few snapshots with a borrowed camera. Butcher warned him that Ike would not like the camera, and Powell put it away. These photographs, which were stolen before Powell could develop the film, might have been memorable, for on that day General Giovanni Messe, who took over from an ailing Erwin Rommel, surrendered his forces. Organized resistance ceased, and Eisenhower's forces were left in undisputed possession of North Africa and of nearly 300,000 Axis prisoners.

NEXT CAME SICILY. At Casablanca, Roosevelt, Churchill, and Stalin authorized the invasion of Sicily to follow the end of Axis resistance in Tunisia. First came a preliminary assault on Pantelleria, a small outcrop of volcanic rock containing a large Axis airbase. NWAAF raids began at once and quickly escalated to a round-the-clock pounding that helped drive the demoralized Italians to surrender shortly after the invasion on June 11. By this time Sicily itself was a familiar target. The object was to eliminate Axis air opposition to the scheduled invasion by intensive bombing of the island's many airfields and the aircraft based there. Additionally, NWAAF sought to block reinforcements by heavy bombing of Messina and of key supply and communications facilities across the narrows in southern Italy. Allied troops landed in Sicily on July 10, and although final reduction of the German land forces took more than a month, air resistance ceased by the fourth day.

To support these operations, Spaatz moved an advance command post from Constantine to La Marsa, a resort on the coast near Tunis. He took with him a small intelligence staff consisting of Colonel George C. McDonald and four subordinates: Harry Bowers, the Georgia lawyer who had recruited Powell to NWAAF and who later died in the crash of a cargo plane (Powell wrote Bowers's mother of having visited the grave site); Bill Ballard, a young New York architect; Leavitt Corning, a petroleum engineer from Texas; and Lewis Powell.

The four men shared a small house on the beach; since one had to be on duty at all times, they ended up working almost around the clock. With such a small group, they were all necessarily generalists, but Powell's particular responsibility was to monitor the disposition and capabilities of the German Air Force.

August 17, 1943, found Patton and Montgomery in Messina, and the Allies in possession of all Sicily. At NWAAF the air campaign against Italy was well underway. Suddenly and mysteriously, Powell was ordered back to the States. He did not have the service overseas to warrant rotation and no explanation was given for the recall, but he had been overseas for nearly a year and was overjoyed to go home, whatever the reason. He left Africa on August 23, took his first transatlantic flight, and reported as ordered at the War Department in Washington, D.C., on August 26.

THE YEAR AWAY

Powell had been overseas almost exactly one year. This and an absence of similar duration later in the war were the only occasions in more than fifty years of marriage that Powell spent significant time apart from Jo. His correspondence during those periods provides a rare glimpse into the inner feelings of an exceptionally private man.

When Powell left home, one concern was money. There was no prospect of privation, but Powell expected to live on Army pay. In fact, he never had to. Shortly after he entered the service, his partners offered to make up the difference between his government pay and what he would have drawn from the firm. The gap was large. In 1942, Powell earned $8,735.94. If his Army income, including base pay and various allowances, were annualized (he served from May through December), it would have come to less than half that figure. As Powell's pay increased with rank, the firm's contribution declined, but throughout the war, it roughly doubled his government income.

This kind of private contribution to the men in uniform was not uncommon immediately after Pearl Harbor, but Powell thought it would not outlast the initial enthusiasm for the war effort. He predicted to Jo: "I feel very definitely that the present very good arrangement can't last long. It isn't human, as law business contracts (as it will) & taxes increase, for my partners to continue making *donations*." He insisted that the family live within his Army income, "except *only* for insurance premiums and a part of our taxes." He also engaged in small economies, such as returning a wristwatch that Eleanor had bought in New York and buying a cheap one instead ("we can save at least $15") and offering to cut down the list of couples to whom Jo might give wedding presents. He even rebuked Jo for spending twenty-five dollars on a tricycle for Sunny's Christmas present—a stinginess he shortly regretted.

Prudent to the point of pessimism, Powell fretted about money throughout the war, but the "miracle" of the firm's generosity continued much longer than he or his partners would have predicted, to the point that Powell became embarrassed by it. In March 1945 he wrote Mr. Gay suggesting that the salary supplement be stopped retroactively as of the first of the year. He was not, he said, merely making a polite gesture, but was "urging on you what I consider to be sound and just." Gay wrote back that the partners wanted to keep up the payments. Powell professed himself "frankly somewhat troubled" but did not protest overmuch, and the payments continued throughout his service.

THOUGH POWELL'S FINANCIAL FEARS proved groundless, he vastly underestimated the psychic cost of separation from Jo and his family. Indeed, he was shocked to discover how much he missed them. From the beginning, Powell begged for letters from home. He wanted tidbits of Jo's life, anecdotes about the children, word of friends and relatives—"homey news of those I love and miss so much." Since the mail usually arrived in batches, he took to rationing his consumption of letters, reading one or two each night before he went to sleep: "It surely takes superhuman will power to do this, but it is grand to have this to look forward to *every* day."

When the letters did not come, he grew churlish. He was vexed by the irregularity of delivery. Some letters would speed to him in a week or so; others would take months. He and Jo began to number their letters so that gaps would be identifiable, and this procedure allowed him to calculate that from September 30 through October 26, 1942, Jo had written only seven letters, or one every fourth day. "I do think I am entitled to feel slightly neglected on the above basis," he complained.

He complained about V-Mail, a process of photographic reduction designed to speed overseas delivery by saving weight. A letter written on a V-Mail form would be microfilmed, then sent overseas as a miniature photographic negative, which would be blown up to approximately half the original size and delivered. The results were often illegible. If the author had a cramped hand, as did Powell's mother, V-Mail letters sometimes could not be deciphered even with a magnifying glass. Powell's dislike of them escalated. First he said that they should be sent only as extras, then not at all. When they continued (they were supposed to be faster), he again admonished against them, then exploded: "Can't you all understand plain English? *I would rather have no mail whatever than photographed* V *mail*—and I never meant anything more."

Such outbursts were rare. Most of his letters to Jo were supportive and fond, but they were not romantic. The courtliness and reserve so often remarked on in Powell's later life seemed in this context oddly formal. His famed reticence was never more in evidence than in matters of the heart. He never mentioned sex nor did more than hint at physical longing. When Jo wrote that his sister Zoe and her husband had gone walking in the moonlight at Bear Island, Powell found himself "more homesick than ever." "We will surely have a lot of 'walking' to catch-up on," he wrote Jo, "and I am more than willing." In another letter, he said, "I have your lovely picture beside my bed, and thus you are the first person I see each morning and the last before I go to bed. . . . If only this were true in person."

Certainly, Jo had no reason to fear that he was involved elsewhere. Powell never indulged in the psychic liberation of being at war and overseas. On the contrary, he struggled to maintain the connectedness of his former life. Loyalty, reserve, and preoccupation made him unable even to enjoy the company of other women. As he wrote Jo:

> I didn't realize what a "family" man I am. I utterly lack the quality, possessed by most of my fellow officers, to have a gay time with whoever happens to be available. For example, there was a dance here last night and I attended with a group of other American officers. . . . We were all given the opportunity ahead of time to have "dates" arranged for us. Most of the officers wanted dates, and got them. I went "stag," and after surveying the situation carefully I did not dance a *single* time! After listening to the music and chatting with a couple of Scotch officers (in their full dress skirts) about the Valley Campaign in 1862 (Second Battle of Bull Run, etc.), I came home alone and went to bed at 11:30. Most of my friends straggled in much later. I am not reciting this little story to prove how "good" I am, because under the circumstances I think it really desirable to be sociable. My real point is that I compare every girl I see with you and the comparison is so utterly devastating that I can't even develope [*sic*] enough interest to dance with some one else."

Jo longed for more. When she complained that he did not write "love letters," his response was pure Powell: "I am a conservative soul by nature, and would never think of putting in black and white how much I love you. It makes me blush to think of writing what I really feel in my heart. I've always loved you dearly, but this war and our separation have accented and strengthened my love beyond expression."

Intimacy did make Powell blush. His constraint in matters of sex and desire extended, in lesser form, to all questions of personal feeling. This was a man who characteristically referred to his eldest daughter, of whom he was vastly proud, as "a very satisfactory child." Even coarse language embarrassed him. In North Africa, the young flyboys of the 319th named him "Great Heaven Above Powell" for his reluctance to say anything stronger. The only time he included profanity in a letter home, he reduced it to the letter "h" followed by a demure blank. Against this pattern of fastidious understatement, his statements of love for Jo seem less reserved.

The overriding aim of Powell's correspondence was a ferocious desire to stay in touch and in control, despite physical separation. All his life, Powell sought security in friends and family. The complete protection of his mother's love could not reach beyond childhood, but it could, perhaps, be replaced by an encircling web of affection and friendship. At the center was Jo, and Powell demanded constant evidence of his presence in her life. He wanted letters and more letters, various items (the sleeping bag, prescription sunglasses) that he could not get overseas, and "innumerable small packages of things" from home. Their contents mattered less than their frequency, for every letter or package received was a tangible reassurance that he had not been forgotten. He compared his mail to others and was chagrined to find that there were "dozens of enlisted men and of course many officers who beat me on every mail. I don't admit that their wives love them any more."

The relationship was demanding but not one-sided. He averaged a letter to Jo every second or third day, and most were long and chatty. He often took pains to describe in laborious longhand events that she might find funny or interesting, such as the discovery and purchase of seventy-one eggs concealed in an Arab's baggy pants or the dinner of "plus grand rabbit" that was suspected of being cat. Powell also wrote his friends and partners and urged Jo to keep up with them: "Friendship, like flowers, requires constant attention and nourishment—otherwise they fade and die. One of your main jobs, my precious, is to keep our circle of friends reasonably intact."

Powell's intense desire to keep his world intact was never more evident than in the letters to his children. Little Jo was four and Penny only two when Powell left home. He fought desperately to avoid being reduced to a mere abstraction in their lives. Sitting in a cold hut in England or squatting on his helmet in the mud of North Africa, Powell wrote letters for Jo to read to their daughters—letters that the older girl, at least, could understand and associate with the absent man who wrote them. Often he spoke of other children, as in the stories of Pierre and Robert, whose home he shared on arriving in North Africa, and Mo (for Mohammed), the shoeshine boy who became the child entrepreneur of the American base in Constantine.

Mo, Powell wrote Sunny, was different from the other boys: "He is smart, with a nice bright face and brown eyes that always smile and sparkle. He loves people (*like you do*) and is friendly with everyone; therefore all the soldiers liked Mo from the very first." They bought him shoe polish and brushes from the PX and set him up in business, where he made two or three dollars a day—enough to be "really rich." Mo used some of his money to buy more polish and brushes and hired other Arab boys to work for him at stations around the post. Like many of Powell's stories, this one had a moral: "And thus little Mohammed has now become a capitalist, a businessman, and a great success—all because he was smart, clean, friendly, and attractive, as well as diligent."

Other letters told the children things they could understand—about a nest of baby birds on the wall of the officers mess, about a crippled hen whose inability to lay eggs led her to the stewpot (scarcely shocking to young girls raised on a farm), about the funny little Frenchman who followed Powell around the apartment near Oran insisting that "baths should not be taken."

Sometimes Powell wrote to allay childish concerns. When he learned that little Jo was afraid to go to sleep for fear of wolves, Powell wrote:

> Sunny, you know your Daddy has never told you anything but the truth. Now I am going to tell you the *truth* about wolves, and I want you never to forget it. There are *no* real or live wolves in the part of America where we live—*not even a single one*. Wolves are only in *books*—like the book about Little Red Riding Hood and the Three Little Pigs. But there are no real wolves in Virginia.
>
> Therefore, darling little daughter, you must never worry about wolves. It is foolish to worry about something that doesn't exist, and you don't want to be foolish. You are too smart for that.
>
> Also remember this—there is *nothing* to be afraid of when you go to bed at night. There are no bad animals or people in America or Virginia. . . .

So, when you go to bed at night take this letter with you, have Mother read it to you, and then put it under your pillow (do you have a pillow yet?) so you will remember what I've said.

Long-distance fathering was frustrating, but Powell kept at it. He worried about where Sunny should ride her new tricycle (a high hedge shielded the driveway from the street) and so gave her painstakingly detailed instructions on tricycle safety. He wrote birthday notes in time to arrive on the special day and promised extra birthday parties to make up for the celebrations he missed. Always, he tried to recall himself to his children: "I think every day of the fun we have had—on the beaches at Nags Head and Florida, where we swam and fished together; at Bear Island, where we played tag in the yard, and went with Mammar and Pops to see the chickens and the cattle; at Rothesay, where we played on the lawn and rolled down the hill together; and [at a rented house in Richmond] where you and Mother would run to meet me, and I would read to you while you sat on my lap."

In these letters, Powell struggled against his own absence. When he arrived in Washington on August 26, 1943, Jo was there to meet him, and he resumed, with as little interruption as he was forced to allow, his life in his family. Afterward, he would always say that family came first. Those who witnessed his prodigious devotion to work may question whether he actually lived according to that rule, but Powell himself never doubted or forgot that his happiness was grounded in the love of his wife and family.

WHEN POWELL REPORTED to the office of the A-2, the Assistant Chief of Staff, Intelligence, for the Army Air Forces, he was assigned temporarily to the intelligence school at Harrisburg, where he was to update Army manuals and recount his combat experience. Powell thought nothing else was intended. He had served with one of the earliest medium bomber groups to see combat and had witnessed the painful evolution of suitable tactics for the B-26. He could speak with authority on the need for thoroughness in interrogating combat crews and on the right way to give briefings and lectures. He also had served on the staff of a combined Anglo-American headquarters and thus had some sense of the political context of Allied intelligence work. His experience made Powell a valuable instructional resource.

In fact, however, he never taught a class at Harrisburg. Almost certainly, he was slated from the start for something more exciting. From Harrisburg he was repeatedly summoned to Washington for temporary duties and extended conversations that look in retrospect like interviews. He spent ten days in Washington in early November, then departed on a twenty-day trip to Air Force installations in Florida and New York. For most of December, he was in California, investigating poor morale in the intelligence sections of Air Force units stationed there.

The new year brought two important changes. First, Powell was made a major. He had been recommended for promotion in the ordinary course in December 1943, but the Adjutant General rejected the recommendation in the mistaken belief that he did not have sufficient time in grade. This error was corrected, and the promotion came through on January 18, 1944.

At about the same time, Powell was initiated into the most secret of Allied military intelligence. On February 2, Powell was relieved from duty at Harrisburg and assigned to the Military Intelligence Service, War Department. Although Powell always thought of himself as an airman, in fact he no longer was. He had been transferred out of the Army Air Forces altogether and brought directly under the authority of the Secretary of War in the most elite and unusual of all military intelligence services—the so-called Special Branch.

CHAPTER IV

ULTRA SECRET

THE ENIGMA

On July 24, 1939, as Hitler's shadow lengthened across Europe, three British agents flew to Warsaw. They were met by Colonel Stefan Mayer, head of Polish intelligence, and by Lieutenant Colonel Gwido Langer and others from the Polish cryptology section. Arriving the same day by train from Paris were Captain Gustave Bertrand and another French intelligence officer. The British were persons of consequence. Commander Alastair Denniston was a veteran of Room 40, the Admiralty's famous World War I cryptological section, and now head of its descendant, the Government Code and Cipher School. Dillwyn Knox, also a graduate of Room 40, was a classics scholar and brilliant cryptanalyst.* The third man, introduced as Professor Sandwich from Oxford, said very little. He was, in fact, Colonel Stewart Menzies, then deputy head, but soon to become "C," of the British Secret Service, an office so secret that its holder was never named.

The next morning, the Poles took their guests to a cipher center deep in the Kabacki Woods near the small town of Pyry. There Colonel Langer and his colleagues told their French and British counterparts of Polish progress in deciphering the most secret of German radio communications—those enciphered on the machine "Enigma."

Neither the word nor the machine was unknown to the Allies. Indeed, "The Glow-lamp Ciphering and Deciphering Machine 'Enigma'" had been sold commercially in Berlin in the 1920s, and the United States of America had been one of its purchasers. The British knew of the Enigma and may even have possessed the commercial

---

* Within the general field of "cryptology," modern usuage distinguishes between "cryptography," which is the making of codes and ciphers, and "cryptanalysis," which is the breaking of them.

prototype, but there is no evidence of effective knowledge of the much more complicated version used by the German military. The French were further along. Bertrand had bought from a German, code-named "Asche," several documents about Enigma, including the actu-al settings at which the machine had been operated for a time by the German Army. Estimates of the value of these documents vary, but at the least they confirm that the French were familiar with the design and operation of the German machine.

Even so, neither Bertrand nor the British were prepared for what the Poles had to say. They had an Enigma—not the early commercial ver-sion but a reconstruction of the German military model. By itself, the machine would have allowed the Poles only to encrypt and decrypt their own messages, not to read someone else's; but the Poles had also learned how, with time and effort, to penetrate the German Enigma ciphers. Unfortunately, this capability had lapsed in December 1938, when the Germans modified the machine, but the Polish cryptanalysis would provide the foundation for a future attack on Enigma ciphers. Best of all, the Poles had made two extra machines, which they pro-posed to donate to the British and French. Transportation was han-dled by the French, and on August 16, 1939, Captain Bertrand arrived at Victoria Station and there handed over to "Professor Sandwich" the Enigma machine. Two weeks later, Germany invaded Poland.

THE ENIGMA WAS an electromechanical device that substituted one letter for another. It looked like a complicated typewriter. At the bot-tom was a board of twenty-six keys, one for each letter in the alphabet. These keys were connected in a very elaborate way to twenty-six trans-parent windows located over small electric bulbs (hence "glow-lamp"). Each window displayed a letter of the alphabet. When the Enigma operator depressed a letter key (say, A), a different letter (say, M) would light up. The operator would enter every letter of the message, and an assistant would note the Enigma substitutions. The cipher-text could then be transmitted by radio in Morse code. At the receiving end, each letter of the cipher-text would be typed into an Enigma with the same settings, and the original letter would light up. The alpha-betic substitutions worked both ways, so that if the Enigma converted A to M, a machine *with exactly the same settings* would convert M to A and reveal the original message.

Of course, any code in which one letter consistently stood for another could easily have been broken. The frequency with which let-ters appear and the emergence of patterns would have made quick work for cryptanalysts. The Enigma, however, was polyalphabetic. That is, it made a different substitution each time a given letter appeared. So, if the first A produced M, the second might produce P, the third G, and so on. This array of alphabetic substitutions would stretch out until the full sequence of substitutions had run its course. Only then would the sequence repeat, and a pattern begin to emerge. The larger the sequence of substitutions before the pattern repeats, the greater the difficulty of cryptanalysis; and the sequence of polyalphabetic substitutions produced by the Enigma was very, very large.*

To decipher intercepted messages, the British had to figure out the initial settings of the Enigma machine on which the message had been encoded. Most of the settings were changed daily, and some were selected at random by the enciphering clerk and changed for every message. Full description of cryptanalysis of Enigma ciphers would require mathematical sophistication and more than a little patience, but the crucial point is that it had to be done again and again. There were several series of Enigma settings in use at once. The German Air

---

* To explain why this was so requires a look at the mechanism that linked the alphabetical keys to the glow-lamp letters. The electric current generated by depressing a key would pass through three rotors, through a reflector, back through the three rotors, and then to a letter. Each rotor had twenty-six positions. The positions were connected by wires, so that current entering a rotor at position A would exit that rotor at a fixed position other than A. The first rotor advanced a position after each keystroke, thereby triggering a new set of connections between input and output. After the first rotor had made a complete revolution, the second rotor would move a step. After the second rotor had come full circle, the third would advance one position. The reflector remained fixed. This mechanism enciphered each letter in a new configuration of rotors, with a total sequence of twenty-six times twenty-six, or 17,576 possible configurations.

In the world of cryptology, even this is not a large number. Other features increased the possible configurations. The rotors could be taken out and placed in any order. There are six possible ways to arrange three rotors, which increases the total possible substitutions to six times 17,576 or 105,456. In 1938 the Germans increased the number of rotors to five. Although only three were used at the time, the five rotors allowed any of sixty possible arrangements of three. This change increased the configurations tenfold. Finally, the German military had added to the commercial Enigma yet another layer of complexity in the form of a plugboard. The plugboard resembled a telephone switchboard with twenty-six holes. The holes were connected by wires with plugs at each end, and the wires could be moved to connect pairs of letters. So at the plugboard, A could be paired with H, B with Z, and so forth. These pairings produced an automatic swapping of letters, both before the current entered the rotors and after it emerged from them. Superimposing the array of possible plugboard configurations on all the other variations in the machine produces a total of possible configurations in the billions of trillions. Even in cryptology, the number is very, very large.

Force, for example, used one series of settings (called Blue by the British) for practice purposes, another (Red) for general operations, another for North Africa, and so on. The German Army had its own settings, as did the Navy, the Abwehr (military intelligence), Heinrich Himmler's Sicherheitsdienst (security police), and other agencies. In a sense, all of these settings had to be broken repeatedly, as daily changes and the initial rotor positions for individual messages presented new problems for solution. The result was not a single, quick victory, but a continuing, painstaking, and sometimes unsuccessful effort to decrypt Enigma intercepts while they might still be useful. All this took place at Bletchley Park, "a ghastly late Victorian mansion" northwest of London, to which the Government Code and Cipher School had been removed shortly before war began.

The success of these efforts depended not only on the sophistication of British cryptanalysts but also on the carelessness of German operators. The number of possible Enigma settings was so enormous and the time required to sift through them so prohibitive that the correct settings would rarely be found unless the cryptanalysts knew where to look. They tried to find a "probable word"—some known word or phrase that they could use to deduce the Enigma settings used to encode the message. Although a good cipher clerk could defeat the "probable word" attack by stratagems designed to make communications unpredictable, a careless operator was the cryptanalyst's best friend. A bad clerk might select the settings in some nonrandom way, so that the cryptanalyst knew what to look for. Some used the names of girlfriends. Or the clerk might phrase messages in a stereotyped way, as, for example, by always beginning daily reports with the same formal salutation to the commander. Anytime the same message is transmitted in two different ciphers, there is the cryptanalyst's chance. One expert has concluded that the Enigma "would have been impregnable if it had been used properly." Fortunately, it was not.

This dependence on German mistakes meant that the various Enigma networks were not equally hard to penetrate. The Luftwaffe was the first and the easiest. Perhaps Hermann Göring's megalomaniacal confidence infected his men. In any event, the Luftwaffe's use of Enigma was "helpfully insecure and slapdash" throughout the war. Indeed, at Bletchley Park it came to be expected that the daily settings for the main Luftwaffe network would be available before breakfast. Cipher discipline was far better in the German Army and better still in the German Navy, which presented problems all its own.

So it was that by luck, insight, and the massing of resources, the

British came to be able to decipher the most secret of Germany's wartime communications. This ability was never perfect. There were delays, interruptions, and blind spots. Over time, however, British capabilities improved, and as thousands upon thousands of radio intercepts poured into Bletchley Park, more and more of them could be quickly deciphered and read.

THE CODE WORD for Enigma decrypts was Ultra. The name suggested something beyond "most" or "top" secret and had complementary implications. Ultra intelligence was immensely valuable but also immensely vulnerable. If the Germans had discovered the success at Bletchley Park, they could have redesigned the Enigma, tightened communications discipline, and taken other steps to defeat cryptanalysis. The challenge, therefore, was simultaneously to use and to protect Ultra intelligence.

This required first that Bletchley Park itself be secure. Everyone who worked there was carefully chosen. RAF personnel patrolled the perimeter. Those assigned to Bletchley Park usually came for the duration; once admitted to the secrets of Ultra, transfer to another post became virtually impossible. They swore to keep their mouths shut, and they did—not only during the war but for decades thereafter. Churchill called them "the geese who laid the golden eggs but never cackled."

Second, Ultra intelligence had to be communicated to those who could use it. Within Britain itself, distribution could easily be accomplished to the few authorized recipients. Throughout the war, Bletchley Park's most satisfied customer was Churchill himself, who received his "eggs" in a locked box despatched daily by "C" to his chief. Graver problems arose for distribution to commanders in the field. They had to be indoctrinated into Ultra and given the latest Enigma decrypts, but the content and source of those communications had to be zealously guarded.

For this, a special system was devised. Its creator was RAF Group Captain F. W. Winterbotham, whose 1974 best-seller *The Ultra Secret* first gave wide currency to knowledge of Ultra. Winterbotham distributed Ultra to field commands via Special Liaison Units, or SLUs, attached to the headquarters of Ultra recipients but not under their command. Instead, the SLUs reported to the British Secret Service in London. An SLU consisted of an officer (usually kept at junior rank to avoid any indication of importance) and two or three technician sergeants to operate the radio. (Their transmissions often were enciphered on the Typex, a machine not unlike the Enigma, but more tight-ly controlled. Reportedly, their communications were monitored by British cryptographers to assure strict cipher security.) The SLU officer had to decipher the Ultra radio signals, deliver the messages to the commander, and recover them afterward for destruction. Recipients were not allowed to keep Ultra signals nor to repeat, transmit, or refer to them in any way.

Furthermore, any action taken on the basis of Ultra had to be so contrived that the enemy could not guess the source of the information. Sometimes this was as simple as leaking word that the information came from the Italians—an explanation that the Germans found infinitely plausible. A more elaborate example comes from the air campaign to interdict German shipments to North Africa. Ultra often revealed the precise dates on which tankers would leave Italy to cross the Mediterranean. Reconnaissance aircraft would then be sent out to see—*and be seen by*—the target vessels. The visual sighting would be reported to bomber command which would sink the tanker. In this way, low-level intelligence served as a cover for Ultra.*

All this was laid down to the Special Liaison Unit officers by Winterbotham. Controlling senior commanders was something else again. It could be a delicate business for SLU officers to insist that strong-minded generals follow the rules. When problems arose, Winterbotham himself would fly out to set things right. Ultimately, breaches of Ultra security could be reported to the Chiefs of Staff or, on his order, to Churchill personally.

The SLUs succeeded in maintaining a low profile for Ultra and for themselves. This was so even at American commands, where unexplained British personnel might have aroused curiosity and suspicion. As an intelligence officer at a largely American headquarters in North Africa in 1943, Powell never heard of Ultra. Of course, he had seen the

---

*   A famous nonexample of the role of Ultra cover is the bombing of Coventry. The story is often told that the British knew of the impending attack but deliberately sacrificed Coventry to save Ultra. This was the version broadcast on "60 Minutes" on August 1, 1982, and reported by Anthony Cave Brown in his thrilling book *Bodyguard of Lies*. The conventional story, however, is at least an exaggeration. The British did know of a huge impending raid on one or more of three cities, including Coventry, but correct identification of the targets was delayed by use of code names. Moreover, the British did take countermeasures, although they proved largely ineffectual. For a vigorous attack on the "monstrous distortion" that Churchill deliberately sacrificed Coventry, see Ronald Lewin, *Ultra Goes to War*, pages 99–103. A careful sifting of the evidence, together with specific corrections of published views and reproduction of original sources, appears in F. H. Hinsley, *British Intelligence in the Second World War*, volume I, pages 528–48.

SLU unit—two or three British soldiers and a truck partly concealed by camouflage netting—but he did not know who they were or what they did. He assumed that they were involved with low-level radio intercepts. The same was true at other American headquarters, where the "secret Limeys" quietly went about their work, revealing neither their identity nor their mission.

EVEN BEFORE PEARL HARBOR, the British and Americans had exchanged signal intelligence. After the United States entered the war, closer cooperation was sought, but proved difficult to achieve—especially where Ultra was concerned. The British may have feared that their own efforts might be swamped by American resources, and in any event they distrusted American security. They dispatched British SLUs to service American commanders* but did not encourage direct American involvement. This policy irked the American intelligence officers, who did not want to be merely clients of Bletchley Park. The resulting negotiations were protracted and difficult, but on May 17, 1943, agreement was reached: The U.S. cryptology effort would concentrate on Japanese ciphers; the reading of German and Italian military ciphers would remain at Bletchley Park; and each side would share all decrypts. An appendix spelled out elaborate precautions for the use and handling of these materials. The American delegation to Bletchley Park would be strengthened, and American officers would work alongside the British in the decryption of Enigma ciphers and in the selection of messages to be sent to Washington and to the theater commands. Finally, although communication of Ultra decrypts remained in the hands of the British SLUs, American commanders would also be given an American officer, trained at Bletchley Park, to serve as Ultra adviser or representative. It was this position for which Colonel Alfred McCormack recruited Powell.

COLONEL McCORMACK WAS not Regular Army. He was a Wall Street lawyer, recruited to government service in the aftermath of Pearl Harbor. In outcome, Pearl Harbor was a naval defeat; in origin, it was

---

* Most American commanders made good use of Ultra. An exception was General Mark Clark, who showed a foolish and costly indifference to Ultra intelligence. One other American, Eighth Air Force commander Ira Eaker, had his staff make use of Ultra, but obstinately refused to allow himself to be indoctrinated into its secrets. Eaker resisted personal knowledge because he was unwilling to accept the restriction, placed on every Ultra recipient, that he not voluntarily place himself in danger of capture by the enemy.

an intelligence disaster. Decrypted Japanese communications that gave lavish warning of the impending attack went unheeded. Complacency, interservice rivalry, and inadequacy of personnel were factors, but most important was the lack of any effective system for the evaluation and use of signal intelligence. McCormack was brought in to solve this problem.

Brilliant, successful, and hard-working, McCormack was intolerant of failure and impatient with routine. He did not suffer fools gladly, even when they wore a general's stars. After two months of investigation, McCormack reported to Secretary of War Henry Stimson that "there was a very large job to be done all along the line." He wanted a new organization and new personnel. The new organization was to bring all of radio intelligence (then lodged in the Signal Corps) under G-2, the intelligence division of the General Staff. The Special Branch, as it came to be known, would see that enemy radio communications were not only intercepted and decrypted, but also analyzed, distributed, and properly used. For these tasks, McCormack insisted, Special Branch needed special personnel. Because of its "reputation as a graveyard for Regular Army careers," military intelligence had not attracted the Army's best talent. New men were required. The challenge facing Special Branch, said McCormack, could be met "only by imaginative persons of absolutely first-class ability and suitable training, and not simply by any reserve officer or college graduate who happened to be available."

Stimson approved McCormack's proposals and seduced him into uniform to help put them into effect. McCormack became Deputy Chief of Special Branch, second to Colonel (later Brigadier) Carter W. Clarke, one of the few Regular Army officers able to handle McCormack. During the investigation, McCormack had fired a brigadier and three colonels detailed to assist him. Clarke was next. He later recalled that his assignment was to "go down there and get along with that goddamned man"—and he did.

Clarke and McCormack made a good team. Clarke covered the military side of military intelligence—security, administration, and political infighting. McCormack set about recruiting Ultra advisers. The concept was entirely American. British SLU officers did not share normal intelligence duties; they communicated Ultra signals and left the recipients to form their own judgments. In American commands, however, an American Ultra representative would receive the decrypts from the SLU, evaluate them in light of other intelligence, and interpret them for his superiors. He also would monitor security to ensure that no action taken on Ultra information would reveal the source. In short, the adviser would see that Ultra intelligence was used and not misused. In the words of one historian, an Ultra adviser would have to be "a clear-headed diplomat, capable of assimilating detailed information rapidly and of expounding it lucidly; persuasive, independent, authoritative."

Lewis Powell was an obvious choice. Like most of the twenty-eight men McCormack selected, Powell was a lawyer. He knew how to assemble evidence and to make a lucid presentation. Unlike many others, he had only a glancing connection to the Ivy League (and none to Princeton, where McCormack had gone), but he had done well at school. His age and standing outside the military would nourish independence, and his instinctive tact and ingrained courtesy would smooth relations with senior officers.

In these ways, Powell was broadly typical of American Ultra advisers, but in another he was almost unique. Unlike most others, Powell had combat intelligence experience. He had an uncommon familiarity with the other intelligence sources that made up the background for interpreting Ultra decrypts, and he had worked for a commander who was soon to play an even larger role. Spaatz had left the Mediterranean and was now back in Britain as commander of the United States Strategic Air Forces (USSTAF). It was that command to which Powell now returned as Ultra Secret representative.

RETURN TO EUROPE

On February 25, 1944, Josephine Powell saw her husband board a DC-4 transport for a night flight to Europe. He carried a locked canvas pouch to be delivered to General Eisenhower. Also on the sparsely filled airplane was the Polish ambassador to the United States from the London government in exile. The plane refueled in Nova Scotia and took off again about midnight in cold, snowy weather. After a few hours, the passengers were told to put on oxygen masks, as the pilot was trying to fly above a storm. This proved impossible, and by the next morning, they were flying just a few hundred feet over the Bay of Biscay, low on fuel and hundreds of miles off course. The pilot warned that they might have to ditch in the ocean or land in the neutral Republic of Ireland, where military personnel would have been interned for the duration. In preparation, Powell tied the courier pouch to his service revolver to make sure it sank, but the fuel held out until they reached an inactive RAF field in Northern Ireland. When they tried to take off again the next morning, they knocked the tip off a wing. A new plane was sent, and on February 28, Powell finally made London, delivered the pouch to Eisenhower's headquarters, and reported to the office of Special Branch. Josephine learned of his arrival from a tiny newspaper article noting the return to London of the Polish ambassador.

At Special Branch, Powell reported to McCormack's London deputy, Colonel Telford Taylor. Taylor, former general counsel to the Federal Communications Commission and future Nuremberg prosecutor. In between, Taylor headed the Military Intelligence Service, War Department, London—a deliberately vague title for the senior Ultra representative in Europe.

Taylor sent Powell to Bletchley Park for training. Arriving at about the same time were three other Ultra advisers. Major James Fellers, an Oklahoma City lawyer, was one of the few Ultra advisers from west of the Mississippi and, like Powell, a future president of the ABA. After indoctrination, he was sent to advise Powell's friend, General "Pete" Quesada, commander of the IX Tactical Air Command. Major Adolph G. "Rosey" Rosengarten, a Philadelphia lawyer described as more military than the West Pointers, was assigned to General Omar Bradley. Finally, there was Captain Alfred Friendly, future Pulitzer Prize winner and managing editor of the *Washington Post*, who was billeted near Powell in the small town of Bedford, from which they commuted by train each day to Bletchley. Friendly remained at Bletchley Park to help translate Enigma decrypts.*

Powell's training at Bletchley Park was one part Ultra and three parts German Air Force. Of Ultra itself, the Americans were shown everything. Powell "had no feeling whatever of any restraint on what we saw" and found the British totally frank. "They told us things that I don't think Americans would have told us." This was good policy, as it encouraged a sense of identification with the community at Bletchley Park to offset, if need be, the natural instinct of loyalty to an American field commander. Powell said later that his "own personal experience with the British, at and after Bletchley, could not have been better."

At Bletchley, Powell met the brilliant mathematician Alan Turing and many others, but the bulk of his training came from two young

---

*   In 1983 Friendly shot himself after a long illness. Powell wrote several wartime friends with the news of Friendly's death but did not mention the immediate cause.

RAF officers destined for postwar careers in publishing, E. J. B. "Jim" Rose and Peter Calvocoressi. They were Bletchley Park's leading experts on the German Air Force. After decryption, Enigma intercepts were translated from the German, assessed, and annotated for the recipients. Points of interest were noted on index cards. The cards recorded all sorts of information—names of German officers, location of units, production plans and estimates, damage and casualty reports, and technical information of all descriptions. As the index grew, it became an encyclopedia of Allied intelligence. Given the Luftwaffe's necessary reliance on radio communications and its poor cipher discipline, the index was especially detailed in its coverage of the German Air Force. Rose and Calvocoressi certainly knew more about the organization and operation of the German Air Force than anyone else in the West and, as Powell believed, may have known more than many high-ranking Germans.

Powell emerged from their training, as he thought, "an authentic expert on the German Air Force." Some confirmation of that claim comes from a small buff notebook containing fifty sides of closely written notes on Luftwaffe organization, training, operations, and tactics. Only a much later annotation connects these notes with Bletchley Park. In 1944 they were identified merely as belonging to Lewis F. Powell, Jr., Maj. A.C., Office of the Military Attache, American Embassy, London. Nothing reveals the source of this information, although its accuracy and detail would surely have been cause for German alarm.

AFTER THREE WEEKS at Bletchley Park, Powell was sent to the Mediterranean. He left London on April 4 and three days later arrived in Algiers, where he delivered sealed documents and explained his mission. Two days thereafter, he flew to Italy and toured U.S. operations in Caserta, Monte Cassino, and Bari, before returning to Algiers. On these travels, Powell interviewed British SLU personnel, met American intelligence officers, and sat in on their briefings. He made detailed, but elliptical, notes on personnel and operations.

On May 14, 1944, Powell submitted a report on his investigation. In its final section, he made a number of recommendations, including increasing Air Force representation in Special Branch. He proposed that every American and every joint American-British command should have an American Ultra representative, in addition to British SLUs, and that senior officers, who assumed that Ultra was a purely British product, should be advised of the growing American participation (taking care, of course, "not to minimize the magnificent efforts of the British"). Most important, he insisted that Ultra advisers should be given more training in other sources of air intelligence: "While the importance of those other sources will usually be conceded, there seems to be a tendency in practice to rely too heavily upon Ultra to the exclusion of all else. Officers trained by Special Branch must avoid this tendency, and this can best be accomplished by greater emphasis during the training period on what may be described as general combat intelligence."

Obviously, this recommendation reflected the lessons of Powell's pre-Ultra experience in North Africa. Less obviously, it also reflected his determination not to confine himself to a narrow mission, however important it might be, but to make himself broadly competent to participate in a wide range of intelligence decisions. He carried that determination with him, when, on May 14, 1944, he reported to General Spaatz.

USSTAF

Spaatz commanded the United States Strategic Air Force (known by the unlovely acronym USSTAF), which was headquartered in Bushey Park, near the palace of Hampton Court on the outskirts of London. Bushey Park was also home to SHAEF, Supreme Headquarters of the Allied Expeditionary Force, under General Eisenhower. The propinquity was no accident. Spaatz and Eisenhower were old comrades, and Spaatz "liked to be close enough to Eisenhower's headquarters to coordinate plans personally." Powell stayed at Bushey Park until the success of Normandy was assured and USSTAF established advance headquarters in France. For some months, he shuttled back and forth between the two locations, and at the end of the year moved permanently to the new main headquarters in St. Germain.

The intelligence staff to which Powell reported was already a sizable operation. The chief was Brigadier General George C. MacDonald, an easygoing fellow whom subordinates called "Uncle George." He delegated work to others and "never wrote anything himself." His deputy was Colonel Lowell Weicker, a Yale man whose father had built E. R. Squibb & Sons into a pharmaceutical giant and whose son would later serve as a United States Senator from Connecticut and later Governor of that state. Weicker was, in Powell's words, "extremely attractive, extremely generous, and very engaging," but he was also hot-tempered and self-indulgent. Though Weicker's quick anger when confronting disagreement hurt his ability to deal with others, he and Powell became close friends.

Of the several groups working under Weicker, the largest was the Operational Intelligence Section, headed by Lieutenant Colonel Julian Allen. Before the war, Allen had joined the Paris banking affiliate of J. P. Morgan. He had an apartment in Paris and a country house in Normandy, which the Germans occupied when they overran France. They drank the rather ordinary wines found there and, when they withdrew, left Allen a polite thank-you note, never having discovered the rare wines and precious silver buried halfway down an abandoned well. Allen had joined the British Army, where he served until the United States entered the war. Allen was ideally suited to his job in intelligence, as he spoke French and German fluently and, said Powell, "knew Western Europe as well as I know the state of Virginia."

Under Allen were some seventeen officers and various enlisted personnel divided among the several functions of operational intelligence. McDonald, Weicker, and Allen were "in the know" on Ultra, but none had been to Bletchley Park or received formal training.

Powell's integration into this organization was surprisingly quick. Technically, he was not even under Spaatz's command—"although if he spoke, I listened." As a member of Special Branch, Powell was commanded by Telford Taylor but detailed to Spaatz as Ultra representative. As such, he was a special concern of Chief of Staff General George C. Marshall. On March 15, 1944, Marshall had set out the duties of Ultra representatives in a directive to General Eisenhower: "Their primary responsibility will be to evaluate Ultra intelligence, present it in useable form to the Commanding Officer and to such of his senior staff officers as are authorized Ultra recipients, assist in fusing Ultra intelligence with intelligence derived from other sources, and give advice in connection with making operational use of Ultra intelligence in such fashion that the security of the source is not endangered." The letter set forth safeguards for the use of Ultra and concluded by reiterating the particular importance that Ultra representatives be given "facilities and opportunity . . . to enable them to perform their duties fully and effectively." This direction was to be passed on to all Ultra recipients. To make absolutely sure that Eisenhower understood the importance of these instructions, Marshall appended a cover letter directing him to "give this matter your personal attention" and "take all necessary steps" to see that the requirements were "meticulously observed."

Marshall had given the Ultra representatives a charter of responsibility and independence. He had defined their mandate broadly and had charged Eisenhower personally to see that others would cooperate. All this Powell knew, but he seems to have relied most heavily on another, and quite innocuous, sentence in Marshall's letter. "If at any time," Marshall noted, "the flow of Ultra intelligence is not sufficient to occupy fully the time of these officers, they may be used for other related intelligence assignments."

Powell exploited this invitation. Virtually his first task was to assess the workings of the Operational Intelligence Section and report to Julian Allen, which he did in a memorandum revealing his usual effective combination of deference and ambition. Powell found the section "on the whole, functioning most efficiently" but offered several comments and suggestions. Then he addressed his own agenda: "In considering the manner in which I can be of greatest value to you as your Assistant, I suggest the gradual delegation to me of the following duties." There followed a long list of specific suggestions, which closed with a bid for responsibility buried in a promise of cooperation: "In general, learn to 'pinch-hit' for you on all matters whenever you are away, and at all times endeavour to relieve you of as much detail as possible."

In fact, Allen needed an alter ego. Known for his loose administrative style, General Spaatz spent little time at headquarters. As he preferred to work in his residence, where he used Allen as his personal briefing officer, someone had to stand in for Allen back at the office. Powell must have done so effectively, for plans were soon laid for Powell to take over as Director of Operational Intelligence when Allen followed Spaatz to France.

In this position, Powell would command senior officers and routinely deal with American and British officers of exalted rank. A promotion was therefore needed. Spaatz sent a personal letter to the Assistant Chief of Staff for Intelligence, saying it was "absolutely essential" that Powell's rank be brought "more in line with his responsibilities" and requesting waiver of minimum time in grade. McDonald and Weicker followed with letters to Telford Taylor and Alfred McCormack. This three-pronged attack succeeded, and Powell was promoted to Lieutenant Colonel on August 30, 1944, the same day that advance headquarters were established in France and Powell became head of the Operational Intelligence Section.

In January 1945, Powell's unit was given additional responsibilities and reorganized as the Operational Intelligence Division. The expanded operation comprised four branches, one headed by a full colonel, employing in all about forty officers and an equal number of enlisted personnel. Another early promotion was recommended. Spaatz, McDonald, and Weicker again wrote everyone in sight, emphasizing Powell's daily representation of USSTAF at Eisenhower's morning briefing and arguing that "the rank of Lt. Colonel is too light for this responsibility." Taylor agreed, but the proposal was too much for Washington. Despite continuing pressure from USSTAF, the promotion to full colonel hung fire until July 26.

As the wrangling over promotion reveals, Powell's USSTAF superiors regarded him as their own. Indeed, McDonald originally recommended Powell to the theater commander for the Legion of Merit, only later to remember that the recommendation had to come from Powell's official boss in Washington. McDonald, Weicker, and Allen would hardly have been so concerned for Powell's advancement had he insisted on the independence authorized by Special Branch. Powell's successful integration into USSTAF intelligence owed much to Spaatz and his staff, who welcomed Ultra and used it responsibly. But it was also a tribute to Powell's own drive and adaptability. His instinct for team play and desire to play an active role led Powell to seek major operational responsibility in USSTAF intelligence.

THE CENTERPIECE of Powell's USSTAF duties was the daily briefing. Spaatz was often briefed separately by Julian Allen, and on these occasions the senior officer at the headquarters briefing would be Spaatz's deputy, Major General Frederick L. Anderson, Jr. Powell and Anderson built a close working relationship. When all those present were "in the know," Powell could describe Ultra decrypts directly. Otherwise, Ultra information would be merged with intelligence from less sensitive sources or withheld for more private communication. Ultra was by no means the only source. Intelligence also came from the British Air Ministry, which employed several thousand persons in collecting, analyzing, and evaluating information on the German Air Force. Additional information came from photographic reconnaissance, aerial observation, low-level "Y" radio intercepts, agents and collaborators, prisoners of war, and captured documents and equipment. Powell's job was to integrate information from all these sources into a coherent summary for daily presentation to Spaatz and Anderson.

As Powell's responsibilities grew, delegation to others became more and more necessary. Especially after the reorganization of the Operational Intelligence Division, Powell's duties became increasingly

administrative and supervisory. Just as he would years later in law practice, Powell quickly saw the value of well-trained subordinates, who
could step in when needed. For their benefit, he wrote a long memorandum on the etiquette, style, and content of war room presentation.
He insisted on "thorough and painstaking preparation." Time pressure
required the use of notes prepared by others, but "the briefing officer
must study these notes with sufficient care . . . to know and understand them thoroughly." Certain items had to be read word for word,
but since it was "more difficult to read material effectively than to
speak in the ordinary way," these items also had to be studied carefully
in advance. It was much like a lawyer's preparation for trial.

There was also a lot of writing. In addition to the regular reports
and appreciations issued daily or weekly, Powell's unit made special
studies of such topics as the impact of American air power on the
German war machine, the effectiveness of carpet bombing of German
troops in the front lines, and the role of Allied air power in checking
the Ardennes offensive. At one point, Powell prepared a plan to isolate
the Ruhr by bombing lines of communication and transportation.
There was a special report on the German oil industry as a target for
strategic bombing and another on all feasible target systems, focusing
especially on "the time factor between an air attack and its actual
effect on the fighting front." In all these efforts, the premium was on
the lawyerly skills of accuracy, clarity, and logical presentation.

Among Powell's most interesting duties was the task of representing
USSTAF at SHAEF. In early 1945 Powell often represented General
McDonald at Eisenhower's briefing, held daily in the Petit Trianon at
Versailles. He also sometimes represented USSTAF at deliberations of
the SHAEF Joint Intelligence Committee. Most important of all was
the SHAEF Weekly Air Commanders Meeting, where the Allied air
commanders met to discuss the past week's operations and to plan for
the future. McDonald himself attended this meeting, but he was usually accompanied by Powell and Allen.

THE CHIEF OBJECT of all these efforts was the selection of bombing targets. Both the British and the Germans had abandoned daylight
bombing. Grievous losses had driven both forces into bombing at
night, when the only targets they could find were enemy cities. The
Americans, by contrast, practiced "precision bombing." They had aircraft that could fly above the level of preclusive flak and a bombsight
that promised accuracy from high altitude. Even the heavily armed
American planes were subject to appalling losses if sent without fight-

er protection, but if properly escorted, and given fair weather (which was rare indeed in the winter of 1944–45), American heavy bombers could hit specifically identified targets with considerable accuracy. Choosing the targets to be attacked was, and remains, controversial.

For American airmen, first priority was the destruction of the German Air Force. This could be attempted directly, by attacking airfields and destroying aircraft manufacture, or indirectly, by bombing strategic targets of such importance that the Luftwaffe would have to risk their dwindling assets to defend. The former approach culminated in February 1944 in the famous "Big Week" of massive bombing raids against virtually every known source of German fighter production. Great claims were made for these raids at the time, but it soon became plain that they did more to disperse than to destroy German fighter production. The indirect strategy focused on oil. Oil was crucial to the German military machine and especially to the Luftwaffe. Destruction of natural and synthetic oil production would not only be debilitating in itself; it would force the German fighters to take to the air in defense of oil and, in so doing, to risk their own destruction.

Spaatz urged the oil campaign on Eisenhower in the planning for the invasion of Europe, but Ike opted instead for a plan to bomb railroads. Attacking transportation was the best way for air power to make an immediate contribution to the land battle in Normandy, which was Eisenhower's overriding concern.

After the landings at Normandy, the oil strategy quickly resurfaced. In a letter to his subordinate commanders dated September 1, 1944, Spaatz reported that the Germans had successfully dispersed and hidden airframe production but that the attacks on oil had cut deep: "The German Air Force, Ground Forces, and economy, are all imminently faced with collapse for lack of fuel." Therefore, oil was the top priority. Direct assault on the German aircraft industry would be limited to engine factories and the fledgling production of rockets and jet fighters. Excess bombing capacity could be devoted to ordnance depots and the production of tanks and motor transport or to enemy transportation.

From Powell's point of view, these priorities partly came down from on high and partly evolved upward from USSTAF intelligence reports. Ultra provided a particularly rich account of the success of the oil strategy. From September 1944 until the German surrender, Ultra decrypts were "an almost continuous chronicle of oil shortage everywhere." Through Ultra, Powell received and reported the nearly daily German complaints of fuel trouble, the difficulty of dispersing or disguising synthetic oil manufacture, and the progressive enfeeblement of the German Air Force as operations of all sorts were curtailed for lack of fuel.

Years later, Powell recalled a spectacular instance of the campaign against oil: "[W]e knew almost as soon as Albert Speer did that we had found the vital organ of the German economy in the synthetic oil plants. . . . They had all been located back in East Germany, so that until we had fighter escorts, it was just too dangerous to attack them. We usually had damage assessment reports from Ultra following an attack. I remember one from Leuna advising Speer that we had reduced its capacity to some twelve to fifteen percent, and it would be six weeks before they could get production back to a significant level. The great beauty of that was that we knew when to attack again."

In fact, the Allies attacked synthetic oil plants again and again. The largest was Leuna, which was bombed heavily on May 28, 1944, and (after the six weeks mentioned by Powell) again on July 7 and twenty times after that. The campaign was expensive and dangerous but effective. From the first raid until the end of the war, production at Leuna averaged only 9 percent of capacity.

Equally critical was the wastage of German pilots. The Luftwaffe spent itself in defense of oil and other targets, and although Speer was able to build more planes, he could not manufacture experienced crews. The fuel shortage meant that they were never adequately trained. Through Ultra, Powell chronicled the terrible attrition of German pilots. By September 1944, USSTAF would know that "[p]ilots and gasoline shortages have become the limiting factor in G.A.F. operations, *not* aircraft." Strategic bombing exploited this knowledge.

OF THE INNUMERABLE TARGETS of Allied strategic bombings, none is so controversial as Dresden. On the night of February 13, 1945, British bombers dropped more than 2,500 tons of bombs, both high-explosive and incendiary, on Dresden and left that small, crowded city engulfed in flames. American bombers arrived the next day with instructions to bomb the railroad marshaling yards, only to find the target obscured by smoke. They bombed by radar (with what accuracy one can only guess), dumping nearly 700 additional tons of explosives. A second American raid on the 15th, followed that night by still more British bombing, suggests a prenuclear use for the word "overkill." Estimates of the dead have gone as high as 135,000. Although that figure is unsubstantiated and extreme, even the more careful estimates of 35,000 dead are quite high enough to evoke horror. Among historians, the decision to bomb Dresden remains in bitter dispute, but among the public at large, "the city has become a symbol for Allied brutality and mindless destructiveness."

To these great events, Powell was little more than a bystander. Dresden came to him as a decision, not a proposal. Its first mention was a request from General Anderson for target information and maps—a request that Powell could not immediately meet, as Dresden had been thought "off-limits so far as any objectives of the American Army Air Forces were concerned."

Another Bletchley Park veteran was more actively involved. Powell's friend and former instructor, Wing Commander Jim Rose, was now Powell's counterpart in operational intelligence at the British Air Ministry. Rose learned of the intention to bomb Dresden and tried to head it off. He called Spaatz, who was amenable to canceling the mission, and the British commander, Sir Arthur "Bomber" Harris, who was not. As Telford Taylor later recalled, "Sir Arthur was adamant and General Spaatz was unwilling to stand aside if the British were insistent on going ahead." Dresden was bombed as planned.

Forty years later, Rose thought of publishing his story and asked Powell for information. Powell was eager to respond. For years he had chafed at Soviet and East German propaganda portraying Dresden as evidence of Anglo-American atrocity far beyond the damage inflicted by the Russian occupiers. In 1978, after an exhibit at the National Gallery entitled "The Splendors of Dresden," friends asked Powell why this jewel of the Northern Renaissance had been destroyed. Powell put that question to General George S. Brown, recently retired as Air Force Chief of Staff, who showed the letter to General Ira Eaker, former commander of the Fifteenth Air Force, then living in retirement in Washington. Eaker's response to Powell included a scholarly article on the subject, as well as a draft of his own introduction to the American edition of David Irving's *The Destruction of Dresden*. Subsequently, Powell and Eaker corresponded with each other and with Robert A. Lovett, former Assistant Secretary of War for Air. Additionally, Powell wrote or spoke to several others—to Spaatz himself, who died in 1974; to Spaatz's biographer, David R. Mets; to General Pete Quesada; and to John J. McCloy, former Assistant Secretary of War. Therefore, in March 1985, when Powell got Rose's letter, he was able to present Rose with the collective memory of several witnesses.

POWELL AGREED THAT Dresden was "a dreadful mistake." When first told of the plan by General Anderson in 1945, Powell had said he thought Dresden was "'off-limits'—as an historic city target of no military significance to us." Anderson replied that the attacks had been requested by the Soviet Union. Some years earlier, Powell had checked with Spaatz, who "stated briefly that he understood that the Soviets wanted Dresden bombed, that the British had agreed, and that the U.S. Air Force would never had attacked it otherwise." Eaker had agreed that "none of the senior American air commanders viewed Dresden as a proper target" and was "unequivocal in his recollection that Soviet pressure prompted the attacks." Quesada had heard the same story, and Lovett and McCloy confirmed the "common understanding in the War Department" that the Russians had insisted on bombing Dresden because of its "importance as a communications center for troops and supplies moving to the Eastern front."

The idea of a Russian request for the bombing of Dresden has general currency in U.S. Air Force circles. Powell is not the only, or the most important, source of such speculation. Such a request might have been conveyed in one or more of three ways. First, the Soviets might have made a specific request through Washington. This was Powell's first surmise, but it is almost certainly untrue. It is clear that the Soviets were informed of the plan and did not object, but there is no record of a request made by them to Washington.

Second, the request could have been made when Roosevelt, Churchill, and Stalin convened at Yalta. In fact, there is evidence that it was. On February 3, 1945, General Antonov, Deputy Chief of Staff of the Red Army, asked for Anglo-American air support to interdict reinforcements to the eastern front. As described by Churchill's biographer, Martin Gilbert: "The British and American Chiefs of Staff at once agreed . . . to an attack on the German army's lines of communications in the Berlin-Dresden-Leipzig region. They also agreed, at Antonov's suggestion, that these three specific cities should be 'allotted to the Allied air forces,' leaving Russian bombers to attack targets further east." According to Gilbert, the bombing of Dresden was "a direct result of the agreement reached at Yalta by the British, United States, and Soviet Chiefs of Staff, to make emergency use of Anglo-American air power in order to disrupt German reinforcements moving eastward to the Russian front." This may well have been the basis for Anderson's remark to Powell that the Soviets had requested the bombing, for Anderson had been at Yalta and surely would have learned of plans made there for American strategic bombing.

The Yalta explanation is good as far as it goes, but it fails to account for earlier identification of Dresden as a target by the British. A week before Yalta, the British Joint Intelligence Committee suggested that the war could be shortened decisively if Anglo-American bombers could give "assistance to the Russians during the next few weeks." "Bomber" Harris, "a commander of coarse singlemindedness" in pursuit of the destruction of German cities, nominated Berlin, Leipzig, and Dresden as "focal points of the German system of communications in front of the Red Army." Urged on by a blustery Churchill, who only later doubted the wisdom of bombing German cities "simply for the sake of increasing the terror," the British made plans for bombing Dresden, consulted with Spaatz, and forwarded these plans to Yalta. Thus, however much Antonov and the other Soviets may have wanted the bombing, their request at Yalta did not originate the idea; the British had already conceived a plan to bomb Dresden and other eastern cities as a way of helping the Russian offensive.

The third and least noticed opportunity for a Russian request to bomb Dresden was the experiment with shuttle bombing. The idea was that American bombers might reach targets otherwise beyond their range by flying straight across Europe, refueling and rearming at Soviet bases, and returning to the west the next day. The Russians agreed in principle but were obstructionist in practice. Their attitude—and German success in counterattacking the Russian bases—caused the scheme to be dropped after a few trips. Ira Eaker led the first shuttle bombing mission on June 2, 1944. He later reported to Powell that he had been asked by Marshal Novikov, head of the Soviet Air Force, to bomb Dresden, as it was "the principal logistic and communications center supporting the German defense against Marshal Zhukov's advance." Eaker also said the same request had been made to Fred Anderson when he headed the second shuttle mission a few weeks later. According to Eaker, "Both Anderson and I communicated these requests to General Spaatz and they were passed on to the combined Chiefs of Staff."

These events also could have supported Anderson's statement that the Russians had asked for the attack, but they do not link up well with the actual sequence of events, as the shuttle missions came several months before Dresden was targeted. Nevertheless, the Russian requests made to Eaker and Anderson may help to explain why Spaatz so readily agreed to the British proposal and why the American airmen believed that the Russians were responsible. The truth about Dresden is probably the conventional story of British instigation of, and American acquiescence in, a plan that was consistent with Soviet wishes but that the Soviets later found convenient to disavow.

For present purposes, the curious thing about the decision to bomb Dresden is Powell's abiding interest in it. No one claimed that he had personally influenced the decision. Yet years later, his time otherwise fully occupied at the Supreme Court, Powell busied himself collecting evidence, interviewing witnesses, reading secondary sources, and urging others to write for publication. Powell's letters confirm that he was annoyed by the Soviet propaganda, yet the intensity of his reaction remains surprising. After all, whether the Soviets actually asked for the bombing of Dresden was not the crucial issue. If such a request had been proved beyond doubt, it would have merely demonstrated that the postwar Soviet accounts were not constrained by a punctilious regard for factual accuracy. That would have surprised no one, least of all Powell. And if a Soviet request to bomb Dresden had been indisputably shown, that would not have absolved Western leaders from responsibility. The decision to bomb Dresden may or may not have been justified by the exigencies of warfare in an industrial age, but the judgment of history—whatever it may be—will not turn on who first came up with the idea.

For Powell, the controversy over Dresden implicated something more personal and more important than proof of Soviet cynicism. For him, as for so many others, Dresden had become a symbol. It was a symbol of the postwar attack on the morality of strategic bombing. American airmen had long taken comfort in the fact that their equipment and technology allowed them to attempt something more precise than area bombing. They did not condemn the British, who, lacking the option, found a virtue in necessity and responded in kind to the German assault on London. Indeed, in the partisanship of war, many took grim satisfaction in the reduction of German cities. Powell himself at first shared this view. "The American Air Forces have, it is true, directed their efforts against industrial targets," he wrote a friend a few weeks after the attack, "but with blind bombing conditions on most days you can imagine the widespread destruction inevitably resulting. Personally, I consider this very fortunate indeed as the German people are being taught for the first time in modern history what it means to have war on their own soil."

But his more fundamental and durable reaction was relief, commingled with a subtle sense of superiority, that the Americans did not have to resort to area bombing. Of course, Powell knew as well as anyone that precision bombing was often not precise. When weather or smoke made bombing visually blind, radar would be used, with appreciable loss of accuracy. Military and industrial targets located in populated areas were fair game despite the civilian loss of life. Still, it was one thing to accept the inevitability of civilian casualties in modern warfare and quite another to set out with the goal of killing as many civilians as possible. Powell was always afterward to maintain this distinction: "It was not the policy of the Army Air Forces to bomb cities indiscriminately. We sought to attack military targets in the daytime. . . ." Powell often noted that American bombing of Dresden was aimed at the railroad marshaling yards—by any definition an acceptable military target.

There was a real difference between area and precision bombing, but the distinction was never as clear on the ground as it seemed in the air. In the case of Dresden—massive blind bombing of a target wholly obscured by smoke—it seems almost theoretical. That is why Powell was so anxious to insist that the attack originated elsewhere. If so, it would be possible to preserve, at least in the main, the belief in American restraint. If, as Powell insistently (and plausibly) believed, Spaatz, Anderson, Eaker, and others "would never have attacked Dresden on their own initiative," they—and he—had maintained an important reserve against the degradation of modern war. He wrote Jim Rose that the senior American officers with whom he dealt were "with occasional exceptions . . . strongly opposed to bombing civilians or cities indiscriminately. Our *primary* targets almost invariably [Berlin being the acknowledged exception] were military ones." When Rose wrote back a closely reasoned letter fingering Churchill and Harris but suggesting that Spaatz at least acquiesced, Powell gave a little ground: "There is probably enough blame for all concerned. My own view is that without the request of the Soviet Union and Churchill's desire to impress our 'ally,' USSTAF under Spaatz would never have targeted Dresden."

Still later, Powell wrote fellow USSTAF veteran Bill Haines, bringing him up to date on the Rose correspondence and relating evidence of Russian involvement. By this time, the issue had begun to wear. Powell again distinguished area from precision bombing but with a trace of nostalgia for a clarity that the distinction no longer seemed to have: "Apart from historical curiosity, I suppose there is little purpose in spending time on this now. We do know that Tooey [Spaatz] was opposed to the type of indiscriminate bombing that was the specialty of British Bomber Command. Marshaling yards are a legitimate target but where they were located in the middle of a large city—particularly an historic one like Dresden—I can't believe Tooey relished this."

Nor did Lewis Powell.

*   *   *

Dresden was not the only mission specifically directed from above. In the spring of 1945, the head of the Manhattan Project requested, through Chief of Staff George Marshall, the destruction of certain facilities in Oranienburg, a town eighteen miles north of Berlin. German prisoners of war and other sources had revealed that Oranienburg was the site for processing certain ores used in producing atomic energy. Fred Anderson told Powell that they had been ordered to bomb a "heavy water" plant in Oranienburg. Powell made a hectic trip to London to find the necessary maps, and a raid was launched on March 15. All above-ground facilities were destroyed, but since the site was occupied afterward by the Russians, no more detailed assessment is available.

In April, "Hap" Arnold, Commanding General of the Army Air Forces, visited the European theater. Powell was detailed as his personal intelligence officer. By this time USSTAF had nearly run out of targets, and Arnold's visit had the relaxed and joyful air of a victory tour. Nonetheless, elaborate arrangements were made to keep him informed of latest events. A war room was set up in the Ritz Hotel in Paris, where Powell gave twice daily briefings. After a few days, they went to Cannes. Communication with USSTAF headquarters was maintained by twice daily telephone calls, backed up by a teletype link for sensitive messages and a courier service for the most secret information. The events were serious, but Powell enjoyed lush steaks, rare wine, crisp pastry, and diligent waiters on a veranda overlooking the Mediterranean. He even found time for two pleasure trips: one to Monte Carlo, where he displayed a "conspicuous lack of skill" at roulette; and another to tag along on a PT boat mission, which he thoroughly enjoyed though it netted nothing. Despite these escapades, Powell continued twice daily briefings, answered Arnold's "innumerable questions," and "developed a very warm affection" for the affable commander.

When Powell returned to St. Germain, the end was well in sight. Shortly before the German surrender, Powell, McDonald, and Weicker flew to Salzburg and drove to the Berghof, Hitler's retreat near the village of Berchtesgaden. Their mission was to contact and recruit German General Staff officers who specialized in the Soviet air force. Accompanied by 101st Airborne troops, the American airmen found their German counterparts and made their offer: If the Germans came to England and shared all they knew about Soviet air capabilities, they would be allowed to return to Germany within a year. The Germans

were only too happy to accept, as they rightly feared capture by the
Soviets. They were flown back to England, housed outside London,
and debriefed at the Air Ministry. Though Powell doubted the utility
of this project, he came away with a nice souvenir. A recent RAF raid
had left the Berghof in shambles, but the basement housed a well-pro-
tected kitchen, dining room, sitting room, bedroom, and throat clinic.
In the disordered dining room, the three airmen found Adolf Hitler's
long-stemmed champagne glasses. These were liberated and given a
new home on Rothesay Circle in Richmond, Virginia.

VICTORY IN EUROPE

On May 7, 1945, only hours after Colonel General Jodl signed documents
of unconditional surrender, General Spaatz had a buffet luncheon in his
residence. The event was dominated by mixed emotions. Deep satisfaction with the victory over Nazi Germany was marred by a sense of lost
opportunity. Powell recalled a "consensus that we had the capability to
take Berlin and much of the territory that is now in East Germany."

The German surrender put operational intelligence out of business.
Powell now had three options. First, Spaatz was slated for the war in
the Pacific and offered to take Powell along. Since McDonald was
remaining in Europe, Powell would presumably have been Spaatz's
chief intelligence officer. Second, Powell was invited to Washington to
head the General Staff section on Japanese air intelligence. Third,
McDonald suggested that Powell might prefer to stay in Europe as
U.S. liaison to the British Air Ministry in London.

Ironically, Powell's decision to accept the third option sprang from
his desire to go home. The job in Washington would have allowed him
to rejoin his family but only at the cost of months—or years—of additional service in the war against Japan. The cleanup projects in Europe,
by contrast, were scheduled for completion by mid-September, so
Powell focused on September 19, his thirty-eighth birthday, as the target for getting out of uniform. McDonald agreed to let him go at that
time *and* to help him get out of the service.

The latter assurance was valuable, for Powell heard from every quarter that the Army was hoarding lawyers. They were needed to prosecute war criminals and to renegotiate government contracts, and the
Army was keeping them in service. The "latrine rumor" to this effect
was confirmed by the unfortunate experiences of some lawyer friends
and by the word from Robert A. Lovett "that it was extremely difficult

for a qualified lawyer to obtain a discharge at this time." Powell was not at all inclined to wind up his Army career "pursuing some petty war criminal or trying to squeeze a few dollars out of a government contractor." He would remain with McDonald in Europe and hope for an early out.

Powell's London duties were of two sorts. First, he had to oversee completion of various studies to document the air campaign against Germany and to support air force planning for the war against Japan or for any future conflict (including the unarmed but deadly earnest inter-service competition for postwar resources). One such effort was the Coffin Report, an extensive study under the direction of Lieutenant Colonel Caleb Coffin to document the contribution of air power to the defeat of Germany. Another study, for obvious reasons not mentioned at the time, was the Haines Report, written by William Wistar Haines (later author of *Command Decision*, a novel turned into a Broadway play and a feature film) to record the role of Ultra intelligence in strategic bombing. When the Haines report was declassified in 1979, the National Security Agency sent Powell a copy, which he then shared with its author. Eventually published in a series on classified studies and attributed only to the U.S. Army Air Force, the Haines Report is by far the most detailed and concrete account of the uses and limitations of Ultra intelligence in strategic bombing.

Second, and no doubt more fun, was Powell's work as liaison to the British Air Ministry. Part of his job was to establish good relations with the British personnel, including a new Air Vice Marshal. For this mission, Powell was ideally suited. He liked and admired the British, and his impeccable manners and slight reserve appealed to them. By late summer, he was able to report to McDonald "strong liaison" with Air Ministry and "wholesome relations" with its new chief.

WITH CHARACTERISTIC UNDERSTATEMENT, Powell described the circumstances of these labors as "entirely comfortable." In 1944 he had lived in a flat at 43 Lowndes Square owned by the Queen of Yugoslavia. He shared the place with Lowell Weicker and Lieutenant Colonel Stewart McClintic, a Yale graduate and Mellon banker who eventually took charge of the London-based headquarters of USSTAF intelligence. When Powell began to spend time in France, he kept his flat in London and left clothes in each place, a convenient arrangement but so expensive that he had to write home for financial reinforcements. When Powell was posted to the Air Ministry, he simply moved back full-time to 43 Lowndes Square.

Weicker soon decamped to the States, leaving Powell and McClintic to the care of their landlady and housekeeper, Mrs. Dawson. These unusual accommodations had been justified by Powell's need for a suitable place for entertaining British dignitaries, and they were sometimes put to that use. The queen's apartment was also used for less official entertainments, especially by Stewie McClintic, who came in for a good deal of kidding for high life and late parties, despite "the example of prudence and sobriety" that Powell claimed to set for him. The merriment pleased Mrs. Dawson, who thought the apartment "now almost as exciting as when Colonel Weicker was here."

But the comforts of England were nothing compared to the luxuries of France. When the Germans left Paris, McDonald, Weicker, Powell, and two other officers moved into a small mansion in the suburb of Neuilly, a short drive from the Allied headquarters at St. Germain. The house had formerly been occupied by a German military commander with a taste for the best. It had several large bedrooms, each with its own bath, and a huge drawing room that became a center of entertainment. The impresario of this establishment was Captain René deChochor, who got the house, recruited one of the great chefs of Paris and two assistants to run the kitchen, found three chambermaids to keep the place clean, and assigned an American staff sergeant to supervise. DeChochor himself was a world-class scrounger. Coffee, cigarettes, and fresh eggs (stowed away on B-17s coming from the States) could be swapped for almost anything. Equipped with a jeep and trailer and a C-47 cargo plane to transport them, deChochor flew to Burgundy and returned with one of Europe's best wine cellars.

Here, amid otherwise unobtainable luxuries—when bananas flambé was served for dessert, a countess begged for a fresh banana on the ground that her children had never seen one—Lowell Weicker entertained. Having lived in Paris before the war, he seemed to know everyone. The elegant drawing room was always full of famous people, invited by Weicker and lured by the fruits of deChochor's expeditions.

It was here that Powell found himself dining with Gertrude Stein and Alice Toklas. The joke among the Americans was that Stein had taken up with Toklas only to prove that she, Stein, was not in fact the ugliest woman in Europe. Powell later thanked Weicker for "the honor you did me . . . when the charming Alice (mustache and all) was assigned as my dinner companion," but confessed it had been "a rough evening." He also remembered—painfully—"trying to sustain my end of a conversation with Gertrude Stein on the subject of Pablo

Picasso." It is unlikely that Powell found any of his wartime duties more difficult.

Despite these amenities and the gratifying promotion to full colonel on July 28, Powell was anxious to go home. Though the end of the European war had naturally produced a "let down feeling," morale remained fairly high until the appearance of the atomic bomb. Then Powell confessed to thinking "that the technique employed against Hiroshima and Nagasaki by two aircraft renders rather obsolete anything that can be said about the activities of our thousands of planes in the German war." The departure of old comrades deepened the gloom. At one point Powell wondered sardonically whether the best chance to escape the Army might be retirement at age sixty-five.

Most of all, Powell missed his family. He had been abroad eighteen months, and his daughters were growing up without him. He wrote daughter Penny, now four, that Mrs. Dawson had a little girl "just your age" named Diana. "Diana has blond bobbed hair (not long and curley like yours), and very pretty blue eyes. She is a shy little girl but I have gradually made friends with her by giving her chewing gum. I hid it under her sweater as I used to do with you." When Jo cut Penny's hair and mailed Powell the clippings, he sent Penny a USSTAF shoulder patch* to bolster her morale, adding, "I certainly needed something for my own morale when I received that envelope full of your hair." It took two months to get a second patch for little Jo. When it arrived, Powell sent it off with a long letter: "I think of you every time I see a little French girl riding a bicycle, and this means that you are in my thoughts rather constantly."

At the end of August, Powell put his case to General McDonald. In a month or so, Powell could leave Europe "without affecting adversely any of the matters which you have entrusted to my care." His law firm had lost two partners, one to death and another to ill health, and needed his return. Also, "three and a half years away from my law practice at this stage of my life is beginning to cause me considerable personal concern." McDonald agreed, and Powell received the necessary War Department orders on October 8. He arranged passage on the *Queen Mary* but at the last minute got space on an Army transport, which flew from Prestwick to Iceland to the States. He arrived in

---

* The patch itself was described in an aside: "I think this patch is a nightmare. It looks sort of like a barber pole with a bad hangover. It has taken exactly one year to design, which is not exactly a credit to the artistic talent of our Air Forces. I have not put one on and frankly don't intend to."

Washington on October 28 and was released from assignment a week later.

SHORTLY BEFORE DEPARTING from Europe, Powell went to see firsthand the effects of Allied bombing. He toured Germany for six days, visiting most of the major cities in the west. The results were sobering. The great Krupp works in Essen were gone, and the destruction of Cologne seemed nearly complete. "[Y]ou could not see a single building standing in Cologne, not a single one," Powell recalled. (In fact, the great cathedral itself stood virtually unscathed amid six hundred acres of ruin and devastation.) Indeed, the city was so filled with rubble that one "had a hard time moving about," save for a couple of streets that had been bulldozed clear. These sights confirmed what anyone in Powell's position would already have believed—that Allied bombing campaign had been devastatingly effective.

Reality, however, did not yield so readily to casual inspection. Conditions for precision bombing were rarely ideal, and many bombs missed their targets. The targets themselves were not always well chosen, and the injury done to them was sometimes more apparent than vital. In particular, machines and machine tools were often damaged far less than the factory structures that housed them. In such cases, the equipment could be repaired and reassembled elsewhere. Most important, the German economy had been greatly undermobilized. Until surprisingly late in the war, plant and machinery were plentiful and only incompletely used. Given the redundancy of industrial capacity, Allied air attacks did not quickly cut to the bone. This was notably true of the massive assault on German airframe manufacture culminating in the Big Week attacks in February 1944. Production sagged, but only briefly; within a few months, the number of new German fighters reached and surpassed former levels.

These facts—and a great many more—were reported by the United States Strategic Bombing Survey, a massive postwar investigation of the results of strategic bombing conducted under civilian leadership at the direction of President Roosevelt. The Strategic Bombing Survey detailed key shortcomings of the air offensive but also noted achievements. Most important was the defeat of the German Air Force. When Allied bombers threatened vital targets, German fighters were forced to defend, and when they did, they were engaged and destroyed by Allied escorts. The wastage of experienced pilots and disruption of combat organizations were crippling. On D day the German Air Force had only eighty operational aircraft with which to resist the invasion.

No factor contributed more to the success at Normandy than the absence of the Luftwaffe. Powell was not wrong in thinking that "Our victory in the air made the land invasion possible."

After Normandy, strategic bombing turned to oil, again with great effect. Powell knew this also. No one who had been privy to Ultra intercepts needed to be told of the strangulation of German military power by the dearth of fuel, as the Germans themselves constantly complained about it. As Ultra reported, and as the Strategic Bombing Survey confirmed, the Germans viewed the attacks on oil as "catastrophic."

The best known part of the Strategic Bombing Survey is a paragraph labeled "conclusion." Its characterization is so controversial that it is best quoted in full:

> Allied air power was decisive in the war in Western Europe. Hindsight inevitably suggests that it might have been employed differently or better in some respects. Nevertheless, it was decisive. In the air, its victory was complete. At sea, its contribution, combined with naval power, brought an end to the enemy's greatest naval threat—the U-boat; on land, it helped turn the tide overwhelmingly in favor of Allied ground forces. Its power and superiority made possible the success of the invasion. It brought the economy which sustained the enemy's armed forces to virtual collapse, although the full effects of this collapse had not reached the enemy's front lines when they were overrun by Allied forces. It brought home to the German people the full impact of modern war with all its horror and suffering. Its imprint on the German nation will be lasting.

Although both the wording of this conclusion and the supporting data have been subject to varying interpretation, the verdict seemed generally favorable. Nevertheless, doubts persisted. In time, the issue of the effectiveness of strategic bombing in Germany became entangled with American air policy in Vietnam. In many minds, the two campaigns were linked in failure.

To Powell this casual equation of World War II and Vietnam was grievous error. In 1977 Edwin Yoder wrote a column about arms control containing a single vagrant sentence: "And we know the story of strategic bombing both in World War II and Vietnam." Powell reacted with a four-page letter and an invitation to lunch. He admitted that the air campaign against Germany had been "far from flawless." There had been wasteful misjudgments and folly, but he thought the successes of Normandy and the oil campaign "far outbalanced the failures."

After explaining all this in detail, Powell added a "footnote" on Vietnam: "There probably never has been a greater misemployment of weapons and men than the attempt to bomb the labyrinth of Ho Chi-Minh trails in those jungles. [The Air Force] was allowed only rarely to attack the enemy where the effects could well have been decisive: the air fields, ports, factories, dams, the few railroads, and yes, the cities themselves of *North* Vietnam. Undertaking a war in Southeast Asia was the major blunder, but this was compounded by a 'no-win,' 'no-attack' the enemy's home base policy—unique in the annals of warfare." "There is," Powell insisted, "simply no 'linkage' whatever between what strategic bombing undertook and accomplished against industrialized Germany, and what it was mistakenly assigned to do in the jungles and paddy fields of agrarian South Vietnam."

Another critic of strategic bombing was less easily corrected. Of all the appraisals of Allied air power, few are as grudging as that of John Kenneth Galbraith. Galbraith was an insider and an expert. He directed the all-important economic section of the Survey and wrote most of the summary report. He might have been expected to stand by its conclusions, but a 1971 review of Albert Speer's *Inside the Third Reich* revealed at least a shift in emphasis. Galbraith's overall judgment was severe: "At best the bombing was a badly flawed performance." True, oil and railroads were effectively attacked, "but these raids had come late." Most surprising was Galbraith's suggestion that, by destroying civilian employment and freeing German workers for the war effort, Allied bombing "might on balance have added to the German labor supply." A few years later Galbraith reiterated these views in his memoirs, detailing the "costly failures" of strategic bombing but admitting as to strengths only that the campaign against oil and railroads "did have military effect." And the astonishing suggestion that the bombing might actually have lengthened the war was sharpened and restated: "It could be argued that the effect of the air attacks was to increase German airplane output."

Read in full, Galbraith's comments suggest that he was less concerned with World War II than with discrediting American bombing in Vietnam. "The purposes of both history and future policy would have been served by a more dramatic finding of failure," he wrote of the Strategic Bombing Survey, "for this would have better prepared us for the costly ineffectiveness of the bombers in Korea and Vietnam, and we might have been spared the reproach of civilized opinion."

Powell thought Galbraith "dead wrong." He believed that strategic bombing had been generally effective in World War II and that air power had been ludicrously misused in Vietnam. In 1971 Powell tried to answer Galbraith's allegations in a letter to *The New York Times* that the newspaper did not see fit to print. A year later his position on the Supreme Court guaranteed a hearing for his views but at the same time made him reluctant to enter public controversy. Accordingly, he kept silent, even in the face of what he viewed as pernicious misstatement.

THE LEGACIES OF WAR

Powell's experience in World War II was partly fixative and partly formative. At thirty-four years of age, married, father of two, and already well launched on a professional career, Powell did not enter the Army a callow youth. Neither was he subject to the extremities of combat or capture that might threaten to break down a personality. To a surprising degree, his military service was dominated by continuities with prewar life.

Operational intelligence was in many respects like lawyering. In both, Powell had to analyze evidence, organize it coherently, and present it persuasively. In a sense, Spaatz and Anderson and McDonald were Powell's clients. They set the agenda and made the decisions but depended on him for information and advice. In intelligence, as in the business of lawyering, Powell had to balance loyalty and independence. The adviser who tries to usurp decision-making authority will soon lose the ear of the boss, but the counselor who says only what the client wants to hear will fail both himself and the client. Good advice is honest advice, even if it is unpleasant. The inevitable tension between discretion and candor was heightened by the special responsibilities of an Ultra representative. In the words of historian Stephen Ambrose, Ultra advisers "had to be diplomatic enough not to offend the senior generals to whom they reported, but firm enough to make sure the generals heard what they had to say." Powell was both.

There was also surprising continuity in the social side of professional life. Powell made many friends among the men with whom he served. Most were not from the South (some were not from the United States), but they were not unfamiliar. First of all, they were male. As in law practice, the few women were secretaries. Moreover, the men shared certain traits. They were white, professional, usually well educated, and often socially elite. The Hollywood image of wartime service as a forced melding of social disparates was, for Lewis Powell, only faintly true. For the most part, he worked with people not dissimilar in class and outlook from the lawyers and businessmen he knew in civilian life.

Yet alongside these continuities, there was growth. In North Africa, Powell faced and surmounted the challenge of a rougher, less organized existence than he had ever known. As an Ultra adviser, he handled enormous responsibility with discretion and skill. He returned from war a full colonel, with the Legion of Merit, the Bronze Star, and the French Croix de Guerre with Palm. He had served with conspicuous success in a winning cause, and although this did not distinguish him from thousands of others, it brought to him the special regard that his generation afterward reserved for those who won the war. Years later, his reputation was enlivened by the disclosure of Ultra. The flurry of books, reviews, and articles that began in 1974 made frequent mention of then Justice Powell, who, although by no means the most important figure at Bletchley Park, was perhaps its most prestigious alumnus.

And there was growth in reality as well as reputation. As head of USSTAF Operational Intelligence Powell directed forty officers and as many enlisted personnel—an organization three times as large as Hunton, Williams. In the Army, Powell learned to manage. He learned to delegate responsibility and encourage initiative without relinquishing control. When he returned home, he longed to put those lessons to work in the practice of law. Although it would be some years before he assumed control of his law firm, Powell returned from war not only with an instinct to govern but also with an awareness of his capacity to command.

World War II also helped fix certain attitudes that were often to surface in Powell's later life. He liked military service. He worked with men he admired in a cause that was undoubtedly right, and their efforts were validated by unqualified success. The attitudes of subsequent generations were more conflicted. Especially during Vietnam, many Americans—especially young Americans—came to regard the military with a disdain verging on contempt and sometimes laced with cruel hostility. These were feelings Powell never shared. For him, as for most of his generation, the armed forces wore the mantle of victory. Mistakes and derelictions were aberrational, not symptomatic.

Powell had a similar reaction to the distrust of intelligence activities. After Vietnam, and especially after Watergate, secrecy fell into bad odor. Many came to doubt both the morality and the efficacy of covert intelligence. Powell, however, knew from experience the enormous advantages that secrecy could bring. World War II also confirmed certain international allegiances. Like Ed Murrow, Powell admired the British war effort. His experiences at Bletchley Park, in subsequent Ultra collaboration, and at the British Air Ministry augmented this respect with affection. Although he recognized the dominant role of the United States in the war effort and in the postwar world, he was always careful "not to minimize the magnificent efforts of the British, both past and present." In later years, Powell would call Winston Churchill the greatest man of the century and in so doing pay homage not only to an irresistible personality but also to the nation that, for Americans, Churchill came to personify.

The war also ratified Powell's dislike of the Soviet Union. Revolutionary Russia had never attracted Powell, and no shedding of illusion was required for him to see that Stalin's regime was violent, cruel, and ugly. In particular, Powell bitterly condemned the Soviet refusal to allow their air bases to be used for relief of the Warsaw uprising. Encouraged by Radio Moscow and by the approach of the Red Army, the Poles rebelled against the German garrison on August 1, 1944, only to find themselves denounced as reckless adventurers and abandoned by the suddenly inert Soviet forces. USSTAF bombers were ready to drop supplies to the beleaguered Poles but needed to land at Russian bases. For the next six weeks, as the Germans systematically crushed Polish resistance, the Russians refused permission. Despite direct appeals by Churchill and Roosevelt, only one relief mission was flown before the Germans reestablished control over what had been Warsaw. Many apologies have been made for the Red Army's immobility, but few can be imagined for the refusal to allow assistance by others. Powell's conclusion was stark: "We were prepared to fly, but the Soviets would not allow us to land . . . nor would they move their own grounds forces. They deliberately wanted the Polish underground wiped out, which the Germans were permitted to do."

Most of all, World War II confirmed Powell as a patriot—not of the sloganeering, flag-waving variety, but as a man wholly convinced of his country's essential rightness. Powell never pretended that things done in the name of the United States were for that reason defensible, but he never doubted the broad alignment of American self-interest with world peace and freedom. This was not a casual assumption; it was an ardent faith. Many years later, Justice John Paul Stevens merely voiced the view of all who knew Powell when he described him as "an extraordinarily patriotic man." "He has," said Stevens, "a feeling for the country that is quite exceptional." For Powell, as for so many of his generation, that exceptional feeling was anchored in World War II.

CHAPTER V

RISING STAR

FAMILY REUNION

On his return from Europe, Powell and Jo went to Sea Island, Georgia, where they had honeymooned a decade before, for three weeks of idle pleasure. This time they had the company of Stewart McClintic, Powell's friend from operational intelligence, who knew the owners of Sea Island and arranged for the Powells to share a house about a mile from the Cloister. More time was needed to reestablish normal relations with the children. Jo and Penny, now eight and six, had not seen their father for twenty months. Powell had done all he could to keep himself alive in their minds, but his actual presence must have been unfamiliar.

The reunited family needed a place to live. When Powell left for the service, Jo and the babies moved in with her parents and lived there during the school year for the rest of the war. They spent summers at Bear Island, which Louis Sr. had purchased from Uncle Ned so that the latter could give the money to the church. When Ned died in 1931, six weeks after his sister Eleanor, the elder Powells took Bear Island as a summer place. After renovating the house to add indoor bathrooms and a new wing, they took up full-time residence in 1937 and lived there until Mary Lewis died in 1964. During the war and for many years thereafter, the Powell children spent summers and holidays at Bear Island with the grandparents they called Mammar and Pops.

When the war in Europe ended, Jo bought a small house on the street named for Confederate General J. E. B. Stuart. For some reason Powell did not like it. They lived there only until the girls were out of school for the summer, then accepted the invitation of Dr. and Mrs. Rucker to live with them while they looked for another place. The reason may have been partly financial, as a sudden postwar jump made home values seem ridiculously high. At those prices, Powell, who always underestimated his future prosperity, was eager to sell. The house on Stuart Avenue for which Jo had paid $8,000 was sold a year later for $14,000.

The Powells looked at houses but found none they liked so well as the Ruckers'. It was no wonder. The house at 1238 Rothesay Circle—named but rarely called Glenelg—is a colonial mansion. It is approached by a circular drive behind the inevitable hedges, but most of the land lies behind the house, where a columned portico overlooks the James River. The vacant lot next door, which Dr. Rucker had given the Powells as a wedding present, adds privacy. Inside the house is spacious, with five bedrooms and three baths on the main upstairs hall and a back staircase leading to two small bedrooms and a bath for servants. On the ground floor are large living and dining rooms, kitchen, pantry, and library. The size and grandeur of the place far exceeded anything the Powells could have afforded on their own. Even with both families present, no one was cramped for space.

Joint occupancy had continued for a year when Dr. Rucker discovered that he had scleroderma. The term, which means hardening of the skin, describes a chronic degenerative disease of unknown origin, characterized first by a tightening of the skin and then by hardening of connective tissue throughout the body, including eventually the heart and lungs. Foreseeing progressive debility for himself and increasing isolation for his wife, Rucker asked the Powells to remain there permanently. After Dr. Rucker's death in 1953, Mrs. Rucker gave Jo a one-half interest. She inherited the remainder on Mrs. Rucker's death in 1981. And though the Powells, who by this date spent most of the year in Washington, considered moving to smaller quarters, the idea foundered on Jo's desire to stay in the house she loved.

In the early years, the senior member of this combined household was Marvin Pierce Rucker. Son of a doctor who eventually settled in the Richmond area, Pierce Rucker began college classes at Randolph Macon at age twelve and later studied at the Medical College of Virginia, Harvard, and Johns Hopkins. After several years in general medicine, he confined his practice to obstetrics, becoming one of Virginia's first specialists in that field. Dr. Rucker was an active and public-minded physician. He taught for many years at the Medical College of Virginia (where he was an early sponsor of prenatal clinics), served on the Richmond Board of Health, and held leadership positions in many medical groups, including the presidency of the American Association of Obstetricians, Gynecologists, and Abdominal Surgeons in 1934. He was editor of the *Virginia Medical Monthly* and published more than 150 articles on obstetrics. At his death, an obituary in that magazine described him as a scholar of wide interests and a man "always ready to contribute his time and talents to the common welfare" of his community.

In his later years, Dr. Rucker's scholarship moved beyond medicine. Having read that twenty-eight flowers bore the names of physicians, he began to write brief histories of flowers named for medical doctors or other scientists. He published more than a hundred of these essays, which he called "Floral Eyponyms," as well as as sixty-eight biographical sketches of contributors to the field of obstetrics.

In 1906, Pierce Rucker married Josephine McRae, who, as her grandchildren delight to mention, was descended from Pocahontas. She grew up in Richmond, where her father ran a retail store selling china, silver, and glassware. A dimunitive woman who seemed physically mismatched with her tall husband, Josephine McRae Rucker was a proper Victorian lady, devoted to home and family, with no independent social life. Even the church, in which both Ruckers were active during his lifetime, became less important after his death. She gave all her time to husband, children, and grandchildren.

Of the Ruckers' four children, three were boys. George Scott died as a young man, but Edwin McRae and Douglas Pendleton joined their father in the practice of obstetrics. (Both Rucker brothers died of cancer in 1979, the same year as Angus Powell.) Daughter Jo was the family favorite, and when she moved back home with her husband and two little girls in 1947, there seems to have been no friction. The only time that Jo and Penny can recall being physically punished by their father was when they irritated Dr. Rucker. Powell himself treated his father-in-law with great respect. Their relationship was aided by mutual admiration and also by brief contact. Powell went to the office six and a half days a week and returned to his bedroom to work after dinner. Dr. Rucker kept an upstairs study where he worked until confined to bed by his illness. Between Powell and Mrs. R., as he called her, there was real affection. As she had been devoted to her husband, so she became to her son-in-law. As one of the Powell daughters recalls, "When Grandfather Rucker was alive, he was King and Daddy was right next to him. And then when Grandfather died, it was Daddy who was King. And Grams [Mrs. Rucker], Mummy, and Mammar were all totally devoted to doing anything that Daddy wanted."

Jo managed the household. That the Powells paid no rent made it easier to afford the servants to whom Jo was accustomed, so she always had the help of a full-time cook and maid. Mrs. Rucker was the babysitter and drove the children where they needed to go. To them, it was almost like having two mothers. Altogether, the collection of three generations under the same roof seems to have been easy for all concerned. As Jo summarized the situation, "Daddy invited us out, and Mother kept the children so I could travel with Lewis, and I kept house, and everybody was happy. It was a very pleasant arrangement."

As A FATHER, Powell was demanding—perhaps in his way as demanding as his father. Unlike Louis Sr., Powell never barked or belittled, but he was no less effective in communicating to his children that achievement was expected and mediocrity not esteemed. Powell seems to have been a large and constant presence in the lives of his children, despite his devotion to work. A few idle hours would come on Sundays, when the family would drive out to Bear Island and spend the afternoon swimming and playing tennis, but for most of week, Powell monitored every minute. Even Sunday mornings were subject to meticulous time management. Powell went downtown to the office, then joined his family at the Grace Covenant Presbyterian Church—but only for the last twenty minutes. He consistently arrived just in time for the sermon, after the opening hymns and—his daughters insist—after the collection plate had been passed.

Powell's chief opportunity for contact with his children was the evening meal. Every evening, the Rucker-Powell household sat down to dinner in the large dining room. Powell sat at the head of the table; Mrs. Rucker sat at the opposite end, with (in the early years) Dr. Rucker on her left. There was no radio or television during dinner, no jumping up and down to fetch things from the kitchen, no welter of competing voices. There was one conversation, and it was conducted by Powell. Often the subject was work. As the children grew older, they heard of their father's law practice and his involvement in community affairs. In turn, they were questioned about their own activities. What had the girls done at school? What grades did they get? How were they doing at tennis? Had they helped out at Bear Island? By his own example and by the directions of his interest in them, Powell established an expectation of excellence.

Fortunately, Powell's formidable demands on his children were softened by a gentle and supportive side. When Jody, as he called his first child, was afraid to swim in a meet, Powell knelt down in the parking lot of the Country Club of Virginia to reassure her. It was perfectly normal to be nervous, he said. He himself was often nervous. "I remember being genuinely amazed," Jo recalled, "that he said he always got butterflies in his tummy before making a presentation or arguing a case or giving a speech." Heartened by his example, Jo agreed to swim. He guaranteed that she would not be hurt, that no matter what happened there was no risk of injury, and that even if she came in last, that was no disgrace. As it happened, Jo did get hurt. A false start down the line caused the girls to lose their balance, and Jo hit her chin on the concrete wall along the outside lane. She climbed out and started again, swam trailing blood, and won the race. Only then did she go to the emergency room to have the cut stitched up. Both in her private anxiety and in the public determination to succeed, Jo was her father's daughter.

Jo's principal sport was tennis, which Powell had taught her to play on the court at Bear Island. Though she won city and state championships, she was reluctant to let her father see her compete. Once she asked Powell to stay away from a fifteen-and-under tournament in Byrd Park, only to spot him watching the match from behind a parked car.

When he could not be personally on the scene, as when the children spent weekends with his parents at Bear Island, Powell made lists of things for them to do. They earned points for each activity—for helping with household chores, for picking up sticks in the yard, for serving a basket of tennis balls, for thirty minutes of practice against a backboard. He hated idleness.

When Jo was thirteen, she spent six weeks with Eleanor and Frank Dewey in New Mexico. Shortly after she arrived, her father sent an elaborate chart of daily athletic activities to be completed during the vacation, with the incentive of a weekend at the Farmington Country Club in Charlottesville if she kept to the schedule. Eleanor tore up the list and took Jo on a tour of the West, including the Grand Canyon, Carlsbad Caverns, and a week on a dude ranch. Powell must have thought these activities worthwhile, as he treated both Jo and Penny to the weekend at Farmington despite the uncompleted charts.

Powell's high expectations worked with Jo. In so many ways she was like her father—controlled, disciplined, and eager to excel. As Eleanor said, "Jo tried hard to please her father in every way. And she did. She really did." But Powell's approach worked less well with Penny. Part of the problem was that she was a second child. "In thinking about the children," said Powell's wife, "he thought of them together—and Jo always came first." Penny competed with her elder sister and, at a disadvantage of two years, rarely equaled her performance. "Looking back on it," Penny recalls, "I bet I was very puzzling and probably somewhat embarrassing to Daddy. I think that Daddy has always cared about doing things well, and there I was doing things very badly."

This self-judgment is not strictly true. Penny was a good athlete. Until she quit the sport at age fourteen, she played tennis well. Her real shortcoming was school. Burdened with a mild dyslexia, Penny had a hard time learning to read. The nature and cause of her difficulty were not immediately apparent, and though her parents took her to the University of Virginia and engaged specialists in remedial reading, progress was slow. No doubt this curious lack of performance was in fact puzzling, perhaps even embarrassing, to her accomplished father. Though Powell would never have admitted playing favorites, his focus on his firstborn and the eagerness with which Jo responded to his attentions may have increased the problems of the younger sister.

In time, Penny surmounted her learning disability. She attended St. Catherine's in Richmond, majored in philosophy at Sweet Briar, and eventually obtained a master's degree from Harvard. There was, however, a legacy of self-doubt that for a time was turned against her parents. In her college years, she began to feel that she had been neglected as a child, and the criticism leveled at her privileged background by her two faculty advisers helped fuel her resentment. At an age when most young people are returning to a more comfortable relationship with their parents, Penny was asserting her independence. Eventually, she did find her way back to the family, but that is getting ahead of the story. In the immediate postwar years, Penny was an attractive and vivacious little girl in the midst of a not untroubled childhood.

ON JULY 1, 1947, the Rucker-Powell household was enlarged by the birth of Mary Lewis Gwathmey Powell, called Molly. With a gap of seven years between the second child and the third, Molly seemed to begin almost a new generation of Powell offspring. Five years later, Lewis F. Powell III was born. Knowing it was her last pregnancy, Jo had hoped for twins. Powell was so ecstatic at the birth of a son that he could not quite believe his good fortune and asked the nurse if she were sure of the sex. "I have been looking at naked babies for twenty years," she answered disdainfully, "and have not yet made a mistake."

Though sure of the baby's sex, the nurse was embarrassed at the mother's age, which she listed on the birth certificate as forty-one. In fact, Lewis III was born on Jo's forty-second birthday. The completed family now had six members but only three birthdays. Daughters Jo and Molly were born on July 1, Penny and her father on September 19, and Lewis III and his mother on September 14. Jo said the arrangement saved on cake.

THE DRIVE FOR THE TOP

When Powell returned to Hunton, Williams in December 1946, he found himself on a collision course with Thomas Benjamin Gay. It had fallen to Gay to keep the firm together when two of the eleven partners and all but one of the six associates went off to war. Gay found new associates, only to see them called into service within a few months. The remaining lawyers were placed under enormous strain. As a survivor recalled, "We had an undiminished number of things to do with a greatly diminished number of people to do them." The situation worsened in the spring of 1945, when Edmund Preston died of a heart attack at age forty-six, and Irvin Craig, who had never fully recovered from the strain of the annexation case, withdrew from the firm for reasons of health.

The war also put a cap on Gay's ambitions outside the firm. In 1936 he had been elected Virginia's state delegate to the American Bar Association, a post he would occupy for twenty-one years. In 1939–41 Gay was chairman of the ABA's House of Delegates, the organization's second most important office. He wanted to run for president of the ABA but felt he could not do so with Hunton, Williams so shorthanded. "This," he said, "is my war contribution."

When hostilities ended, Gay wanted Powell back in harness. For Gay, the ideal situation was the status quo ante, with Powell as Gay's senior assistant and Merrill Pasco (who had served on General Marshall's personal staff and emerged from the war a full colonel at age twenty-nine) completing the team.

Powell had other ideas. Reentry into the humdrum world of civilian law practice would have been hard enough in the best of circumstances. It may have been an exaggeration to say, with George Gibson, that Powell "had been hurling thunderbolts on three continents," but the war had been the most challenging and exciting time of his life. Having commanded forty officers and as many enlisted men in operational intelligence, Powell was now to return to Hunton, Williams and find himself in charge of nothing. In the words of the firm's historian, Powell was "back where he had been four years earlier, at the beck and call of an exceedingly harassed and demanding senior partner."

Not only had the war whetted Powell's appetite for command; it had also increased the urgency of his ambition. He was nearly forty and more anxious than ever to make his mark in the world. It would not be long before Powell began to see that his military service had actually enhanced his prospects in postwar America. He had the prestige of rank and, more important, the confidence that went with it.

But for the first few months back in the office, Powell saw only that his real career had been on hold for nearly four years. He was now a man in a hurry.

One option was to leave Hunton, Williams for advancement elsewhere. On the recommendation of Special Branch chief Alfred McCormack, he was offered the post of general counsel to the Marshall Plan, but that would have required time overseas. More tempting was an offer from wartime colleague Lowell Weicker. At Weicker's instigation, Powell had been named to the board of directors of E. R. Squibb & Son in March 1946. Now Squibb invited Powell to become vice president and general counsel. In favor of this proposal were immediate responsibility, salary and benefits tripling his current income, and the long-range prospect of considerable wealth. But Powell did not wish to leave Richmond, and he was reluctant to give up the independence of law practice for the life of a corporate executive. In private practice, as he later told Bill Moyers, "if I really didn't like the way that things were going in the firm, I could always put my hat on and walk out."

For this kind of independence, Powell needed clients. The railroad reorganization work that originally came to Colonel Anderson was increasingly turned over to George Gibson. The power company and other business clients attracted by Justin Moore were handled by his team of lawyers, including Gibson and Moore's longtime lieutenant Archibald Robertson. Gay was the firm's chief litigator. With the important exceptions of the Southern Railway and Standard Oil of New Jersey, he attracted cases, not clients. So long as Powell worked on Gay's cases, he would be under Gay's control, and Gay had no intention of relinquishing his control or sharing his clients. He wanted to keep Powell as his own private workhorse, while he signed the letters, met the clients, and took the credit. In Powell's words, "Mr. Gay was *not* an unselfish person."

The solution to his problem was as obvious as it was daunting. Powell needed clients of his own. He needed to back up the implicit threat that if he put on his hat and walked out the door, the business would go with him. In this, he was spectacularly successful. Within three years, he had won his independence from Gay, and by 1953, when Powell reached irreconcilable differences with a more senior lawyer, he was able to drive his rival from the firm. By that time there was no doubt that the future of Hunton, Williams lay with Powell. He had become the dominant lawyer in his generation, as he would eventually become the leading "rainmaker" in the history of the firm. How he won that position is the story of Powell's drive to the top.

*   *   *

IN 1977, AT THE REQUEST of his former firm, Powell wrote a memorandum on how to build a law practice. "As a basic pre-condition," he said, "one must merit recognition as a quality lawyer. This recognition comes to a lawyer with a high degree of professional skill and dependability, a capacity for unremitting work, and a genuine dedication to serve the clients' needs or cause (even when the cause seems rather forlorn), common sense in dealing with people, and the capacity to inspire client confidence." Powell had these qualities; yet he recognized that many able attorneys do not attract business. "The problem is that the young lawyer must become known."

But how? A good place to start is with the organized bar. "After all, a lawyer's reputation—in no little degree—is in the hands of other lawyers. . . ." Powell was active in the Richmond Bar Association and in 1949 was elected its president, but he wanted something more. "I decided early on that there were tens of thousands of able local and state lawyers in our country. I wanted to establish a national reputation." In 1937, when money was scarce, he paid his own way to Kansas City to attend the annual meeting of the American Bar Association. He joined the Junior Bar Conference (now called the Young Lawyers' Section) and became its chairman in 1941. This position carried with it a seat in the governing body of the ABA, the House of Delegates.

Powell's ABA activities would eventually lead to a web of contacts with leading lawyers across the nation, but in the early postwar years, he relied chiefly on connections at home. These he developed through charity work and public service. Immediately after his return to Richmond, Powell began making speeches on behalf of the Community Fund, ending up as an officer of the organization and a member of its board of trustees. He provided pro bono—from "pro bono publico," meaning unpaid—legal services to the Viginia Home for Incurables, the Retreat for the Sick Hospital, and the Red Cross. He also became involved in a cause that would later bring him fame and credit—the provision of legal services to the poor. This was done through the joint efforts of the local bar association and the Family Service Society of Richmond. Powell became president of that organization and served on its board. He even became the lawyer for the Garden Club of Virginia. These activities earned Powell a reputation as the leading "free" lawyer in Richmond—a reputation, he said, that was "not given the highest rating by partners concerned with cash flow." Performing such services, Powell later declared, "is a duty of citizenship that should be undertaken quite apart from the possibility of establishing broader personal recognition," but it also had the "positive by-product" of making a young lawyer well known in the community.

Powell also threw himself into local business and political affairs. He joined the Richmond Chamber of Commerce and in 1952 was elected its president. He led Virginians for Eisenhower, the committee through which the Byrd organization channeled its support of the Republican candidate. And he played a leading role in the movement to reform Richmond's cumbersome form of government. At that time, the city had a government on the federal model, with a bicameral city council and a mayor armed with the veto power. Since both houses and the mayor had to agree on any action, the system inclined toward gridlock. Shortly after Powell returned from the war, Thomas Boushall of the Morris Plan Bank (later the Bank of Virginia) led a delegation from the Richmond Citizens Association to recruit him to their effort to replace the old structure with a city-manager form of government. Thus began Powell's only venture into electoral politics.

State law authorized election of a charter commission, which would propose a new form of local government and submit its recommendation for approval by the people in a city-wide referendum. The Citizens Association endorsed a slate of seven candidates, all of whom won. Powell came in fourth in the field of seventeen candidates and was selected by the winners as their chairman. The commission proposed at-large election of a unicameral city council, selection of a mayor (who would not have the veto power) from among that group, and delegation of executive responsibilities to a city manager. Despite bitter opposition from those who felt that more responsive government would mean higher taxes, the new scheme was approved by a large majority of the city's voters in a referendum on November 4, 1947.

In the first election under the new regime, Powell was urged to run for city council, but he refused. Again the Richmond Citizens Association endorsed a slate of candidates, most of whom won. One candidate who won without RCA backing was Oliver Hill, who became the first black elected to the Richmond city council. Ironically, two years later, Hill ran *with* RCA support but lost by forty-four votes, despite a record of able service.

By far the most important of these commitments—both in the time Powell devoted to it and in its impact on his future career and reputation—was the Richmond School Board. Powell was appointed to that body in 1950 and was elected its chairman in 1952, a post he held for the next eight years. (The details of that service are recounted in the next chapter.)

These activities represented the confluence of public-mindedness, personality, and self-interest. That Powell sincerely felt an obligation to his community cannot be doubted. Neither can it be doubted that he liked working with city leaders and took pleasure in the respect they showed for his efforts. In postwar Richmond, as at Washington and Lee, Powell was a joiner. But it is also true that Powell's public service helped him professionally. Charitable and civic activities brought him into contact with a broad sampling of lawyers, businessmen, and other citizens of standing. Already by the end of the 1940s, Powell was well and widely known in Richmond as a leading member of his generation.

THE TURNING POINT in Powell's drive for clients came on September 8, 1950, when Richmond lawyer and former U.S. Commissioner of Internal Revenue Royal Cabell died of a heart attack. Cabell's death was, as Powell said, "as favorable event in my life as anything that ever happened to me." At the time of Cabell's death, there were only two other lawyers in Cabell's firm. Wallace Moncure handled litigation, and Cabell's son, Royal Jr., was only two years out of law school. As a consequence, Powell inherited Cabell's clients.

First to arrive was the Albemarle Paper Company. Acting as counsel for a local investment firm, Powell had handled a small financing for the company a few years earlier. Within a week of Cabell's death, Albemarle's president, Floyd D. Gottwald, asked Powell to take over the representation and to go on the firm's board of directors. Powell later described Gottwald as "an ideal client from a lawyer's viewpoint. He was determined to build Albemarle into a national, and later an international, corporation. Moreover, he was imaginative, immensely resourceful, and also willing to take risks that more conservative businessmen would have considered imprudent." The connection to Floyd Gottwald proved enormously valuable to Hunton, Williams and to Powell personally.

A few days after Gottwald called, Powell was approached by the Chesapeake Corporation of Virginia. As Chesapeake was also in the paper business, Powell asked Gottwald for permission to represent both and, on receiving his approval, accepted the offer. Chesapeake was controlled by the Olsson family, who were not as expansion-minded as Gottwald. As a consequence, it remained a small, well-run company and a valuable Powell client.

The third of Cabell's clients to come to Powell was the Richmond retailer Miller & Rhoads. The key figures in the company were Powell's friends Webster S. Rhoads and Edwin Hyde, who invited him to become general counsel. In the 1960s when Miller & Rhoads merged into a larger company, Powell joined them on its board of directors. It is a measure of Powell's extraordinary way with clients that he—not the senior lawyer of the acquiring firm—became general counsel of the combined company, Garfinckel, Brooks Brothers, Miller & Rhoads, Inc.

These clients made Powell an independent force in Hunton, Williams. His success in drawing new business freed him from Mr. Gay and increased his influence and prestige. Collectively, these clients were responsible for the creation of the Powell team. The Albemarle Paper Company, the Chesapeake Corporation, and Miller & Rhoads—together with occasional work from David M. Lea and other clients—provided Hunton, Williams with far more work than Powell could handle alone. By 1951 he had assembled a team of younger lawyers who worked directly for him.

In 1952 Harvie Wilkinson became executive vice president and the following year president of State Planters Bank. Gay would remain general counsel until his retirement, but Powell was clearly in line to succeed him. Prospectively at least, State Planters also counted as a Powell client.

THIS SUDDEN INFLUX of new business from Powell's clients provided the economic foundation for the most dramatic incident of Powell's career as a practicing lawyer—the termination of Wirt Marks. Fourteen years Powell's senior, Wirt Marks had been a partner of Hunton, Williams since 1925. By 1953, with Randolph Williams dead and Henry Anderson nearly so, Marks was second among active partners only to Gay and Moore in the firm hierarchy and in the distribution of income. He was a workhorse and an extremely effective lawyer, described by his associate Larry Blanchard Marks as "one of the, if not *the* most able lawyer in Virginia." He was also one of the most combative. Marks was the "kind of person that you'd want to be your lawyer and dread seeing on the other side. . . . It didn't matter what the case was, big or little, he'd just beat it to death and beat the other side to death. He was just *mean.*"

Marks was scarcely more agreeable to his colleagues. George Gibson described him as "a remote person with only one idea, which was the one *he* preferred." John Riely thought him an "awful bastard." Powell himself described Marks as "a *very* able lawyer" but "*not* a team player." At least he was not on Powell's team. Marks had long resented Justin Moore, who came to the firm after Marks but had his name in the title and a larger share of the profits. Now that Powell's star was rising, Marks became jealous of him too. Given the clash of the personalities and the conflict of ambitions, confrontation became inevitable.

The precipitating event was advice given by Marks to the Virginia-Carolina Chemical Corporation. Company president Joseph A. Howell wanted a long-term employment contract. Marks opposed the idea, as he was certainly entitled to do as a member of the corporation's board of directors. Marks, however, did not stop at expressing his business judgment; he also gave the opinion that the proposed employment contract was illegal under Virginia law. This statement was doubly wrong. It misstated the law and, what was worse, attempted to control business decisions by manipulating legal advice. Howell went straight to Justin Moore to say that although he was happy to retain Hunton, Williams as his lawyers, he would have no more to do with Wirt Marks.

When Marks refused to back down, Powell insisted that he leave the firm. Not only was Marks wrong on the law; he had directly contradicted the position taken by Hunton, Williams when a similar question had been raised by another client. Now the firm found itself in the embarrassing situation of having advised one client to go ahead with a plan that another client had been told was illegal. Big-time law practice could not tolerate such free-lancing.

No doubt Marks was in the wrong. No doubt also that his standing in the firm was weakened by his personality and by his feud with Moore. It was weakened still further by Howell's determination to find a new lawyer. Still, Marks had other clients, and it should have been clear, as events were to prove, that his departure would mean lost business. Nevertheless, he was driven from the firm. The partners were called to an emergency meeting at two o'clock on a Sunday afternoon in late 1953. As the firm did not have a written partnership agreement, there were no complicated procedures. The partners simply dissolved the firm and immediately reconstituted it—without Wirt Marks.

The author of this drastic remedy was Lewis Powell. John Riely tried to smooth things over and got his "head cut off" by Powell. George Gibson later could not remember that he had even discussed the underlying issue. "Amazingly enough," he said some years later, "I never knew the difference that provoked the altercation. The resulting difference was so fundamental that Lewis wouldn't discuss it. He simply said, 'I am going to leave unless the firm backs me up on this. . . .'"

Faced with Powell's ultimatum (and Moore's acquiescence), the partners agreed that Marks was out. He took with him two important clients, the Bank of Virginia (now Signet Bank) and the Richmond, Fredericksburg & Potomac Railroad. The former eventually returned to the firm, but the latter was lost forever.

Among the remaining lawyers at Hunton, Williams, regard for Powell was laced with new respect. No wonder the younger lawyers thought him cold and calculating, a man with "a very steely outlook." The ghost of Wirt Marks told them that Powell had clout—and that he was prepared to use it.

ONE YEAR LATER Powell acquired an especially interesting and prestigious client, the foundation that owned Colonial Williamsburg. Since the immense fortune expended on the restoration of Colonial Williamsburg came from the Rockefellers, the enterprise was represented by New York lawyer Vanderbilt Webb, a personal friend of John D. Rockefeller, Jr. Hunton, Williams handled purely local matters.

Two events drew Powell to Rockefeller's attention. The first was Powell's successful defense of a local ordinance requiring new construction within the historic area to conform to what had been there in the eighteenth century. As a wholly private operation, Colonial Williamsburg lacked the power of eminent domain. In consequence, Rockefeller had to pay handsome prices for the houses and other buildings that he had so meticulously restored. The owner of one important property—the site of the *Virginia Gazette* (now the Printer and Binder Shop) on the Duke of Gloucester Street—resolutely refused to sell. She wanted to construct an inn on that site to accommodate the expected horde of tourists. Of course, the presence of nonconforming structures in the midst of the colonial restoration would have defeated the whole purpose. When Powell challenged her action in court, he won "an absolutely essential victory." Defeated in her plan to make her own fortune, she eventually agreed to lease the property to Colonial Williamsburg for ninety-nine years, and the site was included in the restoration.

A second issue involved the removal of Eastern State Mental Hospital from downtown Williamsburg to a more remote location. Justin Moore was engaged for that purpose and asked Powell to appear before the appropriate committee of the Virginia General Assembly. So it was that when Rockefeller wanted to meet Moore personally, Powell went along. The meeting was held in Bassett Hall, the

Rockefeller residence in Williamsburg, with John D. Rockefeller, Jr., the director of Colonial Williamsburg Kenneth Chorley, his assistant (and successor) Carlisle Humelsine, Moore, and Powell. The question was a bond issue to fund construction of a new home for the state mental hospital. Rockefeller proposed to underwrite the issue so that the state could finance the new facility at a very modest rate of interest, but that, said Moore, was impossible. Under Harry Byrd's famous "pay as you go" policy, Virginia would not issue bonds. Borrowing money on any terms or for any purpose was absolutely ruled out.

After listening patiently to this explanation, Rockefeller said quietly, "Mr. Moore, I don't like your Senator Byrd's philosophy, and if my father had followed it, I wouldn't be sitting here tonight discussing the matter."

Eventually the idea of the bond issue was dropped, but so was Justin Moore. Rockefeller did not like being lectured to, but he did like "that young fella Mr. Powell." As Humseline later recalled, "if Mr. Rockefeller liked that young fellow, so did we." Powell was invited to go on the board of Colonial Williamsburg and become its Virginia counsel and, when Vanderbilt Webb died two years later, to become its general counsel. John D. Rockefeller III became chairman of the board of trustees, followed by his brother Winthrop. In 1973 when Winthrop died, Powell became the head of the Colonial Williamsburg Foundation, the only position of that sort he retained while on the Supreme Court.

ON JANUARY 7, 1954, the last of the firm's founders died. Henry W. Anderson had suffered from colon cancer for four years, but unlike Randolph Williams, who had reduced his percentage of the firm's income long before his death, Anderson continued to take a share equal to that of other named partners. In 1951, for example, Anderson, Gay, and Moore each drew $58,651.61, as compared to $37,089.27 for Powell. Anderson's death not only freed up a lot of income; it also made available a space in the firm's title.

By this time, the firm had existed for more than half a century. Hunton, Williams had become a kind of brand name, which could not be altered without loss of recognition. Anderson's name, however, was dispensable, and so was dropped in favor of Powell's. As the firm's second leading business-getter after Moore, Powell seemed a natural choice. The only question was whether George Gibson's name should also be added.

Gibson was slighty ahead of Powell in seniority, widely acknowledged as the firm's most brilliant mind, and successful in *retaining* the business of important clients. At this stage of his career, however, Gibson did not *attract* business. Powell asked whether Gibson should also be added but was told by Gay and Moore that as six names were too many, Gibson would have to wait for another space. Powell did not press the point.

Thirty years later, as Powell lay recovering from major surgery, his mind turned to the embarrassment he felt at having allowed his name to go in before Gibson's. "Following the death of Henry Anderson," Powell wrote Gibson, "I did think it was appropriate for my name to be included but I cannot say that I focused then on how selfish it was for me to accept this preference over you. I do recall how generous you were in this respect, and detected no feeling of resentment on your part."

One other person was consulted. Henry Anderson had never married, but he had a niece, Frances Shield, whom Powell now visited to explain the contemplated change. As Powell recalled, "she couldn't have been nicer about it" and said she fully understood.

Accordingly, on June 1, 1954, the name of the firm was changed to include its rising star. It was now Hunton, Williams, Gay, Moore & Powell.

CHAPTER VI

A HARD-LINE
MODERATE

BROWN V. BOARD OF EDUCATION

Brown may be the most important political, social, and
legal event in America's twentieth-century history. Its great-
ness lay in the enormity of injustice it condemned, in the
entrenched sentiment it challenged, in the immensity of
law it both created and overthrew.

—J. Harvie Wilkinson, III
From Brown *to* Bakke (1979)

The beginning of the end for the Old South came on May 17, 1954. "We
conclude," said a unanimous Supreme Court, "that in the field of public education the doctrine of 'separate but equal' has no place. Separate
educational facilities are inherently unequal." With these words, the
Justices launched a revolution. Or rather, they edged toward one. They
did not order instant integration but invited further argument on how to
begin. A year later, they asked for "a prompt and reasonable start," then
watered down this demand with the famous oxymoron that desegregation should proceed "at all deliberate speed." In the years that followed,
there was ample deliberation but precious little speed. More than a
decade after the original pronouncement, southern schools remained
almost completely segregated. Yet even if the full extent of this caution
had been plainly visible in 1954, few would have doubted the momen-
tousness of the Court's decision. For *Brown* did much more than overrule
a legal precedent; it condemned a way of life.

In Virginia, as throughout the nation, reactions varied. Black
Virginians accepted the promise of *Brown* warily but with thanksgiving.

For them, *Brown* was a goad to reform. As Thurgood Marshall later said, *Brown* "probably did more than anything else to awaken the Negro from his apathy to demanding his right to equality." White Virginians reacted with disbelief—disbelief that was partly an act of will but partly a genuine incredulity that a system so long sanctioned by law and custom would really be overthrown. Ironically, this denial may have been prolonged by the Court's statesmanlike gradualism. The policy was designed to give the South time to prepare for the wrenching changes in store, but in some places, especially in Virginia, delay nurtured opposition.

Virginia's leaders at first responded sensibly. A few hours after *Brown* was announced, Governor Thomas B. Stanley issued a statement: "It had been hoped the provisions of our State Constitution would be upheld, but the court came to a different conclusion. . . . I contemplate no precipitate action, but I shall call together as quickly as practicable representatives of both state and local governments to consider the matter and work toward a plan which will be acceptable to our citizens and in keeping with the edict of the Court." In the same vein were comments by the state's Superintendent of Public Instruction: "There will be no defiance of the Supreme Court as far as I am concerned." And Attorney General J. Lindsay Almond, Jr., who had argued one of the several desegregation cases heard with *Brown*, now acknowledged that the "highest court in the land has spoken" and voiced the hope "that Virginia will approach the question realistically and endeavor to work out some rational adjustment."

Then everything changed. By late June, talk of voluntary compliance had all but disappeared. Governor Stanley abandoned moderation and pledged to "use every legal means at my command to continue segregated schools in Virginia." He even hinted that the state might withdraw altogether from providing public education. Gone was Lindsay Almond's hope for a "rational adjustment" in Virginia's laws; in its place came denunciation of *Brown* as an invasion of states' rights and a violation of the Constitution. The question for Virginia's elected leaders became not how to live with the Court's decision, but how to resist it.

What had turned reasonableness into refusal? The answer lies in the character of Virginia's senior Senator and political patriarch, Harry Flood Byrd, and in the structure of the organization over which he presided. Harry Byrd was a figure unlike anyone in public life today. Elected Governor in 1925 and United States Senator in 1932, Byrd controlled Virginia politics for four decades. His "organization"—critics called it a "machine"—grew from the county courthouses scattered across Virginia and the local politicians who worked there. At the state level, the organization commanded enough support to overwhelm both Republicans and antiorganization Democrats,* but its strength was not uniform in all regions. It was concentrated in the rural areas, especially in the broad swath of peanut farms and tobacco fields arching across the state's long southern border. The Southside was rural, poor, and 40 percent black, nearly double the figure for the state as a whole. In Virginia, as elsewhere, the crucial factor determining the reaction of whites to school desegregation was the proportion of blacks in the local population. Enthusiasm for *Brown* came easily where the problem was someone else's, and diehard resistance flourished where whites approached minority status. In this, as in some other respects, the Southside was more like Alabama or Mississippi than like the rest of Virginia, and it greeted *Brown*'s threat to white hegemony with the same intransigence. Whatever counsels of moderation might have prevailed in the Washington suburbs or in the Shenandoah Valley or even in Richmond, the Southside simply said "no." And its voice was greatly amplified by its power and prominence within the Byrd regime. In essence, the political structure of the organization enlarged the influence of rural, black-belt whites, and thus tilted the entire state toward a policy of immoderate opposition.

So did the state's acknowledged leader. Harry Byrd was not a dictator (there was a good deal of internal democracy within his organization), but neither did he merely echo the sentiments of his supporters. Byrd's was a voice of unequaled influence and prestige. Had it been raised in support of compliance, however partial and grudging, things would have gone differently. But Byrd set his face squarely against accommodation of any sort. This attitude was not a foregone conclusion, for Byrd was no race-baiting demagogue. His public presence was dignified and respectable; his style more patrician than populist. Byrd's political clout did not depend on his ability to arouse or exploit animosity, nor was white supremacy the centerpiece of his personal philosophy. He might have been expected to join others of his class, who disliked vulgarity and extremism almost as much as integration. Yet Lindsay Almond reported that "the top blew off of the

---

* From 1926 until 1970, all but one of Virginia's governors were Byrd loyalists. The exception was James H. Price, who served from 1938 to 1942 and was endorsed by the organization only to avoid embarrassment. Byrd's sway over the state's vote in national elections was almost complete. The only clear defeat came in 1948, when Harry Truman carried Virginia despite Byrd's obvious distaste. The next Democrat to carry Virginia was Lyndon Johnson, who succeeded without an explicit Byrd endorsement but with the active support of key Byrd lieutenants. The Senator himself remained "majestically and enigmatically silent" throughout the 1964 campaign.

U.S. Capitol" when Byrd heard of Stanley's initial moderation, and the Governor's quick about-face was evidence enough of the Senator's reaction. From the beginning, Byrd personally championed defiance. Together, Harry Flood Byrd and the political organization aligned with his name set the Commonwealth of Virginia on a doomed and fateful course.

MASSIVE RESISTANCE

The phrase came from Senator Byrd's statement on February 24, 1956: "If we can organize the Southern States for massive resistance to this order, I think that in time the rest of the country will realize that racial integration is not going to be accepted in the South." Virginia's resistance was not only massive but total. For the next three years, the state allowed not one black child to attend public school with white children. The full force of the state's resources were arrayed against even token integration. As future Governor Lindsay Almond proclaimed in his 1957 campaign, "We will oppose, with every facility at our command, and with every ounce of our energy, the attempt being made to mix the white and Negro races in our classrooms. Let there be no misunderstanding, no weasel words, on this point: We dedicate our every capacity to preserve segregation in the schools."

As a final measure, the state stood ready to shut down its schools altogether rather than permit black and white to sit together. It is hard to imagine a policy more shameful in origin or disastrous in consequence. It was also quite plainly unlawful.

Earlier, the state had sought a lawful means to avoid integration. This was the goal of the Gray Commission, a group of state legislators appointed by Governor Stanley, chaired by state Senator Garland Gray, and charged with the task of responding to *Brown*. After deliberating for more than a year, the Commission produced a plan. Pupil assignment would be delegated to local school boards, who could consider, among other factors, the availability of facilities and transportation and the health, welfare, and aptitude of each child, "*as well as the welfare and best interests of all other pupils attending a particular school*" (emphasis added). This last phrase authorized discrimination in all but name. If, contrary to plan, localities assigned black children to white schools, there would be an escape hatch. Any child assigned to an integrated school could withdraw and receive a public tuition grant to help pay for private education.

It is quite clear that this plan aimed to maintain separate schools and that eventually it would have been struck down by the courts, but at the time there was a respectable argument that it met the letter of the law. Later the Supreme Court went much further, but *Brown* itself did not actually require integration; it only condemned enforced segregation. The Gray Plan would have dropped the legal requirement of segregation and theoretically allowed integration to occur, although under arrangements making it avoidable. At the time, it seemed possible that the Gray Plan might satisfy Virginia's constitutional obligation.

But there was a problem. The proposal to spend public money for use in private schools required an amendment to the state Constitution. Accordingly, the General Assembly convened in special session and scheduled a popular referendum to authorize the change. This produced the first major split among Virginia's whites. Though an important minority, led by northern Virginia delegate Armistead Boothe, opposed the tuition grant plan as a threat to public education, the organization rallied behind the slogan that "no child be required to attend an integrated school," and on January 9, 1956, the measure passed by a stunning margin of over two to one.

Everything seemed to be set. Virginia had a plan for dealing with the Supreme Court. It stopped short of outright defiance but promised no substantial inroads on the institution of segregation. Several years earlier the University of Virginia had begun admitting a few blacks, and the world had not come to an end. The state's race relations—described by V. O. Key as "perhaps the most harmonious in the South"—remained largely placid, and the experienced, dignified, and respectable followers of Senator Byrd continued in control. Neither the Congress nor the President had taken up the issue, and the parade of court orders that eventually dismantled segregation throughout the South had not yet begun. At this point, a knowledgeable observer might have predicted that desegregation would proceed in Virginia as it did throughout the upper South—token integration followed by foot-dragging gradualism, grudging compliance fueled by an appreciation of inevitability.

But this was not to be. The Gray Plan became irrelevant almost as soon as it was approved, and the politics of desegregation lurched further to the right. Reluctance gave way to defiance, as Virginia took its stand with the radical resisters: "Segregation now, segregation tomorrow, segregation forever!"

How did this happen? Why did the leader of the upper South become the leader of extreme reaction? Three factors played a part. First, in a strange way the referendum endorsing the Gray Plan helped seal its fate. The only issue actually on the ballot was the tuition grant proposal. Its overwhelming approval in the face of an energized opposition from defenders of the public schools not only showed support for tuition grants; more broadly, it encouraged diehard resisters to believe that Virginians would rather sacrifice than submit. The referendum's success was misread as "a mandate from the people for the utmost resistance to school integration." Second, the personal convictions of Senator Byrd and of his inner circle again led the way. As one historian of this period concluded, "instead of being hog-tied in constructive impulses by the prejudice of their constituents," Virginia's leaders "were actually more extreme in their opposition to school desegregation than the people of the state as a whole." Third, the surge toward massive resistance was greatly aided by the discovery of a purported intellectual justification for this position. The doctrine of "interposition," as it was called, made massive resistance respectable.

IN THE MIDST of the referendum campaign, Senator Byrd endorsed the tuition grant proposal but ominously withheld comment on the other half of the Gray Plan—namely, local control over pupil assignment. Organization leaders were already thinking of scuttling local option once tuition grants were secure. Some months later, when it became clear that a few localities (voluntarily or under court order) would begin admitting black students to white schools, the organization acted. In a special session held in August 1956, a divided General Assembly approved a plan proposed by Governor Stanley and supported by Senator Byrd. Control over pupil assignment was withdrawn from the localities and given to a staunchly segregationist state Pupil Placement Board. No voluntary integration would be allowed. If the courts ordered desegregation, the schools would be shut down. The Governor was required to close schools subject to desegregation orders, and if a locality tried to remain open, the state would cut off funds. The locality could then attempt to fund integrated schools on its own or it could cease public education altogether. In the latter case, children could attend (segregated) private schools with tuition grants to help pay the cost. The mechanics of massive resistance were now in place.

Measures so reckless and extreme might have been thought mere bravado, but they were not. Though delay and evasion postponed the issue for nearly two years, by the fall of 1958 the day of reckoning had arrived. In Charlottesville, in Norfolk, and in little Warren County, schools were actually closed by the state. (The best-known school closing, involving Prince Edward County, came later and was done locally.) Some black schools remained open, and in Charlottesville and Warren County, most white students found makeshift private education; but the school closings in Norfolk affected nearly ten thousand students, and the problems there were severe.

IF HARRY BYRD was the political impresario of massive resistance, James Jackson Kilpatrick was the theoretician. Only thirty-one years old when he succeeded the legendary Douglas Southall Freeman as editor of the *Richmond News Leader*, Kilpatrick was a brilliant publicist and an ardent segregationist. Casting about for a means to oppose *Brown*, Kilpatrick discovered "interposition," the doctrine that a state could interpose its own sovereignty to defend against illegal acts by the national government. This idea was not new. Indeed, part of its appeal lay in the illustriousness of its progenitors. In 1798 and 1799 James Madison and Thomas Jefferson had toyed with interposition in the Virginia and Kentucky Resolutions opposing the Alien and Sedition Acts. In Virginia these names carried great weight, but the chief architect of interposition was not Madison or Jefferson, but John C. Calhoun. Calhoun took the idea of interposition and crafted a full-blown theory of state's rights. "The great and leading principle," said Calhoun in 1831, is "that the Constitution of the United States is, in fact, a compact to which each State is a party" and "that the several States, or parties, have a right to judge of its infractions." In case of a "deliberate, palpable, and dangerous" abuse of federal power, a state could interpose its own sovereignty in opposition.

In other words, each state could act as its own Supreme Court, deciding for itself what was the law of the land. If a state found that the federal government had exceeded its powers, it could simply nullify the usurpation.

Whatever merit this theory may have had in 1798 or 1831, by 1955 it had none. The modern revival of interposition somehow overlooked the Civil War. Southerners might insist on calling it the War Between the States—or in Richmond, so the joke goes, the Late Unpleasantness—but they remembered the outcome. The ultimate claim of state sovereignty had been tried and lost. It died on the fields at Antietam Creek and in Pickett's charge at Gettysburg. The power of nullification, like the right of secession, ended forever at Appomattox.

In consequence, Kilpatrick tried to avoid the term "nullification," but he worked the same theme under the banner of "interposition." For two months beginning in November 1955, the *News Leader* campaigned for "Interposition, Now!" Readers were treated to lengthy discourses on the Virginia and Kentucky Resolutions and to a steady stream of editorials quoting Madison, Jefferson, and Calhoun. The newspaper also proposed for the General Assembly an interposition resolution, which, after various moderations, was adopted on February 1, 1956. Between Virginia and the Supreme Court of the United States, said the resolution, lay "a question of contested power." The Supreme Court claimed that school segregation was unconstitutional; Virginia said it was not:

> And be it finally resolved that until the question here asserted by the State of Virginia be settled by clear constitutional amendment, we pledge our firm intention to take all appropriate measures, legally and constitutionally available to us, to resist this illegal encroachment upon our sovereign powers and to urge upon our sister states, whose authorities over their own most cherished powers may next be imperiled, their prompt and deliberate efforts to check this and further encroachment by the Supreme Court, through judicial legislation, upon the reserved powers of the States.

What, exactly, did this resolution commit the state to do? Arguably nothing, since the only "legally and constitutionally available" measure to resist a Supreme Court decision was to seek a constitutional amendment, which was plainly impossible. Indeed, the whole interposition hullabaloo might be dismissed as merely blowing off steam, were it not for one thing. Interposition energized massive resistance. It gave intellectual support and a patina of legality to an otherwise indefensible position. It is hard to imagine the gentlemen of Byrd's Virginia flying all flags for white supremacy. The vulgarity of overt racism might have given some of them pause,* but interposition

---

* Perhaps not. A pamphlet prepared for the Committee for the Courts of Justice of the State of Virginia did not pull many punches in stating the rationale for segregation:

> [The Committee record] their profound conviction that the two races ought not to be mingled in the intimacy of the public schools of this Commonwealth. The schools offer an experience that is not educative alone, but social also; they bring together young people in the formative years of their adolescence, before they have an opportunity to fashion a bridle of maturity by which the passions and impulses of inexperience may be governed. The palpable differences between white and Negro children in intellectual aptitudes have been demonstrated repeatedly by careful examinations conducted by responsible educational authorities.... To bring together such disparate groups in a massive integration of classrooms ... would be to create an educational choas [sic], impossible of satisfactory administration, which would lower the educational level for white children and inevitably create race consciousness and racial tensions.... Beyond these problems of teaching and curriculum lie other problems stemming from generations of custom, tradition, and perhaps from anthropological considerations also, which figure heavily in the reasoning of the State in decreeing continued segregation in the schools. [The report then discussed racial disparity in illegitimacy, crime, and venereal disease.]

Thus did the partisans of the organization marry racism and respectability in defense of massive resistance.

spared them this embarrassment. It changed base motive into high principle. Hostility to integration was not merely a matter of color and prejudice; it was a question of political liberty and state's rights.

THE RICHMOND SCHOOL BOARD

Lewis Powell was a child of the Old South. Looking back years later, across the gulf of social revolution, Powell found it "very hard to believe that I accepted the conditions in the South without any question." But at the time, racial segregation—and the assumption of black inferiority on which it rested—was a fact, not an issue: "[I]t never occurred to me to question it." Powell's experiences typified his class and generation. Growing up, he lived with black servants and played with black children; relations were friendly and familiar, but unself-consciously unequal. He attended all-white schools and churches and never met a black as equal. Neither had his background been challenged in the military; the Army in World War II was as segregated as civilian society. Elsewhere in postwar America, civil rights became an issue, but there was little change in Richmond, Virginia. Where Powell lived and worked, the institution of segregation—not only in schools, but in churches, restaurants, movie theaters, and public buildings—was alive and well.

Though Powell later said he was "shocked" by *Brown v. Board of Education*, in retrospect, the assertion seems hard to credit. The decision did not come out of the blue but was the culmination of a long litigation campaign by the NAACP. As Roy Wilkins said, the South "had nearly twenty years to see the train coming down the track." Powell had particular reason to be informed. *Brown* itself was one of five school desegregation cases heard together. In another, Powell's partners Justin Moore and Archibald Robertson represented Prince Edward County, Virginia. Powell did not work on the case, but he knew of its progress and must have foreseen some risk of defeat. The legal edifice of "separate but equal" had begun to crumble long before *Brown*, and though many sophisticated observers foresaw its end, Powell did not. Like most others in the South, Powell thought the constitutionality of segregation was conclusively established by long acceptance. As the attorney for South Carolina, former presidential candidate John W. Davis, told the Justices: "[S]omewhere, sometime, to every principle comes a moment of repose when it has been so often announced, so confidently relied upon, so long continued, that it passes the limits of judicial discretion and disturbance." Like Davis, Powell thought that "separate but equal" had passed beyond judicial disturbance. He was, in truth, shocked to be wrong.

Powell's reaction was nevertheless restrained. His earliest comment was merely to remark, "We particularly need level heads and sound judgment now that the Supreme Court has held segregation to be unconstitutional." A subsequent letter records his opinion that "the school decisions were wrongly decided." He thought them wrong not only as a matter of constitutional precedent, but also as a matter of social policy: "I am not in favor of, and will never favor compulsory integration." These comments were not elaborated, and both said what the addressees wanted to hear; but there is no reason to doubt that they accurately reflected Powell's views at the time. Many years later Powell would praise "the moral and constitutional force of the *Brown* decision" and celebrate the Supreme Court's "leading role in the movement towards true racial equality," but in 1954 his attitudes on race awaited the instruction of future events.

As it happened, this education did not take place on the sidelines. In 1950 the death of lawyer Guy Hazelgrove left a vacancy on the Richmond School Board. The city council, which appointed school board members, turned to another lawyer—a partner in the town's largest firm, veteran of World War II, recently elected president of the local Chamber of Commerce, and sensible supporter of Senator Byrd. Most important, Powell had been chairman of the Richmond Charter Commission, which had reformed the city government, and a member of the Richmond Citizens Association, which had backed the slate of candidates elected to city council under the new charter. The members of the city council owed their positions in part to Powell, and they repaid their debt (or perhaps transferred their burden) by appointing him to the school board. Powell filled the remainder of Hazelgrove's term and was reappointed in his own right in 1951. The next year the school board made him chairman, a position he held for eight years. At the time of his appointment, the *News Leader* had welcomed Powell's selection and praised his "admirable balance of mind" and "rare talent for calm and judicious reasoning." In the aftermath of *Brown*, these qualities were to be sorely tested.

BY SOME LIGHTS, Powell failed the test. Richmond did not admit black children to white schools until the fall of 1960. The next spring, when Powell resigned from the school board on appointment to the State Board of Education, only two of Richmond's 23,000 black children attended school with whites.* Under Powell's leadership, school segregation in Richmond remained virtually complete. The short answer to this complaint, as Powell claimed, was that the school board lacked authority to do otherwise. Virginia had withdrawn pupil assignment from local school boards and lodged that power in a state agency. The Richmond School Board had no power to assign black students to white schools and therefore could not be faulted for failure to do so.

This explains the lack of progress, but it does not entirely meet the case of Powell's critics. It is true that only the state Pupil Placement Board could assign black students to white schools, but it does not follow that the local school boards had no role in maintaining segregation. Obviously, the state board did not consider individually the appropriate school for every child in Virginia. Special requests came to the Pupil Placement Board, but the patterns of pupil assignment were set by local practice. In Richmond, the directory of public schools explicitly grouped "White Schools" in one division and "Negro Schools" in another. There was one set of geographic attendance zones for the white schools and another set of attendance zones for the black schools. In places the zones overlapped, so that some black children had to walk past white schools to get to the black schools. Once assigned to a particular school, a child progressed through a pattern of feeder schools: from white elementary to white junior high to white high school, or from black elementary to black junior high to black high school. There was no mixing. This system of dual attendance zones and feeder schools existed before 1954 and continued throughout Powell's tenure on the Richmond board.

One instance clearly revealed the local role in maintaining segregation. Changes in the school-age population of Richmond during the 1950s resulted in overcrowding at black schools and less-than-capacity enrollment at several white schools. The obvious solution was to transfer black students to white schools, but the school board made no such request. Instead, it attempted to meet the problem by building additions at black schools. When further steps were needed, the board proposed to

* At Powell's confirmation hearings in 1971, his critics charged that only thirty-seven black children attended previously all-white Richmond schools when Powell left the school board. Their objection was better than they knew. The figure of thirty-seven comes from the Fourth Circuit Court of Appeals's *Bradley v. School Board of the City of Richmond*, which specifies the number of black students assigned to white schools in the *fall* of 1961. The only black children attending school with whites when Powell left office in the *spring* of 1961 were the two teenage girls assigned to a previously all-white junior high school in the fall of 1960.

convert one white school to the use of black students. On September 15, 1958, the Richmond school board asked the state Pupil Placement Board to transfer all white students out of an underutilized facility and replace them with black students from two overcrowded black schools.

What emerges from these details is a picture of local collaboration in maintaining segregated schools long after they were declared unconstitutional. It is likely true, as Powell later claimed, that any local attempt to desegregate would have been "a futile act," but it is also clear that no such attempt was made. Under these circumstances, it is hard to absolve the Richmond School Board or its chairman of all responsibility for the snail's pace of change. That, at least, was the conclusion of the United States Court of Appeals for the Fourth Circuit. In *Bradley v. School Board of the City of Richmond*, that court declared:

> Notwithstanding the fact that the Pupil Placement Board assigns pupils to the various Richmond schools without recommendation of the local officials, we do not believe that the City School Board can disavow all responsibility for the maintenance of the discriminatory system which has apparently undergone no basic change since its adoption. Assuredly it has the power to eliminate the dual attendance areas and the "feeder" system which the District Court found to be primarily responsible for the discriminatory practices. . . .

This history did not commend Powell to civil rights activists. A decade after he left the Richmond School Board, his nomination to the Supreme Court was opposed by Representative John Conyers, Jr., speaking for the Congressional Black Caucus, and by Richmond civil rights lawyer Henry Marsh, later the city's first black mayor. Conyers charged that Richmond's continuation of separate schools was not entirely coerced by state law and that Powell had followed "his own segregationist policies."

These words must have been painful to Powell, who did not then think of himself as a segregationist, but that was not the worst of it. Conyers also claimed that Powell had been lawless: "Obviously, Mr. Powell's sanction of the maintenance of a dual system of attendance zones based on race offended the constitutional rights of the black schoolchildren who were entrapped by Powell's policy decisions. . . . In fact, the record reveals that Mr. Powell participated in the extensive scheme to destroy the constitutional rights that he had sworn to protect." Henry Marsh hammered at the same theme. Marsh brought a statement from the all-black Old Dominion Bar Association charging that Powell had "consistently voted to resist or ignore the decisions of the Supreme Court requiring racial integration of public schools" and "supported measures and schemes which frustrate compliance with the law." Marsh saw in Powell's school board years a record of "continual war on the Constitution." His conclusion was scathing: "While calling for law and order in his public statements, [Powell] has repeatedly and consistently demonstrated by his public deeds a wanton disrespect for law. . . ."

No accusation could have hurt more. No charge could have cut more deeply into Powell's conception of himself than a charge of "wanton disregard of law." It was not merely that he was trained as a lawyer. In an old-fashioned way, Powell thought of himself as an officer of the court, a public servant, and a faithful defender of the rule of law. Yet as hurtful as Marsh's allegations were to Powell, they were not altogether unfair. They were, in fact, a plausible interpretation of the public record of Powell's years on the Richmond School Board. The private record was far more complex.

BEHIND THE SCENES

On June 9, 1955, shortly after *Brown II* ordered desegregation to begin, the Richmond School Board issued a press release. It was designed to say precisely nothing. The statement began by noting that public schools were governed by state law and that the Gray Commission had been convened to consider necessary changes in state law. "In view of the foregoing," the statement continued, "it would, in our opinion, be premature for the Richmond School Board to take any action on this subject until such time as it is known what policy will be established on the State level." The board, however, would continue to study the issue "with the greatest care." And so to the ringing conclusion: "The solution of these problems, in the best interest of all of our people and in a manner which will preserve the public school system under law, is a matter of the utmost concern to the School Board, the Administration, and we believe to all citizens of Richmond."

The high-minded indefiniteness of this pronouncement was anything but inadvertent. The school board had decided to duck. State law was in flux, and a majority of the Richmond City Council, which owned the school property and controlled the school budget, were staunchly segregationist. The Supreme Court's endorsement of "all deliberate speed" might mean almost anything. In the circumstances, Powell thought, the best course was to do nothing. Equally important, the board should say nothing. Under Powell's leadership, the Board "agreed (i) not to discuss the desegregation issue in public meetings of the Board, as this would further inflame the high emotions existing in the community, (ii) similarly, not to discuss the problem in public meetings with the City Council, upon which we depended for approval both of our operating and capital budgets, and (iii) to refrain individually from making public statements which might contribute to the tension between the races." All members agreed to this plan, including Booker T. Bradshaw, the sole black member. The chief administrator of the Richmond schools, H. I. Willett, and his subordinates followed suit. No one said anything on desegregation.

As an initial response to the uncertainties of the situation, this code of silence was not surprising. What is surprising is that it continued, month after month and year after year, as the crisis developed. It continued through the debate on the Gray Plan, the campaign for interposition, and the plunge into massive resistance. It continued through the legislative approval of the mechanics of defiance and through the actual school closings in Norfolk and Charlottesville. It continued until massive resistance tottered and fell. The temptation for Booker Bradshaw to speak out against these maneuvers must have been enormous. The pressure on white board members to declare themselves in support must have been great. But no one defected.

The test came in 1956, when Powell's five-year term expired. Twice the city council met in secret session to discuss his reappointment, but the matter was held up when one councilman demanded to know Powell's attitude toward desegregation. Two other councilmen agreed. Powell himself said nothing, simply referring to school board's press release of the previous year, but his supporters moved into high gear to prevent public questioning. One council member sounded the theme: "Mr. Powell is a man of integrity, and I don't think it would be right to ask him to pledge himself on what he might do in years to come." Another added: "We have no right to doubt the good judgment of Mr. Powell, and any attempt to pledge him to any particular course could cost the community the services of one of its ablest citizens." These arguments proved persuasive, for on June 4, Powell was unanimously approved for another five-year term. (The reluctant member was in the hospital but sent word that he favored reappointment.) The newspapers said very little. The whole thing was accomplished without *any* public discussion, either by the chairman of the school board or by the members of the city council, of what was plainly the crucial issue for both.

*   *   *

Behind his public silence, Powell argued privately against tuition grants, interposition, and massive resistance. His correspondence from the period leaves no doubt as to his position. In October 1954, he praised Armistead Boothe, who had defected from the Byrd organization's hard-line stance and had called on Virginians to proceed in good faith to implement *Brown:* "Armistead's moderate view may not be the most popular one politically at this time, but I believe it will prevail in the long run." In a letter to David J. Mays, a prominent Richmond lawyer who served as counsel to the Gray Commission, Powell endorsed the local-option pupil assignment procedure, despite reservations, but opposed the tuition grant proposal: "I, personally, do not approve of the idea of allocating public funds for so-called 'private' education. I am confident this will not work in Richmond, and I doubt that it will work anywhere else constitutionally for any length of time."

By January 1956, when the voters approved the tuition grant proposal, public debate had shifted to something more extreme—the doctrine of interposition. Powell attacked interposition in a dramatic confrontation with James J. Kilpatrick on January 16, 1956. The exchange occurred at a meeting of the Forum Club, one of those private institutions of public power so characteristic of the Old South. The Forum Club was a legacy of Douglas Southall Freeman. Long the intellectual leader of Richmond, Freeman twice won the Pulitzer Prize.* He was a dedicated and conscientious scholar, but he was also a man of affairs and eager to make his influence felt. He was editor of the *News Leader* and pontificated on a variety of subjects in daily radio broadcasts. He also gave a monthly class on public events. In Freeman's day, it was a class, not a club. Freeman did most of the talking, and he did not reward disagreement. He invited only those he liked, and most of those he liked were persons of prominence. Freeman made it a point to get to know promising young men who might eventually warrant an invitation to his class.

Lewis Powell and Harvie Wilkinson were readily identified as rising stars. After the war, Freeman asked them to join his class, which of course they did—it was prestigious. The Powells were even favored with dinner in the Freeman home—evenings that ended early, when the host retired in order to return to work on his books before dawn of

---

* He won first for his magisterial biography of R. E. Lee and again (posthumously) for his seven-volume study of George Washington. He also wrote *Lee's Lieutenants,* a three-volume study of generals and generalship in the Army of Northern Virginia.

the next day. A few years later when the great man died, the two friends helped organize the Forum Club to continue Freeman's tradition. Meetings were now chaired by the editor of one of the daily papers and featured more debate and discussion, but the focus stayed on current events and the membership remained influential and exclusive. It was at a regular monthly meeting of this group, held at the Commonwealth Club in downtown Richmond, that Powell and Kilpatrick crossed swords over interposition.

The *News Leader* was nearing the end of its desperate campaign. It urged on the General Assembly adoption of a resolution of interposition drafted by Kilpatrick and phrased in the most uncompromising terms. Kilpatrick hotly defended his proposal; Powell coolly demolished it. Powell thought he would have won, had a vote been taken, and he was probably right. H. I. Willett was there and said afterward that Kilpatrick "must have thought he'd gotten into a den of rattlesnakes." Virginius Dabney agreed that Powell had "laid him out flat." And at least one listener was even more impressed. "Dear Lewis," wrote Alfred Thompson:

> I am so proud of you! What you did last night, over and above your eloquent and so logical presentation of the issue involved, was to me a tremendous tribute to your honesty, character and courage. Few men could have or would have done what you did and say the things that must have made many people think.
>
> When I went home, I [said] that I had heard a George Washington, Patrick Henry and Abraham Lincoln all blended into one man and that man, as well as being a Virginian, was truly an American who stood for law and order and the continuation of our country's greatness.

The greatest compliment came from Kilpatrick himself. According to Harvie Wilkinson (who may be a partial witness, as he thought interposition "the most farcical damn doctrine ever thought up"), the next morning Kilpatrick confessed: "Good God, did I get chewed up last night!"*

Powell's remarks were not transcribed, but they can be reconstructed from another source. In the days immediately following the debate, Powell wrote a letter to Governor Stanley on interposition. The speech at the Forum Club must have been a version of the argument addressed to Governor Stanley. The letter not only records Powell's views at the time, but also shows the logic, clarity, and power of his advocacy.

---

*   Mr. Kilpatrick has no recollection of these events.

Louis F. Powell at twenty-five.
(Collection of Mrs. Frank L. Dewey)

Mary Lewis Gwathmey Powell at forty.
(Collection of Mrs. Frank L. Dewey)

Lewis Jr., Eleanor, Angus, and Zoe.
(Collection of Mrs. Frank L. Dewey)

Leading the Opening Figure of the 1929 Fancy Dress Ball with Miss Sally Barrett. *(Washington and Lee University, Lexington, Va.)*

On the Grand Tour with Edward R. Murrow.
(Collection of Mrs. Frank L. Dewey)

Lewis and Josephine at a bridal luncheon on their wedding day, May 2, 1936. *(Collection of the Supreme Court of the United States)*

Powell with Angus (*standing*) and Harvie Wilkinson.
(*Collection of the Supreme Court of the United States*)

Josephine with Little Jo.
(*Collection of Lewis F. Powell, Jr.*)

Two views of Bear Island. *(Dementi-Foster Studios; Collection of Mrs. Frank L. Dewey)*

The interposition debate centered on the resolution originally proposed by the *News Leader*. It contained an astonishing assertion:

> Be it further resolved, that . . . the General Assembly of Virginia declares the decisions and orders of the Supreme Court of the United States relating to separation of races in its public institutions are, *as a matter of right*, null, void, and of no effect; and the General Assembly declares to all men that *as a matter of right*, this State is not bound to abide thereby. . . . [Emphasis in original.]

"As you can see," Powell addressed the Governor, "this is no less than a proposal of insurrection against the Federal Government. It is an attitude of lawlessness which would be tolerated in no individual. . . . [I]n my opinion, no responsible party of our State Government should espouse it."

Powell then launched into a four-point argument. First, he said, let us call a thing by its proper name: "Interposition" was simply a euphemism for the long-repudiated doctrine of "nullification." Second, Powell asked, what does interposition mean?: "It is the remarkable assertion that any state—i.e., *each* of the 48 states—has the *right* to decide for itself whether action of the Federal Government is constitutional. Under this doctrine each state is itself the judge whether an act of Congress, an act of the President or a decision of the Supreme Court, as the case may be, is binding upon the state. It takes no imagination to see that this would produce utter chaos."

Third, Powell attacked the historical foundation of this supposed state power: "The *News Leader* has emphasized that Jefferson and Madison supported Nullification in 1798. This is true. But the *Leader* has not pointed out that George Washington did not support it; that John Marshall vigorously opposed it; that Patrick Henry recognized that it would mean the end of the Union; that Madison later retreated from the doctrine when South Carolina attempted to invoke it in 1832; that President Jackson, a Southerner, threatened to send the United States Army into South Carolina over this doctrine; and that the doctrine of Nullification was finally one of the contributing causes of the Civil War." This explained, said Powell, why no competent historian had endorsed nullification since the Civil War.

Finally, Powell advanced "compelling reasons why Virginia should disassociate itself from this radical proposal": "In the bitter emotion of the present school crisis, it is the hope of the Nation that Virginia will set an example of dignity, restraint and respect for law and order."

Moreover, interposition would undercut the Gray Commission, which attempted a lawful accommodation of *Brown v. Board of Education*. Most important, the campaign for interposition would damage the Supreme Court:

> [The] attack on the Court has, I think, assumed disquieting if not positively dangerous proportions. I hardly need say that I personally do not agree with the decision of the Court. I concur in the briefs filed on behalf of Virginia. Indeed, I personally think that we now have an exceptionally weak Supreme Court, with many members possessing few qualifications other than "political" ones. Nor do I consider that the Supreme Court should be protected from fair criticism. But the Supreme Court, as an institution, is one of the great bulwarks of our cherished American form of government. During most of our history it has well protected the personal liberties of the people, and it has been a conservative and steadying influence in times of violent emotion and political passion. Nowhere has this been better recognized than here in Virginia. You will, of course, remember how alarmed we were in 1937 by the proposal to "pack" the Court with judges amenable to the Executive's wishes. The very same newspaper which now proposes Nullification and leads a most vicious attack upon the Court, was in 1937 one of the greatest champions of the Court. It seems obvious that we cannot expect to preserve our cherished institutions and maintain their positions of public respect and confidence, if we praise them only when their actions please us and defy and denounce them when their actions displease us.

The next day Powell wrote a lengthy addendum to take account of the revised wording of the interposition resolution that had just been introduced in the General Assembly. The resolution was more temperate than Kilpatrick's original proposal. The ugly "null and void" language was deleted and the defiance of the Supreme Court was phrased more politely, but it still referred to the Court's decree as "illegal." To Powell, this suggested "that disobedience of the decree is perfectly lawful, as one does not act unlawfully in disregarding an 'illegal' decree." In short, said Powell, while the authors of the resolution had "gained many fine sponsors" by moderating the language, the rephrased version was "only mildly less dangerous than the form originally proposed." The reformulation, however, carried the day politically, and the interposition resolution passed substantially as introduced.

Powell sent a copy of this letter to Senator Byrd and also went to see him. Powell had known Byrd since 1948, when the Senator asked him to head a veterans committee in his reelection campaign. Powell accepted and had been on a first-name basis with him ever since. Powell had many reasons to like Harry Byrd. He was nationally influential, fiscally conservative, and personally honest. Moreover, he was aristocratic— "the quintessence of the Virginia gentleman, with blue-blood ancestry, impeccable integrity, refined manners, and an almost mystic identification with Virginia's past." As one wag said, Byrd provided government "of the gentry, by the gentry, and for the gentry," but leavened by the gentry's "dutiful awareness that it has an obligation to keep the common people happy too." The organization's premium on service and integrity meshed with Powell's values, and its suspicion of change matched his own. Both the policy and the style of the Byrd organization appealed to Powell, who counted himself a loyal supporter.

Now he made a great effort to turn Byrd away from interposition, but the old man would not budge. "He totally disagreed with my view," Powell later recalled. "And I don't think he'd ever heard of the Virginia Resolution until Jack [Kilpatrick] told him about it, but now he just loved to tell me about it. He said: 'Look who drafted the Resolution. It's got to be right.'" The two parted as friends, but Powell had made no headway.

POWELL WAS NOW OBSESSED with interposition. The arguments he had made at the Forum Club and summarized in his letter to Governor Stanley soon found their way into a draft article, entitled "'Interposition'—A Twentieth Century Revival of 'Nullification.'" The typescript runs to nearly thirty pages. It is replete with scholarly reference and historical example, but the tone is not that of disinterested scholarship. Powell was plainly appalled by the threat to the rule of law. On the supposed right of each state to decide for itself the extent of federal power, Powell came out swinging: "On its face, this is a doctrine of chaos—not of law. There can be no such 'right' as this if the Union is to survive. No court is known to have sustained this doctrine as a legal right, and no court is likely to do so. It is simply legal nonsense."

On March 30, 1956, Powell sent the article to F. D. G. Ribble, dean of the School of Law at the University of Virginia and advisory editor of the *American Bar Journal*. The letter of transmittal contained this reservation: "In view of the participation by my firm in the Virginia School case, I will also have to discuss this with Justin Moore and Archie Robertson. . . . The article itself, of course, has nothing whatever to do with the litigation now pending in the District Court, but I would nevertheless want to be sure that the gentlemen actually trying the case are agreeable to the publication of an article along these lines."

The litigation referred to involved Prince Edward County. The desegregation suit brought against that county's school board had been heard in the Supreme Court with *Brown v. Board of Education*. On remand to the District Court, the case bogged down in a series of hearings, decisions, and appeals that continued until 1959, when the county closed its schools altogether. The county had been represented by Powell's senior partners, Justin Moore and Archibald Robertson, in collaboration with the state attorney general. Now he sought their permission to publish. Back came the word: Powell's article might prove embarrassing to the firm. Of course, neither Moore nor Robertson took interposition seriously, but their clients did. It was possible that interposition might be referred to in the pending litigation, and Powell's article would be hard to explain away. Powell therefore asked Ribble to tear up the draft. This letter crossed one from Ribble, so Powell wrote again with yet another lengthy attack on the doctrine, concluding: "Well, this is getting serious and long-winded! Please forgive me, and put this in the waste basket too. Perhaps the Union will survive after all, and anyway I've got to get back to practicing law."

Thus did the politics of law practice invade the politics of desegregation. In any event, there was nothing Powell could have done. By this time, the Byrd organization had a full head of steam and was racing toward the cliff. That summer the General Assembly met in special session to preclude all possibility of integration by lodging the power to assign students in the state Pupil Placement Board. The only local school board to appear in opposition was Richmond's, represented by superintendent of schools H. I. Willett,* but his objections had no effect. By the end of the summer, Virginia was irrevocably committed to massive resistance.

FOR THE NEXT THREE YEARS, Powell kept a low profile. He dealt with many matters concerning the administration of the schools and educational

---

* Willett later recollected in a letter to Powell: "You may recall that I was the spokesman for the school board but that you assisted in the preparation of what I should say and that my appearance before the General Assembly had the approval of the school board. There was one other superintendent of schools that had been scheduled to appear with me but his school board opposed his appearance and it seemed that he would probably lose his job if he did appear, and I advised him in light of the circumstances to acquiesce to their wishes because I did not feel that he could help the situation by being fired at that point in history."

policy, but he made no public comment on desegregation. Indeed, the crisis seemed to ease, as Virginia's public schools remained segregated and open. Then, in the fall of 1958, Harry Byrd's chickens came home to roost. Desegregation orders triggered school closings in Charlottesville, Norfolk, and Warren County, and the brave rhetoric of massive resistance collapsed into a brutal reality.

Political support for radical resistance began to fray. Local citizens formed Committees for Public Schools to oppose school closings. In the annual convention of Virginia Parent-Teacher Associations, a motion to endorse massive resistance failed by a tie vote, 557 to 557. Virginia's newspapers, which had overwhelmingly defended massive resistance, now grudgingly sounded retreat. Powell's friend Virginius Dabney, editor of the *Richmond Times-Dispatch*, admitted: "We must now find another position from which to fight, with ground for maneuver, to gather our strength and renew the battle." Even Jack Kilpatrick had an attack of good sense: "I believe laws we now have on the books have outlived their usefulness, and I believe that new laws must be devised—speedily devised—if educational opportunities are to be preserved and social calamity is to be avoided." Finally, Virginia's business community began, very quietly, to deploy its immense political strength against massive resistance.

The Virginia Industrialization Group consisted of ninety members of the state's business community organized under the chairmanship of Stuart T. Saunders, president of the Norfolk & Western Railway. Harvie Wilkinson, by then head of the State Planters Bank, was vice chairman. Other members included top officers from A. H. Robins, Dan River Mills, Reynolds Metals, Virginia Electric & Power Co., Newport News Shipbuilding & Dry Dock Co., and the Richmond, Fredericksburg & Potomac Railroad, as well as from the state's major banks. The newspaper industry was represented by Frank Batten, publisher of the *Norfolk Virginian-Pilot*, and Tennant Bryan, publisher of the *Richmond Times-Dispatch*. The group also included two practicing lawyers, Charles L. Kaufman of Norfolk and Lewis Powell.

It did not take this group long to conclude that massive resistance was the greatest single obstacle to industrial development. It was said that not a single new industry had come to Virginia in 1958, and, although not literally correct, the statement was largely accurate. Compared to the sensational industrial progress across the border in North Carolina, Virginia looked stagnant, and no one expected an infusion of new capital until the school crisis was resolved. On December 19, 1958, members of the group sat down to dinner at the stately Rotunda Club in Richmond. Their guests were the Governor, Lieutenant Governor, and Attorney General of Virginia. The occasion was private. Despite the presence of their publishers, reporters were not invited, and the press made no mention of the event.

Though Powell missed the meeting because of business in New York, he helped prepare the presentation. A memorandum of December 15 outlined for Stuart Saunders and Harvie Wilkinson the points Powell thought should be made. The businessmen should focus on "the relationship between the school crisis and the future economic welfare of Virginia" and "ways of extricating Virginia from its present impossible position." Powell's tactical directions reveal political acumen: "If there should be such a discussion, it must of course be done without recrimination or blame—express or implied. While I have felt that massive resistance was sheer folly from the outset, we must now take the position that it is time for responsible community, business and political leaders to devote their best thought to sound and practical solutions without regard to past mistakes." Powell then addressed several specific points, including the need for a fundamental change in attitude: "[T]he basic posture of Virginia has undoubtedly been one of defiance. . . . There can be no satisfactory solution of the problem so long as this attitude continues." Once again he expounded the authority of the Supreme Court: "Responsible public officials and leading newspapers have continued to take the position that the Supreme Court usurped the authority to decree de-segregation. This view attacks the very foundation of our system of government. . . . I doubt that enlightened business leaders elsewhere would consider Virginia an attractive place to move until we decide to rejoin the Union."

The target of all this persuasion was the new Governor of Virginia, J. Lindsay Almond, Jr., a complex and tragic figure. He came up as a Byrd loyalist, but was never a Byrd confidant. He was a spellbinding orator whose "greatest political asset was his ability to impress crowds of ordinary people—a talent of which Byrd and his associates were instinctively suspicious." Almond the politician sounded four-square for massive resistance, but Almond the lawyer—and he was a good one—strongly suspected that Virginia's statutes would never survive a court challenge. He spoke fire-and-brimstone segregation, but he, more than most of the state's leaders, recognized some justice in black demands. By late 1958, Lindsay Almond was a torn man—torn between the intractable Senator Byrd and the mounting pressure to abandon massive resistance, between a desire to live up to his own rhetoric and the looming prospect of disaster and defeat.

The Lindsay Almond that the businessmen encountered that night at the Rotunda Club was the fire-and-brimstone version. Everyone spoke to the same purpose: Massive resistance would fail, and it was grievously hurting Virginia. But Almond stood firm. He shook his finger and vowed that he would never accept integration in Virginia's public schools. Yet if Almond fumed, he also listened, and so did his chief adviser, Attorney General Albertis S. Harrison, Jr. They left the room with a clear understanding that the business community opposed massive resistance.

A month later, three federal judges, including future Supreme Court nominee Clement Haynsworth, declared Virginia's school-closing laws unconstitutional. Almond gave one last never-say-die speech, then made a dramatic about-face. On January 28, 1959, he spoke to the General Assembly and bowed to the inevitable. Five days thereafter, twenty-one black children entered formerly all-white schools in Arlington and Norfolk. Massive resistance was over.

Powell was not alone in thinking, as he later said, that the businessmen's cabal had a major influence on Lindsay Almond. Others in the know shared that view, though the event itself was rarely mentioned. Many years later, the *Norfolk Virginian-Pilot* opined that "possibly Mr. Powell's outstanding contribution to Virginia was his leadership in the quiet sabotage by a business-industrial-professional group of Senator Byrd's Massive Resistance."

INTO THE LIMELIGHT

The collapse of massive resistance did not mean instant integration. On the contrary, Virginia's public schools remained mostly segregated for years to come. The handful of black children admitted to white schools in February 1959 were subject to court order. In most other schools, desegregation would begin no sooner than the fall of 1960. Governor Almond had appointed a commission to recommend ways to extricate the state from massive resistance. The school-closing and fund cutoff statutes had been struck down as unconstitutional. Now the commission proposed that local school boards, acting under rules to be prescribed by the State Board of Education, be allowed to resume control over pupil placement—in other words, a return to the Gray Plan three years later. After a bitter fight, the General Assembly agreed; but as it was already well into spring and the State Board of Education had to promulgate regulations, the lateness of the hour was thought sufficient reason (or excuse) to delay the effective date of local option to March 1, 1960.

Moreover, return to local control did not guarantee moderation. The most notorious example was Prince Edward County, where the schools were closed at local insistence *after* the Governor's change of heart and were kept closed until the Supreme Court forced them open in 1964. Richmond was not Prince Edward County, but neither was it a hotbed of integration. The city council was dominated by segregationists. By comparison, the school board seemed moderate; it was willing to accept desegregation, but not to fight for it. The two black girls who entered previously all-white Chandler Junior High School in the fall of 1960 were assigned there by the state Pupil Placement Board, after that body had been reconstituted by Governor Almond. Nevertheless, 1959 saw the breakdown of behind-the-scenes management of Richmond's schools and the school board's first public comment on desegregation. The question was not the immediate admission of black students to white schools but an issue with a longer time frame—the construction of new schools.

THROUGHOUT THE 1950s Richmond's school population was growing—and changing. In 1949 the city's schools were 59 percent white and 41 percent black. In the ensuing decade, the number of white students remained almost constant, while black enrollment soared. By 1958 blacks were a majority of the city's public school students. Everyone agreed that new schools were needed, but their location proved controversial. Under the old dual school system with its overlapping geographic attendance zones, site selection would have been simpler. New schools would have been specifically designated as black or white and would have been located to serve the population of that race. But by 1959, any clearheaded observer could see the dual school system was doomed. Sooner or later, segregation would give way to some racially neutral means of assigning students to schools.* Therefore, the logical place to build new schools was wherever racially blind population surveys showed they were needed. The trouble was that choosing school sites on this basis would facilitate integration. Simply put, putting new schools in racially mixed neighborhoods would make it easier to have racially mixed schools. Thus site selection for the new schools became a stalking horse for acceptance of integration.

---

* Court decisions disapproving color blindness and requiring race-conscious pupil assignments to promote integration were still many years away.

In 1958 the Richmond School Board proposed construction of two new high schools: John Marshall (succeeding to the name of an existing building that would be retired from service) and George Wythe. The city council appropriated $6 million but refused to release the money due to fears that the new facilities would accelerate desegregation. In fact, they were right; the new schools had been planned and their locations selected on the assumption that desegregation was inevitable. One school would be built in Richmond's north side, near the border of suburban Henrico County; the other would be the only Richmond high school south of the James River. Both would be situated in white neighborhoods adjacent to areas of growing black population. Therefore, if one simply looked at a map and imagined that each of the proposed high schools would serve all students in the surrounding areas, one could see the potential for racial integration. As Powell later admitted: "It was perfectly obvious if we built them in the locations recommended by the school board, that they would become integrated in a fairly short period of time." But if this prospect were publicly acknowledged, the proposal would be doomed.

At first, Powell tried private negotiation. Some council members agreed to go forward, but others opposed building any new schools that might facilitate integration. Said one opponent: "I don't want white children sitting beside smelly Negro children in any school in Richmond." Eventually, Powell despaired of private persuasion; he had to go public.

On May 6, 1959, he appeared before an open meeting of the city council to plead for the two new schools. He aimed to rally moderate opinion in support of the proposal and to provide reassurance, or at least political cover, for its opponents. He began with the fact that two new high schools had been planned for many years. The need for them had not disappeared. "This brings us to the fundamental question of whether general public education will continue in Richmond.... [T]he question is no longer whether there will be integration in Virginia. There is in fact already some integration in Virginia, and under the rules of law established by the courts there will continue to be some integration—unless public education is abandoned. This is an unwelcome situation to a large majority of our people, but the time has come to put aside wishful and emotional thinking and face realities." The reality that Powell saw was the choice of "some integration or the abandonment of our public school education."

As Powell reported, the school board "unanimously and with deep conviction" believed in education. Those who, "through understandable resentment at an unwelcome social change forced upon us by

law," believed the schools should be closed, should consider the consequences. These would include juvenile delinquency, deterioration of
the economic health of the community, and "a warping and corrosive
effect upon the personality, aspirations and opportunity of each individual child in our community." There was no alternative but to go
forward with long-range plans for the education of Richmond's children, including the two new high schools.

Finally, Powell reached the critical question of the relation between
the location of the proposed schools and desegregation. The new
schools would not accelerate racial mixing, he asserted. In fact, they
"will actually ameliorate the integration problem." The board believed
"that the new schools would appreciably improve both the short and
long range prospect for minimizing the impact of integration." This
astonishing conclusion was exactly contrary to the expectations of
Powell's listeners. What was the basis for it? Powell's argument was
that construction of the two new white high schools would free existing facilities for use by black students; failure to build the new schools,
he said, would increase overcrowding at existing black schools and
accelerate the pressure for integration.

Powell's explanation may have sounded plausible, but it was in fact
disingenuous. The notion that new schools could be reserved for
whites and old schools turned over to blacks made sense *only* on the
assumption that Richmond would be allowed indefinitely to keep
whites and blacks in separate schools. Powell knew better. Soon the
federal courts would order the admission of black students to white
schools. Eventually, Richmond schools would move—or be forced to
move—toward color-blind attendance zones. When that happened,
the new schools would facilitate integration, for they were to be situated where they could easily serve residential areas of both races.

Disingenuous or not, it is easy to see why Powell made this argument—it was the only way to get the funding. It is harder to understand why the council's segregationists accepted it. Perhaps they
lacked the imagination to foresee that the world they had always
known would soon end. Perhaps their vision was clouded by emotion.
Or perhaps they realized that integration was inevitable and merely
wanted the political protection of public reassurance that they had not
collaborated in its coming. In any event, the argument prevailed, and
the city council approved construction of the two new schools, as proposed, by a vote of seven to one.

Two years later, when Powell resigned from the Richmond School
Board, the *Times-Dispatch* ran an editorial praising his service.

Mentioned among his accomplishments was the building of "two new white high schools." Ten years thereafter, Powell's critics cited this as further evidence of why he should not be confirmed to the Supreme Court. Congressman Conyers quoted the editorial and concluded: "There were those in Richmond who had good cause to be justly proud of the masterful way in which Mr. Powell had perpetuated the antiquated notions of white supremacy through a clever institutionalization of school segregation." Conyers may have had legitimate grounds for complaint, but here he missed the point. The two new high schools did not institutionalize school segregation. In fact, they had the opposite effect. In 1970, after operating for several years under a "freedom of choice" plan, the two new "white" schools were the *only* high schools in the city of Richmond with substantial representation of both races.* Contrary to Powell's public assurance, but consistent with his private expectation, the construction and location of the two new schools actually facilitated desegregation.

AT THE TIME of the campaign for the new schools, Powell also disclosed plans to convert Chandler Junior High School from all-white to all-black once the new high schools were completed. Powell knew that such solutions would not be viable long-term, but the worsening overcrowding of black schools required short-term relief. In retrospect, transferring black students to white schools would seem to have been the obvious remedy, but this was never considered. The majority of school board members had no enthusiasm for that result, and in any event they lacked the political capability. Legally, the state Pupil Placement Board retained exclusive control until March 1960. Powell knew the state pupil placement law was constitutionally "shaky," but it had not yet been held invalid. More important, the school board had to deal with the city council. The council held the purse strings, and the dispute over the new high schools had made unmistakably plain that the council opposed desegregation. The board's solution was to transfer Chandler's students to underutilized white facilities and turn the school entirely over to blacks.

This proposal upset both races. Black leaders objected to the attempt to maintain segregation. Local white residents decried the encroachment of blacks into their neighborhood. In deference to the latter opin-

---

* John Marshall was 68 percent and 32 percent white. George Wythe was 19 percent black and 81 percent white. One other high school was integrated to a lesser degree (92 percent white): another was 99 percent white; and the remaining three were 100 percent black.

ion, the mayor of Richmond, Scott Anderson, introduced a resolution asking the school board to take no action without consulting the city council and asserting the council's right to control the use of school property. This put Powell in a ticklish situation. On the one hand, he wanted to protect the authority of the school board. On the other, there was nothing to be gained from a fight with the city council. As always, Powell tried compromise. The school board adopted a resolution reaffirming its authority over the use of school property but promising to consult the council privately before making any decisions.

At first this conciliation seemed successful. Powell appeared at a council meeting on September 14, 1959, to reiterate the school board's position. Mayor Anderson was ready to withdraw his resolution when Oliver Hill, chairman of the Legal Committee of the NAACP and the state's premier civil rights lawyer, intervened. Hill was not happy with the city council or the school board, but he knew which group he liked less. The city council, he said, should stay out of school board affairs and appoint a committee to study desegregation problems "so that they could be considered factually and rationally." Powell leapt to his feet to say that the school board did not consider that the question of Chandler Junior High School had anything to do with desegregation, but it was too late. The effect of Hill's intervention was to link the school board with integration. Once the issue was framed in that way, a majority of the council insisted on taking a stand, and the resolution passed by a vote of five to four.

The resolution did not settle the proposed conversion of Chandler, and with the breakdown of relations between the school board and the city council, it was no longer possible to proceed by behind-the-scenes negotiation. On February 24, 1960, the school board held a public hearing—its first ever on the subject of desegregation. Although both whites and blacks objected to the proposal, the whites were more numerous and better organized. Nearly a thousand of them had met the preceding Thursday in the Chandler auditorium. They heard a rousing speech by Joe T. Mizell, Jr., a lawyer and local community leader. Mizell bemoaned the decline in property values that would result from blacks in the school and called for concerted resistance to black expansion in the neighborhood. Mizell pointed out that the city council owned the schools and controlled the budget. The jurisdictional turf of the school board meant nothing to him: "When the homes of widows and orphans will be cut in value by 25 per cent by the stupid actions of the School Board, then it's time to get another School Board." Mizell urged his audience to show up en masse to protest the conversion.

Show up they did: nearly sixteen hundred people crowded into the auditorium of the old John Marshall High School and spilled out onto the school's front lawn. An array of white speakers reiterated Mizell's points. One had already been "forced" to move once to escape black encroachment and saw no end to the proposed accommodation: "You'll never be able to give them enough schools," he said. "You'll never satisfy them even if you give everything on God's green earth." Another complained of the effect on property values: "I don't think I have to tell you what happens to real estate values when Negro schools come in. . . . I beg of you to reconsider." And one woman said that her area housed many elderly persons "who would have to move if Negroes occupied Chandler." Applause and cheers greeted these remarks.

The first black speaker was Oliver Hill, who later described what happened: "[W]hen I rose to speak, there was an uproar of boos, catcalls and epithets. It was obvious that this audience had no intention of permitting me to speak. A typical moderator would have suggested that I retire hastily for my own safety, but Lewis stood up beside me and, with calm demeanor and a steady voice, insisted upon the restoration of order. His doing so reminded me of depictions of Jesus calming the stormy Sea of Galilee." Whether others were put in mind of the Deity is not recorded, but the audience quieted down and there was no further disorder.*

The school board decided to reconsider. A statement issued on April 22, 1960, announced the decision to continue Chandler for one more year as a white junior high school and candidly gave the reasons. First, the conversion of Chandler "would become a divisive political issue in the current councilmanic campaign. The issue would probably be framed as a contest between council and the board over basic questions of responsibility for public education." The board was prepared to fight if forced to it, but was "convinced that political controversy over our schools is not in the public interest." Moreover, the board had been impressed with "the overwhelming public sentiment," from both whites and blacks, against the proposed conversion. Finally, continuing Chandler's current use gave some insurance against the possibility that the new John Marshall High School would not be completed in time for fall classes.

That fall Chandler remained all white, save for two black teenagers.

---

* This courtesy was richly rewarded when Powell was nominated to the Supreme Court. Faced with the opposition of Congressman Conyers and others, Powell needed black support. Oliver Hill spoke out publicly and privately on his behalf. Among those Hill contacted was his old friend Thurgood Marshall, who was assured that Lewis Powell was all right.

By the time the issue came up again, Powell had left the school board for a position on the Virginia State Board of Education. The demographic changes that had prompted the proposed conversion of Chandler continued, and in time Chandler became largely black.

EDUCATIONAL REFORM

Two powerful family influences combined to put education at the forefront of Powell's sense of civic duty. From his mother's side came the example of Uncle Ned—learned and gentle, disciplined and caring, a teacher in the best and fullest sense of the word. Through his and his mother's devotion to Uncle Ned, Powell gained a deep veneration for learning and scholarship. He would often compliment the academic attainments of persons whose worldly achievements might have been thought more important. For Powell, calling someone "a fine scholar" was always high praise. From Louis Sr., who came by education the hard way, Powell heard a different but no less earnest perspective on the value of schools. From this hard-driving, self-made man, Powell learned to see education as the key to economic success.

Powell willingly undertook school board service. It gratified both his admiration for education and his ambition to play a leading role in his community. Moreover, the community valued his participation. No one seemed to mind that he had no children in public school (both Jo and Penny attended St. Catherine's, an Episcopal girls' school). Also, no one objected that Powell continued as chairman of the Richmond School Board while his law firm defended Prince Edward County against desegregation. The latter point troubled Powell. In 1955, he wrote the superintendent of Richmond schools, with copies to all school board members: "I have never had any part personally in this litigation, but I am concerned over the possibility that my membership in this firm may cause questions to arise, particularly in the minds of our Negro citizens, as to whether it is appropriate for me to remain as Chairman of the School Board." He offered to resign and asked his colleagues to convene in his absence "and exercise your collective best judgment as to what will best serve the public interest." They advised him to stay, and he did—again, without arousing public comment.

The most important act of Powell's early tenure concerned personnel. In 1952, a few months after Powell became chairman, New Orleans tried to hire the superintendent of Richmond schools, Henry I. Willett. "Hi" Willett, as he was called, was a man of extraordinary energy and infectious enthusiasm who was already developing a national reputation. New Orleans had a larger school system and promised Willett more money. Powell had to meet the challenge. He did so in part by engineering a substantial raise (from $15,000 to $18,000 a year), but also by orchestrating a show of personal and political support from the entire school board, the mayor, the city manager, and every member of the city council. Willett was made to know that Richmond cared about public education and cared about him. In his statement on Willett's decision to remain in Richmond, and on every appropriate occasion thereafter, Powell made a point of praising his chief administrator. Willett, said Powell, was "the best school superintendent in America. . . . We do not know where we could replace him with a superintendent of equal capabilities at any price."

Powell and Willett had an effective partnership. Willett ran the schools, handling the usual matters of personnel and administration without micromanagement from the school board. Powell carried the ball with the city council, making the case annually for increased funding and for new school buildings. In this endeavor, Powell was markedly successful. Between September 1950 and September 1960, the enrollment in Richmond schools rose from 30,142 to 40,155, an increase of one third. Fifteen new buildings and twelve major additions were constructed, at a cost of over $18 million. During this period, the total number of teachers increased at a slightly faster rate than the number of students, and their compensation rose steadily. In 1950 the starting salary for a teacher with a B.A. degree was $2300; by 1960 it had risen to $3900, an increase of 70 percent in nominal dollars and approximately 36 percent in constant-dollar equivalent. During the same period, the maximum salary advanced from $3600 to $5400 per annum, again an appreciable real-dollar increase. Most impressive of all, the system's operating budget doubled during the decade. If all figures are adjusted for changes in the consumer price index, the real value of per capita expenditures by the Richmond schools rose slightly more than 20 percent during the 1950s. Not only was Richmond educating more students; it was spending more per student on education.

To obtain these resources, Powell acted as advocate and lobbyist for the city's schools. The school board had the authority to set teachers' salaries, but not the funds. The money had to come from outside sources, chiefly the city council. Since teachers' salaries were by far the largest item in the budget, increases required the council's support. Powell's job was to convince the elected officials to take the heat for the increased taxes needed to fund public education. On the whole, he was successful. He approached council members as partners, recognizing the problems they faced and applauding their past support. He tried to show that the money appropriated for schools was well used. Always, he appealed to civic pride: "I think we would all agree," he said in 1954, "that the people of this community are not satisfied with an *average* school system or with *average* quality teachers. . . . We have traditionally taken pride in the cultural advantages and educational assets of Richmond. It is certainly not desirable, and we hope not necessary, to break with this tradition."

Powell also lobbied the state legislature. In 1960 he appeared before the Finance Committee of the state Senate "as an individual who believes deeply that we are doing too little in Virginia for public education." He asked for more money for teachers, even at the price of higher taxes: "The end formerly sought by education was confined primarily to values of the mind and spirit, to the intangibles of culture and a full and satisfying life. No literate person would deny any of these." But in the competitive modern world, there were "harder and more realistic" goals for education—to increase local productivity, to enable Virginia's graduates to compete favorably with those from other states, and ultimately to sustain America's position internationally. "I do not like taxes any better than anyone else," he added. "But I do prefer increased taxes to the awesome consequences of not remaining competitive in the world in which we live."

Not all of Powell's advocacy was aimed at public officials; sometimes he appeared in the court of public opinion. In August 1960, Powell took on Hyman G. Rickover, the Navy legend who made a second career out of attacking American education. "Admiral Rickover," said Powell, "father of the atomic submarine, is a great naval officer and a great American. . . . It is not equally clear that he is a careful and thorough student of American public education." Rickover had ridiculed high school instruction on "life adjustment," "leisure time," and "how to play canasta." Powell said that generalizing from bizarre examples was "exaggeration which exceeds the limit of fair argument." In a country as large as the United States, with thousands of local school boards acting on their own, some "awfully silly things" were taught in school, but "it is manifestly unfair to condemn the entire American system, without reservation, on the basis of the weird examples which usually make the headlines in the press." The people of Richmond could be sure that "the Admiral does not know about the exacting curriculum and standards of the Richmond public schools, where little, if any, of his specific criticisms would be remotely applicable."

*   *   *

BUILDINGS AND BUDGETS did not occupy all Powell's attention. He increasingly used his position as school board chairman to promote educational reforms. Especially after October 1957, when Sputnik exploded America's easy faith in its own scientific superiority, Powell linked public education to international politics. The Soviet Union threatened world domination. America's response could not be limited to military preparedness; it had to include improved education.

Powell voiced these opinions in a statement supporting President Eisenhower's proposal of a billion dollars in federal aid for science education. Though two Virginia Congressmen had objected to the plan as unnecessary, Powell thought it did not go far enough. America needed to reorient and improve education in order to regain scientific leadership. The "deadly national peril" demanded a national response: "It would be the gravest folly to wait and vainly hope for the requisite action from forty-eight states and thousands of localities while the Soviets continue to out-distance us in this race for survival."

He elaborated these ideas in a major speech delivered to Richmond public school teachers in February 1958 and later distributed as a pamphlet. Sputnik was America's "scientific Pearl Harbor." Soviet technological leadership meant "that the ultimate fate of the free world may well depend upon whether American education . . . responds successfully to the Soviet challenge." He then launched into a detailed review of comparative military capability, including inter-continental ballistic missiles, and concluded that America must con-tinue this "senseless weapons race" for "so long as Russia wishes to impose its will upon the world by force." Perhaps in a decade, or more likely half a century, the Russian people would have "leaders whom the world can trust." In the meantime, prepare and educate.

By comparison with Soviet education, American schools were weak in science and math and in overall academic quality: "Our schools and colleges have generally failed to prescribe a sufficiently challenging curriculum and insist upon a sufficiently high level of performance by faculties and students." Richmond should reject "more diplomas and less learning" in favor of higher standards. Greater emphasis should be placed on science and math, and instruction in the Russian and Chinese languages should begin as soon as practicable. Additional pro-posals covered a wide range: requiring more credits for high school graduation; prescribing more mandatory subjects and curtailing elec-tives; augmenting programs for gifted students; and creating a three-year terminal program "for the approximately 50 percent of our pupils who drop out before graduation." All this, of course, depended on teachers, and Powell reiterated his conviction "that the soundest investment we can possibly make in the future of our children is to have the highest quality of teachers." This was not possible "with salary levels lower than those of truck drivers." The ultimate question, as Powell saw it, was whether "luxury-loving, easy-going America" would "make the sustained effort and sacrifice" necessary to meet the educational challenge.

A few months after this speech, Powell dictated a "Check-List to Determine Extent of Progress Actually Being Made in Up-Grading Education in Richmond." This list of extraordinarily detailed questions was designed to keep administrators and faculty focused on his agenda. He wanted to know what additional courses in mathematics, science, and languages would be required for the next year; what additional electives would be available in these subjects; and what new or additional steps were planned "to identify the gifted or talented pupils in math, science and languages and to facilitate their advancement beyond the average." And there was much more. He wanted to know, for example, what new textbooks were available; whether Richmond schools were "really progressive" in taking advantage of television, films, and other new teaching aids; whether Richmond was providing proper in-service training for teachers; and whether progress was being made on gradually increasing homework, requiring more outside reading, tightening up on grades, raising the standards for new faculty, and moving toward some type of merit system for teachers. This formidable array of demands was sent to Hi Willett with the palliative assurance that it was "not a formal request from me as Chairman of the Board" but merely an effort to "be sure that something tangible is being accomplished."

Having stirred things up locally, Powell left on July 19, 1958, for two weeks in Moscow. He went as a member of an ABA delegation to study the Soviet legal system, but he was more interested in Soviet education. When he returned, he made a report to the school board, also reprinted as a pamphlet, entitled "Soviet Education—A Means Toward World Domination." The Soviet Union had "committed itself to the most intensive and extensive educational program ever attempted by any government or people, and with an incredible emphasis on science." There were deficiencies in Soviet schools, notably in failing to produce culturally well-rounded persons, but in the vital areas of mathematics and science, he found Soviet education "considerably superior to that generally provided in America." In response, Powell called again for greater emphasis on math and science; instruction in Russian and Chinese; more attention to the gifted and talented student; and more demanding standards of performance for both faculty and students. Also, he suggested lengthening the school year. Finally, he returned to the problem of political support: "Everyone seems to agree that we should have the finest education in the World. But many vocal supporters of this essential objective tend to melt away or make excuses whenever the subject of increased taxes for educational needs is raised." The ultimate question was whether a free people would make the sacrifices necessary to meet the Soviet challenge.

In the next few years, Powell returned to these themes again and again. Increasingly, his views put him at odds with professional educators. He criticized standards proposed by the Virginia State Board of Education because they required only two units each in science and math—the same number required for Virginia history. He also disparaged the proliferating of electives: "In their natural anxiety to avoid being charged with 'regimentation,' educators and parents have often timidly abdicated their own best judgment in favor of the immature judgment of teenagers who—quite naturally—are disposed to choose the easier subjects." He thought educators should have the courage to *require* a more difficult curriculum: "We have had too much faith in the capacity of inexperienced young people to choose their courses, and too little faith in the capacity of these pupils to carry successfully a prescribed quality program in the fundamentals of English, mathematics, science, history, and foreign language."

The state board of education did not have to follow Powell's ambitious agenda, but Richmond did. In February 1959, the city adopted a curriculum incorporating Powell's reforms. Three kinds of diplomas would be offered: college preparatory, business, and general (supplanting an earlier vocational degree). In accordance with state standards, all three programs required five years of English (counting grades eight through twelve). In other respects, Richmond required substantially more than the state. College preparatory students were told to take four years of mathematics, and business and general students three years, as compared to the two years required by the state. All diplomas required three years of science, while the state demanded only two. History was raised from three years to four, with new emphasis on world history and geography; and college preparatory students were required to take at least three years of a foreign language, with four recommended. Finally, physical and health education (or high school R.O.T.C.) was required for the first time. To make way for all this, the number of elective credits was reduced from eight to three. The whole program bears Powell's imprint, as does the school board's explanation that the new curriculum was designed to combat the "tendency toward mediocrity" sometimes evident in universal free education.

EVEN AS POWELL'S views on educational reform triumphed in the Richmond schools, he moved on to the more controversial design of a course on communism. He broached this proposal in a 1960 speech to the Chicago convention of the National School Boards Association. Existing courses in government and history were inadequate. In most, the textbooks were simply obsolete. In the rare cases where communism was treated at some length, the texts erred in treating communism and fascism as equally dangerous: "Nothing could be more misleading or superficial than thinking which equates communism with fascism. As repugnant as fascism should be to all Americans, it is now a spent force in the world." Communism, by contrast, was a virulent international conspiracy backed by atomic weapons. Instruction should begin on the history of communism—Marx, Lenin, Stalin, and Khrushchev—and on understanding its major characteristics. These he summarized as follows:

> (1) That communism requires a totalitarian dictatorship, in which the instrument of power is the small minority within the party which imposes its will upon the masses.
> (2) That it also requires an "iron curtain" of censorship which insulates the minds of hundreds of millions of people against the truth from the free world.
> (3) That the foreign policy of the Soviet Union (and Red China) is in fact a "war policy," despite its elaborate disguise as an instrument of peace.
> (4) That communism is a world-wide conspiracy which changes its techniques from time to time, but which has never deviated from its imperialistic purpose of world conquest—by force and violence if necessary.

Obviously, this was education to a purpose, but Powell did not want mere propaganda. At least he did not want crude propaganda. As he explained to Hi Willett, a course on international communism would be closely scrutinized. Critics on the right would object to any such instruction, while "fuzzy minded gentlemen" on the left would on the lookout for red-baiting and McCarthyism. Powell was not worried about such criticism, "so long as we develop and present a really excellent and scholarly course," one with "academic quality and accurate historical content."

Ultimately, Powell got his way. The state board of education appointed a committee to develop a course on the fundamentals of a free system, including its contrast with communism, and these ideas were incorporated into the high school course on government. Richmond went further. In the spring of 1961, city schools began a six-week course on the history, philosophy, objectives, and techniques of international communism. Subsequently, it became part of the required curriculum. Teachers seemed to regard the program as worthwhile, but it suffered from the lack of a good text. The only suitable book that had been found was criticized as preachy and repetitious. Eventually, the separate course was dropped, and instruction on communism was relegated to the general course on government.

IN OCTOBER 1960, Powell made his last appearance before the convocation of Richmond teachers. His second term on the school board would expire the next spring, and state law did not allow reappointment. The relatively young man who had taken over as chairman eight years before was now fifty-three years old, and the low profile of his early years had given way to public cheerleading for educational reform. In his swan song before the teachers, Powell had many things to say, though, as usual, nothing at all about desegregation.

Powell began by detailing the progress in the last ten years. He reviewed not only buildings and budgets, but also the new curricular requirements and the performance of Richmond's students. Having worked hard to change aspects of American education, he exited on a note of support and approval: "I believe deeply in the basic soundness of the American public school system. I am unmoved by those who urge that the European or Soviet system is better. . . . I say to Admiral Rickover, and other detractors of American education, that this country's unparalleled attainments—both spiritual and material—are hardly the product of an inferior educational system."

Powell then turned to what he called "one of my pet subjects"—the weakness in teaching "how to speak and write our own language." He had brought this up the year before, when he described the "shockingly inadequate training which the average American receives in speaking and writing." Now he asked again, as he had then, that all teachers, not merely those teaching English, insist on higher standards of oral and written expression.

Powell's "final aspiration" for the Richmond schools was a theme near to his heart: "That is, that we train and inspire our young people to have a sense of duty and devotion to America. In a word, we must *inspire patriotism.*" He knew it was "thought by some to be old-fashioned even to speak of patriotism," but he did not care. He then told the story, as reported in the press, of the "comment book" maintained by the Soviets in Red Square, where the wreckage of the downed U-2 spy plane were on display for many weeks. Tourists were invited to make comments in the book. Many wrote platitudes on peace and friendship, but "not one American defended the necessity of seeking intelligence information on a country which has threatened to destroy us by hydrogen attack!" "The most sickening example," Powell continued, "came from the pen of some warped American mind who wrote: 'The U-2 flight was a wanton act of aggression which is deplored by peace loving Americans.'" "Let us hope," Powell concluded, "that the Richmond Public School System will never produce a spineless Judas of this kind."

Powell had done all he could to prevent it.

STATE BOARD OF EDUCATION

In January 1961, Lindsay Almond began his last year as Governor. The break with Harry Byrd and the continuing trench warfare with Byrd stalwarts in the General Assembly had made his term difficult. One of the opportunities remaining to him was to name two members of the state board of education. The all-black Virginia Teachers Association planned to meet with the Governor to plead for a black board member, but Almond would have none of that. On January 3, 1961, three weeks before the scheduled conversation with the black teachers, Almond announced the appointment of Lewis Powell. A few days later, Almond named Powell's new colleague. Colgate W. Darden, Jr.

Colgate Darden was one of the most remarkable and engaging persons ever to hold public office in Virginia. He had been Governor from 1942 to 1946 and thereafter served twelve years as the third president of the University of Virginia. When Darden arrived in Charlottesville in 1947, neither faculty nor students welcomed a mere politician, but many came to applaud the choice. Darden's formidable political skills secured for the University a trebling of the private endowment and a quadrupling of the annual state appropriation. Moreover, although Darden campaigned for the tuition grant proposal of the Gray Plan, he vehemently opposed closing the public schools. Throughout the

1950s, Darden kept the University aloof and disengaged from the extremities of massive resistance.

Newspapers applauded the appointments. The *Times-Dispatch* called the choices "spectacularly good": Darden and Powell were "so eminently qualified for the board that two more competent men could not have been found." Other editors praised Powell as a person from "outside the realm of pure politics and factionalism" who was "demonstrably dedicated to the cause of education itself." Originally, Powell planned to serve out the remaining months of his term on the Richmond School Board, but when a question arose as to the legality of holding both positions, Powell resigned the local post. The *Times-Dispatch* lauded his chairmanship: "Few men of this generation have served Richmond as ably and conscientiously as Lewis F. Powell, Jr." He had built new schools, raised scholastic requirements, increased emphasis on sciences and foreign languages, demanded greater proficiency in reading and writing English, introduced instruction on international communism, and secured better salaries throughout the school system. One reason he had been so effective was "the respect in which he is held, not only by City Council, but by members of all races and creeds."

The last comment was an oblique way of saying what everyone knew but no one cared to trumpet publicly—that Darden and Powell were willing to accept desegregation. Reporter Guy Friddell termed them "progressive," which may have been an overstatement. Darden himself said they were "middle-grounders," which, given the ground then occupied, was undoubtedly true. Wags called Powell a "hard-line moderate." Whatever the label, both Darden and Powell were, and were known to be, more interested in quality education for all Virginians than in keeping black Virginians out of white schools.

VIRTUALLY POWELL'S FIRST act on the state board of education was to join in issuing regulations authorizing local school boards to resume control of pupil placement, as directed by the General Assembly. The board listed the criteria that localities should consider. Race was not mentioned, but one provision endorsed "maximum continuity in pupil placement by avoidance of any general or unnecessary reallocation or reassignment of pupils heretofore entered in the public school system." In other words, it was all right to go slow. Whether Virginia localities actually needed to be cautioned against rushing headlong into massive integration may be doubted, but in any event the board was reassuring. The board's attitudes were also revealed by its sponsorship of separate statewide conferences for black and white educators. This practice was continued until 1965, when the separate conferences were suspended under an agreement with federal authorities. Interestingly, this was not the policy in Richmond, where Powell and Willett had desegregated the annual convocation of teachers back in the early 1950s. There is no record, however, that Powell objected to separate meetings at the state level or even that the matter came up for discussion.

All evidence points to the same conclusion: The state board of education of which Lewis Powell was a member was willing to accept desegregation, but was also supremely tolerant of the status quo. Until 1964, no one in the state department of education was assigned to work on desegregation. In simple truth, the problem was not on the board's agenda. In itself, this was not surprising. The lack of a statewide policy followed the plan of the General Assembly when it abandoned massive resistance in favor of local option. It also fit the existing pattern of local control over public education. Although the state board had general supervision of Virginia's schools, local control predominated. Major questions of finance and administration were determined locally. In particular, local school boards reacquired control over pupil placement. The state board concerned itself chiefly with such matters as curriculum content, teacher certification, school accreditation, textbook selection, and classroom construction. Desegregation was left to the localities.

In the localities, desegregation progressed about as fast as it did elsewhere in the South—which is to say, almost not at all. Localities adopted pupil placement ordinances, which evolved into so-called freedom of choice plans. Under these schemes, students went to the same schools as before—that is, to segregated schools—until someone requested a change. Since whites did not ask to go to black schools, the burden of going forward fell entirely on blacks. Few made it all the way. Bureaucratic complexity could make reassignment difficult. Various pretexts could be invoked to refuse valid requests. Some blacks were intimidated by threat of retaliation. Even where "freedom of choice" was more or less real, many black parents were reluctant to send their children to white schools. The only black face in a white classroom would have had a hard time under the best of circumstances, and circumstances were not the best.

The upshot of all this was desegregation at a snail's pace. In the fall of 1961, most localities had not even begun. Of the eleven states of the old Confederacy, only Texas had as many as 1 percent of black students in school with whites. Virginia had virtually none (0.25 of 1 percent). Three years later, on the tenth anniversary of *Brown v. Board of Education,* only 5 percent of Virginia's black students attended school with whites.*

Both the pace of desegregation and the extent of state involvement picked up after the 1964 Civil Rights Act. That statute authorized withholding federal money from schools that failed to desegregate. In January of the following year, the state board of education assured HEW that it would comply with federal guidelines. Specifically, the board agreed to make no new commitments of federal funds to school districts without federally approved desegregation plans. Thereafter the state performed various functions of advice and coordination, but did not itself undertake to guarantee desegregation. Rather, each locality acted on its own to comply with federal guidelines or lose federal funds. HEW issued guidelines in the spring of 1965 and toughened them considerably the following year. The effect was to allow freedom of choice to continue, but only if it actually produced results. Increasingly, federal officials judged desegregation plans not by paper promises or expressed intentions but by the degree of integration actually achieved. Under this pressure, the numbers began to rise. In the fall of 1965, one in nine of Virginia's black students attended school with whites; the next year, the figure was one in four.†

The movement was real, but it was too little and too late. In 1968, the Supreme Court ran out of patience. In *Green v. County School Board of New Kent County,* a case from rural Virginia, the Court shifted the burden of going forward with desegregation from black parents to white school boards. No longer was it enough for school officials merely to *allow* integration; now school boards had an *affirmative obligation* to desegregate. In the words of the Supreme Court: "The burden on a school board today is to come forward with a plan that promises realistically to work, and promises realistically to work *now.*" The time for "all deliberate speed" had come and gone; the new watchword was "Now!" Desegregation would be judged by results, and the results had to show in the numbers. And what exactly would local

* Low as it was, this figure was far from the worst. Of the eleven states of the South, only Texas and Tennessee did better, with figures of 7 and 5 percent respectively. Five states—South Carolina, Georgia, Alabama, Mississippi, and Arkansas—still had only a fraction of 1 percent of black students in school with whites. By way of comparison, the border states of Kentucky and Missouri had 62 and 44 percent respectively.

† In the South, only Texas did better. Virginia was far ahead of neighboring North Carolina, which, because it had preferred tokenism to outright defiance in the 1950s, now enjoyed a reputation for racial progress.

school boards have to do to get the right numbers? *Green* implied the answer: School boards should do whatever it takes. From this time forward, federal courts moved rapidly to eliminate racially identifiable public schools.

In the next few years, desegregation gathered steam throughout the South. In the fall of 1968, 42 percent of Virginia's black students attended school with whites, but in most cases the nonminority presence was quite small. By 1970 wholesale changes were underway in Virginia and throughout the region. But by this time, Powell was out of public education. His second term on the state board expired some months after *Green*, just as lower federal courts began to translate the message of that decision into specific demands for immediate action. Luck and circumstance contrived to keep Powell away from the action. He served locally during years when the state forbade any desegregation, and he moved to the state level just as responsibility was returned to the localities. This fortuity—as well as his formidable political instincts—enabled Powell to negotiate his way through shoals that wrecked many lesser reputations.

TWO LARGE CRITICISMS can be made of Powell's service on the state board of education. The first concerns a sin of omission. In his two terms on the state board, Powell never did any more than was necessary to facilitate desegregation. He never took a leading role. He never spoke out against foot-dragging and gradualism. He never really identified himself with the needs and aspirations of Virginia's black schoolchildren. His attitude and that of his colleagues on the state board were reflected in the approach of the deputy superintendent assigned by the state department of education to monitor compliance with federal desegregation guidelines. The description of that official by Powell's friend and admirer, District Judge Robert R. Merhige, Jr., also fits Lewis Powell: He complied with the law, but "found it diplomatically sound not to do any more than absolutely required."

As the 1960s progressed, Powell became increasingly concerned about the poor education of poor students, many of whom were black. In Virginia, many of the worst schools were rural. Powell supported consolidation of rural school districts, higher standards, more money, and greater state supervision to ensure that even in remote and backward locations, schools would be minimally adequate. He also grew to appreciate the special problems of the inner city. In a statement delivered to the state board of education at the time of his retirement, Powell spoke feelingly of the "injustice, as well as potentially disastrous social consequences" of failing to educate the inner city child: "The problem is most acute in the pre-school years. The disadvantaged child, often with little home environment, simply never catches up if his formal education is deferred until normal school age." The predictable result was a teenage dropout. "Then, at best, society has another unproductive citizen to support. At worst, and with increasing frequency, the drop out becomes a juvenile delinquent and then an habitual criminal." Powell suggested preschool programs for the disadvantaged to supplement federal Head Start and continuing special education for those at risk of dropping out. Mostly, he emphasized commitment. The vicious cycle of poverty, illiteracy, and crime "must be broken at all costs. In view of the eroding influence of the home and church, the primary responsibility now rests with the school. This we are beginning to recognize, but the awareness must have a deeper sense of urgency."

Yet despite this sense of urgency about the education of Virginia's blacks, Powell did not try to speed up the pace of desegregation. He did not treat that as his responsibility. Control over pupil assignment had been returned to localities, and it was their job (and that of the federal courts) to see that the schools were desegregated in accordance with the law. All that was true, and yet the predominance of local control did not mean that state officials were wholly insulated from desegregation concerns. There were so many points of contact between state and local decisions, so many intersections between the two spheres, that it is unrealistic to speak of them as entirely separate. In fact, state laws provided the framework for local control, and state officials helped to implement local policies. Thus, although desegregation decisions were made locally, the state board of education and state school officials were involved, although usually in a passive and secondary way, in a wide variety of local acts that affected desegregation in Virginia.

While it is entirely plausible that a more committed state board might have hastened the pace of change, it also seems clear that the effect would have been marginal. Dollars tell the story of control. Figures from the end of the decade reveal that Virginia's localities furnished 60 percent of the funding for primary and secondary public education. The state kicked in almost 30 percent, but the great bulk of that was spent according to formulas spelled out in the appropriations statutes. The money actually disbursed by the state board of education amounted to something less than 3 percent of total expenditures. Given limited financial clout and local control over pupil placement, it seems unlikely Powell or the other members of the state board of education could have greatly eased or hastened desegregation. In any event, they did not try.

THE OTHER CRITICISM of Powell's years on the state board of education concerns the tuition grant program. Statutes originally passed in 1956 to enable white children to leave desegregated schools placed administration of the program with the state board. For some years, the program remained tiny, but in 1959, when the first black children actually entered white classes, many whites left the public schools. Tuition grants and scholarships facilitated this white flight, as they were designed to do. Under the statute, the state board adopted regulations governing the eligibility and payment of tuition grants in 1959 and revised them periodically thereafter. Powell's votes approving such regulations were later cited as evidence that he supported the tuition grant strategy as a way of evading *Brown*. In 1965, this strategy was curtailed by a federal court order barring tuition grants for use in segregated academies maintained predominantly by such grants. Under that order, state officials were supposed to monitor private schools to see whether they discriminated against blacks and were supported predominantly by tuition grants and scholarships from state funds, but there is no evidence that the state board made any serious effort to investigate the recipients. This also was criticized. Finally, Powell was faulted most bitterly for his participation on July 1, 1964, when the state board unanimously extended the deadline for tuition grant applications from Prince Edward County. In effect, the board authorized retroactive reimbursement of white parents who had sent their children to all-white private academies the preceding year. Powell's vote on this matter was later cited in support of the charge that he was in fact a "champion" of segregation.

Insofar as these criticisms track the general proposition that Powell and his colleagues did not push desegregation, they are surely correct. But the specific claim that Powell personally favored the tuition grant strategy, while a reasonable inference from the public record, is at least partly mistaken. As has been noted, his private correspondence records his opposition. When Ed Murrow had a special show on massive resistance, entitled "The Lost Class of '59," Powell voiced his support. "A climate of intolerance now exists in the South which, in my opinion, far exceeds, both in intensity and danger to our country, the type of intolerance which came to be known as McCarthyism," Powell wrote. He hoped, he said, that Murrow's program could help "restore reason to the point were we do not in effect abandon public education for most, if not all, of our children."

Powell's votes adopting regulations to administer the tuition grant program in fact do not reflect personal support for that tactic. For the state board of education, the use of public money to support private schools was a duty, not an option. Members of the state board were not asked whether they thought tuition grants were a good idea; they were told to implement legislative policy. Insofar as Powell and his colleagues merely approved plans for administering that program, they did no more than follow the directions of the General Assembly.

But in one important instance, they did do more. By far the most damning criticism of Powell's years on the state board of education concerns the decision to waive the deadline for tuition grant applications from Prince Edward County. It is easy to see why this episode was singled out for complaint. Any link to the wretched experience in "rural, remote, and resolute" Prince Edward County would naturally excite suspicion, and Powell's vote to resume payments to residents of this recalcitrant backwater seems a flat contradiction of his often-stated belief in the primacy of public education. The issue requires a brief excursion into the extraordinarily tangled history of desegregation in Prince Edward County.

The facts were these. In 1959, some months after Lindsay Almond had abandoned massive resistance, Prince Edward County shut its schools. They remained closed for five long years, as litigation raged over the legality of the county's action. During this time, white students went to hastily created private academies. An offer was made to fund similar facilities for blacks, but they refused, lest the existence of all-black private schools undermine their case for integrated public schools. Most of the county's black children went without formal education until 1963, when Governor Albertis S. Harrison asked Colgate Darden to do something about Prince Edward County. Darden organized a private committee that coordinated federal, state, and local resources and held classes in the buildings formerly occupied by the public schools. The following year, the public schools reopened under order of the United States Supreme Court.

In their first year of operation, Prince Edward County's private academies were funded entirely by private contributions. By 1960–61, they depended on public money, including both state tuition grants and additional funds and tax credits from the county. In August of that year, the federal District Court ordered these payments stopped. Specifically, the court enjoined state officials from "receiving, processing or approving any applications for state scholarship grants from persons residing in Prince Edward County *so long as the public schools of*

Prince Edward County remain closed" (emphasis added). Three years later, when the Supreme Court ordered the schools reopened, the county board of supervisors appropriated money for the public schools *and* resumed the local tuition grant program. The state board of education then asked the attorney general whether it should follow suit. The attorney general replied that the injunction against processing scholarship applications from Prince Edward County was no longer in effect (because the public schools were no longer closed), and the state board voted to accept applications for the immediately preceding school year. In fact, no state funds were paid, as they were almost immediately prohibited by the federal court as "transparent evasions" of constitutional duty.

Powell's support of these payments is difficult to understand. On the one hand, the board's action cannot be explained away on the ground that it was coerced by state law. Even if the state board was required to resume tuition grants to Prince Edward County residents once the injunction had lifted, there was no compulsion to approve them retroactively. That decision looks like an effort by the state board to do what it could to support Prince Edward County's private academies and thus to prevent integrated public schools in that community. In this view, the vote to authorize retroactive tuition grants does seem the act of a champion of segregation.

On the other hand, this interpretation is contradicted by Powell's private complaint to Governor Albertis S. Harrison that "Prince Edward is increasingly becoming a serious reflection upon the good name of Virginia" and perhaps also by his donation of $100 to the privately supported schools for black children. More important, the view of Powell as an ingenious supporter of Prince Edward County overlooks his entire history. Powell had devoted much time and energy to Richmond's public schools. On desegregation, he did no more than the law required, but when forced to choose between segregation and education, he always chose education. Throughout the state's long descent into massive resistance, he fought to keep the schools open. It is not credible that Powell would consistently oppose massive resistance during the heyday of its popularity, only later to embrace the heedless intransigence of Prince Edward County. Neither is it believable that such late-blooming extremism was shared by Colgate Darden.

On all the evidence, it seems clear that Powell's vote of July 1, 1964, represented not a change of heart but a failure of leadership and perception. He and the other members of the state board seem to have viewed this vote not as declaring their support for the diehards in Prince

Edward County, but as more or less routinely carrying out state policy. Whether wisely or not (Powell thought not), the General Assembly had authorized the tuition grant program precisely to enable white parents to escape integrated schools. The applications from Prince Edward County were squarely within the intention of the General Assembly. For a time that policy had been frustrated by the federal court injunction, but once that impediment was removed, the proper course was to implement fully the policy of state law. Allowing retroactive applications did just that. This casual view of the matter underlay the unanimous decision in July 1964. The lack of wisdom in this action was sufficiently proved by the severe and immediate reaction of the federal court, but it goes too far to see this episode as a window into Powell's soul. The vote on July 1, 1964, was not the unmasking of a hidden agenda, but rather a particularly striking example of Powell's general disengagement from the problems of desegregation.

POWELL'S MORE CONSIDERED VIEW of Prince Edward County surfaced in a different forum. A year before he left the state board of education, he was named to the Commission on Constitutional Revision, a group asked by Governor Mills E. Godwin to draft a new constitution for the state of Virginia. The commission worked in subcommittees, and Lewis Powell and Colgate Darden were assigned education. They began with the existing Constitution, which required the General Assembly to "establish and maintain an efficient system of public free schools throughout the State." According to the state courts, this provision prohibited the state from closing public schools to avoid integration, but did not prevent localities from doing the same thing. The "system of public free schools" contemplated by the existing Constitution was a "system" of local option. Virginia could not force its localities to close their schools (as had been done under massive resistance), but it had no duty to keep the schools open if a locality refused to support them. Under this dainty reasoning, the educational shutdown by Prince Edward County was— as a matter of state law—perfectly legal. Of course, this result was overridden when the Supreme Court of the United States ruled that the closed schools violated the federal Constitution. But although that decision superseded state law, it did not change it. *Insofar as the Commonwealth of Virginia was concerned*, a local determination to quit public education remained entirely permissible.

Powell and Darden changed state law. First, they strengthened and enlarged the state's obligation. The new Constitution of Virginia, which took effect in 1971, mandates that the General Assembly "shall provide for a system of free public elementary and secondary schools for all children of school age throughout the Commonwealth" and further that the state "shall seek to ensure that an educational program of high quality is established and continually maintained." Next, they added a provision requiring local participation. The new Constitution allows the General Assembly to apportion the costs of education between the state and localities, and provides: "Each unit of local government *shall* provide its portion of such cost. . . ." (emphasis added). The debacle in Prince Edward County would never be allowed to recur. Moreover, the state board of education was given greater authority over local school boards, so that the quality of local education, especially rural education, could be more carefully monitored.

Finally, Powell and Darden added education to the Virginia Bill of Rights. This was quite unconventional. In most constitutions, the Bill of Rights forbids interference with specified personal freedoms; it is a list of governmental "Thou Shall Not"s. The Virginia Bill of Rights includes such restrictions but also fixes on government the affirmative duty of education. The language may be flowery, but it exactly states Powell's personal creed: "That free government rests, as does all progress, upon the broadest possible diffusion of knowledge, and that the Commonwealth should avail itself of those talents which nature has sown so liberally among its people by assuring the opportunity for their fullest development by an effective system of education throughout the Commonwealth."

THE CENTRAL INTERPRETIVE PROBLEM of Powell's years in state and local education is his steadfast silence on desegregation. In eighteen years of public office, amid a wide variety of public statements on teachers, funding, curricular reform, and the Soviet threat, Powell said almost nothing on race. Even when events forced his hand, as in the breakdown of negotiations with city council over the new high schools, he was as unforthcoming as possible. Powell never gave any explanation for this policy, other than to repeat that public comment would have damaged his effectiveness, and there is no evidence that he unburdened himself more fully in private. He was silent on desegregation and on the reasons for his own silence.

One inference is that Powell did not talk about desegregation because he was not committed to it, that he was content to let the post-*Brown* future unfold without his aid or encouragement. This was undoubtedly true. Powell's record is consistent on the point (despite occasional revisionism in later life) that he acquiesced in desegregation, but did not actively support it. Had he been as committed to racial justice as he was to national security, he would have said more. Yet interpreting silence as unconcern has obvious limitations. No matter what his preferences in the matter, Powell could scarcely have been indifferent to the fact, pace, or tactics of desegregation. No one in his position could have been as uninterested in these issues as Powell's public record would suggest.

A more sinister interpretation is that Powell actually opposed racial progress but was too smart to be caught on the wrong side of history. Under this view, which surfaced in the opposition to his confirmation, Powell did what he could to maintain segregation but knew that ultimately it would fail. He therefore kept his mouth shut, so that no one could later quote him against himself. Of course, this view attributes to Powell astonishing discernment and foresight. For a lawyer in Richmond, Virginia, in the 1950s to guide his actions according to national sensibilities of a different generation would have been remarkable. Still, as an inference from this sparse public record, this interpretation is not wholly implausible. Powell was ambitious, more ambitious than he would confess, and he wanted to play a role outside Virginia. Moreover, he was always protective of his reputation and never careless of his future prospects. If anyone could have played the farsighted game alleged by his critics, it might have been Lewis Powell.

However plausible these interpretations may seem on the public record, they are flatly inconsistent with the private history. Powell may not have been an early convert to desegregation, but he was genuinely and passionately opposed to massive resistance. All evidence from all sources agrees on that point. As a lawyer and a student of history, Powell knew that defiance of the Supreme Court was a losing proposition. Indeed, by the late 1950s, everyone knew it. Prince Edward County became a statewide embarrassment. Anyone who sought only to position himself for the future could have identified this relic of massive resistance as a useful target, yet Powell said nothing. Just as Powell refused comment throughout the 1950s, just as he pulled his letter to Governor Stanley and withdrew his article from Dean Ribble in 1956, Powell continued into the 1960s without public comment on massive resistance. At the same time, he was very active behind the scenes—first in the debate with Jack Kilpatrick, then in the futile mission to Senator Byrd, and most important in his support of the businessmen's cabal to convert Governor Almond. In these circles, Powell's views were no secret. In fact, he was appointed to the state board of education precisely because he opposed massive resistance.

Why, then, did Powell not speak out? Why did a man so careful of his reputation compile a public record so useful to his enemies? Why did he hide his resistance to Harry Byrd and his contempt for Prince Edward County behind a mask of public silence? The reasons are several. First, Powell's own explanation is true. Especially in the early years, and to a lesser degree thereafter, Powell feared that public comment would undermine his effectiveness. Second, Powell had a pronounced distaste for public discourse on issues of race and desegregation. The public comments of Virginia's leaders were occasionally vulgar, often hurtful, and almost always insensitive to black aspirations. Powell's sense of courtesy and decorum, if not his heartfelt political conviction, dissuaded him from entering such a debate. As Powell knew from Oliver Hill's encounter with the angry whites at the debate over Chandler High School, emotions ran high. In that meeting Powell wanted to have as little public discussion as possible. He was finally forced to take a stand, not by political conviction, but by his felt need to preserve, individually and personally, the courtesy and good manners for which he was always known. On this one occasion, his desire to avoid discourtesy and hurt demanded speech; in most situations, it counseled silence.

At bottom, Powell's habitual silence on desegregation also reflected his strong sense of group allegiance. Powell supported Harry Byrd. He was a friend and ally of many of the major figures pushing massive resistance. He was willing to try to change their minds—as he twice attempted with Byrd himself—but he would not break rank in public. Powell's powerful instincts for duty and loyalty pulled him toward cooperation with a political community with which, on massive resistance, he fervently disagreed. The broader opinions of the public at large mattered little. He looked rather to his social and professional peers for confirmation of his standing in the community. Within that group—as in his confrontation with Kilpatrick at the Forum Club—he was ready to debate. But outside that group, he was reluctant to speak out in a way that would impair the influence of the natural ruling class. In short, Powell's silence on desegregation was explained as much as anything by his social and political solidarity with the establishment of segregation. Even when he wanted change, he worked only from within.

EPILOGUE

Amid too many reminders of the incompleteness of racial justice, there are also public acts of reconciliation and affection. On June 20, 1987, the Virginia State Bar presented special awards to Oliver Hill and Samuel Tucker, longtime civil rights lawyers and activists. Between them Hill and Tucker had appeared as counsel in most of the state's desegregation cases—including of the original cases heard with *Brown* and the later return to the Supreme Court to force a reopening of the schools in Prince Edward County. Three decades earlier, the state bar had treated Hill and Tucker very shabbily. Honoring them now was an act of celebration and apology. The event came late in the Supreme Court's term, and Powell as usual was immersed in efforts to complete the Court's business before the end of the month. He also had things on his mind—mostly, the agonizing question of his own retirement. Yet he flew down to Virginia Beach to present the awards to Hill and Tucker and lent his unequaled prestige among Virginia's lawyers to that event. In reply, the recipients made gracious reply to the presenter. One would have thought they had always pulled on the same oar.

Two weeks later Lewis Powell left the Supreme Court. Among the many accolades triggered by his retirement was a resolution of the Richmond School Board. Now with a majority of black members, the board was proud to claim Powell as an alumnus. The resolution did not mention desegregation but praised his "unquestioned devotion to quality education" and acknowledged "with pride and appreciation" his dedication to excellence. Of all the public tributes to a lifetime of achievement, this was his favorite.

More than two years later, on January 13, 1990, L. Douglas Wilder was inaugurated as the sixty-sixth Governor of Virginia and the first black elected to that office anywhere in the nation. The juxtaposition of person and place was richly symbolic. The man who stood before the Capitol of the Confederacy had grown up in Richmond, walking past all-white John Marshall High School to reach the all-black school which he attended, before going on to a black college and black law school. Now, on a cold winter Saturday many years later, he stood facing the statue of Stonewall Jackson to take the oath of office. The judge who stood across the family Bible and administered the oath of office was there at Wilder's invitation. Hatless in the cold wind, a thin old man delivered the constitutional oath: "I, Lawrence Douglas Wilder, do solemnly swear that I will support the Constitution of the United States and the Constitution of the Commonwealth of Virginia and that I will faithfully and impartially discharge all of the duties incumbent on me as Governor of Virginia according to the best of my ability, so help me God."

As applause greeted Wilder's last words, Lewis Powell leaned into the microphone to call above the rising sound, "It's a great day for Virginia!" For the sea of young black faces raised in pride and triumph, the good wishes of a frail old white man may have meant very little, but to those with long memories, it was a gracious benediction from the best of the old order.

CHAPTER VII .

NATIONAL CITIZEN
1955–1971

HUNTON, WILLIAMS, GAY, POWELL & GIBSON

On December 29, 1955, the fifteen partners of Hunton, Williams executed a partnership agreement. The opening paragraph defined the philosophy of the firm. "The practice of the law is a service to society. While an aid to business, it is concerned also with the public welfare. It is informed by the past, dedicated to the future and governed by justice."

Though the prose was George Gibson's, the ideas came from Powell. The second paragraph, in particular, stated a belief close to Powell's heart. "The client cannot be served by an individual so well as by a team. It is only a team that can offer special abilities in innumerable fields and coordinate them for the discharge of important responsibilities. Promoting in this way the interest of clients, the partnership promotes also the interests of partners and renders a broader public service. It strengthens each with the judgment of all. . . ."

The team concept became Powell's creed. It meant, first of all, that free-lancing of the sort Wirt Marks undertook would not be tolerated. It also implied that the firm was willing to hire specialists to meet all the needs of its clients. The team concept even governed the firm's internal organization. While most large firms were arranged by functional specialty—such as corporate law, tax law, and litigation—Hunton, Williams was organized around the leading lawyers and the clients they represented. The Powell team was not merely a concept but an established group of practicing lawyers. When Powell went to see a client—and he always went to see the client rather than have the client come to him—he took another lawyer along. This practice ensured that when Powell was unavailable, someone else could fill in.

It also meant that junior executives in client organizations had someone to talk to. As Powell became more senior and more prominent, he
realized that only top management felt comfortable picking up the
phone and calling him personally. By bringing a younger lawyer with
him, Powell opened a second tier of communication with the client.

Though team-oriented, the partnership was not democratic.
Modification of the agreement required a vote of a "majority in interest" of the partners, meaning that each partner had a number of votes
equal to his percentage of the firm's income. Younger partners could
leave to seek their fortunes elsewhere, but there was no chance of revolution from within. Governance was lodged in an executive committee, which was also weighted toward the top. Gay, Moore, Powell, and
Gibson were made permanent members, while two others were elected
from the partnership.

The partnership agreement also provided for gradual retirement
beginning in the year after a partner reached seventy; three years later,
he would be made "of counsel" and would then be relieved of the
obligation to work but could keep the use of an office and a reduced
share of the firm's profits. This provision applied immediately to Gay,
who turned seventy in 1955. Three years later, he retired from the
executive committee, and although he continued to preside at firm
meetings, he no longer played an active role in firm management.
During this period, Gay's draw declined from 15 (actually 14.875) to 5
percent of the firm's profits, where it was scheduled to remain until
his death. This deal proved better for Gay than for his partners. As
Gay lived to an advanced age, 5 percent of the profits of a rapidly
growing firm became an extraordinary pension. In 1970 he was persuaded to reduce his share to 3½ percent, which was still more than
twice the income of many active partners.

Gay's retirement coincided with the death of Justin Moore, who in
1958 succumbed to a heart attack at the age of sixty-seven. These two
events freed up fully a quarter of the firm's profits. Surprisingly, Powell
and Gibson did not take a larger share for themselves. Under the partnership agreement, each received 10.875 percent of the firm's net
income. This percentage never increased and in fact began to decline
as they neared retirement. Of course, a nearly constant percentage of
the profits of an expanding firm meant a rising income, and Powell's
share increased from $37,000 in 1951 to more than $250,000 dollars
twenty years later.

Although Powell and Gibson allowed a progressive decentralization
of the firm's income, they did not relinquish control. From the time of

Moore's death, Powell and Gibson dominated the firm. The fact was reflected in the firm's title, which on January 1, 1960, was changed to Hunton, Williams, Gay, Powell & Gibson.

GEORGE DANDRIDGE GIBSON was three years older than Powell. He had come to the firm in 1931 as an assistant to Henry Anderson and three years later became a partner. Though Gibson professed himself "impressed and exhilarated by the breezy hauteur with which the Colonel . . . managed to propel himself through the Universe," in fact he disliked Anderson, whom he insisted on calling "Mr." Even so, it was through Anderson that Gibson became a nationally known expert in railroad reorganization, including the long and complicated reorganization of the Denver & Rio Grande Western, which Gibson argued twice before the Supreme Court. But the core of Gibson's later practice came through Justin Moore. Not long after Moore came to the firm, he asked Gibson to handle the Virginia Electric and Power Company's first public offering, a sale of $10 million in bonds. As VEPCO made many public offerings over the years, Gibson became increasingly active in corporate finance. He was made general counsel of the power company, at that time the firm's largest client.

Gibson was a brilliant lawyer. He had a penetrating intelligence, a prodigious memory, and formidable command of the language. He especially excelled in oral argument. He wrote down everything in advance, memorized his statement, then spoke in court with a seemingly effortless clarity and elegance. Gibson's widow described him as "a perfectionist—never content with anything, not things that he did or things that others did." Unfortunately for Gibson's subordinates, he did not hide dissatisfaction. What he said of Henry Anderson also applied to Gibson himself: "He did not suffer fools gladly. Indeed, he was not disposed to suffer them at all."

The effect on younger lawyers ranged from intimidation to terror. Associates who could not meet his standards quickly left the firm. Others stood outside his office polishing the doorknob until they were sure of exactly what to say and how to say it. Eventually, Gibson himself recognized the need for a change. In the late 1950s he took a Dale Carnegie course in "how to win friends and influence people." When his fellow self-improvers elected him valedictorian of the class, Gibson had his first taste of personal popularity.

But even Dale Carnegie could not completely transform George Gibson. He remained apt to skewer associates for the slightest departure from his standards. When young George Freeman appeared in the office wearing a new brown suit, Gibson coolly looked him over and said, "In the future, George, when you are planning to go on holiday, I hope you will let me know in advance." Yet overall Gibson's attempt at midlife correction worked, and he became appreciably more humane and approachable.

Years later, Powell said he was Gibson's best friend. Yet Gibson's second wife, Pearson (an earlier marriage had ended in divorce), thought otherwise. "I wouldn't say they were *good* friends," she concluded. "They had great admiration and respect for each other, but when George wanted someone to talk to, it wasn't Lewis."

This is not surprising. For two enormously successful men, practicing law at the same place and time, Powell and Gibson could not have been more dissimilar. Powell always put work first; Gibson celebrated other interests. Powell liked sports, politics, and military history; Gibson liked theater, ballet, fine homes, and beautiful furnishings. Powell disliked spending money and adventurous travel, both of which Gibson loved. While Powell paid no attention to dress, wearing his Brooks Brothers suits as a conservative uniform, Gibson was a bit of a dandy. At fifteen he carried a cane and as an adult wore handmade shoes and bespoke suits. The two men sounded as different as they looked. Powell spoke in a Virginia drawl that stretched common diphthongs into wobbly syllables. Gibson's clipped speech seemed almost British. Powell's words were sturdy and serviceable, aimed more at clarity than at style. Gibson use of language was fastidious, laconic, witty, and elegant. Even their affections were different. Powell formed fast friendships with other men; Gibson was, in the words of his wife, "not intimate with men, [but] much more relaxed with women."

What Powell and Gibson had in common was the firm. Both chose Hunton, Williams as the vehicle of their ambition. By the time their generation came into its own, they had been practicing law together for twenty years. Powell recognized Gibson as a brilliant intellect and a master craftsman. Gibson saw in Powell sound judgment and an almost magical ability to attract clients. Now they forged an alliance. From the mid 1950s until Powell left for the Supreme Court, Lewis Powell and George Gibson *were* Hunton, Williams. Each had his own team of lawyers, his own constellation of clients, and his own partisans within the firm. Although their collaboration ripened into genuine affection, in origin it was a sharing of control. Over time, the division of responsibility was so well settled, the commonality of objective so complete, and the awareness of mutual advantage so entrenched, that it came to resemble a business marriage.

*   *   *

THE POWELL-GIBSON ALLIANCE can be seen most clearly in the operation of the firm's executive committee. When Moore died and Gay
retired, the committee was reduced to five. Powell and Gibson
remained permanent members. One of the three rotating members
was Eppa Hunton IV, son of the founder and by this time the firm's
senior lawyer (he had joined the firm in 1927). Hunton was more than
a figurehead but less than a force. In the words of Merrill Pasco, who
became managing partner, Hunton "had a lot of common sense and a
lot of influence." Described by Powell as the firm's "social chairman,"
Hunton was the custodian of its traditions. In deference to his seniority (and perhaps also because he was neither Powell nor Gibson),
Hunton was made chairman of the executive committee and periodically reelected to that post until his retirement in 1974.

Therefore, a younger partner elected to a three-year term on the
executive committee anytime between 1955 and 1971 would have
faced the following situation: At the table sat the genial chairman, one
other junior partner serving a three-year term, and the two senior partners and permanent members who controlled the firm's business. The
only opportunity for an elected member of the executive committee
to influence the course of events was when Powell and Gibson disagreed—*and they never did*. None of their colleagues can recall a single
instance when Powell and Gibson disputed firm management. The
disagreements that must inevitably have arisen between them were
invariably settled in private. When Powell and Gibson came to the
executive committee, they had already discussed and decided whatever there was to discuss and decide. And although the formalities were
meticulously observed and courtesies flawlessly maintained, the ratification of their actions by the other members of the committee was
only slightly less predictable than the politburo's agreement with
Comrade Stalin.

In their private counsels, Powell had the final say. In the words of
John Riely, "George would do anything that Lewis said. . . . If Lewis
told him to jump through hoops, George would jump through hoops.
They conferred and talked, and I am sure that Powell listened to
Gibson, but Powell was the guy who made the decisions." Norm Scher
agreed. "Powell had plenty of flexibility. He'd listen to people. It would
be debated. He had patience." But ultimately, "it would be the way
that Lewis Powell wanted it."

Only rarely was Powell's power unmasked. Scher remembers one such
incident, when Warwick Davenport had charge of a matter that Powell

chose to look into. Davenport rejected Powell's comments, and they stood in the hall for what seemed like hours, with Davenport just "yakking" away, until finally Powell's patience ran out. "Warwick," he said, "we have discussed it enough. We will do it *my* way." And they did.

POWELL'S POWER INSIDE the firm reflected his power outside the firm. He had the strongest base of personal clients of any lawyer in the state and a growing national reputation.

Although Powell's practice remained centered in Richmond, he increasingly moved in a broader sphere. Colonial Williamsburg brought him into contact with Rockefeller interests and many notables around the world. In December 1955, Powell and fellow trustees of Colonial Williamsburg traveled to London for a dinner honoring Winston Churchill. Nearly two hundred British and American notables gathered in white tie and decorations to see Williamsburg board chairman Winthrop Rockefeller present Churchill with a town crier's bell, "a symbol of the people's vigil," and ten thousand dollars as recipient of the first (and only) Williamsburg award. Powell sat between the "father of the Royal Air Force," Viscount Trenchard, and the Lord Chief Justice of England, Baron Goddard, and chatted across the table with Field Marshal Montgomery, by then Viscount Montgomery of Alamein.

An increasingly important Virginia client was the State-Planters Bank. In fulfillment of Harvie Wilkinson's long-term plan, Powell succeeded Gay as the bank's general counsel and in 1959 was elected to the board of directors. At that time, Virginia law restricted banks to their own localities. As a result, the state's banks were small, and large-scale financings had to be handled elsewhere. When Wilkinson led the drive to liberalize the banking laws, Powell drafted the necessary legislation and supported it before the General Assembly. Once that legislation was passed, Wilkinson masterminded the combination of State-Planters and five other banks into Virginia's first statewide bank holding company, United Virginia Bankshares. (In 1987 the name was changed to Crestar to facilitate interstate operations.) The acquisitions vastly increased the size of the bank and brought Powell into close contact with financial leaders from around the state.

Another existing Hunton, Williams client also became closely associated with Powell. Philip Morris was a Virginia company that had long used Hunton, Williams for certain kinds of corporate work. By acquiring Benson & Hedges in 1954, it became a major presence in the domestic cigarette industry, and three years later embarked on a spectacularly successful program of international expansion and domestic diversification. By 1963, when Powell joined the board of directors, Philip Morris was a major national corporation with headquarters in New York. Thanks in part to intensive lobbying by Powell and fellow board member Harvie Wilkinson, a huge new Philip Morris plant was located in Richmond.

In solidarity with his client, Powell took up smoking. At least he tried to. In fact, he never learned to inhale. He simply went through the motions on certain social and public occasions, notably the Philip Morris board meetings, where photographs would be taken of the directors holding or smoking cigarettes. (The wife of one of Powell's partners said, "It's a good thing they don't sell condoms.")

Despite the national prominence of Philip Morris, the statewide presence of United Virginia Bank, and the famous figures linked to Colonial Williamsburg, Powell's most interesting and demanding work came from a most unlikely source—the Albemarle Paper Company. Organized in 1887 by Richmond businessmen, Albemarle manufactured "World"-brand blotting paper. In 1918 a young man of twenty came to the company with the announced intention of becoming its president. He learned the operations of the company, invested every spare dollar in Albemarle stock, and in 1941 succeeded to that post.

Underneath Floyd Dewey Gottwald's straightforward, no-nonsense demeanor beat the heart of a dreamer. He was always looking for opportunity. Although Gottwald's company expanded in the 1950s and included both his sons in management, it did not have a staff lawyer. Instead, the company relied on Powell, who was elected a director in 1953 and became "an intimate member of the business family, enjoying the confidence of the Gottwalds and sharing in the discussion of important plans and decisions." As Albemarle grew, so did its legal business and so did its contribution to Powell's career.

At Powell's side was Lawrence E. Blanchard, Jr., a Columbia Law School graduate who came to Hunton, Williams in 1948 and was assigned to Wirt Marks. When Marks left the firm, Blanchard was immediately made a partner and assigned to Powell's team. He became the second lawyer on the Albemarle account.

In the summer of 1962, Gottwald mentioned to his lawyers that he was interested in acquiring the Ethyl Corporation. At first they did not take him seriously. As Blanchard recalls, "Hardly a month went by that Mr. Gottwald didn't come over to the office to sit down and bat around with us some major deal." Ethyl seemed an extremely unlikely prospect. Albemarle Paper Company had annual sales of only $50 million and a net worth of approximately half that amount. Ethyl was much larger. What Gottwald had in mind was to borrow enough money to buy a company many times the size of his own.

Besides, why would Gottwald want to buy Ethyl? Despite its size, Ethyl was a one-horse shay, deriving virtually all its revenue from the antiknock gasoline additive, tetraethyl lead. Competition in that field had increased with the expiration of Ethyl's patents, and demand for the product slackened as gasoline refiners produced higher octane fuel. (The health and environmental problems that later doomed domestic lead sales were not then foreseen.) Over the preceding five years, Ethyl's profits had declined by 39 percent. The owners—Ethyl was a joint venture of General Motors and Standard Oil of New Jersey—wanted to sell but had not been able to find a buyer.

Against these negatives, Gottwald saw two great attractions. First, Ethyl had a large cash flow that could be used to repay the money borrowed to finance the acquisition. Gottwald figured that "the antiknock business was a good foundation for ten years anyway." Second, the company had outstanding research and development capabilities. Gottwald had more faith than Ethyl itself in the company's ability to diversify. In Powell's words, Gottwald "had the vision, imagination, and determination that made his dreams a reality. He not only believed the acquisition was feasible when no one else did; he also thought of Ethyl not as a static, ever shrinking tetraethyl lead company but as a base for a great chemical empire."

By September 1962, it was clear that Gottwald was going to make a serious attempt to buy Ethyl. General Motors and Standard Oil were receptive, chiefly because Albemarle Paper was so far removed from the automobile and refining industries that there was no possibility of antitrust problems. An investment banker negotiated the purchase price of $181 million, but since the surviving company would require working capital, the deal was premised on Albemarle's ability to raise a full $200 million.

For tax reasons, Standard Oil wished to complete the sale offshore. Its executives refused to meet with Albemarle's representatives or even to discuss the matter by telephone anywhere within the United States. Accordingly, the crucial meeting to agree on the terms of the transaction was scheduled for September 13, 1962, in Halifax, Nova Scotia. Representing Albemarle were Floyd Gottwald, his two sons, and the firm's financial officer; a New York investment banker named James H. (Jimmy) Miller; and the lawyers, Powell, Blanchard, and tax specialist H. Brice Graves. They arrived in Halifax to find that noisy Kiwanians had rented virtually every room in the town's only first-class hotel. The sole remaining room went to Floyd Gottwald and Jimmy Miller. Powell and the others were housed across Halifax Bay in the seafaring town of Dartmouth, where they found quarters in a wooden, barracks-type hotel that looked as if it could burn to the ground in a second. The large rope tied to the radiator in each room as a fire escape did not provide much reassurance.

The Halifax meeting revealed enormous obstacles. Albemarle not only had to raise $200 million but to do so by means not involving a public stock offering. (Since Ethyl was owned entirely by General Motors and Standard Oil, its stock had never been publicly traded, and the owners did not wish to undergo the elaborate disclosure required to register securities for public sale.) Moreover, General Motors and Standard Oil insisted that transaction had to be completed by the end of November—a breakneck schedule.

Everyone went into motion at once. Blanchard took up residence in New York, where lawyers from Debevoise, Plimpton were recruited to help. Powell returned to Richmond, where he added Joe Carter and John Riely to the Albemarle team. Meanwhile, furious negotiations were begun to borrow the $200 million. A team of four insurance companies lent the bulk of the money and took back senior notes. General Motors, Standard Oil, and Chase Manhattan Bank took junior securities. Last came $50 million of subordinated notes with attached warrants—jokingly called the "junior-junior" notes—which were sold to a variety of institutional investors. All of these groups had their own lawyers, all of whom had to be satisfied on myriad details before the transaction could be completed. If any lender pulled out at the last moment, the entire deal would collapse.

Base of operations for the Albemarle team was suite 42-H of the Waldorf Towers, consisting of a living room, a dining room, three bedrooms with twin beds, and a former maid's room with a single bed. Powell chose the maid's room so that he would not have to share. At night they dined in the Bull and Bear restaurant in the Waldorf, where the outlook was often bleak. Powell thought that "not . . . a single lawyer, familiar with all of the problems that confronted us—and with an inflexible time schedule—expected the deal ever to be consummated."

The gloom deepened on Monday, October 22, when President Kennedy announced a naval blockade to force the withdrawal of Soviet missiles from Cuba. As Powell recalled, "We went to bed that night at the Waldorf, separated from our families, keenly aware that a nuclear exchange before morning was a possibility."

As it happened, events worked out favorably not only for the United States but also for the Albemarle Paper Company. On November 30, a crowd of lawyers gathered in a conference room on the twenty-third floor of the Chase Manhattan Bank building to close the transaction. Everyone had to identify himself or herself on entering the room, including the Gottwald wives, who were asked whether they represented the lenders. "Oh no," one replied, "we are the *spenders!*"

Not present were representatives of Standard Oil, which insisted that its share of the proceeds be paid in Nova Scotia. Brice Graves had been dispatched to Halifax to hand over the check when everything went through. He was supposed to remain in touch by telephone throughout the closing procedure, but the Canadian operators insisted on disconnecting a silent line. In desperation, Graves picked up a Gideon Bible and began to read Old Testament genealogy. Every now and then someone would pick up the phone to confirm that Graves was "still begatting" on the other end.

Finally, everything was done. The Albemarle Paper Company acquired Ethyl, then immediately changed its name to that of its giant subsidiary. Today, the financial press sometimes call the deal the first leveraged buy out. At the time, they said Jonah had swallowed the whale.

Surprisingly, the meal proved readily digestible. Before the merger, Albemarle had less than $1.50 in annual profit per share of common stock. After the merger, the new Ethyl Corporation had annual earnings of more than $11 per share. But the Gottwalds now faced two crucial challenges. First, they had to reduce the mountain of debt incurred to finance the acquisition. At the same time, they had to diversify operations to reduce the company's dependence on the declining market for tetraethyl lead.

They did both. Aided by Larry Blanchard, who became executive vice president and chief financial officer, and advised by Powell, who remained general counsel, the Gottwalds transformed Ethyl from a highly leveraged tetraethyl lead company to a financially sound chemical empire. By the end of 1971, when Powell resigned from the board of directors to sit on the Supreme Court, annual profit had risen 263 percent to nearly $35 million. During the same period, long-term debt as a percentage of total capital fell from 82 to 45 percent. And sales of lead antiknock compounds declined to only 36 percent of the company's total revenue.

For Powell and his law firm, Ethyl's success was an extraordinary stroke of good fortune. By skill, resourcefulness, and dedication, Powell and his team retained the loyalty of their client, but it was the vision and courage of Floyd Gottwald that transformed the client from a small local company to a large multinational corporation. With Colonial Williamsburg, United Virginia Bank, Philip Morris, and the new Ethyl Corporation, plus a number of smaller accounts, Powell became the premier rainmaker and most powerful lawyer in his firm.

AMERICAN BAR ASSOCIATION

Powell did not rest his ambition solely on the growth of his clients. He aimed for prominence not only in the business side of law practice but also in the political arm of his profession, the organized bar. As chairman of the Junior Bar Conference in 1941, Powell was a member of the American Bar Association's House of Delegates. It was to that body that he aspired to return after the war as the Virginia state delegate.

In the organization of the ABA at that time, each state had several general delegates (mostly chosen by local bar associations), but only one state delegate. State delegates were elected for three-year terms. Together they constituted the nominating committee for ABA officers. Since the full House of Delegates consistently approved these nominations, state delegates controlled the leadership of the organization.

Since 1936 Virginia's state delegate had been Thomas Benjamin Gay. Despite Powell's growing impatience, Gay held this position for seventeen years. In 1953, when he finally decided to step aside, he did try to have Powell succeed him. On March 7, Gay (and other partners) sent letters to thirty-five of the state's ABA members, asking them to circulate nominating petitions on Powell's behalf. Many petitions were immediately completed and returned, yet within three days Powell withdrew his name from consideration.

Early reaction had revealed objections to Powell's candidacy. "I can well imagine the howl that would go up from Virginia Beach to Cumberland Gap," wrote Roanoke lawyer Frank Rogers, if Gay were succeeded by another Richmond lawyer, let alone another member of the same firm. Faced with this protest, Powell stood down, and the post went to Stuart Saunders, general counsel of the Norfolk & Western Railway.

Three years later Saunders became president of the railroad and resigned as state delegate. This time geography was no bar to Powell's candidacy, but opposition came from Richmond rival William L. Zimmer III. If any of Virginia's younger lawyers could equal Powell's ability as a rainmaker, it was Billy Zimmer. Able and appealing, Zimmer counted among his clients both the Reynolds Metals Company and A. H. Robins. (He later became president of Robins, a position he occupied when the firm foundered in the sea of personal injury claims resulting from use of a faulty contraceptive device known as the Dalkon Shield.)

Zimmer could not complain about Powell's hometown, but he did object to electing another state delegate from Hunton, Williams. "I have always felt and still feel," Zimmer wrote Powell, "that this influential representation of Virginia lawyers in the A.B.A. has been unduly monopolized by your firm." Zimmer's campaign made much of Gay's long tenure as state delegate and of his continued presence in the House of Delegates "in another capacity." This statement, which Powell thought "somewhat disingenuous," referred to the fact that as a former chairman of the House of Delegates, Gay was an honorary life member of that body. As a Powell supporter wrote in answer, "The distinction attained by this senior member in Lewis Powell's firm honors all lawyers in Virginia. It seems to be a frail reason for rejecting the experienced and capable representation of Virginia which Lewis Powell offers."

Beneath the gentlemanly veneer was a hard-fought contest. As the balloting neared, Powell feared that he was "underplaying" the campaign. "The truth," he wrote a supporter, "is that the contest is distasteful to me, and I would not have been a candidate if this sort of campaign had been anticipated by me." Yet Powell's idea of "underplaying" came close to all-out effort. His files contain five fat folders of correspondence on the state delegate election, plus a huge stack of membership rosters, probable vote tallies, and lists of local contacts. His partners helped with the state's ABA members and urged other lawyers to join the organization in time to vote. At the last minute, Zimmer began a telephone canvass, which Powell countered by calls and notes from his side. When all the ballots were counted, Powell had 683 votes to Zimmer's 493. Accordingly, he became the ABA state delegate from Virginia for the remaining two years of Saunders's term.

The 1957 race for state delegate was Powell's last contested election. He was returned without opposition in 1959 and again in 1962. In February of the next year, he was elected president-elect of the ABA, an office he assumed at the end of the annual meeting that August. One year later he automatically became the eighty-eighth president of the ABA.

Becoming president of the ABA put Powell on the national map.

More than any other office or event, this victory accounted for the growing prominence that by the end of the 1960s made him a plausible candidate for nomination to the Supreme Court. Yet despite its crucial importance to Powell's career, the selection was accomplished very quietly.

The choice lay with the fifty state delegates, who always chose one of their number. It was, said one observer, "almost like apostolic succession, except that the former Pope was still alive and lobbying the Cardinals." Since most state delegates served more than one term, the group had great continuity. Over the years of attending meetings, they became personal friends as well as political allies. Potential candidates began jockeying for position two or three years before the actual decision, by which time, if all went well, there would be consensus in favor of one candidate.

So it happened with Powell. He was a master of small-group politics. No note went unanswered; no courtesy unremarked; no request unfilled. He had the same balance of pride and deference that made him attractive at Washington and Lee, the same willingness to make himself useful, and the same talent for making others feel valued. His friends were organized well in advance and included lawyers from around the country. Their efforts persuaded prospective rivals to wait for a better time, leaving Powell with an uncontested election as ABA president for the year 1964–65.

As ABA PRESIDENTS are selected on personality rather than policy, most arrive in that office with no real agenda. Yet Powell's term was notable for substantive achievement. In a Waldorf-Astoria ballroom on August 14, 1964, the incoming president outlined his priorities.

First, Powell called for comprehensive reform of legal ethics. The Canons of Professional Ethics, which had been adopted by the ABA in 1908, needed to be brought up to date. In particular, Powell advocated clear standards of conduct for lawyers caught in the widening conflict between free press and fair trial, stronger ethical obligations to represent unpopular clients, and relaxation of rules (against soliciting clients, use of lay intermediaries, and the like) that limited the availability of legal services. He also lamented a lack of enforcement. The bar, he said, had shown "a spirit of marked lenience" in disciplining its own members. As a first step toward weeding out unethical lawyers, Powell insisted on canons capable of effective enforcement. "They must lay down clear, peremptory rules in the critical areas relating most directly to the duty of lawyers to their clients and to the courts.

This sharpening and clarification of the canons will facilitate more effective disciplinary action and also increase significantly the level of voluntary compliance."

To this end, Powell appointed a special committee, charged with the need for comprehensive study. The project took several years and culminated in the Code of Professional Responsibility adopted by the ABA in 1969.

Second, Powell committed the ABA to a massive project on standards for the administration of criminal justice. The idea originated in 1963. It was partly a response to Warren Court decisions requiring far-reaching changes in the behavior of police and prosecutors. It was also partly a product of what Justice Tom Clark described as "a climate of deep concern over the burgeoning problems of crime and the correlative crisis in our courts occasioned by overwhelming caseloads, recidivism, and a seeming incapacity of the system to respond to the challenges of the Sixties." A pilot study conducted during Powell's year as president-elect concluded that the project was ambitious but feasible, and the undertaking was approved by the House of Delegates at the annual meeting in August 1964.

The basic idea behind the project was to bring together knowledgeable judges, lawyers, and academics under the auspices of the ABA, ask them to study the administration of criminal justice, then publish their findings in a series of concrete standards that would provide practical guidance for participants in the system. There were several audiences. The principal target was the courts, which could refer to the standards as authoritative, if nonbinding, pronouncements on how certain problems should be handled. Some recommendations, such as those on sentencing of convicted offenders, were intended chiefly for legislatures. Others were addressed to police administrators. The consistent aim was to bring intelligent, informed, and balanced views to bear on problems of criminal justice.

The key factor was the quality of the participants. Chief Judge Edward J. Lumbard of the Second Circuit Court of Appeals became overall chairman. With his advice, Powell appointed the members of Lumbard's committee and of six advisory committees, each assisted by a law professor serving as secretary and draftsman. It was essential not only that the committee members be persons of ability, but also that they represent all legitimate views and interests so that collectively they would possess the prestige to make their pronouncements matter. These goals were met. A measure of the prominence of those who volunteered their time is the fact that they included four future

Supreme Court Justices. Powell himself joined Lumbard's committee after completing his year as ABA president; Warren Burger chaired an advisory committee and followed Lumbard as overall head of the project; Abe Fortas sat on the committee dealing with the clash between fair trial and free press; and Harry Blackmun served on a committee on the role of the trial judge. The high quality of the work done by the ABA standards committees and the weight given their recommendations by the courts owe much to the caliber of persons recruited to that effort.

Powell's third priority, as announced in his inaugural address, was to expand legal services for the poor. He endorsed legislation guaranteeing lawyers for all criminal defendants. On the civil side, he reiterated the ABA's long-standing support for privately funded legal aid offices. Within a few months, an agency of the federal government proposed to attack the problem with tax dollars as part of Lyndon Johnson's war on poverty. Despite the common objective, the two movements were soon at loggerheads. That direct conflict was avoided and a link of cooperation forged between the public and private sectors was Powell's greatest achievement as president of the ABA.

THE LEGAL AID MOVEMENT began in the 1920s. By 1964 there were 246 legal aid offices, financed by private contributions of about $4 million a year, heavily dependent on volunteers, and closely allied to local bar associations. The Family Service Society of Richmond, to which Powell devoted many hours in the 1930s, was typical. Such organizations were led by establishment lawyers. Their goal was not to eliminate poverty but to assure equal justice for those who happened to be poor. They aimed to provide competent counsel so that poor persons could protect their rights under the law. The economic and social deprivations of poverty were a different concern.

Running through this movement was the idea that legal aid was necessary to maintain faith in the legal system on the part of the poor. Powell's remarks to the ABA's annual meeting in August 1964 were in that vein. "It has been correctly said," he told the delegates, "that respect for the law is at its lowest with underprivileged persons. There is a natural tendency for such persons to think of the courts as symbols of trouble and of lawyers as representatives of creditors or other sources of 'harassment.' It matters little," he continued, "that these critics, through ignorance and poverty or for less excusable causes, are often responsible for their own difficulties with the law. They badly need competent counsel, at reasonable cost, who will provide the advice and assure the just treatment that will engender increased respect for the law."

Powell's speech perfectly illustrates the overall philosophy of the legal aid movement. In the words of one historian, the assumption was that "Legal aid discharges its responsibility and satisfies its ultimate goal if a poor man is provided reasonably qualified legal counsel." The underlying social and economic problems of poverty were not addressed.

The government's program had a radically different agenda. It came from Lyndon Johnson's "antipoverty warship," the newly created Office of Economic Opportunity. The OEO hoped to eliminate poverty. It focused not on equal access to the legal system, but on economic betterment of the poor. The idea of including a legal services program under the antipoverty umbrella originated with Jean Camper Cahn, a black Yale Law School graduate who worked for Sargent Shriver at OEO. Cahn and her colleagues profoundly distrusted the establishment lawyers of the ABA. Within OEO, she later recalled, "negotiations with the bar were a priori assumed to be the equivalent of consorting with the enemy."

So suspicious were the antipoverty activists that they not only did not invite the ABA to a Washington conference on legal services for the poor, but actually refused a request that two ABA leaders be allowed to attend. Fortunately, this rebuff was circumvented, and Powell sent William McCalpin to the conference as an ABA representative. McCalpin returned with an earful of criticism of the legal aid movement and the news that the OEO planned to launch its own legal services program.

On November 17, 1964, Sargent Shriver endorsed the idea in terms that alarmed many lawyers. He spoke of "supermarkets of social service" that would include legal assistance. Laymen would serve as "legal advocates for the poor," handling tasks previously thought to require a lawyer. These words aroused many fears. "What is big brother up to now?" lawyers asked. "Are we going to be 'socialized' by snooping 'Feds' from Washington?" "Will the Federal program help or hurt our legal aid society?" And most important, "Will the Federal program compete with . . . the struggling neighborhood lawyer?" Letters poured in to the ABA's Chicago headquarters demanding that Powell mobilize the organization's resources against the incipient federal program.

Powell refused. Instead, he ordered an in-depth study of the OEO proposal and began negotiations with its backers. In retrospect, the case for compromise seems clear. The "Feds" had more money than legal aid societies could ever hope to raise from private contributions. Moreover, they enjoyed the confidence of the poor, most of whose leaders distrusted the organized bar. On the other side, the legal aid movement had existing organizations that could be put to good use. They also had working relationships with local bar associations, whose support would prove crucial when antipoverty lawyers represented unpopular causes. Local community action agencies, on which OEO chiefly relied, could not be expected to fund legal services lawyers without attempting to control what they did. As Jean Cahn had discovered when she tried to represent a young black man accused of raping a white girl in New Haven, local antipoverty agencies were not immune to political pressure. The bar, however, accepted the need to provide representation for even the most unpopular clients. Alliance with the organized bar could help legal services lawyers establish their independence within the antipoverty movement.

Although in hindsight the advantages of agreement are apparent, at the time the possibility of collaboration seemed remote. Differences in background, outlook, and politics separated the two sides. And, as Jean Cahn recalled, the "distance to be bridged could hardly have been cast more symbolically than to ask a white lawyer from the ranks of Southern aristocracy leading the then lily-white ABA and a black woman lawyer representing the 'feds' to hammer out a relationship of trust and cooperation."

But they did. The ABA leadership agreed to endorse the OEO program and to bring the formidable clout of the organized bar behind it. The OEO agreed not to exclude existing legal aid societies from government funding and to accept some shared management of local organizations. The ABA secured the OEO's commitment to maintaining traditional professional standards in providing legal services to the poor, and the OEO gained the participation of the existing legal aid attorneys in a greatly expanded federal program.

Now came the hard part. Powell had to persuade the House of Delegates to go along. In committing the ABA in support of the federal program, Powell was far ahead of the prevailing sentiment in the organization. The members of the House of Delegates almost certainly would have rejected the idea had they been left on their own, but they were not. In the words of the historian of the OEO Legal Services Program, "no president could have worked any harder or more artfully to influence a decision than did Lewis Powell." He drafted the resolution of support introduced at the midwinter meeting in New Orleans, solicited the backing of leading ABA members, persuaded the organization's board of governors to endorse the resolution before it went to the House of Delegates, and arranged who should speak on its behalf and in what order. On February 7, the ABA endorsement that many OEO officials believed an "impossibility" was passed *without dissent*.

Nor was that all. In the ensuing months, OEO became embroiled in an internal dispute over who should be director of the Legal Services Program and what its place should be in the OEO bureaucracy. Jean Cahn resigned on April 1. Six months later, the OEO had not found a director or begun to implement the program. Within the legal community, support began to crumble. Many questioned whether OEO officials really intended to collaborate with the bar or whether, having garnered the ABA's endorsement, they would now go their own way. According to Cahn, "there was every sign of a major revolt by a reactionary element within the bar—emerging at the state and local level—which threatened to lead to a total severance of all relationships and a withdrawal of endorsement."

In June, the ABA, the OEO, and the Department of Justice co-sponsored a national conference for legal aid lawyers. It succeeded as a "symbolic public handshake" between the legal aid movement and the new government program, but only after tough, behind-the-scenes negotiations. At issue was the OEO's insistence that all recipients of federal money, including legal aid societies run by lawyers, had to give at least one third of the seats on their boards of directors to representatives of the poor. Another touchy question was how the federal agency would value the volunteer services of local lawyers in calculating whether local agencies had met their requirement of contributing one tenth the cost of federally funded projects. On both questions, OEO officials voiced a newfound flexibility. In return, bar leaders reiterated their support.

During the ABA annual meeting that August, Powell chaired a special plenary session at which Sargent Shriver addressed the delegates. Shriver apologized for the delay and promised early action. He announced formation of a National Advisory Committee, which he described as "one practical method of guaranteeing the independence of the OEO legal services program from crass political pressures and of assuring the quality and integrity of the services offered the poor. . . ." Powell and other ABA leaders had agreed to serve on the committee. Their presence reassured the organized bar and kept the agreement intact until the Legal Services Program could get underway.

Powell's role in these events earned him high praise—and in some unusual quarters. When Powell was nominated for the Supreme Court,

Jean Cahn, then director of the Urban Law Institute at Antioch College, recounted these events in a letter of support. Powell, she said, had shown himself to be a man of principle, who pledged his word and kept it. "As a black person," she continued, "who has seen many promises made and not kept, it has been all too rare an experience to find a man who not only holds to such a belief—but who is prepared to back that belief with all the resources and stature and skill at his command." Powell, she predicted, would "go down in history as one of the great statesman of our profession."

THE THREE PRIORITIES Powell articulated on taking office were not his only areas of concern as ABA president. He also played an unexpectedly crucial role in amending the Constitution to deal with the long-standing problems of presidential disability and succession.

With the assassination of John F. Kennedy on November 22, 1963, Lyndon Johnson became President of the United States. As the Constitution then stood, there was no mechanism for replacing Johnson as Vice President. Next in line for the Oval Office came John McCormack, the seventy-one-year-old Speaker of the House of Representatives, and after him, Carl Hayden, the eighty-six-year-old President pro tempore of the Senate. Neither seemed an inviting prospect.

Proposals were made to amend the Constitution to provide for selection of a new Vice President. A related problem was presidential inability. Could a disabled President relinquish his powers to the Vice President, then reclaim them on recovering his health? What if the President became unable to carry out his duties but refused to step aside? Who should have the power to declare the President incapacitated, and how could such authority be secured against abuse?

The ABA, which had long been interested in these matters, convened a special conference of twelve prominent lawyers to hammer out a consensus proposal. The members gathered at the Mayflower Hotel in Washington, D.C., on January 20–21, 1964. Among them were Herbert Brownell, who had been Attorney General when President Eisenhower was incapacitated by a heart attack, Harvard law professor Paul Freund, ABA President Walter Craig, and President-elect Lewis Powell.

A month later, Powell appeared before the Subcommittee on Constitutional Amendments of the Senate Judiciary Committee to present the ABA proposals. The conference endorsed a constitutional amendment on presidential inability and suggested that the President be empowered to nominate a new Vice President, in the event of a vacancy, subject to confirmation by both houses of Congress. "It is true," Powell explained, "that this procedure would give the President the power to choose his potential successor." That, of course, was the "modern practice of both major parties in according the presidential candidate the privilege of choosing his running mate subject to convention approval. In the proposed amendment, the President would choose his Vice President subject to Congressional approval."

Since the sudden death of Estes Kefauver the previous August, the subcommittee had been chaired by a young Democrat from Indiana, Birch Bayh. Senator Bayh shepherded through the Senate a resolution proposing a constitutional amendment along the lines of the ABA recommendation. The Senate acted on September 28, 1964. The House of Representatives was reluctant to diminish its Speaker, who then stood next in line for the presidency, and so sat on its hands until the November elections returned President Johnson and a new Vice President, Hubert Humphrey.

At the outset of the new Congress, the proposed constitutional amendment was reintroduced in both houses. The Senate renewed its approval on February 19, 1965, and two months later a slightly altered version passed the House. Five members of each body were named to the traditional conference committee to iron out the differences between the two proposals, which seemed quite minor. The leader on the Senate side was Birch Bayh. The head of the House delegation was Representative Emanuel Celler of Brooklyn, longtime chairman of the House Judiciary Committee. Negotiations between them quickly resolved most of the differences, but one remaining problem threatened to defeat the entire undertaking.

At issue was a time limit of ten days. Both the House and Senate versions of the amendment said that the President could be relieved of his powers if the Vice President and a majority of the cabinet formally declared him unable to discharge them. Both versions provided that the President could reclaim his powers by declaring that his inability had ended, unless the Vice President and a majority of the cabinet renewed their contrary finding. In that event, the Congress would decide. If the Congress found by a two-thirds vote of both houses that the President was unable, the Vice President would continue as Acting President. Otherwise, the President would resume his constitutional powers.

This elaborate procedure was the same in both versions. The only difference was the timing of Congressional action that would allow the

Vice President to continue as Acting President in the face of presidential objection. The Senate said merely that Congress should act "immediately." The House said that action had to come "within ten days" or the President would automatically resume his powers.

It is probably impossible for anyone who does not share the jealous regard of Senators and Representatives for the dignity of their respective houses to understand why the difference mattered. To an outsider, the thought that a proposed constitutional amendment overwhelmingly supported by both parties would founder on such a detail seems absurd. Apparently, some Republican Representatives feared that without an explicit time limit, a simple majority of the Congress might prevent a President from reclaiming his powers by simply refusing to act. Senators who prided themselves on membership in the "world's greatest deliberative body" reflexively opposed time limits of any sort. Bayh proposed a compromise of twenty-one days; the House delegation insisted on ten. Both sides dug in their heels, and on May 27, 1965, the conference collapsed.

In desperation, Bayh called Don Channell, the director of the ABA's Washington office, who was attending an ABA regional meeting in San Juan, Puerto Rico. The next morning's first flight brought Powell from San Juan back to Washington, where he met with Emanuel Celler and all five House members of the conference committee. He then went to see Senator Bayh, who was just leaving for Indiana. Powell rode with him to National Airport, following him inside the terminal to continue the conversation. There Bayh and Powell ran into Celler, who was headed back to Brooklyn for the weekend.

Powell brought the two legislators together on National Airport's upper observation deck and pleaded for compromise. Bayh volunteered to call on Celler early the next week, and Celler agreed to reconsider his opposition to the twenty-one-day limit. In a letter written only a few hours after the event, Powell called the success "not so much the result of my efforts at mediation as the wholesome effect of 'cooling off.'" Whatever the cause, Celler reconsidered, and the House conferees decided they could live with twenty-one days.

On February 10, 1967, Minnesota and Nevada became the thirty-seventh and thirty-eighth states to ratify the proposal, bringing the total to the necessary three fourths of the fifty states. Two weeks later, the Twenty-fifth Amendment to the Constitution was proclaimed in a White House ceremony. Its provisions were first put to use in the fall of 1973, when President Nixon nominated Gerald Ford to succeed Spiro Agnew, who resigned as Vice President. Ten months later, when

Nixon himself was forced out of office by the scandal of Watergate, Gerald Ford became the thirty-eighth President of the United States.

HOME AND FAMILY

By 1963, when Powell became president-elect of the ABA, his eldest child had graduated from college and married. Jo entered Smith College in the autumn of 1956. At that time, Powell had just been released from seven weeks hospitalization for repeated hemorrhaging following bladder surgery. Too weak to come downstairs, he watched from an upstairs window and wept as his first-born left home.

Jo's adulthood did not end her father's penchant for running her life. The guidance he so generously bestowed on his sister when growing up he now visited on his offspring. As the child who "came first to his mind," Jo received more than her share. On every conceivable subject, he had something to say. A 1960 letter, for example, discusses Jo's plans following graduation. Powell thought she should come back to Richmond and look for a husband. "The opportunity for the greatest happiness of a girl normally lies through marriage. . . . If you were able to marry the right man in Virginia and live in your native state, I am completely convinced that you would have achieved the maximum opportunity for a happy and useful life." Jo had to remember that "every girl faces the problem of diminishing supply. If one is to compete successfully for the 'supply' that is available," Powell wrote, "she can obviously do better if she is on hand and concentrating on the competition."

Jo, however, wanted to live in Boston or New York. Though Powell disagreed, he urged her to "back your own judgment. . . ." If you do not, he added, "you will always have regrets, and you will always blame your mother and daddy for frustrating your heart's desires. This would be most unwholesome, and most unwelcome to mommy and me." He declared himself completely reconciled to her decision and announced his intention to support enthusiastically any choice she might make.

Jo chose New York. Powell's wish that she marry a Virginian was frustrated when Lowell Weicker, Jr., invited her to a house party in Connecticut and introduced her to a young investment banker named Richard S. Smith. Married in 1962, the Smiths eventually returned to his home state of Texas. Their son Elliott and daughter Quincy, destined respectively for Harvard and Yale, became the first Powell grandchildren.

In 1958 Penny entered Sweet Briar College. Her four years there helped bring about a belated declaration of independence from her family, with a resulting undercurrent of unease in their relations. After graduation Penny moved to Cambridge, Massachusetts, where she took a job grading papers at the Harvard Business School. There she met Basil Carmody, whom she married in the summer of 1963. The next year she enrolled in Harvard as a graduate student and earned a master's in the art of teaching. The Carmodys moved to Arlington, Virginia, where Penny taught elementary school, then spent one year in London and three in Brussels before settling in Richmond in 1972. Their children, Lycia and Nathaniel, both of whom would later attend the University of Virginia, were born respectively in 1969 and 1972.

Powell's two younger children remained at home. Molly had just turned sixteen when Powell took office as president-elect of the ABA, and Lewis was almost eleven. Most glamorous of the Powell daughters, Molly was also the most rebellious. Lively and popular at school, at home she was—by her own description—moody, argumentative, and rude. However normal such behavior may be for teenagers generally, it was disconcertingly new to the Powells. "If Molly had been the first," her mother said, "she might have been the last."

Powell contemplated sending Molly to boarding school, but she refused to leave St. Catherine's. Her academic performance remained excellent, even as she bedeviled her parents by dating "just *awful* guys," including one high-school dropout. From Molly's point of view, her teenage rebellions were never serious. "I was going to do what my parents expected me to do, but I wanted to have a little fun before I got there. They were worried, and I never was, because I knew I wasn't going to cross over the line."

As the baby of the family and the only boy, Lewis might have been expected to be spoiled by his sisters, but that is not what he remembers. Jo and Penny left home before he was six, and Molly was not the sort to spoil anyone. "Molly's highest priority as a youngster was to kill me," Lewis recalls, "and my highest priority was to grow up to be big and strong enough to kill her. Fortunately for both of us, when the time came I had lost interest in fulfilling that wish."

Though not indulged by Molly, Lewis was favored by his father. As soon as Lewis was old enough to toss a ball, Powell lost all interest in his daughter's sports. He taught his son to hunt and to play baseball, even coaching Lewis's Little League team, the Rothesay Rebels. Lewis remembers that both his parents were "very involved in my life," regularly attending sports events and helping to drive the St. Christopher's basketball and baseball teams to games around the state.

Powell was involved in his son's life in other ways as well. In September 1964, when Lewis was entering sixth grade, a seven-page memorandum spelled out "Rules for LFP III" for the coming school year. Most related to Lewis's *"primary duty* and *responsibility"*—to do well in school. He was to begin homework immediately after dinner and complete it by 10:00 P.M., with lights out promptly at 10:15. He had free time before supper, but only if he kept his grades up. He was to watch no television on school days and only a limited amount on weekends, but he could earn additional TV time equal to the time he spent reading an approved book. Comic books did not count; any time spent reading them had to be deducted from TV time. Other instructions covered eating and exercise, care of his bicycle, places and activities that were off-limits (the river, a nearby quarry, and the railroad tracks), and hours when he was expected home. A more comprehensive set of regulations could scarcely have been devised.

The surviving copy of this memorandum is marked for Mrs. Rucker. Like so many of Powell's wartime letters, the rules for Lewis III reflect Powell's effort to maintain control even when absent. From 1963 to 1965, he traveled across the country, giving hundreds of speeches to state and local bar organizations and other groups. At the end of his term as ABA president, Jo, who accompanied him only for important occasions, estimated that she had been away from home for a quarter of the year. Powell was away much more. His children joked that when they ran into him into the hall, they needed to be introduced.

When school allowed, the children went along. The day after Molly graduated from high school, she and Lewis accompanied their parents to London for the celebration of the 750th anniversary of Magna Carta. Powell had written the Master of the Rolls to ask about proper attire. "We are not really very particular," Lord Denning replied, "but it would be very nice if, at the service in St. Paul's Cathedral, you had a morning coat and top hat because the Queen is to be present, and at the Mermaid Theatre in the evening a white tie and tails." Her Majesty was indeed present on the morning of June 9, along with the robed judges, the Archbishop of Canterbury, members of the House of Commons, and Molly and Lewis. Their parents saw the Queen again that evening at the performance of a specially commissioned play on Magna Carta, and three days later, all four Powell had seats in Whitehall Palace for the Trooping of the Colours on the Queen's birthday.

The anniversary itself was commemorated in a ceremony at the Royal Courts of Justice on June 15. Powell delivered a graceful speech on the meaning of Magna Carta in American law. "Whatever the Barons and Bishops who forced King John to sign the Charter may have intended, Magna Carta now stands for many of the cherished rights of free men—for trial by jury, for due process of law, and for limitation of the powers of government." He complimented Britain on a system of law under which "the ideal of individual liberty has been preserved for perhaps the longest sustained period in all history."

After two days touring Oxford and Stratford, the Powells returned to London for the weekend. On June 20 Powell left to resume the ABA circuit back in the United States, while Jo, Molly, and Lewis spent an additional nine days in England and France.

A month later Molly and Lewis joined their parents in Miami for the ABA's annual meeting. This event marked the end of Powell's term as president. His address on the state of the legal profession recounted the accomplishments of the past year—undertaking a revision of the ethical code for lawyers, launching and financing a long-term project to improve the administration of criminal justice, and forging an alliance with the federal government to provide legal services to the poor. Any one of these achievements would have been sufficient to claim a successful year. All three produced a chorus of praise.

Immediately after returning to Richmond from the Miami meeting, Molly began to pack for her first year at Hollins College. Lewis III was now the only child at home.

AS HIS CHILDREN MOVED away and he spent more time traveling, Powell increasingly communicated with them in writing. His letter approving Jo's New York plans and his "Rules for LFP III" are but two entries in the thick files of family correspondence from the 1960s. The letters cover everything from national politics to detailed accounts of his own activities to the inevitable advice to his offspring.

Two selections illustrate the range of his concerns. The first is a letter written to Lewis III shortly after his thirteenth birthday. Moved to some intimation of mortality by the hours logged on airplanes, Powell began a testament for his son. Lewis should read more, especially the classics of history and literature and biographies of great men, such as Lee, Jackson, Washington, and Churchill. He should begin to think about a profession, perhaps medicine, which was Lewis's current interest. He should be prepared to help defend his country, but Powell counseled against a military career. "[I]n the modern world, I think being a professional soldier, airman, or sailor would be frustrating and unattractive. There is no such thing as a glamorous war or battle. It is one thing to read about fighting or to see 'thriller' type movies or TV shows. But the real thing is quite different—misery, discomfort, loneliness, despair, and often wounds which result in permanent disability or death."

In general, Powell supported any worthwhile aim. "You know," he wrote, "that I am deeply ambitious for you, as you have been a *special person* since the happy day when you were born. But the form of your success is for you and circumstances to determine. It need not follow at all the pattern of your father. The really important thing is to *be* somebody and *do something* worthwhile in this one life each of us is given by God. This doesn't mean making the headlines or making the most money. Many who succeed in both of these are actually quite contemptible. It *does* mean using your ability in some profession or calling in a way which contributes something to your generation. It also means being a man of honor, character, patriotism, civic consciousness—and of some leadership of your fellow men."

A second letter shows Powell's taste for detail. It was addressed not to Lewis but to his college friend Mike Brittin, whom the Powells suspected of enticing their son from his studies. When Brittin broke his back in a nasty fall, he too fell behind in his work. Powell, by then a Supreme Court Justice, favored the young man with his views on time management. "I have a strong conviction," Powell wrote, "that most men in college handicap themselves by being pretty unsystematic and uneconomical in the use of their own time." As a corrective, Powell offered the discipline of "study rules":

> 1. Go to breakfast *each day* as if you had an 8:20 class. Then proceed, immediately, to the library or some other place where you can study until you do have a class.
> 2. Utilize periods between classes to work.
> 3. Do not return to the fraternity house, or leave the campus, between 8:20 A.M. and lunchtime. If you devote this entire period every day to your work, you are off to a running start.
> 4. Have a regular plan for afternoon exercise, recreation and study.
> 5. Have regular study hours each evening.

Any of the Powell children would have instantly recognized the style—concerned, sensible, and meddlesome. No subject was too small or too obvious for Powell's advice. Lewis III was treated to admonitions against borrowing money; to detailed instructions on the proper accoutrements of white tie and tails; to a check for a hundred dollars so that he could purchase a sign identifying his street address ("It is best to have this done in numerals that reflect light at night"); and to the suggestion that Lewis, a poised and witty public speaker, take lessons to "break the bad speech habits even of educated southerners." Few are the instances where Powell's advice was unsound, and rarer still the cases where it was ungenerous, but the recipients of so much attention may well have wished for a little less.

Fortunately, both Molly and Lewis devised ways to benefit from Powell's parental zeal without being overwhelmed. Molly fought back, spending much of her adolescence establishing her independence. By the time she left for college, she felt no need of further demonstration. After graduating from Hollins in 1969, she followed her father into law. At the University of Virginia Law School, she met Christopher J. Sumner, whom she married in 1971. Five years later, Powell stood before his fellow Justices and moved that Kit and Molly Sumner be admitted to practice law before the Supreme Court, then donned his robe and resumed his place on the bench. Powell took great pride in this ceremony, which was thought to be the first time a sitting Justice had sponsored his children for admission to the Supreme Court bar.

Warm, intelligent, and energetic, Kit Sumner soon became Powell's favorite son-in-law. After brief stints in California and Utah, the Sumners settled in Kit's hometown of Salt Lake City, where they raised their son Ryland and daughter Kendall, born respectively in 1975 and 1978.

Lewis responded differently. Uncommonly poised and self-possessed, Lewis took his father in stride. At the reception following Powell's investiture in 1972, nineteen-year-old Lewis—who had just learned that the pretty young blonde to whom he had been paying particular attention was the fourth wife of Justice William O. Douglas—was approached by Hugo Black, Jr. "It's tough," said the son of Powell's predecessor, "going through life with the same name as a famous father." But if having his father's name was tough on Lewis, it never showed. Blessed with his mother's cheerful imperturbability, Lewis avoided both intimidation and conflict. As Molly recalls, "Lewis didn't talk back the way I did. He would say 'okay, okay, okay,' and then do exactly what he wanted."

Fortunately for his parents, what Lewis wanted to do was completely acceptable. After graduating from St. Christopher's in Richmond, he went to Washington and Lee, where he played quarterback on the football team. In 1975 he entered law school at the University of

Virginia, and unlike Molly, who graduated shortly after Powell joined the Court, Lewis spent much of his time reading his father's opinions—and hearing them roundly criticized by young professors. No one could have handled the situation better. As Robert Scott, first holder of an endowed professorship contributed by Powell's friends, wrote Powell of his son, "You should know that his conduct, both intellectual and personal, set a standard the sum total of which has not been exceeded in this Law School."

NATIONAL PROMINENCE

For Powell, the ABA was a bully pulpit. Ranging far beyond the agenda of the organized bar, he spoke on everything from the risk of having no president to the false facade of peaceful coexistence. Mostly, he talked about crime. The first statement to draw national attention was a March 1964 address on the "Crisis in Law Observance." "[W]e live," said Powell, "in an age of excessive tolerance." Tolerance was a virtue when it meant the absence of prejudice but not when it signified the acceptance of misconduct. "Can anyone doubt," Powell asked, "that juvenile crime is caused, in part at least, by parents who permit early drinking, unregulated use of automobiles, [and] uncontrolled absences from home at night . . . ?" America had also grown tolerant of illegal gambling, drunk driving, insurance fraud, and other malefactions. In a sentence widely quoted in approving editorials, Powell argued that "a root cause of the crime crisis which grips our country is excessive tolerance by the public generally—a tolerance of substandard, marginal, and even immoral and unlawful conduct." It had reached the point of "moral sickness."

In the ensuing months, Powell sounded variations on this theme. When law-abiding citizens felt unsafe in their homes and afraid to venture onto public streets, Powell cautioned, there was a breakdown in the first duty of government, which was "to protect citizens in their persons and property from criminal conduct—whatever its source or cause." He worried that the pendulum may have swung too far in favor of the rights of criminals. Even *Little Orphan Annie* quoted the ABA chief: "There are valid reasons for criminals to think that crime does pay, and that slow and fumbling justice can be evaded."

Always and everywhere Powell insisted on the rule of law. Civil rights demonstrators and student activists who claimed a right to violate unjust laws drew his rebuke. "It was seriously argued following *Brown v. Board of Education*," he reminded college graduates, "that massive disobedience of court orders and decisions was a proper form of protest. Today, there are others—with quite opposite goals—who insist with equal fervor that civil disobedience of laws deemed to be unjust is a legitimate means of asserting desired rights." Powell disagreed. "Many centuries of human misery show that once a society departs from the rule of law, and every man becomes the judge of which laws he will obey, only the strongest remain free."

In his farewell address to the Miami convention in August 1965, Powell returned to familiar themes. While the rights of suspects should be protected, the "first priority today must be a like concern for the right of citizens to be free from criminal molestations of their persons and property." He also condemned civil disobedience. "An ordered society cannot exist if every man may determine which laws he will obey and if techniques of coercion supplant due process. . . . The courts and legislative halls, rather than the streets, must be the places where differences are reconciled and individual rights ultimately protected."

These words drew thunderous applause from the lawyers of the ABA and from conservative elements across the nation. Unlike some "law and order" advocates, Powell took pains to show that his insistence on obedience to law was not simply a question of whose ox was being gored. He denounced the "small and defiant minority in the South . . . that still uses violence and intimidation to frustrate the legal rights of Negro citizens," and he publicly congratulated the Mississippi State Bar for encouraging representation of civil rights workers and other unpopular defendants. At the August 1965 annual meeting, Powell gave a special award to Richmond lawyer George E. Allen, Sr., who had represented a black Harvard law student charged with assaulting police at a desegregation hearing in Prince Edward County. Though some, including Harvard Law School Dean Erwin Griswold, thought that Powell laid too much stress on the fault of civil-rights demonstrators and not enough on the fault of the government officials, Powell's speeches established him as a tough but fair-minded proponent of public order.

It was this reputation that Lyndon Johnson wanted for his crime commission. Sporadic rioting in the summer of 1964 cracked the foundations of the Great Society. The murder of Kitty Genovese, overheard by thirty-eight witnesses who did nothing to help her, scared the country even more. Barry Goldwater's promise to do something—he never said precisely what—about crime in the streets was the most successful issue in the 1964 Republican campaign. At first, Johnson dismissed the crime problem as inappropriate for federal action, but the depth of popular concern convinced him otherwise. In a message to Congress on March 8, 1965, he declared that "Crime has become a malignant enemy in America's midst" and announced formation of the President's Commission on Law Enforcement and the Administration of Justice.

Johnson asked Powell to chair the commission, but Powell refused. After two years in the leadership of the ABA, he had to get back to practicing law. He did, however, agree to serve as a member on the ground that "There is usually a marked difference between the duties of the Chairman and those of the members of a large Commission." Accordingly, Powell's name was included in the list of nineteen members announced by the President on July 26.

Attorney General Nicholas Katzenbach served as chairman. Members included a former Attorney General of the United States, a state attorney general, a former mayor, a police chief, a prosecutor, two state cabinet officers, three judges, and four past or future presidents of the ABA. The other four places went to the director of the Urban League, the president of Yale University, a representative of the League of Women Voters, and a distinguished law professor. Sufficiently diverse to represent a broad spectrum of opinion, the commissioners were also sufficiently like-minded to have hopes of agreement. Consensus was the order of the day. Aided by executive director James Vorenberg, a full-time staff of about forty professionals, and ten times that many consultants and advisers, the commission eventually issued a widely praised report, *The Challenge of Crime in a Free Society.* Its prestige derived from the fact that the report itself and the more than two hundred specific recommendations it contained were unanimous.

Unanimity, however, had costs. Most obvious was the commission's silence on such divisive issues as the decriminalization of marijuana, the use of criminal laws to enforce sexual morality, and, above all, the death penalty. A more subtle cost of unanimity was the commission's failure to rank its recommendations. Hard choices were finessed by proposing that everything be fixed at once. The commission called for enormous increases in the resources devoted to juvenile crime, more police with better training, new technologies for law enforcement, expanded community relations programs, less crowded court systems, more community-based correctional programs, improved housing, and even guaranteed minimum income. The comprehensiveness of these recommendations suggested that the only "solution" to the crime problem was to remake the whole society.

Behind the scenes, consensus did not come easy. In reviewing successions of draft documents, Powell played tug-of-war with the commission staff, who wanted to make more liberal pronouncements than Powell would accept. Two of these disputes boiled over into public view. The first was wiretapping. Everyone agreed that bugging and telephone interceptions by private parties should be outlawed, but a majority of the commission wanted to allow wiretapping when authorized by court order for legitimate purposes of law enforcement. Lyndon Johnson disagreed. In the State of the Union address scheduled for January 10, 1967, he would call for a complete ban on all electronic eavesdropping save in a narrow category of national security cases. Ten days before the President's speech, commission member (and Johnson friend) Leon Jaworski said he would dissent from the final report unless his colleagues rescinded their approval of police wiretaps. Objecting to this political interference, Powell and some others said they would dissent if the recommendation were changed. Under heavy pressure from Chairman Katzenbach not to embarrass the President, the commission finally compromised by deleting the formal recommendation on wiretapping but including in the text of the report the statement that "a majority of the members of the commission believe that legislation should be enacted granting carefully circumscribed authority for electronic surveillance to law enforcement officers." Though Powell continued to regret the "weak and ineffective stance we are taking on electronic surveillance," legislation of the sort he supported was enacted the following year.

The other dispute concerned the Supreme Court. Had the liberal Justices handcuffed the police? Had the spate of pro-defendant decisions under Chief Justice Earl Warren gone too far in making it harder to get criminals off the streets? Johnson and Katzenbach tried hard to avoid such questions. In his original charge to the commission, the President pointedly did not ask whether the Court's decisions had undermined law enforcement. Instead, he directed the commission to what steps could be taken to promote "greater understanding" of the Court's decisions by its critics. Under Katzenbach's leadership, no staff work was devoted to the impact of the Court's rulings on law enforcement, despite the sustained attention given virtually everything else. In January 1967, barely a month before the report was to be published, Powell's discontent with this policy of silence "finally boiled over." He wrote two like-minded colleagues that he had been "deeply concerned about the Commission's Report—perhaps not so much by what it recommends as by its tone, and perhaps most of all by what it does not say." To remedy that defect, Powell had drafted a separate statement criticizing Supreme Court decisions "which in my judgment unduly limit reasonable law enforcement activities." As revised by Powell and Ross Malone (partly to accommodate objections from staff director James Vorenberg), this document was published over the names of seven commission members.

The "Supplemental Statement on Constitutional Limitations"— Powell was careful not to call it a dissent—focused on confessions. Its main thrust was to ask whether *Miranda v. Arizona*—which required that suspects be told of their right to remain silent and not be questioned by police until provided with a lawyer—had gone too far. Quoting Justice Frankfurter's admonition that "Questioning suspects is indispensable in law enforcement," the statement concluded that an "adequate opportunity must be provided the police for interrogation at the scene of the crime, during investigations and at the station house, with appropriate safeguards to prevent abuse." If a constitutional amendment were required to turn the Court around, so be it. In the meantime, said the signers, "We support all decisions of the Court as the law of the land, to be respected and enforced unless and until changed by the processes available under our form of government."

Although Powell's supplemental statement received a good deal of (mostly favorable) publicity, the proposal to amend the Constitution went nowhere. Five years later, when Mr. Justice Powell was in a position to "amend" the Constitution by overruling *Miranda*, he no longer showed much enthusiasm for doing so—but that story is best left to a later chapter. Ironically, the chief impact of the supplemental statement may have been on Powell's reputation. It established him as a critic—a respectful and responsible but unmistakably conservative critic—of the Warren Court. When the administration of Richard Nixon looked for potential Supreme Court nominees, Powell's name naturally made the list.

IN 1968 POWELL TURNED his attention back to Virginia. In January he began service on the Commission on Constitutional Revision, chaired by state Supreme Court Justice and former Governor Albertis S. Harrison. Its membership was a roster of distinguished Virginia lawyers, including Colgate Darden and civil rights attorney Oliver Hill. The immediate concern was the need to relax restrictions on the state's ability to borrow money, but the commissioners were asked to undertake a thorough revision of an outdated document. The existing constitution had been drafted in 1902. It ran to 35,000 words—as compared to 6,000 in the Constitution of the United States—and tied the hands of the legislature by making detailed pronouncements on many subjects. The commission was asked to cut unnecessary verbiage, update anachronistic provisions, and produce a document of style and dignity.

One area of substantive reform was education. Powell and Darden introduced provisions to increase the primacy of the Virginia Board of Education in setting standards of educational quality throughout the state. Also at their insistence, Virginia's localities would now be required to keep their schools open. Another Powell intervention occurred in redrafting the Virginia Bill of Rights. In language handed down from George Mason's original draft in 1776, the Constitution declared "That no free government, nor the blessings of liberty, can be preserved to any people, but by a firm adherence to justice, moderation, temperance, frugality, and virtue. . . ." Powell wanted to remind Virginia's citizens that they had responsibilities as well as rights, but Oliver Hill objected to enjoining people to obey the law when the law did not protect their rights. Powell agreed, and both points were included in the new Constitution, which endorses "the recognition by all citizens that they have duties as well as rights, and that such rights cannot be enjoyed saved in a society where law is respected and due process observed."

In this and other respects, the commission's work was well received. The General Assembly made relatively few alterations, and after the required two trips through that body, the proposal was submitted to the voters in November 1970. Unlike in New York and Maryland, where similar efforts failed at the polls, Virginians overwhelmingly approved their new Constitution, which took effect on July 1 of the next year.

SIX MONTHS AFTER the constitutional commission finished its work, Powell left on his longest vacation since the end of the war—a three-week African safari. The idea came from Lewis III. When Lewis was nine, Powell gave him a twenty-gauge shotgun. Soon Lewis was shooting "anything that wasn't walking on two feet." Father and son hunted ducks and geese, and watched a Sunday afternoon television program featuring celebrity hunters. The boy never lost interest, so in the summer after his sixteenth birthday—the age required for a license to shoot—Powell took him to Kenya on safari.

Jo, Molly, and Lewis III left first for a cruise through the Greek islands, after which Molly returned home. Powell met his wife and son in Athens, then took an overnight flight to Nairobi. Two days later they were on the East African veld, in the company of a British guide and a staff of natives. Though they lived in comfort, the hunting itself was hard work. Big game meant long stalks in the daytime heat. Fowl flushed by the vehicle had to be chased on foot, perhaps several hundred yards, to the point where they next went to ground. A tracker ran along with a heavy-caliber rifle in case the activity stirred up an angry rhinoceros. At sixty-two, Powell was not up to a steady diet of such exertion, so Lewis did most of the shooting. The carnage was plentiful. In two days, he bagged two pheasants, three guinea fowl, a Thomson's and two Grant's gazelles, a gerenuk, an impala, an oryx, and a wildebeest served up in patties for lunch. Toward the end of the trip, Lewis shot a lion, whose skin returned to Rothesay Circle eventually to become the favorite bed of his daughter Emily.

Twice daily the expedition made radio contact with Nairobi. Though Powell had directed that cables be opened and read over the air, the outfitter was reluctant to broadcast a message from the Secretary of Defense. Consequently, on the night of July 4, 1969, Powell rode the eighty tortuous miles to Nairobi to have a telephone conversation with Melvin Laird. Would Powell serve on a committee to study the Department of Defense? Yes, he answered, provided that he did not have to cut short the safari. Laird said that was no problem, so Powell returned to the States as scheduled on July 23 and shortly afterward attended his first meeting of President Nixon's Blue Ribbon Defense Panel.

The announced purpose of this body was to recommend reforms in the structure and operations of the Pentagon. It was not to involve itself in questions of broad national policy—such as whether American troops belonged in Southeast Asia—but to evaluate the organization and management of the Department of Defense, including procurement practices. The actual purpose, or at least part of it, was public relations—to answer mounting criticism of cost overruns in new weapons systems and the continuing stalemate in Vietnam.

After a year's study, the panel delivered 113 specific recommendations, covering everything from defense contracting to minority recruitment to the duties of the Joint Chiefs of Staff. In the area of procurement, Secretary Laird used the committee to bolster support for a decision he had already reached. He abandoned Robert McNamara's package procurement concept—"under which manufacturers, for a single, fixed price, would undertake to carry out all phases of a weapons system from research through actual production"— because of huge cost overruns. Instead, he installed a "fly before you buy" policy of contracting in stages, with testing and evaluation before entering each phase.

In some areas, the panel's recommendations were politely ignored. Most important was a call for far-reaching reorganization of the Defense Department's top management. The panel wanted to remove the Joint Chiefs of Staff from direct control of military operations and lodge that responsibility in a single top officer. Beneath him would come three commands organized by function rather than by military service: a strategic (i.e., nuclear) command for long-range bombers and missiles, a tactical command for all other combat forces, and a logistics command for support. None of this happened. Beset by critics of the war in Vietnam, the Nixon administration was not eager to provoke the opposition of the military services and their congressional allies by attempting to impose unified commands. The proposal quietly died.

Even before he learned of the administration's unresponsiveness, Powell became frustrated with the panel's mission. In his mind, questions of military bureaucracy and procedure paled beside the overriding issue of the Soviet threat. Working at night and on weekends, without staff assistance of any kind, Powell put his fears on paper. The product, entitled "The Shifting Balance of Military Power," was styled a supplemental statement to the Blue Ribbon Defense Panel Report to the President and signed by seven of the panel's sixteen members. It identified dangerous trends. Most important was the evidence, which Powell termed "reasonably conclusive," that the Soviet Union was aiming at a first-strike nuclear capability. While American defense dollars went down the drain in Vietnam, the Russians spent money on more and better nuclear weapons. They also devoted large resources to research and to deployment of a modern fleet. At home, public hostility toward the military and national defense had reached an unprecedented level. "[I]f these observable trends continue," Powell wrote, "the United States will become a second-class power incapable of assuring the future security and freedom of its people. The road to peace," Powell concluded, "has never been through appeasement, unilateral disarmament or negotiation from weakness. . . . Weakness of the U.S.—of its military capability and its will—could be the gravest threat to the peace of the world."

On September 30, 1970, Powell and his co-signers submitted their thirty-five-page statement on the "Shifting Balance of Military Power" to the President and the Secretary of Defense. Although its avowed purpose was to rally public opinion behind a strong defense, the report was immediately buried. Nothing was heard of it for six months. The White House intervened through Henry Kissinger, who asked the Deputy Secretary of Defense to have his staff "review the Report in some detail for substantive accuracy and for consistency with our other public statements before further consideration is given to releasing it to the public." In other words, never was soon enough.

Finally, on March 12, 1971, the statement was released without fanfare by low-level defense officials and given almost no circulation. Even Blue Ribbon Defense Panel's members were not sent copies. That it was released at all was not due to late-blooming enthusiasm on the part of the administration but to increasing pressure from Powell. Once the document was (however grudgingly) made public, Powell sent copies to everyone in sight, but virtually the only useful publicity appeared in *U.S. News & World Report,* which reprinted the five-page summary under the headline "U.S. Superiority Has Ended."

Powell expected President Nixon and Secretary Laird to applaud his statement. He failed to realize that his alarming attack on strategic preparedness against the Soviet threat was as unwelcome to the administration as it was to their liberal critics. More by implication than by explicit argument, Powell made a hawk's case against administration policy in Vietnam. The war drained resources, provoked domestic opposition, and diverted attention from the Soviet threat. The conclusion was obvious if unstated: Continuing American military involvement in the "limited" war in Southeast Asia was undermining national defense.

Powell's own views on Vietnam were conventionally hawkish. In 1966 he wrote President Johnson in support of a "more normal employment of air power" against North Vietnam. Four years later, these views hardened on a ten-day tour of Vietnam, during which Powell and selected members of the Blue Ribbon Defense Panel interviewed senior commanders on the organization of the war effort. In the field, they visited the headquarters of General Creighton Abrams and of every officer with as many as two divisions under his authority. Everywhere they heard one theme—"Let us fight the war to win it." Military men were rankled by the refusal to invade North Vietnam, by the limitations (later relaxed) on pursuit of the enemy into Laos and Cambodia, and most of all by the on-again, off-again approach to bombing north of twenty degrees latitude. Bombing was controlled from Washington, and the most inviting targets—those in the immediate vicinity of Hanoi and Haiphong—were often denied. Air Force General George S. Brown told Powell that his planes could cripple North Vietnam by bombing dams and other inviting targets but that permission had been refused due to the risk of civilian casualties. Powell's reaction was cold and warlike. Better that the North Vietnamese should suffer than that American servicemen die in a no-win war. Overall, his judgment was scathing. "I saw enough of the war," Powell later recalled, "to reinforce my view that Kennedy, Johnson, and Nixon all should have been impeached"—first, for the "stupidity" of fighting a land war in Asia, and, second, for not doing what was necessary to win it.

Powell offered a more constructive reaction to the debacle in Vietnam in "Political Warfare," a confidential paper that he asked panel chairman Gilbert Fitzhugh to deliver to the President. "Military strength is only one element of national power," Powell began. "The confrontation which has kept the world in turmoil for a quarter of a century is basically ideological," and the United States had gravely neglected "the critical war of words and ideas." "Much of the world has come to believe the lies that it is America—not the Communist superpowers—which is repressive, militaristic and imperialistic. Much of the world no longer believes there is a significant difference between totalitarianism and a free democracy." Powell proposed a national commission—one would have thought he had had enough of these—to study means of "political warfare," including propaganda, political, and psychological measures to discredit Communist regimes. The country could no longer afford the luxury of dismissing such actions as "a dirty business to which we should not stoop. . . . We must put aside the self-deception that the techniques of political warfare are unethical or immoral. The fact is that on the domestic scene we employ many of these techniques against each other with considerable savagery." Powell urged that the same skills be turned against our enemies abroad.

This time Powell received a polite letter from Nixon aide Alexander Haig, but there was no national commission on political warfare and no apparent change in U.S. policy. As in the case of his supplemental statement on the shifting balance of military power, his efforts came to nothing.

Altogether, Powell's relations with the President were distant and disappointing. With other allies of the Byrd organization, Powell had helped Nixon carry Virginia against John F. Kennedy in 1960 and against Hubert Humphrey in 1968. (Only in 1964 did "Virginia

Democrats" support the national ticket.) Yet as President, Nixon showed no interest in Powell's ideas. When Powell wrote a plaintive letter asking whether the President had seen his paper on the Soviet threat, Nixon did not answer. The only time Powell even met the President was at a White House dinner for Lord Mountbatten in the fall of 1970. Yet his standing with the President may have been higher than he knew. Nixon later said that he remembered the "Political Warfare" memorandum and considered it "profoundly perceptive." Of more importance were Powell's record as a conservative critic of the Warren Court and his reputation as one of the nation's premier lawyers. In any event, the next time Powell saw the President was on December 22, 1971, when Nixon presented Powell his commission as a Justice of the Supreme Court.

IN THESE ENDEAVORS, Powell showed a characteristic combination of ambition and reserve. On the one hand, he sought to extend his influence. In the organized bar, as in his law firm and his family, Powell wanted leadership and control. He used the presidency of the ABA as a platform, not only for promoting programs of value to the profession but also for amplifying his own views on a broad range of political and social issues. The crime commission and the Blue Ribbon Defense Panel seemed to offer similar opportunities. For Powell, their chief attraction was not prestige but the chance of having a say in public affairs. When this prospect failed—as in the crime commission's unwillingness to consider criticism of the Warren Court—Powell grew frustrated. His separate statement on constitutional limitations on law enforcement attempted to fill the gap. His essay on the shifting balance of military power reflected a similar impatience with the narrow focus of the defense panel. These publications were aggressive efforts to change the course of public affairs. They revealed an appetite for power.

Yet Powell's forwardness was hedged by a peculiar reticence. He did not, as president of the ABA, publicize his own achievements. As usual, he did his best work behind the scenes; only years later did the full story of his crucial role in securing ABA endorsement of the Legal Services Program become widely known. Powell concentrated on what was done, not who got the credit. His approach was the antithesis of a cult of personality—a style of leadership so decorous as to seem almost self-effacing. Powell's presentation of his separate views on the crime commission and the defense panel was equally restrained. He studiously avoided the term "dissent," though its use would have attracted attention, and kept silent for six difficult months while the White House sat on his report on the Soviet threat.

This balance of ambition and reserve was deeply ingrained in Powell's character. It was that same combination of pride and deference that had made him so popular in college, now transferred to a larger sphere. Powell's aversion to self-promotion was partly good manners. In his code of gentlemanly conduct, drawing attention to oneself was vulgar and rude. It implied a disrespect for others whose contributions were also deserving of notice. More fundamentally, Powell's restraint in disagreement reflected his idea of himself as a team player and as a member in good standing of a meritocratic ruling class. His penchant for compromise was never stronger than when confrontation threatened the solidarity of the elite.

Powell's sense of belonging, his instinctive loyalty to the groups and traditions of which he was part, could easily have degenerated into an empty conventionality. That it did not was due chiefly to his devotion to excellence. He asked for excellence from the associates in his firm and from the members of his family, but most of all, Powell demanded excellence in himself. For a man with a deep aversion to flamboyance and self-promotion, the only road to recognition lay through achievement. Powell hated mediocrity, or rather the acceptance of mediocrity. Underneath the modesty of his demeanor lay a fierce pride—pride in the quality of his work, in the integrity of his ideals, and in the correctness of his behavior. By 1971 these qualities had brought Powell a national reputation, as a lawyer and as a citizen.

CHAPTER VIII

APPOINTMENT

NOMINATION

On August 18, 1969, President Nixon nominated Clement F. Haynsworth, Jr., of South Carolina, to the Supreme Court. Born into one of South Carolina's oldest families, Haynsworth attended Furman University and the Harvard Law School, then returned to Greenville to practice law in the family firm. In 1957 President Eisenhower named him to the Fourth Circuit Court of Appeals.

As a judge, Haynsworth was distinguished for scholarship, industry, and craftsmanship; and as a person, for dignity, courtesy, and kindness. He left an impression of shyness and diffidence, heightened by a slight stutter and by his old-fashioned way of addressing his wife as "Miss Dorothy." In a sympathetic history of the Haynsworth nomination, lawyer John Frank called him "perhaps the most perfect gentleman I have ever known." Southern lawyers shared this view. In the eyes of the region's legal establishment—no less than for a President who wished to encourage and reward the newly Republican South— Haynsworth seemed the perfect choice. But neither the nominee nor the administration had any inkling of the calamitous effect on Haynsworth's nomination of the circumstances surrounding the departure of the man he had been picked to succeed.

Abe Fortas had been the adviser, friend, and confidant of Lyndon Johnson. He gave up none of these roles when Johnson inveigled Arthur Goldberg to resign from the Supreme Court—Goldberg went to the United Nations where, he believed, he would make peace in Vietnam—and put Fortas in his place. As a sitting Justice, Fortas counseled Johnson on everything from campaign finance to the Detroit riots. Most important, he advised the President on Vietnam, speaking in the White House inner circle as Johnson's alter ego in support of the ever-increasing commitment of military force. Although Fortas later tried to downplay it, his second career as presidential adviser was partly known, otherwise suspected, and widely criticized.

When Chief Justice Earl Warren announced in the summer of 1968 that he would retire as soon as the Senate confirmed a successor, Johnson turned again to his faithful friend. He would promote Fortas to Chief Justice and replace him as Associate Justice with a former Texas Congressman and longtime Johnson ally, Homer Thornberry. Like Fortas, Thornberry owed his nomination to personal friendship with the President, but unlike Fortas, he had no great reputation as a lawyer to help offset that impression. The package invited the charge of double cronyism.

Fortas's role as adviser to Johnson made some Senators uneasy. Their discomfort increased when it was disclosed that Fortas's friend and former partner Paul Porter had raised money from wealthy businessmen so that Justice Fortas could be handsomely paid for teaching a seminar at American University. For nine weeks of seminars, Fortas received $15,000, a sum greater than many professors earned for full-time work and at least seven times more than had been paid to any other part-time lecturer. But the chief source of the opposition to Fortas was politics. In March of that year, Lyndon Johnson had announced that he would not seek reelection. Now a lame duck, Johnson no longer had the clout to force his will through Congress, and the Republicans smelled victory in November. Even before Fortas had been selected, Republican Senator Robert Griffin announced that he would vote against *any* Johnson nominee on the ground that "the decision should be made by the next President . . . after the people have an opportunity to speak in November." Legally, this was sophistical. As Everett Dirksen said, "There's nothing about lame ducks in the Constitution." But politically, late nominations are particularly vulnerable, and it behooves a President facing the door to select someone who commands bipartisan support. Fortas did not.

On September 25, 1968, the Republicans began a filibuster. A week later, a vote of cloture fell woefully short. That night Fortas asked Johnson to withdraw his name, thereby becoming the first Supreme Court nominee in nearly forty years to fail to win confirmation.

But there was worse to come. Richard Nixon won that fall's election, and the following April the new administration learned that *Life* magazine planned an exposé on Fortas. The article focused on his dealings with Louis Wolfson, a high-flying financier recently jailed for securities crimes, who had been dropping Fortas's name with increasing frequency as his legal troubles mounted. Wolfson had agreed to pay Fortas $20,000 a year for the rest of his life (and that of his wife's) in return for services to the Wolfson Foundation. Fortas had received the first payment in January 1966 but had returned it that December after Wolfson was indicted.

The *Life* article ran on May 4. In response, Fortas issued a statement so mincing and guarded as to seem disingenuous. It was, said Fred Graham, "a triumph of lawyerlike craftsmanship over personal credibility." The most damaging of Fortas's evasions was his failure to mention that the $20,000, which had been reported as a single payment, was intended to continue annually for life. When that fact came out, Fortas looked all the worse for having tried to hide it.

Meanwhile, Attorney General John Mitchell was conducting his own investigation. He was acting on the advice of his legal counsel, William Rehnquist, that if Wolfson's money was payment for Fortas's help in the SEC investigation, the Justice had violated federal law and should be prosecuted. On May 7, Mitchell met privately with Chief Justice Earl Warren. He carried with him documents that confirmed the *Life* story and showed that the $20,000 payments had been intended to continue for life, but that did not prove Fortas guilty of any criminal wrongdoing. When *Newsweek* reported Mitchell's "backstairs call" on Warren, Mitchell would say only that he felt obliged to inform the Chief Justice of "certain information known by me which might be of aid to him." The country was left to speculate on the dark secrets Mitchell might have unearthed.

What was found a few days later was enough to meet all expectations. In a sworn statement dated May 10, Wolfson reported that Fortas, while visiting him in Florida in 1966, had said that Wolfson need not worry about the SEC investigation, as the violations were merely technical. Then came the bombshell. "Fortas," said Wolfson, "indicated that he had or would contact Manuel Cohen of the Security and Exchange Commission regarding this matter. Fortas indicated that he was somewhat responsible for Cohen's appointment to the Commission as Chairman."

Whether Fortas actually made such statements will probably never be known. In any event, on May 12 Mitchell sent Warren copies of Wolfson's affidavit and certain other documents marked "Personal and Confidential—For Eyes Only of the Chief Justice." The next day Warren convened the Justices to discuss the matter, and the day following Fortas resigned.

For Senate liberals, the result was mortifying. Not only had Fortas been denied promotion to Chief Justice, he had been forced to resign from the Court. Worst of all, his lapse of judgment was so extreme that even his admirers were thankful that he had not been made Chief Justice. Now Richard Nixon would have *two* appointments to the Supreme Court, one to succeed Warren as Chief Justice and a second to replace Fortas.

One week after Fortas resigned, Nixon nominated Warren Burger as Chief Justice. Burger had no political vulnerabilities, and besides, the liberals were "still too stunned by the Fortas debacle to make serious objection." The new Chief Justice was quickly confirmed with only three dissents. The second nomination went to Haynsworth. As Rehnquist later recalled, the administration completely failed to anticipate the reception in the Senate: "Nobody realized the determination on the part of some of the Democrats to do to a Republican what they thought had been done to Fortas." All the rage and resentment at the (self-)destruction of Abe Fortas was about to come down on the unprepared and unsuspecting head of Clement Haynsworth.

THERE WERE, OF COURSE, better reasons to oppose Haynsworth. He was said, with some justice, to be antilabor, and it was the determined opposition of organized labor that derailed the early movement toward confirmation. Although his labor record was in fact mixed, Haynsworth had voted for management in several important cases later reversed by the Supreme Court. He was also denounced as a "laundered segregationist" determined to slow down progress on civil rights. In fact, Haynsworth was a "laundered segregationist" only in a sense that was true of most white southerners of his generation, including his friend Lewis Powell. Despite his South Carolina origins and the support of former Dixiecrat Strom Thurmond, Haynsworth was no obstructionist on civil rights. It is, however, a fair criticism of his record on the appeals court that he failed to appreciate the need for strong judicial response to local recalcitrance. Those who looked for judicial leadership were legitimately disappointed.

The centerpiece of the attack on Haynsworth, however, was not labor law or civil rights but judicial ethics. Matching Haynsworth's cases with his stock holdings, opponents discovered that he had decided a case in favor of the Brunswick Corporation and at about the same time accepted a recommendation from his investment manager that he purchase stock in that company. This was doubtless unwise, perhaps even negligent, but it was not plainly unethical. Then-prevailing standards for judicial disqualification (at least in the Fourth Circuit) required a judge to recuse himself only where his interest was "substantial" and permitted participation in cases involving small stock-holdings. There was no indication that Haynsworth's actions as a judge had in any way been affected by his investments.

Another attack concerned Carolina Vend-a-Matic, a corporation in which Haynsworth and his former law partners held substantial interests. In 1963 Haynsworth sat in a case involving the Darlington plant of the Deering-Milliken company, which owned a large number of other textile plants in the southeast, in a few of which Vend-a-Matic had won competitive-bid contracts to supply vending machines. Again, there was not the slightest ground to think that this distant connection in any way influenced Haynsworth's judgment, but the novel claim was now made that he had been under an ethical duty to disqualify himself from any case involving a company *that did business with* a company in which he held a substantial interest.

These difficulties were masterfully exploited by Indiana Senator Birch Bayh. Bayh moved from one ethical problem to another and back again, generating enough smoke to create the vivid impression of fire. He never rested on any one incident, but spun them all together in an encompassing charge of "insensitivity" to ethical concerns. Bayh's argument was in terms unanswerable. He said that a Supreme Court nominee should be "beyond reproach" and that Haynsworth's participation in cases touching his financial interests had created an "appearance of impropriety." This argument caught and amplified the reverberations from the Fortas affair and lent an air of fine impartiality to the calumniation of Clement Haynsworth. On November 21, 1969, the Senate rejected the nomination by a decisive vote.

POWELL AT FIRST EXPECTED Haynsworth to sail through. He had argued appeals before Haynsworth, knew him from Richmond (where the Fourth Circuit heard cases), and saw him annually at the Fourth Circuit Judicial Conference (a three-day convocation of lawyers and judges that alternated between the Greenbrier and the Homestead). The two men were similar in style and outlook, and Powell applauded the nomination. The subsequent disclosure of ethical problems did nothing to shake his support. "The amounts involved," Powell wrote, "when translated into possible effect on Judge Haynsworth's security holdings, were absurdly trivial. No one could fairly suggest, I think, that he would have been influenced in his judicial decisions by such inconsequential economic benefits." That left only the charge that Haynsworth had been "insensitive" to appearances. "Knowing him personally," Powell added, "I am satisfied that a far more accurate characterization would be 'inattentive'—in a way which involved nothing more than thoughtlessness at the time."

As the nomination headed for trouble, Powell went into action. He organized a telegram of support from sixteen past presidents of the American Bar Association (only one refused to sign), and encouraged similar efforts by the state bar associations in the Fourth Circuit. He worked the telephones to contact people who might help. Lawyers and businessmen in other states were urged to speak to their Senators. Powell himself lobbied Virginia Senator William B. Spong, Jr. (who voted for confirmation), and Maryland Senator Joseph D. Tydings (who had called for Fortas's resignation and felt he owed Haynsworth the same harsh judgment).

When these efforts failed, Powell sent letters of condolence to Haynsworth and to Johnnie Walters, the Assistant Attorney General who had guided the nomination campaign, a note of appreciation to Senator Spong, and a telegram asking President Nixon to urge the defeated nominee to remain on the appeals court. Haynsworth wrote back that he had considered resigning but was "tremendously reassured and encouraged by messages from good friends like you, who have my respect and admiration, and by an unbelievable flood of letters from every state in the union." He even thought some good might come of his defeat: "If it resulted in your appointment, I would be tremendously pleased."

But Haynsworth was again to be disappointed. Powell's name was bruited in the *Richmond Times-Dispatch* and elsewhere and he heard from friends that his name was "high on a small list under active consideration at the White House," but Powell discouraged all efforts on his behalf. It was at this time that he wrote John Mitchell asking that his name be withdrawn from consideration.

With Powell apparently unavailable, the administration turned elsewhere. In consequence, the injustice done to Clement Haynsworth by the Senate of the United States was now compounded by Richard Nixon, who forever linked Haynworth's name with that of his next nominee, G. Harrold Carswell. Professionally and intellectually, Carswell was as undistinguished as Haynsworth was able. William Van Alstyne, a liberal law professor who had supported Haynsworth, put the case exactly: "There is, in candor, nothing in the quality of the nominee's work to warrant any expectation whatever that he could serve with distinction on the Supreme Court of the United States." (Senator Roman Hruska supported him anyway: "Even if he were mediocre, there are a lot of mediocre judges and people and lawyers. They are entitled to a little representation, aren't they?") Moreover, as the hearings plainly revealed, Carswell was a racist, a man of uncertain character and doubtful honesty. On April 8, 1970, the Senate rejected his nomination by a vote of fifty-one to forty-five.*

Twice rebuffed with southern nominees, Nixon turned to Warren Burger's friend, Harry A. Blackmun of Minnesota. This nomination was politically uncontroversial and was confirmed without difficulty after a one-day hearing.

IN LATER YEARS, Powell rarely missed a chance to record his admiration for Clement Haynsworth. He said more than once that the reasons for the Senate's action were "political—in the least creditable sense of that word." In 1983 Congress named the federal building in Greenville, South Carolina, for Haynsworth. At the dedication Powell praised the defeated nominee as a "special kind of hero," who "bore the disappointment, unjust criticism, and unfair publicity with the equanimity of a Robert E. Lee" and by his subsequent career "demonstrated for all to see that the Senate had made an historic mistake." And in a Bill Moyers interview in 1987, Powell dryly etched his view of the "mindless misjoinder" of the names of Haynsworth and Carswell as defeated nominees. After paying his customary compliment to Haynsworth—"I'm glad to say publicly that I think Clement Haynsworth was eminently qualified to serve on this Court"—Powell added that after Haynsworth's defeat, the President nominated "a man named Carswell—[pause]—whom I did not and do not know."

Though Haynsworth's name may be tied to Carswell's in the footnotes of history, the more important connection is between Haynsworth and Powell. If Haynsworth—or for that matter Carswell—had been confirmed to the Court, Powell would not have been selected in 1971. In an odd twist of fate, Powell owed his eventual place on the Supreme Court to the defeat of the man he had done so much to support.

CONFIRMATION

The first call Powell returned on October 22, 1971, the morning after the President announced his nomination to the Supreme Court, was that from Clement Haynsworth. After fencing over who would do the

---

* Astonishingly, seven Senators—including Republican leader Hugh Scott and assistant leader Robert Griffen—voted against Haynsworth but for Carswell.

courtesy of walking three blocks to the other's office, Haynsworth arrived to offer not merely congratulations but advice. Haynsworth had not been ready for the ordeal of confirmation. He had come to Washington with misplaced confidence in his own reputation and had relied on the administration for support. His cousin Harry came up from South Carolina thinking that the proceedings would last a week and ended up spending three months as researcher and staff for the embattled nominee. They were always on the defensive, always one step behind the opposition, responding to one point just as the attack—and the headlines—moved on to something else. Powell, said Haynsworth, must not make the same mistake. He must prepare for the confirmation as if he were preparing for major litigation.

There was double irony in this advice. Unlike Haynsworth, Powell faced no real risk of rejection, as every aspect of the political situation conspired to his advantage. The instinct to avenge Abe Fortas was spent. The charge of antisouthern bias made after the back-to-back rejections of Haynsworth and Carswell made many northern Senators eager to prove that they would vote for a qualified southerner. Nixon's dalliance with Herschel Friday, Mildred Lillie, and West Virginia's Robert Byrd enhanced respect for Powell's professional qualifications. Best of all there was Bill Rehnquist, Powell's conservative co-nominee, to draw the fire of liberal critics. Even Powell's age worked in his favor. As savvy old Jim Eastland, chairman of the Senate Judiciary Committee and one of Rehnquist's strongest backers, explained: "You know why all those liberals are for Powell? Because he's old. They think he's going to die."

Moreover, Powell had many friends. He could draw on contacts from the ABA, from the American College of Trial Lawyers, from the National Legal Aid and Defender Association, from corporate board-rooms and Rockefeller-funded foundations, from speeches and conferences and presidential commissions, from all the activities that had filled forty years of private practice and public life. Unlike Haynsworth, who was little known outside the Fourth Circuit, Powell knew lawyers in every state in the Union. Unlike Robert Bork, who was the darling of conservatives but anathema to liberals, Powell's supporters came from both parties and represented many points of view. And Powell's friends were persons of influence. Indeed, his contacts reached even into the Senate itself. In addition to Virginia's two Senators, Powell knew young Lowell Weicker, who had grown up to be a Senator from Connecticut and who appeared before the Senate Judiciary Committee to say that Powell "had always lived for the America that was dreamt to be." He knew Birch Bayh of Indiana, whom he had helped in drafting the constitutional amendment on presidential succession. Powell was also on what he called "a first-name basis" with Senators Charles Percy of Illinois and John V. Tunney of California and with Senator David Gambrell of Georgia, son of former ABA president and Powell supporter, E. Smythe Gambrell.

The sum of these influences can only be guessed. Powell's files bulge with copies of his supporters' letters to Senators, but it seems likely that a great many more were not sent to him. Except perhaps for the most trusted and senior friends, the request for help rarely came directly from Powell. Influential practitioners were asked to recruit other lawyers to write their Senators, so that overlapping networks of personal contact spread across the country. The emphasis was not on the number of letters—in fact, some concern was expressed to avoid the appearance of an organized campaign—but on bringing to bear influential voices whom the Senators might know and respect.

A small fragment of this effort is visible in a letter from Frederick P. Bamberger of Evansville, Indiana. Bamberger had organized letters from twelve prominent Indiana lawyers, both Republicans and Democrats, including six past presidents of the state bar. These twelve had written (and sometimes called) their Senators on Powell's behalf.

This was the same sort of work that Powell had undertaken for Clement Haynsworth, but multiplied many times over. Especially active were fellow ABA Presidents Whitney North Seymour, Orison S. Marden, and Ross Malone, who left a thick file of correspondence with well-placed lawyers on Powell's behalf. The cumulative effect is unmeasurable, but it is certain that the Senators heard from many different sources, from home-state lawyers whose judgment they respected and whose support they valued, that Lewis Powell should be confirmed to the Supreme Court.

Haynsworth's message was ironic for another reason as well. It was advice that Haynsworth needed and suffered for the lack of, but that Powell never required. Preparation was Powell's creed. He had made his way in the world by diligence, discipline, and attention to detail, and all these qualities would be brought to bear as he made ready for the confirmation.

Powell had not only the instinct for preparation but also the resources. Though he politely accepted assistance from the Department of Justice, he relied chiefly on his own staff. The senior members were Joe Carter and George Freeman. Carter, a so-called Virginia Democrat, dealt with conservative southerners, such as

Eastland and his venerable Mississippi colleague John Stennis, the Republican minority in the Senate, and the Department of Justice. George Freeman worked the other side of the political street. He was a Yale Law School graduate, a former clerk to Justice Hugo Black, and what Virginians called a "national Democrat." Freeman had helped Powell achieve a political balance in his campaign for presidency of the ABA and now served a similar function in the campaign for confirmation. He was especially useful in getting prominent members of the ABA to contact their Senators on Powell's behalf.

The legwork was done by two of the firm's associates. John Shenefield and Allen Goolsby complied with the Senate's various requests for information. They collected and indexed Powell's articles, speeches, and public statements, and prepared files on potentially troublesome issues. Goolsby read the Haynsworth and Blackmun confirmation hearings so that he could see what kinds of questions might arise. He became particularly worried about the all-white Country Club of Virginia, to which Powell belonged and of which he had once been an officer. Goolsby found an old copy of the bylaws, which contained "horrible language" spelling out the circumstances in which personal maids could enter the club. Fortunately, the current bylaws imposed no racial restriction, so that the all-white membership could be portrayed as a fact, not a policy. Despite Goolsby's fears, the issue "never generated any heat."

The effort to uncover and prepare for potential problems sometimes went to absurd lengths. When the *Richmond Afro-American* published a scurrilous letter accusing Powell of everything from racism to the persecution of Christians and of critics of the power company, inquiries were launched to identify its author. When a search of the telephone directory, the city directory, and the VEPCO customer lists revealed neither the author nor the organization he purported to represent, the Powell team knew that the letter would carry no weight. In fact, it was never mentioned.

Completing the confirmation team were a lawyer in the firm's Washington office, recruited because he was on the scene, and Powell's redoubtable secretary, Sally Smith. Smith had worked for Powell since 1962, occasionally traveling with him to ABA meetings so that Powell could keep up with his work. The morning after Nixon announced the nomination, Smith walked into Powell's office and asked, "when do we leave for Washington?," and was from that moment fully engaged in the confirmation effort.

Powell himself helped collect the necessary information, particularly on his personal finances, and consulted with knowledgeable sources (including Warren Burger and Potter Stewart) on how to restructure his investments to avoid ethical problems. He responded to the flood of congratulatory letters and telegrams, returned hundreds of telephone calls, and made courtesy calls on several Senators. He told Carter and Freeman whom to contact, made lists of supporters who could be asked to help, and chose the witnesses who would be invited to testify on his behalf. He endured practice sessions where Carter and Freeman tried to anticipate the toughest questions they could think of. He wrote out in longhand his beliefs on the role of the Supreme Court and dictated brief statements on matters ranging from his service on the Richmond School Board to the concept of a "strict constructionist." He even oversaw the logistical arrangements, including reserving a whole floor at the Hay-Adams Hotel in Washington, with a large suite for work by the confirmation team and separate rooms for its members.

In short, everything was done that could be done to prepare for the confirmation. If there were defeat or disappointment in store, it would not be due to lack of effort.

POWELL APPEARED before the Senate Committee on the Judiciary on November 4, 1971. He was accompanied by Virginia's two Senators, Harry F. Byrd, Jr., and William B. Spong, Jr., by the state's entire congressional delegation, and by the attorney general of Virginia, a national Democrat who carried a letter of support from the state's Republican Governor. Also scheduled to be present (a last-minute change in schedule caused some of them to be late) were nine ABA presidents, the deans of three Virginia law schools, former Senator Joseph D. Tydings of Maryland, Richmond civil rights lawyer Oliver Hill, and assorted other worthies. As Harvie Wilkinson said: "It is not recorded whether a choir of angels actually made an appearance on Powell's behalf, but one seasoned Senator was heard to mumble under his breath, 'Hell, he don't want to be confirmed. He wants to be canonized.'"

The committee received the statements of support from Powell's backers and immediately turned its attention to Rehnquist. In doing so, Committee Chairman James O. Eastland of Mississippi was following the administration's plan to treat the nominations as a package. He knew that opposition would focus on Rehnquist and that delay would be a tactic. Therefore, Rehnquist would go first. There would be no opportunity to bring Powell to a vote before Rehnquist was ready, so that pressure to go forward with the confirmation would necessarily benefit both nominees.

Rehnquist did indeed prove controversial. Few doubted his ability, but many feared that he would bring to the Court an ideologically doctrinaire conservatism, an inflexible hostility to defendants' rights, and an insensitivity to concerns for racial justice. The American Civil Liberties Union broke a long-standing tradition of silence on judicial nominations by condemning Rehnquist as "a dedicated opponent of individual civil liberties" and publicly calling for his defeat. Others supported him just as stoutly. When all was said and done, Rehnquist won approval in the committee by a vote of twelve to four and in the Senate as a whole by a margin of forty-two.

Powell's progress through confirmation was by contrast almost stately. There were minor missteps, as when Powell told Senator Bayh that he had not supported the (relatively moderate) proposals of the Gray Commission, which Powell had confused with the more radical agenda of massive resistance (later supported by Garland Gray). He wrote a letter explaining the error and offering to correct it on the record, but was told that it was not necessary.

On another occasion's Powell was backed up against the wall of the Senate Office Building by a group of women's rights activists. "Ladies," he ventured, "I've been married for thirty-five years and have three daughters. I've got to be for you." The levity was not appreciated. In fact, Powell was later opposed by the National Organization for Women, not for anything in particular he had said or done but because of the "absence of any documented evidence of his affirmative action vis-à-vis women." (Luckily for Powell, the NOW president was not a persuasive witness. She began by telling the Senators of her "considerable doubt" that they had the desire or the capacity to understand her testimony, and later suggested to this panel of lawyers that Supreme Court Justices did not need law degrees. It would be better, she thought, to appoint a behavioral scientist—as she, no doubt coincidentally, happened to be.)

In any event, the crucial issue was not gender but race. The attack was led by Congressman John Conyers, Jr., of the Congressional Black Caucus, and by Richmonder Henry L. Marsh III on behalf of the all-black Old Dominion Bar Association. They pressed four points.

First, Powell belonged to all-white organizations, including the Country Club of Virginia and the Richmond Commonwealth Club. This was true but not disqualifying. It was sufficient that he resign from such clubs, as he had done. Second, Powell sat on the boards of several large corporations, including Philip Morris, that had been sued for employment discrimination. This also was true but scarcely damning. Most large companies had had the same experience, and the connection between a member of the board of directors and hiring decisions was remote. Closer to home was the third allegation, that Powell's law firm refused to hire blacks. Hunton, Williams in fact had no black lawyers, though at the time that was by no means rare. Additionally, there was an allegation that the firm had a policy against blacks, but the charge was double-hearsay (a Yale law student reporting what a Hunton, Williams associate allegedly said about what Hunton, Williams partners had said) and had been denied by the firm. Again, there was no direct evidence connecting Powell to any act of discrimination.

These charges were incidental to the main target, which was of course Powell's role in the (non)desegregation of the Richmond schools. Here there was ground for attack—though not in anything Powell had said. Throughout those turbulent years, he had remained steadfastly silent. The sum of his public statements on the subject of desegregation amounted to almost nothing, and what little he did say ran strongly to vagueness and platitude. Of necessity, therefore, Powell's critics focused on what he did—or did not do—to facilitate desegregation.

The numbers condemned him. When Powell left the Richmond School Board in 1961, after eight years as its chairman, only two of the city's 23,000 black children attended school with whites. Conyers and Marsh inferred an evil motive. Powell, they said, had not done battle with massive resistance but had followed "his own segregationist policies" for the Richmond Schools. He was a "champion" of segregation, who had simply been ingenious and sophisticated in his efforts to keep the races apart.

Most damaging of all, Conyers and Marsh claimed that Powell had violated the Constitution and laws of the United States. According to Conyers, Powell had "participated in the extensive scheme to destroy the constitutional rights that he had sworn to protect." He was described by Marsh as "a man who has for much of his life waged war on the Constitution of the United States" and "has repeatedly and consistently demonstrated by his public deeds a wanton disrespect for law."

The Senate would have overlooked a segregationist past. Most southern leaders of Powell's generation—including those who sat in the United States Senate—had such a background. That a Richmond lawyer in 1971 belonged to all-white clubs or worked in an all-white law firm was far from unusual; it proved only that he had accepted the world as he found it. This the Senators could understand. But the charge that Powell had subverted the law and flouted the Constitution was something else again. If it were believed that Powell had actively sought to obstruct and evade the clear mandate of the Constitution, his nomination would have been in jeopardy.

Powell answered these charges in the language best known to politicians—endorsements. The confirmation team assembled a packet of statements and made copies available to everyone in sight. The first endorsement came from Senator Spong, a respected moderate who in 1966 had become the first statewide candidate in many years to defeat the Byrd organization. Powell, he said, acted in "very turbulent and confused times" to "keep the schools of Virginia open and to preserve the public education system for all pupils." Next there was a letter from the school board's only black member. "I served on the Richmond City School Board under the chairmanship of Lewis Powell from 1953 to 1961," wrote Booker T. Bradshaw. "During that period I did not observe any evidence of racial prejudice on his part. On the contrary, I always found him to be fair, calm, and objective in his approach to the many problems which confronted us." Third came the dean of Virginia's civil rights lawyers, Oliver Hill. Hill pointed to Powell's role in rewriting Virginia's Constitution to guarantee free public education of high quality for all the state's students. He was, said Hill, "a man whose heart is right." There followed an endorsement by Dr. Ferguson Reid, the first black elected to the Virginia legislature since Reconstruction.

Most eloquent of all was the statement of Armistead Boothe, public leader of the opposition to massive resistance. Unlike Conyers and Marsh, Boothe knew of Powell's behind-the-scenes role in persuading Governor Lindsay Almond to back the plan that ended massive resistance and that passed the state Senate by only one vote. "Perhaps today," said Boothe, "there are some younger people who do not remember the '50s or the humanity, the regard for law and the far-sightedness of a few people like Lewis Powell, who helped Virginia, in a Virginia way, to survive the Commonwealth's severest test in this century." Boothe ended with a message for the Congressional Black Caucus: "If the distinguished members of that group could remember the 1950s and could get all the available facts, they would not oppose him. They would approve of his selection and thank the good Lord they would have him on the Supreme Court."

The last item in the packet of supporting materials was a statement by former school superintendent Hi Willett detailing Powell's successful efforts to keep the schools open, to build new schools in the face of extremist opposition, and to prevent the Richmond City Council from insisting on total segregation as a condition of city funding. "In the climate that is generally accepted today," Willett concluded, "progress may appear to have been slow, but the position taken by the School Board and the administration in Richmond was vigorously attacked as being entirely too liberal. . . . Men of goodwill and integrity may differ on what should or should not have been done in retrospect. However, no one can fairly deny the important role that Lewis F. Powell, Jr., played in upholding the law. . . ."

These endorsements were important not only for what they said about Powell, but also for what they allowed him not to say. Powell kept his distance from the desegregation controversy. He did not directly answer Conyers and Marsh or enter into the sort of detailed explanation that would have been scrutinized for distortion or error. Instead, he relied on others, profiting from their credibility and holding himself above the fray.

The high point of this strategy was an extraordinary letter from Jean Camper Cahn. In eighteen typed pages she recounted Powell's role in steering the Legal Services Program through the ABA, in committing his prestige to the project, and in overcoming the opposition of those alarmed by federal funding. She told how Powell had worked closely with the all-black National Bar Association and how he instigated an invitation that made her the first black lawyer, male or female, to address a plenary session of the ABA annual meeting. She closed with a moving tribute:

> . . . I am drawn inescapably to the sense that Lewis Powell is, above all, humane; that he has a capacity to empathize, to respond to the plight of a single human being to a degree that transcends ideologies or fixed positions. And it is that ultimate capacity to respond with humanity to individualized instances of injustice and hurt that is the best and only guarantee I would take that his conscience and his very soul will wrestle with every case until he can live in peace with a decision that embodies a sense of decency and fair play and common sense. In that court of last resort to which I and my people so frequently must turn as the sole forum in which to petition our government for a redress of grievances, it is that quality of humanity on which we must ultimately pin our hopes in the belief that it is never too much to trust that humanity can be the informing spirit of the law.

*   *   *

There were of course other issues. Powell had worried a good deal about what to do with his investments. He, Jo, Lewis III (the only minor child), and various trusts created by him owned $1.5 million in publicly traded stocks. Sooner or later most of these companies would be involved in litigation before the Supreme Court. At first Powell thought of putting his investments in a blind trust, where securities would be bought and sold without his knowledge, but a problem was found in the new Code of Judicial Conduct then scheduled for adoption by the ABA. Its requirements would not have the force of law, but they seemed to state an ethical duty for a judge to take affirmative steps to know of any financial holdings that might cause a conflict of interest. A blind trust would not do. Another option was for Powell to sell all his holdings, but in some cases that would trigger a substantial tax on capital gains. This was especially true of the Sperry & Hutchinson stock he had received on the sale of his father's business. Additionally, Powell had invested in some companies—such as Philip Morris and the Ethyl Corporation—for which he would have to disqualify himself because of past association whether or not he owned stock. The eventual plan, therefore, was to sell most of his securities and concentrate his holdings in a few former clients for which he was already disqualified. To the committee, he promised merely to do whatever was necessary to avoid conflicts of interest.

Powell was also asked about legal issues. He was for free speech, against crime, and in light of the personal publicity of the last few weeks, thought that a right of privacy "would be a very fine thing." He gave short answers when possible, spoke longer when necessary, and refused to be drawn into issues he did not understand. Senator Fong, for example, was very concerned about a question of grand jury procedure. Was it proper for the prosecutor to invite someone to testify as a witness when that person was really a target of the grand jury investigation? Powell could not say. "I have never been before a grand jury in my life," he explained. "I am not really familiar with the procedure you described. In fact, I never heard of it before." Fong tried again: "Well, do you think it is fair to subpoena a person before a grand jury as a witness for the Government after the prosecution has presented evidence to that very grand jury sufficient to warrant an indictment of that person without his testimony and then ask him a lot of questions?" "I wouldn't want to express a legal opinion," Powell answered, "but I would say it is very unfriendly." Amid the laughter, Fong withdrew the question.

Powell's soft manner and careful preparation saved him from difficulty. A good example is a long exchange with Senator Edward
Kennedy on the subject of civil disobedience. In 1966 Powell had
given a lecture at Washington and Lee entitled "A Lawyer Looks at
Civil Disobedience." Some months later he republished these views in
less scholarly form in *U.S. News & World Report*. There Powell condemned civil disobedience as a precursor of "organized lawlessness
and even rebellion." "This heresy," he wrote, "was dramatically associated with the civil rights movement by the famous letter of Martin
Luther King from a Birmingham jail. As rationalized by Dr. King, some
laws are 'just' and others 'unjust'; each person may determine for himself which laws are 'unjust'; and each is free—indeed even morally
bound—to violate the 'unjust' laws." Powell then rebutted King's
"rationalization" at some length. He acknowledged the need for racial
justice and social reform but cautioned against rewarding extremists.
"[T]hose who preach, practice and condone lawlessness are the enemies of social reform and of freedom itself. In short," he concluded,
"the one indispensable prerequisite to all progress is an ordered society
governed by the rule of law."

Though Powell's reference to King was merely incidental to his
main theme, it was quite misleading. Powell implied that King had
claimed a *legal* right to violate "unjust" laws, which was not the case.
King had always been ready to bear the legal consequences of his
moral claim. Senator Kennedy proved the point with an excerpt from
King. "In no sense," said King, "do I advocate evading or defying the
law, as would the rabid segregationist. That would lead to anarchy.
One who breaks an unjust law must do so openly, lovingly, and with a
willingness to accept the penalty. I submit that an individual who
breaks a law that conscience tells him is unjust, and who willingly
accepts the penalty of imprisonment in order to arouse the conscience
of the community over its injustice, is in reality expressing the highest
respect for law." What on earth, asked Kennedy, was wrong with that?

What indeed? King's position was in fact entirely consistent with
Powell's cherished regard for the rule of law. Now Powell turned his
considerable lawyer's skill to putting the most agreeable face on his
remarks without changing his position. He ignored the *U.S. News &
World Report* redaction and spoke instead of the longer and more careful article in the Washington and Lee law review. As that article
showed, he was "not talking about the testing in good faith, usually on
a lawyer's advice, of specific laws deemed to be both unjust and
invalid," as had been true in the sit-in demonstrations of the early civil

rights movement, which had been upheld by the Supreme Court. Powell's concern was not violating a law to test its validity but defying the law to defeat the government.

As this answer made no specific mention of King, Senator Kennedy tried again. Powell responded that King had been "entirely within his rights" to bring the early civil rights cases and that, "it need hardly be said that he will be recognized as one of the great leaders of his people." Then came the Powell touch. When he had written on civil disobedience, Powell noted, he could find only one article applicable to the modern situation, and that was by (Kennedy friend and adviser) Burke Marshall. Since then, he had seen another article by (Kennedy friend and adviser) Archibald Cox, a copy of which he happened to have with him. "I think that [Cox] expressed his views far better than I did," Powell explained, "but in terms of the philosophic content and approach I would agree with him." Apparently satisfied, Kennedy let the matter drop.

Of all the issues in Powell's long career, the most persistent and pointed questioning concerned a newspaper article. Less than three months before being nominated to the Supreme Court, Powell had written "Civil Liberties Repression: Fact or Fiction?," an uncharacteristically savage rebuttal to the charge of widespread repression in American society. Here Powell's usual reserve and moderation gave way to a shrill attack on "standard leftist propaganda" about violations of civil liberties. Issues included wiretapping ("[l]aw-abiding citizens have nothing to fear"); the mass arrests at the 1971 May Day demonstrations in Washington (the alternative was "to surrender the Government to insurrectionaries"); the charge of a police conspiracy to kill Black Panthers (Powell found "no evidence whatever" of such a plot); systematic suppression of dissent (which Powell called "sheer nonsense"); and judicial persecution of radicals ("[n]o country in the world has done more to insure fair trials").

Yes, of course there were violations of civil rights, but the real test, said Powell, was "whether these are episodic departures from the norm, or whether they are, as charged, part of a system of countenanced repression." On that issue, his conclusion was clear: "America is not a repressive society. The Bill of Rights is widely revered and zealously safeguarded by the courts. There is in turn no significant threat to individual freedom in this country by law enforcement."

At one level, these sentiments were unobjectionable. Few Senators would be oppose a Supreme Court nominee on the ground that he had too *much* faith in the legal system or because he had criticized the

radical left. Yet there was something about Powell's civil liberties article that liberals found hard to swallow.* It showed just how deeply
Powell abhorred the chaos and discord of the late 1960s, how far
removed he was in sympathy from the young demonstrators who
crowded Washington streets on May Day, how ready he was to dismiss
the concerns of those, including Senator Kennedy, who saw a pattern
of law enforcement directed against the left. The article revealed him
as a man of profoundly conservative instincts, as least when confronting a threat to public order, and of a hard-edged reaction to
attacks on the rule of law. Liberals wondered whether perhaps they
faced a wolf in sheep's clothing.

But unease did not translate into opposition. Powell was too well
known and too widely supported to make a tempting target, and his
appearance before the committee left no opening for attack. He was
poised, measured, calm, evidently open-minded, and obviously well prepared. The strident and alarmist tone of his civil liberties article was
contradicted by a lifetime of balanced and moderate opinion and by his
demeanor before the committee. In the end, Powell won unanimous
approval by the Judiciary Committee and nearly unanimous confirmation by the full Senate. Ironically, the single "nay" vote was based not
on Powell's record in desegregating Richmond's schools nor on his views
on civil liberties. Senator Fred Harris of Oklahoma opposed the confirmation on the ground that Powell was "an elitist [who] has never shown
any deep feelings for little people."

THE MONTH THAT INTERVENED between Powell's confirmation and his
swearing-in was a busy time. To the usual social events of the
Christmas season, Powell's friends now added various celebrations,
including a testimonial dinner in Richmond and lunch in his honor at
the 21 Club in New York. He had a huge backlog of correspondence to
answer and supporters to thank. Never had Powell's wide circle of
friends and acquaintances been more valued—or more demanding.

There were also more serious tasks. Powell had to arrange to withdraw from his firm. Professionally, the transition proved remarkably
easy, as Powell had always worked with his team, bringing junior partners and associates along so that they were well known to his clients.
The fruits of this policy were now shared by Powell, who could hand
over his responsibilities to lawyers well-trained to assume them, and

---

* Many questions concerned wiretapping, an issue that came before Powell on
the Supreme Court and is covered in that context in Chapter XII.

by Hunton, Williams, which retained Powell's clients after he left. Financially, Powell was owed his share of the firm's income earned through January 3, 1972, when he formally withdrew from the partnership. The firm also bore the costs of the confirmation effort. The long hours spent by Carter, Freeman, Shenefield, and Goolsby, and by Powell himself, were accounted for as work for the firm and thereby allocated to the entire partnership as foregone income.

Additionally, the Powells had to find a place to live. This problem was solved by Jo's friend Georgine Biggs, who recommended Harbor Square, a modern condominium complex in southwest Washington. Southwest is the smallest quadrant of the city, bounded on the north by a line stretching from the Capitol down the Mall to the Lincoln Memorial and on the east and south by the incurving arc of the Potomac River. Recently revitalized through urban renewal, the area sprouted several large apartment buildings, the best of which, such as Harbor Square, overlooked the river. Georgine and Bill Biggs had moved there with their friends Muriel and Hubert Humphrey. The Humphreys took the penthouse closest to the river, with living and dining rooms facing south toward Potomac Park and Fort McNair, and the Biggs lived one floor below. The Powells moved into the penthouse next door to the Humphreys, with whom they soon shared an unlikely friendship. Georgine Biggs recalls that Humphrey "was very friendly and very forward" and that no one else treated Powell "with quite the same informality."

In addition to the neighbors, Harbor Square had an excellent location. It was not more than ten minutes away from the Supreme Court, even in heavy traffic. Sally Smith took an apartment across the street and drove Powell to and from work. Harbor Square also had easy access to the interstate to Richmond, where Jo expected to return perhaps twice a week. Her mother's reaction to her daughter's departure had not been enthusiastic. "I never thought I would be asked to give up my life for my country," said Mrs. Rucker, but she grew accustomed to living alone, and Jo made the trip south less often than she had thought. The Powells quickly fell into a pattern of returning to Richmond for two months after the Court's term ended in late June and for the Thanksgiving and Christmas holidays. Though they spent most of their time in Washington, they still regarded the house on Rothesay Circle as home.

Powell also had to hire a staff. On the night of Powell's nomination, Justice Black's widow called George Freeman to say that Powell's appointment would have pleased Hugo very much and that Powell should feel free to approach Black's staff. As Sally Smith had already announced her intentions, Powell came with a secretary,* but he also needed three clerks and a messenger. Two of Black's clerks agreed to stay on with the new Justice, and Harvie Wilkinson's son Jay, who by fortuity was scheduled to graduate from law school that January, completed the team. Powell also took Black's messenger, Spencer Campbell, who was a loyal and genial member of the team for several years.

With these arrangements, Powell was ready to undertake his new responsibilities. On January 3, 1972, Powell took the constitutional oath that put him on the federal payroll at sixty thousand dollars a year. Over the years, his salary rose to more than a hundred thousand dollars but never exceeded a small fraction of what he would have earned at Hunton, Williams. Yet, as he was eventually to learn, the nonmonetary compensations of Powell's new job far outweighed any sacrifice he had made to accept it.

---

* Shortly after he arrived at the Court, Powell was authorized to hire a second secretary. An early occupant of that job was an exceptionally able and attractive young Richmonder named Gail Galloway. Galloway became a close friend of the Powells and remained very much a part of the Powell chambers "family" long after she had left to become the Curator of the Supreme Court.

CHAPTER IX

THE SUPREME
COURT

THE CONFERENCE

Immediately after being sworn in on January 7, 1972, Powell attended a reception with family and friends in the East Conference Room. Rehnquist had a similar event in the matching West Conference Room. Neither honoree could stay long. After barely thirty minutes, a buzzer summoned the new Justices to their first Conference.

Powell stopped by his office to pick up his Conference book—a large black notebook with the items for discussion filed in order—and continued down the corridor to the chambers of the Chief Justice. When the Justices rise from the long mahogany bench at which they hear cases and disappear through the red velvet curtains behind them, they descend three steps, cross a corridor, and enter the anteroom of the chambers of the Chief Justice. An opening to the right leads to the Chief's private offices. An opening to the left leads to the Justices' robing room, where nine lockers with brass nameplates house the robes when not in use. Straight ahead through double doors lies the Justices' Conference Room.

The room has the look of an exclusive club—oversized but understated, dominated by wood and leather, arranged more for comfort than for visual effect. Most of the furniture dates from 1935, the year the Supreme Court building opened. The walls are a mellow white oak, and a large rose-colored rug leaves a decorative border of inlaid flooring visible on all sides. The original two-tiered crystal chandelier still hangs from the ceiling, though fluorescent lights now provide illumination. The nearly forty-foot wall opposite the entrance is punctuated by three floor-to-ceiling windows draped in a dark rose brocade. Bookcases stand in the intervals between the windows, and more bookcases line the near wall. On the left as one enters is a fireplace with a black marble hearth and mantel, above which hangs a portrait of Chief Justice John Marshall.*

On the morning of January 7, as at the beginning of every Conference, each Justice shook hands with all the others. Powell took his seat on the near side of a long walnut table, surrounded by high-backed, black leather chairs with plaques bearing the names of the Justices. A wooden pencil tray, a green felt blotter, and notepads of various sizes mark each place.

Other than starting an hour late, Powell's first Conference fit the usual schedule. Traditionally the Conference convenes on Friday mornings—at nine thirty in those weeks when the Court hears oral argument and a half hour later when it does not. Oral argument is scheduled on Mondays, Tuesdays, and Wednesdays from October through May. Most cases are decided the same week they are argued, though the votes taken at Conference are not binding and occasionally change after the Justices see the draft opinions. A Justice who writes for a Conference majority that later falls apart is said to have "lost a Court," meaning that the draft intended as the opinion of the Court became a dissent. Usually, however, the Conference vote holds, and the decision made in the week of oral argument emerges several months later in the published opinions of the Supreme Court.

On that day, the Justices had no business of this sort, as that week they had not heard oral argument. They were occupied instead with the other major category of the Court's work—deciding which cases to hear. Though people often threaten to take a case all the way to the Supreme Court, the option is rarely available. Of the several thousand cases that the Court is asked to hear each year, fewer than two hundred are accepted for briefing and argument. The selection is made by the Justices themselves, who examine preliminary documents called cert petitions—more formally, petitions for a writ of certiorari. If at least four Justices wish to hear a case, they grant the petition and issue a writ of certiorari, and the case is scheduled for oral argument. If they do not wish to hear a case, they deny the petition, and the decision of the lower court is left in place. Though an individual Justice may choose to comment, the Court itself does not explain its reasons for

---

* The portrait, by John Martin, is said to have been the family's favorite. The Chief Justice's daughter gave it to his granddaughter on her wedding day. In 1889 Justice Joseph B. Bradley bought the portrait from the granddaughter for the princely sum of $1,000.

denying review. It simply issues a one-line order recording that the petition for a writ of certiorari is denied.

Contrary to some newspaper accounts, the Justices' refusal to hear a case does not signify that they agree with the lower court's decision. In lawyer's terms, the denial of a cert petition is not precedent; it cannot be taken as approval of the lower court's action. That the Justices refuse to hear a case usually means that it was not thought important enough to warrant their attention.

Deciding which cases are important enough is governed by the "rule of four." By long-standing custom, four votes suffice to grant review. Thus a minority of the Justices can force the Court to decide a case that the majority would rather avoid. Rarely, however, do the votes for and against review precisely track the Justices' views on the merits. Often the Justices who agree that a case should be heard do not agree on how it should be decided.

Virtually every Conference deals with a batch of cert petitions; most also resolve argued cases. Under Chief Justice Burger, whose style of presiding leaned toward the discursive, Friday Conferences proved inadequate for both tasks, and the Justices began meeting briefly on Wednesday afternoons after oral argument. For almost all of Powell's tenure, the Justices met on Wednesdays in argument weeks and on most Fridays throughout the term. Wednesday Conferences dealt with the cases argued that Monday; Friday Conferences handled the cases heard that Tuesday and Wednesday and the weekly crop of cert petitions.

Even before he took the formal oath of office, Powell had busied himself with the cert petitions to be discussed at the January 7 Conference. At the end of the day, the Court had granted review in ten of the 150 cases before it.

Exactly what was said about these cases—or the thousands considered at other Conferences—is known only through the Justices' handwritten notes. No transcript exists. Indeed, no outsider is allowed to attend a Supreme Court Conference. No secretary, law clerk, or messenger is ever present. In the unlikely event that it becomes necessary to interrupt a Conference, a note is handed to the guard standing outside in the hall, who knocks on the door. The Court's most junior Justice answers the door and receives the message.

At Conference, the Justices sit and speak in a certain order. Seating at the Conference table is said to be by seniority, but it actually is determined by a kind of seniority auction. A place that becomes vacant is taken by the most senior Justice who wants it. If, as each vacancy occurs, every Justice chooses to move to the next most senior location, an exact progression is maintained; but if, as sometimes happens, a Justice prefers to stay put, the scheme is changed.

In general, however, a certain pattern prevails. The Chief Justice sits at the head of the table. At the opposite end sits the most senior Associate. Three (usually senior) Justices take their places on the Chief's right, and four (usually junior) Justices sit on his left. As Justice Rehnquist once explained, "there are three levels of elbow room about the conference table"—excellent for the Chief and the most senior Associate, good for three senior Justices arrayed on one side, and "fair to middling" for the four who sit opposite. On January 7, Powell and Rehnquist took the two middle seats on the Chief's left, facing the three more senior Justices who sat on his right.*

THE JUSTICES ALSO SPEAK in order of seniority. At Powell's first Conference and for almost all of his career, the first to speak was the man at the head of the table, Chief Justice Warren Burger.

Born the same year as Powell, Burger grew up in less favored circumstances. After graduating from high school in St. Paul, Minnesota, he had to turn down Princeton, because even with a partial scholarship he could not pay the cost. Instead he spent two years at the University of Minnesota, then sold life insurance during the day to support four years of night classes in law. As a practicing lawyer in St. Paul, Burger entered Republican politics as a supporter of Harold Stassen (before Stassen's national aspirations became a perennial joke). At the 1952 Republican convention, Burger worked for the nomination of General Eisenhower over the more conservative Robert Taft and in the process came to know the man who ultimately put him on the Supreme Court, Eisenhower's running mate, Richard Nixon.

After three years as Assistant Attorney General in the Eisenhower administration, Burger was appointed to the United States Court of Appeals for the District of Columbia Circuit. The D.C. Circuit, as it is called, was one of the nation's most prestigious courts—and one of the most liberal. Burger's conservatism stood out, especially in criminal cases, where his devotion to law and order put him at odds with his defendant-minded colleagues. In 1969 newly elected President Nixon named Burger to succeed Earl Warren as Chief Justice. He had held the post for three years when Powell and Rehnquist joined the Court.

---

*   This statement is based chiefly on a detailed account by Justice Blackmun. Inquiries to the other surviving Justices did not always produce consistent recollections.

At sixty-four, Warren Burger was a handsome, heavyset man, with regular features and a broad forehead topped by a wave of white hair. He spoke in a mellifluous baritone and carried himself with self-conscious dignity. As Senator Everett Dirksen once said, Burger looked, sounded, and acted like a Chief Justice. In fact, he so well fit the part that some said he had come from central casting. On the bench and in the many ceremonial duties of a Chief Justice, Burger performed to perfection.

The Conference was another matter. In reviewing petitions for certiorari, Burger's role was to summarize each case scheduled for discussion. The Justices review all cert petitions, but most are denied without being addressed at Conference. A few days beforehand, the Chief circulates a "discuss list." It includes many more petitions than will actually be granted, as the Chief's job is to list all plausible candidates for Supreme Court review, not just those he wishes to hear. Each Associate Justice may add to the discuss list. If none of the nine thinks a case warrants discussion, the cert petition is automatically denied. If a case makes the discuss list, the Justice who put it there—usually the Chief—presents the case orally before the Justices vote on whether to hear it.

Burger's presentations were anything but crisp. Over time they congealed into set speeches having more to do with the Chief's predispositions than with the merits of the particular case. In criminal cases especially, Burger tended to hold forth on the general theme of law and order rather than to focus on the specific question at hand. Moreover, he often interrupted the others. This habit proved particularly irksome to the junior Justices, who had to listen to the Chief's reiterations while they waited for the chance to have their say. It is doubtful that such trifles made much of an impression at Powell's first Conference, but as the years passed, Burger's windy vagueness became harder to bear.

Also annoying were Burger's passes. When the Justices met to decide argued cases, Burger was expected to announce his vote at the end of his opening statement,* but he sometimes withheld his vote until the others had cast theirs. Though honest indecision would not

---

*   It is often said that at Conference the Justices speak in order of seniority but vote in reverse sequence. This must have been true at one time, for when Powell arrived at the Court, the printed forms used by the Justices to record Conference voting listed the Justices in reverse order of seniority. At no time during Powell's tenure, however, did the Justices actually vote in that sequence. They consistently followed the more economical practice of casting their votes at the end of their statements. Eventually the forms were changed to reflect that practice. Today they list the Justices in order of seniority.

have been faulted, Burger was suspected of manipulation. By custom, the senior Justice in the majority decides who shall write the Court's opinion. By virtue of his office, the Chief Justice is always senior and is therefore entitled to assign the opinion whenever he is in the majority. Since some cases are destined for the history books and others are, in Powell's term, "dogs," the assignment power is valuable. Burger was suspected of postponing his decision so that he could end up in the majority and assign the opinion, even if it meant voting against his real preferences. The practice aroused suspicion and resentment, especially among the Court's liberals, even though Burger's passes usually reflected nothing more than inadequate preparation.

In personal relations, Burger usually maintained a hearty geniality. Powell's thick file of correspondence with the Chief reveals many acts of generosity and helpfulness, many friendly notes and small courtesies. Rehnquist later said that Burger had been "a warm and considerate friend" since the day he arrived at the Court. Powell said much the same thing—and in the main he meant it.

But Burger was also heavy-handed and insensitive. A good example is the case of the stolen footnotes. In 1966 Congress authorized the Tennessee Valley Authority to build a dam on the Little Tennessee River. Twelve years, one statute, and $100 million later, the Supreme Court ordered the project abandoned because of a newly discovered fish. The Endangered Species Act of 1973 ordered federal agencies (including the TVA) to avoid any harm to endangered species. Congress may have had the grizzly bear and whooping crane in mind, but the statute applied equally to the snail darter—a tiny fish of no particular distinction found only in one short stretch of the Little Tennessee. Closing the gates of the dam would raise the water level in the river and destroy the home of the newly discovered snail darter.

After much internal wrangling, the Court decided that the dam could not be used. Burger wrote for the majority: "It may seem curious to some that the survival of a relatively small number of three-inch fish among all the countless millions of species extant would require the permanent halting of a virtually completed dam for which Congress has expended more than $100 million." But, said the Chief Justice, the Endangered Species Act required "precisely that result."

Powell did not think it "curious"; he thought it "absurd." His dissent argued that the statute could not sensibly apply to projects that had been largely completed before the law was enacted and before any endangered species was found. One footnote culled from the trial record information on the insignificance of the little fish. (There were

130 species of darters, Powell reported, with more than forty known species living in the Tennessee River system and new ones discovered every year. The various kinds of darters were so similar that even ichthyologists had trouble telling them apart.) A second footnote quoted a secondary source on the extraordinary breadth of a law construed to protect all endangered species at whatever cost. ("The act covers every animal and plant species, subspecies, and population in the world needing protection," including approximately two million full species, of which perhaps 200,000 are endangered.)

To Powell's astonishment, both footnotes showed up, virtually unchanged, in Burger's next draft of the majority opinion. Thinking there had been some mistake, Powell's clerk went to Burger's clerk, who said that the Chief felt entitled to take from a dissent any material that he thought belonged in the majority opinion. Powell's clerk returned and suggested adding to the dissent a nasty line explaining the origin of the stolen footnotes, but the Justice refused, saying that, "It's no time to get into a pissing contest with a skunk."

Although anxious to avoid a public tiff, Powell was sufficiently perturbed to write a private letter. "Normally, there would be no question about my deferring to the Chief Justice," he wrote Burger. "But I must say that this is the first time in my experience here when another Chambers lifted verbatim language that I had written in an opinion previously circulated. As your opinion for the Court will precede my dissent in the U.S. Reports, a reader will think—contrary to the fact—that I plagiarized yours." In deference to the Chief, Powell agreed to revise his footnotes to eliminate the duplication but added, "I do raise this private flag of gentle protest."

Burger responded that same day with a cheery note telling Powell to "Relax!" While no doubt good advice, Burger's comment completely missed Powell's sense of injury. Anyone who knew Powell would have realized that how extraordinary his "private flag of gentle protest" actually was. Anyone who valued Powell's friendship should have rushed to admit error. Burger's cordial unconcern left Powell with a kind of emotional paper cut—trivial and temporary but nonetheless irksome. Multiply such trivialities many times over, pile them up for years on end, and one has some understanding of the way Burger's personality undermined his leadership.

And if the Chief's high-handedness annoyed Powell, with whom he enjoyed generally good relations, how much more irritating it must have been to the Court's liberals. For them, Burger's failings were not submerged in a broad current of agreement on the cases. For them,

Burger's occasional misstep aggravated an antagonism that was to some degree inevitable. Not only had he replaced the immensely popular Earl Warren, not only was he senior in rank to Justices of longer service and, it must be said, of greater ability, but he opposed what they held dear. Burger came to the Chief Justiceship as an outspoken critic of the Warren Court, and it is scarcely surprising that the enthusiasts of that era greeted his leadership with something less than open arms. To this predictable incompatibility, Burger's personality added an unfortunate irritant.

Perhaps the most fundamental division between Burger and his colleagues grew out of the conflicting conceptions of the nature of his job. Burger was not merely a Justice of the Supreme Court. He was the Chief Justice of the United States. To Burger, the distinction made a world of difference.

Powell's entire responsibility, and that of any Associate Justice, revolved around deciding cases. Burger had that responsibility and many others besides. In deciding cases, the Chief Justice is merely the first among equals. Except for the power to assign opinions, he has no more control over his colleagues than one United States Senator has over another. In other areas, however, the Chief has powers and duties unique to his position. Not only must he preside on the bench and lead the discussion at conference; he must also make innumerable decisions about the Supreme Court building and personnel. Correspondence with Burger during Powell's first few months on the Court hints at the wide-ranging demands on the Chief's time. He had to arrange a memorial service for Hugo Black, select a new Court librarian, approve a standardized "docket sheet" for use in all the chambers, set fees for appointed counsel, and handle countless details of budgets and staffing. And Powell (no doubt his colleagues also) bombarded Burger with special requests. Could the Chief Justice do something about the poor lighting in Powell's office? Did he know that retired Justice Stanley Reed had no one to drive him to and from the Court while his messenger was ill? Could Burger arrange for someone else to fill in?

Burger threw himself into such tasks. A man of varied interests, including sculpting and gardening, Burger handled the daily diet of small problems and undertook improvements in Court life. He redesigned the bench, changing it from a straight line to a shallow "U" so that the Justices on either end could see each other. He renovated the four interior courtyards on the Court's main floor, installing tables and chairs and attractive plantings to make them inviting spaces in

good weather. He redecorated the Supreme Court cafeteria, even helping to select the new glassware and china. He oversaw the maintenance of the aging building, taking an active interest in its appearance
and furnishings.

Burger was further diverted from the business of the Court by a
daunting calendar of public events. Every Justice is deluged with invitations—to dedicate buildings, deliver lectures, receive awards, swear in
officials, and write appreciations of deceased or retiring lawyers and
judges. Most are declined. For the Chief Justice, however, some invitations were almost command performances. Every year, for example, he
made a State of the Judiciary address to the ABA; no one else would have
been suitable. Burger liked pomp and ceremony and perhaps gave such
matters too much time, but to some extent they came with the job.

Burger also served as spokesman for the entire federal judiciary, especially in matters before Congress. He pushed hard for more judges and
for better pay. (For many years even cost-of-living increases were stalled
by legislators' embarrassment at giving themselves a raise and their
insistence that judges be paid no more than they.) Burger encouraged
judicial education programs and lobbied against outmoded procedures
that placed unnecessary burdens on the federal courts. On top of all this
were Burger's nonjudicial responsibilities, such as serving as a regent of
the Smithsonian Institution and a trustee of the National Gallery of Art
and of the Hirshhorn Museum and Sculpture Garden.

Such matters distracted Burger from the business of deciding cases.
The work that Powell and his colleagues saw as the most important
nonpresidential responsibility in the nation was to Burger only part,
and perhaps not the greater part, of the role of Chief Justice. His
slackness in the work they cared about owed something to the fact
that he cared about so much else.

In later years, Powell often said that Warren Burger had done more
to improve the administration of the federal courts than any Chief
Justice since William Howard Taft. The comment is perfectly true. It
is also true that the most consequential decision of Burger's long
career was to devote himself so freely to the administrative, supervisory, and ceremonial activities that competed with his work as a judge.

WHEN WARREN BURGER took his seat at the head of the table that
Friday morning, he must have felt great satisfaction. With two new
conservative Justices, the fifteenth Chief Justice might prevail as well as
preside. Under his leadership, the Burger Court would pull back from

the adventurous egalitarianism of Earl Warren and restore self-restraint to the business of judging. It would reaffirm faith in the popularly elected branches of government and in the competence of local institutions to address local problems without the oversight of federal judges. Most important, it would redress a dangerous imbalance in the criminal law. Burger saw in the rulings of the Warren Court a soft-headed preoccupation with the rights of accused criminals and a neglect of the rights of their victims and of the need for social order. Strengthening the hand of law enforcement was Burger's top priority.

Of course, Burger needed five votes. Looking down the table to his left, he saw two likely prospects. Without prior judicial experience, Powell and Rehnquist were expected to follow their Chief. Besides, both were known to share Burger's concerns, especially on questions of law and order. In speeches and articles, Powell had railed against criminals, radicals, and the New Left, specifically criticizing the Warren Court decisions that Burger found most objectionable. Rehnquist was even more conservative. A disciple of Barry Goldwater and a veteran of John Mitchell's Department of Justice, Rehnquist could be relied on for support. As allies in counterrevolution, Powell and Rehnquist seemed ideal.

On his right, Burger counted another friendly vote. Harry A. Blackmun was a childhood friend. They grew up together in St. Paul, and Blackmun was best man at Burger's wedding. Blackmun took both undergraduate and law degrees in six years at Harvard, then practiced in a large Minneapolis firm until 1950, when he left to become house counsel to the Mayo Clinic. In 1959, President Eisenhower named him to the Eighth Circuit Court of Appeals. It is likely he would have remained there if the Senate had confirmed Haynsworth or Carswell or if Powell had been persuaded to accept an earlier nomination. In his characteristically self-effacing way, Blackmun called himself "old number three"—because he was Nixon's third choice after Haynsworth and Carswell. (Years later, when Justice Anthony Kennedy had a similar experience, Blackmun gaily welcomed him to the number-three club.)

Blackmun was nearly Powell's age, a slight, soft-spoken, fiercely dedicated man. He did his work so carefully and insisted on handling so much of it himself that he soon fell behind in his opinions, earning from the clerks the nickname Fast Harry. Blackmun rarely held forth in Conference (except in tax cases where, as Justice Brennan said, "the rest of us are so stupid"), and even more rarely did the intensity of his feelings break through his calm veneer. Most of the time, he was gentle, kindly, and unassuming.

In a few years, Blackmun would begin a migration to the left and would end up (after Powell retired) as an aging liberal on an increasingly conservative Court, but there was no sign of that future in 1972. When Powell took his seat at the Conference table, Blackmun seemed to be all that President Nixon could have wanted in a Justice—personally upright and professionally competent, a safe, sane, and sensible alternative to the liberal activism of the Warren Court. Outwardly, at least, Blackmun also seemed quite willing to play second fiddle to his friend and sponsor, Warren Burger. He was called the Minnesota Twin, a double reference to his favorite baseball team and to his apparent subservience to the Chief Justice.

With Powell and Rehnquist, Burger and Blackmun would have four votes—only one short of a majority. It would have been ludicrous to suppose that the Nixon appointees would always agree, or that any of them would abandon his own better judgment in favor of solidarity with the others. On the contrary, the natural impulse might have been to distinguish oneself by taking a different line. But on the crucial issues, the Nixon Justices could be expected, more often than not, to end up on the same side. Each of them was more conservative than any of the holdovers from the Warren Court. Together they formed a bloc of four, loosely united by outlook and sympathy, and—apparently— poised under the leadership of Chief Justice Burger to remake American constitutional law.

AGAINST THESE FOUR stood three outspoken liberals. Remote and distracted at the opposite end of the table from Chief Justice Burger slouched the enigmatic, inspiring, and infuriating figure of William O. Douglas. Although only nine years older than Powell, Douglas seemed, by reason of his early fame and longevity on the Court, to be of an entirely different generation. Before Powell had a law degree, Douglas was Sterling Professor of Law at Yale and was called the "most outstanding law professor in the nation." In 1934, when Powell was coming early and staying late at the offices of Andrew Christian, Douglas was a member of the powerful Securities and Exchange Commission. And in 1939, while Powell endured the tutelage of Thomas Benjamin Gay, William O. Douglas came to the Supreme Court.

He arrived during the Chief Justiceship of Charles Evans Hughes, the man who had resigned from the Supreme Court in 1916 to run against President Woodrow Wilson, but returned fourteen years later as the nation's eleventh Chief Justice. Hughes was succeeded by Harlan Fiske Stone, Stone by Fred M. Vinson, Vinson by Earl Warren, and Warren by Warren Burger. Now in Burger's third year, Douglas was by a margin of seventeen years the Court's most senior Justice—and surely its most controversial.

Douglas was renowned as an indomitable individualist, an invincible human spirit who triumphed over adversity, defied conventional expectations, and "dared to be different." Before Douglas was six, his father died, leaving an impoverished widow and a child so weakened by polio that he was expected to lose the use of his legs and to succumb by forty. Douglas did neither. He fought his affliction by walking, always alone, in the foothills of Washington's Cascade Mountains, trying first to go up without stopping, then without changing pace, and finally to climb while whistling. Douglas conquered his frailty and came away with a lifelong love of the wilderness and of the idea of himself in heroic struggle against great odds.

Easily the Court's quickest intellect, Douglas wrote with a lightning facility that Powell could only envy. When Douglas expected to be in the minority, he would often dictate a dissent on the same day as oral argument, before his colleagues had even voted, and put it aside for several months. When the majority opinion was eventually circulated, Douglas's dissent would immediately follow.

When Powell knew Douglas, the old man retained his dazzling speed, but by this time the full force of his brilliance rarely came through in his opinions—at least not in conventional lawyerly style. Douglas wrote with the looseness of a journalist. He scorned the accepted conventions of legal reasoning and peppered his opinions with quotations, sociological observations, and personal comments. While admirers thought his work refreshingly free of cant, critics found it slapdash; but all agreed that Douglas's voice was uniquely his own. Indeed, that may have been partly the point. Rehnquist later said that Douglas seemed disappointed if others agreed with him, "because he would therefore be unable to write a stinging dissent."

After thirty years on a collegial court, Douglas was anything but collegial. He seldom joined in questioning the lawyers during oral argument, but instead worked away at his own writing from his place on the bench. In Conference he rarely said more than was necessary to record his vote. When he did say more, it was often worse. After Burger explained at length his vote to affirm, Douglas might follow with, "Chief, for the reasons you have so well expressed, I vote to reverse."

In ways great and small, Douglas discomforted his colleagues. When the Court had a single car for use by all eight Associate Justices,

Douglas treated it as his own. He never apologized, never explained, and never gave any thought to the inconvenience of others. Of far greater moment, he routinely left town before the end of the Court's term. Douglas—who said publicly that his job required only four days a week—typically finished his opinions in early June. As his colleagues struggled to complete theirs, he moved for the summer to his mountain home in Goose Prairie, Washington. There was no phone. If another Justice needed him, he could write and ask Douglas to call from a pay phone nearby, but otherwise Douglas was out of town and out of touch during the Court's most hectic season. Sometimes his absence was consequential, as when he told Powell that he would have joined Powell's dissent of the previous summer if only he had seen it in time. Douglas's premature departure infuriated his colleagues. As one said, "If every justice had done that, the Court couldn't have functioned."

Douglas had great magnetism. He could, when it pleased him, be relaxed, loquacious, and charming. He delighted Powell with a note from China saying that the Chinese disliked Powell's decision allowing rich school districts and poor school districts, but that they applauded his opinion giving aliens the right to practice law. He inspired in others not only admiration but affection and fierce devotion. Yet Douglas could also be brutal. Revered outside the Court as a protector of the powerless, Douglas in person despised weakness and often made life miserable for those under his control. Law clerks were routinely "fired" for incompetence, including one poor fellow cashiered by telephone before he had even met the Justice (though he, like the others, was allowed to return after a few days). A year with Douglas was said to be like fifty-two weeks of boot camp. Douglas used a buzzer to summon his clerks to consultations they rarely approached without dread. As one recalled, "It is difficult to convey, unless you went through it, the absolute terror that a Douglas clerk felt at the thought of making a mistake." Secretaries, messengers, and elevator operators also felt the sting of his disdain.

To his credit, Douglas showed the same face to those who were not defenseless. He feuded with Felix Frankfurter and delighted in needling Chief Justice Burger. Douglas even quarreled with fellow liberals. There was strain between Douglas and Hugo Black, and for two or three years Douglas barely spoke to Chief Justice Warren. Most hurtful of all was his attitude toward Thurgood Marshall. Douglas said in print that Marshall was put on the Court "simply because he was black" and in private treated Marshall with an abruptness approaching contempt. Many years later, Justice Brennan recalled that Douglas "never liked" Marshall and that Marshall, in light of his own experience, "could never really believe it wasn't race."

In view of this record, it is surprising that this irascible old liberal got on well with the Court's newest members. Rehnquist and Douglas were much alike—smart, quick, and confident, with an open, informal personal style. The two hit it off so well that the Rehnquists spent several days with the Douglases at their retreat in Goose Prairie. Douglas's relations with Powell, while more reserved, were nevertheless cordial. Although much too conservative for Douglas's taste, Powell was an accomplished lawyer and free of the pompous self-importance that Douglas could not resist deflating. By Douglas's standards, he treated Powell well.

For his own part, Powell's view of his senior colleague fractured into two quite different reactions. Privately, he thought Douglas "a real SOB." The incident that stuck in his mind occurred two years before Powell joined the Court, when he and Jo and daughter Molly attended an ABA meeting in Dallas. Douglas and his fourth wife, Cathy, were also present. Molly became friendly with Cathy, whom all the Powells thought a "really wonderful person." The two young women discovered that each was headed for law school in the fall, Cathy Douglas to American University and Molly Powell to the University of Virginia. At one point, Cathy introduced Molly to her husband, explaining, "She's Lewis Powell's daughter, and she's starting law school this fall at the University of Virginia." Without acknowledging Molly, Douglas merely growled to his wife, "That is a helluva lot better school than the one you're going to." Cathy may not have minded the remark, but for the Powells, it came to typify Douglas's bullying and rudeness.

On the other hand, Powell admired Douglas's intellect—and perhaps feared his tongue. Douglas had been a Justice so long that he became linked in Powell's mind with the Court itself, and some of the reverence that Powell felt for the institution rubbed off on his most senior colleague. These reactions combined in a wary respect, a veneration that was entirely genuine though unaccompanied by affection.

DOUGLAS HAD NO close confidants on the Court, but Justices Brennan and Marshall were frequent allies. In 1972 William J. Brennan, Jr., was in the sixteenth of thirty-four years on the Court. When he retired he would quite plausibly be thought "the most influential Justice of the Supreme Court since John Marshall." Even his critics at the conservative *National Review* admitted that "no individual in this country, on or off the Court, has had a more profound and sustained impact upon public policy in the United States" than Justice Brennan.

The directions of his influence were liberal and humane. He championed civil rights and civil liberties, especially the freedoms of speech and press, and supported expanded procedural protections for persons accused of crime. He favored federal power over states' rights and judicial authority over the elected branches of government. Brennan's genius lay in his systemic perspective. He devised mechanisms for federal courts to second-guess state criminal convictions and created avenues for federal judicial oversight of government at all levels. Not all of Brennan's innovations have survived, but it is nonetheless true that his legacy is writ large across the face of American constitutional law.

Brennan was born to Irish immigrants in Newark, New Jersey, where his father was a brewery worker, labor activist, and local politician. After attending the Wharton School at the University of Pennsylvania and Harvard Law School, the son returned to Newark to practice law. He went on the state bench in 1949 and three years later was promoted to the New Jersey Supreme Court. As a state judge, Brennan became known for efforts to speed up trials and relieve court congestion. As is so often true, his appointment to the Supreme Court of the United States owed much to chance. In 1956 the Chief Justice of New Jersey, Arthur Vanderbilt, was scheduled to give the keynote address at a large Washington conference on the problem of overburdened courts. Two days before the meeting, Vanderbilt fell ill, and Brennan went in his place. His speech impressed U.S. Attorney General Herbert Brownell, who, when a Supreme Court vacancy opened four months later, contemplated the electoral advantages to President Eisenhower of appointing an Irish Catholic Democrat from the Northeast and recommended Brennan.

When the civil rights movement gained ground in the late 1950s and early 1960s, Bill Brennan was the right man in the right place at the right time. He espoused equality and human dignity at a time when they were the most insistent and compelling demands in the nation. He believed in the broad reach of federal power at a time when the defaults and malefactions of many states (especially in the South) were there for all to see. He believed in judicial activism (in desegregating schools, reforming prisons, restraining police) at a time when no one else was willing to act. Whether Brennan's beliefs preceded the events or were spawned by them, in the 1960s Brennan was a judge in tune with the times.

Brennan's influence arose not only on the power of his ideas and the acuity of his intellect, but also from the warmth of his personality. Unlike Douglas, who relished the lonely protest, Brennan had an instinct for coalition. Except in his later years, when the habit of strident dissent sometimes overcame him, he rarely missed an opportunity to agree. If ever there was an effective Court politician, it was William Brennan. At five feet six inches, he reminded people of a leprechaun—buoyant, irrepressibly optimistic, so vivacious and lively that he was often described as twinkling. In Brennan's presence, even those who knew better found it hard to resist feeling that they were special.

Personal relations at the Supreme Court are not always easy. Holmes is said to have described the Justices as "nine scorpions in a bottle." They have also been compared to partners in an arranged marriage with no possibility of divorce. The tensions of collective decision-making have been said (though not by a Justice) to generate "debilitating personal rivalries, resentments, apathy, burnout, idiosyncrasy, and a shrill and nasty rhetoric of invective." Yet Brennan could say at the end of his career, "I have sat now with about a fifth of all the Supreme Court Justices there have been, and I have never had a cross word with one of them. Not with a single one of them." Taken literally, the statement strains credulity, but it evidences Brennan's determination to get along. Though the effects of his personality are hard to trace, it is impossible not to believe that Brennan's success as a Justice owed something to his warmth as a friend.

Most important, Brennan had the votes. During the 1960s, the liberal majority on the Warren Court grew increasingly secure. By the beginning of the last year of that decade, there were six Justices who could more or less safely be described as liberal.* It is no accident that Brennan's most important victories came in the years when the mastermind of the Warren Court had a host of allies. By the time Powell took his seat on the opposite side of the conference table in 1972, the prospects for judicial liberalism had dramatically dimmed. The number of outright liberals on the Court had declined to three. Though Brennan had triumphs yet to come, from this time forward, he was more and more often in dissent.

THURGOOD MARSHALL WAS the Court's third liberal. Although Powell knew Marshall only as a Justice of the Supreme Court, the weight of his achievement lay elsewhere. Alone among the Justices, Marshall's reputation reached beyond the law and lawyers. Only Marshall was so often accosted by admirers that he found it difficult to dine in public.

---

*   Chief Justice Warren and Justices Black, Douglas, Brennan, Fortas, and Marshall.

Only Marshall would find himself played by the elegant Sidney Poitier in a television mini-series (though a former clerk told him it should have been Redd Foxx). Only Marshall would have claimed the attention of biographers and historians if he had never been named to the Supreme Court. To call him "the most important lawyer of the 20th century" was not at all far-fetched.

The roots of that judgment lay not in Marshall's work on the bench but in his work before it—in the masterful twenty-year litigation campaign, conducted by the great-grandson of a slave, to defeat racial segregation. Before he became Solicitor General of the United States, Marshall appeared before the Supreme Court in thirty-two cases. He won twenty-nine. More than with any of the hundreds of cases decided by Justice Thurgood Marshall, his name will forever be linked with the victory in one case argued by lawyer Thurgood Marshall—*Brown v. Board of Education*. In the words of a fellow civil rights activist, Marshall brought his people the Constitution of the United States "like Moses brought his people the Ten Commandments." He was an authentic American hero.

For these prodigious labors, Marshall eventually received establishment recognition. In 1961, President Kennedy named him to the Second Circuit Court of Appeals. In 1965, President Johnson made him Solicitor General and two years later appointed him to the Supreme Court. (Johnson liked to complain to Marshall of the "political hell" Marshall's nomination had caused, saying that Vietnam was "an excuse" used to get back at him for putting the first black on the Supreme Court.)

Marshall's appointment to the Supreme Court proved a curiously mixed blessing. On the one hand, it crowned his career and cemented his place in history. After years of knocking at the door of southern courthouses, Marshall sat on the country's highest bench. After years of asking whites for simple justice, Marshall could now command it. The southern judges and lawyers who had humiliated and tried (unsuccessfully) to intimidate Thurgood Marshall now had to do what he said. The Constitution those judges swore to defend was now construed by him. It is hard to imagine a transformation more complete—or more gratifying.

On the other hand, Marshall's elevation to the Supreme Court placed him in a situation for which he was not ideally suited. On the great questions of equality and racial justice for which Marshall had so long fought, he spoke with a force and passion that never dimmed. He always championed the underdog. But the Court also deals with lesser questions, matters of securities or tax or environmental law, technically complex issues embedded in intricate, sometimes labyrinthine, federal statutes. In these cases, Marshall seemed not much interested. For him, the law was a battering ram to break down barriers to the constitutionally guaranteed rights. His success as a litigator owed more to perseverance and courage than to an intellectual interest in the law. And Marshall was a master of anecdote, always ready with a telling story or earthy image to drive his point home. He was dramatic, often humorous, sometimes caustic, and stunningly effective.

Marshall's style was not ideally suited to his new role as a Justice. He faced too many problems that did not yield to analysis by anecdote. In the arcane world of administrative law or state taxation of interstate businesses or the jurisdiction of the federal courts, Marshall's broad commitments seemed out of place. His tendency to see every issue in bright lines and stark contrasts seemed crude and escapist when attention shifted to the many shades of gray.

In time, Marshall became bored. In voting, he followed the lead of Justice Brennan, to whom he grew closer as the years went by. In most terms, they voted with each other more regularly than did any other two Justices. Sometimes, their percentage of agreement reached astonishing heights. "Brennan and Marshall" became almost a hyphenated entity, predictably aligned in the general run of cases and almost certain to vote together on the really important ones. Marshall's dependence on his senior colleague became more apparent as he lost his hearing. He would lean over to Blackmun, who sat next to him at conference, and ask, "Harry, how did Brennan vote?" If told that Brennan had voted to affirm, Marshall would say simply, "Chief, I vote to affirm."

Opinion writing did not interest him. He turned more and more of it over to his clerks, who were, year in and year out, exceptionally talented young lawyers. Marshall himself spent hours each day telling stories and watching daytime television. He told his clerks precisely and emphatically what to do, then let them do it. As the results were often impressive, he enjoyed a reputation outside the Court for scholarly opinions, but inside the Court, he often seemed uninformed and disengaged.

To some of his colleagues he also seemed withdrawn and vaguely hostile. Within two years of Marshall's appointment to the Supreme Court, the tide of judicial liberalism had begun to ebb. From 1972 until his retirement in 1991, Marshall saw support for the values he held dear steadily eroding, and he could not suppress his indignation. In race cases particularly, Marshall grew increasingly bitter. He stopped short of calling his colleagues racist—but just barely. At the least, he thought them insensitive. "What do they know about Negroes?" he asked in 1990. "You can't name one member of this Court who [knew] anything about Negroes before he came to this Court." Most of all he resented the unwillingness of some of his colleagues to embrace minority preferences as a way of redressing past injustice. "There's not a white man in this country who can say, 'I never benefited by being white,'" insisted Marshall. "There's not a white man in the country who can say it."

Although frustrated by his colleagues' views, Marshall did little to try to change them. His style was more confrontational than persuasive. In Conference, he told tales of prejudice in the segregated South, funny stories that invited his colleagues to laugh with him but that also left an aftertaste of rebuke. Sometimes Marshall abandoned humor for caustic sarcasm. What he did not do was to attempt to engage the sympathies of other Justices in one-on-one conversation. Quick to take offense, he was too proud to try to educate his colleagues to his point of view—and too suspicious of their motives to think it worthwhile to try.

Marshall's relations with Powell fit this pattern. In nearly sixteen years of joint service, Marshall came to Powell's chambers only once (and that on a family matter) and never asked Powell to visit him. The Powells invited the Marshalls to dinner in their apartment, which was a pleasant occasion, but the invitation was not reciprocated. In the words of another Justice, "Thurgood held Lewis at a distance."

And Marshall's dealings with Powell were further burdened by memories of the Old South. Powell's courtly ways and soft Virginia accent reminded Marshall of the educated and impeccably well mannered southerners who for so long had maintained the subjugation of blacks. Powell once made the mistake of saying in Conference that only he and Thurgood would understand a certain point because they were the only southerners. Marshall's head snapped up in dismay. He came from the border state of Maryland, but in a more fundamental way than geography, he and Powell came from different worlds.

Despite these crosscurrents of politics and personality, Marshall and Powell maintained a cordial relationship. In an interview after he retired, Marshall happily recalled the time in January 1987 when a two-foot snowfall left large areas of northern Virginia without electricity. Included was Marshall's home in Lake Barcroft, a small community surrounding a 140-acre private lake eight miles from D.C. Lake Barcroft was not high on the power company's repair list. As the hours turned into days, Marshall began telephoning everyone he could think of, including the local representative of the power company, until finally his clerks suggested that he call Powell. When he did, Powell called his former partner T. Justin Moore, Jr., by that time chairman of the Virginia Electric and Power Co., who promptly called Marshall. "The next thing I knew," said Marshall, "there were *three* trucks in front of the house." Not only did Marshall get his electricity restored, but he had one more confirmation of the power of Lewis Powell and all the other rich white men who ran the South to get whatever they wanted by private contacts.

In January 1972, when Marshall and Powell first sat down on opposite sides of the conference table, this relationship lay in the future, but already they faced a great divide in background and outlook. Marshall could see that his views would not flourish in the changed climate of the Burger Court.

AT TWO CORNERS of the Conference table but in the political center of the Court sat Potter Stewart and Byron White. From Powell's first day, Stewart was his closest friend among the Justices. Though younger than Powell, Stewart was fourteen years his senior on the Supreme Court, having been appointed in 1958 at the age of forty-three. Born to a prominent Ohio family with a tradition of public service, Stewart was superbly educated at Hotchkiss, Yale, Cambridge, and the Yale Law School. After taking his law degree, Stewart served as a naval officer in World War II before returning to Cincinnati to practice corporate law.

Like Powell, Stewart took an active interest in his city's affairs and held local office. Like Powell, Stewart had not only the skills but also the cast of mind of a good lawyer. With a penetrating intelligence and a eye for detail, Stewart paid careful attention to briefs and oral argument. Though a fine writer with a gift for pungent expression, Stewart avoided runaway rhetoric. He approached his job in terms of cases, not causes, and disdained sweeping generalities. In the words of a former clerk, Stewart's "most consistent philosophy was his skepticism about the virtues of apparently consistent philosophies." Like Powell, he would often earn praise as a lawyer's lawyer and a judge's judge.

Stewart and Powell were alike not only in temperament and background but also in politics. Stewart was a moderate Republican. While Powell called himself a Virginia Democrat, he voted for Republicans in national elections. Both were friendly with George Bush, favoring him in 1980 over the more conservative Ronald Reagan. Stewart and

Powell even had the same judicial hero. As a junior Justice on the Warren Court, Stewart allied himself with John Harlan. Though Powell never sat with Harlan, he took him as the model of what a judge should be—a fair-minded arbiter of disputes, carefully adapting past precedents to present realities in a process more pragmatic than ideological. This tradition was handed down from Harlan to Stewart to Powell. Stewart and Powell did not always agree, but they shared a style of judging and a conception of their responsibilities that made it easy for them to understand and respect differences of opinion. As Powell later recollected, "I felt particularly free to talk to Potter, and when I was having difficulty making up my mind on a case, whether Potter and I voted the same way or not, I felt free to talk to him."

Personally, Stewart was hard not to like. He was affable and witty, with an infectious interest in sports and politics and a keen sense of fun. He was robust in friendship and secure in his own abilities but genuinely modest and solicitous of others. Later Powell remembered that they had never exchanged a harsh word. The wives were as compatible as their husbands, so that the two couples traded dinner invitations every few months. Potter Stewart was as close as Powell came to replicating in Washington the intimate friendship that he enjoyed in Richmond with Harvie Wilkinson, and Stewart's retirement in 1981 left a gap in Powell's life.

Powell's relations with the other centrist Justice were more complicated. Byron R. White was one of the most impressive individuals ever to sit on the Supreme Court and, as a judge, one of the most difficult to characterize. White grew up in a small Colorado town where he learned the virtues of hard work. He graduated from the University of Colorado with one of the highest grade point averages ever achieved there and with ten varsity letters in three sports. His All-American performance at tailback earned him the nickname "Whizzer" and a shot at the National Football League. As a rookie with a last-place team (the future Pittsburgh Steelers), he led the NFL in rushing. White left football to accept a Rhodes Scholarship to Oxford, then entered the Yale Law School, where he led his first-year class. He interrupted law school to make money in football, and in 1940–41 he again led the NFL in rushing (this time with the Detroit Lions). Pearl Harbor ended White's football career. After four years as a naval officer in the South Pacific, he graduated from Yale, clerked for Chief Justice Fred Vinson, and returned to Colorado to practice law.

Along the way, White repeatedly crossed paths with Jack Kennedy. They met in Europe in 1939, when Kennedy's father was Ambassador to the Court of St. James's, again in the South Pacific, when Kennedy commanded PT-109, and again in Washington, when Kennedy was a freshman Congressman and White a clerk at the Supreme Court. White organized Kennedy's Colorado campaign and after the victory over Richard Nixon became Deputy Attorney General under Robert Kennedy. Fifteen months later, the President named White to the Supreme Court, saying, entirely without hyperbole, that the forty-four-year-old nominee "has excelled in everything he has attempted."

As a Justice, White was expected to be more or less liberal. Reports at the time said that he had been preferred over Powell's friend and Harvard classmate Paul Freund on the ground that Freund was politically less reliable. Once on the Supreme Court, however, White proved anything but predictable. He has been described as everything from a "Kennedy liberal" to a "fierce conservative" to a "loner," "maverick," and "mystery man." The confusion resulted partly from White's disparate views in various areas of the law. He was liberal on school desegregation and busing but conservative on affirmative action, energetic in attacking sex discrimination but opposed to a constitutional right of abortion, broad in his support of government regulation of the economy but narrow in his conception of free speech. This range of opinions is difficult to comprehend under any one label.

White's views also changed over time. Relative to other Justices, White's long career on the Court showed a drift to the right. In the 1960s White agreed most often with Justice Brennan, but by the early 1980s he voted most regularly with Chief Justice Burger. In between was a decade of "swing" voting that defies easy description.

When Powell and Rehnquist arrived in 1972, they found Byron White at the statistical center of the Court. In that first year, the Justices split five–four in twenty-one decisions. White was in the majority in eighteen. The most common pattern was a standoff between the Nixon appointees on the one hand and Justices Douglas, Brennan, Stewart, and Marshall on the other, with White holding the balance of power between them. Eight times he voted with the four Nixon appointees against his colleagues from the Warren Court. Seven times he voted with the holdovers against the Nixon four. In both directions, White's vote was decisive. Statistically, at least, he was "leading from the center."

But although White could have been a superb military commander, he did not have the conviviality for leadership on the Supreme Court. At the time of Powell's first conference, White was fifty-three years old, broad-shouldered and lantern-jawed, with an iron grip that made grown men wince. On the basketball court tucked away in the attic above the courtroom, White held his own with law clerks half his age. He made up for a loss of speed with toughness and an intensely competitive spirit. The same traits surfaced in the Conference room. White could be gracious and charming—Jo Powell thought he was "lovely"—but he could also be abrupt, even abrasive, intolerant of weakness, and scornful of indecision.

Years later, Powell insisted that he and White had always been friends, but to others it was not clear that the warm relationship between them had a fast start. It may have taken some time for White to discern the strength that lay beneath Powell's gentleness, and it is clear that White's patience was occasionally exhausted by Powell's fastidious interest in all sides of every issue. Once White grew so exasperated with Powell's carefulness that he snapped his pencil in Powell's face and said he should make up his damn mind. For his part, Powell sometimes resented the contentiousness of White's opinions. In 1974 when the White clerks took Powell to lunch, one of them said that the invitation was in part an attempt to make amends for the hard feelings that had arisen between the two chambers. Powell "graciously—but pointedly—replied that it would take more than one lunch to do that."

But if at first personality differences kept White and Powell apart, time drew them together. As they grew accustomed to one another, the regard each felt for the other deepened into genuine fondness, and by the time Powell retired, he was happy to count White as a close friend. In 1972, however, it was Stewart, not White, who elicited Powell's affection and to whom Powell looked for guidance. Powell regarded White with more distanced admiration.

SUCH WAS THE MEMBERSHIP at Powell's first Conference. While no knowledgeable observer expected bloc voting, in the main the alignment seemed clear: four conservatives against three liberals with two Justices in the middle. This lineup supported three predictions about the future course of the Supreme Court. First, there would be no strong charge to the left or right but many close decisions clustering in the middle of the political spectrum. This forecast proved accurate. The era that began in January 1972 was neither consistently liberal nor consistently conservative but decidedly mixed. It was an era of judicial balance.

Second, there would probably be a slight overall tilt toward the conservative side. This much seemed implicit in the numbers. Against the three liberal holdovers from the Warren Court stood the Nixon four. In order to prevail, Douglas, Brennan, and Marshall would have to attract *both* of the Court's swing votes. Burger, Blackmun, Powell, and Rehnquist could win with only one. This prediction also held true, at least in the main, although the picture looks different depending on where one chooses to focus.

A third prediction was that the decisive voices on the Burger Court would be those of Justices Stewart and White. The political alignment of their colleagues as well as their own substantial talents marked Stewart and White as key players, as in fact they were. What was not apparent in 1972 was that Stewart and White would share the middle ground with Powell and also with Blackmun. Ideological movements within the Court and the addition of new Justices over the years produced currents and crosscurrents that no one could have foreseen. The voice that emerged from the mixed messages and split decisions as the most nearly determinative member of the Burger Court was neither Stewart nor White, but Powell.

LIFE IN THE MARBLE PALACE

From this time forward, Powell's professional life centered on his fellow Justices. The broad circle of lawyers and clients who had populated the world of Powell's private practice was now replaced by an inner sanctum of nine jurists. And for nearly a generation the group remained remarkably stable. Of the eight other Justices present at Powell's first Conference, five attended his last Conference nearly sixteen years later. On average there was only one new face every five years.

This select and nearly unchanging fraternity worked in a fitting style and setting. There was no hurrying back and forth across the American landscape to win support for their positions, no currying favor with this group or that, no campaigning or electioneering to disrupt their deliberations. The Justices simply worked and waited. Sooner or later the great issues of the day would come to the Supreme Court. They would come not hastily but at the measured pace of appellate litigation, and they would be heard when the Justices chose to hear them. The ultimate decisions would be far removed from the clash and clamor of political debate, for the traditions and methods of adjudication are as insulated as possible from considerations of partisan advantage or personal gain. It seems appropriate, therefore, that the Justices' physical surroundings are as grand as their responsibilities—and as carefully screened from the stresses and pressures of daily life. Given the detached and Olympian perspective that the Justices seek to attain, it is fitting that they work in the splendid isolation of a marble palace.

For most of the nation's history, the Supreme Court heard cases in the U.S. Capitol and worked chiefly in their homes or lodgings. Before the Civil War, the Justices sat in a courtroom in the building's basement. When two new wings for the House and Senate were added to the Capitol in 1861, the Supreme Court moved upstairs to the old Senate chamber. Not until 1935 did the nation's highest court have its own building.

Construction on the new facility began in 1931. Amid the declining prices of the Depression, the building was completed *and* furnished for $500,000 less than the $9.75 million appropriated by Congress. Facing west toward the Capitol, the structure presents an imposing facade of sixteen Corinthian columns supporting a sculptured pediment. The central portion of the building rises four stories above the surrounding plaza, with three-story wings on either side. The whole of the exterior, including the plaza, is clad in white marble. The overall effect rivals the grandeur of a Greek temple.

Inside, restraint yields to opulence. Massive bronze doors open into a vestibule leading to the Great Hall, a room of monumental proportions. Marble columns, interspersed with busts of former Chief Justices, line the walls. At the far end are the doors to the courtroom, which is also of grand scale. Here different shades of Spanish and Italian marble lend a subtly decorative touch. Above the columns that line the walls of the courtroom are carved marble panels and above them, over forty feet from the floor, an elaborately ornamented plaster ceiling in terra-cotta, baby blue, and white medallions with gold leaf. The bench sits at the far end of the courtroom against the backdrop of white marble and red velvet.

The Great Hall and the courtroom are aligned on the east-west axis. A transverse corridor forms a cross, with a courtyard and fountain in each quadrant, and two wings have the effect of enclosing the central core and its courtyards in a large rectangle. It is here on the outer perimeter of the north and south wings that the Justices have their chambers.

Originally, the rear of the building accommodated all the Justices' chambers, providing each with a suite of three rooms (for the Justice, his secretary, and one law clerk). The front half, which was open to the public, housed various Court officers. As the Justices's staff increased, they took over the space occupied by the administrative offices, which were moved to a lower floor. For the first few months of his service,

Powell used Justice Black's former rooms in the rear of the building, but in the summer of 1972 he moved into one of two new chambers created in the southeast corner of the building, a space previously occupied by the Clerk of the Court. (This remodeling allowed the expansion of existing chambers and the use of two smaller suites by retired Justices.)

Powell's new chambers, which he kept until retirement, were on the front of the building in the south wing. He had one large room for himself, another for Sally Smith (soon to be joined by a second secretary) and Spencer Campbell, and two smaller rooms for three clerks. (The suite had two bathrooms, one in the Justice's private office and another shared by the rest of the staff.) In these new quarters, Powell had to do without a working fireplace, but he had much more space and a splendid view of the U.S. Capitol.

To get to the robing room or the Justices' Conference Room, Powell would walk to the back of the building by the means of the long corridor leading around the south wing. Along the way he would pass the chambers of Justices Blackmun, Douglas, Brennan, and Marshall. If he continued around the north wing, he would come to the chambers of Justices Stewart, White, and Rehnquist, and retired Chief Justice Earl Warren, whose rooms were directly opposite Powell's on the other side of the Great Hall.

Powell sometimes made this circuit for exercise in bad weather, though more often he would walk around the outside of the building. There he was rarely recognized.* In Richmond, he could not walk down the street without being stopped and greeted, but in Washington but he could go almost anywhere without attracting notice. Even at the Court, he was sometimes anonymous. *New York Times* reporter Linda Greenhouse once saw tourists hand Powell their camera and ask him to take their photograph, which Powell did and "went on his quiet way." Court personnel were another matter. Guards stationed at the intersections of the corridors would rise, if seated, to greet an approaching Justice. Other Court employees showed the

---

*   Even when Powell identified himself as a Supreme Court Justice, it sometimes did no good. On his appointment to the Court, Powell resigned from the University Club (because he would rarely be in New York) but was told that he could continue to use the club as an honorary member. When the Powells stayed there some years later, they were awakened after retiring by a clerk who said that he could find no record of membership, honorary or otherwise, and that, Supreme Court Justice or not, Powell would have to leave. Luckily, Powell remembered the name of a lawyer on the club's board, who successfully intervened with the clerk.

same courtesy, and since Powell treated everyone with friendly respect, he was soon a staff favorite. The calm, unhurried civility that prevailed inside the Supreme Court provided a suitable atmosphere for the Justices' deliberations.

Although in the 1970s the rising threat of terrorism made everyone more conscious of security risks, mostly the guards kept their eyes on the tourists waiting in the Great Hall for the chance to watch oral argument. Every now and then a protester would have to be removed from the courtroom, but many incidents were avoided by careful observation of those standing in line. If someone was overheard threatening disruption, he or she would be questioned before entering the courtroom. If an individual looked unstable or unruly, the guards would save an adjacent seat for one of their number, who would sit down next to the potential troublemaker. There were of course always a few groupies who tried to slip down the corridor to the Justices' chambers for a private chat. One woman of catholic taste fell in love first with Douglas and then with Burger, showing her devotion to both by faithful attendance at all Court sessions. Eventually wooden gates were erected to bar access to the private areas, and an airport screening device was installed at the public entrances. Such precautions focused on the Supreme Court building itself, as it was considered the likely scene of any disturbance or threat. Outside the building the Justices, secure in their anonymity, rarely had to give a thought to personal safety.

In Powell's case, the only exception had from the outset the quality of an opera buffo. On October 2, 1978, a young Briton named David Robson wandered into the Virginia Supreme Court in Richmond, where he told a police officer that he would like to see Justice Powell. On discovering that the long, wrapped object protruding from the man's knapsack was a loaded high-powered rifle with a telescopic sight, the officer put Robson under arrest for carrying a concealed weapon. Since Robson had been looking for Powell, the FBI and the Supreme Court security were immediately notified and tried (unsuccessfully) to get Powell to agree to twenty-four-hour guards.

It turned out that Robson's mother had worked with Powell in London during the war and had renewed the acquaintance when she and her husband ran into the Powells in Kenya in 1969. Their son, accustomed to the less regulated environment of Kenya, had been hitchhiking across the United States and had purchased the rifle for protection while sleeping outdoors. The five days it took to verify these facts young Robson spent in jail. (He was treated deferentially

by the other prisoners, who thought he was a professional—if inept—
"hit man.") When Robson was released, he went to the Court to apol-
ogize for all the trouble and was received by Powell under the watchful
eye of Lt. James Zagami, who stood in the open door and made sure
the young man was always "within arm's reach."

WORKING IN THE MARBLE palace was comfortable and civilized but also
slightly antiquated. Powell had only one secretary, who was barely able
to keep up with his dictation. She had no time for the clerks, who used
the hunt-and-peck method to do their own typing. Reduced to working with scratched-out and hand-edited drafts that he would never
have tolerated in private practice, Powell successfully lobbied for
authorization to hire a second secretary. His three law clerks seemed a
sufficient number to the Justices who had long worked with two, but
to Powell, fresh from managing a large team of partners and associates
at Hunton, Williams, it seemed a distressingly small staff. In 1974
funds were approved for a fourth clerk. Not only personnel was wanting. The lights in Powell's office were so dim that he had to read next
to a window. At Powell's instigation, Burger ordered the installation of
fluorescent lighting throughout the building. A few years later Powell's
chambers (specifically his then second secretary, Linda Blanford) took
the lead in introducing word processors to the Court and creating an
electronic link to the print shop in the basement.

Unlike his colleagues, most of whom had been judges for years,
Powell functioned like a senior partner. If the staff is inadequate, hire
more. If modern equipment could improve office efficiency, buy it.
Powell was shocked to learn that only a year before he came the Court
acquired its first photocopier. Until then, the Justices either had their
drafts and memos set in type and printed or relied on onionskin carbon copies known as "flimsies." The junior Justice who received the
blurry ninth carbon often had no choice but to rely on the views of his
elders. One of the reasons for such slow modernization was Congress,
which had to review expenditures and which often took an inordinate-
ly detailed interest in Court's budget.

By far the most important of Powell's suggestions was the creation
of what has become known as the cert pool. When Powell came to the
Court, every chambers had its own way of dealing with the steady flow
of petitions for certiorari. Brennan, for example, did his own sorting.
After fifteen years on the Court, he knew all the arguments and all the
precedents, many of which he had written. Most important, he had a
clear idea of the claims he wished to hear and those he preferred to

ignore. After a minute or even less with each petition, Brennan could throw most of them aside. Such speed would have dismayed those who labored to make their petitions attractive to the Justices, but it was essential to keep up with the work.

For Powell, this approach was impossible. He followed the lead of most chambers in asking his clerks to prepare memos summarizing the cert petitions. These memos had several advantages over the original papers. First, they were shorter. They could be very short indeed if, as was often true, the claim was frivolous or "fact-specific." This dismissive label meant that the petition was important only to the litigants and should be denied on that ground. An arsonist from Albuquerque who said he had been framed would get no hearing from the Supreme Court, because even if his claim were true, it raised no issue of national importance. Second, cert memos were often much better than the original papers in identifying the right argument. This situation arose especially in prisoner cases, where indigent prisoners were allowed to proceed in forma pauperis—that is, without lawyers—and present their claims in documents of their own devising. The rare kernel of merit in such petitions usually had to be discovered and restated, a time-consuming task better suited for a clerk than a Justice. Third, cert memos were written after the clerk had considered both sides. Some petitions looked meritorious until a reply brief or the opinion of the court below gave a conclusive reason why it was not. In such instances, the cert memo saved time by stating the crucial point first, no matter where it appeared in the original documents.

The pattern therefore in Powell's chambers and elsewhere was for a clerk to summarize each cert petition in a memo of one to several pages. In a particularly difficult or interesting case, Powell might go back to the original papers, but mostly he worked from the clerks' memos.

The problem was duplication of effort. The same cert petition would be summarized for Powell by a Powell clerk, for White by a White clerk, and so forth. Why not divide all the cert petitions among the chambers and circulate the memos to all the Justices? If the cert petitions were divided among the nine chambers, the burden on each clerk would fall from thirty or more a week to a mere handful. Overall the process would take less time, and each clerk could give more careful attention to the few petitions for which he or she had primary responsibility.

The scheme seems so obvious that one wonders why it had not been adopted long before, but Powell's suggestion ran counter to the traditional independence of each chambers. If White relied on a memo by a

Powell clerk, perhaps there would be some loss in the individuality of the Justice's reactions. In addition, the burden of drafting memos fell more heavily on the junior Justices. As Justices became more experienced, they tended to have firmer ideas about what cases they wanted to hear. They could handle the petitions themselves, as Brennan did, or at least give their clerks a good sense of what to look for.

When Powell persuaded Burger to propose a cert pool, the idea was received enthusiastically by the Court's newcomers. The four Justices who chose not to participate—Douglas, Brennan, Stewart, and Marshall—included the three most senior Justices. All four of the Nixon appointees joined the pool, as did Justice White. The resulting alignment looked like a liberal-conservative split but probably owed as much to differences in the length of Court service.

Begun on an experimental basis in the fall of 1972, the cert pool continues to this day. The petitions are allocated among the pool chambers, and the memos circulate to each of the participating Justices. The original holdouts never joined, but most new Justices have done so. In 1993 eight Justices participate in the cert pool, with only Justice Stevens' clerks handling the petitions on their own.

It is in the cert process generally and in the cert pool in particular that the law clerks have the greatest sway. The influence of the clerks is much exaggerated—not least by the clerks themselves—but it is probably true that the way a case is presented in the pool memo can affect its chances of being heard by the Court. Of course, even if a clerk has an axe to grind, there are built-in limits on the opportunity to do so, including the risk of embarrassment if a case is found to be misdescribed. Since any Justice can put a case on the discuss list, it seems likely that almost all plausible candidates for a full hearing receive the focused attention of the Justices themselves. More important, the clerks' role changes once the petition is granted. When the case comes back several months later for oral argument, the Justices will study the lawyers' briefs. At that point, at least in Powell's chambers, any memo by a clerk would be ancillary to Powell's own preparation and not in any sense a substitute for the direct personal attention of the Justice. In most important respects, the Justices do their own work.

POWELL AND THE PRESS

To the reception following his swearing-in, Powell invited family and friends and a few reporters whom he knew personally, such as CBS's

Fred Graham. Left off the list were Charlie McDowell, who was rescued by Josephine Powell as a guard turned him away, and a young reporter named Nina Totenberg.

One of the first women to cover the Supreme Court, Totenberg was "driven nuts" by older male colleagues whose personal relationships with the Justices gave them what she thought was an unfair advantage. Totenberg upbraided Powell for excluding her from his reception, which only served to make him think her unbalanced, but it was not long before he agreed to have lunch with her and she began to establish a personal relationship of her own.

Such was Powell's introduction to the Supreme Court press. Over the years, he enjoyed generally favorable coverage—especially for a conservative. Generalizations about the political proclivities of the press are always subject to counterexample, but most reporters who covered the Supreme Court identified more readily with the Warren Court liberals than with the four new Nixon appointees. The difference in sympathy showed up not so much in the coverage of decisions as in the comments and asides about the Justices' personalities. Rarely was publicity given to Justice Douglas's less attractive behaviors, though the stories circulated widely. Many journalists so admired the grand old man of judicial activism that criticism seemed like lèse-majesté. Neither did the press dwell on Justice Marshall's progressive estrangement from his duties, although that also was well known.

Warren Burger, by contrast, rarely got a break. His foibles and vanities were often remarked on, sometimes unfairly, as in the Jack Anderson column deriding Burger's imperial pretensions in having "a length of gold carpet rolled out for the august jurists to cross as they make their way through a rear hallway to take their seats on the bench." In fact, Burger had thoughtfully covered the marble steps coming down from the bench with a carpet remnant to provide better footing for the aged Hugo Black and the nearly blind John Harlan. Burger responded to such publicity with a distrust of the press verging on paranoia, which only exacerbated bad relations. Blackmun, in these early years, was dismissed as an appendage of the Chief Justice, and Rehnquist, too, had his share of unfriendly notices, including an unusually bare knuckled attack in the *Harvard Law Review*.

Alone among the Nixon appointees, Powell enjoyed a good press. When Jo was asked why she thought the media were so nice to Powell, she said at once: "Because he is so nice to them." It was a habit of long standing. Thirty years earlier, when Powell was a junior lawyer for Henrico County in annexation litigation, reporter James Latimer found him "a man of great patience, sympathy, tact, and understanding. No matter how stupid the question, he'd give you a listening, courteous answer." As a Justice, Powell continued this policy, shunning personal publicity but often providing background interviews to reporters who covered the Court. As a result, most of the Court regulars came to know him personally.

It is not entirely coincidental, therefore, that the most hurtful personal criticism Powell endured in nearly sixteen years on the bench originated far away from the coterie of Washington-based reporters who covered the Supreme Court. In the late spring of 1980, Powell began receiving inquiries from Gilbert Cranberg, editorial-page editor of the *Des Moines Register*, concerning his investments. Cranberg objected to the fact, as revealed in the annual financial disclosure statements required by a recent statute, that the Powells owned shares in publicly traded companies. On June 11, the *Register* ran an editorial accusing the Justices of "playing fast and loose with their responsibilities" and urging them to sell their stocks.

Cranberg's facts were accurate. Following his confirmation and after determining that the blind trust used by many lawmakers would likely not satisfy the ABA-endorsed ethical standards for judges, Powell rearranged his holdings to minimize potential conflicts of interest. He sold shares in certain large companies (such as AT&T, IBM, and General Electric) that were likely to have litigation before the Supreme Court, kept his shares in companies (such as Ethyl and Philip Morris) for which he would be disqualified in any event by past association, and purchased shares in several Canadian companies that he thought unlikely to appear before the U.S. Supreme Court. Then he turned the management of his portfolio over to a Richmond bank.

These measures did not eliminate the possibility that Powell would have to disqualify himself because of his investments, but after several years on the bench, the problem had arisen only rarely. Cranberg's insistence that the Justices divest themselves of all investments was a solution in search of a problem. The law plainly did not require anything so radical, and the suggestion initially received little attention or support.

But Cranberg had just begun. Frustrated by distance and the lack of informal access that a "Court regular" would have had, he asked to see the list of companies that Powell's clerks used to screen for potential conflicts of interest. Powell declined to release these "internal personal papers" on the ground that the annual public accounting of his investments should suffice. He also explained to Cranberg that most of his disqualifications resulted not from securities he owned but from the involvement of Hunton, Williams or his former clients. When Cranberg responded with an editorial condemning "Supreme Court Secrecy," Powell told Sally to open a file on the Cranberg correspondence, remarking that "we have not heard the end of this gentleman's crusade."

Powell was right. Cranberg set out to prove that the Justices should not own stocks by catching them in a case where they should have recused themselves. Recusals were noted on the record, as in the statement, "Mr. Justice Powell took no part in the consideration or decision of this case," but the reasons were not explained. Cranberg began to match Powell's recusals with his published stock holdings. He applied this technique not only to cases heard and decided on the merits, but also to the much larger number of cases that the Justices refused to hear, often after the most cursory consideration of petitions for certiorari.

Eventually Cranberg found what he was looking for. Although Potter Stewart and Josephine Powell owned stock in Johnson & Johnson, both Justices Stewart and Powell participated in the Court's refusal to review a ruling involving Ethicon, Inc., a wholly owned subsidiary of Johnson & Johnson. "It is appalling," thundered the *Des Moines Register*, "that high-court justices would create a situation in which they can be suspected of illegal and unethical conduct. . . . Powell and Stewart were negligent at best in their handling of the Ethicon case."

The problem, not surprisingly, was that the Justices had not noticed who owned Ethicon. The connection to Johnson & Johnson was not apparent from the name of the subsidiary, and the cert pool memo, which was all that Powell had seen on the case, did not mention it. Moreover, unknown to Cranberg, both Justices sided against their supposed financial interest by denying the review that Ethicon wanted. In any event, neither vote mattered. There was only one vote to grant review, and if both Justices had recused themselves, there still would have been the same one vote. There could scarcely have been a smaller molehill.

Three weeks later Cranberg struck again. This time he found a case Powell should have recognized, a cert petition involving Avon Products, a stock that Powell owned under that name. The case was a pip-squeak, an outlandishly trivial dispute that belonged, if anywhere, in a small claims-court. It did not make the discuss list. That the petition was therefore automatically denied no doubt accounted for Powell's failure to recuse himself from its "consideration."

Cranberg, who discovered a similar but unrelated oversight by

Stewart, reported both instances in an editorial entitled "Law violation by justices," claiming that "U.S. Supreme Court Justices Potter Stewart and Lewis Powell each violated federal law and the Code of Judicial Conduct at least once last year." Cranberg did not emphasize the distinction between decided cases and the many thousands of cert petitions that the Court declined to hear. Nor did he mention that voting not to hear a case would have exactly the same effect as a recusal, since neither would contribute to the four votes needed to grant review. Instead, the editorial resurrected the troubles of Clement Haynsworth and called for an official investigation: "The Senate will be guilty of hypocrisy if it ignores the nature of Powell's and Stewart's investments and the impropriety and appearances of impropriety associated with them. . . . U.S. Supreme Court Justices cannot be above the law. They, too, must be held accountable."

Having mounted his high horse, Cranberg proceeded to ride. He supplemented his editorials with articles in other publications and peppered Powell, the other Justices, and the Court's information officer with letters asking why the Justices did not publicly state their reasons for recusal. Rehnquist responded with a letter explaining that the question whether to remove oneself from a case was not cut-and-dried but often involved personal judgment. Was a party represented by a Justice's former law firm? How long ago? Did the Justice's former firm represent only a "friend of the court"—a nonparty who wished to be heard? And if a Justice had practiced in a large firm, should he disqualify himself only when he had personally worked for a litigant or whenever anyone else in the firm had done work for that client? Given the variety of circumstances and the subjective nature of the question of bias, Rehnquist concluded, "I have simply thought it best not to publicly announce a reason, because it might well be a reason with which some of my colleagues would agree and some would not."*

Rehnquist did not specifically mention Powell, but his examples were well chosen—and probably consciously intended—to edge Cranberg toward some understanding of Powell's situation. Powell himself was by this time fed up with Cranberg. The letter he drafted was unusually pointed: "If these questions were asked me by any reporter who regularly covers this Court, I would be happy to respond for background information purposes. On the basis of what you have

---

* In fact, one of the few criticisms Rehnquist ever made of Powell was that he was "a little overly fastidious about disqualification," which put pressure on his colleagues to conform to his extremely conservative standard.

written, however, it is evident that your understanding of the Court, and the way it operates, is limited. Nor can one have confidence that your primary interest is accurate and fair reporting."

Second thoughts prevailed, however, and Powell wrote a longer and gentler reply emphasizing the myriad issues in recusal and his willingness to provide an informal explanation of his reasons for disqualifying himself to any reporter who regularly covered the Supreme Court.

CRANBERG'S CRUSADE yielded at least one benefit. In October 1980 the Court announced a rule requiring that briefs and other documents filed on behalf of corporations list all parent companies, subsidiaries, and affiliated corporations. This useful innovation, for which Cranberg could claim credit, would prevent another Ethicon. It would not, however, preclude the possibility of oversight by a law clerk, who, facing the weekly stack of cert petitions, might fail to match each name carefully against the recusal list. This risk could only be minimized by Powell's meticulous instructions, repeated to each year's incoming clerks, to check every litigant and any affiliated entity for potential conflict of interest.

Another offshoot of Cranberg's campaign was less constructive. On December 3, 1980, he published another editorial bemoaning the "mindless secrecy" of the Court's disqualification procedures and listing the number of recusals by each Justice for the past four and a half years. The calculations purported to exclude instances when a Justice was absent from the Court, probably due to illness, and therefore could not participate. Powell led the list with 196 disqualifications.

A few months later this figure showed up on the CBS Evening News. CBS had apparently been waiting for the right time to run the story. They found it when Stewart's recusal in a case involving Bristol Myers left the Court divided four to four, resulting in automatic affirmance of the lower court. In such cases, the Justices do not address the legal issue but simply note that the judgment below is affirmed by an equally divided Court. After Dan Rather recounted these facts, legal correspondent Fred Graham discussed the "nagging problem of Supreme Court ethics, involving Justices who own stock in corporations." Focusing on Powell and Stewart, two "millionaire justices with extensive stock holdings," Graham cited the "study" showing 196 disqualifications for Powell in the past five years. "[I]t seems inevitable," Graham concluded, "in these days of giant corporate conglomerates, that justices with extensive stock holdings are bound to be disqualified from doing their jobs in a substantial number of cases."

Powell was furious. He had always been thin-skinned on matters of personal honor or dedication to duty. Graham had impugned both, implying that it was somehow unethical for Powell to own stocks and that he was shortchanging his job as a Justice. And Graham was not a misguided outsider but a knowledgeable Court regular, whom Powell knew personally and who knew or should have known that the story was grossly misleading. Powell had his clerk compile a list (using the same sources available to Cranberg) documenting all the Justices disqualifications for the period in question. Powell then sent Graham a letter recounting the results.

First, the number of disqualifications in the category described was not 196 but 109, "an error of almost 50%." Cranberg got the wrong figure by counting some cases twice (once when review was granted and again when the decision was handed down) and by including cases that Powell missed for health or other personal reasons. (He missed cases due to colon surgery in 1979 and a few more when he attended Lowell Weicker's funeral.) Second, Graham gave the figures out of context. The total of 109 disqualifications came not only from the few hundred cases that the Court had decided on the merits, but also from the vastly more numerous petitions for certiorari. Altogether, the Court had considered more than eighteen thousand cases, of which Powell's recusals were far less than 1 percent.

Most important, Graham had not said, as Cranberg had been careful to note, that most disqualifications did not result from stock ownership. A case-by-case tally showed that Powell had recused himself in eighty cases because of participation by Hunton, Williams or because of the interest of a former client. He disqualified himself in an additional twenty cases involving friends or entities with which he had been associated, such as the city of Richmond. In only nine instances had he disqualified himself due to securities held by him or his wife or their trusts, and only two of those were argued cases. While Graham could not have known the precise breakdown, it should have occurred to him that many disqualifications would have arisen from Powell's extensive private practice rather than from his investments. And if Graham had not known, he could have asked.

"Finally," wrote Powell, "your broadcast raises questions as to the responsibilities of the media. . . . What public interest are you serving by this kind of misleading criticism?" Powell concluded with a reproof as pointed as any that appears in his voluminous correspondence: "In sum, Fred, the broadcast was seriously flawed by erroneous statements, errors of omission, and wholly unjustified inferences. If we had not been friends and known each other for nearly 20 years I would be writing this letter to the responsible senior officers of CBS. I do not, however, plan to make this letter public and do not authorize you to do so."

Graham responded handsomely. He announced on CBS radio that he was "prepared to eat some crow on the subject of Supreme Court Justices who own corporate stock." Powell and Stewart, he now realized, were "caught in a legal box" by the recent act of Congress that forced judges (but not legislators) to keep track of their financial assets, thus preventing reliance on blind trusts. Moreover, Graham acknowledged that his account of Powell's disqualifications had been wrong. There were in fact only nine recusals due to financial conflicts. "The end result seems to be that the problem of Supreme Court deadlocks due to stock ownership does exist, but it is not a problem of major proportions for the Court. Furthermore, the problem is one created in large part by Congress's 1974 law, which could be amended to let Supreme Court Justices use blind trusts or other means to avoid actual conflicts of interest, without having to take themselves out of cases."

Graham also called Powell with a private apology. He was "shocked and surprised" to learn how unwise he had been to rely on Cranberg's editorial. He did not inquire into the accuracy of the figures because he thought it would be futile to do so. The explanation was self-protective, but in a way it proved Cranberg's point. As Powell wrote the Chief, "by remaining totally silent we give an excuse to media persons who wish to denigrate the Court or Justices individually. We also fail to give the facts to reporters who wish to cover the Court honestly." Even Cranberg had begun his stories only "after he had done—one must admit—a rather careful, though ignorant and hostile, investigation."

Accordingly, Powell placed on file with Barrett McGurn, the Court's press information officer, a twelve-page "background memo" on disqualifications. It was available for review by any reporter who regularly covered Court, so long as it was understood that the document could not be published or anything in it attributed to the Justice. While the memo focused on Powell's experience (including the figures already given Graham), it also addressed judicial disqualifications generally. "My sole purpose," Powell wrote, "is to aid in understanding for the future; it is not to correct previous misinformation or to generate publicity," adding in parentheses that "I have already had more than enough of this!" He appealed to professional responsibility and fair play:

There is not the slightest evidence of a Justice knowingly sitting in a case in which he or his spouse had a financial interest, or in which his participation otherwise would constitute a breach of trust or ethics. Nor, except in a very few cases, has disqualification due to stock ownership at all affected the work of the Court.

It therefore seems fair to ask whether any public interest is served by creating unjustified doubt in the public's mind as to the ethics and impartiality of Justices of the United States Supreme Court—an institution that over nearly 200 years has been faithful to its high responsibilities. . . .

This controversy is revealing on several grounds. From the beginning, Powell had shown himself sensitive to criticism—certainly more sensitive than anyone with life tenure needed to be. He was also characteristically measured in response. His letter to Graham was severe but fair, and was recognized as such by the recipient. Powell dwelt chiefly not on his sense of outrage (though that came through loud and clear) but on the facts, which he presented in convincing detail. Even Cranberg did not receive the reprimand Powell thought he deserved. After Cranberg published one of Powell's letters (the one declining to release his "internal personal papers"), Powell treated the irate editor with wary reserve, cautiously trying to educate him on the disqualification issue.

Most others dismissed the conflict-of-interest campaign as trivial. After a handful of follow-ups and a few rebuttals, the story died. The experience of the *Omaha World-Herald* was probably typical. Not knowing what to make of the Ethicon case "exposé," the editors contacted their Washington reporter who, after nosing around, declared it "about the weakest conflict-of-interest case I've ever heard of." Powell's elaborate memorandum on file in the Court's information office helped ensure that others would have the background to see it the same way.

The imbroglio over stock ownership and judicial ethics revealed something more than Powell's sensitivity to criticism and his deft dealings with the press. As in the Sherlock Holmes story about the dog that did not bark, the most telling aspect of this episode is what did not happen. Despite the investigations of Gilbert Cranberg, the attentions of Fred Graham, and the scrutiny of an alert press, there was, as Powell insisted, "not the slightest evidence of a Justice knowingly sitting in a case in which he or his spouse had a financial interest, or in which his participation otherwise would constitute a breach of trust or ethics." The piddling business of not knowing that Johnson & Johnson owned Ethicon, Inc., or of not disqualifying himself from denying a patently frivolous cert petition involving Avon Products was the only dirt anyone ever found on Lewis Powell. Nor was he unique. The other Justices with whom he sat could also claim spotless records. They might be liberal or conservative, sagacious or shallow, broad-minded or narrow, cautious in imposing their views or seduced into false certitude of their wisdom, but no one could call them corrupt.

This the public understood. Lewis Powell and the Justices with whom he sat had a reputation for honesty so deserved and secure that no one gave it a thought. The Supreme Court owed much of its prestige to this fact. No matter how strongly one disagreed with the decisions of the Justices, no one suspected they were seeking personal gain. If they were wrong, it was not for that reason.

And so the history of Lewis Powell on the Supreme Court is not the story of his investments, or of his extensive personal connections to money and influence. It is not a tale of strife and greed and conflict. It is only secondarily an account of his relations with the other men (and one woman) who shared the supreme judicial power during his tenure. Primarily, the history of Lewis Powell on the Supreme Court is a story of the structured collision of lofty ideal and concrete fact in the litigated case. It is a story of the paradoxical protection of a democratic people by their least accountable and most elite institution, a story of that peculiar brand of American politics known as constitutional law.

CHAPTER X

RACE
AND THE PUBLIC
SCHOOLS

BUSING IN THE SOUTH

In 1968 the Supreme Court finally told the South it had to desegregate *now*, but the Justices did not explain just how that should be done. On the particular facts at hand, there was no problem. New Kent County, the home of *Green v. County School Board*, was a rural area, with blacks and whites dispersed throughout the county. It had only two schools. All the white students attended one school. They were joined there by the handful of blacks who had exercised their right under the "freedom of choice" plan to transfer to the white school. The historically black school remained all black. In these circumstances, desegregation was easy: Divide the county into two districts, each with its own school, and send all children to the school in the district where they lived. This was the rural equivalent of the neighborhood school. In Kent County and throughout the rural and small-town South, neighborhood schools worked to eliminate state-imposed racial segregation.

But what of southern cities? In the cities, blacks and whites generally lived apart. Neighborhood schools in segregated neighborhoods would be segregated schools. Even if attendance zones were drawn to maximize integration, some schools would remain all white or all black. This was especially true of elementary schools, which usually were small and served compact areas. For southern cities, the *Green* decision left many questions: Did every school in a large urban system have to be racially mixed? Was neutrally administered neighborhood education constitutional, or would the cities have to achieve integrated schools even in segregated neighborhoods? This choice implicated the most drastic and controversial of all desegregation remedies—forced busing.

The issue came to the Supreme Court from Charlotte, North Carolina, where an earlier desegregation case was reopened after *Green*. Under the existing "freedom of choice" plan, two thirds of the black students in the combined Charlotte-Mecklenburg school system still attended all-black schools. *Green* required more. Under pressure from District Judge James B. McMillan, the school board came up with a new plan. It redrew attendance zones and allowed student transfers only where they would promote racial mixing. This plan would have fully desegregated the system's ten high schools and would have been almost as successful for the twenty-one junior high schools, but many of the seventy-six elementary schools would have remained one race. Even under this most ambitious of the school board's proposals, more than half the black elementary pupils would have attended predominantly black schools. This was not good enough for Judge McMillan.

Instead, he divided Charlotte-Mecklenburg into pie-shaped wedges extending outward from the center of the city to the suburban and rural areas of the county. He ordered that blacks be bused out and whites be bused in, so that every school in the system would have a mix of races. This plan required the daily transportation, solely to achieve integration, of more than ten thousand children. Critics railed that McMillan required every school to have the precise mathematical ratio of the system as a whole, but he did not go quite that far. While blacks made up 29 percent of the total student population, black enrollment at individual schools would range from 9 to 38 percent. Nevertheless, the plan sought to redistribute the races more or less evenly throughout the system and eliminate all one-race schools. For this, busing was an absolute necessity.

The school board appealed to the Fourth Circuit Court of Appeals, which reversed McMillan's order. The majority thought he had gone too far in requiring the busing of young children. They insisted on "reasonableness" in desegregation, which, for the Fourth Circuit, meant elementary education based on the neighborhood school. Southern school systems would not be forced to counteract the effect of residential segregation through busing.

This was a crucial ruling, for if busing was not reasonable in Charlotte, it would not be reasonable anywhere. In fact, Charlotte was the best possible place for busing. Some years earlier, and for reasons

having nothing to do with desegregation, the city of Charlotte and surrounding Mecklenburg County had merged their schools into one large
system. The merger vastly aided McMillan's plan. First, the combined
Charlotte-Mecklenburg system, unlike many city school districts, had
an overall white majority. Busing in Charlotte-Mecklenburg would leave
no school with minority enrollment higher than 40 percent. Second,
the size of the combined system not only kept whites in the majority
and thus reduced the incentive for white flight; it also made flight more
difficult. Whites determined to avoid integration could try to pay for
private school, but they could not simply move to (or, for new arrivals,
locate in) the suburbs, for the nearby suburbs were also within the busing decree. Finally, busing itself was a familiar activity in Charlotte-
Mecklenburg. Even before McMillan's decree, more than one fourth of
the system's children rode buses to school. This fact led many to agree
with Judge McMillan that busing itself was a red herring. As Jesse
Jackson would later say, "The issue is not the bus; the issue is us."

When the case, *Swann v. Charlotte-Mecklenburg Board of Education*,
came to the Supreme Court, Powell was almost asked to argue the case
for the school board. A delegation approached Charles Rhyne, a nationally known lawyer and former Charlotte resident who lacked the time
and recommended Powell. The Charlotte lawyers did not know Powell
and decided to go it alone, then kicked themselves later when his nomination to the Supreme Court suggested that he might have been a
good choice after all.

Powell nevertheless became involved in the case. Metropolitan
communities throughout the South saw their fate tied to Charlotte's.
They urged their views on the Justices as amici curiae, or "friends of
the court," a courtesy title given interested nonparties who wish to be
heard. Virginia filed an amicus brief on behalf of Richmond and
Norfolk, where busing had also been ordered. The brief was signed by
Andrew Pickens Miller, the Attorney General of Virginia, but listed as
special counsel its principal author, Lewis Powell.

AS LAWYERS ARE PAID to represent their clients' interests, a legal brief
may or may not reflect its author's views. Yet Powell's amicus brief on
behalf of the Commonwealth of Virginia came from his heart and
foreshadowed the positions he would later take as a Justice of the
Supreme Court.

In Richmond and Norfolk, as in Charlotte, the threat of judicial
intervention prompted local school boards to get serious about deseg-

regation *now*. Like Charlotte, Richmond and Norfolk redrew attendance zones and adopted majority-to-minority transfer provisions to increase racial mixing, but, like Charlotte, they were left with largely one-race elementary schools in areas of residential segregation. As Powell claimed, the Virginia cities had (at long last) done all that they could do, short of busing, but one-race schools remained. Was this good enough, or would busing be required?

The question, as Powell saw it, was one of constitutional objective. If racial balance was the overriding goal, busing was indispensable. Nothing else would mix students from racially segregated neighborhoods. But if quality education was the goal, the costs of busing should also be considered. The costs of busing included not only the money, which might be considerable, but also the psychic and educational disadvantages of removing children from familiar environments, of separating them from their parents for more hours each day, and of undermining the institution of the neighborhood school.

Powell believed in the neighborhood school. It assured easy access, facilitated parental involvement, and maximized the opportunity for extracurricular activities after hours. Moreover, neighborhood education fostered political support. As the former school board chairman told the Justices: "A willingness to pay increased taxes and to vote for bond issues can evaporate quickly in the face of enforced busing and dismantling of neighborhood schools where such actions do not contribute to improved education for all."

The crucial words in Powell's sentence are "education *for all.*" Compulsory busing would probably help inner-city blacks. Civil rights leaders certainly thought so, and Powell had no reason to say otherwise. He did not look at it as exclusively a question of black welfare. Like most opponents of busing, he was moved chiefly by fear that it would hurt education in mostly white, middle-class neighborhoods. This was not an idle concern. Years of oppression had degraded the educational achievements of poor blacks. Forced mixing of economically and intellectually deprived black children with middle-class whites might help the former, but not without consequence to the educational environment of the latter. The economic and social separation of neighborhoods could be ameliorated, but not countermanded, by school desegregation. Perhaps the better course would be to desegregate *within* the economic structure of urban housing, preserving good schools in good neighborhoods, even though those neighborhoods remained mostly white.

This was a dangerous argument. It came close to saying that white welfare mattered more than black equality. It would not do, therefore, simply to argue that busing would hurt whites. One had to show also that busing would not help blacks, that it would prove ineffective to redress the centuries of oppression and discrimination now weighing upon black children. This point required careful phrasing. It was hard to build an argument around the harsh realities of disparity and preju- dice without seeming to endorse them, but Powell tried to do so.

Busing was wrong, he argued, not because it attempted integration, but because it would not achieve integration. It was not only costly but futile. The ultimate problem was not the expense or the inconve- nience or even the impairment of learning that would come with dis- mantling the neighborhood school. The ultimate problem was white flight. Whites would stay out of the city schools rather than submit to busing. Some would pay for private education, and many more would choose to live in the suburbs. Of course, urban emigration predated desegregation. Ever since World War II, families who moved up the economic ladder also moved out of the inner cities. This migration would continue with or without busing, but Powell said it would vastly accelerate if all city schools were required to achieve racial balance.

Once begun, white flight would be self-perpetuating. The more whites abandoned city schools, the more intense the pressure on those few who remained. At some uncertain "tipping point"—variously esti- mated at 25 to 50 percent black—attrition would become exodus, leaving behind only those whites without the means to escape. The result would be concentration of whites in the suburbs and resegrega- tion of blacks in the inner cities. Therefore, Powell argued, busing was unproductive, if not actually regressive: "It frustrates the aspirations of *Brown*, namely, the promotion of equal education opportunity; it assures in time the resegregation of most of the blacks in many urban communities. This will result in deteriorating educational opportuni- ties both for poorer blacks and whites who cannot afford to move." In short, the end result was "precisely the opposite of that desired." Resegregation not only defeated integration, it had adverse social and economic consequences: "Property values deteriorate; sources of local taxation shrink; all municipal services—as well as education—suffer; and—worst of all —the quality of civic leadership erodes."

Though Powell was graphic in cataloging the evils of busing, he was much less detailed about the consequences of not busing. There was good reason for the omission, for if busing had unpleasant results, so also did the refusal to bus. Without busing, successful middle-class

schools in predominantly white neighborhoods would remain successful, middle-class, and predominantly white. The black urban poor
would continue to attend virtually all-black, inner-city schools. So long
as urban school desegregation was confined by housing patterns, integration would not be much advanced. True, black children would be
relieved of the stigma of legal apartheid, but the benefits that were
expected to flow from the association of the races would be largely
denied. If and when economic progress and social justice changed
racial housing patterns, school desegregation would follow. In the
meantime, legal segregation would be ended, but actual segregation
would survive in the neighborhood school. At bottom, Powell asked
the Supreme Court to give up on "Desegregate *now*" and adopt
instead a long-run strategy for improving public education by retaining the participation and support of a mobile and resistant white population. This the Court refused to do.

INSIDE THE COURT, consideration of *Swann* was confused and embittered. At Conference, Chief Justice Burger said he thought McMillan
had gone too far. Only Hugo Black agreed. That left Burger in the
minority, and by Court custom, the power to assign the opinion
should have passed to the senior Associate Justice in the majority,
William O. Douglas. But Burger had other ideas. He lived in the memory of Chief Justice Warren's astounding success in guiding a divided
and doubtful Supreme Court to a unanimous opinion in *Brown*, and
he wanted to repeat that achievement. *Swann* would be a crucial test
of his leadership. Besides, nothing he had said at Conference had been
binding; he had voiced only tentative views. Burger announced that he
would write *Swann* himself. More important than the merits of the
case was Burger's desire to write a unanimous opinion for the Court in
the desegregation landmark of his administration.
    There followed a prolonged tug of war, as the Justices who wanted an
unqualified endorsement of McMillan's order sought to extract an
acceptable opinion from the reluctant Chief Justice. The result was a
murky opinion that seemed to look in several directions at once. On the
one hand, the idea that every school had to have the same racial balance was expressly rejected: "The constitutional command to desegregate schools," said the Court, "does not mean that every school in every
community must always reflect the racial composition of the school
system as a whole." On the other hand, mathematical ratios were
expressly accepted, although only "as a useful starting point in shaping
a remedy to correct past constitutional violations." Amid this confu-

sion, one thing was clear: McMillan was affirmed down the line. The result spoke more loudly than the inconsistent explanations. Whatever had been said along the way and despite the personal opposition of the author of its opinion, the Supreme Court had upheld forced busing.

A few months later, the Chief Justice made a clumsy effort to reverse this defeat. The occasion was Burger's refusal to stay a lower court order pending Supreme Court review. For this sort of question, the Justices act individually, with no participation by their colleagues. Given a chance to speak on his own, Burger tried to rewrite *Swann*. He stressed the restrictive portions of the Court's opinion and ignored the equally prevalent comments looking the other way. There is nothing greatly surprising in this, as judges often try to make a precedent say as much or as little as possible, but Burger sent copies of his statement marked "to the personal attention" of the nation's district judges. This was incredibly presumptuous, for it suggested that the lower courts should follow Burger's individual reinterpretation rather than the official opinion of the Supreme Court. As one prominent federal judge quite correctly responded, "I don't work for the Chief Justice." Of course, the maneuver was too transparent to be successful. Aside from ruffling a few feathers, Burger's statement had no effect.

SWANN WAS ANNOUNCED on April 20, 1971. Almost exactly six months later, President Nixon nominated Powell to the Supreme Court. In the hearings on his confirmation, the Senate Judiciary Committee heard extensive testimony about the snail's pace of desegregation in Richmond in the 1950s, the Richmond School Board's plan to build two new "white" high schools in 1959, and the State Board of Education's 1964 decision to fund retroactive tuition grants in Prince Edward County. These events were said to show that Powell was at heart a segregationist, adept at sophisticated stratagems to undermine *Brown*. His more recent brief against busing and the unanimous rejection of his position by the Supreme Court were not mentioned. The reason is not hard to find. While *Brown* had always enjoyed support in the nation and had become even in the South the archetype of morality and justice, busing was never popular. A Gallup poll at the time of Powell's nomination revealed overwhelming sentiment against it. Opposition to busing prevailed in the North and the South, among Democrats and Republicans, even— according to some samplings—among blacks. To campaign for busing was political suicide. Even if the Supreme Court did not, as Mr. Dooley claimed, follow the election returns, the United States Senate certainly did.

Thus, although the Senators questioned Powell on the history of desegregation in Richmond, they hardly mentioned the looming controversy over busing. Powell sidestepped the only inquiry on that subject by blandly saying that such questions "would have to be resolved on the facts and in light of the Supreme Court decisions," and the Senators eagerly accepted this evasion. When the Senators confirmed Powell, they placed on the Supreme Court a Justice whose views on one of the critical issues of the day had been recently, and, to all appearances, unanimously, rejected by his new colleagues.

BUSING MOVES NORTH

From *Brown* through *Swann*, all desegregation cases to reach the Supreme Court came from southern and border states. This was no accident. Not only was the problem most visible in the South, but the legal theory behind the desegregation cases implied a regional limitation. *Brown* condemned state-imposed segregation. It did not create a constitutional right to integrated schools. The difference seems technical but is crucially important. Under *Brown*, racial segregation denies equal protection of the laws only where it is imposed or sponsored by the government. The mere fact of racial separation, in schools or elsewhere, does not violate anyone's constitutional rights. Lawyers capture the distinction in a bit of Latin jargon: De jure segregation—separation by law—is unconstitutional; de facto segregation—racial separation without government responsibility—is not unconstitutional. Under this theory, court orders at first addressed only those school systems that officially required segregation by race as of 1954. Such laws were most notorious in the South.

At the time of *Brown*, this legal theory fit the social facts. Whatever might have been said of racial justice in the North and West, state-imposed segregation was distinctively a southern problem. Indeed, to a degree now difficult to recall or re-create, it seemed to many exclusively a southern problem. Only the South (and a few border states) practiced educational apartheid. Therefore, only the South needed to change. If the South could be brought into line with the rest of the country, if its peculiar moral deficiency could be overcome, the problem would be solved. And the South itself reveled in its distinctiveness and reinforced its isolation. Only in the South did leaders rail against allowing any black child into any white school, ever. Only in the South was racial exclusion elevated from mere fact to high principle.

Southern defiance earned northern contempt, and helped perpetuate the rest of the nation's complaisant belief that desegregation was a regional problem.

By 1972, when Powell joined the Supreme Court, this illusion had crumbled. Racial unrest in the 1960s shifted from the rural South to the urban North and West. Riots hit Newark, Philadelphia, New York, Chicago, Detroit, and Los Angeles, as well as Washington, D.C. Under threat of court order and the cutoff of federal funds, the South now led the nation in desegregating schools. In 1971 the Department of Health, Education, and Welfare reported that 32 percent of black pupils in the South attended schools with minority enrollment higher than 80 percent. In the North and West, 57 percent of black students attended such schools. In the South, 44 percent of black students went to schools with white majorities; in the North and West, that figure was only 28 percent. It was no longer possible to see segregation as exclusively, or even chiefly, a southern problem.

The social reality had changed, but the legal doctrine still aimed at the South. Even *Swann*, which could have arisen anywhere, was written and understood as a specifically southern decision. The Court's opinion defined the problem in terms that were unmistakably, if not inevitably, southern. As *The New York Times* read the case, the issue at the heart of *Swann* was "not busing at all," but "rather the Court's belief that the school authorities of Charlotte, North Carolina, and other Southern districts, have openly defied the 1954 Supreme Court ruling that outlawed the maintenance of dual school systems." Perhaps so. And if *Swann* was just another southern school case, perhaps busing would not be required elsewhere.

THE FIRST CASE to test that assumption came from Denver, Colorado. Denver had never practiced formal segregation. Indeed, the Colorado Constitution expressly prohibited the "classification of pupils ... on account of race or color." Yet Denver's record was by no means pure. As the city's growing black population expanded into an area known as Park Hill, the school board contrived to keep some schools virtually all white. A new elementary school was built in the area of black growth; mobile classrooms were used to accommodate increasing black enrollment without reassignment to white schools; and transition neighborhoods were allowed to use "optional attendance zones" that encouraged students to choose schools according to race. These subtle devices added up to state-imposed segregation in Park Hill.

The question that came to the Supreme Court was whether the

school board's manipulations in Park Hill justified a desegregation order embracing the whole city. Schools in the larger "core city" area of Denver were also overwhelmingly black, but here there was no history of government responsibility. The core city schools had been predominantly black long before the school board's actions in Park Hill and from all that appeared, were products of the same pattern of residential segregation that characterized all of America's urban areas. The issue, therefore, was whether purposeful (that is, de jure) segregation in part of a school system required busing in the whole.

The Court's answer was yes. The Justices told the trial court to consider the question under guidelines that made citywide busing all but inevitable. This ruling cast a long shadow. While northern cities did not practice the explicit apartheid of the South, few would be found altogether free of taint. Searching examination of the history of a city's schools would often uncover official decisions that supported or perpetuated racial separation. After the Denver school case, such acts would be interpreted as illegal de jure segregation.

At least, they *might* be so interpreted, if the judge were receptive and the plaintiffs' lawyers sufficiently energetic and skillful. The Denver school case did not equate North and South. Rather, it invited blacks outside the South to prove, if they could, the sorts of subtle racism found in Denver. This process was arduous and expensive. It required a kind of legal archaeology to chip away layers of legitimate explanation in order to uncover deeper motives. Because the evidence was often equivocal and the question of intent elusive, much depended on the attitude of the particular trial judge. As a result, desegregation in the North and West was far from uniform. The Denver school case thus endorsed busing outside the South, but at the same time perpetuated a regional approach to desegregation.

Powell recoiled from both conclusions. He wanted to treat North and South the same, and he opposed busing in both. These views were fiercely held, yet they brought him into conflict with his new colleagues and, to a degree, with his concept of judging. Powell often said that he believed in precedent. He believed that judges should follow prior cases. As he told the Senate Judiciary Committee at his confirmation: "As a lawyer, I have a deep respect for precedent. I know the importance of continuity and reasonable predictability of the law. This is not to say that every decision is immutable but there is normally a strong presumption in favor of established precedent."

But here the established precedent seemed to Powell grievously wrong. To the consternation of the South and the relief of many northern cities, decisions since *Brown v. Board of Education* had condemned only de jure segregation. The Court had also endorsed busing. *Swann* was unanimous, if contradictory, and only a year old. In such circumstances, Powell's professed respect for precedent surely counseled hesitation. But that was not all. Powell had replaced Hugo Black as the Court's only southerner. His role in the (non)desegregation of the Richmond schools had been picked to pieces in his confirmation. Anything he said on the subject would be read with suspicion. Although his pre-Court experience made Powell think himself particularly knowledgeable about education, he also knew that it left him especially vulnerable to criticism about desegregation. All these factors—his newness on the Court, his regard for precedent, the risk that he would be misunderstood—called for caution. He could simply join the majority and keep a low profile. Yet in the end, Powell did neither. Instead, he waded into the most embittered public debate of the day and produced one of the most creative and controversial opinions of his career.

THE CASE WAS ENTITLED *Keyes v. School District No. 1.* Its history not only reveals Powell's early views on desegregation but also provides a good look at the operation of his chambers during his first full year on the Supreme Court. It shows how Powell wrote opinions and how he used his clerks. Finally, the history of *Keyes* also reveals some surprising, yet characteristic, interactions among the Justices in a case that all of them considered important.

The request for Supreme Court review of *Keyes* came up on January 7, 1972, at Powell's and Rehnquist's first Conference. Neither wanted to hear the case, but their colleagues did and review was granted a week later. Since the spring calendar was already full, oral argument was set for October. After argument, the Justices met at Conference to address the merits. Burger, Powell, and Rehnquist voted against requiring citywide busing; they wanted to order desegregation only in Park Hill. The other participating Justices* coalesced around the views of Justice Brennan. Brennan said that the trial judge had erred in not finding de jure segregation in the core city, as well as in Park Hill. He proposed that the question be reconsidered by the trial court, but under guidelines from the Supreme Court that would virtually ensure citywide busing. This was a diplomatic masterstroke. It granted the broadest possible relief in the narrowest-sounding terms. Brennan knew that this approach would get

---

* After some hesitation, Byron White, whose old law firm had once represented the Denver School Board, recused himself from the case.

the result he wanted without sparking the kind of controversy that might break up a fragile majority.

As the senior Justice in that majority, Douglas had the power of assignment, and he sensibly chose Brennan. In short order, Brennan produced a draft opinion along the lines of his remarks at Conference. Marshall joined the next day, and within a week Douglas and Stewart were also on board. Brennan needed only one more vote, but that last vote was a long time coming. After several weeks of silence, Harry Blackmun said that, although he was "in large part in accord" with Brennan's draft, he would nevertheless withhold his vote "pending other circulations."

Powell now decided to write. In this effort, he had the able assistance of J. Harvie Wilkinson III. Jay, as he was called, had taken off a semester from law school for an unsuccessful campaign for election to Congress. Owing to this escapade, he graduated out of season in January 1972. The timing was perfect. When Powell went to the Supreme Court, Wilkinson went with him. The other clerks, who had been inherited from Hugo Black, at first looked with disdain on this family friend with the fancy name, but there was much more to the choice than friendship and hometown sentiment. Wilkinson was also brilliant. As an undergraduate at Yale, he had written *Harry Byrd and the Changing Face of Virginia Politics*, an impressive achievement for a scholar of any age. He took a law degree at the University of Virginia and published an admiring article on Powell's idol, John Marshall Harlan. The doubts of other clerks were soon laid to rest, not only by Wilkinson's ability but also by his amiable informality and his care never to pull rank.

In fact, Wilkinson's special relationship with his boss did not always work to his advantage. Wilkinson rented an apartment in Southwest Washington and rode to and from the Court each day with Sally and the Justice. As Powell wrote Harvie and Letitia, "Sally provides the transportation, and Jay provides the conversation." With this greater access, however, came a greater exposure to Powell's advice. The reserve that Powell practiced with other clerks fell away, and Jay received the benefit of Powell's views on everything from careers to haircuts. As a co-clerk put it, "Powell was all over Jay" in an affectionate regard that others might view with both envy and dread.

From Powell's perspective, Wilkinson's greatest strength was his prose. His writing was always clean and vivid. At its best, the hours of refinement and polish produced an elegance that seemed effortless and almost conversational. Wilkinson's weakness, if he had one, was a lack of distance from Powell's views. The ideal law clerk is both loyalist and critic—faithful to the judge's instructions, yet alert to any deficiencies of thought or expression. Wilkinson was very like Powell, not only in his southern origin and privileged background, but also in attitude and temperament. Both were politically conservative and socially correct, soft in manner, moderate in judgment, and conventional in outlook. On desegregation and busing, as on most things, they saw eye to eye.

In the summer before *Keyes* was argued, Powell asked Wilkinson to study the case. Wilkinson responded with a preargument memorandum called a bench memo. Wilkinson shared Powell's distaste for the regional approach to desegregation and after some research advised his boss that there was "a legally respectable way to take virtually any position you want" on the constitutionality of segregation in the North. With respect to busing, however, Wilkinson found no room for maneuver: "There is unfortunately no legally respectable way, in light of *Swann*, to take your most heartfelt views on . . . cross-town busing." Wilkinson had reread *Sann* and found the pro-busing language "even stiffer than I remembered. Burger got very little for his vote." Wilkinson's conclusion was gloomy: "From a policy standpoint, this is a very unattractive case because we are faced with the possibility of extending an odious remedy [busing] across the country and victimizing thousands of innocent families and schoolchildren or leaving our own section of the country to suffer in isolation under an inequitable and hypocritical constitutional doctrine."

Powell shared the sentiment but not the helplessness. Wilkinson had read *Swann* as a student, receiving what the Court intended to say. Powell read *Swann* as an advocate. He mined its inconsistencies for room to take his "most heartfelt views" against busing. As an exercise in interpretation, Powell's reading was strained. Ultimately, however, the question Powell faced was not one of interpretation but of decision. Powell would come out against forced busing, no matter what the Supreme Court had said in *Swann*.

Busing, Powell said, was a travesty lacking any constitutional basis. It produced educational chaos and prompted white flight. It would end in futility, animosity, and resegregation. Even his next-door neighbor, Hubert Humphrey, had remarked that the Court had gotten the country into "one hell of a mess" by forced busing. (Powell cautioned Jay not to use this statement; he mentioned it only because no one could "doubt Hubert Humphrey's dedication to racial equality.") Though Powell realized that "many will view an expression from me as reflecting a southern bias, if not southern racism," he insisted on writing. The Justices had not paid any attention to his amicus brief in *Swann*, but now he was a Justice himself. He could be outvoted but no longer ignored.

So Powell took his dictaphone and set to work. Years of practice had made him skilled in the art of speaking the written word. The results were clear, readable, and well organized but not stylistically finished. Nor were they meant to be. Powell's long experience in working with junior lawyers was now turned to his clerks. He did not simply take a clerk's draft and edit it into a final opinion. Rather, there was a sort of written dialogue between clerk and Justice. Typically, the clerk would write a first draft, to which Powell would respond with a memorandum proposing changes great and small: Add a paragraph on this or that, append a footnote on the following, cite this case, make that argument, and so on. The clerk would produce a revised draft, to which Powell would respond with another memorandum, and so on. If all went well, the memoranda got shorter as the opinion moved through successive drafts. Powell did not expect his clerks to follow blindly each instruction. A clerk told to add a certain paragraph to a draft opinion might do so, or make some other change to take account of the point, or suggest why the addition should not be made. Of course, some response was required. If Powell was not satisfied, he would return to the point in next memorandum. By this method, Powell kept several clerks busy on opinions that he in an important sense "wrote," even when he never put pen to paper.

In *Keyes*, Powell began with dictated memoranda, which he gave to Wilkinson with directions to produce a draft opinion. There followed several weeks of back and forth between clerk and Justice. Finally, Wilkinson's effort was sufficiently far along that Powell had it printed as a chambers draft—so called because it would be seen only within chambers and not be circulated to the rest of the Court. He now invited comments from the other clerks. Larry A. Hammond was a University of Texas graduate and former Black clerk who had agreed to stay on an extra year. William C. Kelly, Jr., was a graduate of Harvard College and Yale Law School, who had moved up from an appeals court clerkship the previous summer. Neither was antibusing. As Powell joked in his cover memorandum: "There is a vague rumor floating about that neither of you is totally enchanted with my position on school desegregation." He asked that they read the draft, "accepting my position as reflecting my carefully considered judgment, but nevertheless feeling free to make any and all suggestions which you think would strengthen or improve it."

They responded in that spirit. Hammond had been at the Court at the time of *Swann* and questioned Powell's description of it. The discussion was revised accordingly. Hammond also thought that Powell's tone was unbalanced and that he should say something affirmative about the benefits of integration. Powell added suitable language. Kelly steered Powell away from citing Burger's attempt to recoup his defeat in *Swann* by subsequent reinterpretation. Burger's distribution of his individual statement was a sore spot with the other Justices and with many lower court judges, and there was no point in stirring up hard feelings.

The final product bears marks of intervention by Hammond and Kelly and much of it is couched in Wilkinson's prose, but it is still unmistakably Lewis Powell. No clerk had urged the attack on *Swann*; this was entirely Powell's doing. The argument owes a good deal to Powell's brief in that case and even more to his own soul-searching. The result is quite unlike the impersonal collective voice of many Supreme Court opinions. It is an unusually discursive, intensely personal, and revealing statement by a concerned individual.

AT ITS CORE, Powell's position was simple: Integration was a good thing, but busing was not. He called for "reason, flexibility, and balance" in pursuit of desegregation. Many steps could and should be taken within the framework of neighborhood education.* But forced busing presented a vastly more complex problem: "It promises on the one hand a greater degree of actual desegregation while it infringes on what may fairly be regarded as important community aspirations and personal rights." Foremost among them was neighborhood education. Neighborhood schools were cheap and easy for all concerned, but more than that, they reflected the deeply felt desire for a "sense of community" in public education:

> Public schools have been a traditional source of strength to our Nation, and that strength may derive in part from the identification of many schools with the personal features of the surrounding neighbor-

* "For example, boundaries of neighborhood attendance zones should be drawn to integrate, to the extent practicable, the school's student body. Construction of new schools should be of such a size and at such a location as to encourage the likelihood of integration. Faculty integration should be attained throughout the school system. An optional majority-to-minority transfer program, with the State providing free transportation to desiring students, is also a helpful adjunct to a desegregated school system. It hardly need be repeated that allocation of resources within the school district must be made with scrupulous fairness among all schools."

hood. Community support, interest, and dedication to public schools may well run higher with a neighborhood attendance pattern: distance may encourage disinterest. Many citizens sense today a decline in the intimacy of our institutions—home, church, and school—which has caused a concomitant decline in the unity and communal spirit of our people. I pass no judgment on this viewpoint, but I do believe that this Court should be wary of compelling in the name of constitutional law what may seem to many a dissolution in the traditional, more personal fabric of their public schools.

This statement neared the core of Powell's belief. He venerated the traditional connectedness of home, church, and school. He feared the rootlessness, the anonymity, the impersonality of life in modern cities. In a speech the previous summer, Powell lamented that Americans were being "cut adrift from the type of humanizing authority which in the past shaped the character of our people." Teachers, parents, neighbors, ministers, employers—these were the "personal authorities [that] once gave direction to our lives." Relationships with them "were something larger than ourselves, but never so large as to be remote, impersonal, or indifferent. We gained from them an inner strength, a sense of belonging, as well as of responsibility to others."

Here was Powell the true conservative. For him, the neighborhood school epitomized the values of community, of belonging, of cooperation in a common endeavor for the public good. Of course, the image was undeniably incomplete. The neighborhood school was a fine thing for those with good schools in decent neighborhoods. To others, it might be meaningless, or worse. As Jay Wilkinson later wrote, to many blacks, neighborhood schools "meant confinement, a slow suffocation in the dankness of the ghetto. The school bus might mean hope, escape, the door to a new life of challenge and opportunity." This Powell did not see. His vision was idealized, but it was not entirely false.

Neither was it racist. Powell did not now believe (if he ever had) that white children would be hurt by association with blacks. His attitudes had changed since 1954—changed more radically than he himself recognized. By the early 1970s revisionism began to creep into his recollections. He told Wilkinson: "As you know, I personally supported *Brown* when this was extremely unpopular in Virginia; I opposed massive resistance and interposition, and was regarded by many in Virginia as a liberal integrationist." He went even further in the memorandum asking Hammond and Kelly to review the draft opinion: "To the dismay of many southern conservatives (including old friends), I have honestly believed in the advantages, in our pluralistic society, of the

children of all races and creeds being brought together in public education. I thought the *Brown* decision was long overdue." At the time,
he had thought no such thing. Although he had opposed massive
resistance and interposition, no sane person could have thought him a
"liberal integrationist." Powell's memory edited the past to bring it
more nearly in line with his current values. By this time, he honestly
believed in the value of integration, and it seemed inconceivable to
him that he had ever endorsed or tolerated the regime of segregation.

Powell accepted integration but not busing. He feared that the
"unpredictable and unmanageable social consequences" of forced busing would destroy public education. "No one can estimate the extent
to which dismantling neighborhood education will hasten an exodus
to private schools, leaving public schools the preserve of the disadvantaged of both races, or guess how much impetus such dismantlement
gives the movement from inner city to suburb, and the further geographical separation of the races." Nor was white flight the only evil.
Busing might also "cause deterioration of the community and parental
support of the public schools [and] divert attention from the paramount goal of quality in education to a perennially divisive debate
over who is to be transported where."

Although Powell said that he would not categorically forbid court-
ordered busing, he did not specify when it might be valid. He said only
that it should be approached "with special caution." In his words, the
courts should return to a "more balanced evaluation of the recognized
interests of our society in achieving desegregation with other educational and societal interests a community may legitimately assert."
The language was mild as milk, but the message was crystal clear.
Desegregation was fine, but only so long as it could be done without
forced busing.

ALTHOUGH POWELL'S WAS the first public criticism of busing by any
Justice, it was not the only controversial part of his opinion in *Keyes*.
Equally important was his attack on the traditional distinction
between de jure and de facto segregation—between segregation
unconstitutionally imposed by law and legally permissible segregation
resulting from private choice. Powell argued that segregation was segregation, wherever found and of whatever origin. It was equally damaging to black students wherever they lived. Yet constitutional
doctrine remained fixated on segregation found to be state-imposed or
sponsored in or after 1954.

This focus had a regional application. It put every southern town and county under an affirmative duty to achieve racial balance in their schools, but left the rest of the country largely alone. As a result, northern schools were now *more* segregated than their southern counterparts. This, Powell complained, was "accepted complacently by many of the same voices which denounced the evils of segregated schools in the South." There should be one law for all: "[I]f our national concern is for those who attend such schools, rather than for perpetuating a legalism rooted in history rather than present reality, we must recognize that the evil of operating separate schools is no less in Denver than in Atlanta."

Privately, Powell admitted he was infected by "Confederate emotion." The southern white and the northern liberal each spied more clearly the mote in the other's eye. While the former saw no difference between segregation in North and South, the latter found no similarity. For many northerners, the controlling image of school desegregation was still Little Rock in 1957—ugly, violent, lawless whites who had to be coerced by force to accept what the law decreed and decency demanded. Only when violence moved to Boston did this picture lose its regional coloration. In contrast, many southerners saw the increasingly detailed and demanding desegregation decrees of the late 1960s as a second Reconstruction, carried out by judges rather than generals, but scarcely less oppressive. Busing, in particular, was seen as judicial punishment, visited on innocent white schoolchildren for the sins of their ancestors. That the same regime was not imposed elsewhere (at least not as soon or as thoroughly) was infuriating. Sauce for the goose was sauce for the gander, and no history lesson could convince the South that regional desegregation was anything less than rank hypocrisy.

Theoretically, of course, there was nothing regional about it. State-imposed segregation was condemned wherever it was found, and if it was found more readily in the South, whose fault was that? But this rationalization meant nothing to Powell. Publicly, he termed it a "legalism rooted in history rather than in present reality"; privately, he called it a "constitutional phony." Wilkinson agreed. His bench memo reinforced what Powell already believed—that the de facto–de jure distinction was "bogus legal mumbo jumbo" used to allow in northern cities a degree of segregation not tolerated in the South.

But there was more to Powell's position than the wish to play tit for tat. He showed also that the original rationale for the distinction between de jure and de facto segregation was no longer valid. That argument hinged on developments since *Brown v. Board of Education.* Obviously, the facts had changed. The South had gone from the bastion of educational apartheid to the least segregated region of the country. Equally important, the law had changed. The original command to stop *state-imposed* segregation had been replaced by a duty to eliminate *all* segregation where segregation had once been state imposed. The distinction may sound small, but the practical difference between these formulations was in fact enormous. The Supreme Court's shift from one to the other undermined the logic behind the traditional de jure limitation.

As Powell explained, the distinction between de jure and de facto segregation derived from *Brown*, which condemned only state-imposed segregation. Fourteen years later, the Supreme Court had partly abandoned that limitation. *Green* imposed on southern school boards an "affirmative duty" to eliminate segregation "root and branch." The South could not simply stop requiring segregation; it had to take affirmative steps to undo the past by mixing the races. As translated by *Swann* to an urban setting, this meant large-scale busing to achieve racial balance. But—and this is the key—in urban centers racial separation did *not* result exclusively, or perhaps even chiefly, from historic, state-imposed segregation. The underlying culprit was residential segregation, which prevailed in virtually all of America's cities, North and South. As Powell said, "the familiar root cause of segregated schools in all the biracial metropolitan areas of our country is essentially the same"—residential segregation, "the impact of which on the racial composition of the schools was often perpetuated and rarely ameliorated by action of public school authorities." As Powell concluded: "This is a national, not a southern phenomenon. And it is largely unrelated to whether a particular State had or did not have segregatory school laws."

Thus, the law had evolved to a patent contradiction: School districts with a history of formal segregation were required to eliminate *all* segregation, including segregation not attributable to that history; in districts without such a history, school segregation springing from the same root cause was allowed to continue. No wonder the South saw regional bias. School districts with a bad past (including all of the South) had to tackle a problem that other school districts (including some in the North) were allowed to ignore. Powell's conclusion was simple. The Constitution should be interpreted to require a uniform approach to the national problem of segregated schools.

POWELL'S ATTACK on the distinction between de jure and de facto segregation put him in odd company. On the one hand, Justice Douglas and many civil rights lawyers had long urged that view. They argued that de facto segregation was a myth. They conceded that school enrollment reflected housing patterns but argued that that did not absolve the government of responsibility for segregated schools. Residential segregation was itself the government's fault. It might be true that the segregated housing was not caused by school boards, but so what? Segregated housing was supported by other agencies of government in a variety of ways. There was the overt support for all-white neighborhoods by the Federal Housing Administration through the 1940s; the enforcement until 1948 of racially restrictive covenants requiring subdivision purchasers to resell only to other whites; various zoning restrictions that made it harder for lower-income persons of both races to move into desirable neighborhoods; and the usual location of public housing projects in all-black neighborhoods of the inner cities.

In light of the ever-present hand of government, activists argued, it was ludicrous to speak of urban housing patterns as if they reflected purely private choice. That might be true for middle-class whites in their affluent suburbs, but blacks in the inner-city ghettoes did not choose to live there. They were in fact coerced, if not by zoning laws and housing projects, then by the lack of economic opportunity for which the government, after two centuries of official oppression, could not disclaim responsibility. Racially separate housing in the cities of the United States was "very much the result of longstanding white fears of black-invaded neighborhoods working their way into public law and policy." In short, de facto segregation of schools was a myth, because the underlying problem of residential segregation was itself de jure. This argument did not often prevail in the courts, but in the minds of many it undermined confidence in the traditional de facto–de jure distinction.

On the other hand, southern politicos had an altogether different reason for opposing the de jure limitation. They thought the rest of the country would never stand for the treatment the South had been getting. They wanted to export their problems to the nation at large as a way of rallying support for their position. Listen to Jack Edwards, Congressman from Alabama, explaining his vote *against* an antibusing amendment offered by colleagues from Michigan: "I look at it from a rather cold standpoint. We are busing all over the First District of Alabama, as far as you can imagine. Buses are everywhere. . . . People say to me, 'How in the world are we ever going to stop this madness?' I say, 'It will stop the day it starts taking place across the country, in the North, in the East, in the West, and yes, even in Michigan.'"

Such was the rationale of the southern Senators who, in 1970, moved to require that HEW desegregation guidelines apply across the board or not at all. This effort prompted an act of rare political courage by Abraham Ribicoff of Connecticut, who rose to denounce the "monumental hypocrisy" of condemning segregation only in the South. Powell took pleasure in quoting Senator Ribicoff:

> Unfortunately, as the problem of racial isolation has moved north of the Mason-Dixon line, many northerners have bid an evasive farewell to the hundred-year-old struggle for racial equality. Our motto seems to have been 'Do to southerners what you do not want to do to yourself.'
>
> Good reasons have always been offered, of course, for not moving vigorously ahead in the North as well as the South.
>
> First, it was that the problem was worse in the South. Then the facts began to show that that was no longer true.
>
> We then began to hear the de facto–de jure refrain.
>
> Somehow residential segregation in the North was accidental or de facto and that made it better than the legally supported de jure segregation in the South. It was a hard distinction for black children in totally segregated schools in the North to understand, but it allowed us to avoid the problem.

Predictably, Ribicoff was praised by some for spotlighting the need to do more in the North and condemned by others for playing into the hands of southern recalcitrants.

THE SAME DIVISION of opinion doomed Powell's position in *Keyes*. Internal documents show that there was in fact a majority on the Supreme Court to discard the de jure limitation and condemn even de facto school segregation as unconstitutional. But because the supporters of that position were themselves divided on busing, their position on de facto segregation was never adopted. The facts are these.

The Denver school case first came to the Court a year before Powell got there. The question at that time was merely preliminary: Should the trial court's desegregation order be delayed pending appellate review? The appeals court said yes, but the Supreme Court said no. In the course of these deliberations, Justice Douglas circulated a statement approving court-ordered desegregation for de facto schools. This would have overthrown the de jure limitation. Brennan, Stewart, and Marshall agreed. Douglas then had four votes, but since that deadlocked the Court (Justice White not participating), the opinion was not published.

When Powell arrived the following year, that made five votes for dropping the de jure requirement. In fact, there may have been six, as Harry Blackmun later said that he too was persuaded "that the de jure–de facto distinction eventually must give way." Yet when the opinions were finally published, only Powell and Douglas took this position. How six votes were turned into two gives insight into Powell as a Justice and his surprising ineffectiveness as a Court politician.

As has been noted, Brennan's draft stalled on January 9, 1973, when Blackmun announced that he would await other views. Powell and company labored away until April 2, when his draft opinion attacking the de jure limitation was ready for circulation. Brennan responded the next day with a memorandum to his colleagues. At the original Conference, Brennan recalled, a majority of the Justices were committed to the distinction between de facto and de jure segregation, so he had drafted the opinion in those terms. But, he added, "I would be happy indeed to recast the opinion and jettison the distinction if a majority of the Court is prepared to do so." This was an invitation to Powell to join forces—but only on Brennan's terms:

> Although Lewis and I seem to share the view that de facto segregation and de jure segregation (as we have previously used those terms) should receive like constitutional treatment, we are in substantial disagreement, I think, on what that treatment should be. Unlike Lewis, I would retain the definition of the "affirmative duty to desegregate" set forth in our prior cases, [including] *Swann*. Lewis's approach has the virtue of discarding an illogical and unworkable distinction, but only at the price of a substantial retreat from our commitment of the past twenty years to eliminate all vestiges of state-imposed segregation in the public schools. In my view, we can eliminate the distinction without cutting back on our commitment, and I would gladly do so.

Brennan had offered to take Powell's views on the de facto–de jure distinction but not on busing. The offer, however, was contingent. Brennan would change his opinion *if* he could get majority support— that is, if Powell tendered his vote. Had the situation been reversed, had someone with four votes and good prospect of a fifth offered Brennan half a loaf, he would have jumped at the chance. Powell could have done just that. He could have secured a uniform national approach to desegregation and eliminated the "constitutional phony" that plagued the South. But at what price? Would he have had to give up his opposition to busing? That, of course, he was unwilling to do. But would Brennan have been willing to revise his opinion on the de facto–de jure distinction and let Powell go his own way on busing? There is no way of knowing, for Powell never asked. He never tried to accept Brennan's offer on his own terms or approached Brennan to explore the common ground. He never tried to make a deal.

Given Powell's background, this quiescence is surprising. He was an experienced negotiator, skilled in the arts of compromise and adept at evading disagreement. His enormous success in private practice, not to mention his rise to power in the ABA, testifies to his abilities as a behind-the-scenes politician, yet these abilities were never brought to bear in *Keyes*. The reason was partly inexperience. He was new on the Court and the tactical opportunities of that environment—biding one's time, waiting for the right case, laying the foundation now for an argument to be made later—were unfamiliar. Pride of authorship also may have played a part. To join Brennan in eliminating the de facto–de jure distinction would have required that Powell jettison the opinion on which he and Wilkinson had worked so hard. He would naturally have been reluctant to see such labors go for naught.

Most of all, Powell was concerned about how he presented himself to the public. His opposition to busing was too heartfelt to repress, but he knew that an antibusing tirade from a former school board chairman of a segregated southern school district would be treated with contempt. If Powell had joined Brennan on the de facto–de jure distinction and dissented only on busing, he would have had less opportunity to express, in a personal and individual way, his support for desegregation. Shorn of the discussion of the false limitation on the scope of desegregation, Powell's opinion would have seemed merely and predictably antibusing. As Wilkinson later commented, "Powell was very concerned that his position be seen on the whole and in the round"—that is, in favor of a nationwide obligation to desegregate but against forced busing as a means to that end.

These factors explain Powell's missed chance, but they do not tell the whole story. All were specific to the time and context of *Keyes*, and the striking thing about Powell's failure to negotiate is that it was not atypical. In fact, it was characteristic. Of course, he frequently tried to cast his views in ways that would attract support, and he was often ready to balance conflicting arguments and seek a middle ground. But Powell had no interest in making deals. It seemed to him inappropriate. Powell approached the Court with a kind of reverence. The Supreme Court was the temple of his belief in reason, in moderation, in the worth and progress of the search for a perfect balance of order and liberty. He had this faith long before he became a Justice, and he never lost it afterward. He might, in later years, be dismissive of certain points of view, and privately, even of certain Justices, but he never became cynical about the process of judging. There would have been nothing irregular or unethical in approaching Brennan with a view to getting what he could out of the case, but to Powell, this would have been somehow unseemly. The "substantial disagreement" over busing that Brennan noted in his memorandum of April 3 was, in the final analysis, quite real. Powell would not try to avoid it.

In the silence that followed Brennan's letter, Douglas circulated an opinion saying that he joined Brennan but also that he agreed with Powell on the indefensibility of the de jure limitation. Blackmun said nothing. Finally, on May 30, Burger made a clumsy attempt to derail Brennan's draft by suggesting that the case be put over for reargument the following term. The ostensible reason was to allow reconsideration with a Detroit busing case, which Burger thought was somehow connected, but the suggestion was widely viewed as a stall. Brennan shot back a short but devastating letter. "If you have canvassed the *Detroit* issues, as I have, you might agree that none of them is even remotely connected with any decided in *Keyes*." When Burger responded in turn, the bickering proved too much for Blackmun. In the fourth circulation of May 30, Blackmun gave Brennan the essential fifth vote.

His explanation caused Powell no little anguish. "I am persuaded, as Lewis and Bill Douglas appear to be, that the de jure–de facto distinction eventually must give way. Lewis' opinion—both parts of it—is, for me forceful and persuasive." But, since Blackmun felt that "we need not meet the de jure–de facto distinction for purposes of the Denver case," he would join Brennan—not only on the de jure issue but also, crucially and inexplicably, on the issue of busing. In short, Blackmun agreed with Powell but voted with Brennan.

This left only Burger, who probably agreed with Rehnquist that the desegregation order should be limited to Park Hill but who ended up also voting with Brennan. That is, he went along with Brennan's outcome. He did not join Brennan's opinion but published a statement that reads, in its entirety, "MR. CHIEF JUSTICE BURGER concurs in the result."

And so the Denver school case was handed down on June 21. Powell had been energetic, independent, creative, and even courageous, but wholly unsuccessful. The experience left him wearied but resigned. As he told Wilkinson that afternoon: "Sometimes, Jay, there are things one has to do. I suppose that, to be worthy to sit on this Court, you have to be willing to go it alone."

INTERDISTRICT BUSING

Half of Powell's position in *Keyes* died with that case. Never again did he argue for the unconstitutionality of de facto segregation.* Civil rights activists and southern politicians had once made common cause in criticizing the de jure requirement; now both found reason to let it be. Civil rights lawyers no longer had that much to gain, for the Supreme Court had opened the door to nationwide busing without doctrinal change. Proving de jure segregation was tedious and expensive, but, after *Keyes*, almost certain of success. Then, too, outsiders had no way of knowing the support within the Court for overthrowing the de jure limitation. From all that appeared in the opinions, the Justices were committed to it, and civil rights lawyers saw no future in continuing the dispute.

Powell soon reached the same conclusion. For him, as for other antibusing southerners, attacking the de jure limitation had always been a double-edged sword. Eliminating the distinction between de jure and de facto segregation would end the isolation of the South, but it might also extend compulsory transportation across the land. In *Keyes* Powell had tried to get one result without the other, but he had failed. Increasingly, it was clear that desegregation meant busing, and Powell refused to extend that odious remedy for the sake of regional revenge. Now that he had gotten his "Confederate emotions" off his chest, he settled down to a rear-guard action against forced busing.

Although no one could have said so at the time, *Keyes* was, in retrospect, the high-water mark of the Supreme Court's commitment to busing. Not that there was any quick retreat. Lower courts continued to sift through the actions of local school boards to find de jure segregation and, where it was found, to order system-wide desegregation. The Justices sometimes quibbled with how those findings were made, but they did not curtail the spread of busing.

Cases from Columbus and Dayton illustrate the approach. Ohio had outlawed school segregation in 1888. Nevertheless, local school boards, especially in the years before *Brown*, intentionally kept the

---

* He would have had some explaining to do if he had. Powell's position in *Keyes* was doctrinally inconsistent with later decisions holding that the constitutional guarantee against racial discrimination is violated only where there is a discriminatory purpose. The mere fact that government action affects whites and blacks differently does not make it unconstitutional. Since Powell supported these rulings, he would have had to find some ground for distinguishing his position on de facto segregation of schools.

Cleaning his mess kit in North Africa.
(Collection of the Supreme Court of the United States)

With Brigadier General George McDonald at Hitler's retreat near Berchtesgaden. *(Collection of the Supreme Court of the United States)*

(Caption is on facing page)

Lewis and Jo at the Greenbrier, 1948. *(Chase Studios, Washington; Collection of the Supreme Court of the United States)*

Opposite: Touring France with General of the Army Henry H. "Hap" Arnold, April 1945. *(Collection of the Supreme Court of the United States)*

Powell with his parents and
Lewis III, 1954. *(Dementi-Foster
Studios; Collection of the Supreme Court
of the United States)*

From left to right: Molly, Penny, and Jo with their parents at Jo's Debutante
Ball, 1957. *(J. Etheridge Ward; Collection of the Supreme Court of the United States)*

Powell strikes a characteristic pose, 1965.
(Grauman Marks; Collection of the Supreme Court of the United States)

With Lewis III after a football game at Washington and Lee.
(Collection of the Supreme Court of the United States)

Justice Potter Stewart receiving an award from Powell at the ABA annual meeting, 1970. *(Sievers Photo, St. Louis; Collection of the Supreme Court of the United States)*

President Nixon with his nominees. *(The Nixon Project, National Archives)*

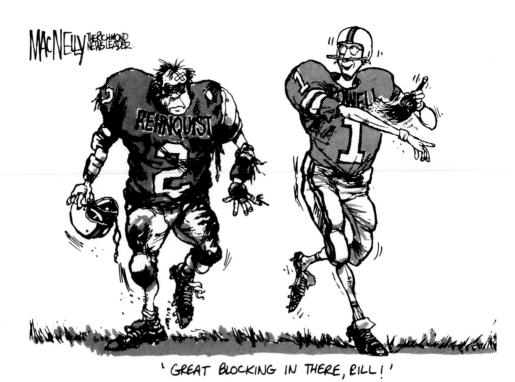

'GREAT BLOCKING IN THERE, BILL!'

Cartoonist Jeff MacNelly's comment on the confirmation.

(Cartoon by Jeff MacNelly. Reprinted by permission of Tribune Media Services)

races apart. This history put the cities under an affirmative duty to desegregate. Neighborhood schools would not do. Instead, children would be bused from one neighborhood to another to achieve racial balance. As in all these cases, court-ordered busing was justified as a remedy for the malefactions of local school boards.

This was *Keyes* all over again, but Powell's strategy was entirely different. This time he did not dispute the requirement of de jure segregation; he used it. If the majority could exploit past sins to justify today's busing, Powell could exploit the lack of connection between the two. He would fight busing by showing that the past acts of local school boards actually had little to do with the racial separation that busing was meant to remedy.

The argument was easy to make. In cities such as Columbus and Dayton, the traditional justification of busing as a remedy for de jure segregation had been stretched beyond plausibility. Powell ridiculed the supposed connection between isolated past acts of local school boards and the widespread existence of predominantly black schools. "I would particularly like to emphasize," he wrote his clerk, "the fallaciousness of the assumption . . . that there has been a system-wide violation of constitutional rights in the sense that but for such violation there would be no predominantly black schools in the school district. No rational human being could believe this to be true."

Powell was right. No rational human being could believe that residential segregation in Columbus and Dayton and other northern cities resulted from the acts of local school boards. Under the de jure theory (which Powell had denounced in *Keyes*), school segregation violated the Constitution *only* if it resulted from government action. Therefore, he reasoned, the separation of the races in urban centers was not unconstitutional, and federal judges could not seek to correct it by forced busing.

His published opinion restated the point as follows: "There are unintegrated schools in every major urban area in the country that contains a substantial minority population. This condition results primarily from familiar segregated housing patterns, which—in turn—are caused by social, economic, and demographic forces for which no school board is responsible." By requiring system-wide busing "without relation to the causes of the segregation found to exist," the federal courts were acting without constitutional justification.

This was not Powell's position in *Keyes*; it was Rehnquist's. Rehnquist had never been swayed by Powell's attack on de facto segregation. He saw, as Powell later came to see, that the de jure limitation could be used to constrain judicial intervention and busing. Now Powell and Rehnquist joined forces. After *Keyes*, they voted together in *every* school desegregation case for the rest of Powell's tenure on the Court. Often, as in the Columbus and Dayton cases, they were in dissent.

NOTWITHSTANDING THESE SETBACKS, the attack on busing was gaining ground. Ironically, the crippling blow was struck by the Supreme Court itself, which with one hand encouraged the experiment of busing and with the other ensured its failure. The decisive event was the Court's rejection of interdistrict busing.

The issue first came to the Supreme Court from Powell's hometown. Indeed, each stage in the long history of school desegregation was recapitulated in Richmond. From total resistance to token compliance, from "freedom of choice" to massive forced busing, Richmond saw it all. The busing order came from Powell's longtime friend, District Judge Robert R. Merhige, Jr.

Born in Brooklyn of immigrant stock, Bob Merhige came to Richmond almost by accident. He took a part-time job there as a football coach, hoping to send himself through law school at the College of William and Mary. On discovering that the school was fifty miles away in Williamsburg, he enrolled instead at the University of Richmond and, after the war, returned there to practice law. He became one of Richmond's best and best-known trial lawyers, despite his refusal to embrace the buttoned-down style of the city elite. Merhige was short, voluble, witty, politically liberal and personally irresistible. He lacked any trace of formality or reserve, with a taste in clothes that made him "look like a sherbet factory."

In manner and appearance Merhige was the antithesis of Lewis Powell, yet they admired each other.* Over the years, Merhige did a good deal of referral work, mostly divorce and minor criminal matters, for Hunton, Williams lawyers who were too silk-stocking for that sort of thing. In his only appearance opposite Powell, Merhige came out on top. He had sued two department stores on behalf of an employee and won a favorable settlement by cheerfully speculating on the how the jury would react to the fact that one of the defendant's officers had recently been convicted of wartime profiteering.

A vacancy on the federal bench arose in the mid-1960s, and a com-

---

*   Their relationship was cemented in 1978, when Merhige hired Lewis III as his law clerk. When young Lewis showed up for work, Merhige feigned surprise and lamented that he thought he was hiring "the real Lewis Powell."

mittee of Richmond lawyers, including partners from Hunton, Williams, organized to support Bob Merhige. When the nomination stalled, Powell and others went to see Ramsey Clark, then Lyndon Johnson's Attorney General. The intervention was providential, as the Justice Department mistakenly thought Merhige had received less than the highest professional rating from the American Bar Association. Powell had the ABA correct the misimpression, and Merhige took the oath of office on August 30, 1967. Richmond would soon learn that the brash confidence of Bob Merhige, the rough-and-tumble trial lawyer, would also animate the Honorable Robert R. Merhige, Jr., District Judge.

The Richmond desegregation suit had lain dormant since 1966, when the court suggested, and the school board adopted, "freedom of choice." Two years later, in *Green*, the Supreme Court demanded desegregation *now*. Surprisingly, the Richmond plaintiffs did not immediately seek to capitalize on that decision. Their lawyer, Powell critic Henry Marsh, had won a seat on the city council and in that position could not very well sue the school board. Eventually Marsh withdrew from the case, and his successors asked for additional relief. In 1971, Merhige ordered busing.

White Richmond reacted with fulmination and outrage. The *Times-Dispatch* inveighed against Merhige's "appalling decision," his "shocking lack of concern" for the welfare of children, his "callous disregard" for quality of education, and his "total contempt" for the legitimate concerns and parents and children. Letters to the editor made this diatribe seem mild by comparison. And harsh words were not the worst of it. Merhige's dog was shot, and a small cottage on his property was burned.

In Powell's circles, lawlessness was deplored, but busing was scarcely less unpopular. In fact, Powell's emotional antipathy to compulsory transportation dates in part from the scalding experience in Richmond, where the community was torn, white opinion outraged, and issues of educational quality shunted aside in the convulsion that followed Merhige's order. Even sympathetic observers conceded that "the busing orders accelerated the perceived as well as the actual deterioration in the school system's discipline, morale, achievement levels and community support." Powell agreed. He watched with dismay as, a few weeks later, the Supreme Court announced its decision in *Swann*, which showed that Merhige had been right in the eyes of the law, if not in the eyes of many Richmonders.

Richmond was like Charlotte, but with one decisive difference.

Charlotte's schools had a substantial white majority; Richmond's did not. The combined Charlotte-Mecklenburg school system encompassed the outlying suburbs as well as the inner city, and the student population when busing began was more than 70 percent white. By 1970 Richmond's schools were 70 percent black. In that year, annexation of a mostly white area briefly brought that number down to 60 percent. In April 1971, when Merhige ordered busing for the coming school year, black enrollment was projected at 63 percent but in fact rose higher. By the end of the first month of school, one in five of the remaining white students had left the Richmond system. The exodus raised black enrollment to 69 percent of the total, and everyone expected it to rise further still. Within a very short time of beginning to bus, Richmond found itself engaged in a costly and bitterly resented program of compulsory transportation to rearrange the races in an increasingly one-race school system.

By itself, there was nothing the city could do. Richmond is surrounded by two counties—Henrico to the north and west, and Chesterfield to the east and south. Both were (and are) overwhelmingly white and largely middle class. In Virginia, unlike other states, cities and counties are mutually exclusive. For a city to expand into an adjacent county requires a judicial annexation proceeding, with compensation to the county for the land and capital improvements lost to it. Such proceedings are protracted, expensive, and often only partly successful. Thus, Richmond could neither stop whites from settling in the surrounding counties nor readily expand to bring those areas within its jurisdiction.

Nor could it realistically hope for blacks to disperse to the suburbs. Richmond's black population was not only racially concentrated, it was also, in the main, economically disadvantaged. Neither Henrico nor Chesterfield was hospitable to low-income residents. Both counties opposed public housing and maintained economically restrictive zoning. Thus, residential segregation prevailed not only within Richmond, but also among the three political subdivisions of the metropolitan area.

Faced with white flight and no means of self-help, the Richmond School Board took an extraordinary step. It asked Judge Merhige to order the consolidation of the Richmond, Henrico, and Chesterfield schools into one metropolitan system. In essence, Richmond asked Merhige to remake the local school districts in order to provide the essential raw materials for eliminating one-race schools—namely, substantial numbers of children of both races.

On January 10, 1972—three days after Powell took his seat on the Supreme Court—Merhige issued his order. Richmond, Henrico, and Chesterfield would be consolidated into a single school system. The metropolitan area would then be divided into geographic subdivisions shaped like the pieces of a pie. Busing would exchange black pupils from Richmond with white pupils from the adjacent suburbs. The plan would eliminate all one-race schools and maintain in every school a comfortable white majority. The proportion of black students would range from 17 to 40 percent, which Merhige hoped would be below the "tipping point" at which "white students tend to disappear . . . entirely." In effect, Merhige tried to create in Richmond by judicial decree the metropolitan school district that existed in Charlotte by community choice.

This order was literally unprecedented. No federal judge had previously required metropolitan consolidation. Merhige knew that his decree would be in trouble in the Fourth Circuit, so he tried to protect against reversal by amassing such a wealth of factual support that his solution would seem inevitable. In 325 printed pages, Merhige made his case. He recounted the history of segregative acts by all three localities and the surreptitious cooperation of state officials. He found that the city-county boundaries were unrelated to educational needs and that they helped maintain residential segregation. He charged that the counties' insistence on local control merely masked their desire to resist integration. All this and much more Merhige detailed, but the heart of his argument was straightforward and plain. Consolidation was justified because it was necessary. No other means existed to eliminate one-race schools.

The Fourth Circuit reversed. For the majority, it was decisive that the city-county boundaries had not been created or manipulated for the purpose of segregating schools. The suburban systems might be havens for middle-class whites who wanted to avoid integration, but there was no evidence that they had been designed for that purpose. The counties, which had existed long before desegregation became an issue, could continue to function as separate localities with their own school districts and could not be forced to consolidate with of Richmond. The appeals court therefore upheld busing within the city but struck down busing to and from the surrounding suburbs.

The Supreme Court split down the middle. Douglas, Brennan, White, and Marshall sided with the imperatives of desegregation; Burger, Stewart, Blackmun, and Rehnquist, with the sanctity of local government. Powell did not participate. The mere fact that he was deeply concerned about busing was no reason to recuse himself from the case, nor did he stand to gain or lose financially. But his role in the long history recounted in Judge Merhige's opinion might have distorted his judgment or at least caused others to think so. It was a clear case for recusal.

With the remaining Justices deadlocked, the Fourth Circuit was upheld by default. As is customary in such cases, the Supreme Court issued no opinion. It published only the usual formula: "The judgment is affirmed by an equally divided Court."

WHEN THE ISSUE of interdistrict busing next came to the Supreme Court, the focus was squarely on Lewis Powell. Everyone knew that he would cast the deciding vote.

This time the scene was Detroit, and the situation there was in many ways Richmond writ large. The city of Detroit was becoming increasingly black and poor and surrounded by suburbs that were overwhelmingly white and largely middle class. Reshuffling students within the city was pointless. Detroit would end up, like Richmond, with "an all black school system immediately surrounded by practically all white suburban school systems." To avoid this fate, the lower courts planned busing to the suburbs. Specifically, they planned the daily transportation of more than 300,000 pupils back and forth between the city and some fifty-three outlying school districts. The sheer magnitude of the undertaking was breathtaking. Also unsettling was the fact that none of the suburban districts had been found guilty of de jure segregation. Both the city of Detroit and the state of Michigan stood condemned for past discrimination, but the suburbs were involved in the decree only because their white students were needed to offset the black majority in Detroit. Again, as in Richmond, the question was whether the drive for racial balance or the integrity of local governments would win out.

For Powell, the question was easy. If some busing was bad, more was worse. He doubted that busing could achieve any durable solution, even if it were expanded to include the suburbs. Moreover, he fervently believed in local control of education. Powell therefore came down against the interdistrict remedy and handed school desegregation plaintiffs their first Supreme Court defeat.

He did not write in the case, at least not for publication. The Chief Justice took the opinion himself and in due course circulated a draft. Astonishingly, it dealt with the wrong issue. Still smarting from his defeat in *Swann*, Burger wrote as if the Court had decided to overrule its endorsement of busing. He said a great deal about the lower court's misguided search for racial balance in every grade of every school but gave scant attention to the crucial question of the interdistrict remedy. This approach was worse than obtuse; it was risky. Burger's general criticism of busing struck a responsive chord with Powell and Rehnquist, but they also needed Stewart and Blackmun, who had joined *Swann* and who, unlike Burger, seemed to have meant what they said there. If by flailing at the wrong issue, Burger lost their votes, the outcome might be so fractured and confused as to snatch defeat from the jaws of victory.

Thoroughly alarmed, Powell wrote the Chief Justice. He tried to deflect Burger from the general attack on busing, which was not a winning issue, to the specific question of interdistrict busing, which was. Powell relied heavily on the brief of Robert Bork, the former Yale professor who had been named Solicitor General of the United States at the end of Nixon's first term. Bork first came to Nixon's attention as an opponent of busing. Now he appeared in the Detroit case as a "friend of the court" to advise the Justices of the views of the federal government.

Bork's argument was crisp and lawyerly. Desegregation decrees were governed by a legal rule of general applicability: The remedy should fit the constitutional violation it was meant to redress. If Detroit was guilty of de jure segregation, Detroit could be required to bus children to desegregate its schools. If the suburbs had collaborated in that violation—as, for example, by manipulating district boundaries in order to keep black students in the city—they also could be made to bus. But courts could not order an interdistrict remedy absent proof of an interdistrict violation. The scope of the remedy was limited by the scope of the violation.

This reasoning might be thought more legalistic than realistic, but it was clear and logical and could win five votes. All Burger had to do was crib Bork's brief and he would gain a Court. Powell pointed the way by liberally quoting Bork's submission, but the Chief made only minor revisions and there was no rush to join his opinion. On June 3, Rehnquist wrote Burger with suggestions for reforming the opinion, but there was still no progress. Ten days later, all five members of the potential majority met to hash out the mess. Powell came armed with a few pages that he meant to substitute for part of what Burger had written, but instead they simply got folded into the mix. Four days afterward Stewart weighed in with a letter restating many of Powell's objections, and the next day Blackmun endorsed Stewart's letter.

Burger responded with yet another draft and the insentient comment that "our differences are essentially semantical."

As the successive drafts crept toward acceptability, time was running out. Ordinarily, the Court would have adjourned by early July and any case not completed would have been put over until the next term. But in the summer of 1974 the Justices had agreed to stay in Washington to hear the Nixon tapes case. Given that opportunity, the Detroit case was continued for some weeks past the end of the usual term and was finally handed down on July 25. Despite the extra time, the Court's opinion was not persuasive. It was clear enough in saying that an interdistrict remedy required proof of an interdistrict violation, but not at all clear in explaining just *why* that should be so. There were a few sentences on the virtues of local control and pertinent remarks on the difficulties of judicial intervention. These were sensible concerns, but the Court's cursory recitation did not make a strong case. Ultimately, the majority came to rest on a legalism: The scope of the remedy is limited by the scope of the violation. From all that appears, the human dimensions of the underlying social problems were simply outside the Justices' concern.

In dissent, Thurgood Marshall called the Court's decision "a giant step backwards" from the great ideal of equal justice under law. The Court had disapproved the only feasible means of desegregating Detroit's schools. In its insistence that the remedy should fit the violation, the majority had provided "no remedy at all." For the dissenters, the boundaries of local school districts were not as important as desegregated schools for the children in those districts: "We deal here with the right of all of our children, whatever their race to an equal start in life and to an equal opportunity to reach their full potential as citizens. Those children who have been denied that right in the past deserve better than to see fences thrown up to deny them that right in the future."

Critics off the Court were more outspoken. NAACP general counsel Nathaniel R. Jones saw the Detroit busing case as "the sad but inevitable culmination of a national anti-black strategy." Derrick A. Bell, Jr., a leading scholar on race and racism, recalled the hapless white boxer who found that he could run but could not hide from heavyweight champ Joe Louis. Unlike that failed "white hope," said Bell, for years white Americans had been "running from blacks in the inner cities and hiding in the suburbs." The Detroit case helped them do it. Judge Skelly Wright said that the Supreme Court had "abandoned the ideals of *Brown* at the sign reading 'City Limits.'" The Court, he charged, had "legitimated and accelerated the national trend toward residential, political, and educational apartheid."

But if these observers were alarmed by the Detroit decision, there was also something traditional and familiar in the Court's approach. The requirement of de jure segregation had always focused on school boards and school districts, not zoning laws and housing patterns. The acts of local school boards were sifted and searched for evidence of discrimination, but residential segregation was usually found to be nobody's fault. This approach walled off school desegregation cases from the broader problems of economic disparity and racial isolation. It made sure that a school case was treated as a school case and nothing more.

The federal courts in Richmond and Detroit had taken on more than *school* segregation. They tried to use schools as the point of attack on a segregated society. The underlying problem that these courts faced was not just one-race schools but the pervasive racism of American society generally. Racism was manifest in segregated schools but also in black poverty and urban housing patterns. As the National Advisory Commission on Civil Disorders had argued: "What white Americans have never fully understood—but what the Negro can never forget—is that white society is implicated in the ghetto. White institutions created it, white institutions maintain it, and white society condones it." Interdistrict busing would have used the school bus as the vehicle for a judicial attack on the racial structure of American cities. With Powell's tie-breaking vote, the Supreme Court turned that effort aside. The requirement of an interdistrict violation ensured that the school bus would be used only to solve school problems.

In this sense, the Detroit school case was, in Jay Wilkinson's phrase, "an act of absolution." It absolved white America of legal responsibility for the ghetto. Because the suburbs did not create segregation in Detroit, they had no duty to relieve it. The concentration of poor blacks in the inner cities was a social problem, not a constitutional violation. Leaving the problem to politicians meant no interdistrict busing. That much was certain. Inner city education might or might not improve, but there would be no forced exchange of pupils between the pleasant white neighborhoods of suburban America and the urban underclass.

Why? What caused the Court that approved busing in *Swann* to reject interdistrict relief? Two obvious answers were Powell and Rehnquist, but they were only two votes. What accounted for the other three? Thurgood Marshall thought he knew. He charged that his colleagues had given in to the strident public opposition to busing.

"Today's holding," he feared, "is more a reflection of a perceived public mood that we have gone far enough in enforcing the Constitution's guarantee of equal justice than it is the product of neutral principles of law."

Marshall did not mean that the Justices followed opinion polls. Those who entertain that suspicion do not understand the splendid isolation of life in the marble palace. Supreme Court Justices are at least middle-aged. There is no possibility of promotion, and none expects to hold a different job. Neither can they be demoted or fired (save by the extraordinary and extraordinarily difficult process of impeachment). As Marshall himself grew fond of saying, "I have a lifetime appointment and I intend to serve it." Of course, a Justice may prefer a life free from criticism, but popular opinion becomes a small matter when it has no practical consequence.

Marshall's point was different. Public opposition to busing mattered, not because it would make the Justices uncomfortable, but because it might make busing fail. The eruption of violence in Boston was still a few months away, but no one doubted in the summer of 1974 that resistance to forced busing from the suburbs to the inner city would be intense, prolonged, and embittered. Violence could be faced down but at what cost? More insidious, more damaging, and more difficult to control was white flight. Ironically, interdistrict busing was supposedly the answer to white flight. The trial judge wanted to bus the Detroit suburbs precisely because he knew that busing only the city would drive whites out. Including the suburbs would mean whites would have to go that much farther to outrun the school bus.

But might they do just that? Powell thought so. Even before *Swann*, he had warned that even "new and enlarged boundaries would not long contain a mobile and unwilling population." At some point, time and distance would curtail busing, and that point might well fall short of where some white parents were prepared to flee. Greater Detroit, for example, had eighty-five outlying school districts. The trial court ordered busing to and from the inner fifty-three districts. What if whites with school-age children simply moved farther out? What if they resorted to private schools? Would they do so? Would they do so in sufficient numbers to defeat desegregation? If so, would forced busing be expanded yet again in an effort to reach the outer suburbs?

Detroit and the surrounding counties had a million public school children in an area the size of Delaware. Would the court eventually find itself trying to construct and maintain a busing plan for the entire metropolitan area? How would the amalgamated entity be governed?

Who would determine tax rates, bond issues, building locations, and teacher salaries? The questions were endless, and the prospect of answering them in a court of law—and of revising those answers repeatedly as the circumstances changed from year to year—was, to say the least, unnerving.

To Powell, busing had always seemed a dangerous experiment. The Detroit case showed how complex and expensive it could become, yet there was no guarantee it would work. In his mind, the Detroit busing case did not condone the ghetto; it merely recognized its resistance to judicial decree. Ultimately, he and the other Justices in the majority shared the rueful comment of the appeals court judge in the Richmond case who said, "A school case, like a vehicle, can carry only a limited amount of baggage."

WAS INTERDISTRICT BUSING in fact doomed to fail? Or could metropolitan remedies of the sort proposed in Richmond and Detroit have saved America's cities from educational decay? Subsequent experience has been cautionary but not conclusive. Interdistrict busing was tried on a smaller scale in Wilmington, Delaware, and Louisville, Kentucky. Things went reasonably well in Wilmington but not in Louisville. The National Guard had to be called out to escort children to school, and the combined Louisville–Jefferson County school district experienced sudden and substantial white flight as soon as interdistrict busing was ordered.

Ultimately, however, the controversy over interdistrict busing boils down to a question of goals. It is the same question posed by Powell's brief in *Swann* and raised in a long succession of desegregation disputes since that time. It is a question that has divided scholars and community leaders, both black and white. What exactly is the constitutional goal? Is racial mixing an end in itself? Or is it merely one ingredient in equal educational opportunity?

The difference is this. If racial mixing is an end in itself, interdistrict busing is essential. Often, there is no other way. The degree of racial mixing that will result from interdistrict busing or any other desegregation plan is often unclear, and generally speaking, results have fallen short of expectations. But despite those uncertainties, this much is plain: In most large urban centers, interdistrict busing would produce greater racial mixing in public schools than could be obtained by any other means. If racial balance is the key goal, the Detroit decision is surely wrong.

On the other hand, if the ultimate goal is equal educational opportunity, the issue is far from clear. Powell believed that busing hurt education. Busing controversies diverted attention from issues of educational quality, divided communities along racial lines, and encouraged abandonment of public schools by the middle class. As Powell suggested in *Keyes*, busing was a leap in the dark. Powell foresaw that attention would be diverted from the paramount goal of education to "a perennially divisive debate over who is to be transported where." Powell saw busing as a disastrously misguided experiment, likely to destroy local support for the public schools without really helping either blacks or whites. These views were and are deeply controverted, but the lamentable history of urban desegregation makes it hard to say that he was wholly wrong.

RACIAL BALANCE OR QUALITY EDUCATION?— THE DALLAS SCHOOL CASE

The law of school desegregation had now reached a dead end. *Swann* ordered busing to achieve racial balance despite residential segregation. *Keyes* extended that requirement to cities across the nation. But the Detroit case said the obligation stopped at the city line. The law was beset with internal contradiction. *Swann* and *Keyes* rejected neighborhood schools in the cities; the Detroit case protected neighborhood schools in the suburbs.

This combination of rulings was a blueprint for disaster. Unwittingly, the Supreme Court had maximized the incentive for white flight. On the one hand, busing within cities eliminated white enclaves and broke down residential barriers between the middle class and the urban poor. This gave middle-class whites reason to leave. On the other hand, the refusal to bus the suburbs protected white enclaves and built up residential barriers between the middle class and the urban poor. This gave middle-class whites a place to go. With both carrot and stick, the Court had encouraged white flight.

"White flight" is a complex social phenomenon not well captured by that simple phrase. In fact, the term is a misnomer, as actual relocation to the suburbs is less important than the nonentrance of new families to the city. The least predictable element is the resort to private schools. Elite boarding schools are largely the preserve of the wealthy, but, if sufficiently motivated, large segments of the middle class find some form of private education within their means.

Despite the anecdotal familiarity of these effects, white flight is much disputed among social scientists. Of course, the steadily, and sometimes sharply, declining white enrollment in city school systems is well documented. What is disputed is the degree to which the loss of white students was caused by school desegregation. On that issue, the inherent difficulties of social science research and variations in the circumstances being investigated are compounded by the tendency of observers to describe what they wish to see. Busing's supporters are reluctant to admit that the practice causes white flight. Its opponents are likely to exaggerate the phenomenon as a sort of scientific scare tactic. The result is a body of research characterized, in the words of one expert, "by dissensus, inconclusiveness, indeterminacy and subjectivity."

Despite the controversies, most assessments would support the following observations. First, school desegregation was not the chief cause of falling white enrollment in city schools. Demographic changes in America's cities and a declining white birthrate led to declining white enrollment in urban school systems, quite apart from desegregation. Second, school desegregation, and especially busing, did exacerbate the loss of white students. The existence of this effect is more or less clear (and in some cases unmistakable), but its magnitude is uncertain. It surely varied from city to city and from time to time. Generally speaking, white flight soared when a new desegregation plan was implemented, and the incremental white departure attributable to desegregation declined thereafter. Thus, although the Supreme Court's desegregation decisions did not in themselves cause white flight or the resegregation of city schools, they did make a bad situation worse.

And the problem was not only racial but social also. The exclusion of Grosse Point Woods and St. Clair Shores from the Detroit busing order brought a class bias to desegregation. The denizens of the suburbs were usually well off. The cities trapped the disadvantaged of both races. The social burden of achieving racial equality was anything but equal. As Jay Wilkinson put it: With busing, the Supreme Court "declared an all-out war" on school segregation, "but then decided that much of the citizenry was not required to participate. Not surprisingly, the necessary national commitment never developed. The chief question among whites became how to avoid the conscription of the courts." Perhaps, he mused, "this is how we handle racial problems in this country: by leaving poor blacks and working-class whites to trench warfare, while most of middle-class America remains comfortably quartered outside the battle zone."

*   *   *

IN RETROSPECT, the Court's policy seems to have been doomed to failure. The Court would have been wiser to fish or cut bait—either to require much more busing or to allow much less. Interdistrict busing would have increased social upheaval, but it also would have inhibited white flight and helped prevent resegregation of city schools. Tolerating neighborhood schools would have stalled racial mixing, but it also would have made white flight less attractive and helped maintain middle-class support for urban education. The choice between these alternatives might be bitterly contested, but there was no point in splitting the difference. The Court had to follow through or back off.

Instead, it adopted a policy of halfhearted coercion. More accurately, it adopted a policy of wholehearted coercion half of the time. The Supreme Court's message to the lower federal courts was nonsensical. Bus the cities but not the suburbs; do whatever is necessary to achieve racial balance *within* a given school system, but do little or nothing to require racial balance *among* school systems. This compromise sacrificed the best chance to achieve racial balance, but did nothing to promote alternative aspects of equal educational opportunity.

By the mid 1970s, debate over the goals of desegregation—a question broached by Powell in his brief in *Swann*—was well underway. The NAACP and the NAACP Legal Defense Fund (which became separate entities for tax reasons) continued to see integration as the goal. Since lawyers from these organizations conducted almost all school desegregation suits, their perspective was pushed on the courts. Typically, the NAACP and the Legal Defense Fund tried to achieve for every school a racial mix close to (within 10 or 15 percent) that of the system as a whole. Racial balance was their top priority, and busing was the means to that end.

Increasingly, however, blacks began to question this agenda. Some civil rights leaders came to believe that racial balance was less important than black learning. They argued that the immediate goal should not be to maximize racial mixing but rather to improve black education.

Theoretically, racial mixing and educational improvement were not incompatible. Indeed, for a time, they seemed perfectly aligned. Putting white children and black children in the same classroom was intended not only to end the massive racial insult of educational apartheid but also to improve black learning. That in fact was the theory of *Brown*. Education would improve naturally, almost effortlessly, once the black child was relieved of the psychic and cultural isolation of segregation. Even as that pristine faith began to falter, other reasons were found for equating quality education with racial mixing. There was the hostage theory. Putting white children in black schools would force whites to care about (and pay for) black education. As NAACP General Counsel Nathaniel Jones quipped, black parents knew that "green follows white."

Yet as the 1970s advanced, some civil rights advocates came to doubt that there was any necessary link between racial mixing and improved learning. In a famous 1976 article, law professor Derrick Bell advanced the heretical view that "court orders mandating racial balance may be (depending on the circumstances) educationally advantageous, irrelevant, or even *disadvantageous*" to black children. There were many reasons. White resistance was obviously hurtful to black children. This was true of the nine black students yelled at and spat upon as they entered Little Rock's Central High School under massive armed guard in 1957, and of the 135 black students trapped by the angry white mob surrounding a South Boston high school in 1974. Not surprisingly, only a fraction of those students ever returned to the white school. Then, too, black children usually bore the greater share of the inconveniences of busing. They started earlier, rode longer, and returned later to their homes and neighborhoods. Once they reached their destination, black students were neither welcomed nor understood. Often, they were confronted by racial insensitivity, or worse, from their teachers. Cultural differences were alienating and isolating. Disciplinary suspensions of black students seemed unaccountably high. Far too often, even fully desegregated systems were "an educational wasteland for black children."

Some black leaders came to believe that integration and education did not necessarily go hand in hand. Rather than strive at all costs for racial balance in the classroom, why not concentrate instead on the quality of education offered there? *Brown* had held that separate education was inherently unequal. But black education in America was not unequal only because it was separate. In almost every respect, in cities and counties, both North and South, black schools were poor schools. The question was whether the immediate target of litigation should be the separateness of black education or its inequality. Which should have top priority? The choice of targets was not freely made, for after the Detroit decision, busing to achieve racial balance seemed increasingly futile. No matter how carefully the declining white enrollment was redistributed, overwhelmingly black school systems remained overwhelmingly black. In many of America's large cities, educational improvement became the only game in town.

*   *   *

A RUDIMENTARY VERSION of this strategy surfaced in Detroit after the Supreme Court struck down interdistrict busing. The trial court rejected an NAACP proposal to bring every school in the city within 15 percent of the overall ratio. Given the large black majority in the system as a whole, this plan had some odd implications. A school with 55 percent black enrollment would have been too white, but a school with 85 percent black enrollment would have been accepted as not racially identifiable. The court approved a plan that required less busing and relied in part on neighborhood schools. No school would have been more than 70 percent white, but some schools would have remained virtually all black. Additionally, the judge ordered various "educational components" to redress the learning deficit left by segregation. These included an in-service training program to assist teachers and administrators in treating all students fairly; revised testing procedures to eliminate cultural bias; special guidance and counseling programs to deal with the problems and tensions arising from desegregation; and, perhaps most important, a remedial reading program. The overall effect was to shift the emphasis from racial balance to educational quality as the immediate goal of desegregation.

Although the Detroit decree took only a modest step in this direction, the intensity of reaction to it revealed deep division within the black leadership. Mayor Coleman Young praised the plan as a sensible step toward better black education. Cornelius Golightly, also black and president of the Detroit School Board, called it "a very reasonable solution to how you desegregate a school system that is predominantly black." But NAACP General Counsel Nathaniel Jones called it "an abomination" and "a rape of the constitutional rights of black children." Nor was this an isolated instance. In Boston, in Atlanta, and elsewhere, the civil rights community split between those who demanded busing no matter what and those who were willing to trade racial balance for educational "sweeteners."

When the Detroit case came back to the Supreme Court, the only question before the Justices was whether the educational components could be included in a desegregation decree. (The extent of intracity busing was being reconsidered by the District Court.) At the Conference, Powell and Rehnquist wanted to reverse the order, and Burger and Stewart were undecided. No one doubted that the educational components were a good idea, but there was doubt that they should be ordered by a federal court. Powell, known inside the Court as "the school board's friend," sided with the local board against court interference. But when it became clear that the school board actually wanted the court order, Powell decided to go along. He did so in a grumpy little opinion stating that only the convoluted and bizarre history of the Detroit desegregation case justified the District Court in "virtually assum[ing] the role of school superintendent and school board."* Ultimately, the Court was unanimous in approving the educational components. This ruling made clear that programs designed to improve learning could legitimately be included in a desegregation decree.

OF ALL THE DESEGREGATION CASES on which Powell sat, none so clearly revealed his personal hopes and fears as the litigation from Dallas. To many, the case seemed unimportant. The Fifth Circuit Court of Appeals had ordered the trial court to reconsider some aspects of a desegregation decree. The Supreme Court merely let that order stand. No new principle of law was announced. No precedent was overruled. The majority did not even issue an opinion. But to Powell, Dallas was the full flowering of a decade of judicial mistakes. All the evils that he had foretold—white flight, urban resegregation, displacement of local control and the stifling of local initiative, preoccupation with racial balance at the expense of quality education—were involved in Dallas. The Supreme Court's refusal to intervene seemed to Powell monumental folly.

In 1971 District Judge William M. Taylor, Jr., ordered desegregation in Dallas. His plan did not comport with *Swann* and was eventually disapproved by the Fifth Circuit in 1975. Judge Taylor now faced an alarming situation. The desegregation plan that had been too little for

---

*   Originally, the Detroit desegregation plaintiffs and the school board had been adversaries, but over time their positions changed. The educational components were first proposed by the school board as part of a package with reduced emphasis on racial balance. The plaintiffs objected to the limitation of busing, but had no quarrel with the various special programs that the school board wanted. The odd thing is that the board had the power to adopt these programs without court order, which is why Powell at first assumed that the school board must have opposed the court order.

What the school board lacked was money. The board's object was to force the state of Michigan to pay for educational sweeteners that would aid desegregation. It did this by persuading the District Court to include these programs in its desegregation decree, which the state of Michigan could not resist. Although the state had no dispute with the merits of the educational components, it simply did not want to pay for them. What distressed and distracted Powell was the spectacle of having these questions of state-local responsibility turned over to a court of law. Ultimately, however, he agreed that the situation in Detroit was so bad that judicial interference was justified.

the Fifth Circuit had been too much for many whites. Between 1971 and 1975, Anglo students (the word was used to identify non-Mexican-American whites) fell from 69 to 41 percent of the total. Anglo enrollment in the Dallas school system had dropped 40 percent and was still falling.

The relation to desegregation seemed obvious. At the least, court-ordered desegregation had intensified underlying trends and converted slow attrition into a sudden, massive, and apparently continuing Anglo exodus. Busing would only hasten that trend. Resegregation of schools was the predictable result, and though Judge Taylor later said that he "never felt we had any potential for violence," the possibility cannot have been far from his mind. The antibusing violence that racked Boston in 1974–75 was too recent and too widely publicized to have been completely ignored. But Dallas was not Boston. It was younger, stronger, and—in the heyday of oil—richer. Dallas would make desegregation work.

In that can-do spirit, Taylor prodded the Dallas business community to get involved with desegregation. He spoke privately to business leaders and, when nothing much happened, delivered a public tongue-lashing. He said it was the "height of shortsightedness" for business leaders to sit on the sidelines. Their aim was "to attract other businesses and industries into this great city and they, of all people, should know that there is little hope of success in that regard if public education here is inferior and if the city is torn by racial strife."

The response was the Dallas Alliance, a collection of business heavyweights and civic leaders who established correspondent relationships with a wide variety of community organizations. The Alliance appointed and funded an Educational Task Force consisting of seven Anglos, seven Mexican-Americans, six blacks, and one Native American. Their job was to produce a consensus school desegregation plan. They did so, and Taylor adopted their plan without major change.

The ethnic map of many cities—including Charlotte and Richmond—looks like a doughnut, with an inner core of black residents surrounded by a ring of whites. In Dallas the configuration was different. Dallas looked like a pie with one entire wedge, from the center of the city to the outermost boundary, populated almost entirely by blacks. Exchanging students from the outer edge of that wedge with whites from the opposite side of a large city would have been a logistical nightmare. In between lay the traffic congestion of the central business district, an area of "naturally integrated" housing that no one wished to disturb, a wide arc of Mexican-American settlements, and two "island" school districts. The islands were former suburbs that had been entirely surrounded by the city of Dallas and the Dallas school district. Their schools were virtually all-white, but under the rule of the Detroit case, they could not be brought into the Dallas plan.

Faced with these difficulties, the Educational Task Force agreed on the following. The Dallas school district was divided into six subdistricts. Four had racially mixed populations. The fifth was a small rural area about which no one was much concerned. The last subdistrict was East Oak Cliff, the black wedge of the city and the chief bone of contention. East Oak Cliff was an area of subdivisions originally developed for whites, but the average Anglo occupancy had been only 2.3 years. In the space of three years in the 1960s, the subdivisions changed from all-white to nearly all-black. By the 1970s, East Oak Cliff was a large triangle of concentrated black population, bounded by the Trinity River and Interstate 35 and not easily meshed with the rest of Dallas. The Task Force decided to leave East Oak Cliff alone. Their schools would remain overwhelmingly black.

The other disputed issue was busing within the racially mixed subdistricts. Here the Task Force plan was unusual. From kindergarten through third grade, neighborhood schools were the norm. Boundaries were drawn to promote integration, but busing was not required. Students in grades four through eight were bused. Their schools were planned to reflect the racial balance in each subdistrict to within 10 percent. Then, on entering high school, students returned to their neighborhoods. This was odd, as in other cities older students were bused more, not less.

In approving a plan without high school busing, Judge Taylor seems to have had three factors in mind. First, high schools had larger attendance zones and therefore allowed slightly greater racial mixing without busing. Second, Taylor was "once burned, twice shy" on this issue. In 1971 he had ordered a thousand Anglo students transported to formerly black schools. Four years later, only fifty Anglo students attended those schools. Taylor hoped that the prospect of returning to neighborhood high schools might induce Anglos to stay in the system. Third and most important, Taylor thought the Educational Task Force had found an alternative to busing at the high school level. The alternative was magnet schools.

A magnet school has a special program or curriculum designed to attract students. Dallas already had one highly successful magnet, offering a variety of career-oriented programs, and planned to build seven more. These would offer specialized training in such fields as

creative arts, business and management, health professions, and avia-
tion. Ideally, magnet schools might achieve voluntary integration.

To be attractive, however, magnets must be special. If a school is
merely given the name magnet and a little curricular window dressing,
it will not entice students to leave their neighborhoods. But if given
sufficient resources and vigorous promotion, magnet schools can aid
desegregation.

Magnet schools are costly, and this was the key to the Task Force
plan. The Dallas Alliance promised money for the Dallas schools. The
opening round was an $80 million bond issue, which the business
community engineered and supported. This funded a major infusion
of resources into new magnets and into the schools of East Oak Cliff.
More money also paid for a training center designed to improve teachers' "ability to perform in a multi-cultural setting" and for more
minority hiring. The plan required the top level of salaried administrators to reflect the ethnic composition of the student population. More
minority principals and supervisors would guarantee the system's fairness to minorities and commitment to desegregation. Judge Taylor
also appointed an independent auditor to monitor the schools and
report regularly to the court.

Also part of this scheme—but not mentioned in Judge Taylor's
order—was a community campaign to defuse opposition to busing.
Wealthy Dallasites agreed to cover any financial losses of business leaders who publicly backed desegregation. The Chamber of Commerce
came up with $100,000 to promote racial cooperation and the new
magnet schools. News media were not so subtly encouraged, often by
their largest advertisers, to take a "constructive" view of the situation.
Taylor himself met with the editors of the two major daily newspapers.
Vocal opponents of busing received telephone calls from local leaders,
and a "silk-stocking Gestapo" discouraged public posturing and resistance.

This then was the Task Force plan. At its heart lay a trade-off: more
money and support for education, less busing to achieve racial balance. Both sides were motivated by a concern for the future of their
city and by a fear of white flight, but the compromise was not easy.
Nor was it universally admired. The division of opinion ran especially
deep among blacks. Some agreed with Yvonne Ewell, an assistant
superintendent of schools who accepted the exclusion of East Oak
Cliff from busing: "The political advances and retreats of the last
twenty years suggest to me that desegregation is not the answer," she
said. "While I affirm desegregation as a principle, I don't worry much

about it.... [I]f the kids get the skills and the knowledge they need, they will desegregate the society." Others sided with the NAACP, which objected bitterly to the compromise of constitutional rights and appealed Judge Taylor's order. The Fifth Circuit followed *Swann* and ordered Judge Taylor to reconsider.

As it emerged from the Fifth Circuit, the Dallas case was not an inviting candidate for Supreme Court review. The Fifth Circuit did not actually order more busing; it merely directed Judge Taylor to consider that option. Powell's first reaction was to wait and see what happened, but that attitude did not last. The more he looked into the case, the more he wanted the Supreme Court to intervene right away.

Powell thought Judge Taylor deserved praise, not reversal. Someone, finally, had faced up to the problem of white flight. The dimensions of that phenomenon might perplex social scientists, but Powell never doubted its reality. The facts of Dallas fairly screamed of it, and Powell's files were full of newspaper clippings that seemed to confirm the Dallas experience. The *Washington Post* described the 31 percent drop in white enrollment in Los Angeles, the 40 percent decline in white enrollment in the six years after busing began in suburban Prince Georges County, and the "unhappy parents nationwide" who were turning to private school. Powell was impressed by sociologist James Coleman, who said, "It is *not* the case that school desegregation, as it has been carried out in American schools, generally brings achievement to disadvantaged children."

The most poignant story came from rural Alabama, where blacks were bused forty-two miles to a formerly white school from which *all* the white students had fled. "It just doesn't make any sense," said one black parent. "We've tried to change things, but we can't seem to get anywhere. Now it's worse. We're afraid that one of those buses is going to wreck and some children will be hurt or killed.... This isn't integration—it looks like outegration to me."

Everything Powell knew—or thought he knew—converged on one point: Busing hurt education. But Judge Taylor's caution in busing was not the only thing he liked about the Dallas plan. There was also the organized outpouring of community support for public education. Dallas had achieved what Powell had always wanted for Richmond—a community-wide commitment to excellence in the public schools. That this plan came from the city's business and professional elite, rather than from professional educators or from a federal judge, seemed to Powell right and proper. Members of the Dallas Alliance were the city's natural leaders, as Powell and his friends had been in Richmond. The behind-the-scenes power brokering did not seem in the least suspicious to a man who had joined in a veritable conspiracy of Virginia businessmen to stop massive resistance. The vast financial commitment that the Alliance had engineered for Dallas was just what Powell had worked for in Richmond but had never so fully achieved. And, whatever the impact on desegregation, magnet schools were the sort of educational innovation that appealed to him.

The Dallas plan was not perfect, but it was the best Powell had seen since coming to the Court. He called it "a serious and comprehensive effort to deal fairly, effectively, and constructively with the infinitely complex problem of structuring a public school system in the eighth largest school district in the United States." It deserved Supreme Court support.

Powell's colleagues did not agree. Only he, Burger, and Rehnquist voted to hear the case—one shy of the four votes needed to grant review. Although the Court does not explain why it refuses to hear a case, each Justice has the right to dissent from the denial of review. Powell rarely did so, but this time he would write. The case was put over for several weeks while he worked on his opinion. The result was a powerhouse of fact and argument. The crucial fact was the rapid and continuing decline in Anglo enrollment: from 69 percent in 1971, to 41 percent in 1975, to 35 percent in 1978, to an estimated 26 percent for 1980. Unless these trends were reversed, there would be too few Anglo children to matter. Powell believed in racial diversity—"certainly where it results voluntarily or from the normal professional decisions of a well-run school system"—but the compulsory "uprooting of children from neighborhoods and extensive transportation to distant schools" led not to diversity, but to resegregation. Busing tended to "frustrate rather than achieve the benefits of children of all races voluntarily attending schools together." And while busing perhaps could be said to produce equal educational opportunity, it also produced poorer educational opportunity. It was time, he said, "for a rethinking of the role of the federal judiciary in public education." Dallas was the place to turn the corner.

This cri de coeur moved Justice Stewart, who, on February 16, 1979, provided the necessary fourth vote to grant review. The case was argued on October 29 of that year. At the Conference two days later, Powell, Burger, Stewart, and Rehnquist sided with Judge Taylor. Brennan, White, Blackmun, and Stevens wanted either to affirm the Fifth Circuit or to dismiss the writ of certiorari as improvidently granted.

Dismissal would simply revoke the decision to hear the case and leave the Fifth Circuit's judgment in place, just as if the Supreme Court had never intervened. Marshall would have agreed with that view, but he had recused himself. That left the Court divided four–four.

Burger now made a thoughtful gesture. If the Court split four–four, the judgment of the lower court would automatically be affirmed. Precisely the same result would be achieved by a majority vote to dismiss the writ. But there was one difference. By long custom, no one issues an opinion in tie cases. By contrast, where certiorari is dismissed as improvidently granted, dissenting Justices are free to speak their minds. Burger therefore switched sides: "Since Lewis has a strong desire to write his views," he wrote, "I will change my vote," thus making five votes for dismissal and giving Powell the opportunity to publish a dissent. Powell did dissent, showing only the agreement of Stewart and Rehnquist in his lament for the loss of local control.

DESPITE POWELL'S SETBACK, the Dallas case coincided with a subtle shift in the law of desegregation. Supreme Court doctrine did not change, but it became less relevant to the litigation in the lower courts. Dallas shows why. The case, which had been appealed to the Fifth Circuit in 1976, was remanded to the District Court in 1980. Judge Taylor now recused himself (because of increased involvement by his old law firm), and Judge Barefoot Sanders took over. By this time, changing demographics made busing to achieve racial balance seem almost pointless. Anglo enrollment, which had been 41 percent in 1975, had dropped to 30 percent by 1981, and was predicted to fall to 23 percent by 1985. No matter how meticulously the dwindling white minority was spread around, racial mixing would be slight.

Even more important was the declining support for busing among blacks. It was one thing to say that white resistance should not defeat black rights. It was quite another to say that black children had to "enjoy their rights" whether they wanted to or not. In Dallas, the original plaintiffs and the NAACP continued to press for more busing. Now, however, they were opposed not only by the school board and the Dallas Alliance but also by a formidable consortium of black groups. Organized as the Black Coalition to Maximize Education, the coalition opposed more busing and supported the shift in emphasis to educational improvement.

After extensive hearings, Judge Sanders ruled that "additional systemwide transportation is not a feasible remedy for the existing constitutional violation." The plan he approved differed only marginally from Judge Taylor's original. However controversial the retreat from busing may have been in the mid 1970s, by the end of the decade it seemed almost inevitable. And by the mid-1980s busing to achieve racial balance (as opposed to a variety of other reasons for transporting students) seemed to have peaked. The long and short of it was summed up by E. Brice Cunningham, Dallas counsel for the NAACP, who reported that "the people who wanted busing in 1976 no longer want it today." By this circuitous route, the Dallas busing controversy came to an uneasy end.

THE LEGACY OF BROWN

Of the several thousand Supreme Court decisions in this century, none is so secure in moral standing or public esteem as *Brown v. Board of Education*. It is universally approved as both right and necessary. But *Brown* is much more than an admired bit of history. It is a continuing source of prestige and authority for the Supreme Court. The image of the heroic Court, stepping in where others dared not, to free an oppressed people and relieve the nation of the crippling legacy of segregation, is cherished in the American memory. That image has become a potent justification for judicial activism. More powerful by far than any academic theory of constitutional interpretation is the legend of *Brown*. Like Winston Churchill in the years before World War II, the Supreme Court was supremely right when it mattered most. All later acts are clothed in that success.

Ironically, the Court's school desegregation cases scarcely warrant this regard. Since *Brown* itself, the Court's record has been decidedly problematic. The very next year the Court started down the wrong path with its license of "all deliberate speed" in achieving desegregation. Some say the tolerance of delay was a mistake from the outset. Certainly, it became so over time. A delay of a year or two may have been necessary. Conceivably, even four or five years of gradualism would have been justified. But the Court allowed the deliberation to stretch out for nearly a generation. In 1958 and again in 1964, the Court faced down outright defiance, but for fourteen long years after *Brown*, it remained aloof and disengaged from the routine problems of enforcing desegregation.

In 1968 the Court finally lost patience. Having quietly indulged inaction and tokenism for an entire educational generation, the Justices now demanded instant action. More important, they demanded a different kind of action. The *Green* decision imposed an affirmative obligation not merely to desegregate the public schools but to integrate the schools wherever segregation had been practiced. The standard changed from the absence of racial barriers to the presence of racial balance.

On the facts of *Green*, this ruling was unimpeachable, but three years later, the Court announced that pursuit of racial balance could, and usually would, include busing. Thus, in only three years, the Court lurched from one extreme to the other and embraced the most disruptive, controversial, and problematic of remedies—forced busing. In some cities busing worked, but in others it produced mostly resentment and strife. The decisions hurried past the intermediate possibility of requiring desegregation by all feasible means short of busing. Instead, the Court veered from passivity and disengagement to total commitment.

When Powell took his seat in January 1972, the Supreme Court's policy on school segregation could fairly have been described as all-out war. But the hostilities were soon curtailed at the city limits. The Justices were now deeply divided, and the internal stalemate on the Court produced a regime of schizophrenic contradiction: Bus the cities but not the suburbs. Attack the effects of residential segregation but only *within* increasingly minority urban school systems. Let neighborhood schools prevail elsewhere. Ironically, a divided Court chose to fight only where the battle could not be won.

There are at least two plausible opinions on where the Court jumped the track. Each can be supported by cogent argument, and even the long view of history is not likely to resolve the bitter disagreement between partisans on each side. Civil rights leaders, dependably represented on the Court by Justices Douglas, Brennan, and Marshall, saw Detroit as the grievous error. If busing failed, it failed because it was not tried on a sufficient scale, because the Court was unwilling to carry the fight to the suburbs.

Powell took the other side. He saw *Swann* as the crucial mistake. In his view, the Court erred when it required that urban school systems attack residential segregation. That required busing, and Powell never deviated from the conviction that busing hurt education and prompted resegregation through white flight.

Ultimately, both sides may have been partly right, but the compromise between them was surely wrong. The noble promise of *Brown* has been—depending on one's point of view—either abandoned or distorted, but on any estimation not achieved.

CHAPTER XI

ABORTION

THE WARM-UP

Three weeks before Powell and Rehnquist were sworn in, the Supreme Court heard argument in a pair of cases involving abortion. The first was brought by Jane Roe, later identified as Norma McCorvey, who said she had been gang-raped but afterward admitted that was not true. She was in fact an unmarried woman with an unwanted pregnancy whose unwillingness to abide the status quo made Jane Roe famous. The second case was brought by Sandra Race Cano, known as Mary Doe, who won for others the right to abortion but only after putting her own baby girl up for adoption. Ironically, the unwilling mother later became a pro-life activist, while the unwanted daughter came to support the right of abortion. In retrospect, these tangled stories seem an apt beginning for the enduring constitutional conflict over abortion.

The first case came from Texas, where a nineteenth-century statute banned all abortion except where necessary to save the woman's life. The second case, from Georgia, involved a more modern law. Georgia allowed abortion in three circumstances: (1) where, in a physician's best judgment, continuation of the pregnancy would endanger the life of the woman *or* seriously and permanently injure her health; (2) where the fetus would likely be born with a "grave, permanent, and irremediable mental or physical defect"; and (3) where the pregnancy resulted from rape. More than a dozen states had similar laws. These "reform" statutes had been thought liberal when enacted, and in practice (through sympathetic diagnosis of risk to the woman's health) had allowed far more abortions than anyone expected. Now they, too, were attacked as unduly restrictive. The campaign for legislative reform had won abortion on demand (for early-stage pregnancies) in four states, including New York, and antiabortion litigation sprang up around the nation.

Still, at first not much was expected from the cases of Jane Roe and Mary Doe. Both involved jurisdictional issues that might derail the cases before the Court reached the merits. And earlier that year, the Supreme Court had rejected a constitutional attack on the Washington, D.C., abortion statute. No one foresaw a complete about-face.

Then something happened. At Conference, Douglas, Brennan, and Marshall declared themselves in favor of some version of a constitutional right to abortion, although what they had in mind at this early stage may have been fairly limited. Unexpectedly, Stewart and Blackmun also seemed willing to strike down these laws, or parts of them, although on narrow grounds. Both worried that the laws interfered with the professional judgments of physicians. They made the vote five–two against upholding the statutes. Or perhaps it would be four–three against, if, as some thought, Blackmun ultimately supported the statutes, or possibly even three–four in favor of the antiabortion laws, if Stewart also went the other way. The discussion was so muddled that no one could tell for sure.

When Burger took advantage of this uncertainty to include the abortion cases in his assignments, Douglas hit the ceiling. Though not the first time the Chief had usurped the assignment power, this was by far the most important. Douglas circulated a curt note stating that he, Douglas, would assign these opinions, but Burger stood his ground. "At the close of discussion," he replied, "I remarked to the Conference that there were, literally, not enough columns to mark up an accurate reflection of the voting in either the Georgia or the Texas cases. I therefore marked down no votes and said this was a case that would have to stand or fall on the writing, when it was done." Burger closed by noting, "That is still my view of how to handle these two . . . sensitive cases, which, I might add, are quite probable candidates for reargument."

The suggestion of reargument only exacerbated liberal fears. Burger had assigned the cases to the most ambivalent member of the apparent majority, his Minnesota Twin, Harry Blackmun. Conspiracy theories abounded. Burger hoped to detach Blackmun from the liberals. Or perhaps he thought Blackmun's draft would scare off Stewart. Or perhaps he was simply playing for time. Burger knew Blackmun would be slow, and delay might give him the chance to press for reargument after Powell and Rehnquist joined the Court.

Despite these suspicions—and the hostility that gave birth to them—the liberals could do nothing but sit and fume. Any attempt to take the cases away from Blackmun would only spur his resentment, and the liberals desperately needed his vote. Douglas had already dashed off an opinion broadly declaring a right to abortion, but first showed it to Brennan. Brennan advised against circulation. Realistically, the liberals had no choice but to wait for Harry.

As HARRY BLACKMUN labored into the spring of 1972, trying to come to grips with the awesome responsibility that had been placed in his hands, Powell was going through his own dark night of the soul. His troubles had nothing to do with abortion. He was simply overwhelmed by work.

When Powell first came to the Court, he told himself he had the advantage of knowing more business and corporate law than all the other Justices put together. That may have been true, but it did him precious little good. His first assignment for the Court was a corporate tax opinion, but he soon found himself adrift in a sea of cases for which his practice left him woefully unprepared. He had to decide whether illegitimate children could be excluded from their father's death benefits (they couldn't); whether jury verdicts had to be unanimous (not always); and whether the ordinary rules for search and seizure applied in domestic security cases (they did). He had to decide whether the right of free speech applied in a privately owned shopping center (it didn't); whether a state college could deny official recognition to the local chapter of the radical SDS (it couldn't); and whether reporters had a constitutional right to refuse to answer grand jury questions (they didn't). He also wrote in cases involving labor arbitration, federal jurisdiction, international law, the right to counsel, equal protection, speedy trial, and the estate tax. Most wrenching of all, he had to vote on whether convicted murderers could be put to death (Powell thought they could).

In most of these areas, Powell knew little. He had to study the briefs to identify the arguments, then go back and read the precedents. His clerks helped, but as they were well versed in contemporary constitutional doctrine, they spoke a kind of shorthand that Powell only partly understood. References familiar to a recent law school graduate often meant nothing to him. Ideas current in the classroom he found entirely new. He had to learn every issue from the ground up.

So he labored away at a mountain of paper that seemed to grow faster than he could digest it. He came to the office seven days a week and was sometimes so tired when he left that he let Sally carry his briefcase to the car. At home after dinner, he lay on the floor with an arm over his eyes as Jo read aloud from briefs and papers. Now and then he would roll over to make a few notes before Jo resumed her recitation. They rarely went out.

As this pace continued, Powell began to wonder. In his own mind, his successes had always been due to his ability to work longer and harder than anyone else. He thought himself exceptional in discipline and dedication, not insight or intellect. Now he had to question whether perseverance was enough. There were only so many hours in the day, and at age sixty-five the effort showed. At the time of life when most men retire, Powell found himself working harder than ever before.

And the work was grueling and lonely. It was one thing to spend long hours as a senior partner—meeting, traveling, and entertaining clients. It was quite another thing to sit alone at a desk from morning until night with stacks of paper and a dictating machine. At Hunton, Williams, Powell had worked chiefly with people; at the Court, he worked chiefly with documents.

The social isolation was as bad as the work load. That spring, Powell called former ABA president Charles Rhyne, and said: "Charlie, I've been up here now for about three months and not a single soul has invited me out for lunch." Rhyne immediately set him straight: "Lewis, none of us in a law firm is going to invite you to lunch because we file petitions for cert up there every year. If the other side sees me taking you to the Metropolitan Club for lunch, it would be embarrassing to you." Powell was off-limits.

After a few months of this regimen, Powell reached his nadir. On the verge of collapse from exhaustion, self-doubt threatened to get the better of him. Perhaps the Supreme Court was too demanding. Perhaps, at his age, success by hard work was out of his reach. Perhaps he was not up to the job. Perhaps he should resign.

How long and how seriously Powell entertained this thought is not known. He never mentioned it to clerks or colleagues, and his reserve hid the unrest within. By late spring, the crisis had passed. In Powell's own words, he "gradually began to learn some law." When he confronted issues a second time, he saw the benefits of experience. Questions that had seemed bafflingly complex on first encounter were much more manageable when revisited. And as Powell got to know his colleagues better, his demands on himself became more realistic. Powell came to the Supreme Court with unfeigned reverence for the institution and exaggerated respect for the intelligence, dedication, and high-mindedness of those who sat on it. Familiarity set him straight. He never lost his veneration for the Court as an entity, but as he came to know the Justices as individuals, each with his own flaws and foibles, Powell thought better of himself. Perhaps he would not be a great Justice, in the manner of his friend John Harlan or his predecessor Hugo Black, but he could do at least as well as some of the others.

By late spring, Powell had regained his bearings. He was still a novice judge who often looked to others for guidance, but he would learn. Though his sense of his own value to the Court remained fragile, he no longer thought of resignation. It would be some time yet before Powell could fairly be said to be relaxed in his responsibilities, but from this time forward, he grew in skill and assurance.

ON MAY 18, 1972, Blackmun circulated a draft opinion in *Roe v. Wade*. It struck down the Texas statute—but for a peculiar reason. Blackmun said that a law banning abortion unless "procured or attempted by medical advice for the purpose of saving the life of the mother" was so obscure and indefinite that no one could tell what was meant. The law was therefore void for vagueness. This was the narrowest possible ground for decision but also the least tenable. Whatever else might have been said of the Texas statute, it was certainly not unintelligible. It was in fact more definite (and more restrictive) than the D.C. statute upheld against the same attack only a few months before. Blackmun knew the vagueness approach had problems and indicated that he was prepared to try again if the others wished. "This may or may not appeal to you," he said in an accompanying memorandum. "I am still flexible as to results, and I shall do my best to arrive at something which would command a court."

One week later Blackmun circulated a draft opinion in the Georgia case, *Doe v. Bolton*. This draft went much further, yet still stopped short of declaring an absolute right to abortion. On the one hand, Blackmun said that "a woman's fundamental personal decision whether or not to bear an unwanted child" came within the constitutional right of privacy. On the other hand, he also emphasized the rights of the unborn: "The pregnant woman cannot be isolated in her privacy. . . . The heart of the matter is that somewhere, either forthwith at conception, or at 'quickening,' or at birth, or at some other point in between, another being becomes involved and the privacy the woman possesses has become dual rather than sole. The woman's right of privacy must be measured accordingly." The opinion then struck down various procedural requirements in the Georgia law without squarely facing the central issue.

Brennan and Douglas wanted Blackmun to go further still. They urged him to condemn all regulation of abortion, save the requirement that it "be performed by a licensed physician within some limited time after conception." Brennan argued this position case in an artful memo congratulating Blackmun on his draft while at the same suggesting that the Georgia statute "be held invalid in full." The liberals backed off, however, when they perceived a threat from the other side. On May 31 Burger revived his suggestion of reargument: "This is as sensitive and difficult an issue as any in this Court in my time and I want to hear more and think more when I am not trying to sort out several dozen other difficult cases." Hence, Burger announced, "I vote to reargue early in the next Term."

The liberals were ready to accept Blackmun's drafts—warts and all—rather than risk reargument. As Powell and Rehnquist had now joined the Court, they would vote if the cases were reargued. Burger felt certain of their support, an attitude that irritated the other Justices. A note from Brennan to Douglas records one reaction: "I will be God-damned! At lunch today, Potter expressed his outrage at the high handed way things are going, particularly the assumption that a single Justice if CJ can order things his own way, and that he can hold up for nine anything he chooses, even if the rest of us are ready to bring down 4-3's for example. He also told me he . . . resents CJ's confidence that he has Powell and Rehnquist in his pocket. Potter wants to make an issue of these things—perhaps fur will fly this afternoon."

As it happened, the liberals did not have a chance to accept Blackmun's draft, because the author himself now asked that the cases be put over, even though "it would prove costly to me personally, in light of the effort and hours expended. . . ." "On an issue so sensitive and so emotional as this one," Blackmun continued, "the country deserves the conclusion of a nine-man, not a seven-man court, whatever the ultimate decision may be." Besides, he added, "[a]lthough I have worked on these cases with some concentration, I am not yet certain about all the details."

Brennan and Marshall acquiesced, but Douglas was furious. Burger had somehow put the arm on Blackmun. He had usurped the assignment power and given the opinions to the Justice least likely to command a Court. He had thwarted the will of the majority (Douglas counted himself, Brennan, Stewart, Marshall, and Blackmun as favoring the right of abortion) and tried to subvert the outcome. On June 1 Douglas wrote the Chief: "If the vote of the Conference is to reargue, then I will file a statement telling what is happening to us and the tragedy it entails."

The statement Douglas drafted was truly shocking. It said flatly that Burger had assigned the opinions from the minority, "an action that no Chief Justice in my time would ever have taken," and that there was "a destructive force at work in the Court." Douglas made a scathing attack on Burger's motives: "The plea that the cases be reargued is merely another strategy by a minority somehow to suppress the majority view with the hope that exigencies of time will change the result. That might be achieved of course by death or conceivably retirement, but that kind of strategy dilutes the integrity of the Court and makes the decisions here depend on the manipulative skills of the Chief Justice."

And there was more. Having accused Burger of playing politics inside the Court, Douglas now charged him with dragging the Court into outside politics: "This is an election year. Both political parties have made abortion an issue. What the political parties say or do is none of our business. We sit here not to make the path of any candidate easier or more difficult. We decide questions only on their constitutional merits. To prolong these *Abortion Cases* into the next election would in the eyes of many be a political gesture unworthy of the Court."* He added that, "Russia once gave its Chief Justice two votes, but that was too strong even for the Russians." With fine economy, Douglas had managed to insult Burger and humiliate Blackmun in a single sentence.

Some of the most inflammatory statements were deleted at Brennan's suggestion, but even the toned-down version was quite enough to set off an explosion within the Court. It occurred just as Powell emerged from his period of self-doubt. He and Rehnquist had previously declined to vote on reargument on the ground that "the other seven Justices were better qualified to make these decisions," but when Blackmun stalled, they were ready to act. After clearing his intention with Blackmun, Powell wrote the Conference: "I have been on the Court for more than half a term. It may be that I now have a duty to participate in this decision, although from a purely personal viewpoint I would be more than happy to leave this one to others." Powell had not read the briefs or Blackmun's drafts ("I am too concerned about circulating my own remaining opinions to be studying cases in which I did not participate"), but he had decided to vote for reargument. He was persuaded "primarily by the fact that Harry Blackmun, the author of

---

* In fact, neither party emphasized abortion as a campaign issue in 1972. Nixon sent a letter to Terence Cardinal Cooke indicating his opposition, but neither he nor his opponent, Senator George McGovern, pressed the issue.

the opinions, thinks the cases should be carried over and reargued next fall. His position, based on months of study, suggests enough doubt on an issue of large national importance to justify a few months of delay."

Immediately after circulating his opinion, Douglas took off for Goose Prairie, leaving the others to wonder if his draft was merely an attempt at intimidation or if he would actually publish this extraordinary document. First Brennan and then Blackmun tried to dissuade him. Blackmun assured Douglas that his vote was firm, the majority would survive reargument, and nothing would be lost by delay. Finally Douglas relented. On June 26, the last day of the term, the Court ordered the abortion cases scheduled for reargument, with only the notation that "Mr. Justice Douglas dissents."

THE DECISION

Things moved quickly when the Court reconvened that fall. Reargument was heard on October 11, and within a few weeks Blackmun had a draft opinion. He had worked on it all summer, researching in the Mayo Clinic library and writing in his summer office in downtown Rochester.

What Blackmun produced differed radically from his original draft. Gone was the claim that the Texas law was void for vagueness. In its place was the broad pronouncement of a constitutional right to abortion. Blackmun's explanation for this conclusion was long on history but short on reasoning. He began with an investigation of the "ancient attitudes" toward abortion* and proceeded through the English common law and English statutes to early legislation in the American states. The point of all this, according to Blackmun, was that until the nineteenth century abortion had been viewed with "less disfavor" than under current statutes. But so what? Blackmun's account did not show a tradition in favor of abortion, but only a condemnation less ancient and less uniform than might have been supposed. The fact that early-

---

*   This point proved unexpectedly controversial. Blackmun cited Persian, Greek, and Roman practices in support of the conclusion that "[a]ncient religion did not bar abortion." Religious critics responded that Blackmun meant ancient paganism, since early Christians had consistently disapproved of the practice. "We would not normally expect the Court to consider the teachings of Christianity and paganism before rendering a decision on the *constitutionality* of a law," said *Christianity Today*, "but in this case it has chosen to do so, and the results are enlightening; it has clearly decided for paganism, and against Christianity."

stage abortion had been a serious crime for "only" a century scarcely made it a constitutional right. On that reasoning, the Constitution would also protect spousal rape or the use of opiates. There was simply no logical connection between the history that Blackmun so painstakingly assembled and his conclusion that abortion was a constitutional right.

The opinion also canvassed the views of the American Medical Association, the American Public Health Association, the American Bar Association, and the Conference of Commissioners on Uniform State Laws. Once again, the purpose was unclear. None of these groups had any particular competence to address the *constitutionality* of abortion laws. The most that could be learned from this institutional head count was that establishment opinion was moving away from an absolute ban on abortion. How that showed that the Constitution now contained a right to abortion remained obscure.

Worst of all, the opinion read as if it were not really the woman's choice that mattered but rather the medical judgment of her doctor. Blackmun did not declare a woman's right to end her own pregnancy but spoke instead of constitutional protection for "the attending physician [who] decides in consultation with his patient that in his best medical judgment her pregnancy should be terminated. . . ." This reasoning reduced the woman to a bit player in her own pregnancy, entitled only to "consult" with her (usually male) doctor. (It was left to Powell, writing ten years later, to recharacterize *Roe* as holding "that the right of privacy, grounded in the concept of personal liberty guaranteed by the Constitution, encompasses a woman's right to decide whether to terminate her pregnancy.")

Other oddities were thrown in. Blackmun discoursed at length on the Hippocratic oath and its relation to the Pythagorean school of Greek philosophers—a topic that the briefs had understandably failed to mention. Occasionally, the opinion descended to the absurd—as in the suggestion that fetuses were not persons within the meaning of the Fourteenth Amendment because they had never been counted in the census.

Underlying all this confused irrelevancy was the central issue of when life begins. "[A]t some point in time," Blackmun stated, "it is reasonable and appropriate for a State to decide that . . . another interest, that of potential human life, becomes significantly involved." But when? Blackmun's response was incoherent. First, he said the question was one a court could not answer. "We need not resolve the difficult question of when life begins. When those trained in the respective disciplines of medicine, philosophy, and theology are unable to arrive at any consensus, the judiciary at this point in the development of man's knowledge, is not in a position to speculate as to the answer." But despite this expression of judicial modesty, Blackmun did in fact resolve the issue—at least partly—by ruling that the state of Texas could not protect fetal life from the moment of conception. By this pronouncement, Blackmun answered the very question he purported to evade.

If life did not begin at conception, when did it begin? At what point did the state's "important and legitimate interest in the potentiality of human life" override the woman's freedom of choice? Was it "quickening," when the fetus discernibly begins to move in the womb? Or viability, when the child is able to live outside the mother's body? Or did the fetus not become a human being until live birth? Each of these stages had some support in history or logic, but Blackmun chose none of them. He said that the state's interest in protecting the life of the fetus became compelling at the "end of the first trimester" of pregnancy. Beyond that point, the state could restrict abortion to "reasonable therapeutic categories"—presumably, circumstances affecting the woman's life or health.

What was the reason for picking the end of the first trimester as the end of the right of abortion? Blackmun gave none. There was no explanation of why the end of the first trimester was crucial either medically or morally, much less constitutionally. In a cover memo to his colleagues, Blackmun defended his choice on the ground that it was no worse than any other: "You will observe that I have concluded that the end of the first trimester is critical. This is arbitrary, but perhaps any other selected point, such as quickening or viability, is equally arbitrary."

OF ALL THESE GROUNDS of objection, only the last bothered Powell. He wrote Blackmun on November 29: "I am enthusiastic about your abortion opinions. They reflect impressive scholarship and analysis, and I have no doubt they will command a court." Powell may have been trying to spare Blackmun's feelings, as he later said privately that the abortion opinions were "the worst opinions I ever joined," but it is not clear whether he thought so at the time or came to that view in light of later criticism.

Powell's chief concern with Blackmun's draft was not its reasoning but the conclusion that the right to abortion lasted only through the first trimester of pregnancy. Powell preferred to continue the right until viability, which more nearly coincided with the end of the second trimester of pregnancy. The woman's right over the fetus should continue while it could not live outside her womb. When it could—at the point called viability—there was an independent human life that the state could insist on protecting. Powell quoted Judge Jon O. Newman, writing in a Connecticut abortion case, in support of drawing the line there: "[T]he state interest in protecting the life of a fetus capable of living outside the uterus could be shown to be more generally accepted and, therefore, of more weight in the constitutional sense than the interest in preventing the abortion of a fetus that is not viable. The issue might well turn on whether the time period selected could be shown to permit survival of the fetus in a generally accepted sense," not just for a few hours or with heroic medical intervention. When the fetus becomes able to live on its own, Powell argued, the interest of the state becomes "clearly identifiable, in a manner which would be generally understood."

Blackmun responded privately to Powell and shortly thereafter put the issue to their colleagues:

> One of the members of the Conference has asked whether my choice of the end of the first trimester, as the point beyond which a state may appropriately regulate abortion practices, is critical. He asks whether the point of viability might not be a better choice.
>
> The inquiry is a valid one and deserves serious consideration. I selected the earlier point because I felt that it would be more easily accepted (by us as well as by others) and because most medical statistics and statistical studies appear to me to be centered there. Viability, however, has its own strong points. It has logical and biological justifications. There is a practical aspect, too, for I am sure that there are many pregnant women, particularly younger girls, who may refuse to face the fact of pregnancy and who, for one reason or another, do not get around to medical consultation until the end of the first trimester is upon them or, indeed, has passed.

Blackmun also saw an argument for the earlier date. After the end of the first trimester the states should be able to require hospitalization. In any event, Blackmun was ready to do whatever was necessary to get a Court: "I would be willing to recast the opinions at the later date, but I do not wish to do so if it would alienate any Justice, who has expressed to me, either by writing or orally, that he is in general agreement, on the merits, with the circulated draft."

Douglas at once answered, without explanation, "I favor the first trimester, rather than viability." This response shocked Larry Hammond. Hammond had brought Judge Newman's opinion to Powell's attention and urged him to press for viability on the purely practical ground that, "[f]or many poor, or frightened, or uneducated, or unsophisticated girls, the decision to seek help may not occur during the first 12 weeks. The girl might be simply hoping against hope that she is not pregnant. . . ." Douglas's insistence on the shorter time was bizarre: "The Justice who more than anyone else on this Court stakes his judicial reputation on protecting the poor and the black . . . cannot fail to recognize that a first trimester rule falls most heavily on those classes."

Justice Marshall had the same thought and intervened to propose a compromise. Viability should be the earliest time when the law could restrict abortion in order to protect the life of the fetus. The right should extend at least to that point. If regulations—such as requiring hospitalization—were needed for *maternal* safety, they could be enforced between the end of the first trimester and fetal viability. Blackmun's timing would be preserved but only for this secondary issue. The crucial boundary of the woman's right would be fetal viability.

Blackmun agreed, and Marshall's compromise became law. The published opinion defines a constitutional right to abortion in three phases:

(1) Until the end of the first trimester, the abortion decision "must be left to the medical judgment of the pregnant woman's attending physician."

(2) During the next phase, a state could regulate abortion "in ways that are reasonably related to maternal health."

(3) Only after viability could the state act to protect "the potentiality of human life." At that point, the state "may, if it chooses, regulate, and even proscribe, abortion except where it is necessary, in appropriate medical judgment, for the preservation of the life or health of the mother."

The opinion, many noted, read like a "model statute."

The abortion decisions were announced on January 22, 1973. The issue of *Time* magazine then at the newsstands already carried an account of the outcome. "Last week TIME learned that the Supreme Court has decided to strike down nearly every anti-abortion law in the land. Such laws, a majority of the Justices believe, represent an unconstitutional invasion of privacy that interferes with a woman's right to control her own body." The article went on to say, again correctly, that prohibition of late-stage abortion would be allowed but that otherwise, "a woman's freedom to end her pregnancy will not be significantly abridged."

The leak caused an explosion in the Supreme Court. It was a source of pride throughout the building that Court personnel routinely handled even the most sensitive cases without leaks. More than decorum was at stake. Publication of preliminary deliberations would inhibit free debate inside the Court and possibly distort outcomes. In many cases, prior knowledge of decisions would be worth money. Fortunes could be made in stock speculation if one could find out beforehand how a particular company or industry would be affected by a pending case. Finally, any lapse of security made others more likely. Given the long history of tight lips, most reporters left Court personnel alone. Some felt it was improper to pry into the Court's business and in any event did not expect to learn much. Most important, so long as the traditional discretion was maintained, no reporter needed to fear being scooped by a rival. Once the press saw that the wall of silence could be breached, restraint would collapse, competitive instincts take over, and spying and snooping increase.

So thought Burger, who was outraged by *Time*'s scoop. That the leak had occurred in the abortion cases only made matters worse. The Chief's sensibilities had already been rubbed raw by a *Washington Post* exposé of the ugly mess surrounding the decision to put the abortion cases over for reargument. (The day the article appeared Douglas wrote from Goose Prairie to say that he had "never breathed a word concerning the case, or my memo, to anyone outside the Court.") As much as Burger might have liked to respond to the *Post*'s portrayal of him as a heavy-handed manipulator, tradition kept him from doing so. The *Time* article was a second offense. This time he would find and fire the person responsible.

Burger sent a confidential letter demanding that the Justices question their clerks and threatening lie detector tests to uncover the culprit. But no such measures proved necessary. The culprit himself opened Burger's letter, as he was instructed to do, even for confidential correspondence, when his boss was out of town. A few minutes later, a shaken Larry Hammond repaired to the upstairs office to call Powell, who was visiting General Pete Quesada in Florida. After several frantic hours, Hammond found Powell and told him this story.

Hammond had talked to Dave Beckwith, a law school classmate working for *Time*. Beckwith had the opportunity to make his career by writing the cover story on the abortion decision. He asked Hammond for help so that he would not make a mistake rushing to deadline after the decisions came down. When Hammond refused, Beckwith persisted. Nothing would be published until the cases were announced. Besides, Beckwith already knew the essentials. He knew that the Court would strike down the antiabortion statutes, and he knew how most of the Justices voted. He only asked Hammond to confirm whether Judge Newman's opinion in the Connecticut case was important to the Court's reasoning. Hammond finally agreed that it was.

Hammond believed that nothing would be published until the decisions were announced, which was expected to be very soon. As it happened, there was a delay of a few days for Burger to write a concurrence. As Powell's Conference notes reveal, Burger voted all along to strike down the abortion statutes but looked for some narrow ground. Now he put off the announcement so that he could draft a short opinion saying that the decisions somehow meant less than they said. The delay gave Beckwith a scoop.

A distraught Larry Hammond told his story to Powell, read the scorcher from the Chief, and recited his own letter of resignation, which he had drafted and redrafted in the intervening hours. Powell at once cut him off. There would be no resignation. Hammond should wait there while Powell spoke to the Chief. A few minutes later, Burger's secretary called Hammond to the Chief's outer office, where he waited until being ushered into the Chief's inner office. To Hammond's surprise, Burger was all grace and generosity. Powell had praised Hammond's ability and character. The Chief ruminated about the terrible things Beckwith had done, congratulated Hammond on his candor, shook his hand, and sent him on his way.

The incident had several sequels. Beckwith called to say that he had been double-crossed by his editors, who had run the story early over his objections. This Hammond did not, and does not, believe. Burger's outrage did not dissipate. He met with senior officials from *Time* and explained in no uncertain terms what he thought of them and their reporter. It was, Burger is reported to have said, the moral equivalent of wiretapping.

The earlier leak has never been identified. Obviously, someone spoke to Beckwith before he talked to Hammond. Even if Beckwith did not in fact know all that he pretended when he spoke to Hammond, someone had told him enough to enable him to make the bluff. Beckwith himself implied that a print shop worker or messenger was responsible, but the fact that he obviously did not have a copy of the opinion (if so, he would have quoted it) argues against that possibility. A rumor later came out of the Chief's chambers that the *Time* editors said their source was a Justice, not a clerk, but that Burger refused to believe it. Other than Larry Hammond, no one ever stepped forward to acknowledge responsibility.

The experience left Hammond chastened. It was, he said, "the most embarrassing and humiliating misstep of my professional career." It also made him fiercely loyal to Powell. It must have been a rare satisfaction when, on leaving Powell's service, Hammond received a letter from his boss: "Although you can hardly have the slightest doubt as to my admiration of you as a lawyer and as a human being, I have wanted—without being too sentimental—to summarize in writing how I feel. In briefest terms, I think you are one of the ablest lawyers with whom I have ever worked. Your capacity for penetrating legal analysis is exceptional. You also write with clarity and precision, and I had complete confidence in the thoroughness and integrity of your research, and"—in the circumstances, the phrase could not have been inadvertent—"in the soundness of your judgment."

OF THE NEARLY three thousand votes in Powell's judicial career, none is at once so easy and so difficult to explain as abortion. At the time, Powell found the decision easy. He returned from Richmond in the fall of 1972 with his mind already made up. He took Larry Hammond to lunch at the Monocle and announced his decision. There was no equivocation, no debate, no exchange of memoranda, no tentative drafts. He would vote to strike the abortion laws because he thought it intolerable that the law should interfere with a woman's right to control her own body during early pregnancy. (Some years later, Bob Woodward and Scott Armstrong said in *The Brethren* that Powell could not find an answer to the abortion issue in the Constitution and "felt he would just have to vote his 'gut.'" Though the locution sounds false, the sentiment rings true.)

Powell was therefore ready to join Blackmun's majority. He delayed only long enough to make sure that the woman's right reached beyond the end of the first trimester, as Blackmun originally proposed, to the point of fetal viability. He did not write separately, although he toyed with the idea, nor did he urge reforms in Blackmun's draft. Despite the bitter passions aroused by the issue of abortion, Powell's initial consideration of it was straightforward, free from doubt, almost routine.

On one level, this was not surprising. That Lewis Powell personally opposed restrictions on abortion was almost predictable. He was a

well-educated, non-Catholic, upper-class male—a group then, as now,
overwhelmingly supportive of freedom of choice. Certain personal
facts reinforced this predisposition. Pierce Rucker had been a leading
obstetrician and chairman of the local board of health, and both his
sons had followed him in that specialty. Dr. Rucker had been exactly
the sort of well-educated, high-minded, socially responsible professional whom Powell admired. It did not seem right that the Dr.
Ruckers of the world should have their hands tied by restrictive laws.
Most important, Powell thought those laws did not in fact stop abortions but drove women outside the law.

A few years earlier, Powell had been awakened by a call from a nineteen-
year-old Hunton, Williams office boy, who was distraught and weeping.
Powell met him at the office, where he learned that the young man had
been seeing an older divorcée who had become pregnant. She decided on
abortion and asked him to help. He tried to follow her instructions but the
woman hemorrhaged and died. By the time he called Powell, the police
knew of the death and its cause but not that the office boy had been
involved. Powell calmed him down and had him stand by, while Powell
arranged to see the local prosecutor. On hearing the story and confirming
the facts, the prosecutor decided not to press charges. This incident
convinced Powell that women would seek abortions whether they were
legal or not and that driving the practice underground led to danger and
death.

These views were reinforced by Molly, the most outspoken of the
Powell daughters, who argued not only that illegal abortion was ugly
and dangerous, but that the birth of unwanted children was also a
cost. Molly saw abortion and birth control generally as part of a
humane policy of concern for child welfare. Powell shared this point of
view. The post-*Roe* debate cast abortion as a head-on conflict between
the woman's right and the child's future, but to Powell, the freedom to
end unwanted pregnancy seemed consistent with the best interests of
both women and children.

All these influences aligned in favor of liberalized abortion. It is not
surprising that Lewis Powell the private citizen favored freedom of
choice. What is surprising is that he would write that position into the
Constitution. As a personal attitude, Powell's support for abortion on
demand is immediately understandable; as a declaration of constitutional law, it is not. The question that cries out for answer is how
Powell, supposedly a fan of judicial restraint, could find a right to
abortion in the Constitution.

*   *   *

ABORTION IS AN ISSUE from which it is hard to achieve a critical distance. Those who view the fetus as a fully human life from the moment of conception treat any justification for the practice with dread and loathing. Those who see the right to abortion as the cornerstone of women's liberation respond to any criticism with impatience and anger. Both reactions make it difficult to see clearly the *constitutional* issue in *Roe v. Wade*.

As constitutional law, the abortion decision was an astonishing act of judicial innovation. One may view the result with regret or thanksgiving, but its creativity cannot be gainsaid. Nothing in the conventional sources of constitutional interpretation pointed to that result. There was nothing in the document's text (even the word "privacy" does not appear), or in its history, or in the preexisting legal traditions that the Constitution might be thought to have incorporated. There was nothing in the usual sources of legal reasoning to suggest that abortion was a constitutional right.

Nothing, that is, *except* the Court's own precedents. The 1965 decision in *Griswold v. Connecticut* announced a constitutional right to use contraceptives, at least within the relationship of marriage. The origins of this right were similarly obscure. (Justice Douglas said it lurked in the penumbra of emanations from the specified rights, a circumlocution that afterward became a figure of fun.) For Powell, as for many others, the constitutionalization of contraception paved the way toward protecting abortion; as both involved sexuality and reproduction, the distance between them seemed not that great. And in many other cases the Supreme Court had declared rights—such as the right to travel or to study German or to send one's children to private school—with no clear basis in constitutional text or history.

Constitutional protection for unspecified rights was not new, and the problem of finding the sources of such rights was by no means confined to abortion. *Griswold* established that the Constitution included a nontextual right to privacy and that it covered at least some individual choices regarding reproduction, at least within the institution of marriage. One could argue that *Griswold* had presaged *Roe* and believe, as Powell always claimed, that his vote in *Roe* was supported by precedent, but the suggestion should not be pressed too far. *Griswold*, after all, was grounded in the traditional privacy of acts within marriage. *Roe* reached far beyond that context. And ultimately, each addition to the Constitution must stand on its own. Recognition of one unspecified right does not mean that all such claims should be accepted, nor does it relieve the Court of the burden of justifying each new action. State legislatures saw a vast difference between contraception (which was routinely permitted) and abortion (which was largely proscribed). Even conceding all the prior precedents, one still must rank the abortion decision as among the most venturesome acts of judicial innovation in the history of the Supreme Court.

Powell did not think of himself as a judicial activist. President Nixon had introduced him to the nation as a "strict constructionist," and although Powell avoided that phrase, he described himself similarly. "I believe," he told the Senate Judiciary Committee, "in the importance of judicial restraint, especially at the Supreme Court level. . . . In deciding each case, the judge must make a conscious and determined effort to put aside his own political and economic views and his own predilections and to the extent possible to put aside whatever subtle influences may exist from his own background and experience." Of course, such statements were pro forma for Supreme Court nominees. At his confirmation hearings in 1970, Harry Blackmun had endorsed a far more restrictive concept of the role of the judge. "I personally feel," said Blackmun, "that the Constitution is a document of specified words and construction. I would do my best not to have my decision affected by my personal ideals and philosophy, but would attempt to construe that instrument in the light of what I feel is its definite and determined meaning."

That such statements are routine does not make them insincere. Powell meant what he said, and no doubt Blackmun did also. In a reflexive, nontheoretical way, Powell thought of himself as a disciple of restraint. He placed himself in the tradition of John Harlan, a Justice known for craftsmanship, clarity, lawyerly reasoning, and a modest conception of the judicial role. Though Harlan was not quick to engraft his personal preferences onto the Constitution, even he had joined in *Griswold*'s finding of a constitutional right for married couples to use contraceptives. Generally, he sought a proper balance between continuity and change. In practice, that meant gradualism, respect for the lessons of history, and deference to legislative choice. In short, Harlan sought to build on the traditions of societal consensus rather than trying to uproot them. Powell saw himself following in Harlan's footsteps as a careful, restrained, lawyerly judge. Yet this self-image is forever challenged by his vote in *Roe v. Wade*.

THE REASONS for that vote are several. Most important, yet least noticed, was the sense of momentum inside the Court. The abortion laws had been struck down the year before by a vote of five to two, and the majority against these statutes remained firm. Powell had no reason to think that his vote would matter one way or the other. That the issue seemed settled was in itself no reason to support the constitutionalization of abortion, but it eased Powell's way into a preexisting majority.

Another reason was the surprising lack of antiabortion sentiment inside the Court. White and Rehnquist voted to uphold the laws but chiefly for the reason that abortion was not covered by the Constitution, not on the ground that it was intrinsically wrong. The Court's only Catholic, William Brennan, supported freedom of choice. So did Powell's closest friend on the Court, Potter Stewart. So, for that matter, did Powell's clerks. In Powell's circle, no one spoke from the conviction that abortion was murder.

Had Powell faced an eloquent and committed opponent of abortion, it would not have changed his private convictions. Powell was not personally religious nor otherwise much given to abstraction. The idea that a fertilized embryo was a fully recognized human life would always seem to him unacceptably remote from ordinary experience. That this belief was closely associated with the Catholic Church only made it easier for him to dismiss. No argument would have persuaded Powell that the disturbing realities of unwanted pregnancy and back-alley abortion should be subordinated to religious dogma.

But if Powell had to override heartfelt objections from a clerk or colleague, he at least would have been alerted to something he entirely missed—the risk that the constitutionalization of abortion would be deeply and durably divisive. Underlying Powell's abortion vote was an appeal to the future. He predicted—or rather assumed—that misgivings about the origin of the constitutional right would be lost in the widespread satisfaction with the result. Alexander Bickel identified the same assumption as the "idea of progress" underlying the decisions of the Warren Court: "Historians a generation or two hence . . . may barely note, and care little about, method, logic, or intellectual coherence, and may assess results in hindsight—only results, and by their own future lights." The Justices, Bickel thought, were betting on the future, "in the belief that progress, called history, would validate their course, and that another generation, remembering its own future, would imagine them favorably."

So it was with Powell and abortion. He did not worry about the deficiencies in Blackmun's opinion or the plunge into judicial activism, because he thought the result so plainly sound. To Powell, abortion looked like *Griswold*. There, too, the origin of the right was obscure. There, too, theoreticians had complained about the Justices injecting their personal preferences into the Constitution. There, too, Catholic hierarchy had objected. But there had been no widespread public outcry. The people generally agreed with Potter Stewart that Connecticut had enacted "an uncommonly silly law," which they were not sorry to see struck down.

In *Griswold*, the Court had not so much overridden the legislative action as updated it. By striking down an old statute, the Court had simply brought Connecticut's legal code into line with the law in other states, with the actual practice in Connecticut (where the ban was routinely unenforced), and with the judgment of future generations. It was as if the Justices had consulted the looking glass of contemporary American society and found there a slight distortion, an outdated, unenforced, and atypical state statute that did not accurately reflect modern values. By invalidating that law, the Court had acted as midwife to the future, hurrying Connecticut along the path taken by the nation as a whole.

But was abortion really the same? Laws against abortion were the norm, not the exception; they were usually enforced, not openly flouted; and there was no clear consensus against them. Nevertheless, in Powell's mind, the comparison held. State legislatures were slowly and haphazardly moving toward a more permissive stance. Constitutionalizing abortion would merely speed that process. Controversy and criticism were expected, but Powell assumed that constitutional protection for abortion, like the right of contraception declared in *Griswold*, would soon command widespread support and acquiescence.

Columnist Shana Alexander made the same comparison in 1972, when she predicted legislative legalization of abortion. "[T]he Catholic hierarchy may have made abortion its last stand," she wrote. "It was not so long ago that most Catholics believed that contraception was equal to murder, and agreed that if a choice had to be made in childbirth between mother and infant, the obligation was to save the child. To look back now at these medieval-sounding positions— the one so foolish, the other so monstrous—is to realize that this present 'last stand' too will shortly fall. A fresh wind is fast blowing away the left-over mists of Victorian sexual hypocrisy, and it seems certain that in a year or two abortion, already legal in eighteen states, will be the universal law of the land."

She was right, of course, but not in the way she expected. The legislative reform in which Alexander had such faith was cut short by the

Supreme Court, in part because Powell and his colleagues had the same vision of the future and the same confidence in their own foresight. By constitutionalizing abortion, Powell meant to anticipate popular sentiment, not to supplant it. By leaping over the current legislative muddle, the Court would achieve—quickly, cleanly, and without wrenching divisions—the solution toward which the country as a whole was clearly aimed.

Prediction, however, is treacherous. Powell's vision of popular acceptance of abortion proved only partly right. The polls confirm that support for freedom of choice is strong and widespread, but also that the opposition to it is committed and unreconciled. The nearly universal acquiescence that now attends the constitutionalization of contraception within marriage never reached abortion. Though the right is secure, the issue remains corrosively divisive. And the profound irony is that Powell's haste toward the future he thought inevitable may have made that future more costly to attain.

THE CONSEQUENCES

Powell sat in eighteen abortion cases after *Roe v. Wade.* On the one hand, the Court confirmed and protected the abortion right, striking down laws requiring a married woman to have the consent of her husband or an underage girl to have the consent of her parents, and rejecting various other attempts to make abortion difficult. In these decisions, Powell joined Brennan, Marshall, Blackmun, and Stewart or Stevens to form a majority. On the other hand, the Court upheld a law requiring that an unmarried minor notify her parents (not that they had to consent) and turned aside repeated efforts to compel government funding. In these decisions, Powell sided with Burger, White, Rehnquist, and usually Stewart. In every case Powell prevailed. By allying first with one group and then with the other, he was always in the majority on abortion.

The abortion funding cases proved especially controversial. They opened Powell to the charge that he was interested in constitutional rights only for the middle class, but he believed that private clinics in fact made abortion readily available without government funds. Moreover, there was a real difference, long established in constitutional law, between forbidding the government to interfere with private activity and requiring the government to pay for such activity. It was one thing to stop the government from outlawing abortions and quite another to make the taxpayers support them. Powell thought that it would unnecessarily inflame abortion opponents to insist that tax dollars fund a practice they abhorred. To that extent, he tried to accommodate antiabortion sentiment, but he never wavered in support of the basic right. To that conviction, he held firm.

The Court, however, did not. During the 1980s, the *Roe* majority dwindled steadily, as Stewart was replaced by Sandra Day O'Connor, Burger by Antonin Scalia, and Powell himself by Anthony Kennedy. By 1989 there were only four sure votes for abortion as a constitutional right.

In that year, a bitter and badly fractured Supreme Court decided *Webster v. Reproductive Health Services*. Four Justices (Rehnquist, White, Scalia, and Kennedy) seemed ready to overrule *Roe*. Another four (Brennan, Marshall, Blackmun, and Stevens) stood squarely behind it. The balance of power lay with Justice O'Connor, who was willing to allow state regulation of abortion so long as it did not impose an "undue burden" on the woman's right. (O'Connor's fence straddling drew a harsh denunciation from Antonin Scalia, who said that her approach "cannot be taken seriously.")

With Brennan's retirement in 1990 and the elevation of David Souter to take his seat and the replacement of Marshall by Clarence Thomas a year later, the unqualified supporters of *Roe v. Wade* shrank to two. Many lamented its demise, but two years later a surprising majority of the Supreme Court reaffirmed the constitutional right of abortion. O'Connor, Kennedy, and Souter joined Blackmun and Stevens in upholding *Roe*. Any other course, they said, would cause "profound and unnecessary damage to the Court's legitimacy, and to the Nation's commitment to the rule of law." The 1992 election of President Clinton and his announced intention to appoint only supporters of *Roe* to the Supreme Court secured the victory. Though the right of abortion came within an eyelash of being overruled, it now appears to be a fixed feature of constitutional law for the foreseeable future.

OVER TIME, the number of abortions settled at about 1.6 million a year, most of them by unmarried women under the age of twenty-five, many of whom had at least one abortion previously. The high rate of abortion suggested that the option was one that many women wanted. In this respect, the experience after *Roe* tended to confirm the practical assessment on which Powell's vote had been based.

Additionally, *Roe* boosted the ideology of choice. The Supreme

Court's decision did not merely expand the practical opportunity for abortion; it declared abortion available *as a matter of right*. It said that there was something fundamentally wrong with compelling a pregnant woman to carry an unwanted child to term. It withdrew the issue from the obscurity that had so long cloaked laws on sexuality and reproduction and placed the enormous authority of the Supreme Court behind a woman's freedom of choice. *Roe* transformed abortion from a dirty secret to a constitutional right—and created a powerful constituency of political support for this pronouncement.*

Powell approved of all this. In other respects, however, the consequences of *Roe v. Wade* contradicted Powell's expectations. Few decisions in the history of the Supreme Court—and certainly none in Powell's tenure—have so profoundly reoriented American politics and law. The constitutionalization of abortion had effects, great and small, that rippled through the society and rebounded in ways unforeseen and still not well understood. For Powell, these consequences were not only unexpected but also unwelcome.

Most important was the rise of antiabortion politics. If the abortion decision created and energized its own constituency, it also, in seeming obedience to the laws of physics, produced an equal and opposite reaction. More than any other single cause or factor, abortion created the Religious Right.

Before *Roe v. Wade*, the right-to-life movement was a scattered, largely Catholic response to legislative reform. It surfaced at Powell's confirmation in testimony from the Celebrate Life Committee of Long Island and other local organizations in New York, where permissive legislation had sparked opposition. With no national following, these witnesses were politely ignored.

Roe v. Wade did not defeat opposition to abortion. On the contrary, it energized the right-to-life movement. Most non-Catholic activists date their involvement from the time of that decision. To them, the constitutionalization of abortion was a sudden assault by the most prestigious and authoritative of secular institutions on traditional values of family and faith. In the days and weeks after January 22, 1973,

---

* The Gallup Poll reported that the number of Americans who think abortion should be legal under all circumstances climbed from 21 to 31 percent in the years 1975–1990. During the same period, the percentage of respondents stating that abortion should be illegal in all circumstances declined from 22 to 12. Throughout, a majority of respondents believed that abortion should be legal in some, but not all, situations.

they reached out to join others who were equally shocked at the Court's decision. They were less well educated than proabortion activists, less likely to come from the professional classes, less likely to have a voice in the kinds of establishment organizations relied on by Justice Blackmun. Many were women, mostly housewives, who were married, had children, and did not work outside the home. And before *Roe*, they were surprisingly disengaged from the communities in which they lived. Not only were they uninvolved in politics (many did not even vote), but they were also not active in church or civic groups, such as scouting or the PTA. If they were not a majority, as Spiro Agnew had claimed, they were surely silent.

Silent, that is, until *Roe v. Wade*. To say that antiabortion activists disagreed with the decision is to put a pale cast on a deep and enduring antipathy. They did not merely dislike the constitutionalization of abortion; they found it threatening. In ways that others found hard to fathom, many right-to-lifers saw the legalization of abortion as an assault on their beliefs, their values, their sense of self-worth. The driving force of the antiabortion movement was not merely conviction, but fear.

First, abortion challenged their belief in the sacredness of embryonic life. Not that antiabortion activists necessarily held any sophisticated theological position on when life begins. The moral standing of the fetus was not so much argued as assumed; it was something everyone knew. What everyone knew was "that the embryo was a human life as valuable as any (and perhaps more valuable than some because it was innocent, fragile, and unable to act on its own)." The Supreme Court now said this belief was merely one point of view and not one that the legislature could cast into law. In fact, as Blackmun showed, disagreement about the morality of abortion went back a long way, but antiabortion activists had not thought the question open. "[I]n America there had been little plain-spoken public debate about the moral status of the embryo since the middle of the nineteenth century, and many mistook a century of silence for a millennium of consensus."

This belief in the moral standing of embryonic life followed the teachings of the Catholic Church and accounted for the prominence of Roman Catholics in the early movement. Before *Roe*, most Protestant denominations, including fundamentalists, had no clearly defined position against abortion. A 1968 symposium of evangelical scholars revealed uncertainty and a wide range of views. In fact, their final statement leaned toward freedom of choice. "As to whether or not the performance of an induced abortion is always sinful we are not agreed," the scholars announced, "but about the necessity and permissibility for it under certain circumstances we are in accord." They concluded that a "Christian physician" could recommend abortion to safeguard the "greater values" of "individual health, family welfare, and social responsibility."

Three years later, another sampling of evangelical opinion showed the same divided views. Most participants did not insist on full moral status from the moment of conception but described the fetus as a "potential" human being. They rejected the "extreme notion" that abortion is morally insignificant, but most agreed that it should be allowed in "hard cases."

This concern for "hard cases" reflected the weight of Protestant opinion on the eve of *Roe v. Wade*. After *Roe*, evangelical and fundamentalist opinion hardened into opposition. The loose consensus that abortion was *sometimes* appropriate increasingly gave way to the view that it was *never* right. Scholars recanted, pastors became aroused, and influential laymen, such as future Surgeon General C. Everett Koop, changed their views. By 1980, fifty-nine of ninety-nine denominations opposed abortion, and the retreat from choice has continued.

What accounts for the decline in religious tolerance of abortion in the face its official validation by the Supreme Court? Why did a decision that Powell thought would solidify an emerging national consensus instead provoke a formidable and durable backlash?

The answer lies in the ways the Supreme Court unwittingly redefined the abortion debate. Before *Roe*, abortion reform went state by state. The focus was local, the compromises varied, and the results uneven. Nationally, abortion was a nonissue. It never arose in the 1968 presidential campaign and barely surfaced four years later. Inflation, Vietnam, drugs, crime, poverty, and busing were hot issues in 1972; abortion was not. It was not mentioned in interviews with the Democratic nominee nor in an explanation of "How Mr. Nixon Woos the Democrats." Of eight commentators asked by *Newsweek* to address the "real issues" of 1972, only Gloria Steinem (foreshadowing the link between abortion and women's rights) spoke of abortion. Elsewhere, it was relegated to a list of such "off-beat" questions as the legalization of marijuana, public funding for the Olympics, and a local ban on hunting doves.

Roe v. Wade transformed this diffuse debate into a national issue. Like a magnifying glass that concentrates the sun's rays on a single point, *Roe* focused all the energies and passions aroused by abortion on presidential elections. The Court's decision changed the content of the debate as well as its location. Before *Roe* the question was whether some abortion should be permitted; afterward it was whether any abortion could be restricted. Religious leaders who could accept abortion in "hard cases" recoiled from abortion on demand. The difference, while perhaps not intelligible in a strictly theological approach to the beginning of life, was central to abortion as a social issue. *Roe v. Wade* approved abortion as birth control. Within the confines of her right to privacy, the woman could abort for any reason—because the pregnancy was inconvenient, or the child had been conceived out of wedlock, or the baby was the wrong sex. Abortion on demand threatened not only—perhaps not even chiefly—the sacredness of fetal life; it also challenged the traditional morality of sex. At the core of the antiabortion movement lay a "set of unmistakably conservative sexual values"—opposition to pornography, premarital sex, homosexuality, even sex education. Increasingly, and especially among fundamentalists, antipathy to abortion had less to do with protecting fetal life than with preventing teenage sex. "God did not ordain sex for fun and games," said one activist, yet the Supreme Court seemed intent on liberating people from the consequences of their own actions. The constitutionalization of abortion became Exhibit A in the modern assault on the traditional family.

This affront to conventional morality was accompanied by a threat to personal identity. The women who flocked to the pro-life movement after *Roe* were mostly mothers who stayed home and raised children. That was not merely what they did; that was who they were. The insult from *Roe v. Wade* was logically obscure but emotionally direct. They felt that the Supreme Court had denied their worth, had reduced the transcendent reason for their existence to a matter of official indifference. Sociologist Kristin Luker reported that, "the new activists were people who had direct experiences with pregnancy. Moreover, they were people whose values made pregnancy central to their lives. Now they were faced with a Supreme Court decision that seemed to devalue not only the status of the embryo but pregnancy itself." To them, abortion on demand not only denied the moral standing of the unborn; it disparaged the worth of the women who gave birth.

The threat posed by abortion on demand to the traditional morality of sex and the family opened the door to the New Right. Originally (and to an extent still), the right-to-life movement encompassed a wide range of political views. The New Right, by contrast, was overtly ideological. It defined itself by linking historically conservative positions on anticommunism, defense preparedness, and the like, to an aggressively "pro-family" (that is, antifeminist) agenda of social issues. Abortion was the point of convergence between New Right ideologues and fundamentalist Christianity, and the alliance between them was perhaps inevitable. The politicians brought savvy leadership and technical sophistication; the antiabortion movement supplied committed foot soldiers and grass-roots organization. Together, they formed the Religious Right, a new coalition of conservative Catholics, Mormons, and the traditionally anti-Catholic fundamentalists of the South and Southwest.

Jerry Falwell's Moral Majority gave the movement a name, but one that was in both parts misleading. The goal was not private morality but public power, and its adherents were never a majority of the political nation or even, as Pat Robertson learned, of the Republican Party. They did not need to be. The crucial importance of the Religious Right lay not in majority status, which it never had, but in its effect on the political balance of power. By bringing Ronald Reagan and George Bush large number of supporters not historically identified with the Republican Party—indeed, often not previously active voters—the Religious Right transformed the nation's politics and cemented the exclusion of Democrats from the White House through the 1980s.*

Of course, election of Republican Presidents did not disturb Powell, but he was upset at the intrusion of abortion into national politics. For a man who sought compromise and valued courtesy, who revered rationality and mistrusted emotion, who spoke in the modulated tones of the corporate boardroom and believed in noblesse oblige, the raw intensity of abortion politics was scary. And the issue would not go away. Fifteen years after *Roe*, a national cover story proclaimed "America's New Civil War." "Say that one word," the article began, "and other words fire like weapons. One side yells bloody murder; the other insists that a woman presides over her own body. . . . The extremes are at an impasse, and the national debate rages relentlessly on."

Activists focused on the President and the Congress, because they had to face the voters, but for both sides the real target was the Supreme Court. Having tried to take abortion out of politics, the Court now found itself a victim of the politics of abortion. Having

---

* Empirical research shows that in 1988 an astonishing 81 percent of "white born-again Christians" supported George Bush over Michael Dukakis. Approximately 50 percent of all other Protestants voted for Bush, as compared to 49 percent of Catholics and 30 percent of Jews. Data from 1984 are similar.

taken it upon themselves to say when abortion would be permitted, the Justices now found that their answer controlled the fate of the Court itself. The flash point was the selection of judges. Powell deplored the centrality of abortion, abhorred the "litmus test" it was said to have become and the subordination of a candidate's personal qualities and professional achievements to reliability on this one issue. The debacle of the Bork nomination dragged the Court even deeper into partisan politics. Bork's confirmation proceedings were the most rancorous, raucous, publicized, and politicized of any in this century (until the later hearings on Clarence Thomas), and abortion was a major reason.

A nadir of a different sort was reached in the Bush administration, when the sudden departure of Justice Brennan led to the nomination of David Souter, a man of intellect and integrity but an unknown quantity elevated to the nation's highest court precisely because he had the supreme good sense never to have voiced an opinion on *Roe v. Wade*. When Thurgood Marshall retired a year later, nominee Clarence Thomas also professed never to have expressed himself on that subject, leaving many to wonder whether it was possible that a thoughtful and outspoken lawyer would have taken no position on the greatest constitutional issue of the time and, if so, whether such disengagement was really healthy.

To Powell, this cat-and-mouse game seemed ludicrous, yet in a way he was partly responsible. The politicization that Powell so disliked was in large measure a consequence of the constitutionalization of abortion.

A SECOND CONSEQUENCE was equally unintended. *Roe v. Wade* not only changed constitutional politics; it also transformed constitutional theory. Its impact on the way the Constitution is taught in the nation's law schools went much deeper than merely adding abortion to the list of protected liberties. *Roe* redirected constitutional scholarship and intensified an the ongoing debate about the nature of the Constitution. Is the Constitution a document or an idea? Is it fixed or flexible? Is its meaning to be derived *from* the words or ascribed *to* them? Is constitutional law really law at all, or is it merely a branch of politics? On these fundamental questions, *Roe v. Wade* has had profound effect.

Owen J. Roberts, best known as the Justice whose "switch in time saved nine" from the Roosevelt Court-packing plan, made constitutional law sound simple. "The Constitution is the supreme law of the land ordained and established by the people." All legislation must conform to it. When a statute is challenged as unconstitutional, Roberts wrote, "the judicial branch of the Government has only one duty—to lay the article of the Constitution which is invoked beside the statute which is challenged and to decide whether the latter squares with the former."

To decide whether a statute squares with the Constitution is sometimes just that simple. The question whether a twenty-nine-year-old could be elected President admits only one answer: "neither shall any Person be eligible to that Office who shall not have attained to the Age of thirty five Years." Similarly, the Constitution specifies that there shall be "two Senators from each State," not three, or five, or some number reflecting the state's population. But in the realm of the Constitution, such clear answers are rare. Even questions that look easy sometimes turn out not to be. Was it true, for example, that George Romney, who sought the 1968 Republican nomination for President, was disqualified from that office because he was not "a natural born Citizen," or might that phrase have been stretched to include a child born to Americans visiting Mexico? The answer was (and is) unclear.

Such small-scale uncertainty pales in comparison with the majestic generalities of the Bill of Rights. "Congress shall make no law . . . abridging the freedom of speech." What, exactly, is "freedom of speech"? Certainly not every use of language. No one has a constitutional right to lie under oath or to solicit another to commit murder, even though these crimes involve words. But if "freedom of speech" does not include all use of language, what does it omit? Does the Constitution protect condom ads, trashy novels, or tabloid exposés? (Generally, yes.) And might "freedom of speech" also reach some conduct? Does it include, for example, the "symbolic speech" of burning an American flag? (Also yes.)

None of these questions can be answered simply by reading the Constitution. No matter how carefully the text is studied, the words remain indeterminate. The "freedom of speech" protected by the Constitution is broad (or narrow) enough to yield any number of interpretations. And so are the guarantees of "due process" and "equal protection" and the prohibitions against "unreasonable" searches and "cruel and unusual" punishments. Different judges will read these phrases differently. When the Constitution and a statute are laid side by side, "whether the latter squares with the former" will often be unclear.

Resolving such questions requires not inspection but interpretation—

not a passive reading of meaning laid down long ago but an active effort to reach a modern understanding. The text is surely relevant, but so are the history of the Constitution, the structure of government it creates, the broader goals and principles that can be inferred from its provisions, and, inevitably, the judge's own sense of what the Constitution *should* mean, the selection from various possible meanings of the one that seems most consistent with fairness and good sense. As Justice Roberts himself well knew, the task of interpretation is more difficult—and more open-ended—than his description implied.

So ran conventional wisdom at the time of *Roe v. Wade*. Constitutional law was widely, though imperfectly, understood as an act of *interpretation*. It was not as mechanical as Justice Roberts made out, but neither was it purely political. Interpretation began with the text and with the history and structure of the Constitution and sought to link results to the document in lawyerly ways. If text, history, and structure were not clear, at least the Court should adopt a reading that the conventional sources of constitutional law did not foreclose. The underlying premise widely (but by no means uniformly) prevailing in the classroom was that the Constitution itself had meaning, which the faithful judge could discover and apply.*

As an act of conventional interpretation, *Roe v. Wade* is next to impossible. As John Hart Ely has noted, the Constitution "simply says nothing, clear or fuzzy, about abortion." Abortion was not *found* in the Constitution; it was *put* there by the Supreme Court. It would take an intellectual contortionist of uncommon pliability to approach the Constitution in historical context, as a "document of specified words and construction" with "definite and determined meaning" (to quote Justice Blackmun), and find there anything resembling a constitutional right to abortion.

Roe therefore does not appeal to the interpretive tradition of constitutional law but to a competing approach, equally old, also venerated, and frequently vindicated—the tradition of *fundamental rights*. This

---

* Readers will recognize that the question is more complicated than this summary suggests. For one thing, the Constitution itself occasionally seems to recognize that its text is not exhaustive. The Ninth Amendment, for example, states that the Constitution's enumeration of certain rights "shall not be construed to deny or disparage others retained by the people." On one reading, this language requires the Supreme Court to define and protect those "other" rights not stated in the Constitution. In other words, the text commands judges to look outside the text. This is the sort of thing that makes one's head swim and leads to endless academic debate.

view holds that the Constitution authorizes the Supreme Court to safeguard rights not specified in the document. The approach is not interpretive. It does not rely on the text but on moral reasoning, extrinsic to the document itself, that identifies certain interests as fundamental to the human personality. The rights themselves may come from moral philosophy or natural law or political theory. Whatever the source, fundamental rights are protected because they are simply too important to leave to legislative control. For a majority of the Justices, abortion is such a right.

For more than a century, these two approaches to constitutional law have co-existed in uneasy tension. *Roe v. Wade* did not invent the idea of nontextual rights, nor did it defeat the ideal of constitutional law as interpretation, but it did shift the balance between them. The change is most evident in the academy. Before *Roe*, interpretation was rarely explicitly rejected in the nation's classrooms. There were other voices and other theories and Supreme Court decisions that were hard to understand in this way, but in most schools interpretation was at least the professed norm of constitutional law. Today that no longer is true. Interpretation certainly survives. Indeed, in reaction to *Roe*, there has been a rebirth of insistence on interpretation, including a particularly constricted doctrine of original intent, but the idea no longer dominates. In many quarters—especially the nation's most elite and influential schools—interpretation has been replaced by a frank indifference to the words of the Constitution and a renewed attention to the moral requirements of a just society. The momentum has shifted away from viewing the Constitution as a law, to be read and interpreted like any other legal document, and toward using the Constitution as a charter for social justice, to be continually re-created by each generation.

Roe was not the first or only decision to create a new constitutional right, but it was at once the most extreme and the most important. It was extreme in its clarity. In no other case in modern times has a declaration of constitutional law been more ostentatiously nontextual. The extreme difficulty of reconciling *Roe* with the traditional notion of interpretation made it a kind of test case—not for abortion only, but for constitutional law as a whole. Is the Constitution a legal document, to be read and interpreted like any other, or is it a charter for judicial construction of a just society? Should the Justices try to be lawyers or statesmen? Abortion made judges and scholars choose sides. Opposition to *Roe* became a kind of loyalty oath for traditional interpretation, while support for *Roe* became the flagship of a vast movement embracing nontextual rights.

The political controversy over abortion made the intellectual issue unavoidable. *Roe*'s break with the tradition of interpretation was not only too obvious to explain away; it was too important to ignore. Earlier decisions in the tradition of fundamental rights were either recognized as mistakes (such as early-twentieth-century decisions striking down government regulation of the economy) that could be safely criticized, or they were politically so nearly uncontroversial (such as *Griswold*) that they could be tolerated, even by those who committed in the main to traditional interpretation.

Roe raised the stakes. The decision was bitterly criticized, both in the academy and on the streets, and the ferocity of these attacks called forth an equally passionate defense. In this free-fire zone, equivocation and compromise gave ground. Students of the Constitution were forced to choose sides, and they overwhelmingly chose *Roe*. A brief filed in *Webster* represented the views of 885 law professors who asserted that "the right of a woman to choose whether or not to bear a child, as delineated . . . in *Roe v. Wade*, is an essential component of constitutional liberty. . . ." And the law reviews, at first full of criticism of *Roe*, quickly moved toward justification. Before long, leading legal scholars were busy proving that *Roe* was right—and therefore that the idea of constitutional law as legal interpretation was necessarily wrong.

This development can be traced in the work of one of the nation's most gifted and prestigious lawyers, Harvard professor Laurence H. Tribe. If he were not so active on so many fronts, Tribe might be said to have made a career out of defending *Roe*. At first he argued that legislators should be barred from regulating abortion because their views might be influenced by religion—as if opinions grounded in religious faith, as opposed to the secular ideologies of the Harvard Law School, were for that reason illegitimate. (One might as well say that antiwar votes should not be counted if inspired by religious pacifism.) Tribe then tried a different tack. In a pair of articles in the mid 1970s, he made the surprising claim that the constitutionalization of abortion was justified not in spite of but precisely because there was no societal consensus on the question—as if judges had a duty to rescue democracy from hard decisions.

More recently, Tribe has anchored the defense of *Roe* in the firmer ground of gender equality. In an influential treatise he argues that laws against abortion deny women "a control over sex and its consequences that men take for granted." That such restrictions are imposed by men, who do not bear the personal costs of pregnancy, turns injury into injustice. "A woman forced by law to submit to the pain and anxiety of carrying, delivering, and nurturing a child she does not wish to have is entitled to believe that more than a play on words links her forced labor with the concept of involuntary servitude. To give society—especially a male-dominated society—the power to sentence women to childbearing against their will is to delegate to some a sweeping and unaccountable authority over the lives of others." Given the "myriad ways in which unwanted pregnancy and unwanted children burden the participation of women as equals in society," laws against abortion operate "to the serious detriment of women as a class" and are for that reason unconstitutional.*

Finally, in 1990 Tribe wrote a book that continued his defense of *Roe*, but for the first time made conciliatory noises about the need for political compromise. Ultimately, however, he again rejected any qualifications of the right.

Tribe's work reveals much more than the workings of an agile mind. It illustrates the preoccupation of modern constitutional scholarship with the justification of *Roe*. The theme that emerges more and more clearly is that abortion is too important not to be in the Constitution. If the Framers left it out, the omission must be corrected. The thrust of Tribe's argument is to show why the right of abortion is essential to a just society; the link between that right and constitutional language or history is pro forma. This is the essence of the fundamental rights approach to the Constitution. *Roe v. Wade* forced a widening gulf between the open-ended, ever-changing Constitution, as taught in today's law schools, and the older and narrower conception of the Constitution as a document of "definite and determined meaning." It was the engine not only of political controversy, but also of intellectual revolution.

A THIRD CONSEQUENCE of the abortion decisions touched Powell more personally. *Roe v. Wade* was the genesis of a phenomenon that has often been remarked but never adequately explained—the greening of Harry Blackmun.

In his first years on the Supreme Court, Blackmun seemed to be what everyone had expected—a colorless, competent, conservative

---

*   Today the gender-equality argument is plainly dominant in the justification of *Roe*. Then Judge (now Justice) Ruth Bader Ginsburg has suggested that the constitutional foundation of *Roe* would have been stronger had the decision been put on this ground. And in a powerful article entitled "Rethinking Sex and the Constitution," Professor Sylvia Law insists that "[c]ontrol of reproduction is the sine qua non of women's capacity to live as equal people" and that restrictions on abortion therefore "plainly oppress women."

judge closely allied with his friend and sponsor, Chief Justice Warren Burger. In Blackmun's first full term, he disagreed with Burger in only one case in ten—not only Blackmun's highest rate of agreement with any other Justice but the closest alignment between any two Justices on the Court that year. This pattern held for some time. For the five terms from 1970 through 1974, Blackmun disagreed with Burger in fewer than one case in five.

But then he changed. During the last five years of their joint service (the 1981 through 1985 terms of the Court), Blackmun split with the Chief more than twice as often. Over the same period, Blackmun's disagreements with Rehnquist also almost doubled.

The statistics document Blackmun's shift to the left not only as a movement away from Burger and Rehnquist but also as an approach toward Brennan and Marshall. During his first five terms, Blackmun disagreed with his liberal colleagues in nearly half the cases. By the last five years of Burger's tenure, that rate had fallen by half. In 1986 Blackmun described Thurgood Marshall as a person of "excellent judicial reactions" who "seems to know the right way to go on most issues." By that time the "right way to go" for Harry Blackmun was distinctly liberal. In both the 1985 and 1986 terms, Blackmun voted most often not with the conservative Chief Justice, or with middle-of-the-roaders such as White and Powell, but with Marshall and Brennan. Over the years, Blackmun had migrated from the conservative orbit of Warren Burger to the Court's opposite extreme.

Blackmun's transformation did not show in numbers only; it also had a human face. In his early years on the Court, Blackmun wrote an opinion refusing to allow one Robert Kras to file for bankruptcy without paying a fifty-dollar fee. The trouble was that Kras did not have the fifty dollars. He lived on welfare with his wife, their two small children (one with cystic fibrosis), his mother, and another child in a tiny apartment in New York. Because he owed money, he could not get a job; and because he had no job, he had no money; and because he had no money, he could not pay the fee required to clear his record of bad debts and become employable. Catch-22. There were sound legal reasons to rule against Mr. Kras (Powell and three others agreed with that result), but there was no reason to be insensitive to the difficulty of his situation. Blackmun said that if Kras really wanted to make a fresh start, he would find the fee "within his able-bodied reach." After all, he could pay in installments of less than two dollars per week, which was "less than the price of a movie and little more than the cost of a pack or two of cigarettes." It was left to Justice Marshall to point out that saving two dollars a week might not be so easy for the desperately poor. As one critic said of Blackmun's performance, "Confronted with a man with no bread, he told him to give up cake. The queen of France could not have done better."

Compare this Harry Blackmun with the Harry Blackmun writing only four years later in the abortion funding cases. Led by Powell, the Supreme Court refused to require the government to pay for abortion, just as it had refused to require the government to pay for Robert Kras's bankruptcy proceeding. This time Blackmun dissented. For the financially helpless woman, Blackmun wrote, "the result is punitive and tragic. Implicit in the Court's holdings is the condescension that she may go elsewhere for her abortion. I find that disingenuous and alarming, almost reminiscent of:'Let them eat cake.'"

Blackmun closing plea for compassion must have surprised Robert Kras. "There is another world 'out there,'" Blackmun wrote, "the existence of which the Court, I suspect, either chooses to ignore or fears to recognize. And so the cancer of poverty will continue to grow. This is a sad day for those who regard the Constitution as a force that would serve justice to all evenhandedly and, in so doing, would better the lot of the poorest among us."

This was a different Harry Blackmun. Gone were the lawyerly disengagement, the conservative caution, the traditional reluctance to see the government's failure to relieve poverty as a constitutional violation. In their place were an emotional directness, an instinct to right wrongs, and compassion laced with outrage at those who disagreed. Blackmun increasingly found this voice. He would never be known as a consummate craftsman. He would continue to produce opinions that sacrificed structure and analysis for seemingly random collections of fact and observation. But Blackmun would also write with genuine force and feeling. Increasingly, his thoughts were not hidden or disguised, not tangled up in technicality, or buried beneath mountains of references, or obscured by ornamental prose. What Blackmun's work lacked in dazzle and sophistication, it made up for in humanity and directness. And this more personal, more engaged, more open and sincere public voice was raised not in service of the values with which Blackmun began his judicial career but in support of the dwindling liberal minority on an increasingly conservative Court.

Blackmun's transformation has never been satisfactorily explained. Liberals were content not to look a gift horse in the mouth. They praised Blackmun's "flexibility" and "open-mindedness," his "sense of fairness" and "capacity for growth." Conservatives thought he had been bamboozled by Brennan. Neither fully understood that the impetus for Blackmun's turn to the left was not political but personal, not intellectual but psychological.

The root of Blackmun's metamorphosis lay in the natural concern of a parent for a child. The parent was Harry Blackmun and the child was *Roe v. Wade*. Blackmun knew that *Roe* would always be mentioned first in any account of his career. It was the challenge of a lifetime, and Blackmun thought he had met that challenge. When he put together a majority of seven, uniting everyone from Douglas to Burger behind his opinion, Blackmun was entitled to believe that his labors had been rewarded. The opinion was more important than any written by his colleagues, even the venerable Justice Douglas. It would establish him in their eyes and allay the doubts he always felt about being in their company.

What a cruel irony it must have seemed when the opinion in *Roe* was greeted not with praise but with derision. Many years later, a Blackmun admirer said *Roe* had become "famous as a humane charter of liberty for women who wish to control their lives and reproductive destinies," but early reaction was largely critical. Many approved the result, but no one liked the opinion. Said one commentator, "It seems to be generally agreed that, as a matter of simple craft, Justice Blackmun's opinion for the Court was dreadful. . . . Insofar as *Roe* gives us evidence, we can conclude that Justice Blackmun is a terrible judge." Such remarks could not fail to wound, and they proved especially hurtful to Justice Blackmun.

And the criticism of *Roe* as a failure of craft was joined by a more vicious attack on *Roe* as a moral statement. Pickets marched across the street from the Court, denouncing both the decision and its author. They showed up wherever Blackmun gave speeches, and they sent him letters, full of anguish and outrage. Often, they included gruesome photographs of aborted fetuses.* Such savagery was at once understandable and unfair. It was understandable that opponents of abortion would lash out at the life-tenured judges who forced legalization upon them, but it was unfair that the hostility should fix on Blackmun, who was no more responsible for the result than Powell or Brennan or Burger or Stewart. That this gentle, caring man should be depicted as a brutal baby-killer was grotesque.

---

* Antiabortion literature sometimes used the same tactic. In *Four Ways to Kill a Baby*, a picture of a dismembered fetus, actually only two inches long, was enlarged to resemble the photo of a baby, to whom it was compared.

Another Justice might have let this go by, but not Blackmun. He read the letters, looked at the pictures, and shared the pain of his critics, almost as if he had a duty to suffer along with them, and he wondered why they could not understand—it was not abortion he favored, but choice. A woman could carry her child to term or free herself of an unwanted pregnancy. No one was forced to act contrary to her beliefs. Was that not justice?

Blackmun's great triumph became an emotional disaster. *Roe* brought him ridicule, not respect. The wound was deep and was soon surrounded by defensive scar tissue.

It was Blackmun's defensiveness about *Roe* that led to his metamorphosis as a liberal. Faced with a barrage of criticism, Blackmun tried to validate *Roe* by vehement reiteration. If the constitutionalization of abortion could be repeated, confirmed, and indeed expanded, it might be made invulnerable. Far from qualifying the right announced in *Roe*, Blackmun wanted to extend that ruling to ever more doubtful territory. He voted not only against the flat prohibition of abortion, but also against laws requiring a husband's or parent's consent; against a ban on advertising for abortion; against a statute directing that the doctor determine whether the fetus was viable and, if so, try to save its life; against a requirement that an unmarried and underage female get the consent if not of a parent, at least of a judge; and even against the rule that the parents of an underage girl be notified that their daughter intended to have an abortion. It was as if by reiterating and extending *Roe*, Blackmun could not only prove its correctness, but also erect barricades to safeguard the citadel of his creation.

For several years, *Roe* seemed in no danger. The 1977 abortion-funding cases first put Blackmun in the minority. His dissent, which has already been quoted, began a long line of increasingly passionate defenses of abortion, culminating in his 1989 dissent in *Webster v. Reproductive Health Services*. His attack on the majority's apparent willingness to reconsider *Roe* has a vehement eloquence not often seen in Supreme Court opinions. He accused his colleagues of deception and cowardice, of "[b]ald assertion masquerad[ing] as reasoning" and "totally meaningless" standards. *Roe*, he insisted, had been decided "as logic and science compelled," and his colleagues had "not one reasonable argument" as to why it should be abandoned. "I fear," he wrote, "for the future. I fear for the liberty and equality of the millions of women who have lived and come of age in the 16 years since *Roe* was decided. I fear for the integrity of, and public esteem for, this Court."

Though the *Webster* majority stopped short of overruling *Roe*, Blackmun feared the worst. "For today, at least, the law of abortion stands undisturbed. For today, the women of this Nation still retain the liberty to control their destinies. But the signs are evident and very ominous, and a chill wind blows." As it happened, however, his pessimism was overdone, for three years later the Court turned back the attack on *Roe* and reaffirmed that decision, though by the slimmest of margins.

For Blackmun, the attack on *Roe* was personal. Those who kept the faith won his trust and support. Thus Blackmun drew closer to Brennan and Marshall, not out of gratitude or even because of Brennan's canny courtship, but because of an underlying sense of rapport on this crucial issue. Those who questioned the right of abortion came increasingly under suspicion. Blackmun pulled back from his conservative colleagues not because he disliked them (Burger excepted), but because of a sense of distance and disharmony. And always the dominant feature of this psychic landscape, dwarfing all else, was *Roe v. Wade*. The decision not only created a constitutional right to abortion, it also, over time, made Harry Blackmun a liberal.

FOR HIS PART, Powell remained loyal to *Roe* and viewed the prospect of its overruling with undisguised regret. When asked to give the 1989 Leslie H. Arps Lecture to the Association of the Bar of the City of New York, he chose as his topic, "Stare Decisis and Judicial Restraint." The Latin phrase means "let the decision stand." Powell used it to speak on the virtues—the *conservative* virtues—of following precedent. Although the message seemed to have special relevance to *Roe*, Powell did not press the implication beyond noting that "there is no secret as to how I would have voted in *Webster*." On other occasions, both public and private, he took every opportunity to say that he stood by *Roe v. Wade*.

To this extent, Powell followed Blackmun. Yet to Powell, abortion was an issue, not a cause. He thought the antiabortion activists were wrong, but he did not regard them as enemies. Indeed, he tried to accommodate their sensibilities—most notably in his persistent refusal to require government funding for abortion. Powell steadfastly supported the constitutionalization of abortion, but he did so in a characteristically balanced way. He thought it not only right in principle that women should have the choice, but also sane and sensible for the law to recognize an option that many women would insist on taking, whether it were legal or not.

In this respect, Powell's support for abortion tied into his core ideological commitment to the rule of law. If, above all else, people had to respect the law, it followed that the law had to respect their beliefs. The law could not, without great cost, condemn a practice to which a sizable fraction of the otherwise law-abiding population were irrevocably committed.

In this way, Powell recognized the passionate demand for freedom of choice, even though he did not fully share the emotion. Intellectually, he believed that abortion was an indispensable condition of human freedom and an irreducible requirement for the equality of women. But he did not have Blackmun's intensity of feeling. Consequently, although he consistently supported *Roe*, he did not follow Blackmun into insisting that every aspect and detail of the law of abortion be resolved in its favor. In the abortion-funding cases and on some other subsidiary questions, the two parted company.

Thus it was that Powell and Blackmun grew apart. Blackmun's drift to the left put political distance between them, but it was nothing compared to the growing psychological estrangement. Blackmun's odd stridency, his tight-lipped resentments, the occasional outbursts that punctuated his normally mild demeanor, seemed to Powell puzzling and childish. Over time, Powell retreated into a wary formality, delicately trying to avoid anything that would set Blackmun off. He did not always succeed. Powell once went through some weeks in which Blackmun did not speak to him, not even to acknowledge a greeting as they passed in the corridor. The reason was never explained, though the clerks thought it resulted from some supposed insult by Powell's secretary to Blackmun's daughter. Whatever the cause, the tension was resolved by Powell's 1985 prostate surgery the Mayo Clinic, when an uncontrolled hemorrhage nearly killed him. Blackmun's concern washed away his earlier resentment, and warm relations were reestablished. From then until Powell's retirement three years later, he and Blackmun were on good terms, but always lurking beneath the surface was Powell's awareness of a gulf between them, a psychological divide that was but one small facet of Blackmun's parental protectiveness for *Roe v. Wade.*

CHAPTER XII

THE NIXON
TAPES CASE

A "THIRD-RATE BURGLARY"

It is hard to know where to begin the story of the Nixon tapes case. The "third-rate burglary," as the White House called it, was uncovered in the predawn hours of June 17, 1972, when five well-dressed men with electronic eavesdropping equipment were arrested in the head-quarters of the Democratic National Committee in the Watergate office complex. On September 15 a grand jury indicted these five, plus former White House staffers E. Howard Hunt and G. Gordon Liddy. One could begin the story there or on February 7, 1973, when the Senate established a committee to investigate the break-in. Or perhaps on June 25, when John Dean, former Counsel to the President, began to spill his guts to the Senators and provided the first direct evidence of Nixon's involvement in the cover-up. At the latest, the story begins on July 16, 1973, when a former appointments secretary revealed that the President had secretly taped the conversations in the Oval Office.

Everyone wanted the tapes. They were subpoenaed by the Senate committee and by the Watergate special prosecutor. The office of special prosecutor had been created by incoming Attorney General Elliot Richardson to hold back the rising tide of suspicion of the President and to persuade the Senate to confirm Richardson as Attorney General. To fill the post, Richardson chose his former Harvard law professor Archibald Cox, a Democrat who had been Solicitor General of the United States under Presidents Kennedy and Johnson.

When Nixon refused to give up the tapes, Cox sought a court order. He asked for tapes of nine conversations between Nixon and John Dean. After a hearing on the President's claim of executive privilege,

District Judge John Sirica ordered the tapes turned over to him. Sirica proposed to inspect the tapes, excise the portions that should remain confidential, and give the rest to the special prosecutor. Nixon refused. He took the case to the Court of Appeals, which, on September 13, made an extraordinary public plea for out-of-court settlement of the dispute. It soon became clear that no compromise was forthcoming, and on October 12, 1973, the appeals court approved Sirica's ruling by a vote of five to two.

The nation waited to see whether the besieged President would comply with the order or appeal to the Supreme Court. In fact, he did neither. In an ingenious "compromise," he offered Cox not the tapes themselves but an expurgated summary of their contents. Accuracy would be assured by Senator John C. Stennis, who would listen to the tapes and verify the summary. This was the carrot, but Nixon also had a stick. He commanded Cox, as a member of the executive branch, not to demand anything more. When Cox refused, Nixon ordered him fired. Richardson, who had promised Cox total independence, resigned rather than carry out the order, as did his deputy, William Ruckelshaus. Third in line was Solicitor General Robert Bork, who at 8:24 P.M. on Saturday, October 20, fired Cox and eliminated the office of special prosecutor. The Saturday Night Massacre, as it was called, sparked a firestorm of criticism so intense that it forced the President's hand. Amid the first serious talk of impeachment, Nixon agreed to turn over the tapes and to name a new special prosecutor.

But the tapes issue would not die. First, the White House announced that two of the nine tapes were "nonexistent." Then came word of the famous eighteen-minute gap, an erasure that to this day has not been satisfactorily explained. And still more tapes were demanded—by the Senate Watergate committee, then by the House committee considering impeachment, and finally by the new special prosecutor, Powell's longtime friend, Leon Jaworski.

On March 1, 1974, Jaworski got a new round of Watergate indictments against more senior defendants. Named in the indictment were former White House Chief of Staff H. R. Haldeman, former Assistant to the President for Domestic Affairs John D. Ehrlichman, and former Attorney General John Mitchell. They were charged with conspiracy, obstruction of justice, and other offenses. Only later was it learned that the grand jury had also named as an unindicted co-conspirator the President of the United States, Richard Nixon.

In connection with these new prosecutions, Jaworski subpoenaed sixty-four additional tapes. The President released edited transcripts but refused to part with the originals. Again Sirica ordered the President to comply with the subpoena, and again Nixon sought review of his order in the Court of Appeals. Jaworski then pulled a surprise. He asked the Supreme Court to bypass the appeals court and hear the Nixon tapes case immediately.

The request was extraordinary. Although the Justices have the power to take a case before it has been heard in the lower courts, they almost never do. But then, Watergate was an extraordinary case. Everyone knew that it would get to the Supreme Court eventually. Besides, what was the point in waiting for the lower court to consider the question a second time? The legal issue was precisely the same as in the first tapes case, which the Court of Appeals had decided against the President the preceding October. The research and reflection of the appeals court judges were recorded in their prior opinions. The Justices would not learn more by waiting; they were as informed as they would ever be.

Powell keenly felt the need to end the crisis in the country. Just how corrosive and degrading the controversy had become had been brought home to Powell the preceding October during the Yom Kippur War, when Soviet leader Leonid Brezhnev sent Nixon a brutal note threatening the destruction of the state of Israel by Soviet forces. Nixon ordered American forces worldwide to a "red alert," last used by Lyndon Johnson on the day President Kennedy was shot. Nixon said the Soviet threat was "the most difficult crisis we've had since the Cuban [missile] confrontation of 1962," but many were suspicious. Both *Time* and *Newsweek* reported "widespread mutterings that it was all a desperate ploy to divert attention from [Nixon's] domestic troubles," and Secretary of State Henry Kissinger had to deny repeatedly that the alert was called for political reasons. "There has to be a minimum of confidence," Kissinger pleaded, "that the senior officials of the American government are not playing with the lives of the American people." For many, that confidence was plainly lacking.

Powell found this defiant skepticism shocking. Never one to underrate the Soviet menace, and genuinely respectful of Nixon's foreign policy, Powell was prepared to credit the President's explanation. At the least, it seemed foolhardy to question that explanation. The thought that the nation's ability to meet the Soviet threat of armed aggression might be paralyzed by domestic divisions brought home to Powell as nothing else could the growing costs of Watergate.

A private letter to Gerald Gunther explained Powell's reasons for supporting expedited review. "I was influenced, perhaps decisively, by a personal conviction that the country was undergoing a prolonged agony which already had diverted attention from pressing domestic problems and, at least arguably, weakened our capacity to influence the dangerous course of international events." "One had to be in Washington," Powell added, "to appreciate the extent to which the atmosphere here was poisoned."

Finally, delay would run into a problem with the Court's own calendar. It was already too late to have the case briefed and argued before the current term ended in July. If the Justices scheduled the case now, they could stay in town for a special session and resolve the case that summer. If, however, they waited for the Court of Appeals, the case would not reach the Supreme Court before it reconvened in October.

This prospect prompted Senate Majority Leader Mike Mansfield to ask the Supreme Court to remain in session "so that there will be no unconscionable delays in the consideration of Watergate and related matters which might be placed before it." Mansfield's rebuke irritated Powell. Apart from the irony of being criticized by Congress for not staying in town, Powell resented the idea that the Court's annual summer recess was a vacation. During most of that time, Powell went to the office daily and maintained a full schedule preparing for the coming term. As Powell pointed out in an irate letter to a newspaper publisher who made the same mistake, he had not taken a full week's vacation in his first four years on the Court.

Besides, some respite was sorely needed. The final months of every term became increasingly hard, with the Justices scrambling to finish their opinions and to draft concurrences and dissents to the late-arriving efforts of their colleagues. By the end of June, Powell was always worn out. A few months on a more humane schedule in Richmond restored his strength.

In the spring of 1974, however, this seasonal exhaustion was swept aside by the press of events and the sense of impending doom in the continuing crisis of Watergate. Powell decided to hear the case now. As so often happened, his was the crucial vote. At the Conference, the question moved around the table in the usual order of seniority. When it got to Powell, there were four votes for expedited hearing (Douglas, Brennan, Stewart, and Marshall, all of whom loathed Nixon) and three votes against (Burger, White, and Blackmun). (Because of his service in the Justice Department, Rehnquist did not participate.) Four Justices could grant review in the ordinary course, but expedited review required five. With Powell providing the fifth vote, on May 31, 1974, the Supreme Court agreed to hear the Nixon tapes case.

OF WARRANTS AND WIRETAPS

By now the nation had lost patience with Watergate. The President's claim of absolute executive privilege had been rejected by Judge Sirica (twice) and by the D.C. Circuit Court of Appeals. Whether Nixon actually believed that the Supreme Court would decide in his favor or whether the appeal was just the final playing out of his combative instinct is anyone's guess, but one thing is clear. The President should have known better than to think that he would be saved by Powell.

The tip-off came in one of Powell's first opinions, a case with the puzzling name of *United States v. United States District Court*. There, as in the Nixon tapes case, the courts faced a direct challenge to their authority. There, as in the Nixon tapes case, the executive claimed to be above judicial scrutiny. And there, too, the Supreme Court stepped in to vindicate the rule of law.

The issue was wiretapping. "Pun" Plamondon, a member of the radical White Panther Party, made the FBI's Most Wanted list after bombing a CIA office in Ann Arbor, Michigan in 1968. When the police finally caught up with him, they found sixty-five pounds of dynamite and maps showing military installations in northern Michigan. At his trial, the prosecution tried to introduce tapes of incriminating telephone conversations involving Plamondon and his allies, the Black Panthers. Plamondon moved to exclude these tapes from evidence on the ground that the wiretaps had not been approved in advance by a judge. The government countered that the warrantless surveillance was "necessary to protect the nation from attempts of domestic organizations to attack and subvert the existing structure of the Government."

Had there been no claim of national security, the illegality of the government's act would have been patent. The Fourth Amendment to the Constitution protects personal privacy, not only in homes, but also in telephone conversations. In both situations, the law requires a warrant. A warrant can be issued only by a judge or magistrate, not by a prosecutor or by any member of the executive branch, no matter how highly placed. The approval of a judicial officer provides independent assurance that the intrusion is not unreasonable, that it is not done for an improper purpose, and that there is probable cause to believe the suspect guilty of a crime. It well may have been that the government agents could have gotten a warrant for the Plamondon wiretaps, but they did not ask. Instead, they relied on the approval of John Mitchell, Attorney General under Richard Nixon, who claimed the unilateral authority to order wiretaps in national security cases. At issue, in the words of the Supreme Court, was the claim of "the President's power, acting through the Attorney General, to authorize electronic surveillance in internal security matters without prior judicial approval."

As it happened, Powell was intimately involved in the history of this question. In 1967 he fought to preserve the crime commission's recommendation of legislation to permit wiretaps. After long and bitter debate, Congress passed a law to that effect. It allowed wiretaps in ordinary criminal cases under stringent conditions, including the requirement of a prior court order. The statute, however, did not purport to restrict or regulate the President's power to obtain foreign intelligence information or to take such additional measures "as he deems necessary to protect the United States against the overthrow of the Government by force or other unlawful means, or against any other clear and present danger to the structure or existence of the Government." Congress did not say what the President's powers were or even whether he had any. It simply left national security cases out of the statute.

Then the American Bar Association took a crack at the issue. In 1968 it proposed Standards Relating to Electronic Surveillance as part of the criminal justice project begun while Powell was president. As approved in early 1971, the ABA standards approved warrantless wiretaps to protect against acts of a foreign power but not to combat domestic subversion. Thus, the ABA supported the President's claim of unilateral authority to order wiretaps in national security cases but *only* against foreign agents. Electronic surveillance in domestic security matters—such as Plamondon's CIA bombing—would require a court order.

Powell sat on the ABA committee that approved this requirement, but by 1971 he had apparently changed his mind. On August 1 of that year, the Sunday *Times-Dispatch* published Powell's views in "Civil Liberties Repression: Fact or Fiction?—'Law-Abiding Citizens Have Nothing to Fear.'" The article savagely rebuked opposition to wiretapping. "There seems almost to be a conspiracy to confuse the public," Powell wrote. "The impression studiously cultivated is of massive eavesdropping and snooping by the FBI and law enforcement agencies." In fact, said Powell, wiretapping was used only in two situations: criminal investigations and national security cases. Wiretapping against crime was limited by procedures designed to safeguard the rights of suspects, including the requirement of prior judicial approval. Wiretapping in national security cases involving foreign agents, by contrast, was done without court order under the "inherent power of the President."

The fighting issue was warrantless wiretaps for domestic security. Powell admitted that "some courts" had distinguished internal security from foreign threats but did not mention that the ABA committee on which he sat had drawn precisely that distinction. He now took a different view. "There may have been a time when a valid distinction existed between external and internal threats. But such a distinction is now largely meaningless. The radical left, strongly led and with a growing base of support, is plotting violence and revolution. Its leaders visit and collaborate with foreign Communist enemies. Freedom can be lost as irrevocably from revolution as from foreign attack."

"[T]he outcry over wiretapping," Powell concluded, "is a tempest in a teapot. There are 210 million Americans. There are only a few hundred wiretaps annually, and these are directed against people who prey on their fellow citizens or who seek to subvert our democratic form of government. Law-abiding citizens have nothing to fear."

Three months later, Powell found himself defending these remarks before the Senate Judiciary Committee. Liberal Senators did not think wiretapping a "tempest in a teapot" and were alarmed by the prospect of warrantless surveillance in domestic security cases. As Senator Birch Bayh remarked—just as a "hypothetical"—"it is possible to envision the chief law enforcement officials in this country . . . being motivated by politics so that criticism per se in essence becomes subversiveness." Where, exactly, did Powell stand?

Despite repeated efforts, Bayh could not pin Powell down. When read the views of the ABA and asked to comment, Powell replied blandly that they "accord with my recollection." When asked to spell out when he thought wiretapping should be legal, Powell said, "Senator, I hesitate, really, to try to get into factual situations." When asked why not require a warrant, Powell dodged by saying that Congress could so legislate if it wished. When Bayh pressed for specifics, Powell declined. To answer "would be speculating to a large extent because I have not studied how this problem might be dealt with." Again and again, Powell sidestepped. He had not studied the matter, did not know enough to express a firm view, and could not be enticed into saying much of anything. He sympathized with Bayh's questions—"I can only say that I share, believe me, I share deeply the concerns that you have expressed and that I know are in your mind"— but he would promise only to "consider the entire case in light of the Bill of Rights and the restrictions in the Constitution of the United States for the benefit of the people of our country."

Having gone nowhere at great length, Bayh played his trump card. He quoted the *Times-Dispatch* article and pounced on the contradiction between its scathing attack on critics of wiretapping and Powell's fence-sitting before the committee. "Aren't you rather specific in an area where you said you had not made up your mind already?" Bayh asked.

Powell began his answer with an entirely advertent digression that enabled him to seize the high ground: "I have four children," he began. "I spend a good deal of time with the young, and one of the things that distresses me most is the widely prevailing view among the young that America is a repressive society." Repression occurred, Powell admitted, but "on balance I have the deep conviction that America is the freest of all lands. I have a deep conviction that the Bill of Rights is revered not only by the citizens but by the courts and the legislative and executive bodies of our country." It was fine for the young people to "fight to eliminate whatever examples of repression or unfairness or injustice exist and there are plenty of them, but to turn against the structure of our whole free society seems to me a disaster."

This, Powell insisted, was the real point of the article, not the incidental remarks about wiretapping. Having recast his message in lofty generalities, Powell gently edged away from the embarrassingly specific language quoted by Bayh. It was, he said, addressed primarily to a "hazy area," where "internal dissidents are cooperating or working affirmatively with, or are very sympathetic to countries, other powers, that may be enemies of the United States. This is a very difficult area. Drawing that line, as I have said, is very perplexing."

With that, Bayh had to be content. Powell could not be induced to join issue. He would neither repeat nor retract his statement in the *Times-Dispatch*. He said only that it was not a "fixed view" and that he would "consider all law and facts that seemed to me to be relevant." Eventually, Bayh let the matter drop. Powell had promised nothing, retracted nothing, and lost nothing, but his published views strongly supported warrantless wiretapping in domestic security cases.

HOW SURPRISING, then, that when that issue came to the Supreme Court Conference on February 25, 1972, Justice Powell voted against warrantless wiretaps in domestic security cases. And so did everyone else (Rehnquist not participating). Though the Justices were unanimous as to the result, they were deeply divided on the rationale. Powell and four others thought the warrantless wiretaps unconstitutional and were ready to say so. Burger, White, and Blackmun wished to duck that issue. White argued that Mitchell's affidavit was not sufficiently detailed to bring the case within the statutory exception for national security cases and that the wiretaps should be disapproved on this essentially technical ground. Of course, the inadequacy of the affidavit could be cured in future affidavits, so the result of White's position was that the Administration would lose this particular case but could still claim that it had the right to act without a warrant in future cases. Powell rejected that result. He wanted to say once and for all that warrantless wiretaps in domestic security cases were flatly unconstitutional. Douglas, Brennan, Stewart, and Marshall agreed.

Since the Justices were unanimous as to outcome, Burger had the power of assignment, but he unwisely chose White, whose views plainly would not command a majority of the Court. Douglas intervened with a letter to the Chief: "I think the assignment to Byron (much as I love my friend) is not an appropriate one. . . . With all respect, I think Powell represents the consensus. I have not canvassed everybody, but I am sure that Byron, who goes on the statute, will not get a court." Burger refused to withdraw the assignment to White but said he saw no reason why Powell should not write also. Douglas seized the opening and made his own assignment to Powell: "I am writing you this note hoping you will put on paper the ideas you expressed in Conference and I am sure you will get a majority. I gather from the Chief's memo that he is not at all adverse to that being done."

Powell was not about to get caught in the middle. On March 9 he sent a draft of his views to both Burger and Douglas. "Byron (to whom I am sending a copy of the memorandum) is clearly better qualified than I am to write, and I assume that he will do so. But I will undertake to enlarge this memorandum into a draft if this seems desirable."

It seemed very desirable indeed to Douglas and the liberals to have this conservative Nixon appointee lead the charge against warrantless wiretaps, so Douglas told Powell to set to work. The opinion went through the usual drafts and redrafts, but the changes were minor and few. The most important was the deletion of a long footnote quoting the ABA's approval of warrantless wiretaps against foreign agents. Brennan thought the draft "squint[ed] toward" approving warrantless wiretaps in such cases, and accordingly the footnote was reduced to a summary reference that could not possibly be perceived as taking a position either way. By the end of May, Powell had five votes and later gained Justice Blackmun. White published his views separately, and Chief Justice Burger concurred in the result without opinion.

Justice Powell's opinion as announced on June 19, 1972, was a far cry from his tirade of the preceding August. In the *Times-Dispatch*, he had barely been able to acknowledge that there could be legitimate concern over warrantless wiretaps in domestic security cases. He admitted only that there was, "at least in theory," a potential for abuse. Less than a year later, this merely theoretical potential for abuse had become concrete and vivid. "History abundantly documents," Powell wrote, "the tendency of Government—however benevolent and benign its motives—to view with suspicion those who most fervently dispute its policies." Far from justifying warrantless wiretaps, the fact that the government's concern was domestic security actually increased the need for a court order. As Powell put it, "Fourth Amendment protections become the more necessary when the targets of official surveillance may be those suspected of unorthodoxy in their political beliefs. . . . The price of lawful public dissent must not be a dread of subjection to an unchecked surveillance power."

The authoritarian apologist for executive power had turned into a civil libertarian. In sharp contrast to his earlier view, Powell's opinion for the Supreme Court reflected a newfound appreciation of political dissent. The change in perspective owed much to self-education. In preparing for the case, Powell went back and read the Court's prior cases on the warrant requirement. Having immersed himself in the language and reasoning of Fourth Amendment precedents, he saw more clearly than before the value of a warrant in controlling executive abuse.

Equally important was the change in Powell's role. In the Richmond *Times-Dispatch*, he spoke as a private citizen, for whom the freewheeling expression of political views was entirely appropriate (though in his case not exactly customary). In the U.S. Reports, he spoke as an Associate Justice of the Supreme Court, with the sworn duty to defend the Constitution. As a private citizen, Powell indulged his distaste for the targets of wiretapping. People "who prey on their fellow citizens or who seek to subvert our democratic form of government" did not excite his sympathy. "Law-abiding citizens" had nothing to fear. Now Powell had a sworn duty to protect the rights of *all* citizens, including the extremists and dissenters he did not like. His new responsibility caused him to rethink the issue.

That, after all, is the model of what a judge should do—lay aside preconceptions and open the mind to argument so that the judgment can be as informed, as dispassionate, and as wise as humanly possible. That judges may fail in this calling, that they may tire of the effort or lack the courage to confront their own prejudices, does not mean that the exercise is empty.

Thus did Justice Lewis Powell contradict lawyer Lewis Powell on the scope of executive power. It is true, of course, that Powell changed the Supreme Court—every Justice does—but it is equally true that the Supreme Court changed Powell. *United States v. United States*

District Court was a marker of his growth—and a clear warning to the President in *United States v. Nixon.*

EXECUTIVE PRIVILEGE IN THE SUPREME COURT

The Nixon tapes case was heard on Monday, July 8. Jaworski and his assistant, Philip Lacovara, spoke for the prosecution, while Boston lawyer James St. Clair represented the President. The Court allowed the extraordinary time of three hours, but the argument was surprisingly flat. Jaworski and Lacovara had an easy time of it; all they had to do was to avoid mistakes. St. Clair had much the harder task and did not rise to the occasion. If anything, he dug himself a deeper hole by baldly insisting that the President had an absolute privilege to withhold evidence from a court of law, even in cases of criminal wrongdoing. This went too far for Powell:

"Mr. St. Clair," he asked, "let us assume that it had been established that the conversations we're talking about here today did involve a criminal conspiracy, would you still be asserting an absolute privilege?"

"Yes, quite clearly," answered St. Clair.

But, Powell followed, "[w]hat public interest is there in preserving secrecy with respect to a criminal conspiracy?"

"The answer, sir, is that a criminal conspiracy is criminal only after it's proven to be criminal."

In other words, the President claimed an absolute right to withhold evidence of criminal wrongdoing, and if that made the crime impossible to prove, so be it.

Under the best of circumstances, this claim would have been a hard sell. In the death throes of Watergate, it was a sure loser. By this time, it was plain for all who cared to see that the protection of criminal wrongdoing was not an incidental by-product of the President's claim of executive privilege but was in fact its purpose and object. The misuse of constitutional authority for criminal purposes was something the Justices could not condone.

On July 24 the Supreme Court announced its decision. The President would have to produce the tapes. Nixon agreed and on August 5 released the transcripts, which in fact contained the "smoking gun" that his critics had so long sought. In a conversation in the Oval Office on June 23, 1972, less than a week after the arrest of the burglars, Nixon approved a plan to thwart the FBI investigation and to involve the CIA in the cover-up. The tape flatly contradicted the President's solemnly made and oft-repeated statement that he had known nothing of the official involvement in the break-in until ten months after the fact. It also proved an obstruction of justice.

The reaction was devastating. The *Washington Star-News*, which had been among the President's staunchest supporters, now brutally answered Nixon's plea that the evidence of Watergate be viewed in its entirety and in perspective. "For anyone who has done so conscientiously," the paper replied, "the picture that emerges is disgusting. The cumulative record for criminal effrontery, negligence, mendacity, pettiness, and stupidity is perhaps without equal in the record of history. Yesterday's final affront to the national sense of decency is simply too much to bear."

Amid the rising clamor for resignation and under imminent threat of impeachment, Richard Nixon resigned the presidency, effective August 9, 1974. Sworn in that day as thirty-eighth President of the United States, Gerald Ford announced that "our long national nightmare is over."

POWELL'S ROLE in these events is traced in three remarkable documents. The first and most revealing is a confidential memorandum dictated six months *before* the Nixon tapes case reached the Supreme Court.

On September 2, 1973, Lewis and Josephine left for two weeks with Harvie and Letitia Wilkinson at their vacation cottage in Portugal. That night Powell had prostate trouble and the next day consulted a non-English-speaking doctor who mistakenly prescribed medication for hemorrhoids. After a second night of agony, Powell resolved to return home. He flew back to Lisbon, spent a miserable night in a nearby hotel, and the next day made his way back to Richmond, where he received appropriate medication.

While recuperating on Rothesay Circle, Powell decided to get a head start on the (first) tapes case, which was then pending in the Court of Appeals. At that time, Powell had before him the various papers filed in the trial court and Sirica's opinion requiring that the tapes be surrendered for judicial inspection. Powell studied those documents and recorded his reactions in a September 13 memorandum marked "LFP's Personal Notes No. 1 (Not Subject to Subpoena)."

The opening comments revealed his disgust at the whole affair:

> Few problems of great national consequence have been handled quite so badly by all concerned as what is called "Watergate." The criminal acts themselves, though felonies, would have been routine crimes of no public consequence but for the incredible involvement

(conceded by some, and still denied by others) of high officials in the White House and the Administration. The cover-up, of course, was more shocking than the initial crimes, especially as it appears to involve a number of these officials. . . .

Despite pious protestations to the contrary, the real thrust of much of the political and media attack has been against the President himself. There have been arguable and legitimate grounds for criticizing much of what he has done or failed to do, and this type of criticism is a wholesome feature of our system. But many who hope to destroy if not impeach the President (as they destroyed Johnson) have long since convicted him of personal responsibility for all of the crimes committed. They now want the tapes to confirm the "hanging."

Despite sympathy for the President, Powell was by no means ready to accept the claim of an absolute and unreviewable right to withhold information from a grand jury. "I instinctively recoil from most absolutist positions, and [this one is] no exception." Sirica had found an intermediate position by recognizing executive privilege but insisting that claims of privilege be reviewed in court. Final say on whether presidential confidentiality should give way to the grand jury's need for evidence would rest with a judge. On first reading Sirica's opinion, Powell found that "the brilliance of his analysis was not self-evident" but on further reflection gave Sirica "a considerably higher mark as to his conclusions (possibly a straight B rather than a C-)." What changed Powell's mind was his own inability to think of any better way to handle "what, in truth, is an intractable dilemma."

On the one hand, Powell reasoned, there was "the possibility that any President"—he fastidiously avoided focusing on Nixon—"could be involved personally in criminal conduct or the deliberate concealment of such conduct by his aides and associates." In such a case, it would be "unthinkable" to "allow the President himself to be the sole judge of what, if anything, to disclose to an investigating grand jury." On the other hand, the President must not be left to the mercy of every rogue prosecutor or congressional committee with the subpoena power. No President "could function effectively if he, and everyone with whom he talked or communicated, were always under the threat that some district judge would be reviewing their most private conversations with that sanctimonious wisdom we all have when we 'second guess' decisions for which others are responsible."

Powell concluded that confidential communications with the President deserved a "unique degree of consideration and protection." Specifically, the President should have to supply evidence to a grand jury but not to a congressional committee, where institutional rivalry and partisan politics would invite excess. Moreover, the grand jury's investigation must relate specifically to "definable criminal conduct by presidential aides or advisers," and there must be a "demonstrated and particularized need" for the grand jury to have the information. Finally, a claim of presidential privilege should be upheld whenever there was "a particularized showing that the President acted in the interest of national security, protection of military secrets, the further-ance of counter espionage activities against foreign powers or their agents, or safeguarding delicate diplomatic negotiations."

In short, Powell wanted simultaneously to protect the power of the presidency *and* to prevent the President from abusing that power. Whether both were possible, he was ultimately unsure. "Despite any-thing said above," Powell concluded, "I remain essentially open mind-ed and indeed deeply troubled, as I see no clear, satisfactory resolution of this unfortunate confrontation. . . ."

AS IT HAPPENED, Powell did not need to resolve his troubled mind, at least not then, as the Saturday Night Massacre and Nixon's subse-quent capitulation derailed the litigation before it reached the Supreme Court. Seven months later, the case returned, and Powell's early view gelled into firm conviction.

When the Justices met at Conference on July 9, the day after oral argument, everyone was ready. Douglas and Powell had already circu-lated memos, and others had expressed themselves in conversation. Though the outcome seemed clear, the Justices nevertheless settled in for a long meeting.

The Chief Justice led the discussion through a carefully planned agenda of preliminary matters to the question of whether the subpoe-na had been properly issued and finally to the President's claim of executive privilege. At each stage, the Justices spoke in the usual order of seniority, which, with Rehnquist out, put Powell last. He occupied his time by taking notes, filling twelve sides of paper with a detailed account of the votes and comments on every issue. The best record of Powell's own views is a previously prepared memo he used as the basis for his remarks at Conference.

The result was easy. The Justices unanimously agreed to enforce the subpoena against the President. There was not one vote in his favor. There were, however, two important issues on which the Justices did not agree, and in both, Powell played a crucial role.

Powell's overriding concern as he came to Conference was not merely that the President lose—that was already certain—but that he not drag the presidency down with him. More than anything, Powell wanted to make sure that the Nixon tapes case did not become a blueprint for the harassment of future Presidents. The first point in his pre-Conference memo was titled *Not Just Nixon*: "We decide and write not just as to Nixon and Watergate, but for the long term. The principles involved relate to the basic structure of our government."

For Powell, the "basic structure of our government" meant a strong executive. He mistrusted Congress's willingness to assume real responsibility and doubted its ability to resist short-term political considerations in favor of the long-range national interest, especially in foreign policy. Leadership, he believed, must come from the White House. Powell was determined, therefore, that the Supreme Court's decision not undercut the legitimate powers of the presidency.

This concern surfaced at two different points in the July 9 Conference. It came up first on the question whether the subpoena to the President had been validly issued. Material sought by subpoena in a criminal investigation generally must be *relevant* to that investigation. Powell wanted to require more. He proposed that a subpoena to the President meet a standard of *necessity*. Though satisfied here, the higher standard would be an important protection in future cases. It would mean that subpoenas would not be issued to the President every time someone merely suspected that confidential conversations might be relevant to possible wrongdoing. In this argument, Powell faced the implacable opposition of Byron White, who insisted that a subpoena should issue to the President on the same terms as to anyone else.

The second issue was executive privilege. Once a subpoena was lawfully issued to the President, could he refuse to comply? Did the President have a privilege not to obey the subpoena if (in his judgment) doing so would impair the effective functioning of his office? Powell insisted that he did have such a privilege but that it was not absolute. It could be overridden, as in this case, by the demonstrated need for evidence of criminal wrongdoing.

On this crucial point—that the constitutional powers of the President included a qualified privilege for confidential communications—Powell was adamant, but here too he faced opposition. Douglas said that when evidence was sought for a criminal trial, there was simply "no such thing" as executive privilege, "even as to state secrets." The President could be forced to reveal confidential communications whenever they were relevant to a criminal prosecution. Marshall agreed, and so, apparently, did White and Blackmun.

Confusingly, these two issues overlapped. In fact, Powell had come to Conference with two ways to skin the same cat. Although he insisted *both* that a special showing should be required to issue a subpoena to the President *and* that the President should have a (qualified) privilege for confidential communications, these contentions were partly alternative. If a special showing were required to subpoena the President, he would have less need for a privilege to protect confidential communications. Conversely, if the President could assert such a privilege to resist enforcement, it mattered less whether a subpoena could issue in the first place. In short, it was crucial that the President be protected at one or the other stage of the process, but perhaps not so important that he be protected at both.

The Justices left the Conference of July 9 with these issues unresolved. The compromise that evolved in the following weeks gave each side the point on which it insisted most. On the standard for issuing a subpoena to the President, White prevailed. The final opinion required no special showing but declared the President subject to subpoena on the same terms as everyone else. The only concession to Powell was the qualifier, suggested by Brennan, that a court should be "particularly meticulous" in directing a subpoena to the President.

On the issue of executive privilege, Powell won. The Court's opinion recognized a "presumptive privilege," rooted in the Constitution, to protect the privacy of communications to the President. When no state secrets were involved and the only thing at stake was the President's "generalized interest in confidentiality," his privilege had to give way to the "demonstrated, specific need for evidence in a pending criminal trial." That took care of Richard Nixon. But the Court also recognized the existence of executive privilege as a protection for future Presidents in the exercise of their powers under the Constitution. On this crucial point, Powell prevailed.

THE THIRD DOCUMENT that traces Powell's role in the Nixon tapes case is an unpublished concurring opinion. It began as a partial draft for an opinion of the Court but ended up in Powell's files as a separate statement.

Two days before oral argument, Powell circulated a draft opinion on the question of executive privilege. Ordinarily, this would have been presumptuous. No vote had been taken, no assignment had been made, and no one had told Powell to write anything. In the context of a special summer session, however, it made sense to volunteer. Unlike the regular term, when each Justice worked on his own opinions, the entire Court was now focused on the same case.* Obviously, it made no sense to sit around and wait for oral argument, so the Justices informally divided the issues among themselves and began work. Douglas, Brennan, Stewart, White, and Powell all circulated memos designed to serve as blueprints for portions of the Court's opinion.

Powell went for the main chance. He circulated an early memorandum on the core constitutional question of executive power. His file copy contains the later notation: "At one point Justices Brennan and Stewart were willing to accept the attached memo as [the] basis for an opinion, but as the decisional process evolved it was clear that the C.J. (properly, I think) wanted to write the Court's opinion."

Whether properly or not, Burger did want to write the Court's opinion and was far from eager to surrender pride of authorship to another. Bits and pieces of Powell's draft, as revised by Stewart, eventually found their way into Burger's writing, but the results were not pleasing. In this case, too many cooks muddied the reasoning and garbled the expression. The tautness and clarity of Powell's analysis were lost. Powell therefore recast his memo as a concurrence that he planned to publish if anyone else wrote separately. As it happened, no one did, and Powell's concurrence remained locked in his files.

Powell's memo began with a statement of his abiding ideal: "We are a nation governed by the rule of law." Nowhere, he continued, "is our commitment to this principle more profound than in the enforcement of the criminal law, 'the twofold aim of which is that guilt shall not escape or innocence suffer.'" In the search for truth, the law was entitled to "every man's evidence," but even this rule was not absolute. "It admits of exceptions designed to protect weighty and legitimate competing interests."

The competing interest here was the President's claim of executive privilege. Powell then summarized, better and more briefly than did the President's brief, the basis for his claim:

> All nations find it necessary to shield from public scrutiny some of the deliberations that constitute the process of government. Those selected to conduct the affairs of state must be free to speak plainly to one another and to seek honest and forthright advice on matters of national policy. Yet human experience teaches that those who expect public dissemination of their remarks may temper candor with a con-

---

* Actually, there were two. When the Court decided to remain in session for the Nixon tapes case, it also put over *Milliken v. Bradley,* a case in which the Chief Justice had some difficulty in producing an acceptable opinion.

cern for appearances. The willingness to advance tentative ideas, to play the devil's advocate, and to reveal the ultimate basis for a particular view may succumb to public posturing and a reticence born of the fear of appearing foolish. That consequence would distort and impair the search for sound public policy. Accordingly, a general expectation of confidentiality for deliberations among the officers of government and their advisors serves the public good.

That did not mean that confidentiality should always prevail. Competing concerns were sometimes more important. The real issue was who had the final authority to decide when this was so. The President claimed that he, and he alone, should decide when confidentiality should be breached. The special prosecutor said that the final decision lay with the courts. Powell's answer—in language that was later criticized—was that "the ultimate authority" should reside in "that branch whose constitutional responsibilities are more gravely affected." In the investigation of criminal wrongdoing, that branch was the courts.

As Powell saw it, the defect in the President's argument was that it focused solely on the interests of the executive branch. It took no account of the deep inroads that an unreviewable executive privilege would make on the duties of the judiciary. When both sides of the issue were considered, it was clear that the courts had more at stake.

On the one hand, the President asserted only a generalized concern for confidentiality, not the preservation of state secrets. The argument for absolute privilege therefore rested on the claim that even "rare and isolated instances of disclosure would negate the general expectation of confidentiality and thus defeat the ability of the President to obtain candid advice." But this, Powell thought, was not true. "The willingness to speak plainly is not so fragile that it would be undermined by some remote prospect of disclosure in narrowly defined and isolated circumstances." Here evidence was sought for a criminal prosecution. "It requires no clairvoyance to foresee that such demands will arise with the greatest infrequency nor any special insight to recognize that few advisors will be moved to temper the candor of their remarks by such an unlikely possibility." Enforcing the subpoena would not, therefore, "significantly" impair the President's interest.

This reasoning fenced the President in. If, as everyone professed to believe, it was rare and unforeseeable that presidential conversations would contain evidence of criminal wrongdoing, disclosure of those conversations would be equally rare and unforeseeable. Enforcing the subpoena would not "significantly" inhibit presidential candor. But if the President or his advisers were routinely engaged in criminal activity, that was all the more reason to ensure that claims of executive privilege could be reviewed by the courts.

The judiciary, on the other hand, had much more at stake. "While the President's interest in confidentiality is general in nature, the courts' need for production of material evidence in a criminal proceeding is not. The enforcement of the criminal laws does not depend on an assessment of the broad sweep of events but on a limited number of specific historical facts concerning the conduct of identified individuals at given times. The President's broad interest in confidentiality would not be vitiated by disclosure of a limited number of confidential conversations, but nondisclosure of those same conversations could gravely impair the pursuit of truth in a criminal prosecution."

The balance, therefore, swung in favor of the judiciary. When evidence was sought for a criminal prosecution, executive privilege was not absolute. Nixon would have to give up the tapes. Powell's analysis was unambiguous on that score, but nothing he said dealt with the problem of state secrets or with the enforcement of Congressional subpoenas. Nothing he said suggested that future claims of executive privilege would be resolved the same way. Perhaps these questions would not soon arise. Perhaps they could be settled by cooperation. In any event, Powell refused to burden future Presidents with the legacy of Watergate. He tried to curtail the President's abuse of power without abusing the powers of the President.

THE STORY ACCORDING TO *THE BRETHREN*

Powell's opinion was not published. The evolution of the opinion that was published, under the name of Chief Justice Burger, is one of the strangest episodes in the history of the Supreme Court. For many years, the story was known only to a few insiders. Then in 1979 the history of the Nixon tapes case and many other stories of the inner workings of the Burger Court were revealed in Bob Woodward and Scott Armstrong's best-selling exposé, *The Brethren*.

The idea began in the final days of *The Final Days*, Woodward and Carl Bernstein's chronicle of the collapse of the Nixon administration. Armstrong, who had worked for the Senate Watergate Committee and then assisted on *The Final Days*, joined Woodward in a new investigative effort aimed at the Burger Court. Their first and crucially important source was Potter Stewart. Woodward had seen Stewart around town and had been "pestering him" for an interview. At a dinner party,

Stewart agreed to see Woodward and spent two evenings in off-the-record conversation about the Supreme Court. As Woodward later recalled, Stewart "kind of outlined the book."

Exploiting Stewart's leads proved surprisingly easy. Woodward, who was the senior of the two and enjoyed the greater reputation, asked to see the other Justices, and four agreed. Woodward revealed Stewart's role after his death and confirmed that he did not interview Chief Justice Burger but has otherwise refused to identify his sources.

One of them was Powell. Powell said afterward that Woodward was "rather charming and very deceptive." According to Powell, Woodward "stated, when requesting the interview and repeated when he arrived, that he was not doing investigative reporting. Rather, he planned a serious book on how power is exercised at the highest levels in the three branches of government." Once the conversation was underway, Powell was surprised to find that Woodward already knew a great deal (presumably from Stewart) about the relations among the Justices and was probing for more. Powell retreated into his customary reserve but did not cut short the conversation. More important, he did not put Woodward and Armstrong off-limits to his clerks but continued to rely on them to recognize the line between general background information about the working of the Court and inappropriate gossip.

This mistake was repeated throughout the building. As Armstrong later explained, "You start with the senior people, and they have trouble remembering enough detail. They then refer you to lower-downs to document their story. Once given permission to speak, the lower-downs will proceed to be totally indiscreet." And so they were. A few clerks—not from Powell's chambers—went all the way, giving Woodward and Armstrong copies of documents that they had not been authorized to reveal. In one case, Armstrong sat up drinking with a former clerk until 4:00 A.M., then left with enough Supreme Court documents to twice fill a shopping cart. In another, Armstrong flew out of town for an interview and had to buy an extra suitcase to transport his booty back to Washington.

The most revealing documents that Woodward and Armstrong saw were the Brennan case histories. These remarkable narratives were compiled by Brennan and his clerks to record the inside political history of the Justices' deliberations. Except for the preoccupation with Brennan and the limits of his perspective, they provide exactly the kind of information that an investigative reporter would most wish to have. Detailed, dramatic, and personal, they focus less on the legal issues than on the behind-the-scenes disputes and exchanges, often featuring Brennan as the Court's master politician.

Although the contents, if not the existence, of these histories have always been secret, they were at one time accessible to a small circle. Today they are securely locked in Brennan's desk, with no one allowed to use them but Brennan's official biographer, Stephen Wermeil. They are expected eventually to go to the Library of Congress, but under conditions that will restrict access for many years.

It is not known how many of the Brennan histories Woodward and Armstrong saw or exactly how they got them, but they did see Brennan's elaborate history of the Nixon tapes case and probably some draft circulations. Once they got this far, the rest was easy. The young clerks who talked to Woodward and Armstrong (only five or six refused altogether) were no match for their interlocutors. As most were fiercely loyal to their Justices, their loyalty could be used against them. They could be lured into rebutting uncomplimentary accounts or correcting unfavorable impressions and thereby providing more information than they had intended. Besides, the reporters knew so much going into these interviews that confirmation did not seem to matter. As Armstrong later said, "From their point of view, they are not really revealing information, but simply refining what you already know."

The product of these investigations was a runaway best-seller, a national topic of conversation, and the target of vicious attack. Constitutional law scholar Philip B. Kurland called the book "a hyped-up stunt for political voyeurs." Jack Kilpatrick dismissed it as "a key-hole compendium of snide gossip, third-hand hearsay, pop analysis, and clumsily reconstructed conversations." Author and columnist Anthony Lewis weighed in with "doubts not only about the authors' understanding but also about their scrupulousness." Some critics focused chiefly on the law clerks and on the massive breach of confidence that *The Brethren* seemed to represent, but others took aim squarely at the authors. Critics objected to the soap-opera style, to the preoccupation with personality, to the glancing attention paid serious legal issues, and to the pervasive lack of attribution. Woodward and Armstrong insisted that they had double-checked everything, but the anonymity of their sources undermined the perception of reliability.

Privately, Powell's reaction was scathing. He called it "a sorry example of the gutter level of what is called investigative reporting" and protested that the "personal criticism of the Chief Justice attributed to me, most certainly did not come from me." Publicly, Powell did not enter into debate over the details but ventured only a gentle rebuttal of two "myths" that traced to *The Brethren*. In a speech published in *ABA Journal*, he insisted that the picture of constant feuding and fighting among the Justices was simply untrue. "The erroneous perception of discord on the Court perhaps is based on a failure to distinguish between personal and professional disagreement. . . . Law clerks, who are at the Court only for a year and usually have not practiced, may take personally the professional disagreements among us. A clerk's loyalty to his or her justice tends to be high. This sometimes may cause a clerk—disappointed by the outcome of a particular case—to think harshly of justices who have disagreed with his or her 'boss.'"

A second misconception was that the Court was leaderless and unpredictable. "Those who write this nonsense simply do not understand the responsibilities either of the Supreme Court or of the chief justice." The Justices did not strive for a "consistent judicial or ideological philosophy" but tried to do justice in every case on the facts and the law as presented. In his view, the independence of the Justices was not a weakness but a strength, and the Court itself not a "rudderless" institution adrift without leadership but a collection of strong individuals reaching their own individual judgments.

Perhaps privately Powell would have admitted that there were situations where the Court needed a strong hand at the helm. As Woodward and Armstrong revealed, the lack of leadership was nowhere more evident than in the Nixon tapes case. Despite all the criticism, *The Brethren*'s extended account of that case was a triumph of investigative reporting. The Nixon tapes case was the highlight of the book, and although it caused acute embarrassment inside the Court and fueled Burger's growing paranoia about the press, it gave the reading public a surprisingly complete and accurate account of the evolution of the Court's opinion.

THE STORY ACCORDING TO *The Brethren* began at the Conference on July 9, when Brennan tried to wrest the case from the Chief Justice by proposing that the Court issue a joint opinion signed by all eight Justices. (This had been done once before, when Arkansas Governor Orval Faubus affronted the Supreme Court with the claim that his state was not bound by *Brown v. Board of Education*. The Court answered that it, not the Governor of Arkansas, was the final authority on the Constitution and lent weight to the rebuke by issuing an opinion signed by all nine Justices.) Brennan had talked up this idea beforehand, but when he raised it at Conference, no one spoke up in support of his suggestion. After an embarrassed silence, the Chief assigned the opinion to himself.

Burger then undertook not only to put his name on the opinion for the Court, which at worst would have been a harmless vanity, but actually to write one. This was a mistake. Douglas, Brennan, Stewart, and Powell had already written memos on various aspects of the case, and White was soon to follow. These memos could easily have been assembled into an opinion acceptable to all. When Burger instead struck out on his own, the results were not well received.

In a conversation on July 11, Stewart and Powell agreed that the Chief's draft was "awful" and came up with a plan. As described by Woodward and Armstrong, the two Justices agreed that "Brennan's suggestion of a joint opinion could be implemented, but they would have to work behind the Chief's back. Each of the other Justices would systematically produce alternative drafts to various of the Chief's sections. They all could then express their preference for the substitute sections. Seeing that he was outnumbered, the Chief would be forced to capitulate."

And that is essentially what happened. Stewart led off with a letter to Burger: "I think, with all respect, that Bill Douglas' draft on appeal-ability is entirely adequate, and would suggest that it be incorporated into the Court opinion." Powell and Brennan chimed in with notes endorsing this suggestion. Then Douglas wrote that he had read Brennan's draft of another portion and "would, with all respect, prefer it over the version which you circulated this morning." White attacked another section of the Chief's draft by offering "the bare bones of an alternative treatment," which Brennan and Stewart endorsed. The final straw came when Burger found out that Blackmun had been enlisted to rework something anyone could get right—the statement of the facts. "Et tu, Harry," the clerks said.

The highlight of these maneuvers was the "conspiracy luncheon" of Saturday, July 13, when Brennan, Stewart, White, and some law clerks went out to lunch and ended up making further plans. (Powell was in Lexington for a meeting of the Board of Trustees of Washington and Lee.) The next Monday, Marshall weighed in with a brutal note saying, without pretense at courtesy, that he preferred each of the four alternative drafts to Burger's original. According to The Brethren, "Marshall's memo went off like a grenade in the Chief's chambers." Later that day, Burger struck back. "My effort to accommodate every-one by sending out 'first drafts' is not working out," he wrote. "I do not contemplate sending out any more material until it is ready."

Meanwhile, work continued in the other chambers. The problem was not merely the quality of Burger's work. Without other decisions to occupy their time, the Justices were itching to get their licks in on the

Nixon case. Burger himself identified that as the source of his trouble. In a private letter to Powell, he commented: "[H]ad we been in the middle of the Term, with each of us absorbed in a host of routine tasks, things might have been easier. But a cluster of Justices for the moment under no pressure save this one case is not the greatest state of affairs."

For his part, Powell was still worried about future Presidents and was anxious to fend off White's effort to rob the presidency of all special consideration, but he knew that Burger's nerves were on edge. Powell's suggestions were advanced with trademark delicacy. "I will deliver to you personally," he wrote Burger on July 19, "a 'marked up' copy of your draft on Executive Privilege. It is presumptuous on my part to have taken such liberties with your draft, especially since you circulated it in 'rough' form and I have not seen the more definitive, polished draft which is to come. Yet, I thought it possibly may be helpful to you to see the sort of editing which I would undertake. . . ." Powell then nudged Burger toward accepting Stewart's alternative draft, although, he added soothingly, "I prefer this as revised and blended into yours." "If you relegate all of this to the waste basket," Powell concluded, "I will of course understand."

From this point, Stewart played the leading role—bridging the gap between White and Powell on whether (and at what stage of the analysis) the President should receive special consideration, writing several paragraphs to supplement the Chief's opinion, and finally crafting a replacement for the key section on executive privilege. The substitute, he said, "borrows generously from the draft of the Chief Justice as well as Lewis Powell's earlier memorandum." With no choice but to accept this revolt, Burger "harmonized" the two versions and came up with what he hoped would be acceptable to all. In fact, the result was entirely adequate—not elegant, certainly, but sound in reasoning, narrow in scope, and clear in result.

The Justices met in Conference on Tuesday, July 23, to thrash out any remaining differences. At first, everyone seemed agreed. Then Douglas, who had been away in Goose Prairie during the later stages, announced that there were too many changes to suit him and that he would file a concurrence. Powell at once jumped ship. All along, he had been more concerned than the others to protect presidential powers but had repeatedly compromised for the sake of unanimity. He had given in to White's view on the standard for issuing a subpoena and accepted Stewart's dilution of the constitutional basis for executive privilege. If Douglas were to write separately, he would also. His concurrence was already set in type and ready to go.

This was the turning point of the Conference. Brennan made a passionate plea for unanimity. When Douglas agreed, Powell followed suit. Neither would publish separately. There would be only one opinion after all.

At this point, Powell suggested that perhaps the announcement should be held up a few days to allow the House Judiciary Committee to vote on impeachment. The final proceedings were scheduled to begin the next day, and Powell feared that the prospect of getting the tape transcripts in a few weeks or months (they would go first to Sirica) would provide an excellent reason for delay. (In fact, the ranking Republican used precisely this argument, but the committee voted him down.)

More than anything else, Powell's proposal for delay revealed his exhaustion. The tapes case came at the end of the regular term, when his strength was already depleted by months of long hours. The strain showed when Powell, contrary to his lifelong habit, said something he had not previously thought out. His off-the-cuff suggestion that the Supreme Court should manipulate its schedule according to its likely political effect was contrary to Court practice, and he was quickly dissuaded.

ALL THIS, AND MUCH MORE, was revealed by Woodward and Armstrong, and their account is largely confirmed by the records. In a few respects, however, the limitations of their method led Woodward and Armstrong astray. Relying as they did on gossip and hearsay, they were sometimes missed the substance. A minor example is their misinterpretation of Powell's unpublished concurrence on the question of executive privilege. Describing Powell's views through Brennan's eyes (presumably as reflected in the Brennan case history), they seize on Powell's statement that "the ultimate authority" for deciding claims of executive privilege should reside in "that branch whose constitutional responsibilities are more gravely affected." According to *The Brethren*, Brennan found that sentence alarming: "Powell's position was more dangerous than the White House's, Brennan believed. In their briefs the President's lawyers said that the President had an 'absolute privilege' and absolute authority to decide. Powell now was suggesting that while the Court had a *right* to consider the claim, it should *not*, but should back off and let the Executive Branch decide, if its responsibilities were 'more gravely affected.'"

This account is accurate so far as it goes, but it does not go nearly far enough. It fails to mention what Powell made unmistakably plain—that criminal prosecution was *not* an area where the executive's responsibilities were "more gravely affected." On the contrary, in that circumstance the judicial branch was "more gravely affected," as Powell had quite clearly said. It may be that Brennan actually did see this argument as more dangerous than the President's, but it would have been a surprising and uncharacteristic misapprehension on his part.

Yet the defect in *The Brethren*'s rendition of the Nixon tapes case ran deeper than small errors of interpretation. Despite their success in penetrating the Court's secrecy and putting together an intensely detailed and largely accurate inside story, Woodward and Armstrong missed something important. By focusing more on personality than on the law, they missed the fact that the real question at the July 9 Conference and thereafter was not whether Nixon would lose but on what terms. The crucial issue was whether Nixon's defeat would prejudice the ability of future Presidents to resist encroachments on their authority. The threat would come not chiefly from the courts but from Congress, where partisan politics, investigative grandstanding, and personal animosity might come into play. The specter that haunted Powell was a Supreme Court decision that would strip the President of constitutional authority to resist congressional harassment.

This the Court did not do. The final version of the Court's opinion nowhere hinted or implied that the President lacked legal authority to resist congressional subpoenas. On the contrary, the Court's recognition of a constitutional basis for the claim of executive privilege—although not as clear and detailed as Powell would have liked—strengthened the hand of future Presidents who have claimed they have no legal obligation to comply with every congressional subpoena.

The result was, as Powell had hoped and worked for, a decision that cast a very small shadow. One commentator described the decision in a law review article entitled, "Mr. Nixon Loses But the Presidency Largely Prevails." Specifically, the President had to cooperate with grand jury investigations when a court so ordered. As to the much more frequent conflicts between the President and Congress, the Court said nothing. It left that issue where it belongs, in the constant and many-faceted political tug of war between the President and Congress—a conflict in which each side has both the means to defend its interests and the need to compromise. This political give-and-take, though untidy and frustrating, is in the long run far more tolerable than a rule that routinely allows Congress to go to court to gain the upper hand in its perpetual battles with executive authority.

Thus, in the Nixon tapes case, it was important not only that the

President's claim of absolute privilege be rejected, but also that the President's claim of privilege not be rejected absolutely. At the Conference on July 9, the Justices came dangerously close to that position. That they ultimately backed away from a decision that would have prejudiced future Presidents in the legitimate exercise of their powers was due in no small measure to Powell.

IN LATER YEARS Powell acquired the habit of the formulaic compliment—ritualistic praise for someone to whom he owed respect. Warren Burger, for example, was always said to have "done more for the administration of justice than any Chief Justice since William Howard Taft." This was perfectly true, and it gave Powell a safe ground for complimenting a man who did not excite unqualified admiration.

For Richard Nixon, Powell's routine remark was not, as one might expect, that for all his faults Nixon was a genius at foreign policy. His standard comment on the fallen President was something much closer to home—that he had spared the nation a "constitutional crisis beyond imagination" by accepting the decision of the Supreme Court and adhering, finally, to the rule of law. One may doubt whether Nixon could have done otherwise, given the prospect of impeachment, but Powell's comment is characteristic, not only in finding something graceful to say but in drawing attention to the real and legitimate pride that every American can feel in a nation whose head of state and commander in chief resigns his office rather than defy a court order. That, in Powell's view, was the real triumph of the Nixon tapes case.

As for Richard Nixon, his initial reaction was bitter. He repeatedly asked Al Haig whether there was any "air" in the Court's decision—meaning was there any room for evasion or debate—and, finding none, asked how could he be deserted by the men he appointed to the bench. But fourteen years later, when Powell retired from the Supreme Court, the former President wrote a gracious longhand letter.

Dear Lewis,

When you were reluctant to accept appointment to the Supreme Court because of your age I observed that ten years of Lewis Powell on the Court was worth twenty years for anyone else.

Your superb service has eloquently demonstrated that I was right. All Americans are in your debt.

Sincerely,
Dick Nixon

CHAPTER XIII

CRIME AND DEATH

"THE COUNTERREVOLUTION THAT WASN'T" *

In the 1964 presidential election, Lyndon Johnson was surprised to find that crime had become a national issue. Four years later, Richard Nixon won the presidency on a campaign whose chief domestic component was "law and order." Resentment focused on the Supreme Court. An avalanche of decisions in the 1960s expanded the rights of criminal defendants and restricted freedom of action by the police. Critics charged the Justices with being soft on crime. In response, Nixon promised "strict constructionists" for the Supreme Court, by which he meant mainly that the new appointments should stop inventing new rights for accused criminals and restore a sense of "balance" to the criminal law. In this, the new President was not disappointed.

With the appointments of Burger and Blackmun and the later addition of Powell and Rehnquist, the conservatives had a decisive majority on most questions of criminals' rights. But to the distress of some and the relief of others, there was no sudden about-face. The conservative majority generally accepted the achievements of the Warren Court—but refined them, constrained them, and reduced their scope. The result was a new synthesis, based partly on the insights and innovations of the Warren Court and partly on the doubts and objections of its critics.

Miranda cases are illustrative. Everyone who watches television knows that, "You have the right to remain silent. Anything you say can be used against you in court. You have the right to talk to a lawyer for advice before we ask you any questions and to have a lawyer with you during questioning. If you cannot afford a lawyer, one will be appointed for you before any questioning. . . ."

---

*   Subtitle of a book by Vincent Blasi on the Burger Court.

These warnings make sure the suspect knows that he does not have to talk to the police and that he can stop the questioning at any time by asking for a lawyer. Before *Miranda*, the police grilled their suspects, and the courts tried to figure out afterward whether a confession was truly "voluntary." But the circumstances of interrogation were so varied and the effects of isolation, intimidation, and ignorance so hard to reconstruct that the task proved almost impossible. The 1966 decision in *Miranda v. Arizona* tried to solve that problem in advance by requiring that suspects be read their rights *before* being questioned.

The remedy for noncompliance was suppression of the evidence. If the police failed to give the warnings, nothing the suspect said—or other evidence discovered as a result of what he said—could be used against him at trial. When evidence is suppressed, prosecution may fail. Then the defendant is set free, not because there is doubt about his guilt but because the police erred in eliciting the confession that proved it. In this way, the guilty profit from police misconduct. In the words of Justice Cardozo, the criminal goes free because the constable blundered.

This result brought howls of protest from law enforcement and from those who thought it looked too much like judicial legislation. Many years later, the drumbeat of criticism was still carried on by President Reagan's Attorney General, Edwin Meese, who campaigned tirelessly to overrule the "infamous" *Miranda* decision. Yet the costs of complying with *Miranda* quickly declined as the police learned to live with the new procedure. By the 1980s prosecutors, judges, and police officers generally agreed that "*Miranda* does not present serious problems for law enforcement."

Perhaps for that reason the Burger Court did not overrule *Miranda*, but it did create exceptions allowing the limited use of incriminating statements made before proper warnings. First, the Justices declared that although the prosecutor could not introduce such statements to prove the defendant's guilt, the prosecutor could use such statements to cross-examine a defendant who voluntarily took the stand and contradicted an earlier confession. To rule otherwise would invite perjury. Another exception applies when giving the warnings would endanger public safety—as in the case where a suspect was asked to locate a loaded revolver he had stashed in a crowded supermarket. The majority found the question justified by the police officer's legitimate concern to find the gun before someone else did.

Though in themselves controversial, such decisions stopped far short of overruling *Miranda*. The result was not a simple backtracking but a new synthesis in which the conservative majority of the Burger Court tried to accommodate both the legacy of the Warren Court and the objections of its critics. This was "the counterrevolution that wasn't."

BUT THAT IS NOT the whole story. In understanding the criminal law decisions that confronted Powell and his colleagues, it is important to see that the question before them was usually not whether a Warren Court precedent would be upheld or overruled, but rather whether it would be extended or curtailed. The issues kept changing. Each innovation in defendants' rights sparked the demand for further innovations along the same lines. Each limitation suggested additional limitations under the same reasoning. The frontiers of legal argument were constantly shifting, as were the underlying realities of police practice that the Court's decisions were meant to control. Thus it was often true that the Burger Court was asked to apply Warren Court precedents to situations radically different from those that gave them birth.

Miranda is again illustrative. The problem at which *Miranda* aimed was described at length in the opinion by Chief Justice Earl Warren. He recounted the facts of an earlier case, where the suspect was kept handcuffed and standing for four hours while being questioned by the police. They refused to let him see anyone and even prevented his lawyer, who had heard of the arrest and come to the station house, from speaking with his client. The *Miranda* warnings were designed to eliminate such tactics by informing the suspect that he had the right to remain silent and by reminding the police that statements elicited after the suspect had asked for a lawyer could not be used in court.

As a reform of police interrogation, *Miranda* was a spectacular success. The Court's decisions sharply curtailed abuse, but they also raised many new questions about the precise boundaries of acceptable conduct. No case better illustrates the changing standards of police interrogation than that of Robert Williams. Williams had recently escaped from a mental institution when, on Christmas Eve 1968, he kidnapped, raped, and suffocated a ten-year-old girl. He was seen removing her body from the YMCA in Des Moines, Iowa, and his abandoned car was found the next day in Davenport, some 160 miles away. On December 26 Williams turned himself in to the Davenport police, who read him his rights and held him for the Des Moines police. It was on the long ride back to Des Moines that the illegal interrogation took place.

Williams's lawyers insisted that there be no questioning in the car, and the police agreed to this restriction (as indeed they had to). But although the detectives did not actually question Williams, they had a great deal to say for his benefit. Addressing the disturbed man as Reverend, one of the detectives made what became known as the Christian burial speech:

> I want to give you something to think about. . . . They are predicting several inches of snow for tonight, and I feel that you yourself are the only person that knows where this little girl's body is, that you yourself have only been there once, and if you get a snow on top of it you yourself may be unable to find it. And, since we will be going right past the area on the way into De Moines, I feel that we could stop and locate the body, that the parents of this little girl should be entitled to a Christian burial for the little girl who was snatched away from them on Christmas Eve and murdered. And I feel we should stop and locate it on the way in rather than waiting until morning and trying to come back out after a snow storm and possibly not being able to find it at all.

Moved by this appeal, Williams led the officers to the body.

By the barest of margins, the Supreme Court ruled that the Christian burial speech was an illegal interrogation and therefore that the jury could not be told that Williams had known the location of the body. To Powell, the result was tragic, but the law was clear. Williams had asserted his constitutional right to have a lawyer present during questioning, and the police had agreed. The Christian burial speech violated that agreement. That Williams responded to it could not be considered a truly voluntary decision to waive his rights, given that he was alone on a long trip with police officers who knew him to be "a young man with quixotic religious convictions and a history of mental disorders." The officers had exploited the isolation of the suspect in a setting "conducive to . . . psychological coercion." The evidence therefore had to be suppressed.

Chief Justice Burger was furious. He lashed out in an opinion so intemperate that his fellow dissenters (White, Blackmun, and Rehnquist) refused to join it. Burger expected this kind of nonsense from bleeding-heart liberals but not from Powell. He gave Powell "unshirted hell" about his vote—and not just in private. He took the unusual step of delivering his opinion orally, glaring down the bench at Powell as he read excerpts from his dissent. "Williams is guilty of the savage murder of a small child; no member of the Court contends he is not. While in custody, and after no fewer than *five* warnings of his rights to silence and to counsel, he led police to the concealed body of his victim. . . . In the face of all this, the Court now holds that because Williams was prompted by the detective's statement—not interrogation but a statement—the jury must not be told how the police found the body." The Court had "regresse[d] to playing a grisly game of 'hide-and-seek.'" The Chief's performance was so obviously personal that Powell's staff tried to pick up his spirits with a note to the bench saying they had "sent out for a bushel of rotten tomatoes."

There was more temperate criticism as well. Columnist George Will charged that Powell and his colleagues were "fastidious to the point of fanaticism. They have distorted, not defended, prior rulings on suspects' rights. They have not served justice."

One may think that Powell was wise or foolish in refusing to let the jury hear how the little girl's body was found, but on any estimate, the police misconduct was relatively minor. Judicial meticulousness about such techniques of interrogation is a luxury. It presupposes the absence, in the main, of the gross excesses of the not-so-distant past. A Court prepared to worry about the subtle coercion of the Christian burial speech is obviously not preoccupied with the kinds of direct physical and psychological intimidation that had previously been so common. Indeed, only a generation before, the interrogation of Robert Williams would have seemed quite restrained. That the conservative Burger Court nevertheless found it improper shows how far the frontier of constitutional law had advanced since *Miranda*.

Largely for that reason, the pattern of the Burger Court in the field of criminal law was far more complex than is generally supposed. In some areas, the cases marked a clear retreat, overruling Warren Court precedents or substantially reducing their scope. In other areas—such as the extension of the right to counsel to misdemeanor cases, the constitutionalization of proof beyond a reasonable doubt, and the long line of cases restricting capital punishment—the Burger Court actually expanded constitutional protections for criminal defendants. Most commonly, the Burger Court refused to extend the precedents of the Warren Court or recast their reasoning in ways that implied limitation.

In the large and important category of cases dealing with illegal police searches, for example, the Burger Court modified but did not abandon the legacy of its predecessor. The Warren Court had ruled that evidence found in an improper search could not be used in court, even though it was clearly reliable evidence that proved the guilt of the accused. As a result, guilty criminals became windfall beneficiaries of police error. Chief Justice Burger railed against this result, but his colleagues would not join him in overturning the rule that illegally found evidence must be excluded from trial. Instead, they kept the rule as an incentive to good police work but made various exceptions designed to minimize its costs.

Many of these decisions were bitterly controversial, but they almost never simply turned back the clock. Instead, there emerged a mosaic of accommodation, highly differentiated and strongly variegated but of a generally conservative hue.

THIS POLICY EXACTLY SUITED Powell. He arrived as a critic of the Warren Court. On President Johnson's Crime Commission, he complained about the Commission's silence in the face of "indiscriminate and unjustified criticism of the police," about the abuse of federal habeas corpus to free persons convicted of state crimes, and especially about the decision in *Miranda*. In his minority report on "the difficult and perplexing problems arising from certain of the constitutional limitations upon our system of criminal justice," *Miranda* came in for particular criticism. The time had come, Powell said, to correct the "present imbalance" between the rights of the accused and "the rights of citizens to be free from criminal molestation of their persons and property." To that end, he suggested a constitutional amendment to overrule *Miranda* and "reestablish" the legitimate use of voluntary confessions in law enforcement.

These words were written in 1967. Yet five years later, when Powell had the opportunity to "amend" the Constitution by interpretation, he proved very cautious. He did not try to uproot *Miranda* or the exclusion of evidence from illegal searches, although he did join efforts to limit their scope. Nor did he encourage Chief Justice Burger's hopes for radical retrenchment. Instead, he moved slowly and carefully to reconsider these questions on the facts of particular cases as they came before him.

In part this caution reflected the political reality of the early Burger Court, which did not then have a clear majority for a sharp turn to the right. In part it reflected the timing of Powell's appointment. The cost to law enforcement of complying with new procedures was greatest at the outset, when novelty bred error and the penalty of excluding evidence was often invoked. Naturally, the police—and not only the police—were outraged to see guilty criminals set free. Over time, however, compliance improved, and the benefits of the new rules were more fully realized. And as the police observed the new requirements more consistently, the occasions for suppressing evidence declined. Thus, it was not inconsistent for Powell to have opposed *Miranda* when it was announced but to have accepted it when he came to the

Court several years later. By that time, much of the price for the reform of police practices had already been paid,* and the benefits derived from the rule were more and more apparent.

More fundamentally, Powell's approach to questions of criminal law reflected his idea of himself as a judge. Powell did not come to the Court with an ideological agenda. He neither had, nor thought it appropriate to have, a commitment to any political program. Nor— and this is more unusual—did he have that implicit faith in the validity of his own first reactions that cuts off second thoughts. Powell's letters, memos, and conversations were filled with disclaimers of certitude. His views were "tentative"; his reactions "preliminary" or "provisional," pending further research. He constantly told his clerks that his judgment awaited theirs, that he wanted to know their minds before making up his own. This was not mere courtesy. The constant caveats reinforced Powell's commitment to an open mind. The habit of waiting for others to speak, of listening to what they had to say, of suspending judgment until he had heard all points of view, had always seemed a private virtue; now it was a public duty. To Powell, his willingness to reconsider, to contradict his own past, to take a position that he himself would previously have disapproved, was not a sign of weakness but of a mature self-confidence.

In criminal cases, Powell's duty to reconsider his earlier views was reinforced by his respect for authority. *Miranda* and all the other liberal innovations that he had criticized were decisions of the United States Supreme Court. Emotionally and intellectually, Powell respected the law as he found it. When the precedents tracked his own views, the effect could be stultifying, but when past decisions contradicted his inclinations, their prestige was a useful counterweight to personal predilections. So it proved with the criminal law. There Powell had to grapple with the legacy of the Warren Court and to work out in his own mind and opinions some accommodation between the liberal precedents and his more conservative approach.

His efforts proved extremely influential. Here, as in so many other areas, Powell was the Supreme Court's center of gravity and its most

---

* This was especially true of *Miranda* itself. In a later decision, the Court said that the requirements of warnings would apply to all defendants *tried* after the date of the decision, even though they had been *questioned* before the new rule was announced. This had the ludicrous effect of punishing the police for a failure of clairvoyance. However silly this may have been—and Powell thought it very silly indeed— virtually all of these cases had worked their way through the system by the time Powell came to the Court. From his point of view, they were spilt milk.

nearly decisive voice. In nearly five hundred decisions involving the criminal law, Powell disagreed with the outcome fewer than one time in ten. Others in the political middle of the Court—especially Stewart and White—also enjoyed high rates of agreement with outcome, but Powell was the Justice most consistently in the majority. Rehnquist, the Court's most rigorous conservative, disagreed with the outcome more than twice as often, while the most stalwart liberals, Brennan and Marshall, dissented in nearly half the cases.

In summary, the overall record of the Burger Court in the field of criminal law was one of cautious retreat and accommodation, not counterrevolution, of mixed results and conservative reinterpretations, not radical retrenchment. In this development, the guiding spirit was Lewis Powell.

"STRUCK BY LIGHTNING"

Ironically, the most wrenching and divisive issue of criminal law that Powell faced had nothing to do with the legacy of the Warren Court. When Earl Warren left the bench in 1969, capital punishment seemed clearly constitutional. It had been practiced since the founding of the nation and had never been seriously questioned by the Supreme Court. Yet within two years, the Justices found themselves embroiled in bitter dispute over when or whether a criminal might be put to death. The outcome was not, as some hoped, an absolute end to capital punishment, but a wholly new body of constitutional law controlling its use, a body of law created not during, but after, the Court's liberal heyday.

The first step was a false start. In 1971, after Burger and Blackmun had been appointed but before they had been joined by Powell and Rehnquist, the Court rejected a constitutional challenge to capital punishment. The case was *McGautha v. California*, and the attack focused on jury discretion. Although carefully instructed by judges on the question of guilt or innocence, juries were given virtually no guidance in the matter of penalty. They were left entirely on their own to determine who should live and who should die—and why. No one really knew what went into these decisions. The utter lack of standards was said to be "fundamentally lawless" and therefore unconstitutional, but the Supreme Court disagreed. "In light of history, experience, and the present limitations of human knowledge," said Justice Harlan, "we find it quite impossible to say that committing to the untrammeled discretion of the jury the power to pronounce life or death in capital cases is offensive to anything in the Constitution." Douglas, Brennan, and Marshall dissented.

Ten days after Powell was sworn in, opponents of capital punishment were back before the Court, arguing (again) that juries had too much discretion in deciding who should live and who should die *and* that execution in any circumstance was a "cruel and unusual" punishment forbidden by the Eighth Amendment. The case involved Ernest Aikens, who had robbed, raped, and killed a pregnant woman in 1962 but escaped execution because he was then only seventeen. Three years later, he robbed, raped, and killed a second woman, and this time was sentenced to die.

The Justices agreed to hear Aikens's case, but it ran aground when the California Supreme Court struck down capital punishment as a violation of the *state* constitution. This ruling ended the death penalty in California, no matter what the United States Supreme Court might have said on the subject, since even if the federal Constitution *permitted* the states to punish by death, California remained free not to do so. Since California had now outlawed the death penalty and Aikens would therefore escape execution in any event, the Supreme Court dismissed his case, and shifted its attention to another, raising the same question, from the state of Georgia. Thus it happened that the lead case for the Court's deliberations in 1972 was *Furman v. Georgia.**

In 1972 the death penalty looked like an idea whose time had gone. The United States was almost alone among western industrialized nations in retaining capital punishment, and even here, support was dwindling. Dr. Gallup reported that those favoring the death penalty for murder declined from 68 percent in 1953, to 51 percent in 1960, to only 42 percent in 1966. Thereafter support rebounded slightly and hovered around 50 percent.

More telling by far was the record of those who actually had the responsibility for capital punishment—the jurors who had to impose

---

*   The decision of the California Supreme Court released more than one hundred persons from death row, including Charles Manson and Sirhan Sirhan, but it did not finally end capital punishment in California. An outraged electorate overruled their highest court by amending the state constitution to restore the death penalty. Nevertheless, the California Supreme Court proved extremely loath to affirm death sentences, so much so that Chief Justice Rose Bird lost her job as a consequence. The main point of attack was Bird's record of voting to reverse the death sentence in every case that came before her. Supporters claimed that she was merely fulfilling the judicial obligation to ensure an error-free trial and sentence. Opponents charged that she had taken the law into her own hands by inventing errors to prevent executions. The voters agreed with the critics and ousted Chief Justice Bird and two liberal colleagues at the next retention election.

death sentences, the judges who had to approve them, and the governors who had to let them be carried out. In a nation of more 200 million, with several thousand homicides a year, only ten persons had been executed since 1965, and none in the five years since 1967. Six hundred convicts waited on death row—beneficiaries of a moratorium on executions pending word from the Supreme Court—but the prospect of so many actually being put to death seemed ludicrous and remote. It looked as if the nation had lost its nerve, as if the system no longer had the confidence to carry out its threats, as if the thought of gas or gallows, though tolerated in the abstract, so oppressed the minds of those involved that they blinked at the vision and shrank from the task.

That so few of the nation's many murderers were actually put to death lent great weight to complaints about jury discretion. For many decades, American juries had enjoyed an unconstrained discretion to pick and choose among convicted murderers. Who could say how they chose or why? In most states, death was authorized for anyone convicted of murder in the first degree. This offense required murder that was "deliberate and premeditated," but these apparently solid terms had lost all meaning. A murder could be "deliberate," even if it was committed in a frenzy, and "premeditated," even if the thought came only an instant before the deed. In the remark of the great Cardozo, the definition of first-degree murder was a "mystifying cloud of words" inviting jurors to do as they pleased.

And what the jurors pleased to do was distinctly unsettling. The preconceptions and prejudices of the society at large inevitably showed up in the jury box, and race was foremost among them. There was a pervasive though not well-documented belief that the selection of persons for execution was racially biased. Certainly that was true for rape. In the years 1930–1965, 452 persons were executed for rape. All executions took place in southern or border states, and nearly 90 percent of those put to death were black. Although these figures fairly screamed racial bias, nothing so dramatic could be shown for the much larger category of persons sentenced to die for murder. Still, the evidence was suggestive. At least in the past and especially in the South, it seemed reasonably clear that the selection of those who should die for their crimes was based partly on race.

But race was not the only factor. Physical appearance also seemed to matter, and most of those sentenced to die were in every respect unappealing. Juries seemed especially likely to condemn those so ugly and frightening that they seemed outside the bounds of human sympathy. And almost always, the losers were poor. As one editorial put it, capital punishment was used "against such abject, unknown, friendless, poor, rejected specimens of the human race that it has not placed much burden on the national conscience."

The intersection of race and disadvantage in the nation's gas chambers and electric chairs became the main point of attack. In the hands of Stanford law professor Anthony Amsterdam, mastermind of a brilliant litigation campaign against capital punishment, the argument came to this: The death penalty was barbaric, indecent, and fundamentally at odds with contemporary morals. If it were regularly enforced across all segments of society, the public would recoil in horror and wipe it off the books. Instead, death was reserved for a selected few—socially unacceptable, personally unattractive, invariably poor, and disproportionately black. "The short of the matter," Amsterdam concluded, "is that when a penalty is so barbaric that it can gain public acceptance only by being rarely, arbitrarily and discriminatorily enforced, it plainly affronts the general standards of decency of the society."

This argument carried the day. When the Justices met at Conference on January 21, 1972, there was—to Powell's amazement—an apparent majority to strike down capital punishment. Douglas, Brennan, and Marshall took that view, as expected. The surprise came from Stewart and White, who now objected to the arbitrariness of executing only a select few. As White put it, when only a "tiny fraction" of those convicted are put to death, "I cannot believe that it is fairly meted out." This made sense—indeed, it was precisely the argument so eloquently made by Amsterdam and others—but it flatly contradicted White's vote only one year earlier in *McGautha v. California*. The same held true for Stewart. The reasons he now gave for finding the death penalty unconstitutional would have been equally valid the year before. The fact was that Stewart and White had simply changed their minds, and neither seemed comfortable about it. If they had trouble coming up with a good explanation, perhaps they would change back.

When the Conference broke up that Friday afternoon, the constitutionality of capital punishment remained in doubt. Five Justices were poised to announce a revolution in the law, but two of the five seemed shaky. No one could say whether the apparent majority would survive the coming months.

ON POWELL'S FIRST DAY at the Court, Marshall joked, "Do you have your capital punishment opinion written yet?" Powell not only had not written an opinion; he actually did not have one. He had never been involved in a capital case and had never really thought about the issue. On the

Crime Commission, Powell rejected the staff's desire to come out against capital punishment, but on grounds that were purely pragmatic and political. "Only a handful of persons were executed in the United States last year," Powell wrote in 1966, "and the number sentenced is decreasing each year. The problem is not one of large dimensions nor of first importance in terms of the administration of criminal justice." Coming out against capital punishment would divert attention from more important issues, make the Commission look soft on crime, and "adversely affect the credibility and weight" of the Commission's proposals.

In truth, Powell was neither enthusiastically for nor categorically against capital punishment. He instinctively recoiled from extreme positions, particularly those nonnegotiable ideological commitments that left no room for compromise or debate. This was especially true of capital punishment. Those who saw the death penalty as an affront to human decency and those who saw it as essential to a just society had nothing to say to each other. The chasm between their beliefs could not be bridged by reason. Powell not only rejected the extremes on either side; he shied away from the debate they dominated. Spared by experience from the necessity of coming to grips with capital punishment and temperamentally disinclined to enter a question so rife with rage and conflict, Powell came to the Court without a fixed view.

Once on the Court and no longer able to avoid the issue, Powell became a fervent partisan of capital punishment—or rather of the constitutionality of capital punishment. His commitment was not to the practice, but to its permissibility. The question as he saw it was not whether the death penalty was a good idea, but whether it was an option lawfully available to the states that wished to use it. The evolution of his views on this question give a clear picture of Powell's early idea of his role as a judge.

POWELL CAME TO THE COURT with a simple faith in the clarity and integrity of constitutional law. Perhaps he was a bit naive. He understood of course that in deciding cases, judges necessarily make law. He knew that law is not a science, that rules laid down in words and phrases cannot cover all situations with mathematical precision, but require for their application a sense of what is wise and right and proper. Powell knew this well enough, but he was still not quite prepared for the wide-open spaces of constitutional law. He thought the Constitution might be construed like a statute—controlled by a close reading of the text, informed by the historical intentions of those who drafted it, with judges resolving only borderline ambiguities. He was not ready for the soaring phrases of the Bill of Rights that suggest so much yet specify so little.

For example, what makes a punishment "cruel and unusual" and therefore unconstitutional? The precedents said punishment was "cruel and unusual" if it offended the "evolving standards of decency that mark the progress of a maturing society." Under this approach, the Constitution was not merely indefinite, but changing. The Justices were not merely allowed, but actually required, to give it new meaning as society evolved.

Over time Powell grew used to that idea. He accepted the limits of text and history and the difficulty of applying the lessons of the late 1700s to a world made different by two centuries of change. And he grew accustomed to power. With each exercise, it became more familiar and less intimidating. In this respect, he would follow the lead of his senior colleagues, who were not greatly concerned—some would say not nearly concerned enough—with the *limits* of their power, but only with the direction of its use. Often quoted was the great Chief Justice Marshall's admonition, "We must never forget that it is *a constitution* we are expounding." This remark was usually taken to mean that the Constitution could not be fixed to its original context but had to evolve and grow.

Though Powell later moved toward this view, he was at the outset of his career a disciple of judicial restraint. The question that dominated his thinking in the spring of 1972 was not whether capital punishment was wise or effective or a good idea, but whether it was forbidden by the Constitution. Did the text of that document, or its history, or the legitimate inferences that could be drawn from the structure of the government it created, outlaw capital punishment? If not, the states were free to do as they pleased, and the Court should stay out of it.

Powell's disposition toward judicial restraint was never stronger than in the 1972 capital cases. For one thing, the question was new. Constitutional restriction of capital punishment was not something that the Court's decisions had already begun. Here Powell was asked to declare *for the first time* that the death penalty was unconstitutional—and in doing so to overrule two centuries of experience and a precedent barely one year old. That this invitation to creativity concerned the criminal law only increased Powell's disinclination. The Warren Court's innovations in this field had not been to his liking. Asked now to embark on another fresh adventure, equally unprecedented and even more radical, Powell refused.

This reluctance was confirmed by the example of John Harlan. As Harlan had said in *McGautha*, the administration of the death penalty might be less than ideal, but "the Federal Constitution, which marks the limit of our authority in these cases, does not guarantee trial procedures that are the best of all worlds, or that accord with the most enlightened ideas of students of the infant science of criminology, or even those that measure up to the individual predilections of the members of this Court." The Constitution required only that the trial be fair and that the procedures set forth for the protection of the accused be scrupulously observed. On that ground Powell took his stand.

The Harlan legacy also suggested a political opportunity. Harlan's closest ally on the Warren Court had been Potter Stewart. Stewart had followed Harlan in *McGautha* but now said he was on the other side. Perhaps he could be induced to return to the fold. The example of Harlan, as well as Stewart's prior vote, gave Powell reason to hope. And so he set out to make the case for the constitutionality of capital punishment and in doing so just possibly to recapture Stewart and turn the Court around.

The opinion Powell produced over the next several months was perhaps less polished and elegant than Harlan's best efforts, but it lacked nothing in force or clarity. The opinion did not speak to the wisdom or efficacy of capital punishment. His argument went straight to the question of constitutionality and to the underlying issue of judicial restraint. The decision, Powell argued, not only would affect the seven hundred persons on death row but also would have "potentially shattering effects" on the role of the Court in a democratic nation. Capital punishment was plainly contemplated by the Constitution, which referred to it in several places. It had been practiced since the beginning of the Republic, and its constitutionality had been assumed in a long line of Supreme Court decisions. To reject it now would be "judicial fiat" pure and simple. It would invade the right of the people to decide for themselves whether the death penalty should be maintained and would reflect "a basic lack of faith and confidence in the democratic process."

If there were defects in the administration of the death penalty, Powell argued, the remedy lay in legislation. "Many may regret, as I do, the failure of some legislative bodies to address the capital punishment issue with greater frankness or effectiveness. Many may decry their failure to abolish the penalty entirely or selectively, or to establish nondiscriminatory standards for its enforcement. But impatience with the slowness, and even the unresponsiveness, of legislatures is no justification for judicial intrusion upon their historic powers." Against the demand for reform, Powell interposed the obligation of restraint.

Powell was proud of this opinion. He thought his argument airtight and his history conclusive. And the intentions of Stewart and White remained tantalizingly unclear. Powell tried not to get his hopes up, but always in the back of his mind was the chance that he could reverse the vote at Conference. When Powell circulated his opinion in early May, both Stewart and White praised his draft. The compliments may have been merely courtesy to a beginner, but they nourished Powell's secret hopes. The longer it took for Stewart and White to circulate their own opinions, the more plausible it seemed that the delay meant indecision and that Powell might eventually prevail.

But it was not to be. Though the other Nixon appointees joined Powell's opinion, Stewart and White stuck by their votes at Conference. White concluded that, "the death penalty is exacted with great infrequency even for the most atrocious crimes and that there is no meaningful basis for distinguishing the few cases in which it is imposed from the many cases in which it is not." Stewart captured the same idea in a memorable sentence: "These death sentences are cruel and unusual in the same way that being struck by lightning is cruel and unusual."

And struck by lightning was just how Powell felt. In his first term on the Court, he had completely committed himself on only two issues. One was his attack on the traditional rule that segregated schools were unconstitutional only where segregation had been state imposed—chiefly in the South. The other was the constitutionality of capital punishment. On both these issues, Powell lost—and for reasons he could not fathom. In the Denver school desegregation case, a majority of the Justices privately agreed with Powell's view, but only Douglas said so in print. In the death penalty cases, Powell had, as he thought, the enormous advantage of Stewart's and White's prior votes in *McGautha*. All he had to do was hold them to their stated views. But again he failed. More than at any time until after his retirement, Powell felt discouraged and depressed by the Court's decisions—and by his own inability to affect them.

STEWART AND WHITE made a majority to strike down existing capital punishment statutes, but they did not join the other Justices in an opinion. Marshall had written his own opinion flatly declaring the death penalty unconstitutional, "because it is morally unacceptable to the people of the United States at this time in their history." But what about the laws then on the books? Did they not prove the contrary? Did they not show that in most states the people and their representatives did *not* think capital punishment "morally unacceptable," as Marshall claimed? No, he answered, because it was only the "informed citizenry" whose opinions counted. "Assuming knowledge of all the facts presently available regarding capital punishment," Marshall concluded, "the average citizen would, in my opinion, find it shocking to his conscience and sense of justice." It was a polite way of saying: "If you knew what I know, you'd think what I think."

What Marshall thought was plain enough: "There is too much crime, too much killing, too much hatred in this country. . . . I cannot believe that the American people have been so hardened, so embittered that they want to take the life of one who performs even the basest criminal act knowing that the execution is nothing more than bloodlust. This has not been my experience with my fellow citizens. Rather, I have found that they earnestly desire their system of punishments to make sense in order that it can be a morally justifiable system."

Brennan wrote his own opinion striking down capital punishment, as did Douglas. The outcome was announced in a one-paragraph opinion for the Court with a lengthy concurrence by each of the five Justices in the majority. Apparently everyone wanted to have his say, for the dissenters soon added four more opinions. Burger, Powell, and Rehnquist authored opinions joined by all four dissenters. Blackmun wrote for himself alone an intensely personal statement saying that, even though "I yield to no one in the depth of my distaste, antipathy, and indeed, abhorrence, for the death penalty. . . ," it was nevertheless constitutional.

This lineup led the New Republic to carp about the "single-mindedness" of the "Nixon team" in voting together and to praise the majority's "show of individuality" in writing separate opinions, as if there were some virtue in the inability of any two Justices to agree on one statement. In fact, the proliferation of opinions revealed a Court in disarray. Though five Justices came out against capital punishment, they could not agree on the reason. All existing statutes were struck down, but the future remained profoundly unclear.

HIDDEN BENEATH THE LAWYERLY style and measured phrases of the Stewart and White opinions was an audacious gamble. These Justices wanted to have done with capital punishment but without taking on themselves the responsibility for ruling it unconstitutional. They hoped a nudge would be sufficient. Executions were increasingly rare, and popular support seemed on the wane. If the Court struck down existing death-penalty statutes, exposed the defects in current practice, and made legislatures start over, perhaps they would simply give up. Perhaps the Court could goad the states into abolishing capital punishment without directly commanding that result. Stewart thought abolition inevitable. At conference he predicted that "someday the Court will hold death sentences unconstitutional. If we hold it constitutional in 1972, it would delay its abolition." Striking down the current statutes would force the states to consider their options. When they did, Stewart guessed, they would end all executions. If they did not, there would be time enough to say for certain whether the Constitution permitted punishment by death.

That time soon came. Popular support for capital punishment, which had declined in the 1960s, had just begun to rebound when *Furman* was announced. The rise thereafter was so sharp that it seems almost certain to have been a negative reaction to the Court's decision. In March 1972, 50 percent of Gallup's respondents favored capital punishment for murder. By November of that year, support had climbed to 57 percent. Four years later, when the Court returned to the issue, 65 percent said they favored death for murder.

This sentiment was soon translated into law. In California, where the state Supreme Court had struck down the death penalty as a violation of the state Constitution, the voters restored it by referendum. Legislatures in other states quickly passed new statutes. Within a year, nineteen states had reenacted capital punishment for homicide, and that number soon climbed to thirty-five. By the spring of 1974, the nation's death rows, which had been cleaned out by *Furman*, had sixty-four occupants under the new laws.

Though these laws varied greatly, all tried to meet Stewart's and White's objections to the caprice and freakishness of prior practice. One strategy was to structure and control the exercise of discretion by specifying the factors that should count for or against a sentence of death. The prototype was the Model Penal Code, drafted by the lawyers, judges, and academics of the American Law Institute. The ALI did not come out officially for or against capital punishment but proposed a model statute for use in those states that decided to retain the death penalty for murder.

The model statute had two innovations. First, the "mystifying cloud of words" of prior law was abandoned in favor of a straightforward list of relevant factors. On one side were the aggravating circumstances that might justify execution. Among them were that the defendant was guilty of a prior murder or crime of violence; that the defendant committed multiple murders or murder by means risking many deaths; that the defendant killed in the course of rape, robbery, arson, burglary, or kidnapping; that the defendant killed for pecuniary gain; or that the murder was otherwise "especially heinous, atrocious or cruel, manifesting exceptional depravity." On the other side were mitigating circumstances. Included were that the defendant had no significant criminal history; that the defendant acted under duress or domination of another or in the belief that his conduct was justified under the circumstances; that the defendant acted under extreme emotional disturbance or suffered from some other impairment short of legal insanity; or that the defendant killed when very young. Sentence of death was authorized only where one or more of the aggravating circumstances were found and where there were no mitigating circumstances "sufficiently substantial to call for leniency."

The other feature of the model statute was bifurcation. Guilt and sentencing were split in two. First, the jury would decide whether the accused was guilty of murder. If so, the proceeding would enter a second phase with new evidence and additional argument on the question of whether the convicted defendant should be sentenced to death. Bifurcation addressed a long-standing complaint about the trial of capital cases. In a unitary proceeding, where guilt and sentence were tried together, the defendant was caught in a dilemma. A plea for leniency was usually based on some variation of "I did it, but . . ." If that evidence were used at trial, it would aid in the defendant's conviction. But if the evidence were withheld in the hope of acquittal, it would make a death sentence more likely if the jury did convict. Bifurcation allowed the defendant to fight conviction as best he could and then, if he lost, to introduce additional evidence on the question of penalty. This ensured that death would be ordered only after the jury heard *all* the relevant evidence and considered and rejected any plea for mercy.

Obviously, the model statute did not eliminate discretion. There were still judgment calls, such as whether a murder was "especially heinous, atrocious or cruel" or whether a mitigation was "sufficiently substantial to call for leniency." Nevertheless, the proposal did make a serious attempt to guide that discretion, to make sure that its exercise would be informed and thoughtful and more nearly consistent from case to case. About half the states that reenacted the death penalty based their laws more or less closely on the model statute. They tried to answer *Furman* by controlling discretion.

The other states followed a different strategy. They tried to eliminate discretion by making the death penalty mandatory for certain classes of offenses. Louisiana, for example, passed a law requiring a death sentence in specified cases of intentional homicide—such as where the defendant was guilty of a prior or multiple murder; where the defendant killed in the course of rape, robbery, or kidnapping; where the victim was a police officer; or where the defendant killed for hire. These circumstances were not unlike the aggravations listed in the Model Penal Code, but with a crucial difference. Under the model statute, proof of an aggravating factor made the defendant *eligible* for the capital sanction; whether it would actually be imposed depended on the judgment of judge and jury, who also considered any mitigating factors that the evidence might present. In Louisiana, by contrast, proof of one of these factors made death automatic.

Still more extreme was North Carolina. Before *Furman*, that state had a traditional statute *allowing* capital punishment for first-degree murder. When such laws were struck down, the North Carolina Supreme Court decided that the problem was the jury's discretion *not* to sentence to death. In an astonishing act of judicial barbarism, the state court concluded that the old statute could continue, except that death was now made mandatory on any conviction under the broad and uncertain category of "deliberate and premeditated" first-degree murder. The state legislature then compounded this mistake by reenacting the death penalty along precisely these lines. Thus, in North Carolina, the category of capital murder was not refined and specified, as in Louisiana. Instead, death became the automatic penalty for a crime still defined in the "mystifying cloud of words" typical of pre-*Furman* statutes. Predictably, the state soon led the way in accumulating candidates for execution.

The proliferation of new death-penalty statutes made clear that *Furman* could not be the Supreme Court's last word on capital punishment. By late 1975, there were nearly four hundred persons sentenced to execution under recently revised statutes in twenty-one states. On January 17, 1976, the Justices met in a special Saturday Conference to decide which cases to hear. They could choose from forty-eight capital cases that had already made their way to the Supreme Court. (By the next summer, the number would be nearly eighty.) More than half came from North Carolina, with the others from Georgia, Florida, Louisiana, and Texas. The Justices chose one case from each state. These cases required an answer to the fundamental question that *Furman* had ducked: Was it ever constitutionally permissible to put criminals to death? The People had called Stewart's bluff.

ROUND TWO

The Court that convened in March 1976 to hear a new round of argument on the death penalty was not the same Court that had decided *Furman*. William O. Douglas came to the bench in 1939 and sat longer than any other Justice. His departure was the saddest chapter in the life of a proud man and a wrenching episode in the history of an august institution.

Alone in a hotel room in Nassau, Bahamas, on the last night of 1974, Douglas had a stroke. His wife Cathy returned to the room to find her husband collapsed on the floor, dazed and partly paralyzed. Douglas was now reduced to the kindness of adversaries. Reached at a New Year's Eve party, Burger immediately called President Ford, who, as House Minority Leader in 1970, had led the drive to impeach Douglas for alleged improprieties. Ford dispatched a plane to Nassau with Douglas's personal physician, and the stricken Justice was brought back to Washington and placed in intensive care at Walter Reed Hospital.

After eleven weeks in the hospital, Douglas had improved very little. His speech was slurred, his mind confused, his left arm paralyzed, and his legs virtually useless. Douglas had always been arrogant about his own abilities. Now the blow that crippled his body also disabled his judgment. He defied his doctors and returned to the Court, determined to resume his duties despite his incapacity. The results were tragic. Slumped in a wheelchair with his arm in a sling, Douglas fell asleep during oral argument or was forced by pain to leave the bench. Still he hung on. On one anguished occasion back in the hospital, Douglas told Brennan that he had been visited by a "black man." Who? The black man who sat on the Court. Did he mean Thurgood Marshall? No, Douglas answered, a "black man" who spells his name with a "u"—Harry Blackmun.

So matters continued through the summer, with Douglas confidently declaring his intention to return to the Court at the start of the new term. He did so, to the sorrow of all who saw him. Racked by pain and unable to maintain his concentration or even to control his bodily functions, Douglas continued to fail.

Eventually, his colleagues reached an extraordinary—and very private—decision. They took away his vote. At the Conference of October 17, 1975, with Douglas absent, seven of the remaining eight Justices agreed that no case would be decided five–four with Douglas in the majority. Technically, this was done by merely putting over for reargument any case in which Douglas cast the deciding vote, but in effect the Justices had stripped their stricken colleague of his power. Court lore recounted earlier cases where a committee of Justices had urged a failing colleague to retire, but none where a Justice had been involuntarily cut out of the Court's business.

In this matter, Powell followed the lead of his senior colleagues. Only Byron White objected. In a letter of protest, White pointed out that the Constitution "nowhere provides that a Justice's colleagues may deprive him of his office by refusing to permit him to function as a Justice." The only remedy, White argued, was to "invite Congress to take appropriate action. If it is an impeachable offense for an incompetent Justice to purport to sit as a judge, is it not the task of Congress, rather than of this Court, to undertake proceedings to determine the issue of competence? If it is not an impeachable offense, may the Court nevertheless conclude that a Justice is incompetent and forbid him to perform his duties?"

White's final point concerned publication. The decision was "plainly a matter of great importance" and should be publicly announced. "I do hope the majority is prepared to make formal disclosure of the action that it has taken." But there was no announcement. The Justices were unwilling to let Douglas cast a decisive vote and equally unwilling to precipitate a crisis by suggesting impeachment. Their action was common knowledge inside the Court and probably discernible to any outside who paid close attention. Perhaps out of respect for the Court's greatest liberal, the press maintained a rare circumspection.

Finally, on the night of November 11, 1975, fully ten months after the crippling stoke, Douglas agreed to go. The next day his friends Clark Clifford and Abe Fortas drafted a retirement letter to the President. The day following, Douglas informed the Chief, who had treated his old nemesis with unfailing kindness and sympathy throughout the long ordeal. Burger told the others after a brief birthday celebration for Harry Blackmun, and each in turn shook the once-vigorous hand of their senior colleague.*

---

* The ordeal was not over. Douglas shortly returned to the Court and behaved as if he were still sitting. He announced his plan to participate at Conference in one case and suggested rehearing in another. He also objected to the reduction in staff customary for a retired Justice, saying that he planned to write a two-hundred-year history of the Court and needed help to "untangle many of the cobwebs . . . spun over that history" by his old nemesis, Felix Frankfurter.

Douglas's former colleagues responded with a formal letter signed by all eight Justices. It explained that Douglas could not act in pending cases nor attend Conference nor maintain a large staff. "No member of the Conference could recall any instance of a retired Justice participating in any matter before the Court and it was unanimously agreed that the relevant statutes do not allow for such participation."

Even this did not end the matter. Douglas continued to try to participate in pending cases until thwarted by Court officials who had been instructed to ignore his orders. Helpless in the face of such resistance, Douglas finally gave up. In a memorandum dated March 30, 1976, he acquiesced in the "new regime" of his retirement.

In Court the next Monday, each Justice took his new place at the bench. Powell, who was senior only to Rehnquist, previously sat in the last place to the Chief's right. Now Rehnquist took that spot, and Powell moved to Blackmun's place, the next-to-last seat on the opposite side. To Powell's right, one place nearer the Chief Justice, sat Marshall. To Powell's left, in the place of the most junior Justice, was an empty chair.

To FILL THIS SEAT, President Ford named a fifty-five-year-old appeals court judge from Chicago, John Paul Stevens. The choice of Stevens came as close to the civics-book ideal of nonpolitical selection as any Supreme Court nomination since Cardozo.

Gerald Ford arrived in the White House in the aftermath of Watergate, with no electoral mandate and the task of restoring the nation's confidence. To head the tarnished Department of Justice, Ford recruited Edward Levi, president of the University of Chicago and former dean of the Law School, and relied on him for judicial selections. When Douglas retired, the President told Levi, "Find me another Lewis Powell."

Levi was well situated to follow this instruction. He knew Powell well,* and two of his assistants were former Powell clerks. (Some years later Levi's son David would also clerk for Powell.) Levi interpreted Ford's instruction as a mandate to put professionalism above politics in selecting a nominee. Both Ford and Levi admired judicial restraint, but they did not insist on a rigorously conservative ideology. In fact, they mistrusted it. Levi's ideal of a Supreme Court Justice was one who took each case on its own merits rather than forcing it into an ideological agenda. Their preference cut against Robert Bork, who had the backing of Barry Goldwater and who Levi said "would provide strong reinforcement to the Court's most conservative wing." Besides, rightly or wrongly, Bork had been tainted by the Saturday Night Massacre. Levi's candidate would be beyond controversy, someone

---

* An incident involving Levi earned the Powells privileged status at one of Washington's finest restaurants. The Powells invited the Levis to join them for dinner at the Lion D'Or. As Levi held the door for his wife, she turned to speak to him and fell down the steps to the restaurant, ending up bloody and unconscious. The restaurant's owner, chef Jean Pierre, rushed out into the street and asked taxicabs to radio for an ambulance, which arrived almost immediately. Powell stayed behind a few minutes to reassure the chef, who was aghast at the accident and "frightened to death that the Attorney General of the United States was going to bring suit." Mrs. Levi recovered, no one sued, and Jean Pierre remembered Powell gratefully.

who was intelligent, lawyerly, pragmatic, and sensible, someone who cared about craftsmanship and did not neglect unglamorous cases. In other words, someone like Lewis Powell.

Levi not only disdained ideology, he also ignored partisan politics. No effort was made—as in the case of Nixon's southern strategy—to find a nominee who would boost the President's electoral prospects. Nor did Levi heed Betty Ford's public urging to name a woman, although her husband might have been helped if he had. And a close personal relationship with the President turned out to be a disadvantage. The desire to avoid cronyism hurt Carla Hills, who served in the cabinet as Secretary of Housing and Urban Development, and Ford's old friend Robert Griffin, now Republican Senator from Michigan, who lobbied aggressively for the appointment. Levi's only political concern was confirmation. Given Ford's political weakness, his nominee would have to be beyond reproach.

Levi and his staff sifted many names and submitted a short list for evaluation by the ABA. His memorandum to the President raised several possibilities but focused on two appeals court judges, Arlin M. Adams of Philadelphia and John Paul Stevens of Chicago. Levi praised both but leaned toward Stevens.

Privately, some on Levi's staff thought Judge Adams wanted the job too much, that he might be writing his opinions as advertisements for promotion. Perhaps that is what Levi had in mind when he told the President that Adams's opinions "have considerable flair and reach, which gives them interest and can suggest an influential member of the Court, but revealing a certain weakness, not so much in analytical skill—which he has—but in being willing to sometimes by-pass or go beyond the most careful analysis." Levi's praise of Stevens was unqualified: "Judge Stevens has proved a judge of the first rank, highly intelligent, careful and energetic. He is generally a moderate conservative in his approach to judicial problems, and . . . is a superb, careful craftsman. His opinions lack the verve and scope of Judge Adams' but are more to the point and reflect more discipline and self-restraint."

Ford pondered the matter, read opinions by the candidates, and asked for additional information. He met Stevens at a dinner for federal judges on the Monday before Thanksgiving and afterward discussed the choice with Levi and Chief Justice Burger. That Friday, Ford called Stevens, who took "about two seconds" to accept the nomination.

The new nominee was a person Powell himself might have chosen. First and foremost, Stevens was a superb lawyer. He graduated Phi Beta Kappa from the University of Chicago in 1941 and served three years in the U.S. Navy. After the war, he graduated at the head of his class at Northwestern University Law School, reputedly with the best record ever achieved there, and clerked for Justice Wiley B. Rutledge. In private practice back in Chicago, Stevens won a national reputation as an antitrust lawyer. He wrote law review articles in that field and taught classes at Northwestern and the University of Chicago. Stevens continued in private practice until 1970, when President Nixon, acting at the suggestion of Senator Charles Percy, named him to the Seventh Circuit Court of Appeals.

When Stevens was nominated to replace Douglas, his appeals court opinions were carefully reviewed by the ABA committee and by a team of six Harvard law professors, including liberal guru Laurence Tribe. They found Stevens's opinions "well written, highly analytical, closely researched and meticulously prepared. They reflect very high degrees of scholarship, discipline, open-mindedness, and a studied effort to do justice to all parties within the framework of the law."

With support from across the political spectrum, Stevens's confirmation was assured. The only opposition came from certain women's groups, who resented Ford's failure to name a woman and claimed Stevens was insensitive to women's rights. No Senator agreed. After three days of hearings, the Senate voted ninety-eight to none to confirm John Paul Stevens to the Supreme Court.

To that Court, Stevens brought many qualities anticipated by his sponsors—and some they did not. As predicted, Justice Stevens was smart, hard-working, lucid, and literate. He was also cocksure, fiercely independent, and not in any sense politically reliable. Ford and Levi thought they had found a moderate conservative, but instead they got an eclectic liberal. Mostly, Stevens defied any attempt at categorization or control. He not only disdained political ideology but also resisted the influence of his colleagues. New Justices are often joiners, following the lead of a senior Justice for a year or two while they learn the ropes. Stevens was not. In his first full term on the Court, he wrote seventeen separate concurrences and twenty-seven dissents, more than any other Justice. Sometimes he pushed independence to the point of quirkiness, looking for an unusual approach to a familiar problem, anxious to put his own twist on existing doctrine.

This habit of mind separated Stevens from Powell. Both sought the middle ground but in sharply different ways. Powell characteristically tried to balance conflicting arguments in an open quest for compromise. Stevens tried to redefine the problem, often implying that the solution was easy if only one looked at it in the right way. While

Powell was inclined to split the difference between opposing arguments, Stevens tended to cut across them from some new angle. The results were sometimes original and creative, sometimes merely odd. His relations with Powell were respectful, friendly, and warm, but the two men were intellectually dissimilar and over time increasingly politically divergent.

ALTHOUGH POWELL AND STEVENS sat together for twelve years, their most important collaboration came at the outset of their joint tenure. It seemed obvious from the start that Stevens had the crucial vote on the death penalty. The eight Justices remaining from *Furman* had split four–four. The next round of cases had been delayed until Douglas's successor was confirmed so that the deadlock could be broken. Once Stevens chose sides, there would be a majority one way or the other.

Or so everyone expected. What actually happened was quite different. Instead of a simple tie-breaking vote by the new Justice, there was movement and countermovement inside the Court as the Justices realigned into three divisions. One group were unalterably opposed to capital punishment, and another were prepared accept it with few limitations. The balance of power was held by a third group, who thought the death penalty was constitutional but only with substantial restrictions, and whose votes set the course for future decisions. That middle group included both Powell and Stevens.

The death penalty cases were heard on March 30 and 31, 1976. Anthony Amsterdam, who had argued so brilliantly in 1972, spoke for three of the five defendants. But after years of struggle, Amsterdam had become so morally and emotionally committed to the fight against capital punishment that he had lost all sense of his audience. "Can you conceive," Powell asked, "of any crime as to which you would consider the death penalty an appropriate response?" Amsterdam could not. Not for air piracy resulting in hundreds of deaths? No. Or for the commandant of Buchenwald? No. Or even "if some fanatic set off a hydrogen bomb and destroyed New York City?" Also no. The exchange served only to persuade Powell that Amsterdam was a "nut." Afterward another Justice was heard to say, "Now I know what it's like to hear Jesus Christ."

At the Conference on April 2, only two Justices supported Amsterdam's call for an outright ban on capital punishment. Brennan and Marshall had taken that position in 1972; they reasserted it now and in every capital case for as long as they sat on the Court. All the others, including Stewart and White, agreed that the death penalty was constitutional for some crimes, at least in some circumstances. On the specifics of the five cases, the votes were divided and confused. There were firm majorities to uphold two statutes, less certain support for two more, and no clear majority one way or the other on the law from North Carolina.

Burger assigned all five cases to White. Having flipped sides from *McGautha* to *Furman*, White had now flopped back again and voted to uphold all five laws. Burger figured that the four *Furman* dissenters plus White would make a stable majority, which Stewart and Stevens could join if they wished.

What Burger did not know—or did not wish to recognize—was that one of the *Furman* dissenters was no longer reliable. Powell now found himself most closely aligned not with Burger, Blackmun, and Rehnquist or with the new convert to their position, Byron White, but with his old friend and adversary, Potter Stewart.

The rapprochement between Stewart and Powell proved surprisingly easy, as each now accepted the other's main point. For his part, Stewart now agreed with Powell that the death penalty was not invariably "cruel and unusual." Stewart had ducked this issue in 1972 but four years later found it easier to face. As he said at Conference, the fact that thirty-five states had reenacted the death penalty after *Furman* struck down the older statutes made it quite impossible to say that capital punishment now contravened the "evolving standards of decency" of this society. To that extent, Stewart joined Powell. For his part, Powell now accepted *Furman*'s judgment that the older death penalty statutes were invalid. As precedent *Furman* was exceptionally confused, but Powell took it as having settled that the Constitution placed some limits on the administration of the death penalty. To that extent, Powell joined Stewart.

Each had some explaining to do. Stewart had to explain why some of the revised statutes satisfied his *Furman* objections but others did not. The laws before the Court represented both of the common strategies for dealing with *Furman*. Georgia and Florida (and to a lesser degree Texas) passed laws based on the Model Penal Code. They tried to solve the problem of jury discretion by imposing statutory control and guidance. The other strategy eliminated discretion by making the death penalty mandatory. North Carolina had simply made death the automatic penalty for all first-degree murder. Louisiana had responded more carefully by drafting narrow categories of intentional homicide for which capital punishment was required. Stewart's inclination was to uphold the first three statutes and strike

down the last two—that is, to approve the effort to guide and structure sentencing discretion (even where, as in the Texas statute, that
effort did not go very far), but to reject any form of compulsory death.

Yet if, as Stewart had said in *Furman*, the death penalty was "cruel
and unusual in the same way that being struck by lightning is cruel and
unusual," mandatory death was the perfect cure. By eliminating the
jury's discretion *not* to kill, North Carolina and Louisiana went a long
way toward making capital punishment routine and regular. But mandatory death meant much more death. No state had enforced a mandatory death penalty before *Furman*, and the apparent rigor of the older laws
had been relaxed by jury sympathy. It may have been true that those
who were "struck by lightning" had a more compelling objection to
their fate because of the infrequency with which others suffered it, but
it was hard to accept that the correction lay in making others suffer
more. Stewart did not want blood on his hands. No matter what he had
said in *Furman*, the mandatory death penalty would have to go.

When Powell joined in this conclusion, he too had some explaining
to do. In *Furman*, Powell had insisted that capital punishment was the
business of the states and their legislatures. The Constitution did not
forbid it, and the Supreme Court should stay out of it. Now Powell
was ready to strike down one of the revised state statutes and perhaps
two. Whatever happened to judicial restraint?

Part of the answer lay in the Supreme Court's own responsibility for
the mandatory death penalties. Such laws were plainly a reaction to
Furman. There were no mandatory death penalties prior to *Furman*,
and there was no reason to think that North Carolina or any other
state would have adopted one except in answer to that decision. Once
the Justices intervened in the question of capital punishment, they
assumed some responsibility for the state of the law. They could not,
thought Powell, sit back and wash their hands of the mess they had
created.

Moreover, Powell's idea of judicial restraint always included a
healthy respect for precedent. In 1972 the precedents supported capital punishment, and Powell railed against departing from them. In
1976 the precedents were mixed, and Powell tried to make sense of the
confusion. Did a true understanding of judicial restraint mean that
Powell should try to turn the clock back to the days before *Furman*? Or
that he should accept that decision and try to sort out its implications? Powell took the latter view. As he wrote in his notes for the
Conference, "I accept *Furman* as precedent."

More fundamentally, Powell was simply less concerned about judi-

cial restraint in 1976 than he had been in 1972. At least his commitment to it was changing. When Powell first came to the Court, the
ideal of restraint seemed shining and clear. Judges should interpret the
Constitution, not expand it. If the constitutional text or history did
not condemn a certain law or practice, the judges should let it alone.
Yet Powell's experience on the Court soon blurred this bright line. In
most areas, Powell realized, the precedents had already—perhaps irre-
trievably—distorted the original meaning of the Constitution. The
judge entered in midstream, with the waters already muddied by prior
decisions and the ever-changing circumstances before the Court. The
course of restraint no longer seemed simple and clear.

Then too, Powell's sensitivity to the forward use of his power dulled
with its exercise. As he gained confidence in his own ability and judgment, he relied on them more readily. The awesome responsibility of
his office, which at the outset had seemed so intimidating, grew familiar—and even welcome. He grew to like his power more than fear it,
and eventually, upon retirement, to grieve at its loss.

With these changes in Powell's experience and outlook came a loos-
ening of his commitment to judicial restraint. He never renounced his
admiration for John Harlan, yet in fact his idea of judicial restraint
became quite contextual. The principle declined into an attitude—not
a rigid ban on judicial innovation, but a presumption in favor of legislative acts, a sense of deference to popular choices and values, and an
habitual hesitation to substitute his own views and inclinations. In this
dilution, the idea of restraint survived as a key ingredient in Powell's
decisions, but not as their base or lodestar.

By 1976 Powell's approach was flexible enough not only to accept
Furman as a given but to use it as the foundation for a new law of capital punishment. It was "fair to say," Powell recorded in his notes, "that
[the] result of *Furman* has been wholesome in prompting states to
focus on [the] problem and enact standards." Whether the new standards were in fact good enough to pass constitutional muster was
debatable, but they were indisputably better than the prior law.
Mandatory capital punishment was a step backward. He therefore
joined Stewart's opposition to the mandatory sentences and abandoned the hands-off position he had taken four years previously.

So Stewart and Powell joined forces. They did not want to fritter
their votes away by concurring or dissenting in White's opinions, and
they realized that in at least one case (the one from North Carolina),
White would not have a majority. If they wrote separately, theirs
would be the decisive opinion in all five cases, charting (so they

hoped) a coherent middle course between the two extremes. But they needed another vote. With White, Burger, Blackmun, and Rehnquist, they could make a majority to uphold any law, but to strike down a statute they needed more help than Brennan and Marshall could provide. They needed John Paul Stevens.

Stewart and Powell invited their junior colleague to lunch at the Monocle, and there, over Powell's customary overdone hamburger, they broached their scheme. The three of them were not far apart. All agreed that the Georgia and Florida laws were constitutional. All agreed that the North Carolina law, which Stevens called a monster, was not. Stewart and Stevens were queasy about the Texas statute, which Powell supported, and firmly against the Louisiana statute, which Powell had been inclined to accept. But these divergences were trivial compared to the common ground. All three Justices shared two overriding objectives: First, to answer the question left open in *Furman* and settle once and for all that capital punishment was not invariably unconstitutional; and second, to make sure that *Furman* did not become the reason or excuse for a vast increase in executions through mandatory death penalties. If they could iron out their differences and author a joint opinion, their views would be controlling on all five statutes, and they could give the country the clearest possible guidance for the future.

Someone had to tell White. After all, he had been assigned the opinions. He would have been furious if, after weeks of labor, he was blindsided by the new alignment and robbed of any chance for success. Stewart, Powell, and Stevens went to see the Chief Justice, hoping that he would reassign the cases to them, but Burger refused. Finally, Stewart went to see White. He dropped first one shoe and then the other: White did not have a majority to uphold the North Carolina statute, and—what was from White's point of view far worse—Stewart, Powell, and Stevens had decided to work out a joint position on all five cases. White had no choice but to relinquish the assignments.

The death penalty cases were now in a sort of limbo, and on Wednesday, May 5, the Justices met in Conference to sort out the confusion. The occasion called for leadership, but Burger merely asked Brennan to reassign the North Carolina case, in which there was now a clear majority to strike down the law. Brennan declined. He and Marshall would never agree with the Stewart-Powell-Stevens position, and there seemed no point in giving anyone the impossible task of uniting these five votes behind one opinion. Besides, everyone knew that if any coherent position could emerge from the fractured Court, it would have to come from the three Justices in the center. After several minutes of desultory discussion and embarrassed silence, Stewart stepped in and took the assignment. He, Powell, and Stevens would write in all five cases, and the others could join as they pleased. Everyone acquiesced in what was a fait accompli.

The troika now had the assignments and a guaranteed majority for whatever results they reached, but they did not yet have an opinion. Indeed, they had not even finally settled among themselves how the two borderline cases (Texas and Louisiana) would come out. After some back and forth, they agreed. Stewart and Stevens would vote for the Texas statute, while Powell would oppose the Louisiana law. They also agreed on a division of labor. Powell would take primary responsibility for the lead case upholding the death penalty, *Gregg v. Georgia*. It was his task to explain why capital punishment was not, as Brennan and Marshall claimed, always and everywhere unconstitutional. This was *Furman* revisited, and Powell recycled his dissent in that case for use here on the winning side. Stevens undertook to write the facts of the other four cases. To Stewart fell the greatest challenge. He would explain why the Georgia, Florida, and Texas statutes satisfied *Furman*'s objection to uncontrolled discretion (this part was easy) and why, paradoxically, the mandatory death penalties from North Carolina and Louisiana did not.

Although these results could not reconcile the Court's prior pronouncements in *Furman* and *McGautha*, they did draw a clear line. Mandatory death sentences would be forbidden, but discretionary capital punishment would be allowed, so long as the states made some effort to articulate appropriate standards. The core of Powell's dissent in *Furman*—that the Constitution could not be interpreted to outlaw capital punishment altogether—had at last been accepted by the Court.

DESPITE THIS SUCCESS in the making, Powell's mind was not at ease. The backlog on death row was large and growing. Roughly half of these sentences had been imposed under laws that would be upheld. When they were, the executions could begin in earnest. Powell feared a bloodbath and was looking for a way out.

His plan was that the decisions upholding capital punishment should be prospective only—that is, the laws would be found constitutional only for future death sentences. Those already on death row would have to be resentenced, even if they had properly been condemned under valid laws.

He explained the reasons for this odd idea in an April 16 memo to his clerk, Christina Whitman: "I think one can at least surmise that some of the sentences were imposed by juries, and even by courts, with a rather strong belief that capital punishment would be totally outlawed by this Court. Indeed, I had no idea myself until the day before Conference how some of my Brothers would vote. In view of this ambiguity, I hesitate to say that every sentence of death in these states would have been imposed had the law been settled rather than quite unsettled."

Two weeks later, Powell wrote Stewart: "No one—no legislator, judge, or juror—could have been certain how this Court ultimately would come down on the capital punishment issue." It was at least possible that the uncertainty might have affected their decisions. Recognizing "the stark fact that the carrying out of several hundred executions, pursuant to validation thereof by this Court, would cause profound shock waves," Powell advanced his plan: "We could hold that the effect of our decision sustaining the laws in some of these cases is prospective so far as existing sentences of death are concerned." Those cases would be remanded for resentencing under the validated statutes. "Those responsible for the resentencing could then act with the certainty that the death sentence, if reimposed, would not be constitutionally flawed."

The trouble was that neither Whitman nor Stewart nor Powell himself could find any authority for saying that a decision *upholding* a law as constitutional should apply only prospectively.* Nor was it logical to say so. A death sentence could be upheld on appeal only if it was valid when imposed. If the sentence was valid, it could be carried out. It seemed preposterous to say that a sentence was valid when imposed but that it could not be carried out despite a decision in its favor. What did it mean to uphold a law as constitutional if it could not be enforced? And how could the Court forbid enforcement if the law was in fact constitutional?

To these questions, Powell had no answer. Resentencing every prisoner on death row would have been costly and, owing to the loss of

---

* There was precedent for the quite different proposition that decisions announcing new constitutional standards that *in*validated current practices might sometimes apply only prospectively. The idea was to avoid applying new rules retroactively to cases where they could not have been anticipated or obeyed. In such cases, police practices valid when engaged in would be upheld despite later decisions declaring them unconstitutional for the future. Powell, by contrast, wanted to vacate sentences on the ground of later decisions declaring the sentences valid when imposed. This was unheard of.

evidence or death of witnesses, in many cases impossible. There was no reason to think that the judges and jurors who condemned men (and a few women) to die did so casually or flippantly or without sense of their responsibilities. They might have been uncertain whether the executions would ever be carried out, but that would be true of all capital cases. Any death sentence might be set aside on appeal or commuted by the governor. If capital punishment were valid only where the judge and jury knew *for certain* that the sentence would actually be carried out, no case would qualify.

Powell eventually abandoned his idea. That he had toyed with it at all showed his uneasiness about personal responsibility for renewed executions. The prospect that several hundred persons might be put to death as a direct result of the position he had fought for in *Furman* and prevailed on in *Gregg* made him squirm. The strange suggestion that the death penalty decisions might operate only prospectively was an attempt to distance himself from the consequences of his own acts.

Much the same thing happened after the decisions were announced, when Amsterdam filed a petition for rehearing on behalf of the condemned prisoners and asked that their executions be stayed while rehearing was considered. This should have been a mere formality. Losers in the Supreme Court routinely seek rehearing and are just as routinely denied, but when this petition came to Powell (in his capacity as Circuit Justice for the states involved), he hesitated. If he denied the stay, the executions could begin at once. Again Powell wavered. He decided to grant the stay so that rehearing could be considered when the Justices reconvened in the fall. That way nothing would happen right away, and the responsibility for going forward would be shared by the Court as a whole.

At this point, Burger intervened. Since rehearing would inevitably be denied, there was no reason to stay the executions. In fact, there was good reason not to. As Burger wrote the other Justices, staying the capital cases would inevitably "arouse a certain amount of speculation as to possible shifts in individual positions. To grant a stay at this time opens a genuine risk that some will read into it a willingness on the part of the Court to reconsider the three cases in which convictions and judgments were affirmed." Burger threatened to call the Court into special session to vacate any stay Powell might grant. Powell's hurried telephone consultations elicited support from Stewart and Stevens and advice from Brennan to show some "backbone." On July 22 Powell granted the stay. The Chief did not call a special session, but, as he anticipated, the stay was vacated when the petition for rehearing was eventually denied.

In fact, the flood of executions did not occur. Each and every case was contested so tenaciously that nearly three years would elapse before anyone was put to death other than Gary Gilmore, who asked to die and thwarted all efforts to save him.

THE DEATH PENALTY cases were announced on Friday, July 2, 1976, near the end of an unusually long and difficult term. A handful of cases still remained, including two search and seizure opinions by Powell that provoked scorching dissents from Brennan. Brennan's feelings had been rubbed raw not only by the successive defeats, but also by a newspaper quote of an unidentified Justice saying that Brennan and Marshall were now so isolated and unimportant that there was no point in responding to their increasingly bitter dissents. "You don't go around chasing rabbits," said the unnamed source. "You don't need to answer every flag they run up."

Powell was not the source, as Brennan must have known, but was nonetheless taxed with the sentiment. At the term's final Conference, Powell announced that one of his opinions was ready to go but added, "I don't know if Bill Brennan is ready. He may have more dissenting to do." "Well," Brennan shot back, "I don't know why you even have to ask me. I take it you don't feel you have to read my dissents or respond to them anyway." The incident was smoothed over, but the combination of exhaustion and hard feelings gave the end of term an edgy, nervous air.

The tension contributed to the naturally somber tone of the death penalty announcements. Stewart's voice cracked as he read the opinions upholding capital punishment. White spoke for himself, Burger, and Rehnquist in voting to uphold all five laws. Blackmun merely invoked his opinion in *Furman*. Marshall delivered an anguished dissent and that night suffered a mild heart attack.

THE NEXT DAY the Powells left for Richmond and George Gibson's annual Fourth of July party. The little talk he gave there to his old (and completely discreet) friends—George and Pearson Gibson, Harvie and Letitia Wilkinson, Virginius and Douglas Dabney, Tennant and Mary Bryan, and Justin and Mary Moore—must have reflected his immense satisfaction at the term just concluded. Not only had the constitutionality of capital punishment been authoritatively established and the thrust of Powell's *Furman* dissent adopted into law, but he had prevailed on the second great issue of that year.

In 1973 Powell had proposed a major change in search and seizure cases. The issue was too technical for newspaper headlines but nonetheless enormously important. It involved the scope of federal court review of state criminal convictions.

State criminal defendants were entitled to raise in state court any federal constitutional claims—such as illegal search and seizure or lack of *Miranda* warnings—they might have, and the state judges were required to hear such claims and decide them fairly. If the state court agreed with the defendant, the evidence was suppressed. If not, the defendant could appeal. If the appellate court rejected the claim, the defendant could seek review in the state supreme court and ultimately in the Supreme Court of the United States.

All this was part of the routine process of trial, conviction, and appeal. But there was more. If all those courts rejected the claim, the defendant could start over by raising the same claim in a federal trial court. Technically, this was done by asking the federal court for a writ of habeas corpus. If the federal judge believed that the state courts had erred, he or she would order that the defendant be released or retried, and the state courts, despite their contrary view of the law, would have to comply. In that way, individual federal judges functioned as "little Supreme Courts," overruling an entire state court system to require that federal constitutional issues be resolved as they thought correct. The defendant's ability to press his claim in the state courts and then, if he lost, start over again in federal court gave him "two bites at the apple" on his federal claims.

Though Powell thought this system of dual review wasteful and insulting to state courts, he was willing to put up with it to avoid convicting the innocent. On balance, it made sense to go the extra mile when the question was whether the conviction might be erroneous or unjust. But that was *never* the issue in search and seizure claims. The fact that evidence might or might not have been seized in violation of the Fourth Amendment had no bearing on its reliability. The heroin found in the defendant's luggage proved beyond all doubt that he was in fact guilty of possession, whether or not the police had been entitled to look there. Unlike most constitutional rights, Fourth Amendment violations were unrelated to factual guilt or innocence. There was, of course, the possibility of *error* if state courts misapplied the law of search and seizure, but there was no possibility of the *injustice* of sending an innocent person to jail.

Powell therefore proposed that the relitigation of constitutional claims on federal habeas corpus be curtailed in search and seizure cases. For other issues, the defendant would continue to get two bites at the apple, but for claims of illegal search and seizure, only one. Federal judges would not hear claims of Fourth Amendment violations which had already been considered and rejected in state court and which the Supreme Court of the United States had declined to review.

When Powell first broached this idea in 1973, it attracted only the support of Burger and Rehnquist. Powell's opinion, however, laid the groundwork, and three years later the Court endorsed his position by a vote of six to three, with Brennan, White, and Marshall dissenting. The case—entitled *Stone v. Powell*—was almost as important as the death penalty, though far less dramatic. Here Powell had not only prevailed but had taken the lead in forging a new position and bringing the Court to his point of view.

Brennan and Marshall might be disappointed by the year's events, but Powell was elated. The anguish and self-doubt of his first few months had long ago been surmounted. The enormous effort required to bring himself up to speed in constitutional law was behind him. He had also learned the ways of the Court—how to know what the others were thinking, how to craft opinions to command support, how to plant the seeds for arguments in future cases, when to fight and when to compromise. Most important of all, Powell now saw himself as a leader on the Court, as he had been in other settings. His lifelong desire for control—of himself, of his family, of his friends, and of his firm—had not ceased with his ascension to the bench. He could begin to see himself as a Justice of real influence.

There were, after all, few competitors. Burger was too self-important to be personally influential and too disengaged from the actual legal issues to be an intellectual leader. Two Justices with the brains and personality to lead the Court were politically isolated. Brennan, who had played the crucial role in crafting the decisions of the Warren Court, now led a coalition of two. With Douglas gone, he and Marshall were the only true liberals left. Sometimes they were joined by Stevens and increasingly by Blackmun, but even with these occasional recruits, the liberals were a distinct minority. On the other side was Rehnquist. Smart, affable, confident, and energetic, Rehnquist was equally ready to join ranks with others or to strike out on his own, as the occasion demanded. Like Brennan, Rehnquist always knew his own mind and rarely missed a chance to further his agenda. Ten years later he would be promoted to Chief Justice and preside over a deeply conservative Court, of which he was both the titular and intellectual leader. But that was far in the future. In 1976 Rehnquist seemed almost a fringe figure, a right-wing mirror image of Bill Douglas, quick and tough-minded but out of the mainstream.

That left Stewart, White, and Powell as the Court's dominant center. Each had the decisive voice in certain situations, but in the term just ended leadership had been shared by those two close friends and kindred spirits, Potter Stewart and Lewis Powell. Powell looked forward to more of the same.

THE SUMMER OF 1976 was a happy time. After the holiday weekend in Richmond, the Powells attended the annual naturalization ceremony at Monticello. Every year immigrants gather on Thomas Jefferson's back lawn to become U.S. citizens. On the two-hundredth anniversary of the nation's birth, they found, instead of the usual local dignitaries, that the oath was administered by a Justice of the Supreme Court and the welcoming remarks given by the President of the United States. Amid all the pomp and spectacle of the bicentennial, this quiet ceremony was the most fitting celebration of the nation's birthday. Facing 106 new citizens from twenty-six foreign lands, Ford acclaimed their diversity. "'Black is beautiful' was a motto of genius which uplifted us far above its first intention," said the President. "Once Americans had thought about it and perceived its truth, we began to realize that so are brown, white, red and yellow beautiful." And he expressed the gratitude of their new country: "You have given us a birthday present beyond price—yourselves, your faith, your loyalty and your love. We thank you with full and friendly hearts."

After the ceremony, the Powells visited with the President, while the crowd moved on to hamburgers and hot dogs on the Monticello grounds. Ford recounted to Powell his direction that Ed Levi "find another Lewis Powell" to fill Douglas's seat. That afternoon, the Powells drove to Washington for the Court's final day of announcements on Tuesday, July 9, and then returned to Richmond.

That Saturday they were back in Charlottesville to lunch with Queen Elizabeth (and about two hundred others) in Jefferson's Rotunda at the University of Virginia. They returned once again to Washington for the Colonial Williamsburg board meeting and a White House dinner for German Chancellor Helmut Schmidt, then to Virginia Beach for the summer meeting of the Virginia Bar Association and three weeks later to Atlanta with the American Bar Association.

Intermixed with these official entertainments were purely private ones. Daughter Jo and her family came for a week in July. Powell saw

them in the evenings, but spent his days in the Richmond office, shut-
tling papers back and forth to his clerks in Washington and keeping an
active social calendar over lunch. Near the end of August, the Powells
and the Wilkinsons spent a weekend in one of the meticulously
restored homes reserved by Colonial Williamsburg for use by the
chairman of the board and special guests. On August 30 the Powells
hosted a party at the Country Club of Virginia, then returned to
Washington the next day.

Back in Washington, Powell's social activities slowed as work
increased. On Sunday, September 12, Powell watched the Washington
Redskins come from behind in the final two minutes to beat the New
York Giants for the eleventh straight time. Work on the certiorari petitions had to be done by September 27, when the Justices began a
week-long Conference to decide which cases to hear. On Sunday,
October 3, Powell had lunch with George Bush, and the next morning
heard oral argument in the first case of the new term.

This whirlwind exactly suited Powell. Even in the summer, he preferred to spend a full day at the office and see friends and family over
lunch and dinner. The richness and variety of his social calendar were
due in part to his lifelong habit of staying in touch, but also in part to
the prestige of his position. Everywhere he went, he was an honored
guest. At a time of life when he had expected to begin a painful disengagement, to turn over his clients and relinquish direction of the firm,
Powell found himself, to his immense relief and satisfaction, once
more at the center of events. The appointment to the Court had not
only crowned his professional achievements, but had opened a new
and enlarged arena for his devotion to work, a fresh challenge for his
ambition to succeed, and a vastly greater opportunity for his instinct
to control. By the summer of 1976, Powell felt once again, on a new
and larger scale, in charge.

RAPE, RACE, AND THE DEATH PENALTY

The 1976 decisions had neither categorically condemned capital punishment nor unreservedly approved it. Instead, the Justices allowed
death as a penalty for some crimes, in some circumstances, under
some statutes. Hard questions soon arose.

Some cases tested whether all mandatory death penalties were now
forbidden. Could death be made mandatory for murder of a police officer? (No, said the Court.) Or for murder by a person already under a

sentence of life in prison? (Again no.) Other cases raised questions about the discretionary regimes. Could the jury be barred from considering certain factors as possible mitigations? (No.) Could a person be put to death for helping another to commit robbery and murder, even if he did not personally intend to kill anyone? (Also no.) Could a sixteen-year-old boy be sentenced to die without consideration of to his history of family violence and emotional distress? (Again no.) Could a death sentence be based in part on a psychiatrist's testimony that the defendant might kill again? (Yes.) Could Florida authorize a judge to impose capital punishment, on proper facts, despite the jury's recommendation for mercy? (Also yes.) Could the prosecutor strike from the jury prospective jurors who opposed capital punishment? (Yes, but only if their opposition was so strong that it would "prevent or substantially impair" the juror's performance of his duties.) And finally, could the state execute a killer who had gone insane? (No.)

In almost all of these cases, Powell was in the majority. In fact, for the period of his tenure Powell agreed with the outcome in capital cases more often than any Justice.* With few exceptions, the twisting course of close distinctions in the Court's decisions tracked the views of Lewis Powell.

The most crucial question in this series was whether death could be imposed for rape. Before *Furman*, sixteen states authorized capital punishment for rape. At that time Powell found it "quite impossible" to declare the death penalty unconstitutional for rape, but the *Furman* decision temporarily mooted the issue by eliminating all existing capital statutes, including those for rape. After *Furman*, only three states reenacted the death penalty for rape of an adult woman, and two of those were mandatory laws, which were struck down in 1976. That left Georgia as the only state in the Union to authorize death for rape of an adult woman. (Florida, Mississippi, and Tennessee allowed execution for rape of children.) To resolve whether that penalty was constitutional, the Justices agreed to hear the case of Ehrlich Anthony Coker.

If ever anyone deserved to die for rape, Coker seemed a good candidate. On September 2, 1974, he escaped through the roof of the chapel of the Ware County Correctional Institution, where he had been confined for a previous rape and murder, and made his way to the two-room home of Allen and Elnita Carver, a pair of sixteen-year-

---

*   Stewart was consistently in the majority in the much smaller number of capital cases heard before he retired in 1981.

olds with a new baby. He robbed Allen, forced his wife to tie up her husband, and gagged him with her underpants. He raped Elnita despite her protest that she was just recovering from childbirth. Afterward, Coker forced her into her car and fled the scene but was apprehended by the police several hours later. For these events, Coker was convicted of rape, kidnapping, robbery, car theft, and escape, and for the first of these crimes, was sentenced to death.

Coker's case was argued on March 28, 1977. At the Conference two days later, the Justices voted in his favor. Brennan and Marshall were prepared to overturn any death sentence. They were joined by Stewart, White, Blackmun, and Stevens on the ground that death was a "grossly disproportionate and excessive punishment for the crime of rape." Powell agreed—to a point. His Conference notes recorded that he joined in overturning Coker's sentence but wanted to leave open the constitutionality of capital punishment for a variety of other offenses, including treason, airplane hijacking, and some instances of especially aggravated rape.

The opinion was assigned to White, who, on May 6, circulated a draft declaring death an unconstitutional penalty for rape of an adult woman. After reviewing the draft, Powell's clerk said: "An excellent opinion. I recommend you join." But one passage in White's opinion set Powell off. White had written: "Life is over for the victim of the murderers; for the rape victim, life may not be nearly so happy as it was, but it is not over and normally is not beyond repair." Powell answered that "life may indeed lose its meaning for the victim so grievously injured physically or psychologically as never again to live normally. There have been surviving rape victims for whom the consequences are worse than death." Execution should be permitted, Powell concluded, but "only for the rare case of a rape so outrageous and so serious in its consequences as to justify society's ultimate penalty." Ehrlich Coker did not qualify.

This was Powell at his most particularistic. His penchant for hairsplitting distinctions and fact-specific decisions had overrun any sensible notion of constitutional standards. It would have been hard to define a crime of aggravated rape in a way that captured the extent of the victim's injury. Mrs. Carver might have been permanently devastated by her experience, or she might have proved miraculously resilient. Either way, Coker was responsible. Perhaps the strangest aspect of Powell's position was his insistence that convicted murderer and repeat rapist Ehrlich Coker could not be executed, but that other, somehow worse, rapists could be. Such nice distinctions might have been feasible if Powell could have personally reviewed every case, but as a legal rule for future cases, Powell's distinction among forcible rapes would have been unworkable.

Perhaps for that reason, Powell's views attracted no support, then or later. White spoke for himself, Stewart, Blackmun, and Stevens in holding capital punishment unconstitutional for rape. Brennan and Marshall concurred, while Burger and Rehnquist dissented. Powell did a little of both.

LURKING BEHIND THE FACTS of this case was an explosive issue that the Court's decision enabled it to avoid—racial discrimination in the imposition of death penalty. Ehrlich Coker was white, as were his victims, but the history of capital punishment for rape had a darker cast. The roster of persons executed for rape was so dominated by blacks that, even without disciplined scientific analysis, the role of race was painfully clear. The conclusion seemed inescapable that the exaction of society's ultimate penalty had been corrupted by fear of black depredation against white women, especially in the South. *Coker* laid this history to rest. The pronouncement that no one could be put to death for rape eliminated the clearest instance of racial bias in capital punishment.

For murder, the connection had never been that plain, and *Furman* made the prior experience more or less irrelevant. Still, the evidence was suggestive, and soon after the death penalty was revived by the 1976 decisions, efforts began to document racial bias in the death penalty. The most sophisticated and persuasive of these studies finally reached the Supreme Court in Powell's last year of service in the case of Warren McCleskey.

In 1978 McCleskey and three others robbed a furniture store in Fulton County, Georgia. His job was to enter the front door and keep the customers in the showroom, while the others came in the back and took the cash. While McCleskey was thus engaged, a police officer answering a silent alarm came in the front door and was killed by a bullet to the head. The jury found McCleskey guilty of murder and also found two of the aggravating circumstances specified in the Georgia statute: (1) he had killed in the course of armed robbery, and (2) his victim was a police officer engaged in the performance of his duties. As there was no mitigation, McCleskey was sentenced to die.

The key objection to this sentence lay in the racial identity of the participants. McCleskey was black, and the policeman was white. The case therefore became the occasion for presenting to the federal courts

an elaborate statistical study known by the name of the chief investi-
gator, Professor David C. Baldus. The Baldus study examined more
than two thousand criminal homicides in Georgia during the 1970s
and used the techniques of multiple regression analysis to assess the
effect of some 230 possible variables on death sentences. Based only
on statistical probabilities, the Baldus study could not say anything in
particular about Warren McCleskey or the circumstances of his conviction but only about the general pattern of capital sentencing in
Georgia and in Fulton County.

Exactly what the Baldus study did show has often been misunderstood. The study did *not* show any strong link between an offender's race
and his likelihood of being sentenced to death. There was disparity in the
raw numbers, but when they were adjusted for the effect of nonracial
variables, the difference disappeared. In terms of bias against black
defendants, the Baldus study tended not so much to indict the administration of capital punishment in Georgia as to support it. That white
murderers were only very slightly less likely than black murderers to be
sentenced to death in the South in the 1970s—only one decade after the
marches and violence of the 1960s—was on the whole reassuring.

What the Baldus study did show was a significant disparity in the
prospect of execution based on the race of the *victim*. Murderers of
any race who killed whites were appreciably more likely to be sentenced to die than those who killed blacks. The size of the differential
could be expressed in a variety of ways. Most misleadingly, it was said
(often in the press) that killers of whites were eleven times more likely
to be sentenced to death than killers of blacks, but these were raw
numbers. Properly adjusted to take account of other variables, killers
of whites were about four times as likely to be sentenced to death as
killers of blacks.

The study also located the greatest disparities in a certain range of
aggravated homicides—that is, those cases where the presence of various factors other than the race of the victim made a sentence of death
more likely than usual. In the low aggravation cases (such as drunken
quarrels between friends), capital punishment was extremely rare and
showed little or no victim-race disparity. In very high aggravation cases
(such as multiple murder or the use of torture), death sentences were
commonly imposed and again showed little or no victim-race disparity.
The problem was found in the intermediate cases, where the facts and
circumstances neither precluded nor strongly indicated execution.

In these cases, 34 percent of those who killed whites were sentenced
to die, as compared to only 14 percent of those who killed blacks. This

calculation led to the often-repeated statement that of murderers of whites in the midrange of aggravation, twenty out of thirty-four would not have been sentenced to death if their victims had been black.

However described, the disparity of results based on the race of the victim was dramatic and unsettling. But was it unconstitutional? As usual Powell cast the deciding vote. The statistics alone did not show (indeed no statistics could have shown), that Warren McCleskey had been treated unfairly in any way. Powell stated his position most succinctly in an early memorandum urging his colleagues not to hear McCleskey's case. First, it was hard to know what to make of statistics. "[S]entencing judges and juries are constitutionally *required* to consider a host of individual-specific circumstances in deciding whether to impose capital punishment. No study can take all of these individual circumstances into account, precisely because they are fact-specific as to each defendant." Of course, taking all factors into account was precisely what Baldus and his colleagues had tried to do, but Powell was uneasy with this kind of evidence. As he said elsewhere, "[m]y understanding of statistical analysis . . . ranges from limited to zero."

He also did not know what constitutional weight to give to the statistical effect of the *victim's* race. "[O]ne would expect that if there were race-based sentencing, the Baldus study would show a bias based on the *defendant's* race," but the "study suggests *no* such effect. . . ." Differential treatment of defendants based on the race of their victims was hard to understand as racial bias against defendants.

Finally, Powell thought the overall picture revealed by the figures was decidedly positive. The "study tends to show that the system operates rationally as a general matter: The death penalty was most likely in those cases with the most severe aggravating factors and the least mitigating factors, and least likely in the opposite cases. The pattern suggests precisely the kind of careful balancing of individual factors that the Court required in *Gregg*."

Anthony Lewis later criticized Powell's decision as "effectively condon[ing] the expression of racism in a profound aspect of our law." Powell did not see the case as condoning racism but simply as recognizing the inevitable variations in any nonmandatory death penalty. At bottom, McCleskey's claim attacked not only the death penalty but the idea of discretion and the role of the jury. It was one thing to say that discretion should be structured, guided, and constrained to the extent possible. *Furman* required as much. It was quite another thing to object to discretion whenever its exercise could not be satisfactorily explained. After all, there was "no perfect procedure" for deciding when to impose death. The "inestimable privilege" of trial by jury at least assured a "diffused impartiality" of judgment and "reflect[ed] the conscience of the community as applied to the circumstances of a particular offender and offense." That the power to be lenient might benefit some more than others was not decisive. Mandatory death penalties had been disallowed precisely because they left no room for individualized discretion and mercy. "Where the discretion that is fundamental to our criminal process is involved, we decline to assume that what is unexplained is invidious."

Powell's was the fifth vote for this position, and he wrote the opinion of the Court. "In light of the safeguards designed to minimize racial bias in the process, the fundamental value of jury trial in our criminal justice system, and the benefits that discretion provides to criminal defendants, we hold that the Baldus study does not demonstrate a constitutionally significant risk of racial bias affecting the Georgia capital-sentencing process." Once again, the death penalty was upheld.

INDIRECTLY, HOWEVER, Powell did respond to the concerns of the Baldus study. His answer had been given the year before, when the Court cleared the way for black defendants to challenge efforts by prosecutors to obtain all-white juries. The issue concerned the use of peremptory challenges. Both the prosecution and the defense have the right to challenge jurors "for cause"—that is, to remove from the jury anyone who knows the defendant or who has already formed an opinion about the case or who for any other reason might not be fair and impartial. Additionally, each side has a limited number of "peremptory" challenges. These can be used to remove prospective jurors without cause or explanation. The lawyer might have a hunch about a particular individual or a prediction that persons from certain backgrounds would be unsympathetic.

But what about race? Could the prosecution use its peremptory challenges to eliminate blacks? Could the prosecutor strike blacks from the jury just to make it less sympathetic to a black defendant? No, said a divided Supreme Court. In an opinion by Powell overturning a Warren Court precedent, the Court ruled that a prosecutor could not strike black jurors because of their race. There had to be a legitimate nonracial reason. The necessity of explaining their acts to a judge would surely make prosecutors think twice before abusing their peremptory challenges.

To the extent that the Baldus study revealed a latent racism in sentencing juries, more black jurors would help. In any event, Powell thought this the right response to the problem of juror bias. If there was racial bias in juror perceptions of a victim's worth, the solution was to change the composition of juries, not to eliminate their ability to impose capital punishment. (Of course, this solution was partial at best; it said nothing about the other decisions that prosecutors might make—such as allowing the defendant to plead guilty in exchange for a noncapital sentence—that would contribute to the problem.)

A different sort of response came in Powell's last month on the Court in a vote that otherwise seemed at odds with long-held beliefs. At issue was the constitutionality of using a victim-impact statement in death penalty proceedings. The victims in this case were Irvin and Rose Bronstein, an elderly couple who were robbed and murdered in their home in West Baltimore. The jury found that John Booth broke into their home to steal money to buy heroin and stabbed the Bronsteins so that they could not identify him. At the sentencing phase, the jurors learned of the reactions of the family. The son said his parents had been "butchered like animals." The daughter did not believe that "the people who did this could ever be rehabilitated." Both were depressed, fearful and suspicious for the first time in their lives, often sleepless at night and exhausted during the day. A granddaughter became hysterical whenever she saw dead animals on the road and even after counseling had to turn off the television when there were reports of violence. She also described how the bride and groom at a Bronstein family wedding had to leave their reception to go to the funeral. The social worker who compiled the report concluded, "as she talked to the family members that the murder of Mr. and Mrs. Bronstein is still such a shocking, painful, and devastating memory to them that it permeates every aspect of their daily lives. It is doubtful that they will ever be able to fully recover from this tragedy and not be haunted by the memory of the brutal manner in which their loved ones were murdered and taken from them."

Powell joined the liberals in preventing the prosecution from presenting this kind of evidence in capital cases. His opinion explained: "[In this case] the family members were articulate and persuasive in expressing their grief and the extent of their loss. But in some cases the victim will not leave behind a family, or the family members may be less articulate in describing their feelings. . . . Certainly the degree to which a family is willing and able to express its grief is irrelevant to the decision whether a defendant . . . should live or die." He was also troubled by the "implication that defendants whose victims were assets to the community are more deserving of punishment than those whose victims are perceived to be less worthy. Of course, our system of justice does not tolerate such distinctions."

The problem raised by the victim-impact statement was essentially the same problem revealed in the Baldus study of juror response to the victim's race, but with this key difference. It was inevitable that the jurors would know the victim's race, but it was not necessary that they should also know the victim's family, the impact of the killing on their lives, and the words they could find to express their suffering. To bring these facts into the courtroom was to introduce an *unnecessary* risk of arbitrariness. Almost certainly, information of this sort would exacerbate the problems revealed in the Baldus study. Powell therefore joined Brennan, Marshall, Blackmun, and Stevens in barring victim impact statements from death penalty proceedings.

In dissent Justice Antonin Scalia took Powell to task: "Many citizens have found one-sided and hence unjust the criminal trial in which a parade of witnesses comes forth to testify to the pressures beyond normal human experience that drove the defendant to commit his crime, with no one to lay before the sentencing authority the full reality of human suffering the defendant has produced. . . ." Scalia thought the jury was entitled to consider not only the defendant's "moral guilt" but also the "amount of harm he has caused to innocent members of society."

Those sentiments sounded like Lewis Powell, and it was surprising that he did not share them. At least in part, his vote reflected an increased sensitivity to the intrusion of class and race bias into capital sentencing. As he demonstrated in the case of Warren McCleskey, Powell was unwilling to strike down the death penalty because the system was not perfect. But as his vote against racial challenges to jurors and victim-impact statements showed, he was willing to require that the system for imposing sentence of death be made as nearly perfect as possible.

SECOND THOUGHTS

It is the most profound irony in Powell's service on the Supreme Court that the 1976 death penalty cases were a victory he came to regret. Several factors conspired to make Powell's attempt at a middle ground less and less tenable as the years went by.

First, the new constitutional law of capital punishment proved an extremely fertile ground for litigation. The question became not merely whether the defendant had been properly convicted of murder but also whether the additional and often complicated requirements for imposing a death sentence had been met. Aggravating factors had to be proved beyond a reasonable doubt. Mitigating factors had to be considered. Since the list of mitigations was not closed, virtually any circumstance thought favorable to the accused could be brought up. The focus of the trial spread out from the specific crime charged to the defendant's background and character. Family history, social setting, mental incapacities, and emotional instabilities—all became relevant in a death penalty proceeding.

As the issues multiplied, so did the opportunities for dispute and error. Was this evidence correctly kept out? Was that evidence properly admitted? Was the jury told precisely what use to make of it? Were the prosecutor's comments inflammatory or misleading? Was the defense lawyer competent in handling all these points? As the range of relevance expanded, the complexity of litigation increased.

More important, the objective changed. The traditional goal of litigation is to win. Effort is expended only where there is prospect of success. In death-penalty cases, winning means not losing. Victory is achieved whenever an execution is delayed. As Powell later testified to Congress, "the incentives in these cases are exactly the opposite of those involving imprisonment. The prisoner serving a term of years seeks to have his case reviewed speedily in the hope of gaining release. For the condemned inmate, delay is the overriding objective." The lawyers who litigated these cases often have deep moral and emotional loathing for capital punishment and are committed to expend every resource and exploit every opportunity to defeat or delay execution. Even if they eventually run out of time, they win months and years of life for their clients and extract a fearful price in time and energy from the society that tries to enforce capital punishment.

The result of these forces was a kind of legal guerrilla warfare, a rearguard action contesting every step from the courtroom to the grave. The process could stretch out for years. The case of Warren McCleskey is illustrative.

McCleskey was originally sentence to die in December 1978. In 1979 he appealed to the Georgia Supreme Court, which affirmed the conviction, and to the United States Supreme Court, which denied review. He then asked the state courts for a new trial and for state habeas corpus and presented some twenty-three claims of error, all of which were rejected. He again appealed to the Georgia Supreme Court and to the United States Supreme Court, both of which again turned him down. It was now 1981.

McCleskey then filed a habeas petition in federal court, raising among other issues the Baldus study of capital punishment in Georgia. Extensive hearings were held at this point, as they had been twice before. The petition was finally granted by the trial court in 1984 (on grounds unrelated to the Baldus study), but rejected by the Court of Appeals in 1985 and by the Supreme Court in 1987. McCleskey then filed a second state habeas petition and a second federal habeas petition. The federal court held further hearings in July and August of 1987 and in December of that year again ordered a new trial (again on grounds unrelated to the Baldus study). The Court of Appeals overturned this decision in 1989, and the Supreme Court agreed two years later, finally clearing the way for McCleskey's execution.

The case of Warren McCleskey was exceptional in twice commanding the attention of the Supreme Court but not in its complexity or duration. In death-penalty cases, the average delay between sentence and execution exceeded eight years. Despite the widespread legislative revival of capital punishment after *Furman* and the Supreme Court's approval in 1976, the next decade saw fewer than a hundred executions. Twenty times that many waited on death row, and even that figure was a tiny fraction of all convicted murderers. The proponents of capital punishment had won in the legislatures but not in the gas chamber. There the battle over the death penalty had reached a kind of stalemate. Each side made furious efforts to counter the exertions of the other in a drawn-out war of attrition only rarely punctuated by clear-cut victory or defeat.

For Powell, this war proved personally costly. As Circuit Justice for Georgia and Florida, he heard more than his share of last-minute requests for stays of execution. Of course, execution was always put off to allow for state-court appeals. After they were concluded, setting a date for execution would prompt a petition for review in federal court and a request that the execution be stayed pending consideration of that petition. The first such request was typically granted, but the second, third, or fourth might not be. Eventually, the lower courts would run out of patience, and the requests would make their way to the Supreme Court, often at the last hour, to ask the Circuit Justice to postpone the execution once again so that some new legal claim or argument could be considered. The possibility that these claims had merit grew increasingly remote as the process was repeated, but with life itself at stake, they had to be taken seriously.

The demand on Powell's attention was not unique to death-penalty cases. Imprisoned defendants by the thousand claimed mistake and injustice, but the Justices were ordinarily not much interested. They could not afford to be. In a nation of more than 200 million, they could not hope to review any significant number of criminal convictions or the countless claims of error they produced. Of necessity, Powell relied on the lower courts to see that justice was done. His interest and that of his colleagues was usually confined to cases that raised issues of national importance. But death was different. Here the demand of each prisoner that his (rarely her) claim be considered could not easily be ignored. In no other area was Powell drawn so deeply into the merits of particular cases. In no other context did the gritty realities of crime and death intrude so far into the calm reserve of the marble palace.

Not only were the requests for stay of execution personally troubling; they led to hard feelings among the Justices. A recurring pattern was to request a stay on the ground that some other case then pending in the Supreme Court might conceivably change the law in the defendant's favor. Often the connection between the two cases would be tenuous, but if the Justices could be persuaded to hold one case for the other, the march to the death chamber could be halted for the time being.

These cases exposed an odd quirk in the Court's procedures. The decision to grant review was governed by the rule of four, which meant that a minority of four Justices could force the Court to hear a case. The lesser decision to hold a case in abeyance while another was considered required only three votes. Any other action required a majority. That meant that four Justices sufficed to grant a petition and review a case on the merits, and three could hold it for later action, but five were required to stay an execution. Since there was obviously no point in hearing a defendant's appeal once he was dead, the stay was crucial.

Brennan and Marshall routinely voted to stay. Often they were joined by Blackmun and Stevens. If these four Justices voted to grant—that is, to schedule the case for full argument and decision—Powell would provide a fifth vote to stay the execution until the case could be heard. But what if there were only votes to hold? Did a minority of three Justices who wanted to hold a case for later review have the right to demand that the execution be stayed in the meantime?

Surprisingly, the answer was no. Conservative Justices felt that the liberals were abusing their power to hold a case solely in order to force a stay of execution. Liberals claimed that their right to hold a case for later decision was defeated by the majority's unwillingness to grant a stay. As one clerk recalled, "the war of the stay memos got very heated, even to the point of questions about bad faith."

The tug-of-war over stays of execution became public in the case of Ronald Straight. The state of Florida proposed to execute Straight for torture and murder. After exhausting his remedies in state court, Straight filed a federal habeas petition, which was denied by the trial court, by the appeals court, and on March 31, 1986, by the Supreme Court of the United States. The day before his scheduled execution, Straight filed a second habeas petition raising similar claims. The case came to Powell, who put it over for one day while his colleagues considered the matter and then voted to deny the stay. His refusal to provide the necessary fifth vote to hold Straight's petition caused Brennan to erupt in anger. "For the Court to deny a stay to a petitioner who is under sentence of death, and whose petition four Justices have determined to hold," was "new and gruesome." It was, said Brennan, "a wrong to which I may not be a silent witness."

Powell answered that Ronald Straight had been to the Supreme Court once before, that his claims had been fully and fairly considered, and that there was no reason to go into them again. The exchange revealed a growing bitterness about capital cases. Brennan continued to fight executions tooth and nail, while Powell grew increasingly impatient with the guerrilla warfare tactics of delay.

THE CONTROVERSY over repetitive review of capital cases followed Powell even into retirement. In June 1988, Chief Justice Rehnquist asked Powell to chair a committee to consider the problem and propose reforms. With him were the Chief Judges of the Fifth and Eleventh Circuits, which heard most of the nation's capital cases, and two experienced District Judges. A year later they completed their work.

According to the Powell committee, as it came to be known, the problems were three. First, death-penalty litigation was marred by unnecessary repetition and delay. That it took an average of eight years to complete one case was an indictment of the whole legal system. As Powell later explained to the Senate, "[t]he hard fact is that the laws of 37 states are not being enforced by the courts."

A related problem was the last-minute filings for stays of execution. The committee found that some "attorneys appear to have intentionally delayed filing until time pressures were severe. In most cases, [the] petitions are meritless, and we believe many are filed at the eleventh hour seeking nothing more than delay."

The third problem was a gap in the availability of counsel. Accused murderers could rarely afford to hire their own lawyers. Mostly they depended on lawyers appointed by the court to represent them. Every defendant had a constitutional right to counsel in the initial trial and appeal. Additionally, a statute authorized a lawyer for the first federal petition in a capital case. That left state collateral review, the round of litigation in between trial and appeal in state court and federal habeas corpus. For this stage, the defendant had no legal right to appointed counsel.

Powell proposed to address these problems by offering something to each side. If a state undertook to provide competent counsel for state postconviction proceedings (as well as at trial and on appeal), the prisoner would be barred from excessive delay and repetitive resort to the federal courts. Specifically, the defendant would have to begin post-conviction proceedings within six months of obtaining counsel and would be barred from second, third, or fourth federal habeas petitions challenging the sentence of death. As Powell explained: "Capital cases should be subject to one complete and fair course of collateral review in the state and federal system, free from the time pressure of impending execution, and with the assistance of competent counsel for the defendant. When this review has concluded, litigation should end."

The heart of Powell's proposal was the idea of the quid pro quo. As his clerk recalls, Powell wanted a solution "that would be perceived as a fair compromise" and thought "the only thing that would be politically acceptable on all sides" was a compromise that gave defendants better counsel in return for procedural bars on repetitive litigation. But this was a miscalculation. As the clerk came to believe, "Death penalty opponents did not want better proceedings, much less speedier ones. They wanted to make death penalty proceedings as costly and protracted as possible." From their point of view, anything that made the system better also made it worse.

The Powell committee's report was finished in August 1989 and transmitted to Chief Justice Rehnquist and to the Judicial Conference of the United States, which made the report public on September 21. The next day Rehnquist sent copies to the chairmen of the House and Senate Committees on the Judiciary. This seemingly innocuous act of transmittal to the House and Senate provoked a storm of protest and plunged the Powell committee's recommendations into public controversy.

The explosive reaction to the Chief Justice's act sprang from a tangled political history. Even before the Powell committee was created,

Senate conservatives were moving to restrict repetitive review of capital cases. When Rehnquist appointed the Powell committee, the Senators agreed to defer action *if* they were guaranteed a fast track for legislative consideration of the committee's proposals. Accordingly, a provision was added to a pending bill directing the chairman of the Judiciary Committee to introduce legislation within fifteen session days of receipt of the report and requiring committee action within the next sixty days. Thus the legislative skids were greased for turning the Powell committee's recommendations into law as soon as they were received.

That prospect dismayed many liberals. They thought the Powell committee too southern, too conservative, and too much influenced by its chairman's "markedly jaundiced attitude" toward federal habeas review of capital cases. To "counterbalance" that influence, the American Bar Association—to Powell's intense irritation—named its own committee to study the same problem. Its report, released in November 1989, was styled as a more liberal version of the Powell committee's approach, but in fact it was rather different. It would have done little to speed up the process and actually would have opened the doors for relitigation of certain claims unavailable under present law. Thus, when Rehnquist sent the Powell committee report to Congress and triggered the time limits for legislative consideration, he knew that there was a liberal alternative waiting in the wings and hoped to forestall it by acting quickly.

Moreover, Rehnquist acted against the wishes of the Judicial Conference. The Judicial Conference was composed of the Chief Judge and one District Judge from each judicial circuit, some of whom were hostile to the death penalty and not at all anxious to improve its administration. On the day that body released the Powell committee report, it also announced that the judges had voted to put the matter over until their next scheduled meeting in March 1990 in order to have more time to study the recommendations (and to compare them with the alternative expected from the ABA).

Although this decision disappointed Rehnquist, he "did not think it unreasonable" in light of the lack of time for study. Of course, some judges were "simply opposed to habeas reform in capital cases," and perhaps Rehnquist wanted to get around them. He consulted the statute, which gave "free-standing effect" to the report of the Powell committee without regard to whether it had been approved or even considered by the Judicial Conference. Armed with the power to force legislative consideration of the proposals no matter what the other judges thought, Rehnquist acted. He sent the report to Senate

Judiciary Committee Chairman Joseph Biden, who on hearing the objections of the Judicial Conference wrote Rehnquist to ask whether he had made a "final transmittal" for purposes of triggering the legislative timetable. Rehnquist replied that he had, and Biden was compelled to begin legislative consideration.

Powell thought Rehnquist's action a mistake, as events soon confirmed. Far from cutting off debate, as Rehnquist had hoped, the early transmittal outraged the liberal judges and fueled criticism of Powell's recommendations. Fourteen judges wrote the House and Senate committees asking for delay. Judge Stephen Reinhardt of the Ninth Circuit Court of Appeals took to the pages of the *Los Angeles Times* to protest what he called "the most radical curtailment of the writ of habeas corpus in our history." Other newspapers joined in, as *The New York Times* derided "the execution express," and the *Boston Globe* reported a "death penalty fumble." Quite apart from the grave issues at stake, these criticisms owed something to the suspicion that Rehnquist had tried to pull a fast one.

On October 16, 1989, the Powell committee proposals were offered as legislation not by Judiciary Chairman Joseph Biden but by his Republican counterpart, Senator Strom Thurmond. Biden introduced a more liberal alternative. Five months later, the Judicial Conference rejected key provisions of the Powell report in an action widely reported as a rebuff to the Chief Justice. No version of the Powell committee's report was enacted into law.

THE INABILITY OF JUDGES or Senators to agree on ways to restrict repetitive review of death sentences was no political accident. It reflected the underlying stalemate on the future of capital punishment. The truth was that streamlining review of capital cases—and in the process hastening executions—were goals that many did not share. For some, the redundancy, inefficiency, and protraction of death penalty litigation were desirable. If the process ground to a halt, so much the better. For others, squeamishness about the enterprise led to an unusual tolerance of evasion and delay. The problem was not so much the subversions of lawyers bent on preventing executions as it was a crisis of confidence in the courts. Beset by doubts and misgivings, judges acquiesced in delay. The crippling indeterminacy of death penalty litigation was the product not only of the extraordinary energies of defense counsel and of the open-endedness of legally relevant factors but also of a crack in the moral self-assurance of the judges before whom these cases were heard.

The result was near-paralysis. The Supreme Court had upheld capital punishment, but executions were rare. It became increasingly clear that the Stewart-Powell-Stevens compromise of 1976 had failed. The middle ground that Powell so dearly loved had been narrowed by decision and undermined by experience. All that remained was the thin edge of vacillation between two extremes. Eventually the choice between them would become unavoidable. Either the Court would condemn all capital punishment and be done with the anguish and expense of endless litigation, or it would accept death as a normal penalty for murder, to be imposed in the usual course and with all due speed. The system could not function if every case was a crisis. For capital punishment to succeed, death would have to become ordinary.

With Powell's retirement, there was little doubt which way the Court would jump. The aging liberals fought on, but their days of influence were past. With the arrival of Anthony Kennedy to take Powell's place, the dominant voice on the Supreme Court became that of Chief Justice Rehnquist. Four years later, after Justices Brennan and Marshall had followed Powell into retirement, columnist Edwin Yoder decried "The Rehnquist Ascendancy." The balance, Yoder wrote, began to shift "when Justice Lewis F. Powell Jr. retired. He had been the court's center of gravity in many ways, and he took with him into retirement his Virginian's sense of public responsibility and noblesse oblige." As Yoder saw it, the Court's new agenda was not conservative but radical.

In death-penalty cases, as in all others, Rehnquist knew his own mind. He rarely voted against capital punishment, consistently supported the right of the states to execute convicted murderers, and often complained of paralyzing delay. "What troubles me," Rehnquist said, "is that this Court . . . has made it virtually impossible for States to enforce with reasonable promptness their constitutionally valid capital punishment statutes." Even when the state won, it took "literally years and years and years."

With Powell's departure, Rehnquist soon had a solid majority to loosen the restraints on capital punishment. The Court upheld the execution of persons who were only sixteen years old when they killed, reaffirmed jury discretion in finding aggravating circumstances, and ruled that the defendant could be required to bear the burden of proof on the existence of mitigation. Powell's decisive vote against the use of victim-impact statements in death penalty proceedings was overturned four years later. Writing for the new majority, Rehnquist noted that the precedent has been "decided by the narrowest of margins and over spirited dissents" and was therefore subject to being overruled.

Moreover, the Rehnquist Court tackled the problem of endless litigation in capital cases without waiting for legislation. This was done by bringing repetitive habeas petitions under a preexisting rule against "abuse of the writ." Under this ruling, most second, third, or fourth habeas petitions would be more or less automatically denied. At one stroke, the Court accomplished the most controversial recommendation of the Powell committee without aid of legislation and without any offsetting obligation to improve and expand the availability of counsel.

The message was clear. The Court's careful balancing act was coming to an end. Powell's legacy of compromise and fine distinctions was giving way to a much harder line.

SURPRISINGLY, POWELL LEANED the other way. In a law review article published after his retirement, Powell surveyed the problems of "excessively repetitious litigation" in capital cases and in the closing sentence gave some hint of the author's gathering doubts: "If capital punishment cannot be enforced even where innocence is not an issue, and the fairness of the trial is not seriously questioned," Powell concluded, "perhaps Congress and the state legislatures should take a serious look at whether the retention of a punishment that is being enforced only haphazardly is in the public interest."

In an interview given in 1990, he went further. "[I]f I were in the state legislature, I would vote against capital punishment. There are approximately 2,500 people who have been convicted of murder and sentenced to death . . . , and there have been only about 125 to 130 executions. Capital punishment, though constitutional, is not being enforced. I think it reflects discredit on the law to have a major component of the law that is simply not enforced."

One year later, he took the final step. In conversation with the author in the summer of 1991, Powell was asked whether he would change his vote in any case:

> "Yes, *McCleskey v. Kemp.*"
> "Do you mean you would now accept the argument from statistics?"
> "No, I would vote the other way in any capital case."
> "In *any* capital case?"
> "Yes."
> "Even in *Furman v. Georgia?*"
> "Yes. I have come to think that capital punishment should be abolished."

Capital punishment, Powell added, "serves no useful purpose." The United States was "unique among the industrialized nations of the West in maintaining the death penalty," and it was enforced so rarely that it could not deter. Most important, the haggling and delay and seemingly endless litigation in every capital case brought the law itself into disrepute. "It brings discredit on the whole legal system, that the sentence upheld by the Supreme Court and adopted by more than thirty states can't be or isn't carried out."

For Powell, this was the heart of the matter. The death penalty should be barred, not because it was intrinsically wrong but because it could not be fairly and expeditiously enforced. The endless waiting, merry-go-round litigation, last-minute stays, and midnight executions offended Powell's sense of dignity and his conception of the majesty of the law. The spectacle of nonenforcement bred cynicism about the law's announced purposes and contempt for the courts that could not or would not carry them out. Better to have done with the whole ugly mess than to continue an indecent, embarrassing, and wasteful charade.

But this cannot be the whole story. It is easy to see that the death penalty cases would offend Powell's sensibilities, but it is not so obvious why he eventually came to oppose capital punishment. His reverence for the law could also have been salvaged by more rigorous enforcement. The path of Chief Justice Rehnquist—and increasingly of the Court he led—was not to abolish the death penalty but to see that it could be carried out. After all, the remedy for nonenforcement was more enforcement, and the cure for delay was dispatch.

Essentially, Rehnquist wanted to make death routine. This was not bloodthirst. No one enjoyed capital cases or wanted death sentences to be given casually or rashly or with anything less than scrupulous fairness. But the conservatives did want to get on with it. If it were to be done at all, better that it be done with reasonable speed and confidence—and without repeated intervention by the Supreme Court.

Why then did Powell disagree? Why did he side in the end with Brennan and Marshall rather than with his traditional allies? Why did the man who worked so hard to preserve the constitutionality of the death penalty in *Furman v. Georgia* come twenty years later to renounce it?

The answer lay partly in the bitter education of the cases. From them Powell learned that the death penalty would never be routinely applied. Lawyers would exploit every chance for delay, and judges would be sufficiently beset with doubts to give them frequent opportunity. This much he learned from himself. After fifteen years of capital cases, Powell knew firsthand their deadly hold on the judge's peace of mind. He knew how hard it was not to take a second, third, or fourth look at rejected claims, how easy it seemed to put the whole thing off for one more hearing, how much courage—or callousness—it took to treat death like any other penalty. Some judges could achieve that emotional distance, but Powell came to believe that the system as a whole would always be plagued by doubt and that doubting itself, it would inspire resentment and contempt.

Equally important was Powell's declining regard for judicial restraint. He came to the Court in 1972 with no fixed political ideology but with a strong belief in judicial self-discipline. Judges could not and should not decide what was wise, right, and proper but only what was unconstitutional. For the newly robed Justice, the death penalty was not an issue of personal morality or public policy, but a question of constitutional text and history. Powell concluded that the Constitution plainly contemplated capital punishment and on that point never really changed his mind. Three years after retirement, he could still say, "I don't think there is any possible argument to the contrary."

Powell did not change his view of the constitutional text and history, but came to think they did not matter—at least not after two decades of judicial inroads on the field. By 1991 the intent of the Framers seemed no longer decisive and not nearly so important as the actual experience under the new law of capital punishment. For the Court as a whole, the crucial step was taken in 1972, when, over Powell's objections, the Justices made death a constitutional issue. For Powell personally, the critical year was 1976, when he accepted *Furman* as a new beginning and set out to work with, rather than against, the constitutionalization of capital punishment. By 1991 those decisions had played themselves out in what Powell now saw as a failed experiment in judicial lawmaking.

Even if it had been possible to turn the clock back, Powell did not want to. The ideal of judicial restraint, which had seemed so clear and perfect to the novice judge, had been muddied by events. Powell's passionate plea in *Furman* that the Court should stay out of the death-penalty debate now seemed not only dated, but faintly unreal. Convinced as he now was that capital punishment would not work, Powell did not hesitate to invoke the Constitution. After all these years, he was ready to join Brennan and Marshall in holding it unconstitutional.

But by then it was too late. It was too late for Powell, who had left the Court in 1987, to make his views felt. It was too late for Brennan and Marshall, who followed soon after. And it was too late for Warren McCleskey, who on September 25, 1991, at two o'clock in the morning, after the usual flurry of last-minute maneuvers and delays, was finally put to death for the murder he committed thirteen years before.

CHAPTER XIV

BAKKE AND BEYOND

THE FACTS

He stood just under six feet tall, with blond hair, blue eyes, and the "Teutonic" appearance of his Norwegian ancestors. He was disciplined in body and mind. He ate wisely, ran daily, avoided vices, lived a healthy life. And he was obsessed by an ambition. More than anything else, Allan Bakke wanted to be a doctor.

His has been called "a storybook life of middle-class virtue." Son of a mailman and a schoolteacher, Bakke majored in mechanical engineering at the University of Minnesota. To help pay for his studies, he joined the Naval Reserve Officers Training Corps. After graduation, he discharged his four-year military obligation in the Marines, including a tour of duty in Vietnam, then went to work at a NASA research center in California. It was here that Bakke developed the desire to become a doctor.

Although already well settled with a good job and a growing family, Bakke set out to prepare himself for medical school. He took courses in chemistry and biology, and worked early mornings and late evenings to make up for lost time. Later he spent off hours as a candy striper, an "incongruous male figure" among the women volunteers. He "took tough assignments, often working late with the battered victims of car accidents or fights," and his passion for medicine grew and grew.

In 1972 and again in 1973, Allan Bakke applied to medical school, but without success. His age was a problem. At thirty-three, some thought him too old to begin the long course of study required to become a doctor. Despite good credentials, strong recommendations, and obvious dedication, Bakke was rejected everywhere he applied, including the new Medical School of the University of California at Davis. Bakke was particularly angry at Davis because the school reserved sixteen of the hundred places in the entering class for minorities. Blacks, Mexican-Americans, Asians, and American Indians could compete for these positions, but Bakke could not. "Applicants chosen to be our doctors," he protested to the admissions committee, "should be those presenting the best qualifications, both academic and personal. Most are selected according to this standard, but I am convinced that a significant fraction is judged by a separate criteria. I am referring to quotas, open or covert, for racial minorities. I realize that the rationale for these quotas is that they attempt to atone for past racial discrimination; but insisting on a new racial bias in favor of minorities is not a just situation."

After his second rejection, Bakke filed suit. He claimed that the minority admissions program violated his constitutional rights. Compared to the minority admittees, Bakke had better grades and higher scores on the important Medical College Admissions Test. His average on the four MCAT categories placed him a fraction below the ninetieth percentile of all those who took the test. The comparable figure for those admitted through the Davis special program was the thirty-fifth percentile in 1972 and thirtieth percentile in 1973. Given Bakke's age, no one could say for certain that he would have been admitted had the additional sixteen spaces been open to him, but it was clear that his chances had been reduced. The California Supreme Court sided with Bakke, and the University appealed.

On February 22, 1977, the Supreme Court of the United States agreed to hear the case. It raised the most important question of race relations since *Brown v. Board of Education* and the most divisive. Even terminology was disputed. Supporters of the Davis program called the issue "affirmative action," an upbeat term suggesting racial sensitivity. Opponents called it "reverse discrimination," an epithet suggesting racial prejudice in reverse. Some compromised on "benign discrimination," an oxymoron whose plausibility depended on one's point of view. Whatever the label, the question was starkly put: Were racial preferences *in favor of* minorities constitutionally equivalent to discrimination *against* those groups? If so, affirmative action plans throughout America would be struck down, and the recruitment of blacks into the learned professions would slow to a trickle. If not, race consciousness would be ratified, and the constitutional ideal of a color-blind society would be lost or at least indefinitely postponed. The stakes were high, and emotions ran higher, as the Supreme Court prepared to hear the case of *Regents of the University of California v. Allan Bakke.*

WHEN POWELL RETIRED from the Supreme Court, he said *Bakke* was his most important opinion. Few would disagree. The case fixed the future of racial preferences, and Powell's was the decisive view. Yet sixteen years earlier, when Powell came to the Senate Judiciary Committee to defend his fitness for appointment, no one bothered to ask about affirmative action. Not one question so much as touched on the issue, nor did any witness. The area of Powell's greatest impact as a Supreme Court Justice was ignored altogether in the confirmation of the nominee.

Race has been so long with us, and the problems seem so intractable that it is easy to forget how quickly the agenda has changed. In 1971 the law of race relations was just emerging from its preoccupation with the South. Less than a decade before, Sheriff "Bull" Connor had horrified national television audiences by turning attack dogs and fire hoses on peaceful demonstrators. Three civil rights workers were killed in Mississippi, and Governor Ross Barnett physically barred the door to keep James Meredith out of Ole Miss. Only seven years had passed since blacks won the right to sit at a white lunch counter or stay at a white motel. The Supreme Court's "root and branch" attack on the segregation of southern schools was only three years old, and busing had barely begun. Against the backdrop of these events, it took rare foresight, if not outright imagination, to see racial preferences *in favor of* blacks as a pressing national issue.

Yet even as the nation labored to make good its promise of equal rights, some came to believe that equal treatment was not enough. At least, neutral treatment was not enough. Given two centuries of oppression, equality required preference. The point was often made in the parable of the foot race. Imagine a foot race between two world-class runners. When the race begins, one runner falls behind, and the officials notice that he has weights attached to both ankles. They stop the race, order the runners to hold their places, and remove the weights. Now, is it fair to resume the race from the positions where the runners were stopped? Obviously not. Some correction is required.

That was the conviction that grew in the minds of many leaders, both black and white, in the late 1960s. By the end of that decade, affirmative action was underway. Not surprisingly, it first took hold and flourished in those autonomous outposts of progressive sensibility— the institutions of higher learning.

"Where are the black students?" wondered President Charles Odegaard as he watched the 1963 commencement exercises at the University of Washington. "Where are the black students?" Odegaard's university resolved to enroll more minorities. The law school's solution was a special admissions program for blacks, Chicanos, American Indians, and Filipinos. Thus it was that Marco DeFunis, like Allan

Bakke after him, came to see himself as a victim of reverse discrimination. DeFunis wanted to attend law school in Seattle, where he lived and planned to practice. Twice he applied to the University of Washington, and twice he was rejected by an admissions program that considered minorities separately. Of the thirty-seven minority applicants accepted in the second year, all but one had numerical qualifications lower than DeFunis, and thirty fell below the line where most applications were summarily rejected. As would later be true for Allan Bakke, no one could say for certain that DeFunis would have been accepted had there been no special admissions, but he clearly had been treated differently on account of race.

DeFunis filed suit in state court. He won at trial and took his place in the first-year class at the University of Washington Law School. When that judgment was reversed on appeal, DeFunis took his complaint to the Supreme Court of the United States, which allowed him to stay in school while his case was pending. This seemingly insignificant accommodation turned *DeFunis v. Odegaard* into a famous nondecision. By the time the case was argued, on February 26, 1974, its protagonist had just begun his last semester of law school. The university had said that it would not kick him out in the middle of a semester, even if it won the litigation. Since DeFunis had now entered his final term, there was no longer any concrete dispute between him and the university. Of course, they still disagreed on the general policy of minority admissions, but Marco DeFunis would graduate one way or the other. The case was therefore dismissed as moot. The brief, unsigned opinion gave no hint of the Justices' view of the merits. Marco DeFunis got his law degree, but three years of litigation had shed no light on the constitutionality of affirmative action.

Several Justices thought the Court should address the merits, but only William O. Douglas did so. Douglas's opinion was as defiantly idiosyncratic as its author. On the one hand, and to the astonishment of many, this most liberal of Justices condemned even benign discrimination as unconstitutional. DeFunis, he said, had the right "to have his application considered on its individual merits in a racially neutral manner." That preferences might be needed to bring minorities into the learned professions did not matter. "The purpose of the University of Washington cannot be to produce black lawyers for blacks, Polish lawyers for Poles, Jewish lawyers for Jews, Irish lawyers for Irish. It should be to produce good lawyers for Americans. . . ." Individual merit was the only issue, and race an illegitimate concern.

On the other hand, Douglas disparaged the usual ways of assessing individuals. He lashed out at the standardized tests on which most blacks scored poorly. The tests might be culturally biased. More than that, Douglas simply hated standardization. He railed against the "mental strait-jacket" of multiple-choice testing, claiming that it did not work for the "strong-minded, nonconformist, unusual, original, or creative" individual—such as William O. Douglas. He wanted admissions decisions that were racially neutral, but at the same time profoundly sensitive to the cultural variation among individuals. Whether such judgments were possible or, if they were, whether they would produce any appreciable number of black lawyers, were questions Douglas could not answer. He called for a new trial on whether racial minorities should be exempt from conventional testing.

DeFunis settled absolutely nothing. In fact, the Court's evasion fueled debate. Proponents were alarmed by the apparent defection of Douglas, and opponents saw a prospect of sweeping victory. All eyes turned to the litigation horizon and converged there on the aggrieved and determined figure of Allan Bakke.

BAKKE HAD BEEN WAITING. He had already contacted a lawyer, one Reynold H. Colvin, who had been in the papers for successfully challenging an affirmative action plan in San Francisco. When *DeFunis* fizzled out, Colvin filed suit. He could have gone to federal court but chose instead the Superior Court for Yolo County, California. That court's ruling against racial preferences catapulted Bakke into national prominence. From this point on, the case became a cause célèbre. The California Supreme Court opted to hear the matter without waiting for intermediate appellate review and on September 16, 1976, ruled in Bakke's favor. In San Francisco, two thousand people marched in protest. Emotions ran so high that they spawned bizarre conspiracy theories about the litigation. Some civil rights activists charged that the University was taking a fall, that it was actually trying to lose the case in order to rid itself of an unwanted program. The nation was treated to the curious spectacle of propreference demonstrators urging the Regents of the University of California *not* to appeal the greatest judicial defeat ever dealt to affirmative action.

The opposition of civil rights leaders to Supreme Court review had many origins. In part, it reflected sensible tactical concerns. The rigidity of the Davis program made it hard to defend. Perhaps a better test case could be found. There was also worry that the factual record developed at trial was too skimpy to support a strong defense of affirmative action, although the Supreme Court, when it chooses, readily looks beyond the limitations of the record. More fundamentally, there was frustration that the beneficiaries of affirmative action were not directly represented in the *Bakke* litigation. The parties to the case were Allan Bakke and the University of California. Bakke attacked racial preferences, and the University defended them—but not necessarily on the grounds that most appealed to civil rights lawyers. In particular, the University had little interest in unearthing evidence of past discrimination *against* blacks that might justify the current preferences in their favor. These and other anxieties erupted in mistrustful second-guessing of the University's litigation strategy and bitter criticism of white "arrogance" and "self-righteousness" in ignoring minority concerns.

Some of these charges had merit; others did not. But more important than the specific complaints about trial tactics were the fears and suspicions they exposed. A vast gulf in perceptions divided the supporters of affirmative action. University officials and their lawyers thought their motives unfairly impugned by hysterical critics. Civil rights leaders saw the *Bakke* litigation as yet another example of black powerlessness and white control.

Ultimately, the Regents had no choice. The California court had not only ordered the admission of Allan Bakke; it had banned race as a factor in admissions to all state schools. The state university system could neither live with nor evade this pronouncement. If enforced, it would virtually eliminate blacks from state-supported higher education. Inevitably, the Regents voted to seek Supreme Court review.

Inside the Court, there was a surprising split on whether the case should be heard. Brennan, who in *DeFunis* had chided his colleagues for straining to rid themselves of the dispute, now wanted to duck. He worried that the explicit reservation of sixteen spaces for special admissions made the Davis plan especially unattractive and wanted to wait for better facts. Brennan was supported by Marshall and eventually by Blackmun. Burger also voted no, as he was happy to avoid a divisive race case. Against this view were the obvious importance of the issue and the enormous impact, in California and elsewhere, of letting the state court judgment stand. On February 22, 1977, the Court agreed to hear the case and scheduled argument for that fall.

THE BRIEFS

The Court that agreed to hear *Bakke* was not the same Court that had ducked *DeFunis*. The only Justice openly to have declared himself in the earlier case was now gone. Douglas had been succeeded by John Paul Stevens, whose position on affirmative action was unknown. But then, neither was anyone else's. According to one supposedly inside account, Thurgood Marshall predicted that the "Nixon four" plus White would line up against the Davis program, while Brennan thought that everyone, except perhaps the Chief Justice, was open to persuasion.

Outside the Court, no one was better situated to assess the probabilities than the lawyers for the University of California. After the defeat in state court, the University brought in legal reinforcements. The Regents hired Paul J. Mishkin, a Berkeley law professor and a nationally recognized expert on the Constitution and the federal courts, as special counsel for the *Bakke* litigation. Mishkin then brought in Jack Owens, a brilliant junior colleague who had clerked for Powell at the time of *DeFunis*. At that time, Powell had been deeply troubled by racial preference in admissions but had been inclined to find a way to allow it. Together, Mishkin and Owens knew as much as could be known about the views of Powell and the other Justices. Still, they had precious little to go on. No sitting Justice had taken a public stand, and there was no way to be sure that the fragmentary views voiced at the time of *DeFunis* would survive the changes of time and circumstance. Mishkin and Owens heard supposedly expert predictions ranging from seven–two in their favor to six–three against. No one really knew.

Their best guess was that Brennan and Marshall would support affirmative action and probably White would too. Burger, Rehnquist, and perhaps Stewart would be against. If these predictions panned out, the balance of power lay with three votes. Blackmun, Powell, and Stevens would decide the issue, and no one could say which way they would go. The question was wide-open.

Mishkin and Owens therefore set out to persuade the middle. Owens in particular kept his eye on Powell. He had a hunch that Powell might go their way, as he had been tentatively inclined to do at the time of *DeFunis*. Thinking the *DeFunis* case moot, Powell never came to rest on the merits, but at Conference he had "tentatively" expressed the view, as recorded in Justice Douglas's notes, that although he was "doubtful of the educational policy" behind the University of Washington Law School's minority admissions, he was inclined to think race a "factor that can lawfully [be] considered." If Powell could be persuaded to take the same line here, perhaps the University could prevail; without him, affirmative action would almost surely lose. On the other side, Reynold Colvin labored to protect Allan Bakke's future in medicine.

Both camps were inundated by a flood of briefs from so-called friends of the court, including all sorts of groups that wished to be heard. Establishment opinion lined up behind the university. The ABA, the ACLU, the NAACP, the Association of American Law Schools, the Association of American Medical Colleges, several universities, and the National Council of Churches supported affirmative action. Opposition was led by prominent Jewish groups, including the American Jewish Committee and the Anti-Defamation League of B'nai B'rith.

Most controversial by far was the brief of the United States. The federal government had its own affirmative action programs, which were put at risk by the lower court's decision in *Bakke*. Protecting that interest was the task of the Solicitor General of the United States, a post then held by its second black occupant (the first was Thurgood Marshall), former appeals court judge Wade McCree. He assigned the brief to Frank Easterbrook, a brilliant and politically conservative young lawyer from the University of Chicago. (In 1985 President Reagan appointed Easterbrook, then thirty-six, to the Seventh Circuit.) Easterbrook concluded that, whatever might be said of affirmative action generally, the strict set-aside of sixteen places was *un*constitutional, and he wrote the brief accordingly. When word leaked out that the United States would oppose the Davis program, the proverbial all hell broke loose. Secretary of HEW Joe Califano met with McCree, Easterbrook, and Deputy Solicitor General Lawrence Wallace to insist that the position be changed. Califano wrote President Carter that the draft brief was "bad law, and pernicious social policy" and warned that "you will make the most serious mistake of your administration in domestic policy to date if you permit the Justice Department to file the *Bakke* brief" in its present form. By this time, the White House staff was involved, and on September 12, 1977, the matter was discussed by the cabinet. Both inside and outside the government, pressure mounted to change the brief. Vice President Walter Mondale and Carter aides Stuart Eizenstadt and Robert Lipshutz carried that message to McCree's boss, Attorney General Griffin Bell. Meanwhile, the Congressional Black Caucus warned Carter that he would "discredit his presidency in the eyes of history" by coming out against racial quotas.

Most of these pressures reportedly never reached McCree. They were intercepted by Griffin Bell, who received the various directives and suggestions and simply put them aside. So while the politicians fussed and fumed, McCree made up his own mind. The most influential voice came from outside the administration. McCree's law school contemporary and former Secretary of Transportation William Coleman came to see him. Coleman believed that the Davis program was far less important than the general question of judicial support for affirmative action. It would be a calamity, Coleman argued, if the California court was affirmed. Better to accept the defects in the Davis program than to risk damage on the larger issue.

McCree agreed. He told his drafting team—Wallace and Easterbrook from the Solicitor General's office and Drew Days and Brian Landsberg from the Civil Rights Division—to change the brief. The final product bore "all the scars of its tortured creation" and pleased almost no one. Abrupt shifts in emphasis marred a document that in any event failed to come to grips with the real issue. On the one hand, the brief endorsed what it called "minority-sensitive" admissions. But when it came to the specifics of the Davis program, with its explicit set-aside of sixteen spaces and its inclusion of Asians among the beneficiaries, the brief backed off. It found various reasons for suggesting that the case be remanded to the lower courts so that the operation of the Davis program, which was really quite well understood, could be investigated further. This gutless waffle persuaded no one. Powell dismissed the government's argument as "simply out in left field." Indecision and compromise had squandered whatever influence the administration might have had.

AMID THE WELTER of contention from all sides, two positions clearly emerged. Both were intellectually coherent, legally tenable, and morally defensible. They were also diametrically opposed.

On one side was the ideal of color-blindness. Mr. Justice Harlan said it first—not the John Marshall Harlan whom Powell knew, but his grandfather of the same name, dissenting in 1896 from the infamous *Plessy v. Ferguson* decision approving "separate but equal" accommodations. "Our Constitution is color-blind," thundered the great dissenter, "and neither knows nor tolerates classes among citizens. . . . It is, therefore, to be regretted that this high tribunal, the final expositor of the fundamental law of the land, has reached the conclusion that it is competent for a State to regulate the enjoyment by citizens of their civil rights solely upon the basis of race." These words leapt across the decades to rebuke race-consciousness and warn the Court of repeating past mistakes.

The early civil rights movement cast itself in the same terms. From the steps of the Lincoln Memorial in 1963, Martin Luther King, Jr., dreamed that "my four little children will one day live in a nation where they will not be judged by the color of their skin, but by the content of their character." The NAACP had condemned race-consciousness, as did Thurgood Marshall. In the long litigation campaign against segregation, he insisted: "There is no understandable factual basis for classification by race, and . . . all courts agree that if there is no rational basis for the classification, it is flat in the teeth of the Fourteenth Amendment." The Supreme Court had been told the same thing. In an early brief attacking segregation, solicited by Marshall and signed by 187 law professors, the Court heard again that the Constitution commanded color-blindness. "Laws which give equal protection are those which make no *discrimination* because of race in the sense that they make no *distinction* because of race," wrote the professors. "Reasonable classifications may be made, but one basis of classification is completely precluded; for the Equal Protection clause makes racial classifications unreasonable per se."

Racial preferences jeopardized this ideal. "If the Constitution prohibits exclusion of blacks and other minorities on racial grounds," said Yale law professor Alexander Bickel, "it cannot permit the exclusion of whites on similar grounds; for it must be the exclusion on racial grounds which offends the Constitution and not the particular skin color of the person excluded." For at least a generation, Bickel continued, the lessons of the great decisions of the Supreme Court and of contemporary history had been the same: "[D]iscrimination on the basis of race is illegal, immoral, unconstitutional, inherently wrong, and destructive of democratic society. Now this is to be unlearned and we are told that this is not a matter of fundamental principle but only a matter of whose ox is gored."

On the other side was a vision of racial justice that was not color-blind but fully sighted. Supporters of affirmative action saw the need for race-conscious remedies to correct a race-conscious past. "[T]here can be no blinking," wrote McGeorge Bundy, "the enormous and unique set of handicaps which our whole history, right up to the present, has imposed on those who are not white." To begin now a fastidious color-blindness would be a cruel joke, a high-minded way of refusing to right past wrongs. Centuries of oppression required compensation. As the wrong itself was race-based, so also was the cure. Racial preferences were simply compensatory justice.

But compensation for whom? And for how long? Everyone agreed that compensation was owed to an individual identified as a victim of discrimination. A minority worker not hired on account of race deserved not only a job but also back pay. But what about other minority workers who applied for work at a later time and were not themselves discriminated against? Did they also deserve preference? Was each generation of whites responsible for the sins of its forebears? Did compensation mean that the long, slow grind of oppression visited on slaves and freedmen should be offset by reparations to their descendants? If so, racial preferences might last forever.

These implications troubled and divided the supporters of affirmative action, but most accepted that the past could not be set right. Racial preferences were urged, not to repay the dead, but to assure justice to the living and to open American society to the advancement of all. No one could argue that this generation of blacks had been free from discrimination and disadvantage. Nor was it possible to integrate the professional classes without taking race into account. Therefore, it was right to prefer minorities—at least for now, at least until the legacy of racism could be overcome. Only by that means could the nation move forward toward the ideal of a racially just society.

AN ENTIRELY DIFFERENT justification for racial preferences emerged from political theory. Legal scholars found support for judicial tolerance of minority preferences in their conception of the proper role of the courts in a democratic society. Understanding this point requires a brief look at the prevailing theories of judicial review.

A large problem in American constitutionalism is how to square judicial review with popular self-government. On the one hand, the Constitution set up a representative democracy. On the other hand, it gave judges the power to upset the results of representative democracy by declaring laws unconstitutional. And life-tenured federal judges are about as well insulated from popular control as the Framers could contrive to make them. Thus, the Supreme Court functions as a decidedly undemocratic institution in a nation committed in the main to majority rule.

Generations of judges and scholars have pondered this inconsistency. One answer (among others) is that the courts should defer to political democracy, *unless* there is a good reason not to. A good reason would be to correct some systemic unfairness in the way democracy is practiced. In this view, judges should abide by the results of the political process (even those they find disagreeable), *except* where the process itself is skewed or distorted. In that event, the courts should step in to see that everyone is treated fairly. Under this reasoning, the courts have a special duty toward those "discrete and insular minorities" who are unable to fend for themselves in majoritarian politics. These groups may be excluded by prejudice from effective participation in the political process. When that happens, the courts should look very carefully to see that the excluded groups are not mistreated.

That, at any rate, is the argument that animates much of constitutional law. It applies most clearly to blacks, who were long denied access to political power. On this theory, therefore, the courts are justified in subjecting to the most exacting scrutiny any law or practice that *dis*advantages racial minorities.

But the argument does not apply in reverse. There is no parallel justification for heightened judicial scrutiny when laws disadvantage those in control. The majority can take care of itself. It does not need the special judicial protection accorded "discrete and insular minorities." The faculty members who approved special admissions at Davis were overwhelmingly white, as were the legislators who permitted such programs and the judges who were asked to overrule them. A society so dominated by whites, so runs the argument, does not need special judicial protection of their best interests.

Under this theory, discrimination against minorities and preferences in their favor are not at all the same thing—at least not in terms of the appropriate judicial response. Discrimination against minorities triggers the judiciary's special concern for those historically unable to protect themselves in the political process. Minority preferences, by contrast, are most unlikely to be products of a political process corrupted by prejudice against whites. The Court can therefore take a relaxed and tolerant view of laws and practices that favor racial minorities. Minority preferences should be allowed whenever there is a good reason for them.

And there were good reasons for wanting to see minorities in the learned professions. Black doctors and lawyers might better serve black communities. In *DeFunis* Justice Douglas had insisted that the purpose of a law school "cannot be to produce black lawyers for blacks, Polish lawyers for Poles, Jewish lawyers for Jews, and Irish lawyers for Irish. It should be to produce good lawyers for Americans. . . ." Well, yes, but many minority communities simply did not have enough lawyers, or doctors either, to meet their needs. The state of black medical care was particularly depressing—higher infant mortality, higher maternal mortality, lower life expectancy than whites. These dismal prospects were almost certainly caused in part by a lack of doctors. In 1970 there was one physician for every 649 persons in the United

The Justices of the Supreme Court, 1972. *From left to right:* Blackmun,
Stewart, Powell, Marshall, Rehnquist, White, Douglas, Burger, and Brennan.
(National Geographic Society; Collection of the Supreme Court of the United States)

Powell in chambers, 1977. *(Okamoto Photographs, Inc., Collection of the Supreme Court of the United States)*

President-elect Ronald Reagan and Vice President–elect George Bush visit the Supreme Court, 1980. Chief Justice Warren Burger stands between them. *(Bob Weaver; Collection of the Supreme Court of the United States)*

With Justice Byron White, 1983. *(Collection of the Supreme Court of the United States)*

Thanksgiving, 1981. *Children, from left:* Josephine Powell Smith, Lewis III, Molly Powell Sumner, and Penny Powell Carmody. *(Collection of the Supreme Court of the United States)*

Justice William H. Rehnquist with
Molly Powell Sumner and her chil-
dren, Ryland and Kendall, 1984.
*(Collection of the Supreme Court of the
United States)*

With Justice Sandra Day O'Connor, 1982.
(Collection of the Supreme Court of the United States)

Justices William J. Brennan, Jr.,
and Thurgood Marshall, 1985.
*(The Washington Post/Ray Lustig,
photographer; reprinted with permission)*

Justices Brennan, White, Marshall, Blackmun, Powell, Rehnquist, Stevens,
and O'Connor at the Hugo Black stamp ceremony, 1986. *(Collection of the
Supreme Court of the United States)*

The Supreme Court in Powell's last term. *Seated, from left to right:* Justices Marshall, and Brennan, Chief Justice Rehnquist, Justices White and Blackmun. *Standing, from left to right:* Justices O'Connor, Powell, Stevens, and Scalia.
(National Geographic Society; Collection of the Supreme Court of the United States)

Farewell to the Supreme Court, June 26, 1987.
(Wide World Photos; Collection of the Supreme Court of the United States)

Lewis and Jo at home in Richmond, August 1987.
(Richmond Newspapers; Collection of the Supreme Court of the United States)

States. In the same year, the ratio of black physicians to the black population was one in 4,248. Of course, white doctors could serve minority patients, but would they? Would they go to the ghettos, to the barrios, to the rural backwaters where medical care was needed most? For that matter, would minority doctors? Perhaps not, but surely minority professionals would be more likely than whites to address the special needs of the minority community.

Then, too, minority professionals might serve as role models for the young. Seeing black adults in positions of prestige and responsibility might enlarge the vision of black youth. Aspiration is fueled by a sense of possibility. And the possibilities suggested by black doctors and lawyers (and bankers and teachers and executives and engineers) are especially potent if close to home. Affirmative action to recruit minorities into the learned professions might prime the pump of young ambition and speed progress toward a truly integrated society.

These and other reasons were advanced to show that discrimination against minorities and preferences in their favor were *not* the same thing. They differed in moral content, in relation to the political process, and in responsiveness to social needs. Arguably, therefore, they differed in constitutionality. The Fourteenth Amendment guaranteed to every person "the equal protection of the laws." It did not demand the false equality of treating differently situated persons the same. It did not demand that the law ignore what Coretta Scott King termed "the obstacles and scars of hundreds of years of racism," or the inequalities they produced. On the contrary, the Constitution should allow minority preferences in pursuit of true equality. As Dr. Joseph E. Lowery, president of the Southern Christian Leadership Conference, saw it: "If parents of five children recognize that two of them are seriously ill, it is not an injustice to the other three to administer medical preference to those who are infected."

THIS, THEN, WAS THE CASE for minority preferences. More precisely, it was the case for judicial tolerance of minority preferences. The claim, it bears repeating, was not that affirmative action is always desirable or wise, but only that it is constitutionally permissible. Supporters called for a hands-off policy by the courts. Judges should not police admissions at Davis or elsewhere. They should allow educators to do as they thought best, without judicial interference, so long as they did not discriminate against minorities. Minority preferences would be allowed, but of course not compelled.

Yet against this reasoning stood the ideal of color-blindness and the long and sordid history of valuing persons by their race. If, as Bickel urged, all racial classifications were illegal, immoral, and inherently wrong, then all should be judged by the same standard. Absent the most extraordinary circumstances, any racial preference should be struck down.

Persons of good sense and good will lined up on both sides. Each camp claimed high moral purpose. Each invoked the Constitution to support its view of racial justice, but the conceptions were diametrically opposed. The choice was stark, and the stakes enormous. Ultimately, the decision lay with the "nine old men" of the Supreme Court.

A PRIVATE DECISION

On Monday morning, July 25, 1977, Bob Comfort left his apartment in northeast Washington and walked up Constitution Avenue to the Supreme Court. He skirted the north side of the building and went in the employees' entrance, tucked away under the broad steps that rise from the plaza facing the Capitol to the great front portico promising "Equal Justice Under Law." He was met by a uniformed guard, who found Comfort's name on the list of law clerks and sent him upstairs. Within just a few days, the guards would learn the faces, if not the names, of all the new clerks. Then they could pass unquestioned through the gates that bar the tourists from the inner sanctum.

As this was Comfort's first day, he was shown to the marshal's office and met there by Sally Smith, who took him past the barricade and down the hall to the Powell chambers. The Justice was in Richmond, but Comfort already knew what to do. Some weeks earlier, the new clerks had held a telephone lottery to divide up the cases for the coming term. Comfort had won first pick and had chosen *Bakke*, "by light years the most interesting case that term." As it happened, the choice cost him a week's vacation. He had left his appeals court clerkship on July 15, intending to spend two weeks on the Jersey shore before coming to Powell. But a co-clerk called to say that the amicus briefs were pouring in. The stack of documents on Comfort's desk was over a foot high and growing fast. Perhaps Bob would like to get started? Comfort gathered his energies and showed up the following Monday to begin work.

He was in many respects an ideal clerk. Superbly educated at Princeton and Harvard Law School, Comfort was reserved, sober, mature, and meticulous—qualities well liked by Powell. Comfort was also open-minded. He had studied *DeFunis* at the Harvard Law School but held no firm view one way or the other on the constitutionality of affirmative action. To the extent that a young lawyer of his time could remain emotionally uncommitted on so divisive an issue, Comfort had done so. He was open to argument.

But, as Comfort soon found out, his boss was not. Powell had already read and reread the briefs, underlining key points and adding marginal comments. He had mulled the general issue and studied the arguments and knew what he would do. Rather, he knew what he would *not* do. Powell had no clear idea of what the Supreme Court should say about affirmative action, but he already had a firm conviction about what it should *not* say. It should neither condemn affirmative action categorically nor approve it unreservedly. Faced with two intellectually coherent, morally defensible, and diametrically opposed positions, Powell chose neither.

On the one hand, Powell concluded, it was simply "too late in the day" to forbid all racial preferences. Outlawing affirmative action would be "a disaster for the country." Even if he were driven into an intellectual corner, Powell would find a way to allow some affirmative action, under some circumstances, at least for the time being. On the other hand, said Powell, it would be equally disastrous to give carte blanche for racial preferences. Public institutions would be vulnerable to the demands of special interests. Benefits would be carved up among competing minorities in an ugly game of racial politics. Powell wanted to allow some affirmative action, but also to constrain it, to keep it in check so that race-consciousness would not become the norm. He wanted to preserve for the future the ideal of a color-blind society.

On the surface, at least, Powell's support for affirmative action was surprising. He had never shown particular concern for racial issues. The subjugation of blacks in the South became an issue for Powell only when it was thrust upon him. Throughout the 1950s and 1960s, he did no more than was required to hasten desegregation. On the great question of busing, he resolutely opposed minority aspirations. If Powell's interlocutors on the Senate Judiciary Committee had pressed him for a commitment to support racial preferences for minorities (which is difficult to imagine), they likely would have been met by incomprehension. For this unresisting heir to the traditions of white supremacy to have endorsed *reverse* discrimination would have been, at the time, inconceivable. Yet on the Supreme Court, he did just that. Even as early as *DeFunis*, Powell was groping toward allowing some racial preferences, and in *Bakke* he explicitly embraced that view.

At this defining moment, Powell was most true to his essential character as a pragmatic conservative. He accepted affirmative action for the same reason that, twenty years earlier, he had accepted *Brown v. Board of Education*—because it was necessary. This was the great point at which Mishkin and Owens hammered away in their brief. Race-consciousness in admissions was the *only* way to enroll minorities in significant numbers. As they said, "The outcome of this controversy will decide for future decades whether blacks, Chicanos and other insular minorities are to have meaningful access to higher education and real opportunities to enter the learned professions. . . ." Banning racial preferences would virtually eliminate minority enrollment and maintain the professions as perpetual white enclaves. Of this, Powell was convinced. Preferential admissions were distasteful, unseemly, perhaps even unfair, but they were also vital to an integrated society. There was no other way.

This pragmatism was reinforced by Powell's innate conservatism. His was not the zealous conservatism of a right-wing reformer but the instinctive caution of a born pessimist. He dreaded chaos and upheaval. Law should serve the cause of social stability, and by the time of *Bakke*, social stability required affirmative action. Had the Supreme Court confronted the question in 1955 or 1965 or even 1970, it might have disapproved racial preferences without forcing any radical change in current practice. By 1977 that was no longer true. Affirmative action had become entrenched throughout the land and especially in the universities. To have rejected it altogether would have meant a wrenching reversal. The prospect of this crisis made Powell more than ever reluctant to say no.

Finally, there may have been a subtle psychological link between Powell's southern background and his support for racial preferences. On one level, affirmative action marked an outright reversal of the racial attitudes of the Old South. But in another sense, it seemed almost a natural outgrowth. Both positions shared a tradition of white paternalism toward disadvantaged blacks. For Powell, as for many white southerners, the progression from *Brown* to *Bakke* brought a revolution in announced conviction, an about-face in articulated belief. Yet remnants of old attitudes survived. Justice Powell still had a gentleman's sense of responsibility for the less fortunate and a southerner's instinct for paternalism toward blacks. No southerner could readily deny that blacks needed help, as the excesses of the past and the region were too familiar to ignore. The upper-class sense of noblesse oblige and the southerner's assumption of white control and responsibility conspired to the same conclusion: Racial justice required racial preference. Thus did the habits of mind of Powell's southern upbringing ease his way toward a new perspective. He had that much less to unlearn.

On the other hand, Powell was not ready to accept the Davis program as a blueprint for the future. He was offended by its rigidity, by the fixed number of spaces formally set aside for minorities and dealt with completely separately. With no direct comparison between minority applicants and others, the victims of affirmative action would fade into the background. The harm done Allen Bakke and Marco DeFunis would become routine, and the sharp sense of regret that should attend any distinction based on race would be dulled with repetition. Special admissions programs would become entrenched bureaucracies, and minorities would come to regard them as perpetual entitlements. What Powell feared most was permanence. For him, racial preferences were a short-term response to a pressing need. Yet unqualified Supreme Court approval of the explicit racial set-aside practiced at Davis might lock in such programs forever.

This concern was bound up with the distinction between a goal and a quota. As usual, partisans struggled over vocabulary. "Goal" was an upbeat term suggesting aspiration toward an ideal. "Quota" was an epithet focusing on the curtailment of opportunity. There was much debate in the briefs and elsewhere over whether the Davis program could properly be characterized as a goal (because it was intended to aid minorities, not to disadvantage whites) or a quota (because it reserved a fixed number of spaces). In principle, the distinction was unimportant. If race-based admissions were legitimate, there could be nothing wrong in specifying a numerical target. And if race-based admissions were illegitimate, the absence of numerical target would not make them less so. That race was "only one factor" in the admissions decision, as the University repeatedly emphasized, could not matter if that one factor was unconstitutional.* In theory, the Constitution's tolerance of minority preferences should not turn on whether race counted a little or a lot. The crucial question was whether it should count at all.

Though Powell halfway recognized the flimsiness of this distinction, he was drawn to it nonetheless. The difference was not one of princi-

---

* One need only imagine what would happen if racial discrimination *against* blacks were justified on the ground that race was "only one factor" in the admissions process, that there was no fixed limit on black admissions but only a preference for whites in close cases. That argument would be dismissed out of hand. Discrimination against blacks is unconstitutional, whether the disadvantage is partial or complete.

ple but of practice. A flexible goal and a fixed quota might be alike in theory but not in consequence. They differed in the way that Powell cared most about—durability. An unspecified goal could be expanded or contracted without public fanfare. Informal programs could be cut back as circumstances allowed. Because Powell saw racial preferences not as morally right, but as socially necessary, he wanted to limit them as much as possible. An indefinite commitment might in the future be more easily undone. A fixed quota, by contrast, would draw a bright line from which any retreat would be hotly contested. Explicit racial quotas went a long way toward permanent entitlements, and Powell opposed them for that reason.

He was also troubled by the question of who should benefit. The Davis program included not only blacks and Chicanos but also Asians. This stuck in Powell's craw. Certainly, Asians had been victims of discrimination. The internment of Japanese-Americans during World War II was only the most egregious demonstration. But Asians were academically successful without special programs, as the experience at Davis clearly showed. In the first five years, Davis had taken seventy students through minority admissions. Of these, eleven were Asians. During the same period, an additional forty-eight minority students were accepted through the regular admissions process. Of these, forty-one were Asians. There was no present necessity for affirmative action for Asians, yet they too were favored by the Davis program.

And if Asians were to be compensated for past discrimination, what about other groups who had been mistreated—Jews, for example, who had often faced invisible ceilings on enrollment at prestigious universities; or women, who had struggled to escape the confinement of social expectations? Were they now to be given special advantages in an attempt to balance the historical record? And there were others—Irish, Italians, Eastern Europeans—who also had suffered discrimination. Could they now get on the list? That Asians were included in the Davis program called to mind all the other groups who could make similar claims for special treatment. Faced with potentially limitless demands for compensation for past wrongs, Powell recoiled from the whole idea.

In fact, Powell thought that the inclusion of Asians called into question the integrity of the whole Davis program. The system of preferences was said to be unavoidably necessary to enroll minority students. This was true for blacks and perhaps for Chicanos. But the inclusion of Asians suggested that the Davis program was not a narrow response to social necessity but a political solution to interest-group politics. Powell foresaw a future in which the resources of higher education would be carved up among racial and ethnic categories, with shifting alliances among the various groups as each tried to maximize its piece of the pie. Universities could not be counted on to resist such pressures. White guilt would leave them vulnerable to minority intimidation. The result, he feared, would be the capture of admission to public universities by coalitions of special interests. The principle of individual merit could not long survive if this kind of ethnic spoils system were allowed to take root.

Powell resolved, therefore, that although some affirmative action was right and necessary, it should not be allowed to take hold in permanent allotments of government benefits based on race. Thus it was that Comfort received the instruction to "find a middle ground." Find a way to avoid the dire consequences of total victory for either side. Find some compromise to a seemingly irreconcilable clash of values. Find a way out.

COMFORT RETIRED to his apartment, laden with briefs and papers, and immersed himself in the contending arguments. He emerged some weeks later with a bench memo that was, he said, "at once too long and too short." At seventy-one pages, it was "an inordinate length for any bench memo," but even so, it was "barely able to skim the surface of many of the problems raised."

At the heart of Comfort's memo was the question of the "standard of review." The phrase is used to signal the level of justification required to sustain an action challenged as unconstitutional. Most laws—such as tax rates, speed limits, welfare standards—are judged under the standard of "mere rationality." They are upheld if *rationally* related to a *legitimate* government interest. In practice, this test is even easier than it sounds. Almost anything can be found rationally related to some legitimate interest. As a result, laws subject to "mere rationality" review are virtually never struck down as unconstitutional.

At the other extreme is "strict scrutiny." This standard of review applies to laws that trench on recognized constitutional rights. The classic example is discrimination against racial minorities. Such laws are almost always struck down. In theory, laws subject to "strict scrutiny" may be upheld if they are found *necessary* to achieve a *compelling* government interest, but justifications of this magnitude are exceedingly rare. In Gerald Gunther's telling phrase, the scrutiny is "'strict' in theory and fatal in fact."

Finally, a few questions (including sex-based distinctions) are handled under so-called intermediate scrutiny. This standard requires that the law be *substantially* related to *important* government interests. This formulation splits the difference between "mere rationality" and "strict scrutiny." In the jargon of the law, an *important* government interest is more than merely *legitimate* but far less then *compelling*. In application, the test is not predictable. Generally, a law subject to intermediate scrutiny will be upheld only if the government shows a real and important justification for drawing the distinction.

Such were the framework and vocabulary for Powell's decision on affirmative action. Of course, in themselves these phrases mean very little. They are shorthand references to the traditions of decided cases. But the choice of terms was anything but inconsequential. Selecting the standard of review would powerfully influence the judicial response to affirmative action. If the test were "mere rationality" or even "intermediate scrutiny," minority preferences would thrive. The desire to offset the nation's long history of discrimination by preferential advancement of racial and ethnic minorities could scarcely be thought either illegitimate or unimportant. Sensible reasons for such programs could readily be found. If that was all the Constitution required, affirmative action would be routinely upheld. If, however, minority preferences triggered "strict scrutiny," most could be expected to fall. At least if the requirement of a *compelling* justification were applied with its traditional rigor, few, if any, affirmative action plans would survive judicial review.

Comfort's solution was simple but cunning. After surveying all the arguments, he urged Powell to stick with "strict scrutiny." This was the test for discrimination against minorities and should also apply to discrimination in their favor. Adopting a lesser test would enshrine in the Constitution the repellent notion "that membership in particular racial or ethnic groups renders some individuals more deserving than others." It would be "better to keep the constitutional test of racial classifications the same for each individual, despite changing political judgments about the relative social and political status of the individual's racial or ethnic group." Also, applying the same test to all would obviate the intractable problem of selecting the law's special favorites: "The prejudice faced by every distinct racial and ethnic group entering this country makes each a potential candidate for compensatory legislation. Consensus as to who needs it and who should bear the burden will be lacking." Of course, lesser scrutiny could be reserved for programs aiding blacks and a few others, but "it is not immediately clear how one draws a bright line between those groups and, say, Jews or Orientals. Both of those groups faced almost hysterical prejudice for decades after first arrival in this country. Both face a quieter, subtler form of prejudice today. A decision that the prejudice facing blacks has been quantitatively more disabling would amount to a judicial leap of faith, I think, rather than a judicial expression of social consensus." (Powell wrote in the margin "quite true," though this was a "leap of faith" that anyone raised in the Commonwealth of Virginia should have been ready to make.) By using the same constitutional standard for all groups, the Court would not have to decide "whose ox has been gored more often and for how long."

This, in brief, was the case for "strict scrutiny." But if that test were applied with its usual rigor, affirmative action would not survive. To avoid this prospect, Comfort implicitly watered down the test. Even under "strict scrutiny," he argued, some minority preferences should be upheld—namely, those that served diversity. College admissions had never been based on grades alone. Universities had long favored applicants with different backgrounds, talents, or life experiences. "Fifteen or twenty years ago," said a statement from Harvard College, "diversity meant students from California, New York, and Massachusetts; city dwellers and farm boys; violinists, painters and football players. . . ." Race should count also. "A farm boy from Idaho can bring something to Harvard College that a Bostonian cannot offer. Similarly, a black student can usually bring something that a white person cannot offer. The quality of the educational experience of all the students in Harvard College depends in part on these differences in the background and outlook that students bring with them."

As a justification for minority preferences, Comfort argued, diversity was better than compensation—better, because more limited. Compensation implied that all groups hurt in the past could now claim offsetting preferences. Diversity reached only those who currently remained unrepresented. Diversity cut against affirmative action for Asians or others who had made it on their own. Also, Comfort favored diversity because of the flexible way that such concerns traditionally had been dealt with: "When Harvard College receives applications from Idaho farmboys, it does not establish a separate admissions track for them. It does not insulate them from comparison with other applicants and guarantee them a number of safe seats. Instead, it takes the fact of geographical origin as one factor weighing in the farmboy's favor when he is compared against all other applicants. . . ." Race should be handled the same way. Since race was "simply one ingredient of educational diversity," it was "unnecessary to isolate racial minorities from comparison with other applicants." This, said Comfort, was the crucial defect in the Davis program. It was not that Allen Bakke fell short when compared to the minority admittees. "Rather, Bakke was not compared with them at all."

In short, Davis had imposed a quota. Many months later, Powell's published opinion dismissed that label as "beside the point," but in fact he had an early and persistent interest in whether the Davis program was in fact a quota. To him it was. Diversity seemed to offer a way to reject rigid quotas without banning racial preferences. According to Comfort, the rationale justified race as "simply one ingredient of educational diversity" but not as a precondition for a fixed number of spaces. Diversity offered "the best opportunity for taking a middle course" between fixed quotas and strict color-blindness.

To critics, this reasoning seemed bogus. If educational diversity justified minority preferences, surely it allowed those preferences to be quantified. If racial diversity was a legitimate concern, state universities should be free to set a percentage for minority admissions, just as they do for in-state students. And in principle it should not matter whether Allan Bakke was not compared at all with minority applicants or whether, if compared, they were preferred on account of race. Either way, admission was based on race, and Bakke was disadvantaged as a consequence. The difference was mere formality.

Bogus or not, Comfort's memo persuaded Powell. Powell had asked for a middle course, and now he had one. The trick was to combine traditional "strict scrutiny" with the surprising discovery of educational diversity as a constitutionally *compelling* reason for racial preferences. Sensible affirmative action plans would be approved, but judicial oversight would be maintained. Diversity would be interpreted to justify taking race into account, but only as "one ingredient" in the admissions decision. Overt quotas would be disallowed.

Powell wanted to reach this result if at all possible. The first step was to vet the solution within his chambers. After Comfort had given copies of his memo to the other clerks, all four were convened for a working lunch in the "Ladies Dining Room." This was the anachronistic name of an elegant panelled room on the ground floor where the Justices' ladies (in a time when it was assumed that no Justice would be one) could meet for lunch. (The custom still survives, and yes, Mr. O'Connor has attended.) Powell and his clerks retired there in mid-September to discuss his vote in *Bakke*.

The other clerks had little in common save academic excellence. Jim

Alt was a quiet Iowan, who studied law at the University of Chicago. Powell had succeeded Hugo Black and tried to follow his tradition of always having a southern clerk. Jim Alt was said to occupy that place, on the ground that he had spent the preceding year clerking for a judge in Georgia. Certainly, none of the others qualified. Nancy Bregstein came from the New York suburbs by way of Yale and the University of Pennsylvania. As lawyers go, Bregstein was something of a free spirit. Sometimes her enthusiasms led her further than Powell wanted to go, but ultimately, of course, she acquiesced in his views. Most interesting was Sam Estreicher. Born in Bergen, Germany, to survivors of the Holocaust, Estreicher grew up in New York City, attended Columbia University, then got a master's degree in labor relations from Cornell before returning to Columbia for law school. Voluble, Jewish, emotionally unconstrained, and politically liberal, Estreicher had precious little in common with his boss. Working together was a challenge for both of them and on the whole successfully met.

The discussion in the Ladies Dining Room was frank and spirited. The chief difficulty was to find an intellectually respectable way to validate race as "simply one ingredient" in the admissions decision but to forbid race as an overt requirement for a certain number of spaces. This contradiction was buried in a peculiar concept of diversity. Quite obviously, ethnic quotas would achieve ethnic diversity. How then could Powell endorse ethnic diversity as a *compelling* state interest, yet disapprove the most direct and efficient way to achieve such diversity? Escape from this box required an intellectual Houdini, but Powell proved sufficiently adept. The state's interest was not, his opinion later stated, in "simple ethnic diversity, in which a specified percentage of the student body is in effect guaranteed to members of selected ethnic groups. . . ." Rather, the diversity that constituted a *compelling* state interest was diversity in which "racial or ethnic origin is but a single though important element." For reasons that were not—and could not be—satisfactorily explained, Powell insisted that fixed quotas "would hinder rather than further attainment of genuine diversity."

Estreicher in particular objected to this sophism. Yet even he came to see some wisdom in Powell's insistence on distinguishing goals from quotas. He came on board and later worked closely with Comfort, trying always to make sure that Powell did not shut the door on affirmative action. Eventually, Estreicher would join Powell and Comfort in looking back on *Bakke* as a great achievement.

Powell emerged from the Ladies Dining Room more than ever resolved to take his stand for diversity but against quotas. He told

Comfort to turn his memo into a draft, which Comfort did on October 6. This draft—though repeatedly revised by Powell, eventually festooned with footnotes, and substantially expanded to cover other issues—was the recognizable progenitor of the opinion that emerged nearly nine months later to make the nation's headlines. In all the long months that followed, Powell never wavered from his original position. Even before oral argument, Powell had made up his mind. The real question in October 1977 was not what Powell would do, but whether it would matter. This depended, of course, on the views of eight other Justices, which were still largely unknown.

ORAL ARGUMENT

First light on Wednesday, October 12, 1977, revealed more than one hundred persons huddled on the steps of the Supreme Court. Some had been there all night, waiting for the chance to hear a bare three minutes of oral argument in *Regents of the University of California v. Allan Bakke*. Many would not make it. By the time the doors opened, at 9:00 A.M., there were four hundred would-be spectators, ringed by others who wanted not to hear but to be heard. Unaccustomed to such crowds, the guards did not police the queue, so there was pushing, shoving, and breaking in line. Those with special passes—each Justice had nine—arrived much later. Among them were Senators, Congressmen and other notables, the Justices' families and former law clerks, and Mrs. Earl Warren. Missing was Allan Bakke himself, who struggled throughout the litigation to protect his privacy and some semblance of normal family life. He wanted to come, said his lawyer, but "felt he couldn't maintain his seclusion from the press."

Inside the Court, anticipation continued to build. The Justices' friends and relatives filled the box to the right of the bench. Law clerks crowded among the large columns along the side of the courtroom. Sections reserved for the press, for members of the Supreme Court bar, and for the general public were equally packed. Every seat was filled when, at precisely 10:00 A.M., the Justices emerged from behind the red velvet curtains and took their places at the bench. They came in groups of three through three hidden gaps in the curtains, so that the entire Court seemed to materialize instantaneously. A gavel brought the room to silence, as the Clerk recited the traditional words: "Oyez! Oyez! Oyez! All persons having business before the Honorable, the Supreme Court of the United States, are admonished to draw near and give their attention, for the Court is now sitting. God save the United States and this Honorable Court."

Oral argument is the most accessible and dramatic event in a Supreme Court decision. Often it is also the least important. The idea that a brilliant argument can turn the Court around is largely fiction. Even seasoned Court-watchers can recall only one or two instances where oral argument plainly changed the outcome. Moreover, the lawyer's chance to affect the outcome goes down as the significance of the case goes up. The Justices are most susceptible to persuasion in out-of-the-way areas where they have no firm views. In a great block-buster case such as *Bakke*, the Justices are more likely to have studied the briefs, considered the issue within chambers, and come to rest before entering the courtroom.

Yet in a more subtle way, oral argument can matter. It is the only occasion prior to the actual vote at Conference for all the Justices to focus on the same case at the same time. Although oral argument looks like a lecture interrupted by questions, its more important function is as a conversation among judges. A question asked by one Justice may be a response to another. Sometimes, the Justices go back and forth, making points to each other as they interrogate counsel. The use of questions is advantageous, as it allows the Justices to raise uncertainty without embarrassment and to venture comments without feeling locked in.

Of course, this process requires a lawyer who is sufficiently alert and knowledgeable to conduct the exchange. When this is lacking, the Justices either lapse into bored silence or take over the discussion. Justice Brennan, for example, would sometimes pull a drowning advocate to solid ground by a series of helpful questions—but only if the counsel was arguing Brennan's side of things. "Isn't your argument thus and so," or "Don't you mean to say this?" The right answer to these questions was always "yes." Only rarely was a lawyer so witless or arrogant as to spurn Brennan's rescue.

Thus, the realistic opportunity available to counsel at oral argument is not to overwhelm the opposition in logomachy, still less to mesmerize the Court with rhetoric, but rather to direct a conversation among judges. Great advocates set the agenda for debate. They cannot control what the Justices think, but they can require, at least for a time, that the Justices focus on their version of what the case is all about.

Unfortunately, even this limited opportunity is often wasted. Counsel are almost always chosen by clients, not by the Court. Too often they know everything there is to know about the case and next to nothing about the institution that will decide it. In particular, they often do not realize—or cannot bring themselves to accept—that the outcome in this particular case, which they may have lived with for years and which may be the pinnacle of a professional career, means very little to the Justices. The Justices may care greatly about the constitutional *issue*, but not about the specific *case*. For correct outcomes in individual cases, they necessarily rely on the lower courts. Indeed, in a nation of 250 million, it could not be otherwise. If the Justices worked around the clock, they could not hear more than a tiny fraction of the litigated cases. By careful selection, the Justices can hear all the great issues, but only a few cases. In their eyes, therefore, the specific dispute may be no more than a convenient vehicle for addressing a broader issue. Yet to the lawyer, whose goal is a particular outcome for a particular client, the broader implications may seem almost distracting. Thus, the lawyer unfamiliar with the Supreme Court often falls into the trap of making what the Justices deride as a "jury speech"—a presentation so preoccupied with the facts and history of the case at hand that it seems to the Court almost irrelevant to the larger issue.

So it was with Reynold Colvin. He opened at a level of prosaic particularity ("I am Allan Bakke's lawyer and Allan Bakke is my client") from which he was loathe to depart. After listening to several minutes of unnecessary history, Justice Rehnquist tried to get things moving, but Colvin would not be put off. He continued with the history and got drawn into a pointless imbroglio about the details of the Davis program. Finally, Powell boiled over. His voice was soft but steely, his pace more deliberate than ever, and his words uncommonly sharp: "[T]he university doesn't deny or dispute the basic facts. They are perfectly clear. We are here—at least I am here—primarily to hear a constitutional argument. You have devoted twenty minutes to laboring a fact, if I may say so. I would like help, I really would, on the constitutional issues. Would you address that?"

Colvin tried, but to little purpose. The exchanges were rarely helpful and sometimes testy. At one point, an aroused Justice Marshall said, "You are talking about your client's rights. Don't these underprivileged people have some rights?" Colvin tried to say that they had the right to compete, but Marshall interrupted "To eat cake." As the argument dragged on, Byron White muttered, "This is unbelievable." In fact, the performance was all too typical of a trial lawyer, transported by luck or circumstance to the rarified air of the Supreme Court and unable to make the transition. As one Justice put it, Colvin was simply "in over his head." His essential error lay in spurning the advice of supporters who urged that he turn the argument over to an expert.

Arguing against Allan Bakke's right to be admitted to medical school were genuine experts. Solicitor General Wade McCree appeared as a friend of the Court on behalf of the United States. He gave a dignified defense of the hopeless muddle of the government's brief, but the Court was not much interested. Colvin's real opponent was the lawyer for the university. Surprisingly, the university's argument in favor of racial preferences was not made by either of the lawyers who had written the brief. The Regents decided to bring in a "white knight," someone whose reputation for excellence and integrity would shield the university from charges that it was willing to lose the case, and selected for this purpose Harvard professor and former Solicitor General Archibald Cox, the Watergate special prosecutor fired by Richard Nixon. His ramrod-straight posture, trademark bow tie, and grey crew cut contributed to the image of Yankee rectitude.

As political cover for the beleaguered university, Cox was perfect. Some talked of "too little, too late," but even the university's critics lavished praise on Cox. In other respects, the decision was a closer call. There were delicate negotiations about his fee and his control of the litigation. Cox was a skilled advocate, but he was late coming to the case and lagged behind Mishkin and Owens in substantive understanding. The situation must have been hard on Mishkin, who was superbly qualified to present the case but deferred to the man with the greater reputation. Cox, for his part, found irksome the grueling practice sessions that the others wanted. As Solicitor General, he had "always steadfastly refused to go through a dry run," yet he did rehearse, in a suite in the Hay-Adams, responding to questions and then enduring criticism of his answers.

By the day of the argument, Cox was ready. He appeared in the traditional cutaway coat, now rarely worn by anyone outside the office of the Solicitor General, donned his reading glasses, and began. There were, he said, three facts—three "realities"—that the Court had to face. "The first is that the number of qualified applicants for the nation's professional schools is vastly greater than the number of places available. That is a fact, and an inescapable fact." A second fact was equally inescapable. Racial discrimination had "isolated certain minorities, condemned them to inferior education, and shut them out of the most important and satisfying aspects of American life, including higher education and the professions." And there was a third fact, most important of all, which Cox repeatedly drove home: "There is no racially blind method of selection which will enroll today more than a trickle of minority students in the nation's colleges and universities."

After a few minutes, Justice White interrupted with the first question, and the formal presentation was pushed aside by give-and-take. The pace was so fast and furious that Cox, as he later remembered, "didn't know what I'd said or hadn't said," but his experience showed in the poise and directness of his responses. Ironically, a point that Cox had been dissuaded from raising on his own was brought up in a question from a Justice. In the practice sessions, Cox suggested athletic scholarships as a simple example of non-numbers-based admissions, but was told that it was outrageous and trivializing to compare racial justice to athletics. "I got it thoroughly drummed into me that I shouldn't bring up athletic scholarships," Cox recalls, but then Justice Blackmun did it for him. In pressing the analogy between racial preferences and athletic scholarships, Blackmun asked whether athletic prowess was not the aim of most institutions. Cox responded, "Well, I come from Harvard, sir." As the laughter ebbed, he added, "I don't know whether it's our aim or not, but we don't do very well."

As counsel for the petitioner, Cox had the opportunity to reserve some time for rebuttal, but that was not his usual practice. In *Bakke*, however, the questioning was so hectic that "in desperation" and "on the spur of the moment," he asked to save time for rebuttal. His purpose was not to answer anything Colvin might say, but simply to have time to collect his thoughts and present a brief summary of points he might have missed. But when Cox rose to begin his rebuttal, he only got out the words "Mr. Chief Justice" before Powell, of all people, interrupted him to ask "whether you agree with my understanding of the Solicitor General's position that the record is inadequate for a constitutional decision and should be remanded?" Cox deftly said that he did and proceeded to give his summary anyway.

After two hours—twice the time usually permitted—the Chief Justice brought the argument to a close: "Thank you, gentlemen; the case is submitted." In the lawyer's antique phrase, the decision now lay "in the bosom of the Court." As one wag noted, it probably rested there no more comfortably than a live fox.

THE DECISION

An attempt at evasion was already afoot. *Bakke* was scheduled for discussion at the regular Friday Conference on October 14. The day before, Justice White circulated a memo suggesting that perhaps the constitutional issue could be ducked. Perhaps the case could be resolved on statutory grounds, as an interpretation of an act of Congress rather than as a construction of the Constitution of the United States. From the Court's point of view, this move would have advantages. It would shift public dissatisfaction (which would be intense no matter how the case came out) from the Court to Congress, and it would buy time. If the Davis program were found to violate a federal statute, the Court would not have to decide whether the Constitution would have permitted such a program. The constitutional question could be postponed, or perhaps avoided altogether, if a legislative prohibition could be found.

The statute White had in mind was Title VI of the 1964 Civil Rights Act. That statute banned racial discrimination in any program receiving federal funds. It was undisputed that the Davis Medical School received federal funds. The only question was whether affirmative action was the kind of racial discrimination banned by the statute. Justice Stevens thought it was, and was already at work on proving the point. The contrary view was that Title VI simply tracked the Constitution, that it was intended merely to extend to all recipients of federal funds the same prohibition—whatever that might be—imposed on government by the Constitution. Under this view, if the Constitution allowed affirmative action, so did Title VI.

White thought the statute unclear and proposed that the Court ask for additional briefs on the subject. Powell responded the next day with an opposing memorandum. Title VI and the Equal Protection Clause of the Constitution were comparably brief and vague. Neither clearly spelled out any position on affirmative action. It was "almost certain," Powell argued, that each Justice's view of the statute would follow his understanding of the Constitution, and the same conclusion would be reached under both. And there were good reasons not to evade the constitutional issue. The arguments on each side were "as fully developed as they will ever be." In *DeFunis*, the Court had already gone once to the brink of decision and backed away. "[D]ucking this issue for a second time in three years would be viewed by many as a 'self-inflicted wound' on the Court."

Despite Powell's plea, the majority agreed to call for additional briefs. This meant that the actual vote would be put off for several weeks while the Justices waited to hear more on Title VI. It also meant that opposition to the constitutionality of affirmative action could masquerade as a restrictive construction of Title VI. Internal Court documents reveal that both Burger and Rehnquist wanted to hold the Davis program unconstitutional, but ultimately neither published that view. Instead, both lined up behind Justice Stevens's contention that the program was in any event barred by Title VI. Thus, it soon became clear that at least three Justices were prepared to affirm the California courts in striking down the Davis plan. Whether this action would be explained under the Constitution or under Title VI was ultimately less important than the result of condemning racial preferences.

Meanwhile, Powell put the finishing touches on a draft opinion allowing racial preferences, which he circulated it to his colleagues on November 22. One feature of this opinion dismayed Powell's clerks. After saying that Davis's fixed quotas would somehow hinder "genuine" diversity, Powell cited Harvard as an approved alternative. In his words, Harvard provided an "illuminating example of an admissions system designed to achieve meaningful diversity in the broad sense of this term." But in reality, Harvard was simply Davis without fixed numbers. At both schools, race or ethnic background was a "plus" in an applicant's file and in some cases determined admission. At Harvard, however, this preference was not quantified. Neither was it formalized in a separate track for minority admissions. Rather, Harvard implemented affirmative action through a case-by-case search for "diversity" rather than through overtly separate consideration as at Davis.

The difference was more form than substance. One did not have to be a cynic to believe that as compared to the Davis quota system, the Harvard plan was "simply a subtle and more sophisticated—but no less effective—means of according racial preference. . . ." Powell's attempt to answer this charge was a transparent failure. The published opinion (which reflects only stylistic revision from the draft of November 22) states:

> It has been suggested that an admissions program which considers race as only one factor is simply a subtle and more sophisticated—but no less effective—means of according racial preference than the Davis program. A facial intent to discriminate, however, is evident in [Davis's] preference program and not denied in this case. No such facial infirmity exists in an admissions program where race or ethnic background is simply one element—to be weighed fairly against other elements—in the selection process. . . .

This was pure sophistry. Harvard did not—and could not—deny that race was a factor in admissions. By refusing to look beyond "facial intent" in situations where the fact of racial preference was open, acknowledged, and indisputable, Powell simply penalized candor. Stripped of legalisms, the message amounted to this: "You can do whatever you like in preferring racial minorities, so long as you do not say so."

The clerks found this embarrassing. Not only was there no important difference between Davis and Harvard, but it seemed undignified and elitist to condemn tiny Davis but praise mighty Harvard for doing the same thing with better manners. Powell was supposed to be interpreting the Constitution, not taking orders from the nation's most prestigious university. (Their concern for appearances was not groundless. One commentator later said Powell had ruled that universities may take race into account in admissions "so long as nothing is done in an un-Harvard-like manner.") But Powell overrode all objections. However flimsy others might find the distinction between diversity at Davis and diversity at Harvard, it was precisely that difference that mattered to Powell. Moreover, the nation's colleges and universities needed to know exactly what they could and could not do. Explicit approval of the Harvard approach gave practical guidance on what was permitted.

This was a legitimate concern, but it was not the only reason—or even the most important reason—for Powell's dogged insistence on discussing Harvard. His distinction between Harvard and Davis was an intellectual failure but a public relations triumph. Powell's canny instinct for public perception told him that he had much to gain by celebrating the Harvard approach. Otherwise, his rejection of the Davis quota would be misunderstood as a rejection of affirmative action generally. The crucial difference between his goals-but-not-quotas position and a flat prohibition of all racial preferences might well be garbled in transmission to the public. The Harvard program gave Powell the means to preclude that misconception by discussing a plan he approved as well as one he rejected.

In effect, Powell used Harvard to create the opportunity to decide two cases rather than one. He struck down one plan but upheld the other. This split decision clarified his position and highlighted the divergence from his colleagues on the right. He joined them in invalidating the Davis quota, but not in disallowing all racial preferences. On that issue, as embodied in the example of Harvard, he stood with his colleagues on the left. The combination precisely described Powell's views; he was squarely in the middle of the Court.

The next day Justice Brennan responded with his own memorandum supporting racial preferences. Not only did Brennan approve the Davis program, but he carefully avoided any suggestion that laws favoring minorities should be subject to the same "strict scrutiny" as discriminations against them. He spoke only of "reasonableness," implying (without being too specific about it) that racial preferences should be routinely upheld.

Decisive for Brennan was the lack of anti-white stigma in the Davis program. Reserving sixteen spaces for minorities might hurt some whites, but it did not brand them as unequal. For whites at least, affirmative action carried no allegation of inferiority. "The constitutional principle I think to be supported by our cases," said Brennan, "can be summarized as follows: government may not on account of race, insult or demean a human being by stereotyping his or her capacities, integrity, or worth as an individual." In other words, he added, "the Fourteenth Amendment does not tolerate government action that causes any to suffer from the prejudice or contempt of others on account of his race."

By this test, the Davis program was entirely unobjectionable. Whatever it might be thought to say about minorities (an issue Brennan did not raise), the Davis plan certainly did not insult whites. On that score, Allan Bakke had no complaint. "It is true that Bakke, like thousands of other applicants who fail of admission, was not admitted to medical school. But he was never stereotyped as an incompetent, or pinned with a badge of inferiority because he is white." This was true, of course, not only for Allan Bakke but for all those disadvantaged by affirmative action. Since no minority preferences—at least not those adopted and approved by the white power structure—could fairly be said to cast a racial slur against whites, Brennan was prepared to uphold them.

ON DECEMBER 9, 1977, the Justices tried to thrash out their differences. Burger and Rehnquist restated their opposition to racial preferences. Stewart now joined their camp. All three based their votes on the Constitution but suggested, with varying degrees of reluctance, that they might follow Stevens in relying on Title VI. Stevens was shaky on the constitutional issue (he said he had "changed his mind several times"), but was convinced that Title VI barred this program. The Court should find Davis in violation of the statute and say nothing at all about the Constitution. Burger, Rehnquist, and Stewart eventually fell in with this approach. That made four votes against racial preferences.

White and Marshall joined Brennan, making three votes to uphold racial preferences. (Harry Blackmun was recuperating from prostate surgery at the Mayo Clinic.)

It may be generally true, as Brennan often claimed, that the importance of the Conference is overstated, but at the Conference of December 9, there occurred two critical exchanges. Ironically, the first involved Brennan. Powell came to Conference with the draft opinion already described—for preferences but against quotas, for Harvard's "diversity" but against Davis's. Since Davis was the only program technically before the Court, Powell announced that he would vote to affirm the California judgment condemning the Davis plan, although on narrower grounds. At this point Brennan made a brilliant intervention: Given Powell's view of the case, shouldn't he vote to affirm *in part* and reverse in part? After all, the California court had not only struck down the Davis quota; it had also barred all racial preferences in admissions. Powell did not support this broader ruling, so why not vote to reverse it? Powell at once agreed. Subsequent drafts show him voting to affirm in part and reverse in part, as Brennan had astutely suggested.

The chief historian of the *Bakke* decision, New York University professor Bernard Schwartz, later described Powell's acquiescence as "a crucial concession." Crucial it may have been, but a concession it was not. Brennan's intervention led Powell to do exactly what he wanted to do anyway—split the difference between goals and quotas. That, of course, was precisely the point of approving Harvard while rejecting Davis. Brennan prompted Powell to split his vote as well as his opinion and thereby to emphasize his own divided view. As Powell later summarized for the Chief, "Thus, at the end of my opinion, the bottom line would be: 'Affirm in part and reverse in part.' Bakke would win his case, but the medical school would be free to consider race as one element in its admissions determinations, with all places open to competition." Of course, this helped Brennan too. If *Bakke* came down in this way, the public would likely focus on the key point of agreement between Brennan and Powell—namely, "that the principle of affirmative action was being upheld."

But if the suggestion of a split vote drew Powell toward his liberal colleagues, another comment pushed him away. In the course of the discussion, Stevens said that preferences might be acceptable as a temporary measure but not as a permanent solution. Powell agreed. The problem was one of transition to a color-blind society. Perhaps, Stevens added, blacks would not need these special programs much longer, but at this point Marshall broke in to say that it would be another hundred years. This remark left Powell speechless. He came away from the Conference with a sharpened sense of the vast gulf that separated him from the liberals. Afterward, Bob Comfort thought it just possible that things might have gone differently had Marshall predicted ten years rather than one hundred. Closer collaboration might have been achieved between Powell and the liberals if the latter had recast their position as support for temporary preferences. But Marshall would not move in that direction, and Powell recoiled from the prospect of generation upon generation of racial quotas.

(The estrangement was not one-sided. One inside source reported that Marshall was "livid" over Powell's opinion and regarded it as "racist." Apparently, his resentment focused on remarks that Marshall thought insensitive to the nation's racial history—chiefly, Powell's statement: "It is far too late to argue that the guarantee of equal protection to *all* persons permits the recognition of special wards entitled to a degree of protection greater than that accorded others.")

BLACKMUN HAD MISSED the second *Bakke* Conference. He wrote from the Mayo Clinic to say that the others should proceed without him, adding, "I can swing into place one way or the other after my return." That blithe assurance carried no hint of the anguish ahead.

The next few weeks saw a flurry of memoranda, which changed nothing. When Blackmun returned to the Court in January 1978, the lineup was still four–one–three, with Powell in the middle. If Blackmun joined the four, he would make a majority against racial preferences. If he joined the three, the Court would be evenly divided, with Powell's split vote controlling the outcome. If he joined Powell, he would strengthen the middle and provide a nucleus that might attract support from the sides. The choice was his.

Blackmun turned to his work. He logged long hours, mostly spent alone in the Justices' library, trying in his driven way to master every fact, every precedent, every argument in the case at hand. This took time, and Blackmun was, as always, meticulous. There was nothing unusual in having the others wait for him. In fact, it was almost routine. So Blackmun worked, hard and long and conscientiously, early and late, worked with strict concentration and painstaking care, worked on every case and problem—except *Bakke*.

The greatest civil rights case since *Brown* hung fire while Blackmun spent himself on trivialities. As the winter dragged on, the other Justices fumed and fretted, but Blackmun did nothing—and said nothing. He would not talk about the case, indeed grew irritable whenever *Bakke* was mentioned. The other Justices tried to prod him into voting. *Bakke* was added to the agenda of a Conference in early March, but Blackmun told the Chief beforehand that he was not ready to discuss it, and Burger let it pass. Eventually, Brennan got Burger to approach Blackmun directly, but that also failed. Spring came, but still there was no word on *Bakke*.

On Monday, April 10, Burger tried a different tack. He came to see Powell and suggested that together they look for a way to break the deadlock. Even without Blackmun, there were five votes against the particular form of affirmative action practiced at Davis. Powell should join a narrow opinion striking down the Davis program and leave it at that. After all, it was customary to decide one case at a time. There was no reason Powell had to go beyond these facts. And the opinion could hint broadly, as Burger himself believed, that milder preferences of the sort practiced at Harvard would eventually be permitted. If Powell would agree to join an opinion for these facts only, the Court could break this embarrassing deadlock, get on with its business, and quit worrying about Harry.

Powell refused. "Generally," he told the Chief Justice, "I am strongly inclined to defer to you. But on this issue I have a conviction that the Court should speak out clearly and unambiguously." If the Court struck down the Davis program without also specifying what kind of affirmative action was permissible, "no university in the country will feel free to give any consideration to race. I simply could not join that result." The only solution was to wait. "Although time is slipping away, I cannot believe that Harry is insensitive to this situation. Nor can I believe that he will want the case reargued. We will never be better informed on the issue. With perhaps a total of 75 or more briefs filed in *DeFunis* and *Bakke,* and with distinguished counsel having argued, carrying the case over would be viewed as an irresponsible failure to do our duty. I therefore have every confidence that Harry will make his decision in the near future, and however his vote may go, the country will then have an answer."

As the Court and the country waited for an answer, *Bakke* became entangled in the decision of lesser cases. One raised the question whether Montana could charge outsiders a higher fee than Montana citizens had to pay for a license to hunt elk. The case was argued before *Bakke* and the opinion (in favor of Montana) assigned to Blackmun, who in due course circulated a draft that quickly got five votes. Then the trouble started. When Brennan decided to withhold his vote until argument of a related case, Blackmun was outraged. At Conference in late March, he erupted in bitter recrimination about the delay in handing down the Montana elk-hunting case and the damage it did to his reputation. A law review had said that he was the Court's slowest author, but, as the Montana case showed, that was not his fault. He even threatened to have a press conference to refute the charge of slowness. No one dared mention *Bakke.*

On April 10 (while Burger was importuning Powell), Blackmun had lunch with Brennan. All was sweetness and light, but a few days later he returned to the attack. At the Friday Conference, Blackmun announced that he would not vote in *Bakke* until the lawfulness of Montana's elk-hunting licenses was finally settled. At this point, Brennan must have been tempted to do something, anything, to satisfy Blackmun, but he did not. The Montana case finally came down, with Brennan, White, and Marshall dissenting, on May 23.

A second incident occurred when the Court prepared to announce a Blackmun antitrust decision. At Conference, Brennan failed to mention that he planned to write a concurrence. His later note to that effect required that the announcement be delayed, and again Blackmun was furious. This time Brennan apologized profusely and put aside other work so that the case could come down as soon as possible.

Powell had much the same concerns. One of the things Blackmun worked on while he was not voting in *Bakke* was a complicated tax case, *Frank Lyon Company v. United States*. On March 16 he circulated a draft. Powell agreed with the result, but the opinion was lamentable. It began with an impenetrable statement of the facts and proceeded to a multifactor analysis of no clear point and very doubtful relevance to the outcome. Privately, Powell passed his strictest censure—"If an associate at Hunton, Williams had done this for me, I would have had him fired"— but he would not be dissuaded from joining. He rejected his clerk's advice to concur in the result but not the opinion, and sent Blackmun a note suggesting two inconsequential changes and saying, "you can count on me as a join." "We don't want to upset Harry in *Bakke*," Powell explained. Others may have felt the same way, for despite its flaws, six others joined Blackmun's opinion. (There were two dissents.)

ON MAY 1, 1978, the wait finally ended. Blackmun announced that he would vote for the Davis program. With the Court now evenly split, Burger and Brennan (the senior Justices in each camp) jointly assigned the case to Powell, who found himself in the odd position of being a controlling minority of one. With one "gang of four" (as the clerks called Burger, Stewart, Rehnquist, and Stevens), he made a majority to condemn the Davis quota. With the other "gang of four" (Brennan, White, Marshall, and Blackmun), he made a majority to approve lesser preferences. Powell stood alone, yet his view would be the law of the land.

One week later, Powell circulated an opinion announcing the judgment of the Court. Lengthy additions covered the facts of the case and the question of Title VI, but the heart of the opinion came from his draft of November 22, 1977. A few words were added here and there, but the substance remained unchanged. As expected, no one joined.

At the beginning of June, Lewis and Josephine left town for a weekend in Birmingham, Alabama. Powell disliked traveling near the end of the term, but this event he could neither miss nor postpone. Lewis III was getting married. His bride was Isabell Mims Maynard, whom Lewis met at the University of Virginia Law School. For the next year, they would have a long-distance marriage, with Lewis clerking for Bob Merhige in Richmond and Mims finishing her last year in Charlottesville.

The night before the wedding, the Powells held a rehearsal dinner for more than ninety guests at the Birmingham Country Club. Despite help on the scene from Mims's family, Powell engaged in meticulous long-distance planning, worrying about the guest list, approving the menu, and specifying a wine suggested by the Chief Justice. His own chief responsibility was a little talk after dinner, for which he prepared as if for litigation. The remarks were an apt collection of fluff and pleasantry. "The form on these occasions," he began, "is for the parents—who probably shouldn't speak at all—to reminisce, trying bravely to be amusing without being maudlin." Powell kidded Lewis (who was strikingly handsome) about women ("He had only three girls who ever gave him more than one date. All three hastened to marry someone else.") and was cordial to Mims ("You can understand, in view of this record, why we are grateful to Mims. We hope it is too late for her to change her mind. . . ."). Yet *Bakke* was not far from his mind. Lewis, he told the guests, had said, "For heaven's sakes, Dad, don't decide *Bakke* until after the wedding. I don't want to be embarrassed." Then Powell deadpanned, "I have been trying to figure out how he thinks I'm going to vote." It was a good line and also a gentle way of reminding everyone that even Lewis would *not* know how Powell was going to vote.

When Powell returned to Washington, the opinion was almost ready, but one footnote stirred up a minor controversy. Brennan had argued all along that the Davis quota was permissible because it carried no stigma against whites. Powell responded as follows:

> The Equal Protection Clause is not framed in terms of 'stigma.'. . . *All* state-imposed classifications that rearrange burdens and benefits on the basis of race are likely to be viewed with deep resentment by the individuals burdened. . . . These individuals are likely to find little comfort in the notion that the deprivation they are asked to endure is merely the price of membership in the dominant majority and that its imposition is inspired by the supposedly benign purpose of aiding others. One should not lightly dismiss the inherent unfairness of, and the perception of mistreatment that accompanies, a system of allocating benefits and privileges on the basis of skin color and ethnic origin.

The original version then continued:

> Moreover, limiting the concept of stigma to the imposition of a badge of inferiority would inhibit appropriate scrutiny of classifications such as the quotas imposed upon admission of Jews to some educational institutions in the early part of this century, which were based upon the belief that by virtue of superior ability that group would come to dominate such institutions.

Powell had a point. The Jewish quotas did not reflect the view that Jews were not good enough to compete, but that they were entirely too good. If the Constitution banned racial classifications only where they imposed a badge of inferiority, as Brennan claimed, it would be hard to explain what was wrong with the Jewish quotas. Yet everyone agreed that they were abhorrent. Was this not a weakness in Brennan's argument?

Brennan called Powell to say that the remark was "personally offensive." As Powell recorded in a memorandum to the file, Brennan said "that his respect and admiration for our Jewish citizens was widely known. He thought my reference to the former mistreatment of the Jews would be quoted against him—and his opinion in this case—to his embarrassment." Powell was surprised by this reaction, but said he "would omit anything from any opinion where a Justice of the Court requested me to do so on the ground that what I had written was 'personally offensive.'" A later handwritten note added: "Neither I nor any of my clerks thought there was any reason to request this change. But I would certainly honor a request like this from Bill."*

Aside from such refinements, Powell's opinion was finished. By late June, so were all the others. Stevens wrote for himself, Burger, Stewart,

---

* Brennan and Powell also exchanged views on how Brennan might describe the common ground between them. Originally, Brennan spelled out "the central meaning of today's opinions" as follows: "Government may take race into account when it acts not to demean or insult any racial group, but to remedy disadvantages cast on minorities by past racial prejudice." When this statement was criticized by Stevens, Brennan called Powell to ask whether he agreed with it. Powell responded in a "Personal" letter on June 23, 1978: "If your statement is read literally, I doubt it does reflect accurately the judgment of the Court. . . . [But] I have not objected to your characterization of what the Court holds as I have thought you could put whatever gloss on the several opinions as you think proper." Brennan then revised his statement to add a phrase from Powell's response: "Government may take race into account when it acts not to demean or insult any racial group, but to remedy disadvantages cast on minorities by past racial prejudice, *at least where appropriate findings have been made by judicial, legislative, or administrative bodies with competence to act in this area*" (emphasis added).

and Rehnquist. Brennan (the principal author), White, Marshall, and Blackmun published a joint opinion in response. Additionally, White, Marshall, and Blackmun filed separate statements. Altogether, the opinions would occupy more than 150 pages in the United States Reports.

Most eloquent of all was the opinion of Justice Marshall. The nation's first black Justice wrote with feeling and dignity of the history of his race. None could dispute his conclusion: "The position of the Negro today in America is the tragic but inevitable consequence of centuries of unequal treatment. Measured by any benchmark of comfort or achievement, meaningful equality remains a distant dream for the Negro." The Court itself was partly to blame. Its decision in 1896 to tolerate "separate but equal" had condemned generations of blacks to a life that was legally separate and anything but equal. For Marshall, that past was decisive:

> It is because of a legacy of unequal treatment that we now must permit the institutions of this society to give consideration to race in making decisions about who will hold the positions of influence, affluence, and prestige in America. For far too long, the doors to those positions have been shut to Negroes. If we are ever to become a fully integrated society, one in which the color of a person's skin will not determine the opportunities available to him or her, we must be willing to take steps to open those doors. I do not believe that anyone can truly look into America's past and still find that a remedy for that past is impermissible.

Of course, four Justices found just that, but Marshall ultimately won more than he lost. Ironically, he owed his victory to the Court's lone southerner, a former segregationist and consistent foe of forced busing, the Justice whose background seemed least likely to produce the decisive vote for affirmative action. He must have appreciated the foresight of Oliver Hill, who, on an intuition from personal contact rather than from the public record, had told him that Lewis Powell was all right.

POWELL NOW BEGAN to prepare for the announcement. In a more leisurely age, the Justices delivered their opinions orally. In Powell's time, the Justice who wrote for the Court would merely announce the result, perhaps add a sentence or two of explanation, and refer to the written opinion made available at that hour in the office of the clerk. Dissenters rarely did more than announce their votes. Of course, a Justice could revert to the earlier practice in an exceptional case, and *Bakke* was such a case.

Powell's object was to guide public perception. The lineup was so complicated that a succession of individual voices might be impossible to follow. Powell therefore undertook to give a road map to the views of all the Justices, even though he was, as he put it, "a chief with no Indians." Moreover, Powell was deeply concerned that his position not be misunderstood. That was why he had insisted on praising affirmative action at Harvard and why he had at once accepted Brennan's suggestion that he vote to affirm in part and reverse in part. The same objective governed his statement from the bench. Above all, Powell wanted the public to appreciate that he—and therefore the majority of the Supreme Court—was neither routinely for, nor categorically against, affirmative action. He was somewhere in between. Conveying the subtlety of this position posed a challenge.

The decision was announced on Wednesday, June 28, 1978. The courtroom was not crowded, as on the day of argument, since there was no notice of the cases to be announced. Cognoscenti might have guessed that something was up when Marjorie Brennan, Cecelia Marshall, Mary Ann (Andy) Stewart, and Elizabeth Stevens came into the courtroom. Josephine Powell was not there, as she had not been told. Three cases came down that day. Burger had originally put *Bakke* first, but Powell objected that the other two cases were "pipsqueaks" and urged that the Court save the best for last. So it was a few minutes after 10:00 A.M. when the Chief Justice recognized Powell to deliver the judgment of the Court in No. 76-811, *Regents of the University of California v. Bakke.*

Powell spoke in a soft monotone. He began with the bad news: "I am authorized to announce only the judgment of the Court. There is no opinion joined in its entirety by five members of the Court." He acknowledged the press and the world outside the Court: "The facts in this case are well known. Perhaps no case in modern memory has received as much media coverage and scholarly commentary. More than sixty briefs were filed with the Court. We also have received the advice—through the media and the commentaries—of countless extra-judicial advocates. The case was argued some eight months ago, and as we speak today with a notable lack of unanimity, it may be fair to say that we needed all of this advice."

When all the votes were counted, this was the result: "Insofar as the California Supreme Court held that Bakke must be admitted to the Davis Medical School, we affirm. Insofar as the California Court prohibited Davis from considering race as a factor in admissions, we reverse."

"I will now try to explain how we divided on these issues. This may not be self-evident," he added, as gentle laughter rippled through the courtroom.

After the road map, Powell explained his own reasoning. All racial classifications were "inherently suspect and must be subjected to the most exacting judicial scrutiny." Nevertheless, admissions preferences could be used to further the *compelling* state interest in educational diversity. The trouble with Davis was that by totally excluding all non-minority applicants from sixteen spaces, it went further than was necessary to achieve a diverse student body. Harvard showed how to do it. The experience elsewhere "demonstrates that the Davis-type program—one that arbitrarily forecloses all competition solely on the basis of race or ethnic origin—is not necessary to attain reasonable educational diversity. It therefore violates the Equal Protection Clause in a most fundamental sense. Yet, the way is open to Davis to adopt the type of admissions program proved to be successful at so many of our universities."

When Powell finished, others spoke. Stevens crisply explained his restrictive interpretation of Title VI. Brennan expounded his permissive view. Marshall gravely recounted the history of racial wrongs against blacks. Finally, Blackmun spoke, simply and eloquently, of his heartfelt conviction that in "order to get beyond racism, we must first take account of race. There is no other way. And in order to treat some persons equally, we must treat them differently. We cannot—we dare not—let the Equal Protection Clause perpetuate racial supremacy."

It required only one hour for the Justices to deliver orally a decision it took them nearly nine months to reach. "I have seen great moments there," said columnist Anthony Lewis, "but nothing to match the drama as five members of the court explained their positions in homely terms." The question now was how these views would be conveyed to the people.

FOR WEEKS, THE PRESS had maintained a *Bakke* vigil, with full camera crews waiting outside the Court on decision days and more than twice the usual number of reporters crowded into the downstairs newsroom. Speed was the top priority, and all kinds of arrangements had been made to assure quick transmission. As one paper reported, "On every day on which decisions are released, television crews position themselves outside the court, preparing to broadcast news of a Bakke ruling. When informed in midmorning that only a few minor tax rulings have been released, the crews pack up and fade away like Dracula before a cross."

A few minutes after 10:00 A.M., on June 28, before Powell had even finished speaking, the networks interrupted regular programming to announce the decision in *Bakke*. In the rush to broadcast and with only a summary of the case from the Court's press office, most reporters managed to say only that Bakke had won admission to medical school. Powell's painstaking effort to avoid misdescription seemed at first to have failed.

By that evening, however, the networks had the basics right, and the next morning's newspapers were sophisticated and accurate. Most used a two-pronged headline, with top billing and larger type usually given to the paper's editorial preference. The conservative *Washington Star*, for example, reported, "BAKKE WINS PLACE IN MEDICAL SCHOOL: However, Supreme Court Says Race Can Be Considered in Admissions," and the *Chicago Sun-Times* trumpeted, "WHITE STUDENT WINS REVERSE BIAS CASE: Justices OK some racial preferences." The liberal *Washington Post*, on the other hand, reported, "AFFIRMATIVE ACTION UPHELD: Court Orders School to Admit Bakke, Curbs Racial Quotas," and *The New York Times* led off with, "HIGH COURT BACKS SOME AFFIRMATIVE ACTION BY COLLEGES, BUT ORDERS BAKKE ADMITTED." *Time*'s cover captured the case most succinctly: "Quotas No, Race Yes."

Perhaps the fragmentary initial reports and Justice Marshall's somber tone accounted for the early outcry by many blacks. They seemed to feel the impact of a bullet they in fact had dodged. Harlem's *Amsterdam News* ran the banner headline, "BAKKE—WE LOSE!" Congressman Ronald V. Dellums fumed that he was "appalled" by the "racist decision of the Nixon court." Jesse Jackson veered toward hysteria. He called for massive demonstrations to protest a decision he compared to the Nazi march on Skokie. Blacks, he said, "must not greet this decision with a conspiracy of silence; we must rebel."

Other blacks were more hopeful—and more accurate. The leader of the Congressional Black Caucus, Representative Parren Mitchell, said, "We have not won total victory, but this is not defeat." Benjamin Hooks, executive director of the NAACP, called the ruling "a mixed bag" which included a "strong ray of hope," and Vernon Jordan, head of the Urban League, thought "the most important thing" was the Court's approval of the principle of affirmative action.

Reaction elsewhere was overwhelmingly favorable. Meg Greenfield of the *Washington Post* had hoped that the Court would "find a way to blur the edges of the controversy and reaffirm the important values raised by both sides. You say that is fudging the issue? Fine. It ought to be fudged." Now Powell's "fudge" drew widespread expressions of relief and gratitude. As the *Post* saw it, "Everyone won." Others echoed that thought. Powell's opinion was called "Solomonic" and praised as an act of "judicial statesmanship." Charles Alan Wright of the University of Texas called it "a very civilized ruling"; future Yale president Benno Schmidt thought it "just about right"; and Harvard professor and media star Alan Dershowitz found it "a brilliant compromise." Paul Mishkin, who at first was disappointed to lose even part of the case, later came to see the "peace-making and calming effect of the Powell position." Attorney General Griffin Bell spoke for the Carter Administration when he said, "I think the whole country ought to be pleased."

But some disliked Powell's compromise. Guido Calabresi, future dean of Yale Law School, bemoaned the "lost candor" in Powell's equivocation. Robert Bork, who would later be nominated to take Powell's place, said the opinion was "at bottom a statement that the 14th Amendment allows some, but not too much, reverse discrimination." As politics, Bork argued, "the solution may seem statesmanlike, but as constitutional argument, it leaves you hungry an hour later." From the other side of the political spectrum, Ronald Dworkin agreed. Writing in the *New York Review of Books*, Dworkin called the opinion "weak" and added: "It does not supply a sound intellectual foundation for the compromise the public found so attractive. The compromise is politically appealing, but it does not follow that it reflects any important difference in principle. . . ."

Others, such as columnist William Raspberry, were troubled not at all by Powell's supposed lack of principle. Raspberry wrote: "I, for one, welcome the ambiguity. A clear-cut decision that race may not be considered would have denied the reality of the American racial experience. Minorities, and blacks most particularly, have been crippled by racism. . . . On the other hand, a clear-cut rule that, because of that racist history, blacks and other minorities could be forever spared the necessity of competing with whites would have struck too many Americans as unfair." The Court, he concluded, had "emerged from a stinking quagmire of a case wearing at least a faint aroma of roses."

Ordinary Americans agreed overwhelmingly with Raspberry—and with Powell. When asked the precise issue of *Bakke* ("What if a school reserved a certain number of places for qualified minority applicants. Would you approve or disapprove of that even if it meant that some qualified white applicants wouldn't be admitted?"), blacks split almost evenly, but whites were largely negative. While blacks supported most forms of affirmative action, a majority of whites opposed anything that looked like a quota. On the other hand, most whites endorsed special efforts to help minorities. The same public that condemned racial quotas approved special treatment. As two experts summarized: "Clearly, a majority of whites are willing to endorse 'special consideration' of race as a factor in hiring and admissions and to approve of programs which channel resources to specific racial minorities. But they draw the line at absolute preference."

According to the *Baltimore Sun*, the Supreme Court's view of affirmative action was "as divided and confused as the American people in general"—and along much the same lines. The distinction that Bork and others found lacking in logic made sense to most citizens, as it did to Powell. No doubt it was the illogic of Powell's position that made it so hard for some to accept. A political scientist who programmed his computer with the voting history of each of the Justices predicted, on the basis of the computer calculations, that all nine would side with Allan Bakke. In this case, at least, popular sentiment proved a better guide than supposedly expert analysis.

As POWELL LEFT Washington for the summer, the popular approval of his stance was heartening. So also were the private letters. Judge Henry Friendly, who should have made it to the Supreme Court but never did, wrote to express his appreciation "for the great service you have rendered the nation. This case had the potential of being another Dred Scott case. . . . Your moderation and statesmanship saved us from that." But, Friendly noted, the margin was uncomfortably close: "It reminds one of Mark Twain's remark that God protects children, drunkards, and the United States of America." Constitutional law scholar Gerald Gunther agreed: "I think your stance was exactly right; your fine opinion is of the greatest significance; and I not only hope but believe that it will be recognized as of the greatest importance long after both of us are gone." Colgate Darden thought Powell's *Bakke* opinion was "John Marshall at his best," a sentiment echoed by other Virginians.

The best praise came from Powell's old friend and fellow member of the Alibi Club, General Maxwell Taylor. *Bakke*, he said, "seems to have accomplished the amazing feat of making all parties reasonably happy," then added: "There's much to be said for the British practice of rewarding military victors by appending to them the name of the site of their triumphs—Montgomery of Alamein, for instance. Analogous justice would make you Powell of Bakke—although your Alibi friends might give a ribbing to such a dubbing."

A perceptive comment came from John Riely, the managing partner at Hunton, Williams. Riely had worked with Powell on one of his last major efforts in private practice—Virginia's friend-of-the-court brief against forced busing. Now he wrote: "Dear Lewis— This is by way of being a fan letter. Having read *Bakke,* I consider that you reached exactly the right result. It was brilliant." Then he mused: "It is a long way back to our arguments about *Charlotte-Mecklenburg;* I question whether you would have reached the same result then."

Riely was right. If Lewis Powell had changed the Supreme Court, it was equally true that the Supreme Court had changed Lewis Powell. Riely knew what Powell would have thought of racial preferences in 1970: He would have dismissed them out of hand. Nothing in his long life or practice would have prepared him to say that whites should be held back to make way for less qualified blacks. He might have seen that blacks needed special help, but it is unlikely that he would have been ready to give it—not if it meant disadvantaging innocent whites. Affirmative action had gained great momentum in the ensuing eight years, but it is doubtful that Powell's views would have changed had he remained in private practice in Richmond, Virginia. The crucial and indispensable ingredient in Powell's acceptance of racial preferences was a sense of personal responsibility for racial justice. That came with the oath of office. Every Justice is in part a product of his past, but for Powell, at least, that past was mediated by a new obligation. His seat on the Supreme Court gave him the occasion, the means, and the duty to reconsider what he had always thought. The judgments of Mr. Justice Powell were not, of course, unconnected to his past, but neither did they simply carry forward his pre-Court views and experiences. His office called on him, not so much to change his mind, as to expand his field of vision. In *Bakke* he did just that. The result had one foot in his past and the other in a future that he was now required—and privileged—to help create.

BEYOND *BAKKE*

In nearly sixteen years on the Supreme Court, Powell never dissented in an affirmative action case. In every instance, his views prevailed— the only Justice of whom that can be said.

Warren Weaver, Supreme Court reporter for *The New York Times,* remarked on this tendency in a column entitled "Powell Either (a) Leads, or (b) Follows Very Well." Powell's usual place in the majority could be explained, said Weaver, by two opposite interpretations: "He could be leader in the Court's private deliberations who strongly influences others to join him to produce a majority, or a follower who acutely senses the majority position early and moves toward it." Neither was true. In affirmative action cases, Powell did not sway others, nor did he rush to take whatever position would ultimately prevail. Powell was consistently in the majority because, as in *Bakke*, the rest of the Court was evenly split and he held the balance of power.

The lineup is seen clearly in the six major affirmative action cases on which Powell sat after *Bakke*. Brennan, Marshall, and Blackmun voted to uphold racial preferences in all six cases. Rehnquist, Burger, and Sandra Day O'Connor (who succeeded Stewart in 1981) nearly always voted against. The Court's odd couple were White and Stevens, who seemed to switch places. White was for the plan in *Bakke*, but afterward usually voted against racial preferences. Stevens, by contrast, increasingly joined the liberals. Their offsetting migrations left Powell in charge. Half of these cases were decided five-four, and Powell was always the fifth vote.

In four of these six cases, affirmative action plans were upheld; in two others, they were struck down. Superficially, these decisions do not seem consistent with each other or with *Bakke*. In particular, the concern for diversity, on which Powell purported to place such great weight in *Bakke*, had no obvious relevance to affirmative action in employment. But Powell had stated that minority preferences would also be proper to redress past discrimination by that particular government or agency. On that reasoning, Powell voted to sustain minority preferences in employment as well. These cases confirmed what alert readers of *Bakke* must already have known—that diversity was not the ultimate objective but merely a convenient way to broach a compromise.

More fundamentally, all these decisions served the same goal—to allow some affirmative action, but not too much; to permit race-consciousness, but only where necessary; to approve minority preferences, but require that they be carried out with appropriate sensitivity to white interests and feelings. This was Powell's policy. It led him to accept some programs and reject others, just as he had done in *Bakke*.

Both of the affirmative action plans that were struck down involved a feature that Powell found particularly offensive—the discharge of senior white workers to maintain black employment. Powell wanted affirmative action in hiring, not firing. The reduction in job opportunity for whites was a disadvantage, to be sure, but the burden was spread among a pool of applicants. No individual would likely have an overwhelming stake in a job not already held. Discharging senior white workers, by contrast, would impose costs on them quite directly and would upset settled expectations of employment security. The difference between hiring and firing was not, as Ronald Dworkin wanted, a distinction of principle, but it did affect how racial preferences would be accepted and received. Like goals and quotas, the difference was a matter not of theory, but of practice. For Powell, that was enough.

That, however, is not all. The true legacy of Powell's vote in *Bakke* was broader, more durable, and more controversial than the outcome in this handful of cases, however important they may have been. The true legacy of Powell's approach to racial preferences lies in the enduring ambivalence of the law's reaction to them. Thanks to Powell, affirmative action is familiar, widespread, and significantly successful. Racial integration of higher education and of the professional classes is underway, and the appreciable progress made in that direction is due in large measure to Powell's approval of minority preferences.

On the other hand, affirmative action is also resented, contested, and sometimes curtailed. Society as a whole is not at ease with racial preferences, and as the country moves toward the twenty-first century, the debate over racial quotas has, if anything, grown more intense. This side of the issue also owes much to Lewis Powell. He approved racial preferences but also preserved the grounds for objecting to them. He assured their operation without conceding their future and in so doing, helped preserve the ideal of color-blindness.

Only time will tell how things work out. Racial preferences may not be needed for the hundred years insisted on by Thurgood Marshall, but they have already lasted longer than the ten years hoped for by John Paul Stevens. At this juncture, the verdict is unclear. Future generations may say that Powell fought a rearguard action against racial progress, or that he took a half step down the road toward a society perpetually divided by racial entitlements, or—just possibly—that by luck and wisdom, he eased the transition to a better world for all.

CHAPTER XV

CHANGING TIMES

THE WOMEN'S MOVEMENT

The match between challenge and experience is always partly chance. In some areas Powell's life prepared him for the issues he faced as a Justice, but in other areas, he came to the Supreme Court not only without strong conviction but almost without background. Given his disdain for ideology, Powell did not force new issues into preexisting categories of doctrine or belief. Instead, he approached unfamiliar questions through the methodology of the lawyer. When reading, research, and debate had run their course, he ultimately fell back on habit and instinct. For Powell, the unforeseen social changes of the 1970s and 1980s proved less a test of politics than of character.

So it was with the women's movement. Powell's family and upbringing had been conventionally male-dominated. His mother's life had revolved around her sensitive elder son. The family was culturally and politically conservative, oriented toward the church, and guided by a Victorian sense of respectability and decorum. The devotion of women to home and hearth seemed as fixed and right and natural as the seasons.

Not surprisingly, Powell foresaw a similar future for his daughters. When he sat down four days before the invasion of North Africa to record his hopes for a daughter he might not see again, he said she should be diligent and conscientious in her studies, loving and unselfish with her friends, proficient in sports, and graceful in dancing. She should go to an excellent college, such as Sweet Briar or Wellesley, then marry and have children. "You should be prepared to do some job in the world," he wrote little Jo, "because all women will work more from now on, but your ultimate career, I hope, will be making a home. I am old fashion[ed] enough to believe still that this is woman's highest calling."

Powell urged his daughters to prepare for work outside the home but, in their words, "sort of for the wrong reason." Training for a career was chiefly a fallback in case of divorce. Years later Molly covered the name on her LSAT score and asked her father if this person could get into a good law school. With that score, Powell said, "he could get into any place he wanted to go." He was amazed when Molly uncovered her own name, as it had not occurred to him that a daughter might wish to follow in his footsteps. (Jo, however, recalled a much younger Molly praying, "Forgive us our debts as we forgive our daddies. My daddy is a lawyer, and I'm going to be one too.")

Powell's law practice was also male-dominated. Hunton, Williams, Gay, Powell & Gibson had no women partners, and none of the female associates who passed through the firm worked directly for Powell. His first substantial experience with a woman lawyer came in 1974, when he hired Penny Clark as a law clerk. She and a male student (whom she later married) had graduated at the top of their class at the University of Texas and had been praised to the skies by the Texas faculty. Having no other grounds to choose between them, Powell opted for the female candidate, but not before calling the appeals court judge for whom she was clerking to find out if she was "the kind of girl who's going to break down in tears when the going gets tough." She was not, and Powell hired her.

It may seem surprising that Powell got along so well with Penny Clark—and with Christina Whitman, Nancy Bregstein, and the women who followed. A sixty-eight-year-old man who had worked only with other men might have been expected, as one clerk said, to reveal "an unconscious underestimation of women's abilities," but, she added, "I sure didn't see any sign of that." The others agree. Powell "treated women differently in trivial things, like opening doors and offering chairs, but not in important things." He was "incredibly appreciative of the work done by his clerks, both male and female, and never expected less from women."

Of course, it was the job of Powell's clerks to get along with him. The women clerks, like their male counterparts, were not eager to find fault with their boss. A better test of Powell's adaptation to the changing times would be his first encounter with a woman as a peer. This did not come until 1981, when Sandra Day O'Connor took her seat as the 101st Associate Justice, and first woman Justice, of the Supreme Court.

O'CONNOR SUCCEEDED Potter Stewart, who announced on June 18, 1981, that he would step down after twenty-three years on the Supreme Court. Powell found the act incomprehensible. Stewart was sixty-six years old and still in good health, but unlike Powell, Stewart actually looked forward to retirement. Neither so vain as to think himself indispensable to the Court nor so mistrustful of Ronald Reagan as to try to outlast his presidency, this balanced and sensible man chose to retire at an age that Powell found shocking but that in any other circumstance would have been quite ordinary.

In mid-March, Stewart told his friend Vice President George Bush of his intention to step down that summer. The early warning enabled the administration to move quickly once the retirement was announced. The Justices did not know whom the administration had in mind, but in the 1980 campaign Reagan had promised that "one of the first Supreme Court vacancies" in his administration would be filled by a woman.

In anticipation of this event, the Justices changed their style. First, they stopped calling themselves the "Brethren." Though they liked the tone of collegiality implied by this term, it would not do for a mixed company. Second, they altered their formal titles. Traditionally, the Chief Justice, like the President or any other unique officer, was not identified by name. He was referred to as "the Chief Justice" and addressed as "Mr. Chief Justice." The Associates were addressed by name as "Mr. Justice Marshall" or "Mr. Justice Powell," or, when the context made it clear, simply as "Mr. Justice." The female version would have been "Madam Justice," but this phrase made the men uneasy. Perhaps they feared some silliness about "Mrs." or "Miss" or "Ms. Justice," or perhaps they were put off by other uses of the word "madam." Whether O'Connor herself would have shared these concerns is not known, as the issue was resolved before she arrived. Over the objection of Blackmun, who sensibly wanted to continue the traditional form "until a woman is on the Court and her particular desires are made known," and of Powell, who agreed with Blackmun, the majority decided to shorten the honorific to the word "Justice."

(The change solved the problem for Associate Justices, whose slightly impoverished form of address was now gender-neutral, but it merely postponed the difficulty of entitling a female Chief. The other Justices address their leader as "Chief" or "Chief Justice," but that is a familiarity. To outsiders, addressing that officer as "Chief Justice" sounds so odd that most people put the "Mr." back in. The first woman Chief Justice—or for that matter the first woman President—will again raise the stylistic issue that Powell's colleagues maneuvered to avoid.)

The woman named to this shortened title was a Republican rancher, former majority leader of the Arizona Senate, and state court judge. Sandra Day O'Connor had graduated third in her class at Stanford Law School, after completing both undergraduate and law degrees in five years. First in that class was Bill Rehnquist, who called the White House with a glowing recommendation once he knew O'Connor was under consideration to join him on the Supreme Court. Burger, who had spent two weeks with O'Connor on an Anglo-American judicial exchange, also weighed in on her behalf. Although clearly conservative, O'Connor attracted support from all parts of the political spectrum *except* the Religious Right, which resented her early vote in the Arizona Senate to soften that state's law against abortion. When Jerry Falwell was (incorrectly) reported to have called on "good Christians" to oppose her nomination, Barry Goldwater said good Christians "ought to kick Falwell right in the ass." Far-right activist Richard Viguerie took a hard line. "We've been challenged," he said. "The White House has said we're a paper tiger. They've left us no choice but to fight." In fact, the tiger was nonexistent, and on September 21 the Senate confirmed O'Connor without a single dissenting vote.

Sworn in barely one week before the beginning of the new term, the new Justice found herself far behind. Huge stacks of paper kept arriving in her office, and neither she nor anyone in her chambers knew exactly what to do with them. Like Powell before her, she found Supreme Court procedures at once exacting and informal, with meticulous customs and courtesies governing every aspect of internal procedure but almost nothing in writing. With no handbook or manual to show the way, the only choice was to find someone who knew how things were done, so O'Connor and her new law clerks—whom she inherited from Stewart—spread out to investigate how the other chambers functioned. Each of them took two chambers, asking what papers went where, what various numbers meant, how the voluminous filings were winnowed for Conference, and so forth. "Altogether," recalls O'Connor, "we were in a bad state."

Powell came to her rescue. His second secretary, Linda Blandford, was a person of exceptional ability. According to the Chief Justice, she was the only second secretary in the building who had not applied for O'Connor's first position. When Burger called Powell to ask whether Blandford was aware of the opportunity, Powell virtually forced her to apply. "I *never* wanted to leave Justice Powell," Blandford recalls; "I was so happy there." But Powell pushed her to consider her career. The job was a substantial promotion; it meant more money, more responsibility, and the opportunity to work for the first female Justice. When Blandford agreed, Powell arranged matters with O'Connor, and the transfer was made. It was, O'Connor recalls, "like cutting off his right arm, but it saved my life. Linda was an absolute jewel, who knew what to do and in what order. She solved all my problems at one stroke."

Thus began a special friendship. If Sandra Day O'Connor had been selected by the President for the particular purpose of providing Lewis Powell with the perfect introduction to professional women, she could not have been better chosen. In obvious ways Powell and O'Connor were alike. At the time of her nomination, O'Connor was "said, by friend and foe alike, to be notably bright, extremely hard-working, meticulous, deliberate, cautious, and, above all, a conservative Republican." Powell called himself a "Virginia Democrat," but the description otherwise fit him as well as her. Both were socially prominent, civic-minded, family-oriented pillars of the establishment. Both impressed acquaintances with their lifelong striving for perfection. They even had the same nonprofessional interests. Although at age seventy-four Powell had given up athletics, O'Connor played tennis, skied (sometimes with Molly and Kit Sumner in Utah), led aerobics classes at the Supreme Court, and accepted a surprising number of the avalanche of speaking invitations that poured in on the first woman Justice. In the pace and style and direction of her life, O'Connor practiced what Powell admired.

They were similar even in ways that at first seemed disparate. In Arizona, O'Connor's strict standards and sometimes stern demeanor earned her a reputation as an "iron lady." Some lawyers dubbed her "the bitch queen." "She does not tolerate nonsense," they said, "or people who don't know what they're doing." But these comments were made against type. Expecting softness in a woman, people were struck by O'Connor's tough side. For Powell, expectations cut the other way. Those who met the Hunton, Williams rainmaker were impressed by Powell's gentleness, but the lawyers who worked for him knew well enough the steel underneath. To them he was the "iceman," and the cold formality of his disapproval was no less unnerving than O'Connor's stern stare.

In truth, both were perfectionists. They set incredibly high standards for both themselves and others. As Blandford recalled, both were "driven to accomplish their duties in the most efficient way humanly—perhaps not humanly—possible." Indeed, their demands on those around them could easily have been overwhelming had they not been clothed in thoughtfulness and good manners. More than with any other Justice except Stewart, Powell and O'Connor shared common ground. It is no wonder that they developed a special affection.

There was, however, one bad moment near the end of O'Connor's first term, when Powell circulated a majority opinion in a knotty statutory case. O'Connor "*strongly* disagreed" with his reasoning and dissented, as was right and proper. But as she still felt sure that her colleagues really had not understood the problem, O'Connor circulated a memorandum suggesting that the case be put over for reargument. This "just wasn't done." A member of the majority is entitled to ask for reargument but a dissenter is not. To do so would be considered an unfair attempt to undermine a colleague's Court. "That upset Lewis dreadfully," O'Connor recalls. "It was the only time I've seen him upset." All was made well when she apologized and explained that she had not known the custom. Thereafter they often talked and visited, both about personal matters and about the Court. As O'Connor recalled, "Lewis was the *only* Justice whom I felt absolutely free to visit with about issues in argued cases." The discussions did not always end in agreement, but she found them "invariably helpful."

In one respect, however, the two friends were different. Powell had always been encouraged to believe that his profession would be at the center of his life and that Jo's job, after raising a family, was to support his career. Powell's hard work was always well rewarded; for him, the doors were always open. O'Connor, by contrast, faced the obstacles of a sexist world. After graduating from Stanford Law School with an excellent record, she was offered a job by one of California's leading law firms—as a secretary. She could not get work as a lawyer in private practice and so by default took a job in the public sector—as a deputy county attorney. She followed her husband to Germany and back to Arizona, where she again entered public service and worked her way up to the relative obscurity of an intermediate state appellate court. By comparison, Powell's career seemed paved with advantage.

The foundation of Powell's good relations with O'Connor, as with his women clerks, was his unfailing civility. O'Connor found him "sweet, kind, courteous, and thoughtful." The clerks remarked his courtly manners. He often said things that might have been resented, as when he asked a female clerkship candidate whether she would pursue a career or raise a family, or when he suggested that she check with her husband before accepting the job. Such remarks were offset by his obvious kindness and decency. Indeed, the habit of courtesy and respect that made Powell such a good listener seems to have been especially valued by his female clerks. As Chris Whitman, who had just completed a less successful clerkship with a liberal appeals court judge, put it: "He really took me seriously and listened to what I had to say. I don't think I've ever worked with anyone who brought me in so comfortably. Yes, he was paternal, and he had no idea of the things that were going on in my life, but he trusted what I had to say."

In later years as Powell got more frail, his paternalism inspired in his women clerks a reciprocal tenderness, as if they were not only working for, but also watching over, an older relation. Fortunately for Powell, his old-fashioned chivalry seems not to have caused offense. O'Connor might have been speaking for these younger women when asked whether she was ever put off by Powell's elaborate courtesies. "No!" she shot back. "I thought he was lovely."

POWELL'S RESPONSE to the issues of the women's revolution paralleled his adaptation to female professionals. A few weeks before he arrived, the Supreme Court struck down an arbitrary preference for men over women as administrators of estates. At the least, said the Justices, a law had to be reasonable, and it was plainly not reasonable to discriminate against women solely on the basis of their sex.

This ground seemed quite broad enough to dispose of the next case, a dispute between the government and Air Force Lieutenant Sharron Frontiero. Frontiero claimed her husband as a dependent in order to obtain the increased quarters allowance and medical benefits paid married officers. Under the statutes then in force, a male officer could claim his wife as a dependent regardless of her income, but a female officer could claim her husband only if she actually provided his support. In total pay and benefits, therefore, women were paid less than men for the same work, based solely on an assumption about their financial responsibilities.

On January 19, 1973, Powell and six others voted to strike down this scheme, with Burger and Rehnquist dissenting. Douglas assigned the opinion to Brennan, who within a month circulated an opinion declaring the pay differential unreasonable and therefore unconstitutional. This opinion would easily have commanded a majority, but two weeks later Brennan circulated a new draft adopting a radically different approach. He did so, he said, at the request of Douglas and White, but it seems likely that Brennan himself was the moving force.

Brennan's revised draft declared sex-based classifications "inherently suspect." In the lexicon of the law, this short phrase had far-reaching consequences. It meant that sex, like race, would be a forbidden distinction, despite biological differences between men and women that have no parallel in race. Declaring sex a suspect classification would have meant that virtually all sex-based rules would have been struck down. Even where there were real differences between men and women, they could not have been reflected in the law, absent a truly compelling justification.

This pronouncement would have revolutionized the law of sex-discrimination, and it would have preempted the Equal Rights Amendment. One year earlier, Congress had approved and sent to the states for ratification a constitutional amendment declaring that "Equality of rights under the law shall not be denied or abridged . . . on account of sex." Although the effect of this language was not entirely clear—the Senate had bogged down in a debate about whether men would have the right to use women's restrooms—its thrust was plain. It would have outlawed virtually all legal distinctions based on sex—essentially the same result as would have been achieved by declaring sex, like race, an "inherently suspect" classification under the existing Equal Protection Clause. In essence, Brennan proposed to adopt the ERA by judicial decision.

Powell objected on precisely this ground. "Dear Bill," he wrote on March 2, 1973:

> My principal concern about going this far at this time . . . is that it places the Court in the position of preempting the amendatory process initiated by the Congress. If the Equal Rights Amendment is duly adopted, it will represent the will of the people accomplished in the manner prescribed by the Constitution. If, on the other hand, this Court puts "sex" in the same category as "race," we will have assumed a decisional responsibility (not within the democratic process) unnecessary to the decision of this case, and at the very time that legislatures around the country are debating the genuine pros and cons of how far it is wise, fair and prudent to subject both sexes to identical responsibilities as well as rights.
>
> The point of this letter is not to debate the merits of the Equal Rights Amendment, as to which reasonable persons obviously may differ. Rather, it is to question the desirability of this Court reaching out to anticipate a major decision which is currently in process of resolution by the duly prescribed constitutional process.

Brennan would not be put off. With Douglas and White already on board and Marshall sure to follow, he needed only one more vote. But he did not get it. "After some struggle," Blackmun wrote Brennan, "I have now concluded that it is not advisable, and certainly not necessary, for us to reach out in this case to hold that sex . . . is a suspect classification."

On May 14, when the Court announced its decision in *Frontiero v. Richardson*, Brennan spoke for only four Justices in seeking to declare sex an "inherently suspect" classification. Powell spoke for himself and two others in striking down the law on the narrower ground that it was unreasonable. He insisted that the Court should not intrude in to the ERA debate by making any broader statement. Stewart agreed without opinion. Only Rehnquist thought the law constitutional.

In future years, the tide ran out both on the ERA and on the attempt to have sex-based classifications declared "inherently suspect" under the Equal Protection Clause. The Supreme Court never returned to the point it almost reached in the case of Sharron Frontiero.

IN RETROSPECT it is hard to say how much all this mattered. Ratifying the ERA would certainly have mattered, as approval by the states would have had a social and symbolic significance far beyond the effect of the legal rule. Declaring sex a suspect classification under the Equal Protection Clause, however, likely would not have changed many outcomes. The surviving laws that discriminated against women were usually so lacking in logic that they would have failed any test. Certainly this was true of the various schemes that paid women less in survivors' benefits and other deferred compensation than men who performed the same work. Discriminations of this sort were easily struck down as unreasonable, without regard to whether sex-based classifications should be deemed inherently suspect.

The same held true for a variety of other sex-based disabilities. The Court invalidated a law excusing women from jury duty unless they volunteered; rejected a distinction in the duration of child support for daughters and sons; and struck down a law allowing husbands to dispose of jointly held property without their wives' consent. In Powell's view, these laws readily flunked the test of reasonableness.

Other issues were more difficult. Powell joined the Court in striking down a requirement that public schoolteachers take five months' unpaid leave if they became pregnant. The requirement, said Powell, was based on "factually unsupported assumptions about the ability of pregnant teachers to perform their jobs" and likely reflected some Victorian concern to "insulate schoolchildren from the sight of conspicuously pregnant women." On the other hand, Powell also joined the Court in refusing to rule that the law required private disability benefits to cover the expenses of ordinary childbirth.

The clearest difference between Powell's approach and Brennan's came in those cases where the law seemed to favor women. Special protections or benefits for women might be tolerated as accommodations to social reality, or they might be opposed as perpetuating outmoded stereotypes of female inferiority. Powell took the former view. Over the years, he voted to uphold a law giving widows but not widowers a partial exemption from property taxes; to support an up-or-out rule of thirteen years for women naval officers, even though men were ousted for lack of promotion after only nine years; to allow a state to punish men but not women for consensual sexual intercourse with an adolescent; to sustain a provision requiring men but not women to register for the draft; and to permit a state to maintain an all-female nursing school. In each of these cases, Brennan and Marshall voted the other way. Their strict view of sex-based classifications as "inherently suspect" did not permit such distinctions, but Powell's more flexible approach did.

Perhaps the most surprising thing about these decisions is what a small and relatively unimportant part of the women's revolution they turned out to be. Though the social, political, and psychological aspects of gender equality have been enormously controversial, the legal issues have been less so. Even the generally conservative Burger Court was nearly united in striking down most legal distinctions between men and women, including all those that straightforwardly disadvantaged women. Powell had no difficulty embracing this view.

GAY RIGHTS

While Powell's response to the women's movement was straightforward and secure, his reaction to the claim of gay rights was tortured and unsure. Never before had Powell faced an issue for which he was by instinct and experience so uniquely unprepared.

Agitation for a constitutional right of homosexual relations began early in Powell's tenure. In 1965 the Supreme Court had held that married persons had a constitutional right to use contraceptives. A few years later, the Court had extended that right to unmarried persons. These decisions gave constitutional protection to nonprocreative sex and set the stage for a far-reaching claim. If unmarried individuals had a right to engage in heterosexual intercourse, why not homosexual also? Were not homosexual acts done for the same purposes of gratification and intimacy as other nonprocreative sex? Were they not similarly far removed from harm to third parties? Were they not therefore equally entitled to constitutional recognition under the newly declared right of privacy?

This line of questions might have remained on the periphery of constitutional argument had it not been for *Roe v. Wade*. The abortion decision showed that the Supreme Court was serious about privacy. Not only were the Justices ready to strike down unenforced legislative oddities such as Connecticut's ban on contraceptives; they were also prepared to uproot history and override current practice in order to guarantee individual autonomy in the realm of sexuality and reproduction. If the Justices were willing to constitutionalize freedom of choice in childbearing, why not also in sexual preference? The analogy seemed nearly exact. *Roe v. Wade* created a vast new structure of personal autonomy, of which homosexual relations between consenting adults seemed a natural part.

Would the Supreme Court agree? Many lawyers and activists were eager to find out, but they could not find the right case. Though sodomy had been a crime for centuries and in most states still was, the laws were not enforced against private acts by consenting adults. Technically, the crime of sodomy—the name comes from the Biblical city of evil practices—condemned all oral or anal sex, even between a married couple, but no one imagined that the law would be, or constitutionally could be, enforced in that context. The laws remained on the books, as in popular understanding, only as strictures against homosexuals. Even in that context, the statutes were largely dormant. Strategists actively searching for the vehicle to mount a constitutional challenge to the sodomy laws could never find the right facts. Actual prosecutions always involved some aggravating factor—the use of force, or sex in public, or with an underage youth. The prospect of going to jail for purely private conduct with a consenting adult seemed entirely hypothetical.

This history of nonenforcement explained the 1975 decision in *Doe v. Commonwealth's Attorney*. In Powell's hometown of Richmond, gay men sued to challenge the constitutionality of the Virginia sodomy law. The plaintiffs had neither been arrested nor specifically threatened with prosecution, but said that since they regularly engaged in homosexual sex, they wished to be relieved of the shadow of criminality. A three-judge court upheld the statute over a vigorous dissent by Bob Merhige. Merhige argued that a "mature individual's choice of an adult sexual partner, in the privacy of his or her own home, would appear to me to be a decision of the utmost private and intimate concern. Private consensual sex acts between adults are matters, absent evidence that they are harmful, in which the state has no legitimate interest."

To Powell, Merhige's conclusion seemed not only controversial but unnecessary. He therefore joined his colleagues in summarily and without opinion upholding the state's law. Although the Court was later chastised for backhanding a question of such importance, in truth the Justices did not intend to resolve the issue but only to avoid it. Obviously the country was undergoing some adjustment in its attitudes toward homosexuality. Powell did not wish to intrude into a difficult and divisive constitutional debate unless it was necessary. There would be time enough to decide the constitutional status of consensual sodomy if and when someone was actually put in jail for doing it. In the meantime, he would let the matter lie.

And so for a decade it did. The case that finally forced the issue began almost by accident. On the morning of July 5, 1982, Michael Hardwick left the gay bar where he had worked all night. A police officer ticketed him for carrying an open bottle of beer. When Hardwick did not show up for his court date eight days later, the policeman got a warrant for his arrest. Three weeks later the officer showed up at Hardwick's apartment to serve the warrant. By this time, Hardwick had paid the fine for drinking in public, but the paperwork never caught up with the policeman. He arrived at the apartment at 8:30 in the morning and was told by a friend who had spent the night on Hardwick's couch that he could come in. He walked down the hall, saw a door ajar, and pushed it open to find Michael Hardwick engaged in sex with another man. Hardwick's arrest for that act finally provided the right facts for a constitutional challenge.

The local prosecutor abhorred "that type of conduct" but never used the sodomy statute for simply having sex. Since no public display was involved, the prosecutor dropped the charge, but by that time Hardwick had been contacted by lawyers from the ACLU and had agreed to serve as the plaintiff in a test case. "God bless the police officer," said an ACLU attorney. After looking for five years, the ACLU lawyers had finally found the right case—sex with a consenting adult in the privacy of one's own home. The fact that Hardwick had actually been arrested and taken to jail—indeed, that he was technically still subject to indictment—showed that the dispute was not purely hypothetical. Of course, from a tactical point of view it would have been better still if Hardwick had been tried and punished, but that had not happened and was not likely to. Hardwick's was as good a case as anyone was likely to see. It would be the vehicle for an all-out attack on the sodomy laws.

Hardwick's lawyers lost at trial but won on appeal. By a divided vote the appeals court ruled that private sexual activity with a consenting adult was an individual decision critical to personal autonomy and was therefore protected by the Constitution against government interference. At about the same time another appeals court reached exactly the opposite conclusion. The conflict between them demanded resolution by the Supreme Court.

Still, Powell did not want to hear the case. On October 11, 1985, he joined the majority of his colleagues (White and Rehnquist dissenting) in refusing to grant review. White then took the unusual step of drafting a public dissent from the denial of certiorari, in which he argued that the conflict in the lower courts required Supreme Court review. This action turned the tide, and a week later the Justices reversed course. Ironically, the decisive votes came from Brennan and Marshall, who joined White and Rehnquist in granting review and thus set the stage for their own defeat. Perhaps they expected to win, or perhaps they thought the case should be heard no matter what the outcome. Whatever their reasons, on November 4, the Supreme Court announced that it would hear the case destined to raise the last major constitutional issue of Powell's tenure—the appeal by Michael Bowers, Attorney General of the State of Georgia, in defense of the constitutionality of the Georgia sodomy law challenged by Michael Hardwick.

FROM THE BEGINNING, Powell found the case deeply troubling. As the arguments mounted and the Justices took sides, Powell felt forced to an unwelcome choice between extremes. As he saw it, neither side was entirely right. While others vehemently asserted one position or the other, Powell shied away from both, instinctively searching for a middle course. But this time he did not find one. Neither his colleagues, nor his clerks, nor the lawyers in the case helped him out of the dilemma. Left to his own resources, Powell waited and waffled, accepting finally what he thought to be the lesser of two evils. He never really came to rest or resolved his inner conflict, which surfaced long after his retirement as lingering vacillation and doubt about the vote he had cast. Most important, Powell did not find the means to translate his moderate impulses into legal doctrine. He failed to craft and publish a clear statement of his own views. In this sense, *Bowers v. Hardwick* was Powell's greatest defeat.

On one side was the argument—ably pressed by Laurence Tribe—

that the constitutional right of privacy encompassed a realm of sexual intimacy with which the government could not interfere. No one doubted that such a right existed within marriage. The controversial question was whether the Constitution protected sexual relations outside marriage and specifically between persons of the same sex. Tribe insisted that it did. His argument was grounded in the precedents on contraception and abortion and the zone of sexual privacy that they seemed to create, but he also emphasized cases restricting police intrusion into the home. The "sanctity of the home" was Tribe's candidate for a limiting principle to his claim of personal autonomy. After all, a constitutional right to do as one pleased had to stop somewhere, or organized society would simply collapse. Tribe's answer—or part of it—was limitation by place. Persons had a right to engage in the thrill of their choice but only, he said, in the privacy of their own homes.

It is an indication of Powell's inner turmoil that Tribe's innocuous argument set him off. "Home," Powell wrote, "is one of the most beautiful words in the English language. It usually connotes family, husband and wife, and children—although, of course, single persons, widows and widowers, and others also have genuine homes." But what exactly did "home" embrace? Would it include a hotel room or "a private room made available in a house of prostitution"? Would it include sex in an automobile or in the "'sanctity' of a toilet in a public restroom"? Here Powell was over the edge. Obviously, sexual relations of any sort could be prohibited in public. As Powell himself recognized, "home" was merely a rhetorically attractive way of describing any "truly private setting." Powell's querulousness did not reflect confusion on the point or even real disagreement. Mostly, it revealed an emotional recoil from an argument that seemed to place homosexual sodomy on a par with the sexual intimacy between man and wife.

Powell also questioned whether Tribe's argument meant that other criminal acts would have to be allowed in the "sanctity of the home." "[I]f sodomy is to be decriminalized on constitutional grounds," Powell asked, "what about incest, bigamy and adultery?" Would they also be brought within the constitutional right of privacy? One answer was that these acts might be differentiated in terms of the strength of society's interest in forbidding them. That the government might have to tolerate homosexual relations between consenting adults did not necessarily mean that it would also have to accept bigamy and incest. Powell acknowledged as much when he later wrote in the margin of his own memorandum: "I realize [that] these examples are not fairly comparable."

The strongest objection to Tribe's argument concerned not its boundaries but its premises. Where exactly did a constitutional right to homosexual sodomy come from? The Constitution did not mention privacy, much less sex, and there could be little doubt what the Framers would have thought of Hardwick's claim. On what basis, other than their personal predilections, could the Justices of the Supreme Court legitimately decide what the people of Georgia could and could not forbid?

An answer was made by the state of Georgia and from within Powell's chambers by the clerk assigned to this case. Mike Mosman was a Mormon by faith, a moralist by disposition, and a hard-nosed opponent of judicial innovation. His bench memo, given to Powell two days before oral argument, argued powerfully for limiting the constitutional right of privacy to those interests firmly rooted in the history and traditions of the people.

"The focus on history and tradition," Mosman explained, "results from the fact that the right of privacy is not intended to be the vanguard of changes in social values. It is intended to protect those values that are imbedded in the fabric of our society," not to add new ones. In this view, "homosexual sodomy [did] not fit within the right of privacy." Even Larry Tribe could not deny that such acts had long been condemned. Instead, Tribe tried to reshape the issue by bringing homosexual sodomy within the long-standing societal regard for other forms of sexual intimacy. Mosman countered by pointing out that Supreme Court had "never recognized a broad-based right of sexual freedom. Instead, it has extended protection to those sexual relationships that have traditionally been protected and recognized in our society—those that relate to marriage and other family relationships. Up through the present time, every one of the Court's right of privacy cases can be explained in terms of a concern for the fundamental right of marital and family privacy."

According to Mosman, even abortion could be explained on that ground. Laws against abortion "have the effect of *forcing* a woman to bring a family into existence. For unmarried women, the abortion decision is not a decision about her commitment to her sexual partner; it is a decision about long-term commitments to her potential offspring." In Mosman's view, therefore, the abortion cases did not protect a woman's "sexual freedom," but rather her interest in "her potential relationship and commitment to a child she does not want to bear—her interest in not having the state require her to become a mother." So interpreted, the abortion and contraception cases extended the right of privacy no further than indicated by the "fundamental values of family and procreation."

"More importantly," Mosman concluded, "I think the fact that the right of privacy cases are limited to marriage, family, and procreation accurately reflects the traditions of our people. Personal sexual freedom is a newcomer among our national values, and may well be . . . a temporary national mood that fades. This may be reflected in the fact that in the 1970s twenty states decriminalized homosexual sodomy, while in the 1980s only two states have done so. . . . The right of privacy calls for the greatest judicial restraint, invalidating only those laws that impinge on those values that are basic to our country. I do not think this case involves any such value."

While this analysis put a plausible conservative gloss on most of the privacy cases, it could not explain abortion. *Roe v. Wade* did not recognize a right already deeply imbedded in the history and tradition of the nation. On the contrary, it uprooted existing law to make way for an entirely new right. Contrary to Mosman's memo, *Roe* put the right of privacy in the vanguard of social change. His argument therefore boiled down to this: Whatever had been done in *Roe*, the constitutional concept of privacy should not again be expanded to create a wholly new right. The bold experiment in judicial innovation should not be repeated. The Court should return to a respect for history and tradition, which did not embrace a right to homosexual sodomy.

In this argument, Mosman had powerful allies. First, there was the ghost of John Harlan, who in *Griswold v. Connecticut* had endorsed the right of married couples to use contraceptives but had specifically rejected a right to homosexual sex. Fundamental rights, said Harlan, did not come from the personal whims of the Justices but reflected "the balance which our Nation, built upon postulates of respect for the liberty of the individual, has struck between that liberty and the demands of organized society." The content of the right of privacy was therefore fixed by the traditions of the people, which clearly did not accept homosexual sex. Harlan concluded: "I would not suggest that adultery, homosexuality, fornication and incest are immune from criminal enquiry, however privately practiced."

Second, Mosman could quote Powell's prior decisions—abortion excepted—in support of his historically grounded view of the right to privacy. In *Moore v. City of East Cleveland*, Powell struck down a single-family housing ordinance that defined single family so narrowly that even some close relatives could not live together in one dwelling. This ordinance, Powell argued, intruded into a "private realm of family life which the state cannot enter." When Justice White objected that no such right appeared in the text of the Constitution, Powell answered in the best Harlan tradition. "There *are* risks," he admitted, in recognizing unwritten rights, but the safeguard lay in "respect for the teachings of history [and] solid recognition of the basic values that underlie our society." Here, he said, "the Constitution protects the sanctity of the family precisely because the institution of the family is so deeply rooted in this Nation's history and tradition." The same could not be said for homosexual sex.

Most important, Mosman could appeal to Powell's emotions. However radical *Roe v. Wade* had been as a matter of constitutional law, it did not require that Powell transcend his private sensibilities. He did not find abortion personally offensive. Sodomy was different. Powell said that if he were in the legislature, he would vote to decriminalize sodomy, but that had to do chiefly with the practicalities of the situation. Even where the practice was prevalent, the laws were not enforced. "Moreover, police have more important responsibilities than snooping around trying to catch people in the act of sodomy." But Powell's intellectual commitment to toleration masked emotional misgiving. Abortion had seemed to him unfortunate but not wrong, while homosexuality struck him as profoundly unnatural. "At a very deep level," thought one clerk, "he found homosexual sodomy abhorrent."

These concerns converged at a point of practical importance. Powell wished, above all else, to avoid a broad declaration of a privacy right that would have consequences outside the field of criminal prosecution. Despite Tribe's effort to circumnavigate these issues, Powell feared that accepting Tribe's argument against criminal punishment for homosexual sodomy would entangle the Court in a continuing campaign to validate the gay "lifestyle" in a variety of other contexts. After all, if homosexuals had a constitutional right to engage in sex, would they not also have the right to object to any form of regulation or restriction disadvantaging them for having done so? Would gays then have a constitutional right to serve in the military or the intelligence agencies? Would they have a right to teach in public school or work in day care centers? Would there be a constitutional requirement that the law allow homosexual adoption or same-sex marriage?

This was not a revolution Powell was ready to lead. The eventualities down the road appalled him, but he could not see how they could be avoided if the Court were to declare a new fundamental right to engage in homosexual sodomy. Against the background of these concerns, Powell found his clerk's hard-hitting memo persuasive. Mosman's caution reinforced his own, and the narrow reading of the privacy cases helped Powell draw a line where his emotions indicated. He would not create a new constitutional right of consensual sodomy. He would not attempt another *Roe v. Wade* on behalf of homosexuals. To that extent Powell sided with the Court's conservatives and against the claim of Michael Hardwick.

But Powell was only partly persuaded by Mosman's memo; he was also pulled the other way. Unlike White and Rehnquist, who consistently opposed privacy claims, Powell had generally been in favor of them. He had never backed off from his support for abortion, so for him the analogy to *Roe v. Wade* was far from fatal. On questions of this sort, Powell voted with the liberals, and if he was not willing to go with them all the way to a new constitutional right, he at least respected what they had to say.

And on one crucial point he thought them entirely correct. Just as creating a new fundamental right went too far in one direction, flatly rejecting that claim went too far in the other. If, as the conservatives contended, consensual sodomy was not constitutionally protected, then presumably the states could regulate such acts as they pleased, including by criminal prosecution and punishment. Powell found this prospect barbaric. Whatever his private sensibilities, he was quite unwilling to see the Michael Hardwicks of the world imprisoned for acting on their sexual desires. It seemed to him senseless and cruel that persons afflicted—that was how he thought of it—with homosexuality should be condemned as criminals. Where there was no public display, no use of force, and involvement with minors, the conduct was essentially harmless. Society did not have to approve such behavior, but it could not constitutionally prosecute and imprison those who engaged in it.

Powell therefore sought a middle course. He hoped to split the difference between sodomy as a major crime and sodomy as a fundamental right. He wanted to avoid approving homosexuality in the name of the Constitution but at the same time to protect homosexuals from criminal prosecution. He wanted to prevent oppression without requiring social revolution. As in *Bakke*, he hoped to blur the edges of the controversy in a compromise that would allow the nation to muddle its way toward a better future.

But this inclination was more an instinct than an argument. Powell needed to translate his intuition into law. He needed some doctrine or reasoning that would differentiate criminal punishment from other kinds of restrictions on homosexuals. He needed a legal theory.

Finding no better candidates, his clerks proposed the Eighth Amendment guarantee against "cruel and unusual punishments." Its attraction lay in the fact that it applied specifically and exclusively to the criminal law and therefore might plausibly be used to erect a doctrinal wall between criminal punishment and any other legal disadvantage imposed on homosexuals. Its weakness lay in the traditional understanding of what constituted "cruel and unusual punishments." The phrase obviously covered torture or confinement in inhuman conditions. Additionally, it had been held to forbid some uses of the death penalty, as in the long line of cases restricting capital punishment for murder and forbidding it altogether for rape. But none of these things had been done to Michael Hardwick. He had not been punished at all, much less threatened with torture or execution.

The clerks therefore invoked a different aspect of Eighth Amendment law, the 1962 decision in *Robinson v. California*. So obscure that a generation of legal scholars had debated its meaning, *Robinson* seemed to say that, while individuals could be held criminally responsible for their *acts*, no one could be punished criminally for a mere *status*. The "status" at issue in *Robinson* was being addicted to narcotics, which the Court said could not be made a crime. This ruling would have been precisely applicable if Georgia had punished the status of being homosexual, but that the state had not tried to do. Rather, Georgia condemned the *act* of homosexual sodomy, which, like the *act* of using narcotics, could be proscribed. Nevertheless, the clerks felt that the act of sodomy was so closely linked to the status of homosexuality that perhaps *Robinson* could be stretched to protect both from criminal prosecution.

That, at any rate, was the theory. It was a debatable use of an isolated precedent that did not fit the situation, but it was the best the clerks could come up with. Nor were these flaws the only problem. Perhaps more important, no Eighth Amendment issue had been raised in the courts below. The failure to litigate the claim in the trial court created a procedural obstacle to considering that issue in the Supreme Court. That problem was perhaps not insuperable, but it did further burden an already weak idea. Small wonder that others thought the *Robinson* argument simply "crazy."

Powell, however, was desperate to find some way out of his dilemma. In the days before the Conference, he increasingly clutched the fragile thesis of the Eighth Amendment and its interpretation in *Robinson v. California* as the means of escape.

*   *   *

POWELL'S SEARCH for a legal theory paralleled a search for personal understanding. Sexual activity between men was something he did not comprehend. Unable to say exactly what he wished to learn, he nonetheless realized that he needed to know more.

Unknown to Powell, one of his clerks was gay. Powell merely identified the young man as the most liberal of the four clerks and so sought out his views as a counterbalance to the conservative Mike Mosman. Powell came into the clerk's office and casually asked him to review the arguments in this difficult case. When told that (as the clerk believed) 10 percent of the population was gay, Powell was incredulous. "I don't believe I've ever met a homosexual," he told his astonished clerk. "Certainly you have," came back the reply, "but you just don't know that they are." In North Africa, Powell said, "not a single episode of homosexuality was reported" despite several months away from women, but the clerk insisted that the behavior would have occurred without Powell's knowledge.

The discussion edged toward Powell's true mission when he tried to find out from his startled clerk just what it meant to be gay:

> "Are gay men not attracted to women at all?"
> "They are attracted to women, but there is no sexual excitement."
> "None at all?"
> "Justice Powell, a gay man could not get an erection to have sex with a woman."

The answer left Powell even more confused. "Don't you have to have an erection to perform sodomy?" he asked.

"Yes," he was told, "but that's because of the sexual excitement."

What Powell found so difficult to grasp was that homosexuality was not an act of desperation, not the last resort of men deprived of women, but a logical expression of the desire and affection that gay men felt for other men.

A few days later he made another run at the same topic. Again the clerk tried to explain that gay men "love other men like straight men love women." Powell still found it hard to follow. In the words of the clerk: "He had no concept of it at all. He couldn't understand the idea of sexual attraction between two men. It just had no content for him."

A third conversation took place just before oral argument. Uncharacteristically, Powell had still not decided how he would vote. In great distress, the clerk debated whether to tell Powell of his sexual orientation. Perhaps if Powell could put a familiar face to these incomprehensible urges, they would seem less bizarre and threatening. He came to the edge of an outright declaration but ultimately drew back, settling for a "very emotional" speech urging Powell to support sexual freedom as a fundamental right. "The right to love the person of my choice," he argued, "would be far more important to me than the right to vote in elections." "That may be," Powell answered, "but that doesn't mean it's in the Constitution."

In the end, Powell remained unsure. The issue was also difficult for his clerks, who, disagreeing among themselves and acutely aware of the high emotions on both sides, walked on eggshells to avoid an open breach. From them Powell received little real help. The middle course they suggested to him had not been well thought out, nor was it supported by any substantial writing. Though Powell had an instinct for where he wanted to end up, he had no sure idea of how to get there. In this unusual state of indecision, he went to the Conference on Wednesday, April 2, and shook hands with each of his colleagues as they prepared to decide the case of *Bowers v. Hardwick.*

BURGER LED OFF with a tirade. Homosexual sodomy had been a crime for centuries. If sodomy were declared a fundamental right, incest, prostitution, and the like would surely follow. Quoting Harlan and Powell on the importance of history and tradition and the sanctity of the family, Burger voted to uphold the law.

Brennan followed with a defense of the right of privacy. He answered the objection to the far-reaching implications of a new fundamental right by emphasizing, as Tribe had, the sanctity of the home. For Brennan, the case involved the question of "sexual privacy in the home" and not any broader questions of the state's interest in regulating such acts as incest and adultery.

The other Justices then took sides. White, Rehnquist, and O'Connor lined up with the Chief. Marshall, Blackmun, and Stevens (with misgivings) agreed with Brennan.

The four–four split gave Powell the controlling vote, which in a sense was also equally divided. On the one hand, he was not persuaded that Hardwick had any fundamental constitutional right to engage in homosexual sodomy. On the other hand, Powell thought it would violate the Eighth Amendment "to punish him criminally (*imprisonment*) for conduct based on a natural sexual urge, privately and with a consenting partner." Powell's views were finely balanced, but the case had to be decided one way or the other. Since his Eighth Amendment theory barred criminal punishment, he voted against the Georgia law.

Powell's speech made no one happy. The liberals thought his theory bizarre and the result distressingly narrow. It did no more than preclude criminal prosecution, a possibility that had never been realistic. That was at best a minor victory. The conservatives, on the other hand, were confused and disappointed. The Eighth Amendment issue had not even been raised in the courts below. Why did Powell raise it now? And if Powell agreed with them that sodomy was not a constitutional right, how could a law against it be unconstitutional?

If others were baffled, the Chief was outraged. On the day after the Conference, he sent Powell a private letter. The missive began cogently. First, Powell's theory had not been raised by the litigants. Indeed, Tribe's brief for Michael Hardwick did not even cite *Robinson*, on which Powell now tried to rely, or so much as mention the Eighth Amendment. Moreover, Powell's theory did not fit the case. "Georgia here criminalizes only the *act* of sodomy," Burger noted. "If the act of sodomy is a 'status,' then what about the acts of incest, exhibitionism, rape, and drug possession?" Of course, Powell did not dispute that sodomy was an act. He claimed rather that the act was so closely linked to the involuntary status of being homosexual that it could not constitutionally be punished as a crime. But this theory, Burger argued, "would swallow up centuries of criminal law," since anyone with a "psychological dependency" would be entitled to "carry out (at least in private or with a consenting partner) whatever is necessary to satisfy his cravings."

Burger then warmed to the theme. "[S]urely homosexuals are not 'sex crazed' automatons who are 'compelled' by their 'status' to gratify their sexual appetites only by committing sodomy. . . . It is extremely unlikely that what Western Civilization has for centuries viewed as a volitional, reprehensible act is, in reality, merely a conditioned response to which moral blame may not attach."

In reality, Burger insisted, the case did not involve punishment of a status or of any involuntary act compelled by that status. Rather, "Hardwick merely wishes to seek his own form of sexual gratification." Others "seek gratification through incest, drug use, gambling, exhibitionism, prostitution, [and] rape." That persons were gratified by such activities did not make them constitutionally protected. "As Justice Holmes put it, 'pretty much all law consists in forbidding men to do some things that they want to do. . . .'"

Burger closed with a personal aside: "April 13, an unlucky day, will mark my 30th year on the Bench. This case presents for me the most far reaching issue of those 30 years. I hope you will excuse the energy with which I have stated my views, and I hope you will give them earnest consideration."

Word of Burger's intervention soon leaked out, and it afterward became an article of faith in some quarters that the Chief had somehow "gotten to" Powell. In fact, the rumor captured only the least part of truth. Burger's devastating attack on the *Robinson* theory did make Powell uneasy, but the Chief's excesses put Powell off. That Burger could regard this as the most far-reaching issue of his thirty years as a judge seemed to Powell incredible. His reaction was summarized when he wrote on the top of Burger's statement: "There is both sense and non-sense in this letter—mostly the latter."

A more influential intervention came from Michael Mosman. A few days after the Conference, Mosman weighed in with a memo urging Powell to change his vote. Even if Powell's Eighth Amendment theory was right, Mosman argued, it did not apply to this case. The only question squarely before the Court was whether homosexual sodomy was a fundamental right. Powell agreed with the conservatives that it was not, and his vote should reflect that view. There was simply no reason on these facts to rush into the difficult question of what restrictions, if any, the Eighth Amendment placed on criminal penalties for consensual sodomy, especially since the issue had not been raised below. There would be time enough to consider the question of cruel and unusual punishments if and when someone actually went to jail. In the meantime, Powell should decide the case before him and leave other questions for another day.

On reflection, Powell agreed. On April 8, he wrote his colleagues: "At Conference last week, I expressed the view that in some cases it would violate the Eighth Amendment to imprison a person for a private act of homosexual sodomy." Powell adhered to that view, but "upon further study as to exactly what is before us," concluded that his "bottom line" should be to uphold Georgia's law. Accordingly, he changed his vote.

Powell's switch was variously greeted with jubilation and dismay. The conservatives would now control the outcome, if not the reasoning, and liberal resentment was bitter and deep. Amid all the recriminations then and later about why Powell changed his vote, the most insightful reaction came from Justice Stevens, who wrote Powell that his change of heart reminded Stevens of a curious case from the 1930s in which the Court, with all nine Justices participating, refused to resolve an issue on the ground that it was "equally divided." The vote, as Powell noted in the margin, must have been "4½ to 4½." A split vote was technically impossible, but it precisely reflected Powell's view.

*   *   *

THAT POWELL HAD REVERSED himself quickly became known. Two weeks after the end of the term, Al Kamen published a remarkably complete and accurate account of the switch in the *Washington Post*. Unnoticed and unremarked was a decision of almost equal significance that occurred some weeks later.

With Powell now voting to uphold the law, the Chief Justice found himself in the majority. He assigned the case to White, who took barely a week to circulate a draft as abrupt in tone as it was quick in origin. In an opinion that struck many observers as "superficial, peremptory and insensitive," White dismissed the claim that sexual freedom was a fundamental right as "at best, facetious." Even more disturbing was White's "failure to acknowledge in any way the human dimension of this issue. Not a single sentence expresses any understanding of the fact that this case involves human beings who have needs for intimacy, love and sexual expression like the rest of us. Not a single sentence acknowledges the human anguish that anti-homosexual statutes can create. . . ." Instead, White dispatched the issue and those affected by it with the same sympathy that he would have shown an opposing tackler in his football days. It was the intellectual equivalent of brute force.

Although Powell now planned to vote with White, his initial instinct was not to join this opinion. On April 22, he told White that he would write separately. Yet a month later, he changed his mind and joined White. This decision made White's opinion authoritative. If Powell had refused to join, White would have spoken for only four Justices, and his views would have been exactly balanced and offset by the four Justices on the other side. If Powell had carried through his intention to speak for himself, his would have been the decisive voice, and though he could not have bridged the gulf between the two positions, he at least would have tried to seek out some middle ground. Lawyers and journalists would have focused on his position, which would have given neither side a clear-cut victory and imposed on neither a total defeat. He would neither have encouraged gays to think that all legal disadvantages could be attacked as unconstitutional nor invited their opponents to seek stricter enforcement of the laws against homosexuals. Instead, he would have attempted to refocus the constitutional debate by distinguishing criminal punishment from all other forms of legal regulation.

But this he did not do. He not only joined White's short-tempered outburst but abandoned his plan for a full-scale opinion of his own and issued instead a two-paragraph concurrence that was justly ignored.

Why he did so is perhaps the greatest mystery of Powell's career. On other occasions, he knew well enough the uses of ambivalence. In *Bakke*, for example, he crafted a compromise that neither categorically condemned racial preferences nor unqualifiedly approved racial quotas. That opinion may have been an intellectual muddle, but it was a political masterpiece. And it was also successful in a personal sense, as it exactly reflected his heartfelt view of the case and the issue. In *Bakke*, Powell found a way to translate his conviction into a legal judgment and in so doing to dominate the decision of a divided Court. But in *Bowers* he did just the opposite, joining an ugly opinion with which he only partly agreed and muffling his own quite different views in a throwaway concurrence.

No single factor accounts for this default. Initially, Powell made an effort to learn what he did not know, to maintain his open-mindedness, and to bring to this emotional issue the dispassion that he thought judging required, but he did not follow through. In the end, he gave up on himself and his own perspective. Age and health played their part, as Powell was now seventy-eight years old and still recuperating from a major illness the year before. Infirmity made it more difficult to summon the sustained mental energy required to translate Powell's uncertain views into law. The unusual situation with his clerks may have mattered as well. Paralyzed by divisions that all of them describe as painful, the clerks were unable to coalesce in support of the Justice's instincts. Their conflict made Powell even more keenly aware of the difficulty of the question before him and forced him to fall back on his own resources.

Another factor—one easily overlooked by those who think the Supreme Court's work entirely political—was the shaky intellectual support for Powell's intuition. Powell went to the Conference of April 2 with an argument based on *Robinson v. California* and its teaching that a mere status could not be made a crime. Eventually, he had to recognize that the theory did not fit the case. Under effective attack from the Chief Justice and from Mosman, this approach was abandoned. Instead, Powell turned to another Eighth Amendment theory based on the idea that criminal punishment is "cruel and unusual" whenever it is grossly disproportionate to the crime committed. On this ground the Court had forbidden execution for the crime of rape and rejected life sentences for minor crimes. The lesson of these cases was that criminal punishment was unconstitutional if grossly excessive—that is, wildly out of proportion to any wrong done.

This last point perhaps could be adapted to this situation. Even if

Michael Hardwick did not have a fundamental right to engage in homosexual sodomy, he did at least have an Eighth Amendment right not to be punished excessively for having done so. The Georgia statute at least raised the possibility of extravagant severity, as it authorized imprisonment for up to twenty years. Powell was prepared to rule that a lengthy prison sentence—indeed, any prison sentence—would be grossly excessive for private sexual activity between consenting adults. Of course, on these facts imprisonment was not an issue, as Michael Hardwick had not been prosecuted, much less imprisoned. Nevertheless, this reasoning allowed Powell—at least in his own mind—to forbid criminal punishment for homosexual sodomy without getting into the more difficult issues (such as same-sex marriage and gays in the military) that he did not want to face.

Unfortunately, Powell kept this conclusion mostly to himself. His position was not well advertised by his vote in favor of the Georgia law. His concurrence said merely that imprisonment for consensual sodomy would create a serious Eighth Amendment issue, which he would not get into as it had not been raised below. The point seemed almost an aside. It did not convey the strength of Powell's commitment to the Eighth Amendment theory or suggest how far he was prepared to go. It did not reveal the gulf that separated him from Burger and White. It said nothing about the doubts and concerns that had led Powell first to vote against the Georgia sodomy statute and only later to change his mind. It gave no hint that anyone in the Court's majority was the least concerned about the "human dimensions" of laws against homosexuals.

In short, Powell failed. He failed to capture the Court and make himself decisive, as he had in *Bakke*. More fundamentally, he failed to act on his own best judgment. He took a position he only partly believed in and submerged his disagreement in an elliptical concurrence. He failed, not because he contradicted someone else's expectations of what the law should be but because he did not bring his own wisdom and reflection to bear on the problem. In one of the most crucial constitutional issues of his time on the Court, Powell's voice was muffled, his position obscure, and the essential humanity of his own reactions hidden from public view.

At bottom, Powell suffered from lack of confidence. In *Bakke*, he knew where he wanted to go and, more to the point, knew how important it was that he get there. He was prepared to hold his ground, whatever the cost. In *Bowers*, Powell's every step was beset by doubt. He was unsure of his legal theory and of the underlying social reality, uncertain how to reach his desired result, and sufficiently unsettled in his own convictions that he did not force the issue to a successful conclusion.

EMBLEMATIC OF POWELL'S difficulty with this case, and the most puzzling element in its history, was the remark that he had never known a homosexual. He said it at least twice, once to his clerk and once at the Conference of April 2. Blackmun later told his clerks that he thought of saying, "Of course you have. You've even had gay clerks." Instead, Blackmun said, "But surely, Lewis, you were approached as a boy?" There is no record of a response.

Was Powell being honest? He had in fact employed gay clerks and had also encountered homosexuals working elsewhere in the Court, as he must have encountered them in school, in private practice, in the army, and elsewhere. Of course Powell knew homosexuals. The question was whether he acknowledged anyone he knew as a homosexual. The answer is that he did not, largely because he did not want to. In his upbringing, homosexuality was at least a failing, if not a sin. He later came to think of it as an abnormality, an affliction for which its bearers perhaps should not be blamed but which was nevertheless vaguely scandalous. He would not make assumptions. He would not infer such misfortune without direct knowledge. Powell would not have known someone was homosexual unless that person told him so.

This willed ignorance was not limited to homosexuality. Powell routinely turned a blind eye to what he considered the failings of others— or at least did not anchor such perceptions in his memory by remarking on them. His recollections of those who worked for him always focused on their abilities and achievements, not on their shortcomings—nor on the embarrassing incidents that others might have relished. In fact, his description of someone often approximated a résumé. He would say that one clerk was first in his class at law school or that another clerk had done good work on a particularly important case or that a colleague from private practice was the best at doing this or particularly skilled at that. For each of his many friends and subordinates, he sought out a ground on which he could base respect. He regularly subordinated observation to friendship, and if forced to recognize potentially corrosive differences, he would often retreat to some ground of explanation that seemed to validate both perspectives.

A small example makes the point. Early in his judicial career, Powell was required to review certain pornographic materials to determine whether they were sufficiently devoid of "redeeming social value" to be legally obscene. The clerk assigned to the case told Powell rather casually that the materials really "weren't all that bad." When Powell saw the pictures, he was profoundly shocked. The illustrated sex acts included some he had not thought possible and many more he could not imagine anyone wanting to do or watch. But he did not think ill of his clerk. Instead, he quickly decided that young people had radically different standards and that the clerk's tolerance of such materials was merely generational. The potential for distance or disagreement was simply put aside, as Powell's mind returned to the common ground. No doubt this habit of tolerance and respect for others accounted for the great affection he often inspired in those who disagreed with him.

So it was with homosexuality. Powell had never known a homosexual because he did not want to. In his world of accomplishment and merit, homosexuality did not fit, and Powell therefore did not see it.

BOWERS V. HARDWICK was announced on June 30, 1986. Both White and Blackmun read at length from their opinions in open display of the bitterness within the Court. Powell said nothing, and the amelioration at which he aimed remained buried in his brief concurrence. That evening he enjoyed the distraction of a dinner at the Phillips Museum, where he sat next to Helen Hayes.

The next morning brought harsh reactions to the decision of the day before. The Boston Globe called it "the most preposterous and contradictory ruling to be handed down in a long time." The New York Times inveighed against "a gratuitous and petty ruling, an offense to American society's maturing standards of individual dignity." Various protests occurred, including one by Alan Dershowitz, who attended and then walked out of Chief Justice Burger's speech to the American Bar Association so that he could announce that Burger would be "remembered in infamy" for his part in the decision.

Powell got a small taste of the same treatment in 1989 when he was awarded an honorary degree from Yale. President Benno Schmidt praised him for helping "to fashion justice, to bring us stability, and to accommodate change. It is with pride that Yale awards you a Doctor of Laws." After these kind words at the university graduation, Powell went to the smaller law school ceremony, where he was asked by Dean Guido Calabresi to make a few impromptu remarks. Though most of the audience applauded respectfully, at least one student rose, turned his back, and remaining standing throughout the speech. Powell heard puzzling boos and hisses. As one graduate later explained, "it was important that he should have to bear some cost for his decision." (Fortunately for Powell's peace of mind, he left the ceremony before the speech by a young man wearing a picture of a condom and before Professor Catharine MacKinnon told the assembled families that "some excited graduates must sit a row or two away from their rapists, relieved to be leaving their sexual harassers, trying not to think about those who molested them as children.")

But the most telling reaction to *Bowers* came from Powell himself. On October 18, 1990, Powell gave the annual James Madison lecture at New York University Law School and afterward answered students' questions. One asked how Powell could reconcile his vote in *Bowers v. Hardwick* with his support for *Roe v. Wade.* "I think I probably made a mistake in that one," Powell said of *Bowers.* When a reporter called to confirm the remark, Powell repeated the recantation: "I do think it was inconsistent in a general way with *Roe.* When I had the opportunity to reread the opinions a few months later, I thought the dissent had the better of the arguments."

One man who might have been embittered by this revelation reacted graciously. "I think it's an admirable thing," said Laurence Tribe. "All of us make mistakes, and not all of us are willing to admit them." Tribe also wrote Powell a personal letter recalling his oral argument, which he thought "one of my best," and praising Powell's "courage and candor" in acknowledging error. Tribe then ventured a sly request for something in writing: "Should you be willing to reply to this letter, my wife and I would count your response among our most cherished mementos." Unfortunately for Tribe, Powell's reply was not suitable for framing. "I had forgotten that you argued *Bowers,*" Powell wrote. "I did think the case was frivolous as the Georgia statute had not been enforced since 1935. The Court should not have granted certiorari."*

This was scarcely the ringing endorsement Tribe had in mind, but it truly reflected Powell's view. As startling as his change of heart may have seemed, it was really no more than his continuing unease at choosing between sodomy as a crime and sodomy as a fundamental right. He had never come to rest on that question—not when he voted at the Conference of April 2, 1986, or when he changed his vote on April 8, or some weeks later when he decided to join Byron White. Neither was he really at rest four years later when he came to think he should have stuck by his original inclination. On this issue, Powell never found the middle ground.

---

* Anthony Lewis made the same point in a column berating the Justices for rushing "to pass judgment on a criminal law that was not pressed against Mr. Hardwick and has not been used against anyone for decades." The result of this "unnecessary" decision, Lewis argued, would be to "legitimate atavistic attitudes in our society."

CHAPTER XVI

A SENSE OF DUTY

THE REHNQUIST COURT

A few days before *Bowers v. Hardwick* was handed down, Chief Justice Burger announced his retirement. The median age of the Court he left was the oldest in the nation's history. Five Justices—Burger, Brennan, Marshall, Blackmun, and Powell—were nearing eighty. At age sixty-nine, White was one of the Court's younger members. Burger's departure marked the beginning of a generational fault line; within five years all but one of his contemporaries would also have left the Court.

To succeed Burger, President Reagan nominated William H. Rehnquist. Although Powell's exact contemporary on the Court, Rehnquist had not yet reached the age at which Powell began his service. On September 17, 1986, the Senate confirmed Rehnquist as Chief Justice by a vote of sixty-five to thirty-three. The large number of negatives reflected objections real and contrived. In the former category was an honest dislike of Rehnquist's policies. Easily the most conservative member of a conservative Court, Rehnquist seemed always to vote no. He was against the right of abortion, against affirmative action, against restrictions on the death penalty, and against extensive federal review of state criminal convictions. He was not, as some thought, a conservative activist who tried to force the nation to conform to his views. He was rather a conservative statist who readily accepted the constitutionality of legislation regardless of its political content. In Rehnquist's hands the Constitution was simply smaller. Fewer laws of any sort would be struck down, as constitutional liberties were contracted to give maximum scope to the popularly elected branches of government. To Senate liberals, mistrustful of the nation's political temper, judicial retrenchment seemed an altogether bad idea, and some opposed Rehnquist on precisely that ground.

Many, however, were discomforted by the frankly political nature of this objection and so found other reasons to oppose the nomination. Charges that Rehnquist had harassed black voters in Arizona in the early 1960s were resurrected, even though they had been fully aired in his 1971 confirmation as an Associate Justice. Much was made of the fact that Rehnquist bought property subject to a restrictive covenant forbidding sale to Jews, even though Rehnquist knew, as any competent lawyer would have, that the restriction was legally invalid and therefore meaningless. Some even talked of Rehnquist's "drug problem"—an habituation to Placidyl that developed in the late 1970s when he took the medication to alleviate persistent back pain. (In 1981 Rehnquist recognized the problem and entered a Washington hospital for treatment of drug dependency. Ever since, he has practiced a rigorous regimen of exercise and stands a few minutes every hour to relieve the stress on his back.) Ultimately, these grounds proved insubstantial. Perhaps equally influential was the fact that as a sitting Justice, Rehnquist would have the same one vote whether or not he was confirmed as Chief. In any event, the Senate approved the appointment, and on October 6, 1986, when the Court convened to hear the first argument of the new term, Rehnquist took the center seat as the sixteenth Chief Justice of the United States.

Powell applauded Rehnquist's appointment, as did most of their colleagues. Those who knew the new Chief Justice only through his opinions supposed him to be harsh and unforgiving, but in fact he was genial and unpretentious. Burger had irked his colleagues with petty dissemblings. If he had not yet read the circulated opinions of other Justices, they were "still being processed." If he got to something only after prompting by the other chambers, he backdated the document to make it appear that he had begun work earlier. He denied that law clerks wrote his opinions, although of course they did and everyone knew it. And armed with a convenient memory, he routinely recalled events and characterized precedents in ways that "bore no relation to reality." Rehnquist, by contrast, was open and direct. Even those who deplored his decisions found him easy to work with.

Nowhere was the change in leadership more apparent than at Conference. As the Chief Justice always speaks first, it is his duty to state the case and frame the issue for decision. Burger often came to Conference without a thorough knowledge of the cases. He would wander around the general subject and end up reserving his vote until the others had spoken. Over the years, his long-winded monologues and puffed-up pronouncements became repetitive and maddeningly predictable. Brennan said that Burger would "drive us all crazy—including Lewis—with the same law-and-order speech in every damn criminal case." According to another Justice, once others began to speak, Burger would freely "interject his own comments and views . . . which might or might not be relevant."

As a junior Justice, Rehnquist endured Burger's loose style. As Chief Justice, he would not make the same mistake. Rehnquist's opening statements were crisp and focused, often opinionated, but never useless or vague. Indeed, Rehnquist may have overreacted to Burger's failings, for he imposed on the Conference a Prussian order to which some objected. One Justice disliked the rigid insistence on going down the seniority ladder with no interruptions, and another thought Rehnquist allowed less time for discussion than the cases required. In general, however, the new regime drew high marks, even from Rehnquist's ideological adversaries. Brennan called him "a magnificent Chief Justice."

The true significance of Rehnquist's promotion, however, was not the shift in style but a change in substance. The custom of identifying a particular Supreme Court by the name of its Chief Justice had never seemed especially appropriate for Warren Burger. In fact, one historian of the era, Professor Herman Schwartz, suggested that the Supreme Court of the 1970s and 1980s might more accurately be called the Powell Court, on the ground that Powell was "probably its single most influential member." (Brennan sent a photocopy of this comment to Powell with a note saying "and so completely the truth.") Yet despite the inevitable distortion in collecting nine strong-minded Justices under the name of the Chief, references to "the Rehnquist Court" seem increasingly apt. Aside from abortion, the post-1986 Court has aligned more and more closely with the policies and politics of the Chief Justice. In fact as well as in name, William Rehnquist leads the Supreme Court.

Powell could see little of this future in 1986. He welcomed Rehnquist's style of leadership and took personal pleasure in the success of his junior colleague. At the outset of their relationship, Rehnquist had treated Powell with a cordial regard that seemed to acknowledge the older man's wider experience and greater reputation. Over the years, respect ripened into affection. Rehnquist never tried to lean on Powell, as Burger sometimes did, although to a man of Rehnquist's strong convictions, Powell's instinct for the middle course must have been exasperating. He never ridiculed Powell's penchant for fine distinctions, although privately he thought Powell too given to deciding cases "on these particular facts." When Powell was sidelined for reasons of health,

Rehnquist shouldered the extra burden of Powell's duties as Circuit Justice, keeping his absent colleague informed with chatty letters about Court business. By 1986 the two colleagues enjoyed the easy familiarity and confident friendship that Powell once had with Potter Stewart.

Rehnquist's promotion seemed to Powell, both then and later, an unqualifiedly sound choice. What Powell could not foresee in 1986 was the extent to which Rehnquist and his policies would dominate the coming years. The future depended not on the elevation of Rehnquist but on the next generation of appointments to the Supreme Court.

THE CHANGE BEGAN with Antonin Scalia, whom Reagan named to succeed Rehnquist as Associate Justice. Nino, as friends call him, was a brilliant former law professor (at Virginia and Chicago) and specialist in administrative and constitutional law who sat on the prestigious D.C. Circuit Court of Appeals. Son of a Sicilian immigrant, a devout Catholic, and father of nine, Scalia became the first Italian-American to sit on the Supreme Court and brought to that staid institution an ebullience and vivacity it has not often seen.

Politically Powell and Scalia were not so far apart, but personally they were like oil and water. Scalia's cheerful lack of deference rubbed his senior colleague the wrong way. His volubility struck Powell as bad manners. In Scalia's first oral argument he asked so many questions that Powell finally leaned over to Marshall and whispered, "Do you think he knows that the rest of us are here?" And if Scalia's behavior proved irksome to Powell, his virtues were undervalued. While Powell admired Scalia's formidable intelligence and obvious ability, he found his intellectual ardor vaguely unsettling. Zest for theory and new ideas did not strike a responsive chord in a man who relied chiefly on experience. Scalia's quick dismissal of conventional wisdom seemed to Powell more suited to an academic than to a judge. Scalia's boundless energy and pugnaciousness, which his many friends admired, struck his quiet, self-deprecating older colleague as almost uncivil. Even Scalia's wit and charm were largely wasted on Powell.

Despite the basic good will that each man bore the other and the cordiality that each successfully strove to maintain, there was little common ground. As one clerk who worked for both Justices put it: "Those two wouldn't agree on whether the sky was blue." After a pause, he added: "On second thought, they would agree, but for different reasons."

Underlying Powell's sensitivity to these personality differences was a tension that Scalia did not create and could not relieve. In Powell's nearly fifteen years on the bench, the membership of the Supreme Court had remained remarkably stable. Douglas, who seemed of a different generation from the rest of his colleagues, had left the Court in 1975. For the next ten years, the Court stayed the same, save for the replacement of Stewart by O'Connor in 1981. Otherwise an unchanging group, most of whom were near Powell's own age, had labored together in agreement and dissent for more than fourteen years. Now that Court was breaking up. Burger's departure marked the beginning of the end for Powell's generation. The promotion of a younger colleague to Chief Justice and the appointment of a man nearly three decades Powell's junior told Powell what he desperately did not want to hear: Soon he, too, would have to go.

RETIREMENT

Powell seriously considered retiring several years before he actually did so. Ever since President Nixon had said that "ten years of Lewis Powell is worth thirty years of most," Powell had aimed at a decade's service. He passed that milestone in 1982 but put off thinking about the matter until the following spring.

The least disruptive time to leave the Supreme Court is when the term ends, usually around the end of June. If all goes well, a new Justice can be selected and confirmed before the beginning of the new term in October. But not every summer is equally suitable. Retirement in a presidential election year would drag the nomination into campaign politics, increasing the risk of a confirmation fiasco. Moreover, Powell preferred that his successor be chosen by President Reagan whose only nomination to date, Sandra Day O'Connor, Powell enthusiastically approved.

Powell therefore faced a dilemma. He could leave the Court in the summer of 1983 and give Reagan an unobstructed shot at naming his successor, or he could remain longer and run the risk of being replaced by a liberal Democrat if Edward Kennedy or Walter Mondale won the 1984 election. Against this background, Powell began to consider his options. Now seventy-five years old, he had already served more than his goal of ten years. Perhaps it was time to go.

To resolve that choice, Powell turned not to Jo, who said she had "wanted him to retire since the day he took the oath of office," but to his children, and especially to Lewis III. "I do need to spend a couple of hours with you, privately and quietly," he wrote Lewis on February 3, 1983. That conversation finally took place, after postponements, on the morning of Saturday, April 9, in the house on Rothesay Circle. A partial record exists in a letter Lewis wrote shortly after their conversation.

"[I]n your typically objective and methodical fashion," Lewis wrote, "you have analyzed the merits of retirement this year against hanging in there for several more years." Powell had considered such factors as his age, his eye troubles, his level of energy, and "the likely occupant of the White House after November 1984," but, Lewis cautioned, "your analysis has failed to take account of what you feel in your heart and soul." Lewis had been "struck by the sense of sadness that seemed to permeate your remarks about the satisfaction you derive from judging (and doing it well), from your association with your clerks, from the give-and-take of the Conference, and from the simple greetings exchanged among the Justices before you ascend the Bench. Whenever you retire, I fear that you will miss terribly these and many other aspects of the life of an active Justice—perhaps far more than you can anticipate."

Three weeks later Lewis again wrote to oppose retirement. He promised to let his father know when Powell was beginning to "lose it" but was satisfied that the time had not yet arrived: "You owe it to the Court, the nation, your family, and yourself not to step down while you are still fit to discharge your duties as magnificently as you have for the last 11 years." Jo Powell Smith said the same thing. She and Lewis in fact had coordinated their responses in a joint effort to persuade their father to stay on the Court.

What his children told him was exactly what Powell wanted to hear. He hated the very thought of retirement. Work had always come first in his life; he had no hobbies, no outside interests to pursue, no wish to travel or to spend his time relaxing at home. In 1983 Powell still wanted what he had always sought from his professional life—an outlet for his prodigious energies, a foundation for his self-respect, and the opportunity for recognition, responsibility, and control. Retirement seemed a partial death.

Nor was there an emergency. At age seventy-five Powell enjoyed relatively good health. In 1979 the doctors at Bethesda Naval Hospital, on discovering a polyp, removed eight to ten inches of Powell's colon, which was found to contain no malignancy. ("Praise be!" wrote Harvie Wilkinson; Powell should eat "calories galore" to "enrich the remaining inches so they will not miss the late lamented segment.") Since that surgery Powell had recovered his strength, though not his weight, and had been several years without a crisis. His eyes remained a concern. He was still bothered by "floaters," vitreous opacities that drifted across his field of vision or showed up as tiny mobile black spots, visible chiefly when reading in bright light. More disturbing was the recent deterioration in the sight of his left eye, but this proved due to a cataract on the lens. (On July 12, 1983, he had the cataract removed and a new lens implanted, dramatically improving his vision in that eye.) Most important, Powell had not begun to fade mentally. As Lewis III advised, Powell was plainly still fit to discharge his duties.

And Powell still derived enormous satisfaction from those duties. He liked the power, the prestige, and the respect he was given wherever he went. He also liked the work itself. Sometimes, as in *Bowers v. Hardwick*, there were great, raw, divisive questions that caused him real distress, but they were rare. Most cases that reached the Supreme Court raised issues of genuine difficulty, but in a more structured context. There were statutes to construe and precedents to apply, principles to discern and interpret, arguments to weigh and counterarguments to consider, and, in the end, the obligation to justify the outcome in writing. The process of decision was a model of deliberative rationality, and if the results owed something to personal preferences and politics, they also reflected the constraints and traditions of the law. All this Powell loved. A zealot might have found the discipline of legal reasoning tedious, but for Powell it was not. For him, no position or undertaking in any sphere of endeavor could possibly equal a seat on the Supreme Court.

Why then did Powell come (as he said) to the "brink" of retiring in 1983, when the decision was not compelled by ill health? The timing may have been partly political, but the motivation was a sense of duty. He owed the Court and the country his best. If he could no longer give it, he would retire. But how would he know? He remembered Bill Douglas, reduced to a pitiable spectacle as he clung to a position he was no longer able to fill, and he could see the effects of age on his colleagues. Powell did not want to stay so long that everyone would be glad when he left.

Uncertain about his ability to assess his own performance, Powell put the question to Lewis III—and did so in a way that ensured an honest answer. He did not require Lewis to carry the argument in favor of retirement. Instead, he shouldered the burden of making the case for his own departure. All Lewis had to do to bring about his father's retirement was to acquiesce in an announced intention. When he did not, when he and his sister fought back, insisting that "[y]ou owe it to the Court, the nation, your family, and yourself not to step down," Powell learned what he needed to know.

The episode highlights Powell's capacity for objectivity. As a lawyer in private practice, he had struck an ideal balance between rapport and remoteness. On the one hand, he sympathized with his clients' problems, adopted their ambitions, and shared their concerns. On the other hand, he kept an emotional distance that allowed him to see defects in his clients' plans, to anticipate the objections of others, and to suggest sensible compromises. He was the perfect counselor, critical of his clients' plans but devoted to their interests. Now Powell applied the same rigorous objectivity to himself. He did not fall into the trap of thinking himself indispensable, nor did he suppose that he would necessarily be better than any successor. He did not indulge in self-flattering comparisons to his aging colleagues. He was too disciplined—and too proud. He had to be able to maintain the standards he set for himself, to do the work as he had always done it, with care and perseverance, or he would step aside. In 1983 Lewis III confirmed what Powell hoped and believed to be true—that he was still up to the job.

THE YEAR FOLLOWING Powell's ruminations on retirement seemed to confirm the wisdom of his decision to stay on the Court. His health remained stable, and though perhaps not at the peak of his powers, he was at the height of his influence. In the term that began in October 1983, Powell sat in a total of fifty-one cases decided by votes of five–four or six–three. In these closely divided cases, Powell was in the majority 80 percent of the time. When that term ended in the summer of 1984, Powell had every reason to be glad he had remained on the Court, and when President Reagan won a landslide reelection in the fall of that year, any worries Powell may have had about being replaced by a wild-eyed liberal were laid to rest. Altogether, it was a good year.

But fate had unkindness in store. An examination at the Mayo Clinic in December 1984 revealed cancer of the prostate, and Powell went home for Christmas under the shadow of surgery early in the new year. Removal of the prostate and surrounding lymph nodes is probably as close to being routine as any truly major surgery can be. The procedure ordinarily takes a couple of hours and requires postoperative hospitalization of a few days. When the Powells flew to Rochester at the end of December, Jo took only a small bag and two dresses. Although they discouraged the children from coming, Jo

Smith showed up anyway to keep her mother company. Despite optimistic assurances about the nature of the surgery, Powell prepared for the worst. After checking with Burger, he told his startled clerks that the Chief Justice had agreed that they could keep their positions even if he did not return.

However exaggerated Powell's pessimism may have seemed, the event almost proved him right. As wife and daughter waited, a procedure that should have taken two to three hours took four, then five, then six, then seven. What on earth could the doctors be doing? In fact, they were fighting desperately to prevent a life from bleeding away. About two and a half hours into the operation, as the surgeons were preparing to close, the area began to fill with blood. The doctors responded with clips and sutures, but as soon as one leak was stemmed, another sprang up. In the words of one surgeon, there were "not enough fingers to plug all the holes in the dike." First a hematologist and then an international expert on coagulation were called in, as the doctors kept Powell alive by transfusions and tried to stop the loss of blood.

Perhaps Powell had some predisposition to bleed, as he had endured two similar, though less serious, incidents before. In 1956 he bled for five weeks following routine surgery to remove an obstruction from the bladder orifice and had two hemorrhages requiring cauterization. In 1974, following a transurethral resection of the prostate, he suffered excessive bleeding requiring two units of blood. Perhaps the scar tissue from prior surgeries made the 1985 procedure more difficult or the blood vessels more vulnerable. But the chief cause may have been the cancer itself, which chemically blocked the ability of the blood to clot normally. Antidotes eventually brought the bleeding under control, but not before Powell had received fifteen pints of whole blood and nine more of plasma—a volume sufficient to replace the body's entire supply twice over. As Powell's chief physician later recalled, "surgeons generally leave an operation with a sense of great accomplishment and satisfaction, but that experience was horrific." When Powell finally came out of surgery, after eight hours under general anesthesia, the cancer was gone and he was alive—barely.

After five weeks in the hospital and another in the adjacent Kahler Hotel, Powell returned to Washington on February 6, 1985. Emaciated, unsteady, and "weak as a kitten," he was in no condition to resume work. He kept to his apartment in Washington, and only after several weeks began spending a few hours a day at the office. It was not until March 25, eleven weeks after the surgery, that Powell returned to the bench. In the meantime, the Court heard cases without him. Three were reargued in April so that he could participate, but Powell missed about a third of the Court's work that term.

Accompanying, if not impeding, Powell's recovery was a blizzard of paperwork concerning the costs of his treatment, which came to nearly $19,000. Inscrutable forms, computer-generated statements, and increasingly plaintive letters flew back and forth from Powell, the Mayo Clinic, Medicare, and Blue Cross. Despite the best efforts of everyone involved to assist a Supreme Court Justice, the correspondence grew ever more confusing as the miscommunications multiplied. At one point, Powell actually had a $1,500 profit, as bills that he had already paid and sent to his insurance carrier were reduced to reflect the level of Medicare coverage, and the difference refunded by the hospital to him and then by him to Blue Cross. Of course, no one reimbursed the cost of traveling to and from Rochester or the more than $4,700 in hotel bills.

But money was the least of Powell's problems. The surgery not only left him fragile and exhausted; it also disrupted his plumbing. Removing the prostate tumor took some of the tissue that surrounds the base of the urethra and squeezes it shut except during urination. The result was persistent incontinence. Trying to pull his weight at the Court despite discomfort and weakness, Powell waited until the end of term before returning to the Mayo Clinic for further surgery. While they were at it, the doctors corrected an inguinal hernia. On July 2, 1985, "in considerable pain," Powell flew from Washington to Rochester. The corrective surgery was successful, but Powell had to begin recuperating all over again.

That summer, for the first time, the Powells remained in Washington so that he could be close to his doctors and to the Court's attentive staff. This time his recovery was less difficult. He soon resumed his summer work schedule and was fully prepared for the opening of the new term in October. Lingering problems were a residual weakness and a stubborn inability to regain weight. At the end of the year, he weighed only 132 pounds. Though frail and gaunt, Powell was in fact on the road to reasonably good health.

Given the crisis in January 1985 and the necessity of returning for additional surgery that summer, it is perhaps surprising that Powell did not retire at that time. In fact, he barely considered it. For one thing, the gravity of his problems caught him by surprise. He did not know that he would require prostate surgery until the term was well underway, nor could he have predicted that the experience would be so devastating. By late spring Powell felt that he again had "the physical strength and energy to participate fully and effectively" in the work of the Court. The follow-up surgery set him back, but again there was prospect of full recovery. In short, his problems were real but not chronic. By the end of the summer, when he got a good report from his doctors, he again felt up to the job.

POWELL DID NOT REVISIT the question of retirement until 1987. At that time he consulted Lewis III and his other children and a former clerk.* The conversation took place on Saturday, June 20, in a Virginia Beach hotel during the annual summer meeting of the Virginia State Bar. Powell had flown there to present an award to Oliver Hill and Samuel Tucker, veteran civil rights lawyers who thirty years earlier had been harassed and bullied by the same state bar that now wished to celebrate their achievements. To bless this event, the bar imported Virginia's most distinguished lawyer to deliver the award. Afterward the Justice, his son, and former clerk met to discuss Powell's future.

Again, the timing may have been partly political. The end of the term was the only time when Powell could step down without disrupting the Court's work, and 1987 was the last year when a Supreme Court vacancy would not be caught up in the partisan maneuvering of a presidential election. Yet that Saturday afternoon in Virginia Beach, Powell seemed indifferent to such concerns. He said that Supreme Court Justices so often surprised the Presidents who appointed them that it was pointless to make political calculations. He cited Brennan, whose liberal activism displeased President Eisenhower, and White, whose conservative drift he assumed would have disappointed President Kennedy. To Powell, these cases showed how difficult it was to predict a Justice's performance and therefore how uncertain it was that the timing of an appointment would affect the direction of the Supreme Court.

It was better, Powell said, to concentrate on his personal situation. Was he still up to the job? How many more strong years would he have left? What about his declining stamina? And what would he do with himself if he retired?

What was crucial in the conversation in Virginia Beach was something left unsaid. In 1987, unlike 1983, Lewis did not urge his father to stay. Instead, he maintained a strict neutrality, neither insisting on his father's duty to Court and country nor suggesting that he had an

---

*   The author.

obligation to go. He graciously, sympathetically, and carefully took no position. Powell returned to Washington with the issue unresolved.

It was against the backdrop of this conversation that the former clerk reviewed the issue in a "personal and confidential" memorandum to his former boss. This memorandum was written on Sunday morning and delivered to the Court the next day. Whether Powell relied on it is not known, but it is the only documentary evidence of the considerations discussed at that time.

"The concerns that you will wish to take into account," the memo began, "fall naturally into three types: institutional, personal, and political." Institutional concerns would require Powell to step down if he were incapacitated, but "all evidence confirms that your ability to discharge the duties of your office remains unimpaired." Powell therefore had "no *duty* to retire." He should feel free to "do whatever you think best, and to consult your own welfare in making that determination."

Personal concerns counseled against retirement. "The sudden withdrawal from power and responsibility would be, at the least, disconcerting. Nothing you could do after retirement would entirely fill the gap in your life. . . . It would be a permanent relinquishment of power and a significant withdrawal from the kinds of commitments that have occupied your adult life and . . . that lie very near the core of your sense of personal identity. You are right to view that prospect with anxiety." (Jo Smith said the same thing more simply. "I think you'll be happier if you keep going. And I think you'll be healthier too.")

As his children knew, Powell's reaction to the thought of retirement was more than dislike; it was fear. Unlike private practice, where an elder lawyer can disengage by degrees, or the lower courts, where a judge's transition to "senior status" means a gradual and self-regulated reduction in case load, the Supreme Court is an all-or-nothing proposition. As Douglas discovered, there is no place for a part-time tenth Justice. A retired Supreme Court Justice may sit by designation on the lower courts (as Powell was later to do), but Potter Stewart reported that it was "no fun to play in the minors after a career in the major leagues." Powell often said that Stewart's retirement had hastened his death. Powell did not say, but no doubt feared, that the same might prove true for him.

The "most delicate" considerations were political. In the summer of 1987, it seemed "at least as likely as not" that the next occupant of the White House would be a Democrat. "What difference would that make?" Potentially a great deal, thought the clerk: "Despite the frequency with which one hears it repeated, the notion that Presidents are politically unsuccessful in their Supreme Court appointments does not withstand analysis. . . . This is emphatically *not* to say," the memo continued, "that Supreme Court Justices attempt to follow the wishes of the Presidents who appointed them." That Presidents would sometimes disagree with their appointees was to be expected. "Indeed, any man or woman truly qualified to serve on the Supreme Court would not be completely predictable. The vigorous and independent intellect that the nation requires in your office is fundamentally inconsistent with slavish adherence to any political program."

The point was, rather, that "on average Presidents have been successful at influencing the nation's course by appointments to the Supreme Court." President Nixon had selected Burger, Blackmun, Powell, and Rehnquist. "Although he was surely disappointed by *United States v. Nixon*," the clerk wrote, "I would guess that all four of his appointments have proved broadly compatible with his expectations." Even Blackmun had remained "largely reliable" in criminal cases, which had been Nixon's chief concern. Presidents Johnson, Ford, and Reagan should also have been largely satisfied with their selections. Supreme Court Justices who completely surprised and disappointed the Presidents who appointed them—such as Brennan and Chief Justice Warren—were the exception rather than the rule.

This history built to the conclusion that rather than stay one more year and risk handing his seat to a liberal Democrat, Powell should "either retire now or . . . plan to serve for several more years." "This suggests," added the clerk, "that you should try to imagine what several more years on the Supreme Court would be like. One possibility is that the next five years would be very like the last five years. Another possibility is that you may grow increasingly tired. . . . I have some fear," the clerk concluded, "that the immense satisfaction and sense of accomplishment that you derive from your position may be increasingly offset by exhaustion. Obviously the best guide here is your own intuition and reflection."

The political calculations in the clerk's memo may or may not have mattered to Powell. He said privately that his true reasons for stepping down had been exactly those stated to the press on the day his retirement was announced. These did not include politics. Whether this statement was strictly accurate cannot be known. What is clear is that the crucial factors were Lewis III's neutrality and Powell's awareness of his own diminishing strength.

Reflection made Powell acknowledge the limits of his energy. In 1987 his clerks thought he kept a remarkable pace—"not just for someone his age, but for anyone"—but Sally, who knew him better, saw the decline. The previous year at least two of his clerks thought he should step down. That summer his internist at the Mayo Clinic reported that Powell suffered from "chronic fatigue." The physician prescribed rest and relaxation to counter an "excessive" work load, which he figured at a minimum of sixty-five hours a week. Though he found no diminution of Powell's "abilities to perform critical functions in his role," he thought Powell was "pushing himself too far each day and each week. . . ."

This, of course, was the story of Powell's life. He had always pushed himself each day and each week to work longer and harder than anyone else. Three months shy of his eightieth birthday, Powell could not maintain that effort. Sometime soon, he would have to retire.

ON WEDNESDAY, JUNE 24, 1987, four days after the conversation at Virginia Beach, Powell told Chief Justice Rehnquist that he had decided to retire. They consulted the statutes to find the correct provision for Powell to cite in his letter to the President. (Since federal judges are appointed for life, a Justice who *retires* rather than *resigns* keeps his salary and his eligibility to sit by designation on the lower courts.) The decision was to be kept secret until the morning of Friday, June 26, the Court's last sitting of the term.

Boston Globe reporter Ethan Bronner, historian of the rise and fall of Robert Bork, wrote that Rehnquist broke his word and immediately called White House Chief of Staff Howard H. Baker, Jr. "As soon as Powell had informed Rehnquist of his definite decision . . . and solicited a solemn promise that no one would be told, the chief justice expressed his sincere regret, agreed to keep it to himself, and called Baker with the news." According to Bronner, Baker said he understood the need for secrecy and at once told the President.

Rehnquist heatedly denies this account, and Baker confirms that he first spoke with Rehnquist "only minutes" before the Court convened for the public announcement. Bronner's error probably sprang from a call placed by Rehnquist's secretary to Baker's office Thursday afternoon to learn where Baker could be reached the following morning. From this, Baker guessed that a Justice might be stepping down and went directly to the Oval Office to share this speculation with the President. No one in the White House knew for certain that a Justice was retiring until Baker spoke with Rehnquist on Friday morning.

On that day Rehnquist convened the Conference at 9:45 A.M., ten minutes earlier than usual, so that he could tell the other Justices.

Minutes before, while Rehnquist was calling Baker, Powell phoned Toni House, the Court's public information officer, to ask that she drop by his chambers. The sight of House rushing upstairs alerted a few savvy reporters that something might be up. When House arrived, Powell gave her a prepared statement. At her request, he agreed to a press conference later that day. He then made the long walk down the outside corridor, past the chambers of Justice Blackmun and the smaller offices long occupied by Justice Douglas, past Brennan's rooms and Marshall's, and around to the Chief Justice's chambers in the rear of the building, where he would attend his last Conference as a Justice of the Supreme Court.

Rehnquist felt he was "dropping a bombshell." None of the other Justices knew what was coming. (Powell informed his clerks the day before, but they told no one.) Sandra Day O'Connor wept, and there were tears in other eyes as well, but not much was said. Then the Justices crossed the hall to the courtroom where they would hand down the term's few remaining cases and hear the Chief announce Powell's retirement to the public.

Later that day, Powell heard from his colleagues. O'Connor wrote that she was "devastated" by the news of his departure. "No one on the Court has been kinder than you. There is no one with whom I have felt as free to discuss our cases. . . . There is no one for whom I have greater respect and affection than you. In short, you are irreplaceable." John Paul Stevens wrote that emotion prevented him from speaking at the Conference, "and now there are so many things I want to say that I don't know how to begin." Powell would be remembered, he predicted, as "one of the select few great justices." And from Byron White, no spendthrift with compliments, came a surprising sentiment: "I have seen a good many Justices come and go, but I'm quite sure that I shall miss you more than any of the others, and that is saying a good deal."

In humbler quarters also, Powell would be missed. Court personnel were sorry to see him go. Typical was the verdict of Justice Marshall's messenger, a wizened old man who usually had little to say. That afternoon, Mr. Gaines was making the rounds of the chambers and happened on a Powell clerk commiserating with Brennan's secretary. "Yes," he interjected, "it's a terrible day. It's like a funeral around here." Then he continued on his way, adding, "And I remember when Burger retired; it was just like Christmas morning."

Among family and friends, sadness prevailed. "I'm still crying a bit," wrote daughter Jo, "—for me, for you, for the Court, and for the country. We've all lost something."

*   *   *

POWELL MET THE PRESS at noon in the West Conference Room. Toni House had distributed his statement giving three reasons for the action. First, he would be eighty years old before the Court reconvened. It would have been wise, he said, for the Founding Fathers to have required retirement at age seventy-five, even though that "would have deprived the Court of the service after that age by a number of the most distinguished Justices ever to sit on this Court. . . . But for me, age eighty suggests retirement." Second, he had already served half again as long as the ten years he had planned. Third, although currently in good health, he had a "concern—based on past experience—that I could handicap the Court in the event of reoccurrences of serious health problems."

The reporters tried to draw Powell out on the political implications of his action. "Justice Powell," said NBC's Carl Stern, "certainly it must have dawned upon you . . . that who comes after you may alter the balance of many important issues. Did that weigh into your consideration?" It did not. Later Stern tried again: "You have been described as a moderate. Would you like to see a moderate take your place?" "I don't characterize myself in any way," Powell replied. Despite repeated invitations, he would not comment on the future direction of the Court or the outlook for *Roe v. Wade* or any other political issue. When pressed to say what "one thing" made him decide to go, he recounted the advice of Lewis III: "Dad, it's a whole lot better to go out when some people may be sorry than it is to wait until when you decide to go out, people say, 'Thank God we got rid of the old gent.'"

Looking chipper if frail in front of the lights and camera, Powell struck one note of regret. When Nina Totenberg asked sympathetically whether there was some moment in the past fifteen years "that you think of as your best or finest," Powell paused: "My best moment? No, I never thought of that. Today is one of my worst moments. I leave the Court with a great deal of sadness."

Indeed, he had suffered an irreparable loss. Nothing could approach in personal satisfaction the position he had just relinquished. Powell had gone onto the Supreme Court when he did not want to, because of a sense of duty, and he stepped down from the Supreme Court when he did not want to for the same reason.

When Powell finished with the questions and started to go, the reporters and others present began to applaud. He turned, smiled shyly, gave a wave of farewell, and was gone.

*   *   *

THAT WEEKEND WAS the Powell clerks' reunion. Held in June of each year, this event had long since fallen into a comfortable routine. On Saturday the clerks hosted a catered dinner in the Supreme Court. On Sunday the Powells invited the clerks and their spouses to brunch at the Alibi Club.

Of all the incidental advantages of life in Washington, none pleased Powell more than his membership in the Alibi Club. The club consisted of fifty men drawn chiefly from the defense, intelligence, and foreign policy establishments, with a sprinkling of Senators, Supreme Court Justices, and other notables. Members in Powell's time included Directors of Central Intelligence George Bush, Richard Helms, and William H. Webster; Secretary of State William P. Rogers (whose predecessors George C. Marshall and John Foster Dulles had also been members); Senators Howard Baker, John Stennis, and Alan Simpson; NATO commander Andrew J. Goodpaster; and arms negotiator Gerard C. Smith. The Supreme Court contingent included Justices Stewart and Powell, Chief Justices Burger and Rehnquist, and Justice O'Connor's husband, John. The Alibi Club offered these men a totally private setting for monthly lunches, plus quarterly dinners for members and wives. Since guests had to be invited by the club as a whole, it was rare that any outsider invaded the privacy of the members' conversations. (One of the rare occasions came on January 24, 1981, when Vice President George Bush brought his boss to lunch.)

The Alibi owns a town house on I Street, N.W., in downtown Washington. Outside it is nondescript, but inside it matches any grown-up boy's dream of what a clubhouse should be. The rooms of dark wood and old chairs have never felt a decorator's touch. Every inch of shelf and mantel is crammed with memorabilia, objects too tasteless to be displayed at home, relics of jokes long forgotten, trophies of past triumphs and travels. On the walls are caricatures of members past and present and photographs of the occasional guest (Ronald Reagan, Lord Mountbatten of Burma). Next to the (unlisted) telephone was a price list for appropriate responses: "'Just Left,' 25 cents; 'On His Way,' 50 cents; 'Not Here,' $1; 'Who?' $5." One Sunday every June these precincts were invaded by the Powell clerks.

The night before, a formal dinner was served in the stately grandeur of the Court's East Conference Room. By common consent, the master of ceremonies was John J. Buckley, Jr. Taking off from some case or incident in the term just ended, Buckley would concoct an irreverent review of the Court's work. Powell came in for much kidding, but somehow the sharpest points always targeted Chief Justice Burger, whose rich baritone Buckley mimicked to perfection. Powell would then speak briefly, and his remarks also took a standard form. After genially rebuking Buckley's impertinence and thanking Gail Galloway and Sally Smith for arranging the dinner, he would praise his clerks for the term just ended and introduce those selected for the next one. Somewhere along the way, Powell would reflect on the events of the past year and close by saying once again how much he and Jo enjoyed the association with their chambers family.

All this was as settled and routine as the dinner service, but this year Buckley did something different. Buckley, his wife Jane Genster, fellow Powell clerk David Boyd, and his wife Suzanne put together a videotape retrospective of Powell's career. Styled as "Masterpiece Theatre," complete with familiar theme music and ungrammatical sponsor ("Mobil Corporation, which invites you to join with them in supporting public television"), the tape collected images of Powell's life. Buckley as Alistair Cooke provided deadpan commentary: "In 1941, Justice Powell invaded North Africa." On the Supreme Court, he "issued more than 500 opinions—not all of which have been dissents." The chronology ended with recent pictures of Lewis and Jo, married more than half a century, accompanied by Paul Simon's "Still Crazy After All These Years." Last came still photographs of all the clerks, from 1972 to the present, each image lingering on the screen a few seconds as if in farewell.

Though Powell had planned to explain his retirement, he did not. When the tape ended, he merely murmured "thank you" into the applause. There was nothing else to say—or entirely too much.

AFTERMATH

The hole in Powell's life was filled for a time by applause. In addition to the customary letter of farewell from his colleagues and a formal appreciation from the President, Powell received hundreds of personal communications. He heard from past and future Presidents, from fellow judges and former clerks, from Richmond friends and relations, from World War II veterans and college classmates, from individuals in all walks of life who simply wanted to commend his service. Erwin Griswold, Solicitor General of the United States under Presidents Johnson and Nixon, wrote that his role in urging Powell's nomination to the Court was the "most important public service I have ever been privileged to perform."

Notes came from people Powell likely would not see again—from

Cathy Douglas, now remarried and practicing law in Boston, from Janet Murrow, and from Eleanor Wilson. Many were melancholy. A retired judge from Texas wanted Powell to know that, "Nothing has saddened me so much since the Second Great War as your retirement from the Supreme Court." Paul Freund wrote: "You will be sorely missed on the Court, because the Court needs you. I hope and pray that in choosing your successor the President will be moved above all by your rare qualities, as President Hoover was moved when he appointed Cardozo to succeed Holmes." Many letters were touchingly affectionate. Powell busied himself for several months in the pleasurable activity of answering this mail.

The public response was also gratifying. On the June 26 "MacNeil/Lehrer NewsHour," the toughest and best of Supreme Court reporters turned soft and gushy. NPR correspondent Nina Totenberg said Powell "was held in the highest respect, the greatest esteem. And the most enormous affection. . . . Sometimes when people retire or die, they say very nice things about them. But that's not really true about this man. This is a person of the most enormous gentility and gentleness. I can't imagine him ever saying a harsh word to anyone. And you can't help but have enormous affection for him."

What was there about Powell that made her feel this way? "[H]e treats everybody with such kindness. . . . It's more than courtliness—it's not simply a polite manner. It is a genuine concern, a genuine niceness, a genuine decency that comes through as a human being."*

The next morning Powell found himself hailed by *The New York Times* as a "model conservative" and elsewhere praised as a "force for moderation" in an era of division and controversy and a lawyer's lawyer who "distinguished the Supreme Court by his presence." Columnist Charles McDowell recalled Powell at Washington and Lee as a "tall, thin young man with a shiny face" and said his "gentle, stub-

---

* On the same show law professor and Supreme Court expert A. E. Dick Howard gave the day's most insightful interpretation of Powell's timing:

> [I]t may well have crossed Lewis Powell's mind that if he did not step down this year and stayed on the bench one more year, he would be stepping down in the middle of a political campaign for the presidency. And I think Lewis Powell takes a very honest and institutional view of the Court's welfare. He could well imagine that a nomination for his successor coming in the middle of a presidential campaign might be a very divisive factor—there might be politics played on both sides of it—both the White House and the Senate. And that the Court would be the loser in that kind of process. If that were Powell's thinking, then he might have decided either step down now or wait two years.

born, independent reasonableness" would be missed on the Supreme Court. Virginia commentator Guy Friddell reminisced about the *Bakke* decision, which showed Powell "at his exquisite best, moving along fine lines to apportion justice precisely and truly."

Attention soon turned from praising Powell to speculating on his successor. History now turned trickster, as this deeply conservative man found himself acclaimed most highly by liberals. Two years earlier an ACLU leader called Powell "the most powerful man in America." (Only, said Powell, in his own home—and then only when Jo went shopping.) Now other liberals took up the cry, stressing Powell's importance and exaggerating his liberalism as they prepared to contest an unwelcome successor. The ACLU compiled a list of twenty civil liberties cases decided five–four in the past term, in every one of which Powell was in the majority. (Of course, he often rejected their position, but in the crucial areas of abortion and affirmative action, they rarely won without him.) Senator Edward Kennedy said Powell had "graced the Supreme Court as one of its most distinguished, respected and intelligent members," adding that the Senate would now be "watching carefully . . . to ensure that President Reagan does the right thing instead of the far right thing in filling the large vacancy that Justice Powell leaves." Ralph Neas, executive director of the Leadership Conference on Civil Rights, took the same line: "Lewis Powell has been a fair and distinguished Justice. He has been a true conservative, not a right-wing zealot."

A national reporter (who wished this sentiment to remain anonymous) said more bluntly, "Yes, Powell's conservative, but not like some of those folks. He's not *insane*." Over and over, liberals struck the same theme: The President would do well to nominate to the Supreme Court someone very like Lewis Powell.

Not everyone agreed. The same votes that made Powell the left's favorite conservative were anathema to the hard-line right. The "movement" conservatives in Reagan's Department of Justice had had quite enough of Powell's moderation. They wanted someone less given to compromise, an intellectual leader for the new conservative majority, someone who would make good on this last best chance to realize the Reagan revolution. On July 1, 1987, the President crowned their hopes by nominating Robert H. Bork to succeed Powell on the Supreme Court.

IN PROFESSIONAL TERMS, Bork was spectacularly well qualified. He was a judge on the influential D.C. Circuit Court of Appeals, a former Solicitor General of the United States, and former professor at Yale Law School.

But Bork's professional credentials did nothing to allay liberal fears. Civil rights activists saw Bork as a threat to all they held dear, a hard-nosed opponent of affirmative action and the constitutionalization of abortion, a trenchant critic of judicial innovation, and a tireless campaigner for conservative values. That he was brilliant, tough-minded, courageous, and honest made him all the more dangerous.

And there was something else, something beyond Bork's beliefs and abilities that made him easy for liberals to hate. Bork loved combat. In the generally muted world of judges, he seemed strident and partisan, his views often edged with anger. As much perhaps as for what he believed, Bork was feared—and admired—for *how* he believed it. He was, some said, like an Old Testament prophet—righteous, wrathful, and uncompromising in devotion to his vision of truth.

There was no honeymoon for the Bork nomination. Minutes after President Reagan announced his choice, Senator Kennedy set the tone for the debate:

> Robert Bork's America is a land in which women would be forced into back alley abortions, blacks would sit at segregated lunch counters, rogue police could break down citizens' doors in midnight raids, school children could not be taught about evolution, writers and artists could be censored at the whim of government, and the doors of the Federal courts would be shut on the fingers of millions of citizens for whom the judiciary is—and is often the only—protector of the individual rights that are the heart of our democracy. . . . No justice would be better than this injustice.

Even Bork's detractors admit that this speech could be thought "reckless and intemperate." More accurately, it has been called "character assassination by calculated lie." But it was also stunningly effective. Kennedy's statement "froze the Senate," preventing Senators impressed by Bork's credentials from coming out in favor of his appointment and putting everyone on notice that this would be an all-out, no-holds-barred campaign for the political future of the Supreme Court.

The campaign that Senator Kennedy began was distinguished not only by its nastiness but also by its focus. Although attempts were made to smear Bork's character—Senator Howell Heflin led the way with complaints about Bork's alleged agnosticism (apparently an effective issue in Alabama) and his "strange life-style" (who knows what the folks back home understood by that)—the main thrust was frankly political. Bork's opponents took aim squarely at his politics—at what the chroniclers of the anti-Bork campaign described as "his passionate, relentless assault on virtually everything the Supreme Court had done in the latter half of the twentieth century to strengthen the equality of citizens before the law and the defense of individual rights against the power of the state." Millions of Americans came to share this perception. Their vision of Bork as "reactionary monster" overshadowed more nuanced views and raised the political stakes for those inclined to vote in his favor.

Especially in the South, where conservatism was not usually a liability, the implacable opposition from African-Americans made supporting Bork far too costly. As Louisiana's Bennett Johnson said to a group of freshman Senators from his region, "I know how you're going to vote, and you, and you, and you"—in each case they would vote against because of fear of losing black support. In the end, only six of the twenty-two Senators from the states of the old Confederacy voted for Ronald Reagan's nominee. (By contrast, four years later when African-American opinion in the South divided on the nomination of Clarence Thomas, fourteen southern Senators voted for the nominee.)

THE ADMINISTRATION never effectively countered the anti-Bork campaign. They relied too heavily on Bork's standing within the legal community and realized too late that the battle was being fought elsewhere. But one tactic failed through no lack of effort. From the opening round, the administration tried every means to persuade Powell to endorse Bork.

First came a call from Senator Strom Thurmond. Powell supported Bork but refused to say so publicly. Then Powell heard from his friend George Bush, who emphasized that the nomination needed support but was, Powell said, "typically thoughtful" in not attempting to press him farther than he wanted to go. On September 25, the White House admitted that Bork did not yet have the votes for confirmation, and the President launched a personal counterattack to try to save the nomination. The next day Reagan called and "strongly expressed" his hope that Powell would testify. Powell agreed to think about it, consulted over the weekend with the Chief Justice and with Byron White, and on Monday called Howard Baker at the White House to say that he still did not want to "go public."

Even the third refusal did not end the matter. On Friday, October 9, after meeting with the President, Bork announced that though defeat was now inevitable, he would not withdraw his name from consideration. That day Powell was in Richmond, where he had been sitting by designation on the Fourth Circuit Court of Appeals. While there, he received a call from Leonard Garment, a Washington lawyer and longtime Bork friend, who had thrown himself into a last-ditch effort to save the nomination. Garment tried for twenty minutes to persuade Powell to intervene. Powell's comment that he had discussed his reservations with the Chief Justice prompted Garment to call Rehnquist (with whom he and Bork played poker) and then to write Powell that "Bill says he sees no problem if you make a statement" endorsing Bork's qualifications without formally recommending a vote for or against him. As it turned out, Rehnquist was by no means pleased to have his name used in this way, and Powell was in no way influenced by the letter. The next Monday Powell called Garment and "made it explicitly clear that I had no intention of making any public statement for or against Judge Bork."

By this time, Garment was grasping at straws. Fifty-three Senators had already committed to vote against the nomination, and it was folly to suppose that they would have reconsidered at a word from Powell. But what about earlier? Would an early endorsement by Powell have slowed the anti-Bork campaign? Certainly no such effect has been ascribed to the testimony of former Chief Justice Burger, who appeared before the Judiciary Committee to support the nomination. As Bork's backers knew, however, there were important differences between Burger and Powell. First, Burger came unprepared. He spoke as if the fact that he was the former Chief Justice was all anyone needed to know, and on crucial issues he seemed "astonishingly out of his depth." This would never have been true of Powell, who, if he had spoken at all, would have been prepared. More important, Burger was disabled by his own reputation from influencing the issue. That Burger supported Bork was in no way reassuring to those who feared that Bork would turn back the clock on civil rights and individual liberties. That, they suspected, was just what Burger himself had always wanted to do. Powell, by contrast, carried weight not only with fellow judges and the organized bar but also—to a degree—with the constituencies alarmed by the prospect of Bork. Powell had become every liberal's favorite conservative. He was the model that President Reagan had constantly been exhorted to imitate. All the compliments that Kennedy and others had paid Powell could now be thrown back in their faces if only Powell spoke out for Bork. At least the Bork team could have scored a few points in the media with a witness who would command the attention of the cameras and whose testimony could not be easily dismissed.

But Powell refused. In a contemporaneous memorandum recording these events and in private conversations then and later, he gave only one reason—that it would be "inappropriate for a newly retired Justice to take any part in the nomination or confirmation hearings of his successor." What appalled Powell in the debates over Robert Bork was not that the nominee might lose, but that the Supreme Court might be tarnished. "If I felt free to make a statement," Powell said, "it would focus primarily on what I think properly has been characterized as the 'politicizing' of the confirmation process, and also to some extent the nomination process." The White House's choice had been politically provocative, and much of the reaction to it "slanderous and irresponsible." Powell deplored the role of the "special interest groups," the use against a judicial nominee of the "massive media and mail campaigning that goes on in presidential elections," and the "racial bloc voting" that doomed Bork in the South. "I am concerned," he wrote privately, "that many in the public will think the Supreme Court is simply another political institution."

Powell never believed that the Court was simply another political institution. He believed that law—especially constitutional law—should be grander, more durable, more high-minded, and more rational than ordinary politics. He acknowledged, of course, that judges' personal values influenced constitutional interpretation, but there was much more to it than that. Powell had faith in the independence of judges and in the way they make decisions. He believed in the traditions of brief and argument, of reflection and respect for precedent, and of reasoned elaboration in written opinions. The process, he believed, could lift judicial decisions above considerations of short-term political advantage and move toward a truer and better conception of the public good. For Powell, it followed that courts and judges should stay above the fray. He agreed with columnist David Broder that in times of extremism and crisis, the independence and integrity of the judiciary were precious to the nation and that the political assassination of judicial nominees, whether by the left or the right, threatened "terrible damage to the underlying values of this democracy and the safeguards of our freedom."

At the time Bork's supporters were making the same argument, and Bork himself put his refusal to withdraw from consideration squarely on this ground. "A crucial principle is at stake," he told a national television audience on October 9. "That principle is the way in which we select the men and women who guard the liberties of all the American people. That should not be done through public campaigns of distortion. If I withdraw now, that campaign would be seen as a success, and it would be mounted against future nominees."

Leonard Garment argued in vain that the character of the anti-Bork campaign justified Powell's intervention, but Powell thought otherwise. When Powell said it would be "inappropriate" for him to endorse Robert Bork, he meant something stronger. He saw it as a misuse of the prestige of his office to advance his personal views. After all, if the Supreme Court were to retain the respect and veneration of the people, the Justices had to remain above politics. Public involvement in the debate on his successor would have profaned Powell's reverence for the institution he loved and sullied his idea of himself as a Justice.

Though Powell never said so, it is possible that the concern for the dignity of his office may have been reinforced by care for his own reputation. While the nation engaged in political trench warfare over the nomination of Robert Bork, Powell basked in his country's acclaim. Many who praised him most warmly were alarmed at the prospect of his successor. Anything Powell might say to advance Bork would impair his standing with Bork's enemies, and even if Powell suspected that their esteem was partly tactical, he enjoyed it nonetheless. It may be that personal concerns influenced Powell's action, or they may have played no part. In any event, despite all the pressures brought to bear against him, he stubbornly refused to lend his name to Bork's cause.

On the afternoon of Friday, October 23, 1987, after sixteen weeks of rending controversy, the Senate voted. The margin was fifty-eight in favor and forty-two against—a resounding rejection of Robert Bork and of all that he had come, rightly or wrongly, to represent.

ON OCTOBER 29 Reagan nominated Douglas H. Ginsburg, a forty-one-year-old former Harvard law professor and Assistant Attorney General for Antitrust who was just completing his first year on the D.C. Circuit Court of Appeals. The nomination lasted barely one week. It was doomed when Nina Totenberg discovered—with a little help from his friends—that as a young professor Ginsburg had occasionally smoked marijuana. (Unlike Bork, who left the bench after his rejection by the Senate, Ginsburg continued a distinguished career on the D.C. Circuit.)

On its third try, the administration found a winner. A twelve-year veteran of the Ninth Circuit Court of Appeals, Anthony Kennedy was politically conservative, personally devout, and socially conventional. In the Senate hearings, the nominee artfully distanced himself from Reagan's unsuccessful first choice. Kennedy came across as "either a markedly more moderate student of the Constitution than Bork or a master of soothing rhetoric." In fact, he was both. The Senate confirmed him without dissent, and on February 18, 1988, he took the oath of office as the 104th Associate Justice of the Supreme Court.

That his retirement had precipitated the political bloodbath over Robert Bork and the public fiasco of Douglas Ginsburg caused Powell no little anguish. Jo kidded that it was all his fault, to which he responded, in deadly earnest, "There's no way I could have known. And if I stayed longer, I still wouldn't have known." What he would have done if he had known, he did not allow himself to consider.

THE POLITICAL AFTERMATH of Powell's retirement was immediate and convulsive, but the effect of his departure on the Supreme Court itself was curiously delayed. The 1987–1988 term, which Kennedy joined already underway, went smoothly and without surprises. In result, the decisions of the Supreme Court were so closely in line with those of the past few years that Powell's retirement seemed not to have mattered.

The next year proved otherwise. The 1988–1989 term seemed almost to have been engineered to spotlight what a difference one Justice could make. In that term, the Court so often split down the middle that Justice White asked the librarians to compile a list of five–four decisions. They counted thirty-two, which was (erroneously) thought to be the highest number ever for a single term. In only three of those cases did Justice Kennedy dissent. In all the others, he provided the essential fifth vote for the an increasingly conservative majority.

There is an obvious danger in comparing Kennedy's votes to those Powell might have cast. The process of briefing, argument, research, and writing in which Powell placed such great store often caused him to modify his initial inclinations. That said, it is clear that in some areas the replacement of Powell by Kennedy did change the direction of the Court. Most obvious was *Webster v. Reproductive Health Services*, where the Court upheld a Missouri statute barring use of public employees or facilities for abortions not necessary to save the mother's life. Powell might have agreed with that particular result, but he would never have joined Rehnquist's opinion attacking *Roe v. Wade* and encouraging legislatures to attempt further restrictions on abortion. Also clearly contradicting Powell's views were the rulings in a pair of capital cases. In one, Kennedy and four others held that the Constitution does not categorically prohibit the execution of mentally retarded defendants. In the other, those same Justices ruled that defendants could be put to death for crimes committed when they were sixteen or seventeen years old. Both cases would have come out the other way had Powell remained on the Court.

It is less clear how the outcomes would have changed in the term's civil rights cases. In two important decisions, the post-Powell Court made it more difficult for civil rights plaintiffs to prove racial discrimination in employment and restricted the range of federal remedies for racial harassment on the job. No one can say for sure whether Powell would have voted the other way in both or either of these cases, but it is not implausible. (In any event, Congress overruled both decisions in the 1991 Civil Rights Act, which legislatively adopted the dissenters' interpretation of the controlling statutes.)

Ironically, Powell's vote, which so often had been crucial for the occasional liberal victory, proved unnecessary for their one great triumph of the 1988–1989 term. On June 21, 1989, the Supreme Court struck down a Texas law against desecration of the American flag. Gregory Lee Johnson set fire to a flag in front of the Dallas city hall and chanted while it burned, "America, the red, white, and blue, we spit on you." An odd mix of Justices—Brennan, Marshall, Blackmun, Scalia, and Kennedy—found this action to be constitutionally protected speech under the First Amendment and therefore beyond the power of the state to punish as a crime. "Our decision," said Justice Brennan, "is a reaffirmation of the principles of freedom and inclusiveness that the flag best reflects, and of the conviction that our toleration of criticism such as Johnson's is a sign and source of our strength. . . . We do not consecrate the flag by punishing its desecration, for in doing so we dilute the freedom that this cherished emblem represents."

Rehnquist, White, Stevens, and O'Connor dissented. They argued that while Johnson remained free to voice his contempt for the country in a variety of ways, the flag was special. "The ideas of liberty and equality" represented by the flag, wrote Justice Stevens, "have been an irresistible force in motivating leaders like Patrick Henry, Susan B. Anthony, and Abraham Lincoln, schoolteachers like Nathan Hale and Booker T. Washington, the Philippine Scouts who fought at Bataan, and the soldiers who scaled the bluff at Omaha Beach. If these ideas are worthy fighting for—and our history demonstrates that they are—it cannot be true that the flag that uniquely symbolizes their power is itself not worthy of protection from unnecessary desecration."

However attractive Powell might have found these words, his position was clear. He had been surprisingly forward in protecting political dissent, even when it was crude and vulgar. In fact, one of the earliest indications that Powell might not fit into the lockstep of reaction that was predicted for the Nixon appointees was his handling of three cases involving criminal prosecution for the public use of the word "motherfucking." The holdovers from the Warren Court voted to set aside all three convictions, despite dissents in all three cases from Burger,

Blackmun, and Rehnquist. Powell alone tried to distinguish the cases. Abusive language, he concluded, could not constitutionally be punished when used against a police officer, who should be "trained to exercise a higher degree of restraint than the average citizen" in the face of such provocation. Nor would prosecution succeed against a Black Panther who was invited to speak at a political meeting, where "language of the character charged might well have been anticipated by the audience." But to use the epithet repeatedly before women and children at a public school board meeting was for Powell a "gross abuse of the respected privilege in this country of allowing every citizen to speak his mind."

Perhaps he was trying to draw too fine a line, but at least Powell was struggling to come to grips with a troubling and distasteful issue. In 1972 Gerald Gunther cited these cases as evidence that the newly appointed Justice Powell, like his predecessor Justice Harlan, "had the qualities not only of intellectual but of moral character to listen, to think, to articulate"—to act, in short, "as the conscience of the Court." "I cannot remember," Gunther said later, "ever voicing an opinion that was greeted with so much scorn among fellow Court watchers and by the press," but he was exactly right. Powell quickly proved himself a sensitive and alert protector of free speech. In Gunther's words, he followed Harlan in crafting a First Amendment jurisprudence "devoid of simplistic rules and categorical answers, but . . . rich in sensitive, candid, and articulate perceptions of competing interests."

Like Harlan before him, Powell had faced cases of flag desecration, and also like Harlan, Powell ruled in favor of free speech despite revulsion at the means chosen. As Powell said then and later, he would have voted (as did Justice Kennedy) to allow Gregory Lee Johnson's noxious act.

Powell's absence from the Court was also felt in personal relations. In an institution that prides itself on cordiality, the 1988–1989 term was notably acrimonious. Not only were there many close cases, but there were at least five "lost Courts," when a Justice changed sides after seeing the opinions. (Naturally, it is frustrating for the Justice assigned to write the majority opinion to discover that it has become a dissent.) These tensions spilled over into the published opinions, which The New York Times editorialists pronounced "Supremely Surly."

The "raucous tone and unruly language" that offended the Times also bothered Powell. In a lecture delivered in October 1989, Powell spoke on the virtues of precedent and judicial restraint. Change, he said, was inevitable but should be tempered by "stability and moderation." And gently, very gently, he rued the rancor that had occasionally crept into the Court's opinions. "Unhappily," he noted, "some opinions—on both sides of issues—included language that in time the authors may regret." "[I]n these times," wrote correspondent Linda Greenhouse, "with the Court so sharply polarized, it is all the more striking to hear, over the din of ideological struggle, the loving but concerned voice of a noncombatant."

Privately Powell was distressed by what he had read. "I am rather glad," he wrote his son, that "I was not on the Court." His former colleagues did not share that view. Sandra Day O'Connor missed his "humanizing influence." It was not, she said, "an easy thing to measure, but for those of us who felt it, it will be impossible to forget." Another Justice said privately that with Powell gone, there was "less civility than formerly." Others voiced the same thought—that Powell's soft words and flawless courtesy might have made less bitter and wrenching the transition from the era of judicial balance to the newly conservative Rehnquist Court.

EPILOGUE

As Powell had foreseen, his health following retirement was by no means robust. In addition to urological problems, he suffered at night from a worrisome pain in his legs. In 1988 a blood infection kept him in the hospital for eight days and on antibiotics for three full months. In February 1989 he contracted pneumonia while sitting on an appeals court in Florida and spent a week in a Jacksonville hospital. At the clerks' reunion that summer, he endured the first in a series of alarming blackouts. He was taken by ambulance from the Alibi Club to the Georgetown University Hospital, where the doctors found "no apparent predisposing cause" for the fainting. Ultimately, it was found that the trouble stemmed from cardiac arrhythmia. When his heart picked the wrong time to skip a few beats, Powell would lose blood supply to his head and pass out. A cardiac pacemaker corrected the problem, but not before Powell suffered a nasty fall and a broken hip. Hip replacement surgery and a long convalescence kept him sidelined through the early months of 1991.

Despite these setbacks, Powell continued to work—so much that Jo wondered why he had bothered to retire. They did not return permanently to Richmond, as she had hoped, but remained for most of the year in Washington, where Powell maintained an office in the Supreme Court, with a secretary, a messenger, and one clerk. Fearful of having nothing to do, Powell at first agreed to do too much—to chair Chief Justice Rehnquist's committee on habeas corpus in capital cases, to deliver lectures, to spend several weeks in residence at the University of Virginia and Washington and Lee, to receive various awards and honorary degrees, and to sit on appeals courts in Richmond and elsewhere.

As the years weighed upon him, less was required to fill his day. Still Powell soldiered on, sitting when he could on the courts of appeals, helping to meet the burgeoning case load of the federal judiciary, and continuing his lifelong devotion to work.

POWELL SAID THAT an advantage of retiring "early" was that he got to read his own obituaries. Not all were raves. Amid the many tributes and appreciations of his work, there were dissents. Yale law professor Paul Kahn, for example, argued that Powell's instinct to "find the center, to strike the balance between competing interests" simply showed that he had "little to say." For the most part, however, Powell was praised as a wise centrist, a moral teacher, and a model judge.

Ultimately, evaluation of Powell's career as a judge depends upon one's point of view. Anyone looking for political consistency would be disappointed. But consistency in judging is most evident when it is most simplistic. The more weight a judge attaches to identity of the litigants, for example, the bolder the outline of that judge's ideology. Is the judge for or against labor unions? Sympathetic or hostile to criminal defendants? Predisposed to favor police officers or those who make claims against them? Such crude preferences can easily be read as a consistent political philosophy, which one may like or dislike according to its content.

Of this kind of consistency, Powell cannot fairly be accused. Though no one is free from preconceptions or immune to prejudices, the conscientious judge struggles against them. And Powell was a conscientious judge. He made the effort to keep an open mind and worked hard to ensure that he was well informed. He gave careful and sincere consideration to the arguments on both sides. As a person and as a judge, Powell was a good listener.

Of course, listening is not value-free. What one chooses to hear or is willing to credit depends on a background of personal and political beliefs. But to say that the process of judging is grounded in subjectivity is not to deny the value of self-discipline or to denigrate the goal of self-education. Both are needed, especially given the longevity of judicial tenure. Judges who do not make the effort to avoid premature closure of the mind descend into sloganeering and knee-jerk reactions.

Judges who do not continue to learn show an increasingly irrelevant preoccupation with the problems of an earlier generation. Those who listen, grow. They not only make decisions that others could not have predicted at the time of appointment; they make decisions that they themselves would not have foreseen. Certainly that was true of Powell, who in areas ranging from abortion to affirmative action to free speech made decisions that he would never have endorsed at the time of his appointment.

Powell had abiding faith in the process of judging. Briefing and argument, reflection and debate, attention to the factual record and the obligation to explain oneself in writing were never mere formalities. To him, the procedures of appellate litigation were logical steps in a search for rationality. Conscientious study and respectful attention to the views of others seemed to him allies of wisdom. In short, Powell believed in reason—and in the orderly and deliberative procedures that allowed reason to flourish.

Powell's ingrained courtesy and ability to listen also underlay his most often remarked judicial attribute—an instinct for moderation and compromise. Genuine respect for the views of others directs the mind toward the common ground. Powell was the opposite of William O. Douglas. Powell had nothing of the fierce iconoclast spoiling for a fight. On the contrary, he characteristically sought to narrow conflict, to accommodate opposing views, and, when that was not possible, to disagree without deepening divisions and precluding future rapprochement. For Powell, compromise was not only a necessary feature of a collegial institution; it was a desirable response to a pluralistic society. As Paul Freund said in a retirement tribute, for Powell moderation did not mean "lukewarmness." It was, rather, a mixture of charity and discretion that allowed him to distinguish flexibility from weakness and fanaticism from belief.

Some issues defeat any attempt at moderation. For those who truly believe that abortion is murder, there can be no compromise. For those who think that the death penalty is always and everywhere a crime against humanity, there is nothing to debate. Such divisive issues are a small part of the overall business of the Supreme Court, but they naturally dominate public opinion.

Remarkably, the great issues that will dominate future evaluations of Powell as a Justice were almost completely unforeseen. The three most important decisions of Powell's nearly sixteen years on the Supreme Court were *Roe v. Wade, Regents of the University of California v. Allan Bakke,* and *United States v. Nixon.* None of these issues played any role in Powell's confirmation. The Nixon tapes case arose from events that had not then occurred and that even today seem slightly incredible. The abortion controversy was beginning to make its way through the lower courts but had not reached the national agenda. Affirmative action also had not yet become a political battleground. Insofar as the President had tried to base his nomination, or the Senators their confirmation, on Powell's predicted votes on the watershed political questions of the day, they inevitably failed.

Some will evaluate Powell's judicial career on a handful of results in the most controversial cases. Was he right or wrong on abortion, affirmative action, capital punishment, and the rest? Only the long run of history will yield anything approaching consensus.

In the meantime, the most balanced and loving assessment of Powell's tenure on the Supreme Court comes from his friend and former clerk, Jay Wilkinson. "He will have his critics," Wilkinson wrote. "Some of his votes are not easy to reconcile. Some of his theory is not seamlessly consistent. . . . For those who seek a comprehensive vision of constitutional law, Justice Powell will not have provided it." But, he added, "For those who seek a perspective grounded in realism and leavened by decency, conscientious in detail and magnanimous in spirit, solicitous of personal dignity and protective of the public trust, there will never be a better Justice."

APPENDIX

AGREEMENT AMONG JUSTICES

BUSINESS LAW

(110 antitrust, banking, and securities law cases)

	Powell	Burger	Douglas	Brennan	Stewart	White	Marshall	Blackmun	Rehnquist	Stevens	O'Connor
Powell	—	90%	30%	62%	86%	72%	72%	78%	86%	69%	84%
Burger	90%	—	30%	60%	77%	73%	74%	74%	83%	69%	94%
Douglas	30%	30%	—	96%	32%	70%	68%	39%	26%	n/a	n/a
Brennan	62%	60%	96%	—	52%	68%	80%	67%	51%	71%	73%
Stewart	86%	77%	32%	52%	—	70%	60%	74%	87%	73%	n/a
White	72%	73%	70%	68%	70%	—	75%	73%	68%	79%	66%
Marshall	72%	74%	68%	80%	60%	75%	—	75%	61%	67%	67%
Blackmun	78%	82%	39%	67%	74%	73%	75%	—	75%	75%	69%
Rehnquist	86%	83%	26%	51%	87%	68%	61%	75%	—	68%	89%
Stevens	69%	69%	n/a	71%	73%	79%	67%	75%	68%	—	68%
O'Connor	84%	94%	n/a	73%	n/a	66%	67%	69%	89%	68%	—

Agreement Among Justices

CIVIL RIGHTS

(160 cases dealing with desegregation, affirmative action, and federal antidiscrimination and civil rights statutes)

	Powell	Burger	Douglas	Brennan	Stewart	White	Marshall	Blackmun	Rehnquist	Stevens	O'Connor
Powell	—	86%	53%	55%	88%	74%	53%	74%	82%	68%	86%
Burger	86%	—	53%	49%	85%	70%	47%	74%	85%	66%	86%
Douglas	53%	53%	—	84%	61%	58%	83%	53%	26%	n/a	n/a
Brennan	55%	49%	84%	—	57%	70%	96%	70%	41%	73%	64%
Stewart	88%	85%	61%	57%	—	67%	58%	83%	78%	73%	n/a
White	74%	70%	58%	70%	67%	—	69%	72%	64%	70%	84%
Marshall	53%	47%	83%	96%	58%	69%	—	72%	37%	73%	54%
Blackmun	74%	74%	53%	70%	83%	72%	72%	—	62%	76%	69%
Rehnquist	82%	85%	26%	41%	78%	64%	37%	62%	—	58%	79%
Stevens	68%	66%	n/a	73%	73%	70%	73%	76%	58%	—	69%
O'Connor	86%	86%	n/a	64%	n/a	84%	54%	69%	79%	69%	—

Agreement Among Justices

CRIMINAL LAW

(596 cases dealing with criminal law and procedure, including the death penalty and federal habeas corpus)

	Powell	Burger	Douglas	Brennan	Stewart	White	Marshall	Blackmun	Rehnquist	Stevens	O'Connor
Powell	—	87%	43%	50%	81%	82%	47%	80%	83%	62%	86%
Burger	87%	—	37%	38%	73%	84%	39%	82%	90%	56%	91%
Douglas	43%	37%	—	85%	60%	49%	87%	44%	35%	n/a	n/a
Brennan	50%	42%	85%	—	66%	51%	92%	55%	34%	71%	36%
Stewart	81%	73%	60%	66%	—	76%	65%	76%	66%	73%	n/a
White	82%	84%	49%	51%	76%	—	48%	77%	81%	61%	84%
Marshall	47%	39%	87%	92%	65%	48%	—	54%	30%	67%	29%
Blackmun	80%	82%	44%	55%	76%	77%	54%	—	75%	65%	68%
Rehnquist	83%	90%	35%	34%	66%	81%	30%	75%	—	52%	91%
Stevens	62%	56%	n/a	71%	73%	61%	67%	65%	52%	—	56%
O'Connor	86%	91%	n/a	36%	n/a	84%	29%	68%	91%	56%	—

Agreement Among Justices

PRIVACY

(56 cases dealing with abortion, contraception, and other privacy claims)

	Powell	Burger	Douglas	Brennan	Stewart	White	Marshall	Blackmun	Rehnquist	Stevens	O'Connor
Powell	—	81%	86%	71%	91%	75%	71%	82%	71%	69%	70%
Burger	81%	—	79%	57%	80%	85%	57%	70%	89%	57%	89%
Douglas	86%	79%	—	79%	93%	57%	79%	85%	57%	n/a	n/a
Brennan	71%	57%	79%	—	66%	54%	96%	85%	46%	79%	45%
Stewart	91%	80%	93%	66%	—	71%	66%	74%	69%	67%	n/a
White	75%	85%	57%	54%	71%	—	54%	64%	89%	54%	95%
Marshall	71%	57%	79%	96%	66%	54%	—	85%	46%	79%	45%
Blackmun	82%	70%	85%	85%	74%	64	85%	—	60%	64%	70%
Rehnquist	71%	89%	57%	46%	69%	89%	46%	60%	—	54%	100%
Stevens	69%	57%	n/a	79%	67%	54%	79%	64%	54%	—	40%
O'Connor	70%	89%	n/a	45%	n/a	95%	45%	70%	100%	40%	—

AGREEMENT AMONG JUSTICES

FREE SPEECH

(184 cases dealing with the freedoms of speech and press and the right of access to the political system)

	Powell	Burger	Douglas	Brennan	Stewart	White	Marshall	Blackmun	Rehnquist	Stevens	O'Connor
Powell	—	81%	49%	57%	69%	76%	56%	77%	72%	61%	89%
Burger	81%	—	37%	45%	65%	80%	46%	81%	85%	58%	86%
Douglas	49%	37%	—	86%	70%	80%	88%	40%	28%	n/a	n/a
Brennan	57%	45%	86%	—	74%	53%	94%	57%	34%	69%	48%
Stewart	69%	65%	70%	74%	—	68%	72%	65%	55%	66%	n/a
White	76%	80%	46%	53%	68%	—	54%	76%	77%	57%	79%
Marshall	56%	46%	88%	94%	72%	54%	—	59%	33%	72%	48%
Blackmun	77%	81%	40%	57%	65%	76%	59%	—	70%	61%	69%
Rehnquist	72%	85%	28%	34%	55%	77%	33%	70%	—	54%	84%
Stevens	61%	59%	n/a	69%	66%	57%	72%	61%	54%	—	58%
O'Connor	89%	86%	n/a	48%	n/a	79%	48%	69%	84%	58%	—

AGREEMENT WITH OUTCOME

FIVE GENERAL AREAS

The number shown in boldface is the highest percentage agreement with outcome among the Justices who sat for at least ten years during Powell's service on the Supreme Court (1972–1987). Justices Douglas, Stewart, and O'Connor sat for fewer than ten years during this period and consequently participated in a significantly smaller sample of cases. If, on the basis of that smaller sample, one of those Justices had a higher percentage agreement with outcome, that number is underlined.

	Powell	Burger	Douglas	Brennan	Stewart	White	Marshall	Blackmun	Rehnquist	Stevens	O'Connor
Business (110 cases)	**91%**	90%	39%	67%	84%	80%	78%	84%	82	79%	84%
Civil Rights (160 cases)	85%	81%	58%	69%	_87%_	83%	67%	85%	70%	80%	_87%_
Criminal Law (596 cases)	**91%**	86%	53%	54%	87%	88%	51%	84%	79%	69%	86%
Free Speech (184 cases)	88%	84%	51%	59%	76%	86%	60%	84%	73%	65%	_89%_
Privacy (56 cases)	**96%**	85%	86%	71%	91%	79%	71%	85%	75%	64%	80%

Agreement with Outcome

Selected Specific Categories

The number shown in boldface is the highest percentage agreement with outcome among the Justices who sat for at least ten years during Powell's service on the Supreme Court (1972–1987). Justices Douglas, Stewart, and O'Connor sat for fewer than ten years during this period and consequently participated in a significantly smaller sample of cases. If, on the basis of that smaller sample, one of those Justices had a higher percentage agreement with outcome, that number is underlined.

	Powell	Burger	Douglas	Brennan	Stewart	White	Marshall	Blackmun	Rehnquist	Stevens	O'Connor
Abortion (20)	**100%**	85%	100%	65%	94%	60%	65%	65%	65%	67%	50%
Affirmative Action (14)	**100%**	77%	50%	64%	57%	62%	62%	79%	57%	73%	71%
Antitrust (65)	**88%**	87%	53%	69%	79%	75%	76%	87%	76%	81%	81%
Death Penalty (66)	**86%**	77%	75%	44%	100%	77%	45%	70%	62%	76%	85%
Desegregation (16)	63%	81%	83%	75%	86%	93%	64%	**94%**	63%	78%	50%
Environmental Law (30)	**93%**	**93%**	100%	83%	67%	93%	72%	73%	79%	76%	80%
Equal Protection (145)	**91%**	82%	59%	61%	89%	88%	60%	83%	70%	75%	87%
Federal Crimes (34)	**94%**	88%	50%	74%	71%	88%	79%	87%	79%	67%	76%
Federal Jurisdiction (30)	93%	89%	67%	73%	81%	89%	82&	90%	90%	95%	100%
Gender Discrimination (46)	80%	71%	63%	78%	84%	80%	78%	84%	54%	**89%**	92%
Habeas Corpus (52)	88%	83%	69%	52%	96%	82%	51%	**90%**	82%	65%	92%
Labor Law (123)	80%	79%	68%	77%	74%	85%	78%	**88%**	76%	80%	78%
Military (19)	**100%**	82%	38%	32%	64%	89%	38%	74%	84%	50%	60%
Obscenity (29)	97%	**100%**	31%	31%	41%	100%	31%	93%	97%	40%	100%
Prisons (33)	**94%**	83%	40%	45%	80%	88%	42%	85%	79%	50%	92%
Religion (44)	**93%**	72%	50%	64%	82%	66%	65%	79%	59%	68%	82%
Search and Seizure (133)	**95%**	90%	40%	40%	83%	88%	40%	87%	84%	69%	86%

Selected Specific Categories (cont.)

	Powell	Burger	Douglas	Brennan	Stewart	White	Marshall	Blackmun	Rehnquist	Stevens	O'Connor
Securities Law (37)	95%	94%	20%	54%	91%	84%	75%	81%	97%	74%	85%
Taxation, Federal (67)	90%	85%	56%	88%	79%	82%	90%	75%	81%	72%	88%
Title VII: Employment Discrimination (61)	85%	80%	50%	65%	91%	85%	63%	86%	79%	78%	81%
Voting Rights Act (23)	78%	86%	50%	87%	77%	87%	76%	87%	61%	84%	80%

NOTES

PROLOGUE: THE RELUCTANT JUSTICE

p. 1 "WORST DAY OF MY LIFE": Josephine R. Powell, interview.
TOLD HIS SISTER: Eleanor Powell Dewey, interview.
CONFIDED TO HIS COLLEGE SWEETHEART: Eleanor D. Wilson, interview.

p. 2 WROTE ATTORNEY GENERAL: LFP to Mitchell, Dec. 12, 1969.
NIXON LATER SAID: Nixon to author, Mar. 15, 1990.
MITCHELL WAS KEENLY DISAPPOINTED: Richard Kleindienst, interview; Rehnquist, interview.
NINETY-EIGHTH JUSTICE: Associate Justices who were later appointed Chief Justice have been counted only once.
TWO NEW VACANCIES TO FILL: Abraham, *Justices and Presidents*, 20–23; Ambrose, *Nixon*, 468–71; Totenberg, "Intrigue and Agony: Nixon and the Court," *National Observer*, Nov. 6, 1971, pp. 1, 18; Beckman, "How Nixon Chose Two for the Court," *Chicago Tribune*, Oct. 24, 1971, p. 16; Evans and Novak, "Nixon and Material for the Court," *Washington Post*, Oct. 18, 1971, p. A23.

p. 3 "NIXON'S NOT SO SUPREME COURT": *Time*, Oct. 25, 1971, p. 12.
"UNIFORM IN BOTH MEDIOCRITY": Evans and Novak, "Nixon and Material for the Court," *Washington Post*, Oct. 18, 1971, p. A23.
EVEN JUSTICE HARLAN: Totenberg, "Intrigue and Agony: Nixon and the Court," *National Observer*, Nov. 6, 1971, p. 18.
"ENTIRELY APPROPRIATE": Burger, interview.

p. 4 "PERSONAL AND CONFIDENTIAL" LETTER: Woodward and Armstrong, *The Brethren*, 159–60.
MITCHELL SAID SHARPLY: Griswold to LFP, Apr. 4, 1987.
"THE ONLY WAY YOU WILL EVER KNOW": *Id.* See also Griswold, *Ould Fields, New Corne*, 283–84.
TRACKED DOWN LEWIS POWELL: The account of Powell's conversations with John Mitchell and President Nixon on October 19 and 20 is based primarily on Powell's contemporaneous notes, provided to the author together with an explanatory memorandum dated January 23, 1989, secondarily on Powell's description of these events in an April 21, 1975, letter to former law partner Eppa Hunton IV, and finally on Powell's recollections in interviews conducted in 1990 and 1991.

p. 5 "DADDY WAS BEING IMPOSED UPON": Josephine Powell Smith, interview.
"I THOUGHT I SAW YOUR PICTURE": *Id.*
"MAINTAIN USEFUL VISION FOR MANY YEARS TO COME": L. Benjamin Sheppard, M.D., to LFP, Nov. 1, 1971.

p. 6 MET WITH THE INNER CIRCLE OF SENIOR LAWYERS: Memorandum of Eppa Hunton IV, July 30, 1975.

WELCOME THE OPPORTUNITY TO DIVIDE HIS SHARE: LFP, memorandum to author, Jan. 23, 1989.

p. 7 HE TRIED TO CHANGE HIS MIND: LFP to Eppa Hunton IV, Apr. 21, 1975; LFP, interview; Josephine R. Powell, interview.

p. 8 "YOU JUST CAN'T DO THAT TO THE PRESIDENT": LFP, interview.
REPEATED THE INTERVIEW: *Id.*

p. 9 ALTHOUGH THERE SEEMED TO HAVE BEEN NO LEAKS: Memorandum to Eppa Hunton IV, July 30, 1975.
"EVERYTHING THAT LEWIS POWELL HAS UNDERTAKEN": *Washington Post*, Oct. 22, 1971, p. A4.
"SOME SAID HE WAS TOO OLD": *Los Angeles Times*, Oct. 22, 1971, p. 1.
"[W]E'RE GOING TO BE TALKING ABOUT YOU": Woodward and Armstrong, *The Brethren*, 161.

p. 10 "EASIER TO GET REHNQUIST THROUGH IF HE WERE PAIRED WITH POWELL": Richard Kleindienst, interview.
"LOOKED LIKE LEGAL GULLIVERS": Lisagor, "Nixon's Revealing Quest for High Court Nominee," *Los Angeles Times*, Oct. 24, 1971, p. G3.
"STUNNED AND FOR THE MOST PART HAPPY REFLEX": *Newsweek*, Nov. 1, 1971, p. 16.

p. 11 WEARING THE GREAT CHIEF JUSTICE'S WATCH: LFP to Jay Johns, Dec. 10, 1971.
LEFT OUT A FEW WORDS: LFP, interview.

CHAPTER I: EARLY LIFE

p. 13 NATHANIEL DIED WITHOUT ISSUE: See generally Lucas, *The Powell Families*.
BECAME SOUTHAMPTON COUNTY: Parramore, *Southampton County*, 29.
RESCUED BY A CONFEDERATE SOLDIER: Powell, *Recollections*, 11.
"IMPRESSIVE CHRISTIAN CHARACTER": *Id.*, 14.

p.14 "GAVE ME THE GLAD-HAND SUNDAYS": *Id.*, 27.
TWO YEARS BEFORE ANYONE INVITED HIM HOME: *Id.*, 72.
SHE CAME FROM BEAR ISLAND: The history of Bear Island and of the Gwathmeys is preserved in the written recollections of family members (most of which date from 1944), together with some historical documents, copies of which were made available to the author by Eleanor Powell Dewey.

p. 15 "KINDNESS OF GENERAL GRANT": Undated handwritten notes made by Mary Lewis Gwathmey Powell.
"ALMOST AS BAD SHAPE" AS THE MULE: LFP to Eleanor Powell Dewey, Mar. 24, 1944.
"BELOVED BY ALL WHO KNEW HER": Powell, *Recollections*, 119.

p. 16 "INFERIORITY COMPLEX": *Id.*, 27, 30.
"MARY LEWIS TOOK IT AS A BIG JOKE": *Id.*, 122.
"LOOKING LIKE A WET TRAMP": *Id.*, 123.
"NOT VERY AGILE ON HER FEET": *Id.*
CHANGED THE SPELLING TO "LOUIS": *Id.*, 5; LFP, interview; Eleanor Powell Dewey, interview.
JOSHUA RAISED HOGS TO SELL AS SMITHFIELD HAMS: Powell, *Recollections*, 33–36.

p. 17 HOUSE AT 206 NORTH BROAD STREET: Duncan G. Groner, editor of the *Suffolk News-Herald*, to LFP, July 3, 1972.
"[I]F I SUCCEEDED," POWELL REASONED: Powell, *Recollections*, 41.

p. 18 REDUCE THE BLACK ELECTORATE BY MORE THAN 70 PERCENT: Wilkinson, *Harry Byrd*, 5.

ONLY THIRTY-THREE MANAGED TO REGISTER: Dabney, *Richmond*, 270.

MANIKINS IN STORE WINDOWS DID NOT APPEAR WITHOUT STOCKINGS: *Id.*, 275.

p. 19 THE ONLY "GOOD NEIGHBORHOOD" THEY COULD AFFORD: Powell, "Reflections," 38.

FOREST HILL AVENUE: LFP, interview. This account of Powell's early childhood and education is based on interviews with Powell and his sister Eleanor Powell Dewey and on her written "Reminiscences." A summary appears in LFP, "Reflections," 315–16.

"IF I DIDN'T GO OUT AND BRAVE THE OTHER BOYS, I WOULD BE A SISSY": LFP, interview.

EARS THAT STUCK OUT SO SHARPLY THAT FOR A TIME HE TRIED TAPING THEM: Eleanor Powell Dewey, interview.

p. 20 PUT HIMSELF TO SLEEP AT NIGHT: Josephine Powell Smith to author, Jan. 2, 1993 (reproducing notes from a conversation with her father).

McGUIRE'S UNIVERSITY SCHOOL: See Dabney, *Richmond*, 214, 326–27; LFP, memorandum on "McGuire's University School," July 10, 1989 (used as the basis for an article in the *Richmond Times-Dispatch*, May 31, 1992, p. B6).

SEGREGATED BY LAW SINCE 1906: Dabney, *Richmond*, 272.

p. 21 "THE PRINCIPLE THAT NOTHING COUNTED SO MUCH AS CHARACTER": *Id.*, 214.

"BE EARNEST, WORK HARD, SPEAK THE TRUTH": "John Peyton McGuire, '94," *University of Virginia Alumni News*, Jan. 1949, pp. 12–13.

"BOYS PREPARED FOR THE UNIVERSITY OF VIRGINIA": *Id.*

REACHED A HEIGHT OF SIX FEET: LFP, memorandum on "McGuire's University School," July 10, 1989.

ALWAYS SHOWING A LARGE GAP: J. Harvie Wilkinson, Jr., interview; J. Harvie Wilkinson, Jr., to LFP, Dec. 29, 1986.

ANOTHER STORY SAYS: J. Harvie Wilkinson, Jr., remarks at LFP Testimonial Dinner, Dec. 1971.

p. 22 NEITHER "WEDNESDAY NIGHT'S WORK NOR SOCIAL FUNCTIONS": Powell, *Recollections*, 71.

"REALLY DID RATHER WELL": Eleanor Powell Dewey, "Reminiscences."

"I AM ALWAYS HERE WHEN LEWIS COMES IN": Eleanor Powell Dewey, interview.

"LEWIS JR. HAS SOMETHING TO SAY": Letitia Nelson Wilkinson, interview.

"VERY IMPRESSED WITH HER SON": *Id.*

p. 23 "SOMETIMES GRUFF ON THE OUTSIDE": Josephine Powell Smith, "Reminiscence of Bear Island," Apr. 10, 1984.

"ONE CAT THAT NEVER CAME BACK": Powell, *Recollections*, 18.

"FOR A GOOD MANY YEARS OF LEWIS'S GROWING UP": Eleanor Powell Dewey, "Reminiscences."

"CLOSER TO MY FATHER THAN I WAS": LFP, interview.

"I AM GOING TO PROVE TO DADDY": Eleanor Powell Dewey, interview.

p. 24 "RATHER MORE OFTEN THAN I THOUGHT NECESSARY": LFP, interview.

"NEVER IN YOUR LIFE HAVE YOU GIVEN ME ONE MOMENT'S WORRY": Louis F. Powell, Sr., to LFP, Sept. 18, 1928.

"TAIL END OF THE VICTORIAN ERA": J. Harvie Wilkinson, Jr., interview.

"WONDERFUL DISCIPLINE": Eleanor Powell Dewey, interview.

"ONE OF THE HAPPIEST DAYS OF MY LIFE": LFP, interview.

p. 25 WHICH HIS MOTHER TAUGHT HIM TO STALK: *Id.*

LOUIS SR. "SHOT FROM THE HIP": Eleanor Powell Dewey, interview.

ONCE HE PROPOSED THAT SHE TRANSLATE LATIN: Eleanor Powell Dewey, "Reminiscences."

"ELEANOR, YOU ARE NOT SMILING ENOUGH": Eleanor Powell Dewey, interview.

"DECISIONS I WISELY MADE CONTRARY TO HIS ADVICE": Eleanor Powell Dewey, "Reminiscences."

"ALWAYS GOT ALONG SUPERBLY WITH LEWIS": Eleanor Powell Dewey, interview.

"DON'T UNDERSTAND WHY I HAVE NO INPUT INTO GUIDING ZOE": *Id.*

p. 26 "A LAW UNTO HERSELF, ALWAYS CHARGING ABOUT": J. Harvie Wilkinson, Jr., interview.

ONLY . . . "WHO WAS NOT DEAD SERIOUS": Letitia Nelson Wilkinson, interview.

SAID THAT HIS CHOICE OF COLLEGE HINGED ON BASEBALL: See, e.g., LFP, "Reflections," 316.

"TO STRIKE OUT ON MY OWN": J. Harvie Wilkinson, Jr., remarks at testimonial dinner, Dec. 1971.

A BUS DEPOSITED HIM ON THE MAIN STREET: LFP, interview.

p. 27 AWARDED ONLY ONE COLLEGE DEGREE: Crenshaw, *General Lee's College,* 141.

"MY GOD, I SHOT THE WRONG ARCHITECT": Hoyt, *Valley Views,* 28.

TRADITIONS AND RITUALS OF STONEWALL JACKSON'S DAY: See generally Turner, *Mrs. Ecker's Lexington,* passim; Letcher, *Only Yesterday,* 28–37.

p. 28 TENSIONS WERE EXACERBATED: Charles R. McDowell, Jr., to author, Sept. 14, 1992.

REQUIRED TO WEAR GREEN BOW TIES TO ALL DANCES: *Ring-tum Phi,* Oct. 10, 1925, p. 1.

"HI, GENTLEMEN": *Ring-tum Phi,* Sept. 22, 1926, p. 3; *id.,* Sept. 29, 1926, p. 2.

FIERY, OUTSPOKEN, WHITE-HAIRED "MAIDEN LADY": *Lynchburg Daily Advance,* Oct. 25, 1971, p. 6.

p. 29 "IT WAS A CONFEDERATE WORLD DOWN IN THAT HOLLOW": Charles R. McDowell, Jr., speech at Washington and Lee, Apr. 4, 1992.

"TRAVELLER AS A COLT": Charles R. McDowell, Jr., interview.

CAMPAIGN TO PREVENT ENLARGEMENT OF THE LEE CHAPEL: Crenshaw, *General Lee's College,* 301–303.

"DEAR, MODEST HONEST LITTLE CHAPEL": *Id.,* 302.

SHE FORGOT ABOUT ROBERT E. LEE: Charles R. McDowell, Jr., interview.

BATTLE OF NEW MARKET: See Catton, *Never Call Retreat,* 351–54; Freeman, *Lee's Lieutenants* III: 515–16.

p. 30 "THE PAST WASN'T OVER": Charles R. McDowell, Jr., speech at Washington and Lee, Apr. 4, 1992, paraphrasing Faulkner, *Requiem for a Nun,* 94.

"I WAS INTERESTED IN HISTORY": LFP, "Reflections," 317.

"BESPECTACLED, SEDATE, PROFESSORIAL": *Lynchburg Daily Advance,* Oct. 25, 1971, p. 6.

"HAD THE URGE TO GRAB HIM": Eleanor Powell Dewey to author, Jan. 28, 1990.

FOURTEEN MEMBERS OF HIS CLASS ELECTED TO PHI BETTA KAPPA: *Ring-Tum Phi,* Mar. 23, 1929, p. 1.

"THE CIRCLE": See Crenshaw, *General Lee's College,* 309–10.

p. 31 "ALWAYS HAD A NICE WAY WITH OLDER WOMEN": LFP, interview.

A "B.M.O.C." MUST: Crenshaw, *General Lee's College,* 313.

RAN UNOPPOSED, POLLED THE HIGHEST NUMBER OF VOTES THEN ON RECORD: *Ring-tum Phi,* Apr. 18, 1929, p. 1.

p. 32 FACE-SAVING VOTE. . . TO "TAKE RESPONSIBILITY FOR THE CONDUCT OF THEIR DATES": *Ring-tum Phi*, Jan. 15, 1930, p. 1.

p. 33 HE WAS HER STEADY BEAU: Eleanor D. Wilson, interview.

"CIRCUMSPECT, EXTREMELY PROPER": *Id.*

"A MODERATE AND MIDDLE-CLASS STUDENT ORGANIZATION": Persico, *Edward R. Murrow*, 63.

"FOSTER UNDERSTANDING AMOUNG THE STUDENTS OF THE WORLD": National Student Federation, *Yearbook*, 27.

p. 34 "AMBROVERTS": *Id.*, 34.

"I DID NOT COME THREE THOUSAND MILES": Eleanor D. Wilson, interview.

TOO PREOCCUPIED WITH "FRATERNITIES, FOOTBALL, AND FUN": Persico, *Edward R. Murrow*, 57.

"ED MADE THE HANDSOMEST PRESENCE": Quoted *id.*, 58.

AT LEAST ONE OTHER NSF REPRESENTATIVE: Powell remembers another male. Although Murrow's biographer (Persico, *Edward R. Murrow*, 64) lists Murrow, Powell, and Dierdre Mason, but not Wilson, Wilson's presence is confirmed by a photograph of her and Powell in Brussels.

CALLED POWELL "JUDGE": LFP, interview; Persico, *Edward R. Murrow*, 64.

FIRST ITEM OF BUSINESS WAS A COMPLAINT BY THE GERMAN DELEGATION: Eleanor D. Wilson, interview.

WHETHER THE GERMANS WOULD BE ADMITTED TO FULL MEMBERSHIP: Kendrick, *Prime Time*, 110; Persico, *Edward R. Murrow*, 65; Sperber, *Murrow*, 34.

p. 35 DESCRIBED THE SHOCK THAT CONFRONTED THE AMERICANS AT BRUSSELS: Persico, *Edward R. Murrow*, 64–65.

p. 36 EASIER TO GET INTO THAN OTHER UNDERGRADUATE PROGRAMS: Stevens, *Law School*, 37.

RAISED ITS "LAW DEPARTMENT" ADMISSIONS STANDARDS: Crenshaw, *General Lee's College*, 344–45.

"THE LARGER ATTENDANCE IN YEARS PAST": Quoted in Bryson, *Legal Education in Virginia*, 468.

"WOULD LEAD YOU CLEAR OUT TO THE END OF THE BRANCH": Quoted *id.*, 719.

"ASSUMPTION THAT THE CASES, ONCE THEY WERE SORTED OUT": Woodard, "The Limits of Legal Realism," *Virginia L. Rev.* 54:699.

p. 37 TALKED LIKE WILL ROGERS: Bryson, *Legal Education in Virginia*, 381.

"PUTTING THE HAY DOWN TO WHERE THE CALVES CAN REACH IT": Quoted *id.*, 384.

McDOWELL'S EXAMINATIONS IN BILLS AND NOTES: LFP, interview; Charles R. McDowell, Jr., interview.

A GRADE ONE POINT HIGHER THAN THE BEST SCORE: LFP, interview.

p. 38 REGRET AT THE DEMISE OF OLD TUCKER HALL WAS "PURELY SENTIMENTAL": LFP to W. H. Moreland, Dec. 20, 1934.

"AN EXHILARATING ENCOUNTER": Bryson, *Legal Education in Virginia*, 347.

p. 39 "HE JUST TOLD ME I HAD TO GO": LFP, interview.

"I WORKED BY TAIL FEATHERS OFF": *Id.*

LEADING CRITIC OF THE PROSECUTION OF SACCO AND VANZETTI: See Frankfurter, "The Case of Sacco and Vanzetti," *Atlantic Monthly*, Mar. 1927, pp. 409–32; Baker, *Brandeis and Frankfurter*, 245–73; Baker, *Felix Frankfurter*, 120–30.

p. 40 HAROLD M. STEPHENS: *Washington Post*, May 29, 1955, p. A10.

"I ALWAYS FELT LIKE A DUMMY": LFP, interview.

TWICE SERIOUSLY CONSIDERED BY PRESIDENT KENNEDY: *New Yorker*, Feb. 24, 1992, p. 27.

AFFECTED "THE WAY GENERATIONS OF STUDENTS": LFP, "Tribute," *Harvard Law Bulletin*, June 1992, p. 18.

p. 41 WHETHER CONGRESS COULD PROVIDE FOR JURY TRIAL IN CONTEMPT PROCEEDINGS: *Michaelson v. United States*, 266 U.S. 42 (1924).

DICK KEETON, WHO BEDEVILED THE OLD MAN BY EATING HARD-BOILED EGGS: LFP, interview.

FOCUSED ON "THE WORKINGS OF LAW": LFP, class notes.

CHAPTER II: YOUNG PROFESSIONAL

p. 44 THE WALL STREET FIRM THAT STILL BEARS HIS NAME: During Davis's absence, his partners renamed the firm Davis, Polk, Wardwell, Gardiner & Reed. The latter two names were later dropped.

ARGUED MORE CASES: Harbaugh, *Lawyer's Lawyer*, 531.

OFFERED HIM AN ASSOCIATE'S POSITION AT $150 A MONTH: LFP, interview; LFP, "Reflections," 317–18.

COULD NOT AFFORD TO PROVIDE AN OFFICE: LFP, interview.

p. 45 "DISLIKED BY MORE PEOPLE THAN LIKED HIM": *Id.*

"I NEEDED SOME LEEWAY IN THE MORNING": *Id,*

T. JUSTIN MOORE: Freeman, *The Style of a Law Firm*, 129–43; LFP, interview.

p. 46 "THE AROMA OF A BITCH IN HEAT": Freeman, *The Style of a Law Firm*, 135 (quoting John Riely).

CONSULTED CHRISTIAN, WHO ADVISED HIM: LFP, interview.

HE COULD PUT UP WITH THE LARGE-FIRM BUREAUCRACY: *Id.*

EDMUND RANDOLPH WILLIAMS: See Freeman, *The Style of a Law Firm*, 58–75. Williams was actually a few months younger than Henry Anderson but was senior to Anderson in the firm hierarchy.

p. 47 "SPECIAL GIFT FOR IDENTIFYING AND THEN NOURISHING": *Id.*, 70–71.

POWELL DESCRIBED HIM AS A "COUNSELLOR": *Id.*, 72.

ONLY TWO PEOPLE IN THE WORLD WHOM RANDOLPH WILLIAMS DISLIKED: *Id.*, 74.

HENRY W. ANDERSON: *Id.*, 76–103.

p. 48 "WOULD CATAPULT [HIM] INTO A WORLD OF HIGH FINANCE": *Id.*, 82.

"LEADING RAILROAD REORGANIZATION LAWYER IN THE UNITED STATES": LFP, interview.

RED CROSS MISSION TO RUMANIA: See Bearss, "Marie of Rumania," *Virginia Country*, Mar.–Apr. 1987, pp. 20–28; Godbold, *Ellen Glasgow*, 120–22.

"REAL COLONELS DON'T": Freeman, *The Style of a Law Firm*, 173 (quoting George D. Gibson).

MARIE "PLACED HERSELF IN STAGED MEDIEVAL SETTINGS": Bearss, "Marie of Rumania," *Virginia Country*, Mar.–Apr. 1987, p. 24.

OFFERED THE CROWN OF ALBANIA: Godbold, *Ellen Glasgow*, 122.

p. 49 "ONLY DEATH KEPT THEM AWAY FROM HIS DINNERS": Glasgow, *The Woman Within*, 219–21, 224–25.

"IF YOU LIKE TO PUT ON DOG": Freeman, *The Style of a Law Firm*, 79.

"PLUPERFECT SNOB": Glasgow, *The Woman Within*, 221.

"LIKE PUTTING A THOROUGHBRED TO THE PLOW": Freeman, *The Style of a Law Firm*, 78.

"[I]T MUST BE RECOGNIZED BY ANY FAIR-MINDED PERSON": *Id.*, 92.

"THE SORT OF PERSON A POPULACE KILLS": Glasgow, *The Woman Within*, 228.

p. 50   "I DON'T SIGN ANYTHING HERE": LFP, interview with Anne Hobson Freeman.

"I CAN BE OF MORE HELP . . . WHILE I SHAVE IN THE MORNING": *Id.*

THOMAS BENJAMIN GAY: Freeman, *The Style of a Law Firm*, 104–28.

RIVALRY BETWEEN GAY AND MOORE SETTLED INTO AN ACCOMMODATION: *Id.*, 115.

"HOGGING THE STAFF": LFP, interview.

"RIDE ROUGHSHOD OVER PEOPLE WITHOUT BATTING AN EYE": Freeman, *The Style of a Law Firm*, 135 (quoting John D. Riely).

p. 51   "BANTAM ROOSTER": *Id.*, 108 (quoting Robert P. Buford).

WHO COULD SEND A MESSENGER TO SHARPEN A BOX OF PENCILS: J. Harvie Wilkinson III, interview.

"IN LIGHT OF THIS RECENT DECISION": LFP, interview with Anne Hobson Freeman.

WROTE THE JUSTICES TAKING THE BLAME FOR A MISTAKE: Author.

"HE HAS NEVER INVITED ME TO CALL HIM ANYTHING ELSE": Author.

p. 52   "I AM A PHI KAPPA SIGMA FROM WASHINGTON AND LEE": LFP, interview.

BROKE CRAIG'S HEALTH: Freeman, *The Style of a Law Firm*, 116.

"A VERY NICE, VERY PLEASANT, SOFT-VOICED, SELF-EFFACING YOUNG LAWYER": James Latimer, interview.

"WE LOST IT": LFP, interview with Anne Hobson Freeman.

p. 53   GAVE UP JURY TRIALS BECAUSE THEY KEPT HIM AWAKE: LFP, interview.

"IT WOULD NEVER HAVE OCCURRED TO ME TO LEAVE HOME": LFP, interview with Anne Hobson Freeman.

"I JUST WANT TO MAKE SURE IT'S NOT ME": Eleanor Powell Dewey, interview.

p. 54   "LORD HIGH POOH-BAH": J. Harvie Wilkinson, Jr., to LFP, Dec. 29, 1986.

"BANKERS WERE NOT THE MOST POPULAR PEOPLE": J. Harvie Wilkinson, Jr., interview.

"WE PLANNED AND PLANNED": *Id.*

"WE WERE BOTH DRIVING FOR THE TOP": J. Harvie Wilkinson, Jr., interview with Anne Hobson Freeman.

p. 55   "LEWIS, IT IS EVER THUS": J. Harvie Wilkinson, Jr., interview; LFP, interview.

"OUR HIGH ESTIMATE, OUR LOW ESTIMATE, OR OUR MEDIUM ESTIMATE": LFP, interview.

ONLY KNOWN INSTANCE WHEN POWELL COMPLETELY LOST HIS SELF-CONTROL: LFP, interview; J. Harvie Wilkinson, Jr., interview.

p. 56   POWELL'S FIRST TALK WAS ON THE SUPREME COURT: LFP, interview.

FOUND THEMSELVES "BORED TO DEATH": Josephine R. Powell, interview.

p. 57   WHO "REALLY THOUGHT HE HUNG THE MOON": *Id.*

"REALLY THOUGHT I HAD IT MADE": *Id.*

FIRST ON A NEWSPAPER ROSTER OF RICHMOND'S TEN BEST-LOOKING WOMEN: *Richmond Times-Dispatch*, clipping later marked as dating from the late 1940s or early 1950s.

p. 58   "SHE'S NOT INTELLECTUAL ENOUGH FOR YOU": Mrs. George D. Gibson, interview.

"JO POWELL HAS THE KNACK": Freeman, *The Style of a Law Firm*, 153.

CHAPTER III: WARTIME

p. 60 LONG BEEN IMPATIENT FOR THE UNITED STATES TO COME TO ENGLAND'S AID: Putney, *Ultra*, 1.

PUBLIC INFORMATION CAMPAIGN SUPPORTING DEFENSE PREPAREDNESS: LFP, "The Conference Plan for National Unity," Aug. 25, 1940 (date supplied by accompanying letter).

HIS DOUBTS ABOUT ACTIVE BELLIGERENCE: LFP to Paul F. Hannah, Sept. 4, 1940.

"ITS PURPOSE WAS TO 'INCULCATE A DEEPER UNDERSTANDING OF'": The statement of the objectives of the Public Information Program is taken from the pamphlet, "—for a More Perfect Union," published by the Junior Bar Conference in January 1941.

p. 61 "YOU MIGHT GET KILLED": LFP, interview with Anne Hobson Freeman.

"THIS WAR WILL IN ALL PROBABILITY BE THE GREATEST EVENT": *Id.*

"I COULD NEVER HAVE LOOKED MY CHILDREN IN THE FACE": LFP to Josephine R. Powell, postmarked Aug. 23, 1942.

THE PLACE FOR EDUCATED GENTLEMEN: LFP, interview.

"NOTHING HE COULD DO ABOUT ME—OR MY EYES": Putney, *Ultra*, 1.

PROCEED ON MAY 1: The Adjutant General to LFP, telegram, Aug. 29, 1942.

FEELING LIKE AN IDIOT: LFP, interview.

"I WORKED HARD": *Id.*

p. 62 "PROBABLY IT IS BEST THAT I BE WITH A COMBAT UNIT": LFP to Josephine R. Powell, postmarked Aug. 23, 1942.

"FLYING PROSTITUTE": LFP, interview; see Mets, *Master of Airpower*, 118 (describing efforts to help crews overcome their aversion to Marauders).

"VERY UNATTRACTIVE" COLLISION IN MIDAIR: LFP, interview; LFP, *Diary*, 4–5.

FLYING IN STAGES: Craven and Cate, *Army Air Forces* I:342–49, 640–45; Mets, *Master of Airpower*, 125-27.

LEAVING DISABLED PLANES AND EQUIPMENT STREWN ALONG THE ROUTE: Craven and Cate, *Army Air Forces* II:60; "The 319th in Action," 15–20.

"JUST STAY IN THE BIGGEST HOTEL": Josephine R. Powell, interview; LFP, interview.

"I SHALL NEVER FORGET MY DEPRESSION THAT NIGHT": LFP, *Diary*, 7.

p. 63 "MY GLASSES ARE SO CLOUDY WITH SUPPRESSED TEARS": LFP to Josephine R. Powell, Sept. 3, 1942.

SEPTEMBER 5: Craven and Cate, *Army Air Forces* II:52; "The 319th in Action," 10; LFP, *Diary*, 8–9.

WONDERED IF HER HUSBAND WERE ON BOARD: Josephine R. Powell, interview.

COULD NOT BEND HIS KNEES: LFP, *Diary*, 9.

p. 64 VIOLENT SHIFTS IN DIRECTION: *Id.*, 12.

CORRECTLY GUESSED NORTH AFRICA: *Id.*, 25.

"AIR RAID ALERT DURING TEA WAS IGNORED BY ALL": *Id.*, 21.

"I DON'T THINK I AM A COWARD": *Id.*, 32.

"EVERY MAN FOR HIMSELF AND GOD HELP THE ABSENT": *Id.*, 36–37.

p. 65 SLEPT IN LONG UNDERWEAR AND PAJAMAS: *Id.*, 16–17.

HE SPENT NEARLY HALF OF HIS SIX-MONTH SUPPLY OF RATION COUPONS: *Id.*, 20.

REST OF THE PLACE WAS LIKE AN ICEBOX: *Id.*, 28.

"NOT 'OFFICIALLY' COLD OVER HERE UNTIL NOV. 1ST": *Id.*

ASKED HIS WIFE AND MOTHER TO SEND TWO SWEATERS: LFP to Josephine R. Powell, Sept. 26, 1942.

WHAT HE REALLY NEEDED WAS A SLEEPING BAG: LFP to Josephine R. Powell, Oct. 8, 1942.

THAT MEN WERE ISSUED SLEEPING BAGS IN COLD CLIMATES: Josephine R. Powell to LFP, Nov. 11, 1942.

"THIS IS LIKE WIRING ME TO COME HOME IMMEDIATELY FOR CHRISTMAS": LFP to Josephine R. Powell, Dec. 14, 1942.

RETURN TO CIVILIZATION: LFP, *Diary*, 23.

p. 66 FROM A SMALL ROOM IN THE BASEMENT: Sperber, *Murrow*, 171, 189.

"WAS THRILLED TO HEAR": LFP, *Diary*, 24. The *Diary* entry is detailed and apparently contemporaneous, but the precise date may be error, as a published catalogue of CBS broadcasts does not include Murrow speaking on the day indicated. See Ryan, *History in Sound*, 254.

WITH A HOUSEKEEPER WHO SOMEHOW PRODUCED ORANGES FOR HIS BREAKFAST: LFP to Josephine R. Powell, Oct. 9, 1942. In August 1990 PBS broadcast a two-part documentary about Murrow in which Powell recalled staying with Janet in the London apartment while Ed went on a British bombing raid on Berlin. Murrow's trip resulted in the famous broadcast of December 3, 1943, by which time Powell had returned to the States. It seems likely that Powell heard the Berlin bombing raid broadcast and later conflated it with an earlier occasion when he stayed with Janet Murrow.

THE *MOULTAN*, AN ANCIENT PASSENGER LINER: LFP, *Diary*, 39.

"WE ARE BACK EXACTLY WHERE WE STARTED": *Id.*, 40.

THE CONVOY REVERSED COURSE: Craven and Cate, *Army Air Forces* II:70.

THE FEINT WORKED: Putney, *Ultra*, 5.

HEAVY AND EFFECTIVE: Ambrose, *Eisenhower* I:203–204.

p. 67 ON THE THIRD DAY, THE MEN OF THE 319TH LANDED: LFP, *Diary*, 49–50.

WITH MODERN PLUMBING: *Id.*, 54–55.

TWO HARD-SURFACED RUNWAYS: Craven and Cate, *Army Air Forces* II:118.

"THESE STUPID FRENCH": LFP, *Diary*, 56.

THERE IS NO SUCH THING AS PRIVACY, AND I NO LONGER CARE": *Id.*, 74.

[RAINS] CAME WITH A VENGEANCE IN DECEMBER 1942: Craven and Cate, *Army Air Forces* II:91, 108, 116.

WHERE THE MUD WAS "DEEP AND GOOEY": *Id.*, 85.

"AN APPALLING AMOUNT OF TIME": LFP to Josephine R. Powell, Nov. 25, 1942.

"MOST USEFUL AND VERSATILE HAT IN THE WORLD": LFP to Mrs. M. Pierce Rucker, Nov. 21, 1942.

p. 68 "IT IS POSSIBLE TO LIVE AND BE HAPPY LIKE THIS": LFP to Josephine R. Powell, Nov. 25, 1942.

ASKED FOR THE "NEWS OF THE WEEK" SECTION OF THE SUNDAY *NEW YORK TIMES*: LFP to Josephine R. Powell, Dec. 7 and 19, 1942.

"THESE PEOPLE ARE UTTERLY STUPID": LFP to Josephine McR. Powell, Dec. 22, 1942.

FOUR PLANES AND ONE CREW HAD BEEN LOST: "The 319th in Action," 21–22.

THE JOURNEY TO NORTH AFRICA HAD COST TWO MORE PLANES: LFP, *Diary*, 57.

SHOT DOWN OVER CHERBOURG: Craven and Cate, *Army Air Forces* II:88; "The 319th in Action," 22.

ORAN HAD BEEN INTENDED AS HEADQUARTERS FOR THE TWELFTH AIR FORCE: Craven and Cate, *Army Air Forces* II:83-85.

p. 69 EARLY RAIDS WERE AIMED CHIEFLY AT TUNISIAN AIRFIELDS: *Id.*, 86.

"I AM CONVINCED THAT *THOROUGHNESS* IS THE PRIME ATTRIBUTE OF WORTH-WHILE INTERROGATION": LFP, "Memorandum of Activities of Intelligence Section of 319th Bomb Group from June, 1942 to March, 1943," reprinted in Putney, *Ultra*, 112–15.

WANTED TO "CLAIM THE EARTH": LFP, *Diary*, 70.

"I REALLY FEEL THAT I AM NOW MAKING A CONTRIBUTION TO THE WAR: *Id.*, 74.

"HOMELY AS MUD HENS": LFP to Josephine R. Powell, Nov. 23, 1942.

"TO DELIVER A MORE SUITABLE PRESENT IN PERSON": *Id.*

LOST SEVERAL PLANES AND ONE COMMANDER: "The 319th in Action," 21-22.

NEW COMMANDER ARRIVED ON NOVEMBER 27, 1942: LFP, *Diary*, 61.

FIRST COMBAT MISSION: "A Short History of the 319th Bombardment Group and 319th Bombardment Wing," 1.

WERE LOST IN THE NEXT WEEK: "The 319th in Action," 25–26.

NEW COMMANDER WHO WAS SHOT DOWN AND CAPTURED: *Id.*, 22, photographs following page 155.

A SUICIDE ALTITUDE WHERE EVEN LIGHT ANTIAIRCRAFT FIRE COULD KILL: LFP, *Diary*, 67.

BUT WHEN THE TACTIC WAS REPEATED: Craven and Cate, *Army Air Forces* II:124; LFP, *Diary*, 73.

p. 70 TWO MORE B-26S WERE LOST IN THE SAME WAY: Craven and Cate, *Army Air Forces* II:124; LFP, *Diary*, 73; "The 319th in Action," 29.

"SKIP BOMBING": Putney, *Ultra*, 6 n. 9; LFP, *Diary*, 85–86.

THE 319TH DID GREAT WORK WITH SKIP BOMBING: Putney, *Ultra*, 6.

SANK AT LEAST ONE FREIGHTER AND DAMAGED SEVERAL OTHERS: Craven and Cate, *Army Air Forces* II:147–48.

BUT LOST TWO PLANES IN THE PROCESS: LFP, *Diary*, 87; "The 319th in Action," 31.

THE NEXT DAY STILL ANOTHER B-26 WENT DOWN: *Id.*, 32.

PLANES FROM THE 319TH PERFORMED BRILLIANTLY: Craven and Cate, *Army Air Forces* II:148. The official history specifies that six B-26s participated in this raid; Powell's diary puts the number at five.

LOSING TWO MORE AIRCRAFT: LFP, *Diary*, 90–91.

A FEW HAD TO BE THREATENED WITH COURT-MARTIAL: LFP, interview.

"A SERIOUS LOWERING OF MORALE": Craven and Cate, *Army Air Forces* II:130, 192 (describing morale as "extremely low").

EISENHOWER CAST AROUND FOR THE MEANS TO RESIST THIS ADVANCE: Ambrose, *Eisenhower* I:229-30.

p. 71 TWO WERE SHOT DOWN: "Bombs on the Target: 319th Bomb Group Operational History," 30; "The 319th in Action," 33.

TO FIND THEIR CLOTHES AND PERSONAL EFFECTS: LFP, *Diary*, 94.

RETIRED TO FRENCH MOROCCO FOR REST AND REFITTING: Craven and Cate, *Army Air Forces* II:130–31; "Bombs on the Target: 319th Bomb Group Operational History," 34.

"FAR BETTER THAN GOING BACK TO ORAN": LFP, *Diary*, 97.

"THE HALF-EXISTENCE OF THE THE TWELFTH": Craven and Cate, *Army Air Forces* II:167.

p. 72 SWIFT TRANSLATION FROM "FOX HOLE TO FEATHER MATTRESS": LFP, *Diary*, 93.

"WITH PROVERBIAL WINE, WOMEN, AND SONG": *Id.*

HE HIMSELF WAS IN ALGIERS: *Id.*, 98.

STEAK DINNER IN THE HÔTEL DE RIVAGE: *Id.*, 100.

RECRUITED TO SERVE AS PROSECUTOR AT A SPECIAL COURT-MARTIAL: Headquarters, NWAAF, Special Order No. 15, Mar. 8, 1943.

"THE CAPT AND FIRST SERGEANT OF THIS COMPANY WERE BRUTES!": LFP, *Diary*, 99–100.

p. 73 SHIPPING TARGETS BECAME POWELL'S PARTICULAR RESPONSIBILITY: "Summary of Military Service of Lt. Col. Lewis F. Powell, Jr.," Dec. 28, 1944.

NEARLY 300,000 AXIS PRISONERS: Ambrose, *Eisenhower* I:236.

THE OBJECT WAS TO ELIMINATE AXIS AIR OPPOSITION: Craven and Cate, *Army Air Forces* II:435–39.

AIR RESISTANCE CEASED BY THE FOURTH DAY: *Id.*, 458.

p. 74 THEY ENDED UP WORKING ALMOST AROUND THE CLOCK: LFP, *Diary*, 103.

POWELL'S PARTICULAR RESPONSIBILITY: "Summary of Military Service of Lt. Col. Lewis F. Powell, Jr.," Dec. 28, 1944.

REPORTED AS ORDERED AT THE WAR DEPARTMENT IN WASHINGTON, D.C.: War Department, Headquarters, Army Air Forces, Special Order No. 206, Aug. 27, 1943.

IN 1942 POWELL EARNED $8,735.94: Josephine R. Powell to LFP, July 16, 1943.

"THE PRESENT VERY GOOD ARRANGEMENTS CAN'T LAST LONG": LFP to Josephine R. Powell, July 6, 1942.

p. 75 HE EVEN REBUKED JO FOR SPENDING TWENTY-FIVE DOLLARS ON A TRICYCLE: LFP to Josephine R. Powell, Jan. 2, 1943.

"URGING ON YOU WHAT I CONSIDER TO BE SOUND AND JUST": LFP to Thomas B. Gay, Mar. 30, 1945.

POWELL PROFESSED HIMSELF "FRANKLY SOMEWHAT TROUBLED": LFP to T. Justin Moore, June 11, 1945; LFP to Thomas B. Gay, Aug. 21, 1945.

"HOMEY NEWS OF THOSE I LOVE AND MISS SO MUCH": LFP to Josephine R. Powell, Nov. 25, 1942.

"IT IS GRAND TO HAVE THIS TO LOOK FORWARD TO EVERY DAY: LFP to Josephine R. Powell, Apr. 13, 1943.

p. 76 "CAN'T YOU ALL UNDERSTAND PLAIN ENGLISH?": LFP to Josephine R. Powell, May 23, 1943.

"WE WILL SURELY HAVE A LOT OF 'WALKING' TO CATCH-UP ON": LFP to Josephine R. Powell, July 29, 1973.

"I HAVE YOUR LOVELY PICTURE BESIDE MY BED": LFP to Josephine R. Powell, Apr. 13, 1943.

"I DIDN'T REALIZE WHAT A 'FAMILY' PERSON I AM": LFP to Josephine R. Powell, Oct. 18, 1942.

"I AM A CONSERVATIVE SOUL BY NATURE": LFP to Josephine R. Powell, Jan. 11, 1943.

p. 77 "GREAT HEAVEN ABOVE POWELL": LFP to Josephine R. Powell, Aug. 2, 1943.

HE REDUCED IT TO THE LETTER "H": LFP to Josephine R. Powell, Mar. 16, 1943.

"INNUMERABLE SMALL PACKAGES OF THINGS" FROM HOME:: LFP to Josephine R. Powell, Oct. 30, 1942.

"I DON'T ADMIT THAT THEIR WIVES LOVE THEM ANY MORE": LFP to Josephine R. Powell, Nov. 19, 1942.

"PLUS GRAND RABBIT" THAT WAS SUSPECTED OF BEING A CAT: LFP to Josephine R. Powell, May 27, 1943.

"FRIENDSHIP, LIKE FLOWERS, REQUIRES CONSTANT ATTENTION": LFP to Josephine R. Powell, Oct. 23, 1942.

p. 78 MO (FOR MOHAMMED), THE SHOESHINE BOY: LFP to Josephine McR. Powell, June 2, 1943.

"SUNNY, YOU KNOW YOUR DADDY HAS NEVER TOLD YOU ANYTHING BUT THE TRUTH": LFP to Josephine McR. Powell, Jan. 28, 1943.

p. 79 DETAILED INSTRUCTIONS ON TRICYCLE SAFETY: LFP to Josephine McR. Powell, Feb. 8, 1943.

"I THINK EVERY DAY OF THE FUN WE HAVE HAD": LFP to Josephine McR. Powell, June 10, 1943.

TO UPDATE ARMY MANUALS: Putney, *Ultra*, 14.

REPEATEDLY SUMMONED TO WASHINGTON: Headquarters, Army Air Forces, Nov. 2, 1943 (assigning Powell to temporary duty with the Assistant Chief of Staff, Intelligence, for three days); Headquarters, Army Air Forces, Nov. 5, 1943 (extending same for an additional seven days); Putney, *Ultra*, 15 ("I had been going back and forth to the Pentagon regularly as there were people there who were interested in talking to me").

p. 80 TWENTY-DAY TRIP TO AIR FORCE INSTALLATIONS IN FLORIDA AND NEW YORK: Headquarters, Army Air Forces, telegram, Nov. 19, 1943.

FOR MOST OF DECEMBER, HE WAS IN CALIFORNIA: Headquarters, Army Air Forces, cable, undated (ordering Powell to California on or about Dec. 6, 1943, for approximately twenty days). In late November the A-2, Major General Clayton Bissel, wrote an elliptical letter thanking the commanding general of the Fourth Air Force, stationed in California, for his frankness in advising Bissell of "certain conditions" in that command. Letter from Maj. Gen. Clayton Bissell to Brig. Gen. William E. Lynd, Nov. 26, 1943. Bissell sent Powell and Lt. Col. Charles H. Hallett, who was permanently assigned to the intelligence school, to investigate. The visitation was completed by Christmas, and Hallett and Powell submitted a report that included summaries of conversations with intelligence officers in that command. Bissell forwarded this report to the commander, with a promise of greater support from Washington.

THE ADJUTANT GENERAL REJECTED THE RECOMMENDATION IN THE MISTAKEN BELIEF: C. S. Tyler, Adjutant General, to Commanding General, Army Air Forces, Dec. 29, 1943.

POWELL WAS INITIATED INTO THE MOST SECRET OF ALLIED MILITARY INTELLIGENCE: It is not clear exactly when Powell first learned of Ultra. Powell later recalled extensive conversations and briefings with the two senior officers on the American Ultra team, Colonel Carter Clarke and Lieutenant Colonel Alfred McCormack. Putney, *Ultra*, 15. These almost certainly took place in January 1944, but the idea may have been broached earlier. This is one explanation for a letter to Powell from a Special Branch officer in late 1943. Maj. Porter R. Chandler to LFP, Nov. 29, 1943. Elliptical comments in this letter refer to a contemplated assignment that may have been Ultra. The only contrary evidence is a later letter from the same source stating that Powell could not be freed from his present job and therefore would not be available for the assignment that had been discussed. Maj. Porter R. Chandler to LFP, Jan. 12, 1944. It is therefore possible that this correspondence refers to something unrelated to Ultra.

ASSIGNED TO THE MILITARY INTELLIGENCE SERVICE, WAR DEPARTMENT: War Department, Movement Orders, Feb. 1, 1944.

CHAPTER IV: ULTRA SECRET

p. 81 ON JULY 24, 1939: The account of this meeting and of its background is taken primarily from Garlinski, *The Enigma War*, 38–45; Kozaczuk, *Enigma*, 56–60; Lewin, *Ultra Goes to War*, 1–50.

SOON TO BECOME "C" OF THE BRITISH SECRET SERVICE: Most accounts have Menzies present, but Menzies's biographer does not place him there. See Brown, "C," 206–207.

"THE GLOW-LAMP CIPHERING AND DECIPHERING MACHINE 'ENIGMA'" HAD BEEN SOLD COMMERCIALLY: Kahn, *The Codebreakers*, 420–22; Lewin, *Ultra Goes to War*, 25–29.

BRITISH KNEW OF THE ENIGMA: Hinsley, *British Intelligence* II:488, and III (part 2): 947; Fitzgerald, *The Knox Brothers*, 230.

p. 82 NO EVIDENCE OF EFFECTIVE KNOWLEDGE: Calvocoressi, *Top Secret Ultra*, 36.

BERTRAND HAD BOUGHT FROM A GERMAN: Bertrand, *Enigma*, 23–29; Paillole, *Services Speciaux*, 63–64. The source has been identified as Hans-Thilo Schmidt, whose motive was not ideological but personal. He needed money to entertain women. Brown, "C," 205.

ESTIMATES OF THE VALUE OF THESE DOCUMENTS VARY: Hinsley, *British Intelligence* III (part 2): 947–48; Calvocoressi, *Top Secret Ultra*, 32–34.

HANDED OVER TO "PROFESSOR SANDWICH" THE ENIGMA MACHINE: Bertrand, *Enigma*, 60–61; Garlinski, *The Enigma War*, 45; Kozaczuk, *Enigma*, 59–60; Lewin, *Ultra Goes to War*, 44–45. The most circumstantial account of the transmission appears in Brown, "C," 207–208.

As it happened, the British captured an intact Enigma from a German submarine in February 1940. Hinsley, *British Intelligence* I:336. This event is described in Garlinski, *The Enigma War*, 1–2, but incorrectly dated as "autumn 1939." For the most informed attempt to make a precise estimate of the advance allowed by the Polish transfer, see Hinsley, *British Intelligence* III (part 2): 955-59.

Two other accounts of the transfer of Enigma from Poland to Britain have been given. Group Captain Winterbotham, who devised the arrangements for distributing Ultra intelligence but was not involved in acquiring the Enigma, reported in an early best-seller that the British had learned of the Enigma by smuggling out a Polish worker in a German Enigma factory. Winterbotham, *The Ultra Secret*, 26–27. In what is likely a variation of the same story, Anthony Cave Brown recounts a decision by Menzies to purchase the Enigma from a Pole in 1938 for £10,000 and a subsequent trip to Warsaw by Dilwyn Knox and Alan Turing to pick up the machine. Brown, *Bodyguard of Lies*, 17–20. Subsequently released information reveals that neither of these accounts is correct.

THE ENIGMA WAS AN ELECTROMECHANICAL DEVICE: The construction and operation of the Enigma are described in varying levels of detail in Bennett, *Ultra in the West*, 3–5; Calvocoressi, *Top Secret Ultra*, 24–31; Garlinski, *The Enigma War*, 192–95; Hodges, *Alan Turing*, 165–70; Lewin, *Ultra Goes to War*, 30–32; Welchman, *The Hut Six Story*, 38–52.

p. 83 FULL DESCRIPTION OF THE CRYPTANALYSIS: Good accounts of the decryption of Enigma ciphers appear in Calvocoressi, *Top Secret Ultra*, 49–53; Garlinski, *The Enigma War*, 198–204; Hodges, *Alan Turing*, 170–85.

SEVERAL SERIES OF ENIGMA SETTINGS: Hinsley, *British Intelligence* I:108–109, 120, 326, 336–38, and II:20.

p. 84 BLETCHLEY PARK, "A GHASTLY LATE VICTORIAN MANSION": Friendly, "Confessions of a Code Breaker," *Washington Post*, Oct. 27, 1974, p. C1.

STRATAGEMS DESIGNED TO MAKE COMMUNICATIONS UNPREDICTABLE: Hodges, *Alan Turing*, 184. Hodges mentions "such obvious devices as prefacing the message with a variable amount of random nonsense, inserting X's in long words, [and] using a 'burying procedure' for stereotyped or repetitious parts of the transmission. . . ."

A CARELESS OPERATOR WAS THE CRYPTANALYST'S BEST FRIEND: Bennett, *Ultra in the West*, 6 n. 1; Calvocoressi, *Top Secret Ultra*, 49–53; Hinsley, *British Intelligence* III (part 2): 953–54; Lewin, *Ultra Goes to War*, 118; Welchman, *The Hut Six Story*, 163–69.

"WOULD HAVE BEEN IMPREGNABLE IF IT HAD BEEN USED PROPERLY": *Id.*, 168.

"HELPFULLY INSECURE AND SLAPDASH": Lewin, *Ultra Goes to War*, 58.

SETTINGS FOR THE MAIN LUFTWAFFE NETWORK WOULD BE AVAILABLE BEFORE BREAKFAST: *Id.*, 118.

p. 85 THE GERMAN NAVY WAS THE MOST SECURE: Hinsley, *British Intelligence* III (part 2): 958–59.

TRANSFER TO ANOTHER POST BECAME VIRTUALLY IMPOSSIBLE: Lewin, *Ultra Goes to War*, 129.

"THE GEESE WHO LAID THE GOLDEN EGGS BUT NEVER CACKLED": *Id.*, 183.

LOCKED BOX DESPATCHED DAILY BY "C" TO HIS CHIEF: Hinsley, *British Intelligence* I:295–96; Lewin, *Ultra Goes to War*, 185–89; Gilbert, *Churchill: Finest Hour*, 609. The most complete description of the mechanics of keeping Churchill informed appears in Brown, "C," 293.

A SPECIAL SYSTEM WAS DEVISED: Calvocoressi, *Top Secret Ultra*, 60–61; Hinsley, *British Intelligence* I:572; Lewin, *Ultra Goes to War*, 138–54.

THE ULTRA SECRET FIRST GAVE WIDE CURRENCY TO KNOWLEDGE OF ULTRA: Apparently, the earliest public mention that German Enigma ciphers had been broken was in Wladyslaw Kozaczuk, *Bitwa o tajemnice: Sluzby wywiadowcze Polski i Rzeszy Niemieckiej 1922–39* (The Battle of Secrets: The Intelligence Services of Poland and the German Reich, 1922–39) (Warsaw, 1967), which did not receive widespread attention in the West. Winterbotham's book gave these matters currency in English-speaking countries.

Winterbotham's account was far more comprehensive than the earlier publications, but it was based largely on memory and was in some respects inaccurate. In particular, Winterbotham gave an unwarranted primacy to the British role in the early penetration of Enigma ciphers. This prompted many corrections. For a survey of the Ultra literature, see David Syrett, "The Secret War and the Historians," *Armed Forces and Society* 9:293–328.

p. 86 REPORTEDLY, THEIR COMMUNICATIONS WERE MONITORED BY BRITISH CRYPTOGRA-PHERS: Calvocoressi, *Top Secret Ultra*, 60.

AN EXPLANATION THAT THE GERMANS FOUND INFINITELY PLAUSIBLE: Putney, *Ultra*, 52.

LOW-LEVEL INTELLIGENCE SERVED AS A COVER FOR ULTRA: *Id.*, 11, 92.

"60 MINUTES": "60 Minutes," vol. XIV, no. 44.

REPORTED BY ANTHONY CAVE BROWN: Brown, *Bodyguard of Lies*, 38–44.

LAID DOWN TO SPECIAL LIAISON UNIT OFFICERS BY WINTERBOTHAM: Lewin, *Ultra Goes to War*, 139–42.

ON HIS ORDER, TO CHURCHILL PERSONALLY: *Id.*, 126. For an instance of Churchill's concern with lax Ultra security by Montgomery, see Hinsley, *British Intelligence* II:409–10, 413–14. An account of the quiet but effective punishment of a loose-lipped senior officer appears in Brown, "C," 463–64.

POWELL NEVER HEARD OF ULTRA: Putney, *Ultra*, 10.

p. 87 THE BRITISH AND AMERICANS HAD EXCHANGED SIGNAL INTELLIGENCE: Hinsley, *British Intelligence* II:55.

THEY DISTRUSTED AMERICAN SECURITY: *Id.*, 56–58.

AN EXCEPTION WAS GENERAL MARK CLARK: Winterbotham, *Ultra Secret*, 134–35, 172; Brown, "C," 429–30.

EAKER RESISTED PERSONAL KNOWLEDGE: Lewin, *Ultra Goes to War*, 239–41.

ON MAY 17, 1943, AGREEMENT WAS REACHED: The agreement is summarized in Hinsley, *British Intelligence* II:57-58, and in Parrish, *Ultra Americans*, 98. The full text is available in SRH-110, "Military Intelligence," 39ff., SRG 457, National Archives.

p. 88 GAVE LAVISH WARNING OF THE IMPENDING ATTACK: See generally U.S. Department of Defense, *The "Magic" Background of Pearl Harbor.*

"A VERY LARGE JOB TO BE DONE ALL ALONG THE LINE": SRH-035, "History of the Special Branch," 7, RG 457, National Archives.

"REPUTATION AS A GRAVEYARD FOR REGULAR ARMY CAREERS": SRH-185, "War Experience," 31–32, RG 457, National Archives. This document is unsigned but was found in McCormack's files and likely was written by him.

"IMAGINATIVE PERSONS OF ABSOLUTELY FIRST-CLASS ABILITY": SRH-035, "History of Special Branch," 7–8, RG 457, National Archives.

SEDUCED HIM INTO UNIFORM: Parrish, *Ultra Americans*, 83.

"GO DOWN THERE AND GET ALONG WITH THAT GODDAMNED MAN": *Id.*, 94.

CLARKE COVERED THE MILITARY SIDE OF MILITARY INTELLIGENCE: *Id.*, 94, 203–204.

THE CONCEPT WAS ENTIRELY AMERICAN: Lewin, *Ultra Goes to War*, 246–52.

p. 89 "A CLEAR-HEADED DIPLOMAT": *Id.*, 248.

TWENTY-EIGHT MEN McCORMACK SELECTED: SRH-006, "Synthesis of Experiences in the Use of ULTRA Intelligence by U.S. Army Field Commands, in the European Theater of Operations," 10, RG 457, National Archives.

JOSEPHINE POWELL SAW HER HUSBAND BOARD A DC-4: Memorandum to Brigadier General George C. McDonald, "Summary of Military Intelligence of Lt. Col. Lewis F. Powell, Jr.," Dec. 28, 1944.

HE CARRIED A LOCKED CANVAS POUCH: LFP, interview.

THE POLISH AMBASSADOR TO THE UNITED STATES: LFP, memorandum to author, Mar. 14, 1989.

p. 90 THEY REACHED AN INACTIVE RAF FIELD: LFP to Diane T. Putney, Dec. 14, 1985.

McCORMACK'S LONDON DEPUTY, COLONEL TELFORD TAYLOR: Putney, *Ultra*, 21–22, 84.

GENERAL "PETE" QUESADA, COMMANDER OF THE IX TACTICAL AIR COMMAND: *Id.*, 20.

MORE MILITARY THAN THE WEST POINTER: *Id.*, 22. See Rosengarten, "With Ultra from Omaha Beach to Weimar, Germany—A Personal View," *Military Affairs* 42:127-32.

TRANSLATE ENIGMA DECRYPTS: Alfred Friendly, "Confessions of a Code Breaker," *Washington Post*, Oct. 27, 1974, pp. C1, C3.

"NO FEELING WHATEVER OF ANY RESTRAINT": Putney, *Ultra*, 26.

"THEY TOLD US THINGS I DON'T THINK THE AMERICANS WOULD HAVE TOLD US": *Id.*, 51.

"COULD NOT HAVE BEEN BETTER": *Id.*, 25.

p. 91 THE CARDS RECORDED ALL SORTS OF INFORMATION: Calvocoressi, *Top Secret Ultra*, 62–63; Lewin, *Ultra Goes to War*, 120–21.

AN ENCYCLOPEDIA OF ALLIED INTELLIGENCE: Calvocoressi, *Top Secret Ultra*, 62.

THAN ANYONE ELSE IN THE WEST: *Id.*, 63.

MAY HAVE KNOWN MORE THAN MANY HIGH-RANKING GERMANS: Putney, *Ultra*, 20.

"AN AUTHENTIC EXPERT ON THE GERMAN AIR FORCE": *Id.*

A SMALL BUFF NOTEBOOK: Reprinted *id.*, 117–67.

POWELL WAS SENT TO THE MEDITERRANEAN: The details of Powell's travels are taken from his "trip diary"—notes entered each day in a pocket-sized notebook which he carried with him from Bletchley Park.

A REPORT ON HIS INVESTIGATION: SRH-031, "Trip Reports Concerning Use of Ultra in the Mediterranean Theater," RG 457, National Archives.

p. 92 "NOT TO MINIMIZE THE MAGNIFICENT EFFORTS OF THE BRITISH": Putney, *Ultra*, 170–71.

"WHILE THE IMPORTANCE OF THOSE OTHER SOURCES WILL GENERALLY BE CONCEDED": *Id.*

"CLOSE ENOUGH TO EISENHOWER'S HEADQUARTERS TO COORDINATE PLANS PERSONALLY": LFP, interview with David R. Mets, Oct. 21, 1982.

WHOM SUBORDINATES CALLED "UNCLE GEORGE": LFP to Col. Julian B. Allen, July 11, 1945.

"NEVER WROTE ANYTHING HIMSELF": LFP, interview.

"EXTREMELY ATTRACTIVE, EXTREMELY GENEROUS, AND VERY ENGAGING": *Id.*

p. 93 "KNEW WESTERN EUROPE AS WELL AS I KNOW THE STATE OF VIRGINIA": Putney, *Ultra*, 29.

"IF HE SPOKE, I LISTENED": *Id.*, 22.

DIRECTIVE TO GENERAL EISENHOWER: SRH-026, RG 457, National Archives.

p. 94 MEMORANDUM REVEALING HIS USUAL EFFECTIVE COMBINATION OF DEFERENCE AND AMBITION: LFP, "Operational Intelligence Section of USSTAF," June 1, 1944, reprinted in Putney, *Ultra*, 173–77.

KNOWN FOR HIS LOOSE ADMINISTRATIVE STYLE: Statement of Spaatz's biographer, David R. Mets, in an interview with Powell, Oct. 21, 1982. Powell rephrased "loose" as "somewhat unorthodox."

USED ALLEN AS HIS PERSONAL BRIEFING OFFICER: Putney, *Ultra*, 31.

SPAATZ SENT A PERSONAL LETTER: Lt. Gen. Spaatz to Maj. Gen. Clayton Bissell, Assistant Chief of Staff, Intelligence, Aug. 16, 1944.

LETTERS TO TELFORD TAYLOR AND ALFRED McCORMACK: Brig. Gen. George C. McDonald to Lt. Col. Telford Taylor, Aug. 17, 1944; Col. Lowell P. Weicker to Col. Alfred McCormack, Aug. 16, 1944.

p. 95 EMPLOYING IN ALL ABOUT FORTY OFFICERS: LFP to Thomas B. Gay, Mar. 30, 1945.

SPAATZ, McDONALD, AND WEICKER AGAIN WROTE: Maj. Gen. Carl Spaatz to Maj. Gen. Clayton Bissell, Jan. 14, 1945 (No copy of this letter appears in Powell's files, but it is specifically referred to in later correspondence.); Brig. Gen. George C. McDonald to Col. Telford Taylor, Feb. 7, 1945 (containing the quotation in text); Col. Lowell P. Weicker to Col. Telford Taylor, Feb. 9, 1945.

DESPITE CONTAINING PRESSURE FROM USSTAF: Maj. Gen. Carl Spaatz to Maj. Gen. Clayton Bissell, Mar. 28, 1945.

McDONALD ORIGINALLY RECOMMENDED POWELL TO THE THEATER COMMANDER FOR THE LEGION OF MERIT: Brig. Gen. George C. McDonald to Maj. Gen. Clayton Bissell, May 10, 1945.

POWELL AND ANDERSON BUILT A CLOSE WORKING RELATIONSHIP: Putney, *Ultra*, 31; LFP, interview with David R. Mets, Oct. 21, 1982.

ADDITIONAL INFORMATION CAME FROM: LFP, "Notes on Operational Intelligence Division of Directorate of Intelligence," June 9, 1945, reprinted in Putney, *Ultra*, 183.

p. 96 THE ETIQUETTE, STYLE, AND CONTENT OF WAR ROOM PRESENTATION: LFP, Memorandum to Maj. J. H. Simone, Jan. 28, 1945.

FOCUSING ESPECIALLY ON "THE TIME FACTOR BETWEEN AN AIR ATTACK AND ITS ACTUAL EFFECT": USSTAF Operational Intelligence Weekly Activity Report, Mar. 16, 1945.

EISENHOWER'S BRIEFING: Putney, *Ultra*, 32; Brig. Gen. George C. McDonald, memorandum to Assistant Chief of Staff, G-2, SHAEF, Jan. 24, 1945.

SHAEF JOINT INTELLIGENCE COMMITTEE: LFP, memorandum to Brig. Gen. George C. McDonald, June 9, 1945, quoted in Putney, *Ultra*, 188–89.

WHERE THE ALLIED AIR COMMANDERS MET TO DISCUSS THE PAST WEEK'S OPERATIONS: *Id.*

p. 97 FIRST PRIORITY WAS THE DESTRUCTION OF THE GERMAN AIR FORCE: *Haines Report*, 75; Mets, *Master of Airpower*, 181, 190–91.

THE FAMOUS "BIG WEEK" OF MASSIVE BOMBING RAIDS: *Id.*, 195–96.

SPAATZ URGED THE OIL CAMPAIGN: *Id.*, 202–13; Ambrose, *Eisenhower* I:286–90.

LETTER TO SUBORDINATE COMMANDERS DATED SEPTEMBER 1, 1944: Quoted in *Haines Report*, 133–34. Strategic bombing priorities were restated later that month and again in November 1944, but oil remained the top priority. *Id.*, 140, 154.

"AN ALMOST CONTINUOUS CHRONICLE OF OIL SHORTAGE EVERYWHERE": *Id.*, 134.

p. 98 OPERATIONS OF ALL SORTS WERE CURTAILED FOR LACK OF FUEL: *Id.*, 134–37, 143, 149, 154, 159, 161, 176.

"WE KNEW WHEN TO ATTACK AGAIN": Putney, *Ultra*, 40–41.

PRODUCTION AT LEUNA AVERAGED ONLY 9 PERCENT OF CAPACITY: U.S. Strategic Bombing Survey, *Summary Report*, 9.

HE COULD NOT MANUFACTURE EXPERIENCED CREWS: *Haines Report*, 156.

POWELL CHRONICLED THE TERRIBLE ATTRITION OF GERMAN PILOTS: *Id.*, 92, 94, 156.

"PILOTS AND GASOLINE SHORTAGES HAVE BECOME THE LIMITING FACTOR IN G.A.F. OPERATIONS, NOT AIRCRAFT": Lt. Gen. Carl Spaatz to commanders of the Eighth and Fifteenth Air Forces, quoted in *Haines Report*, 133.

SUGGESTS A PRENUCLEAR USE FOR THE WORD "OVERKILL": Mets, *Master of Airpower*, 275. Precise figures of bombs dropped are given in Gilbert, *Churchill: Road to Victory*, 1219.

AS HIGH AS 135,000: Irving, *Dresden*, 7.

UNSUBSTANTIATED AND EXTREME: The origin of the 135,000 estimate is David Irving, whose book *The Destruction of Dresden* first appeared in Britain in 1963. On July 7, 1966, the London *Times* published a letter from Irving acknowledging an error in his calculations and citing new evidence in support of a much lower figure.

MORE CAREFUL ESTIMATES OF 35,000 DEAD: For a careful evaluation of death toll estimates and other aspects of Dresden, see Melden E. Smith, Jr., "Dresden Revisited: New Perspectives on a Lingering Controversy," a paper presented for the 1978 Missouri Valley History Conference and available in the Powell Papers, Air Force Historical Research Center, Maxwell Air Force Base, Alabama.

AMONG HISTORIANS, THE DECISION TO BOMB DRESDEN REMAINS IN BITTER DISPUTE: Keegan, *The Face of Battle*, 27 ("The strategic bombing campaign against Germany, its costs and benefits, its rights and wrongs, engages the energies of some of the most powerful minds at work in the field of military history today and has fomented one of the subject's few real intellectual antagonisms. . . .").

p. 99 "A SYMBOL FOR ALLIED BRUTALITY": Pogue, *Marshall: Organizer of Victory*, 546.

DRESDEN HAD BEEN THOUGHT "OFF LIMITS": Putney, *Ultra*, 56; LFP, interview with David R. Mets, Oct. 21, 1982.

ROSE LEARNED OF THE INTENTION TO BOMB DRESDEN: Draft statement of E. J. B. Rose, included in letter to LFP, Mar. 12, 1985.

"BOMBER" HARRIS, WHO WAS NOT: Writing in 1984 Rose recalled that Spaatz had agreed to bomb Dresden in order to reach two Panzer divisions being sent to the Russian front. Ultra, however, had told Rose that the Panzer divisions would not go through Dresden. Once given this information, Spaatz agreed to call off the mission if the British went along. Parrish, *Ultra Americans*, 274.

"SIR ARTHUR WAS ADAMANT": *New York Times*, Jan. 18, 1992, p. 22.

ASKED POWELL FOR INFORMATION: E. J. B. Rose to LFP, Mar. 12, 1985.

POWELL PUT THAT QUESTION TO GENERAL GEORGE S. BROWN: LFP to Gen. George S. Brown, June 27, 1978.

SHOWED THE LETTER TO GENERAL IRA EAKER: Gen. George S. Brown to LFP, July 12, 1978.

EAKER'S RESPONSE TO POWELL INCLUDED A SCHOLARLY ARTICLE: Gen. Ira C. Eaker to LFP, July 11, 1978 and enclosures. The article was Melden E. Smith, Jr., "Dresden Revisited: New Perspectives on a Lingering Controversy," a paper presented to the 1978 Missouri Valley History Conference and available in the Powell Papers, Air Force Historical Research Center, Maxwell Air Force Base, Alabama.

p. 100 COLLECTIVE MEMORY OF SEVERAL WITNESSES: LFP to James Rose, Mar. 22, 1985.

LOVETT AND McCLOY CONFIRMED THE "COMMON UNDERSTANDING IN THE WAR DEPARTMENT": John J. McCloy to LFP, Apr. 27, 1983. Generally consistent recollections appear in a letter from Robert A. Lovett to Lt. Gen. Ira C. Eaker, Aug. 8, 1978, a copy of which was sent to Powell.

THIS WAS POWELL'S FIRST SURMISE: LFP to Gen. George S. Brown, June 27, 1978 ("On other occasions, I know that the Soviets requested—usually through Washington, as I understood it—that we attack certain targets."); LFP to Gen. Ira Eaker, July 25, 1978 ("I understood Fred [Anderson] as saying this was a specific request, communicated through Washington—as we had received such requests in the past.").

THE SOVIETS WERE INFORMED OF THE PLAN: Pogue, *Marshall: Organizer of Victory*, 544.

NO RECORD OF A REQUEST MADE BY THEM TO WASHINGTON: Putney, *Ultra*, 57 n. 80.

AS DESCRIBED BY MARTIN GILBERT: Gilbert, *Churchill: Road to Victory*, 1177–78. Other sources cite an Antonov request for bombing of Berlin and Leipzig, with no specific mention of Dresden. See, e.g., Webster and Frankland, *Strategic Air Offensive* III:105.

BOMBING OF DRESDEN WAS "A DIRECT RESULT OF THE AGREEMENT REACHED AT YALTA": Gilbert, *Churchill: Road to Victory*, 1219.

p. 101 THE WAR COULD BE SHORTENED DECISIVELY IF ANGLO-AMERICAN BOMBERS COULD GIVE "ASSISTANCE TO THE RUSSIANS": Quoted *id.*, 1160; Webster and Frankland, *Strategic Air Offensive* III:55 et seq.

"A COMMANDER OF COARSE SINGLEMINDEDNESS": Keegan, *The Second World War*, 421.

"FOCAL POINTS OF THE GERMAN SYSTEM OF COMMUNICATIONS": Gilbert, *Churchill: Road to Victory*, 1161.

URGED ON BY A BLUSTERY CHURCHILL: *Id.*, 1161, 1165; Webster and Frankland, *Strategic Air Offensive* III:103.

"SIMPLY FOR THE SAKE OF INCREASING THE TERROR": The quotation comes from Churchill's personal minute of Mar. 28, 1945, quoted in Gilbert, *Churchill: Road to Victory*, 1257.

FORWARDED THESE PLANS TO YALTA: These suggestions were telegraphed to Yalta from the Vice Chiefs of Staff meeting in London on the night of Feb. 2, 1945. *Id.*, 1176–77.

SHUTTLE BOMBING: Craven and Cate, *Army Air Forces* III:308–19.

"PRINCIPAL LOGISTIC AND COMMUNICATIONS CENTER": Gen. Ira C. Eaker to LFP, July 11, 1978.

p. 102 URGING OTHERS TO WRITE FOR PUBLICATION: LFP to Gen. Ira C. Eaker, July 25, 1978; LFP to James Rose, Oct. 17, 1985.

"THE GERMAN PEOPLE ARE BEING TAUGHT FOR THE FIRST TIME": LFP to Lt. Col. Osmond T. Jamerson, Feb. 25, 1945.

p. 103 "IT WAS NOT THE POLICY OF THE ARMY AIR FORCES": Putney, *Ultra*, 56.

AN ACCEPTABLE MILITARY TARGET: LFP to Dr. Diane T. Putney, Nov. 19, 1987.

"WOULD NEVER HAVE ATTACKED DRESDEN ON THEIR OWN INITIATIVE": Putney, *Ultra*, 57.

"OUR PRIMARY TARGETS ALMOST INVARIABLY WERE MILITARY ONES": LFP to James Rose, Mar. 22, 1985.

"THERE IS PROBABLY ENOUGH BLAME FOR ALL": LFP to James Rose, Oct. 4, 1985.

"I CAN'T BELIEVE TOOEY RELISHED THIS": LFP to William W. Haines, Jan. 6, 1986.

p. 104 NO MORE DETAILED ASSESSMENT IS AVAILABLE: Putney, *Ultra*, 55 n. 78.

LUSH STEAKS, RARE WINE, CRISP PASTRY, AND DILIGENT WAITERS: LFP to Commander Osgood Roberts, Apr. 26, 1945.

"CONSPICUOUS LACK OF SKILL" AT ROULETTE: *Id.*

THOROUGHLY ENJOYED THOUGH IT NETTED NOTHING: LFP to Josephine R. Powell, May 19, 1945.

p. 105 FOUND ADOLF HITLER'S LONG-STEMMED CHAMPAGNE GLASSES: Putney, *Ultra*, 62–63; statement of Lowell P. Weicker, Feb. 6, 1962, attesting to the origin of these glasses for purposes of valuation.

GENERAL SPAATZ HAD A BUFFET LUNCHEON: Putney, *Ultra*, 46. Powell erroneously placed this event on May 8, when Spaatz was in Berlin for the second surrender ceremony which was officially celebrated as Victory-in-Europe day.

A "CONSENSUS THAT WE HAD THE CAPABILITY TO TAKE BERLIN": *Id.*, 46.

WORD FROM ROBERT A. LOVETT: LFP to Thomas B. Gay, Aug. 21, 1945.

p. 106 "PURSUING SOME PETTY WAR CRIMINAL": LFP to Col. John F. Turner, July 27, 1945.

THE COFFIN REPORT: Putney, *Ultra*, 62; MacIsaac, *Strategic Bombing*, 97–98, 201 n. 52.

WHEN THE HAINES REPORT WAS DECLASSIFIED: Roy R. Banner to LFP, June 4, 1979.

"STRONG LIAISON" . . . AND "WHOLESOME RELATIONS": LFP to Brig. Gen. George C. McDonald, Aug. 27, 1945.

WRITE HOME FOR FINANCIAL REINFORCEMENTS: LFP to Josephine R. Powell, Feb. 22, 1945, requesting transfer of $300 to Powell's London bank.

p. 107 POWELL'S NEED FOR A SUITABLE PLACE FOR ENTERTAINING: LFP to Adjutant General, Headquarters USSTAF (Rear), June 16, 1945.

THEY WERE SOMETIMES PUT TO THAT USE: LFP to Col. Lowell P. Weicker, Aug. 7, 1945 (mentioning dinner in the flat with Air Chief Marshal and Lady Courtney).

"EXAMPLE OF PRUDENCE AND SOBRIETY": LFP to William W. Haines, Sept. 5, 1945.

"ALMOST AS EXCITING AS WHEN COLONEL WEICKER WAS HERE": *Id.*

NOTHING COMPARED TO THE LUXURIES OF FRANCE: Rene deChochor, interview.

CONFESSED IT HAD BEEN "A ROUGH EVENING": LFP to Lowell P. Weicker, May 12, 1964.

"TRYING TO SUSTAIN MY END OF A CONVERSATION WITH GERTRUDE STEIN": *Id.*

p. 108 "LET DOWN FEELING": LFP to Col. John F. Turner, July 27, 1945.

"RENDERS RATHER OBSOLETE ANYTHING THAT CAN BE SAID": LFP to William W. Haines, Sept. 5, 1945.

BEST CHANCE TO ESCAPE THE ARMY: *Id.*

"DIANA HAS BLOND BOBBED HAIR": LFP to Ann Pendleton Powell, Jan. 17, 1945.

"I CERTAINLY NEEDED SOMETHING FOR MY OWN MORALE": LFP to Ann Pendleton Powell, Feb. 24, 1945.

"I THINK OF YOU EVERY TIME I SEE A LITTLE FRENCH GIRL": LFP to Josephine McR. Powell, Apr. 9, 1945.

PUT HIS CASE TO GENERAL McDONALD: LFP to Brig. Gen. George C. McDonald, Aug. 27, 1945.

p. 109 POWELL WENT TO SEE FIRSTHAND THE EFFECTS OF ALLIED BOMBING: LFP, Memorandum to Brig. Gen. George C. McDonald, Oct. 8, 1945.

"[Y]OU COULD NOT SEE A SINGLE BUILDING STANDING IN COLOGNE": Putney, *Ultra*, 42.

UNITED STATES STRATEGIC BOMBING SURVEY: See MacIsaac, *Strategic Bombing*; Craven and Cate, *Army Air Forces* III:789–92.

ONLY EIGHTY OPERATIONAL AIRCRAFT: U.S. Strategic Bombing Survey, *Summary Report*, 7.

p. 110 "OUR VICTORY IN THE AIR MADE THE LAND INVASION POSSIBLE": Putney, *Ultra*, 36.

THE GERMANS VIEWED THE ATTACKS ON OIL AS "CATASTROPHIC": U.S. Strategic Bombing Survey, *Summary Report*, 8.

"ALLIED AIR POWER WAS DECISIVE": *Id.*, 15.

SUBJECT TO VARYING INTERPRETATION: See Craven and Cate, *Army Air Forces* III:791:

[T]he survey's final report affirmed with much more authority than could be claimed by any other agency that the victory in the air was complete and that Allied air power had been decisive in the war in western Europe.

But another sympathetic observer read the report as "at best, a muted endorsement" of strategic bombing. MacIsaac, *Strategic Bombing*, 142.
FOUR-PAGE LETTER: LFP to Edwin M. Yoder, Jr., Feb. 24, 1977.

p. 111 "THE BOMBING WAS A BADLY FLAWED PERFORMANCE": John Kenneth Galbraith, "Albert Speer was the Man to See," *New York Times Book Review*, Jan. 10, 1971, sec. 7, p. 2.
"DID HAVE MILITARY EFFECT": Galbraith, *A Life in Our Times*, 226.
"THE EFFECT OF THE AIR ATTACKS WAS TO INCREASE GERMAN AIRPLANE OUTPUT": *Id.*, 215.
"SPARED THE REPROACH OF CIVILIZED OPINION": *Id.*, 226–27. See also the exchange of letters between Galbraith and W. W. Rostow in *The New York Times Book Review*, Apr. 4, 1971, pp. 20, 22, 24.
POWELL THOUGHT GALBRAITH "DEAD WRONG": Putney, *Ultra*, 59.

p. 112 TRIED TO ANSWER GALBRAITH'S ALLEGATIONS IN A LETTER: LFP to Editor, *New York Times*, Feb. 25, 1971.
"HAD TO BE DIPLOMATIC ENOUGH . . . TO MAKE SURE THE GENERALS HEARD": Ambrose, *Ike's Spies*, 56.

p. 114 "THE MAGNIFICENT EFFORTS OF THE BRITISH": LFP, "Report on Visit to Operational Air Commands in Mediterranean Theater," May 14, 1944, quoted in Putney, *Ultra*, 171.
ABANDONED BY THE SUDDENLY INERT SOVIET FORCES: Craven and Cate, *Army Air Forces* III:316–17.
"WE WERE PREPARED TO FLY": Putney, *Ultra*, 45; LFP, interview with David R. Mets, Oct. 21 1982.
"A FEELING FOR THE COUNTRY": John Paul Stevens, interview.

CHAPTER V: RISING STAR

p. 115 STEWART McCLINTIC, WHO KNEW THE OWNERS OF SEA ISLAND: Josephine R. Powell, interview.

p. 116 SOLD A YEAR LATER FOR $14,000: Josephine R. Powell, interview.
SCLERODERMA: Without mentioning himself, Dr. Rucker described the disease in "Acrosclerosis," *Virginia Medical Monthly* 76:493.

p. 117 "ALWAYS READY TO CONTRIBUTE HIS TIME": *Virginia Medical Monthly* 81:44–45.
PUBLISHED MORE THAN A HUNDRED OF THESE ESSAYS: Rucker, *Selected Writings*, vii–xiv.
"WHEN GRANDFATHER RUCKER WAS ALIVE, HE WAS KING": Pendleton Powell Carmody, interview.

p. 118 "DADDY INVITED US OUT": Josephine R. Powell, interview.
ARRIVED JUST IN TIME FOR THE SERMON: Pendleton Powell Carmody, interview; Molly Powell Sumner, interview.
EVERY EVENING, THE RUCKER-POWELL FAMILY SAT DOWN TO DINNER: Josephine Powell Smith, interview; Pendleton Powell Carmody, interview; Molly Powell Sumner, interview.

"HE SAID HE ALWAYS GOT BUTTERFLIES IN HIS TUMMY": Josephine Powell Smith, interview.

p. 119 WATCHING THE MATCH FROM BEHIND A PARKED CAR: *Id.*

WHEN JO WAS THIRTEEN, SHE SPENT SIX WEEKS WITH ELEANOR: Eleanor Powell Dewey, interview.

"JO TRIED HARD TO PLEASE HER FATHER": *Id.*

"JO ALWAYS CAME FIRST": Josephine R. Powell, interview.

"LOOKING BACK ON IT": Pendleton Powell Carmody, interview.

p. 120 SHE BEGAN TO FEEL THAT SHE HAD BEEN NEGLECTED: Josephine Powell Smith, interview.

"I HAVE BEEN LOOKING AT NAKED BABIES FOR TWENTY YEARS": LFP to Lewis F. Powell III, Sept. 11, 1987.

EMBARRASSED AT THE MOTHER'S AGE: Josephine R. Powell, interview.

p. 121 "WE HAD AN UNDIMINISHED NUMBER OF THINGS TO DO": Freeman, *The Style of a Law Firm*, 116 (quoting George D. Gibson).

"THIS," HE SAID, "IS MY WAR CONTRIBUTION": Archibald G. Robertson, interview with Anne Hobson Freeman.

MERRILL PASCO (WHO HAD SERVED ON GENERAL MARSHALL'S PERSONAL STAFF): Freeman, *The Style of a Law Firm*, 121.

"HURLING THUNDERBOLTS ON THREE CONTINENTS": *Id.*, 158 (quoting George D. Gibson).

"BACK WHERE HE HAD BEEN FOUR YEARS EARLIER": *Id.*

p. 122 OFFERED THE POST OF GENERAL COUNSEL TO THE MARSHALL PLAN: LFP, "Unrecorded Biographical Facts," Dec. 15, 1981, pp. 7–8.

"IF I REALLY DIDN'T LIKE": Bill Moyers, "In Search of the Constitution," PBS, June 25, 1987.

"NOT AN UNSELFISH PERSON": LFP, interview with Anne Hobson Freeman.

p. 123 MEMORANDUM ON HOW TO BUILD A LAW PRACTICE: LFP, memorandum to Joseph C. Carter, Aug. 1977. The quotations in this and several succeeding paragraphs come from this memorandum.

"I WANTED TO ESTABLISH A NATIONAL REPUTATION": Freeman, *The Style of a Law Firm*, 154 (quoting LFP).

p. 124 THE MOVEMENT TO REFORM RICHMOND'S CUMBERSOME FORM OF GOVERNMENT: LFP, interview; LFP, memorandum to Joseph C. Carter, Aug. 1977; Dabney, *Richmond*, 334–35; Zimmer, Davis, and Edwards, *Study of the Effectiveness of a Citizen's Association*, 11–20.

OLIVER HILL: *Id.*, 19; *New Republic*, Apr. 9, 1951, p. 7.

p. 125 THE TURNING POINT IN POWELL'S DRIVE FOR CLIENTS: *Richmond Times-Dispatch*, Sept. 9, 1950, p. 20.

"AS FAVORABLE EVENT IN MY LIFE": LFP, interview.

POWELL INHERITED CABELL'S CLIENTS: LFP, memorandum to Joseph C. Carter, Aug. 1977; LFP, interview.

"AN IDEAL CLIENT": LFP, memorandum to Joseph C. Carter, Aug. 1977.

p. 126 "ONE OF THE, IF NOT *THE* MOST ABLE LAWYER IN VIRGINIA": Lawrence E. Blanchard, Jr., interview with Anne Hobson Freeman.

"A REMOTE PERSON WITH ONLY ONE IDEA": All quotations in this paragraph come from interviews with Anne Hobson Freeman.

p. 127 THE PRECIPITATING EVENT WAS ADVICE GIVEN BY MARKS: Lawrence E. Blanchard, Jr., interview.

GOT HIS "HEAD CUT OFF" BY POWELL: John W. Riely, interview with Anne Hobson Freeman.

"I AM GOING TO LEAVE UNLESS THE FIRM BACKS ME UP ON THIS": George D. Gibson, interview with Anne Hobson Freeman.

p. 128 THOUGHT HIM COLD AND CALCULATING: Joseph C. Carter, interview with Anne Hobson Freeman. (Carter agreed that Powell was calculating but not cold.)

"A VERY STEELY OUTLOOK": John W. Riely, interview with Anne Hobson Freeman.

"ABSOLUTELY ESSENTIAL VICTORY": LFP, interview.

p. 129 "MR. MOORE, I DON'T LIKE YOUR SENATOR BYRD'S PHILOSOPHY": Quoted by Carlisle H. Humelsine in a special session of the Virginia General Assembly held in the House of Burgesses on February 6, 1988.

"IF MR. ROCKEFELLER LIKED THAT YOUNG FELLOW": *Id.*

p. 130 POWELL ASKED WHETHER GIBSON SHOULD ALSO BE ADDED: LFP, interview.

THE EMBARRASSMENT HE FELT AT HAVING ALLOWED HIS NAME TO GO IN: LFP to George D. Gibson, July 24, 1985.

"SHE COULDN'T HAVE BEEN NICER ABOUT IT": LFP, interview with Anne Hobson Freeman.

CHAPTER VI: HARD-LINE MODERATE

p. 131 "BROWN MAY BE": Wilkinson, *From* Brown *to* Bakke, 6.

"SEPARATE EDUCATIONAL FACILITIES ARE INHERENTLY UNEQUAL": *Brown v. Board of Education* (*Brown I*), 347 U.S. 483, 495 (1954).

"AT ALL DELIBERATE SPEED": *Brown v. Board of Education* (*Brown II*), 349 U.S. 294, 301, 330 (1955). The phrase did not originate with *Brown*, but came from Holmes through Frankfurter. See *Virginia v. West Virginia*, 222 U.S. 17, 20 (1911). For an effort to trace its origins, see Kluger, *Simple Justice*, 742–44.

p. 132 ACCEPTED . . . WARILY BUT WITH THANKSGIVING: *Id.*, 710.

BROWN "PROBABLY DID MORE": Williams, "The Triumph of Thurgood Marshall," *Washington Post Magazine*, Jan. 7, 1990.

"IT HAD BEEN HOPED": *Richmond Times-Dispatch*, May 18, 1954, p. 7.

"THERE WILL BE NO DEFIANCE OF THE SUPREME COURT": Muse, *Virginia's Massive Resistance*, 4.

"HIGHEST COURT IN THE LAND HAS SPOKEN": *Id.*, 5.

"USE EVERY LEGAL MEANS": *Id.*, 7.

THE STATE MIGHT WITHDRAW ALTOGETHER FROM PROVIDING PUBLIC EDUCATION: Gates, *The Making of Massive Resistance*, 31. Stanley suggested the possible repeal of that provision of the Virginia Constitution requiring the state to "establish and maintain an efficient system of public free schools."

DENUNCIATION OF BROWN: *Richmond Times-Dispatch*, Aug. 20, 1954, p. 1.

HIS "ORGANIZATION"—CRITICS CALLED IT A "MACHINE": Key, *Southern Politics*, 19–35; Wilkinson, *Harry Byrd*, 9–22.

p. 133 ONLY TO AVOID EMBARRASSMENT: *Id.*, 8.

"MAJESTICALLY AND ENIGMATICALLY SILENT": *Id.*, 256.

RURAL, POOR, AND 40 PERCENT BLACK: *Id.*, 10–11 (reporting population and income figures from 1950). See also Gates, *The Making of Massive Resistance*, 2–5 (discussing Virginia's "black belt," consisting of the Southside, here given a slightly different geographical definition, and Tidewater counties).

THE SOUTHSIDE SIMPLY SAID "NO": *Id.*, 31; Muse, *Virginia's Massive Resistance*, 7. Barely a month after the *Brown* decision, twenty Southside legislators met and adopted a resolution recording their "unalterable opposition" to desegregation.

THERE WAS A GREAT DEAL OF INTERNAL DEMOCRACY: Gates, *The Making of Massive Resistance*, 15–17.

THE CENTERPIECE OF HIS PERSONAL PHILOSOPHY: Muse, *Virginia's Massive Resistance*, 26; Wilkinson, *Harry Byrd*, 152.

p. 134   "TOP BLEW OFF OF THE U.S. CAPITOL": *Norfolk Virginian-Pilot*, June 8, 1964, p. 11.

"IF WE CAN ORGANIZE THE SOUTHERN STATES": *Richmond News Leader*, Feb. 27, 1956, p. 1.

"WE WILL OPPOSE, WITH EVERY FACILITY AT OUR COMMAND": Wilkinson, *Harry Byrd*, 138.

THE COMMISSION PRODUCED A PLAN: Gates, *Virginia's Massive Resistance*, 62–69; Muse, *The Making of Massive Resistance*, 15–16; Wilkinson, *Harry Byrd*, 124–25. The full report of the Commission on Public Education, as it was properly named, was printed as *Senate Document No. 1*, Extra Session 1955, General Assembly of Virginia, and reprinted in the *Race Relations Law Reporter* 1:241 et seq. (1956).

p. 135   REQUIRED AN AMENDMENT TO THE STATE CONSTITUTION: Section 141 of the Constitution of Virginia declared, with some exceptions, that "No appropriation of public funds shall be made to any school or institution of learning not owned or exclusively controlled by the State or some political subdivision thereof." Just days before the Gray Plan was announced, the Supreme Court of Appeals of Virginia ruled, in a case brought to test the issue, that this provision would bar tuition grants to students attending private schools.

SCHEDULED A POPULAR REFERENDUM: Gates, *The Making of Massive Resistance*, 69–72.

RALLIED BEHIND THE SLOGAN: Wilkinson, *Harry Byrd*, 127.

PASSED BY A STUNNNING MARGIN OF OVER TWO TO ONE: The vote was 304,154 to 146,164. See generally Gates, *The Making of Massive Resistance*, 73–99.

THE UNIVERSITY OF VIRGINIA HAD BEGUN: Kluger, *Simple Justice*, 289; Wilkinson, *Harry Byrd*, 136.

"PERHAPS THE MOST HARMONIOUS IN THE SOUTH": Key, *Southern Politics*, 32.

p. 136   "A MANDATE FROM THE PEOPLE FOR THE UTMOST RESISTANCE": Muse, *Virginia's Massive Resistance*, 119. See also Wilkinson, *Harry Byrd*, 127 ("The success of the referendum determined the organization's high priests to lead Virginia into an even more defiant stance.").

"INSTEAD OF BEING HOG-TIED IN CONSTRUCTIVE IMPULSES BY THE PREJUDICE OF THEIR CONSTITUENTS": Muse, *Virginia's Massive Resistance*, 163.

OMINOUSLY WITHHELD COMMENT ON THE OTHER HALF OF THE GRAY PLAN: See Gates, *The Making of Massive Resistance*, 82.

ALREADY THINKING OF SCUTTLING LOCAL OPTION: *Id.*, 82–83.

THE GENERAL ASSEMBLY APPROVED A PLAN: For an extensive history of the origin, support, and passage of these proposals, see *id.*, 117–90.

THE MECHANICS OF MASSIVE RESISTANCE WERE NOW IN PLACE: *Id.*, 167–90; Muse, *Virginia's Massive Resistance*, 28–34; Wilkinson, *Harry Byrd*, 131–32.

p. 137   SCHOOLS WERE ACTUALLY CLOSED BY THE STATE: Muse, *Virginia's Massive Resistance*, 67–75; Wilkinson, *Harry Byrd*, 138–39.

SOME BLACK SCHOOLS REMAINED OPEN: Muse, *Virginia's Massive Resistance*, 79.
ARDENT SEGREGATIONIST: See Kilpatrick, *The Southern Case for School Desegregation*, 96–101 (defending segregation on the ground that "the Negro race, as a race, has not earned equality").
JAMES MADISON AND THOMAS JEFFERSON: Gates, *The Making of Massive Resistance*, 101–104.
"THE GREAT AND LEADING PRINCPLE": Quoted in Jenkins, *The Life of John Caldwell Calhoun*, 162.

p. 138 KILPATRICK TRIED TO AVOID THE TERM "NULLIFICATION": Gates, *The Making of Massive Resistance*, 108. Kilpatrick distinguished interposition and nullification as follows:

> Interposition should not be confused with nullificaton; the former is the genus, the latter a species thereof. Nullification is an act of interposition, but interposition is by no means confined to nullification. All blows are not knockout blows. . . . Similarly, assertions of the right to interpose may range from temperate protest at the one extreme to flat nullification at the other.

"INTERPOSITION, NOW!": *Richmond News Leader*, Nov. 29, 1955, p. 12. The fullest exposition of interposition appears in Kilpatrick, *The Sovereign States*.
"AND BE IT FINALLY RESOLVED": *Journal of the Senate of Virginia*, 1956, 146. For a discussion of interposition theory elsewhere in the South, see Bartley, *The Rise of Massive Resistance*, 126–35.
A PAMPHLET PREPARED FOR THE COMMITTEE OF THE COURTS OF JUSTICE: *The Doctrine of Interposition: Its History and Application*, 23.

p. 139 "VERY HARD TO BELIEVE": LFP, interview.
"[I]T NEVER OCCURRED TO ME": *Id.*
"SHOCKED" BY *BROWN V. BOARD OF EDUCATION*: *Id.*

p. 140 THE SOUTH "HAD HAD NEARLY TWENTY YEARS TO SEE THE TRAIN COMING DOWN THE TRACK": Wilkins, *Standing Fast*, 218.
JUSTIN MOORE AND ARCHIBALD ROBERTSON: For an account of that litigation, see Kluger, *Simple Justice*, 480–507, 575–77.
MANY SOPHISTICATED OBSERVERS FORESAW ITS END: Harbaugh, *Lawyer's Lawyer*, 496–97.
"[S]OMEWHERE, SOMETIME, TO EVERY PRINCIPLE COMES A MOMENT": *Id.*, 514; Kluger, *Simple Justice*, 670.
"WE PARTICULARLY NEED LEVEL HEADS": LFP to Carlisle R. Davis, June 3, 1954.
"THE SCHOOL DECISIONS WERE WRONGLY DECIDED": LFP to Ralph T. Catterall, June 6, 1956.
"I AM NOT IN FAVOR OF, AND WILL NEVER FAVOR COMPULSORY INTEGRATION": LFP to Thomas B. Stanley, Jan. 19, 1956.
"THE MORAL AND CONSTITUTIONAL FORCE OF THE *BROWN* DECISION": Remarks at Virginia Union University, Mar. 7, 1980.

p. 141 PRAISED HIS "ADMIRABLE BALANCE OF MIND": *Richmond News Leader*, Aug. 15, 1950, p. 10.
RICHMOND DID NOT ADMIT BLACK CHILDREN: *New York Times*, Aug. 16, 1960, p. 1.
ONLY TWO OF RICHMOND'S 23,000 BLACK CHILDREN: *Richmond Times-Dispatch*, Aug. 16, 1960, reports that the first two black students were admitted to formerly all-white schools in the fall of 1960. There is no record of change during that school year.

POWELL'S CRITICS CHARGED THAT ONLY THIRTY-SEVEN: *Nomination Hearings*, 371 (testimony of Rep. John Conyers, Jr., on behalf of the Black Congressional Caucus).

VIRGINIA HAD WITHDRAWN PUPIL ASSIGNMENT FROM LOCAL SCHOOL BOARDS: Va. Code Ann. secs. 22-232.1-232.17 (Supp. 1960).

PATTERNS OF PUPIL ASSIGNMENT WERE SET BY LOCAL PRACTICE: For detailed description of Richmond's practices, see *Bradley v. School Board of the City of Richmond*, 317 F.2d 429 (4th Cir. 1963).

p. 142 ON SEPTEMBER 15, 1958, THE RICHMOND SCHOOL BOARD: See pages 157–60, infra.

IN BRADLEY V. SCHOOL BOARD OF THE CITY OF RICHMOND: 317 F.2d 429, 438 (4th Cir. 1963).

WOULD HAVE BEEN "A FUTILE ACT": LFP to Robert R. Merhige, Jr., July 2, 1986.

p. 143 "HIS OWN SEGREGATIONIST POLICIES": *Nomination Hearings*, 372.

"OBVIOUSLY, MR. POWELL'S SANCTION": *Id.*, 372.

"CONSISTENTLY VOTED TO RESIST OR IGNORE": *Id.*, 387.

"CONTINUAL WAR ON THE CONSTITUTION": *Id.*, 390.

"DEMONSTRATED BY HIS PUBLIC DEEDS A WANTON DISRESPECT FOR LAW": *Id.*, 387.

RICHMOND SCHOOL BOARD ISSUED A PRESS RELEASE: Richmond School Board statement, June 9, 1955.

p. 144 UNDER POWELL'S LEADERSHIP, THE BOARD "AGREED (1) NOT TO DISCUSS": LFP, "Richmond School Board, 1950–61," July 3, 1975.

p. 145 WHEN ONE COUNCILMAN DEMANDED TO KNOW POWELL'S ATTITUDE ON DESEGRE-GATION: *Richmond News Leader*, May 11, 1956, p. 23.

"MR. POWELL IS A MAN OF INTEGRITY": *Id.*

"WE HAVE NO RIGHT TO DOUBT THE GOOD JUDGMENT OF MR. POWELL": *Id.*

SENT WORD THAT HE FAVORED REAPPOINTMENT: *Richmond News Leader*, June 4, 1956, p. 1.

ARMISTEAD BOOTHE, WHO HAD DEFECTED FROM THE BYRD ORGANIZATION'S HARD-LINE STANCE: Boothe's views were outlined in a speech to the Virginia Education Association. See *Richmond Times-Dispatch*, Oct. 29, 1954, p. 1. For an account of an interview with Boothe on these matters, see Gates, *The Making of Massive Resistance*, 197–200.

"ARMISTEAD'S MODERATE VIEW MAY NOT BE THE MOST POPULAR ONE POLITICAL-LY": LFP to Kenneth Chorley, Oct. 29, 1954.

"I, PERSONALLY, DO NOT APPROVE OF THE IDEA OF ALLOCATING PUBLIC FUNDS FOR SO-CALLED 'PRIVATE' EDUCATION": LFP to David J. Mays, Dec. 1, 1955.

THE FORUM CLUB WAS A LEGACY OF DOUGLAS SOUTHALL FREEMAN: J. Harvie Wilkinson, Jr., interview.

p. 146 POWELL THOUGHT HE WOULD HAVE WON: LFP, "The Richmond School Board," Jan. 13, 1989.

"MUST HAVE THOUGHT HE'D GOTTEN INTO A DEN OF RATTLESNAKES": Virginius Dabney, interview.

"I AM SO PROUD OF YOU!": Alfred C. Thompson to LFP, Jan. 17, 1956.

p. 147 "GOOD GOD, DID I GET CHEWED UP LAST NIGHT!": J. Harvie Wilkinson, Jr., interview.

POWELL WROTE A LETTER TO GOVERNOR STANLEY ON INTERPOSITION: LFP to Thomas B. Stanley, Jan. 19, 1956.

"BE IT FURTHER RESOLVED": *Richmond News Leader*, Dec. 5, 1955, p. 10.

p. 149 INTERPOSITION RESOLUTION PASSED SUBSTANTIALLY AS INTRODUCED: For various refinements made in the General Assembly, see Gates, *The Making of Massive Resistance*, 110–11.

HAD BEEN ON A FIRST-NAME BASIS WITH HIM EVER SINCE: LFP, interview.

"THE QUINTESSENCE OF THE VIRGINIA GENTLEMAN": Wilkinson, *Harry Byrd*, 173.

"OF THE GENTRY, BY THE GENTRY, AND FOR THE GENTRY": Richard Cope, "The Frustration of Harry Byrd," *Reporter*, Nov. 21, 1950, p. 23.

"HE TOTALLY DISAGREED WITH MY VIEW": LFP, interview.

POWELL MADE NO HEADWAY: Three years later, Powell made another effort to turn the Senator toward a more moderate stance, but he met with an equal lack of success. LFP to Harry F. Byrd, Mar. 10, 1959.

p. 150 "ON ITS FACE, THIS IS A DOCTRINE OF CHAOS—NOT OF LAW": LFP, "'Interposition'—A Twentieth Century Revival of 'Nullification,'" Mar. 29, 1956.

"IN VIEW OF THE PARTICIPATION BY MY FIRM IN THE VIRGINIA SCHOOL CASE": LFP to F.D.G. Ribble, Mar. 30, 1956.

THE DESEGREGATION SUIT BROUGHT AGAINST THAT COUNTY'S SCHOOL BOARD HAD BEEN HEARD BY THE SUPREME COURT: For a fascinating account of the early stages of this litigation, see Kluger, *Simple Justice*, 480–507. The later stages are described in Muse, *Virginia's Massive Resistance*, 11–15, 58–62, 148–54.

POWELL'S ARTICLE MIGHT PROVE EMBARRASSING TO THE FIRM: LFP to F.D.G. Ribble, Apr. 3, 1956.

"WELL, THIS IS GETTING SERIOUS AND LONG-WINDED!": LFP to F.D.G. Ribble, Apr. 9, 1956.

p. 151 "YOU MAY RECALL THAT I WAS THE SPOKESMAN FOR THE SCHOOL BOARD BUT THAT YOU ASSISTED IN THE PREPARATION OF WHAT I SHOULD SAY": H. I. Willett to LFP, July 29, 1975.

A MOTION TO ENDORSE MASSIVE RESISTANCE FAILED BY A TIE VOTE: Muse, *Virginia's Massive Resistance*, 90–91.

VIRGINIA'S NEWSPAPERS, WHICH HAD OVERWHELMINGLY DEFENDED MASSIVE RESISTANCE, NOW SOUNDED RETREAT: *Id.*, 94–98; Wilkinson, *Harry Byrd*, 143.

"WE MUST NOW FIND ANOTHER POSITION FROM WHICH TO FIGHT": *Richmond Times-Dispatch*, Nov. 12, 1958, p. 16.

"I BELIEVE THE LAWS WE NOW HAVE ON THE BOOKS HAVE OUTLIVED THEIR USEFULNESS": Wilkinson, *Harry Byrd*, 143 (quoting *Southern School News*, Dec. 1958).

VIRGINIA INDUSTRIALIZATION GROUP: Detailed information about the group comes from an undated memorandum by Stuart Saunders setting forth its origins and history.

p. 152 IT WAS SAID THAT NOT A SINGLE NEW INDUSTRY HAD COME TO VIRGINIA IN 1958: Muse, *Virginia's Massive Resistance*, 109.

SENSATIONAL INDUSTRIAL PROGRESS ACROSS THE BORDER IN NORTH CAROLINA: *Id.*

ON DECEMBER 19, 1959, MEMBERS OF THE GROUP SAT DOWN TO DINNER AT THE STATELY ROTUNDA CLUB IN RICHMOND: Stuart Saunders, undated memorandum.

THE PRESS MADE NO MENTION OF THE EVENT: Although some of the participants shortly thereafter broke their public silence to denounce integration, the first detailed account of the meeting seems to have been Muse's book, published in 1969. Even then none of the particpants was named. Muse, *Virginia's Massive Resistance*, 110; Bartley, *The Rise of Massive Resistance*, 322.

A MEMORANDUM OF DECEMBER 15 OUTLINED FOR SAUNDERS AND WILKINSON THE POINTS POWELL THOUGHT SHOULD BE MADE: LFP, "Industrial Development in Virginia," Dec. 15, 1958.

p. 153 BUT HE WAS NEVER A BYRD CONFIDANT: Muse, *Virginia's Massive Resistance*, 99. On the complicated history of relations between Byrd and Almond, see Bartley, *The Rise of Massive Resistance*, 270–72; Wilkinson, *Harry Byrd*, 134–36.

A SPELLBINDING ORATOR WHOSE "GREATEST POLITICAL ASSET WAS HIS ABILITY TO IMPRESS CROWDS": Muse, *Virginia's Massive Resistance*, 40.

HE, MORE THAN MOST OF THE STATE'S LEADERS, RECOGNIZED SOME JUSTICE IN BLACK DEMANDS: *Id.*, 82; Kluger, *Simple Justice*, 480–82; Wilkinson, *Harry Byrd*, 144.

HE SHOOK HIS FINGER AND VOWED THAT HE WOULD NEVER ACCEPT INTEGRATION: Stuart Saunders, undated memorandum.

DECLARED VIRGINIA'S SCHOOL CLOSING LAWS UNCONSTITUTIONAL: *James v. Almond*, 170 F. Supp. 342 (E.D. Va. 1959).

"POSSIBLY MR. POWELL'S OUTSTANDING CONTRIBUTION TO VIRGINIA": *Norfolk Virginian-Pilot*, Oct. 23, 1971, p. A12.

p. 154 NOW THE COMMISSION PROPOSED THAT LOCAL SCHOOL BOARDS: For details, see "Report of the Perrow Commission," *Race Relations Law Reporter* 4:392–408.

AFTER A BITTER FIGHT, THE GENERAL ASSEMBLY AGREED: Bartley, *The Rise of Massive Resistance*, 325–26; Muse, *Virginia's Massive Resistance*, 163; Wilkinson, *Harry Byrd*, 148–49.

TO DELAY THE EFFECTIVE DATE OF LOCAL OPTION UNTIL MARCH 1, 1960: Acts of the General Assembly of the Commonwealth of Virginia, Extra Session 1959, chapter 71, codified as Va. Code Ann. secs. 22-232.18 et seq.

UNTIL THE SUPREME COURT FORCED THEM OPEN IN 1964: *Griffin v. County School Board*, 377 U.S. 218 (1964).

ASSIGNED THERE BY THE STATE PUPIL PLACEMENT BOARD: *Richmond Times-Dispatch*, Aug. 16, 1960, p. 1.

IN 1949 RICHMOND'S SCHOOLS WERE 59 PERCENT WHITE: *Bradley v. School Board of the City of Richmond*, 338 F. Supp. 67, 184 (E.D. Va. 1972).

BY 1958 BLACKS WERE A MAJORITY OF THE CITY'S PUBLIC SCHOOL STUDENTS: *Richmond News Leader*, June 29, 1959 (reporting 49 percent white and 51 percent black enrollment for the 1958–59 school year).

p. 155 BUT REFUSED TO RELEASE THE MONEY: *Richmond Times-Dispatch*, May 7, 1959, pp. 1, 4.

SCHOOLS HAD BEEN PLANNED AND THEIR LOCATIONS SELECTED ON THE ASSUMPTION THAT DESEGREGATION WAS INEVITABLE: LFP, "Richmond School Board Years, 1950-1961," July 3, 1975.

IF ONE SIMPLY LOOKED AT A MAP: See the locational map printed in the *Richmond Times-Dispatch*, May 11, 1959, p. 4. The potential for integration was particularly evident in the proposed southside high school if, as seemed likely, the small fraction of Richmond south of the large James River would be one high school attendance zone. In 1959 that area was mostly white but with a sizable black enclave in its midst.

"IT WAS PERFECTLY OBVIOUS": *Nomination Hearings*, 278.

"I DON'T WANT WHITE CHILDREN SITTING BESIDE SMELLY NEGRO CHILDREN": LFP, interview.

p. 156 "THIS BRINGS US TO THE FUNDAMENTAL QUESTION OF WHETHER GENERAL PUBLIC EDUCATION WILL CONTINUE IN RICHMOND": LFP, "Statement on Behalf of the School Board Supporting Construction of the New High Schools Without Delay," May 6, 1959.

p. 157 IT WAS THE ONLY WAY TO GET THE FUNDING: LFP, "Richmond School Board, 1950–1961," July 3, 1975.

THE BUILDING OF "TWO NEW WHITE HIGH SCHOOLS": *Richmond Times-Dispatch*, Mar. 13, 1961, p. 14.

"THOSE IN RICHMOND WHO HAD GOOD CAUSE TO BE JUSTLY PROUD": *Nomination Hearings*, 372.

THE ONLY HIGH SCHOOLS IN THE CITY OF RICHMOND WITH SUBSTANTIAL REPRESENTATION OF BOTH RACES: *Bradley v. School Board of the City of Richmond, Virginia*, 338 F. Supp. 67, 232 (E.D. Va. 1972).

DISCLOSED PLANS TO CONVERT CHANDLER JUNIOR HIGH SCHOOL FROM ALL-WHITE TO ALL-BLACK: *Richmond Times-Dispatch*, May 7, 1959, pp. 1, 4.

p.158 POWELL KNEW THE STATE PUPIL PLACEMENT LAW WAS CONSTITUTIONALLY "SHAKY": LFP to Elliott Drinard, July 20, 1959.

A RESOLUTION ASKING THE SCHOOL BOARD TO TAKE NO ACTION WTIHOUT CONSULTING CITY COUNCIL: *Richmond Times-Dispatch*, Sept. 1, 1959, p. 1.

THE SCHOOL BOARD ADOPTED A RESOLUTION REAFFIRMING ITS AUTHORITY OVER THE USE OF SCHOOL PROPERTY: *Id.*

A COMMITTEE TO STUDY DESEGREGATION PROBLEMS "SO THAT THEY COULD BE CONSIDERED FACTUALLY AND RATIONALLY": *Richmond Times-Dispatch*, Sept. 15, 1959, p. 1.

THE RESOLUTION PASSED BY A VOTE OF FIVE TO FOUR: *Id.*

p. 159 CALLED FOR CONCERTED RESISTANCE TO BLACK EXPANSION: *Richmond Times-Dispatch*, Feb. 19, 1960, p. 6 ("[Mizell said that] Chandler should remain a white school indefinitely. He said white residents north of Brookland Park boulevard have prevented a Negro expansion in that area by concerted resistance for eight years and 'there's no reason why it can't stay that way.'").

"WHEN THE HOMES OF WIDOWS AND ORPHANS WILL BE CUT IN VALUE": *Id.*

AN ARRAY OF WHITE SPEAKERS: *Richmond Times-Dispatch*, Feb. 25, 1960, p. 1.

"REMINDED ME OF DEPICTIONS OF JESUS CALMING THE STORMY SEA OF GALILEE": Hill, "Tribute," *Harvard L. Rev.* 101:415–16.

HILL ALSO CALLED HIS OLD FRIEND THURGOOD MARSHALL: Thurgood Marshall, interview.

p. 160 A STATEMENT ISSUED ON APRIL 22, 1960: "Statement of School Board on Chandler School Problem," Apr. 22, 1960.

IN 1955 HE WROTE THE SUPERINTENDENT OF RICHMOND SCHOOLS: LFP to H. I. Willett, July 21, 1955.

A MAN OF EXTRAORDINARY ENERGY AND INFECTIOUS ENTHUSIASM: *Richmond Times-Dispatch*, Mar. 22, 1986.

p. 161 "THE BEST SCHOOL SUPERINTENDENT IN AMERICA": LFP, Oct. 27, 1952.

BETWEEN SEPTEMBER 1950 AND SEPTEMBER 1960, THE ENROLLMENT IN RICHMOND SCHOOLS: These and other figures are taken from LFP, "Notes for Speech, Convocation of Richmond School Teachers," Oct. 6, 1960.

p. 162 "I THINK WE WOULD ALL AGREE": LFP, "Statement to Council on Behalf of School Board," Dec. 27, 1954.

"AN INDIVIDUAL WHO BELIEVES DEEPLY THAT WE ARE DOING TOO LITTLE IN VIR-

GINIA FOR PUBLIC EDUCATION": LFP, "Statement Before Senate Finance Committee on Needs for Education," Feb. 5, 1960.

HYMAN G. RICKOVER: Rickover presented his views in extensive testimony before the House Committee on Appropriations in 1959 and 1962. Published versions of this testimony appear in his books, *Education and Freedom* and *American Education—A National Failure.*

p. 163 A STATEMENT SUPPORTING PRESIDENT EISENHOWER'S PROPOSAL: *Richmond Times-Dispatch*, Jan. 2, 1958, p. 1.

HE ELABORATED THESE IDEAS IN A MAJOR SPEECH: LFP, "Quality in Education— A National Necessity," Feb. 1958.

p. 165 "NOT A FORMAL REQUEST FROM ME AS CHAIRMAN OF THE BOARD": LFP to H. I. Willett, July 18, 1958.

A REPORT TO THE SCHOOL BOARD: LFP, "Soviet Education—A Means Toward World Domination: Report on Trip to Soviet Union (July-August, 1958)." Powell's views on this subject are reported in some detail in the *Richmond Times-Dispatch*, Aug. 24, 1958, p. 21.

HE CRITICIZED STANDARDS PROPOSED BY THE VIRGINIA STATE BOARD OF EDUCA-TION: LFP, "Memorandum on Proposed Statement of Policy by State Board of Education with Respect to High School Curriculum," Oct. 31, 1958. The same views were expounded to the Virginia Commission on Public Education the following year. LFP, "Statement to Virginia Commission on Public Education," July 15, 1959.

p. 166 THE CITY ADOPTED A CURRICULUM INCORPORATING POWELL'S REFORMS: *Richmond Times-Dispatch*, Feb. 28, 1959, p. 1.

HE BROACHED THIS PROPOSAL IN A 1960 SPEECH: The speech is excerpted in the *Richmond Times-Dispatch*, May 16, 1960, p. 16.

p. 167 AS HE EXPLAINED TO HI WILLETT: LFP to H. I. Willett, July 19, 1960.

STATE BOARD OF EDUCATION APPOINTED A COMMITTEE TO DEVELOP A COURSE ON THE FUNDAMENTALS OF A FREE SYSTEM: *Richmond Times-Dispatch*, Jan. 3, 1961, p. 14.

IT BECAME PART OF THE REQUIRED CURRICULUM: *Richmond News Leader*, Aug. 31, 1960, p. 6.

CRITICIZED AS PREACHY AND REPETITIOUS: *Richmond News Leader*, Mar. 29, 1962, p. 11.

IN OCTOBER 1960: Powell's notes are dated Oct. 6. *Times-Dispatch* coverage of Oct. 14 merely refers to the speech at "last week's annual teachers' convocation at the Mosque."

p. 168 HE HAD BROUGHT THIS UP THE YEAR BEFORE, WHEN HE DESCRIBED THE "SHOCK-INGLY INADEQUATE TRAINING": LFP, "Notes for Speech, Convocation of Teachers," Sept. 2, 1959.

CONTINUING TRENCH WARFARE WITH BYRD STALWARTS IN THE GENERAL ASSEMBLY: Muse, *Virginia's Massive Resistance*, 166–68; Wilkinson, *Harry Byrd*, 149–50.

p. 169 TREBLING OF THE PRIVATE ENDOWMENT AND A QUADRUPLING OF THE ANNUAL STATE APPROPRIATION: Dabney, *Mr. Jefferson's University*, 418.

VEHEMENTLY OPPOSED CLOSING THE PUBLIC SCHOOLS: Darden, *Conversations*, 160; *Richmond Times-Dispatch*, Dec. 18, 1955, p. 4, and Dec. 21, 1955, p. 5.

"SO EMINENTLY QUALIFIED FOR THE BOARD THAT TWO MORE COMPETENT MEN COULD NOT HAVE BEEN FOUND": *Richmond Times-Dispatch*, Jan. 31, 1961, p. 10.

"DEMONSTRABLY DEDICATED TO THE CAUSE OF EDUCATION ITSELF": *Norfolk Ledger-Dispatch*, Jan. 6, 1961. See also *Norfolk Virginian-Pilot*, Jan. 5, 1961, p. 4.

POWELL RESIGNED THE LOCAL POST: LFP to Honorable Claude W. Woodward, Mar. 9, 1961. See also *Richmond Times-Dispatch*, Mar. 17, 1961, p. 18.

"FEW MEN OF THIS GENERATION HAVE SERVED RICHMOND AS ABLY AND CONSCIENTIOUSLY": *Richmond Times-Dispatch*, Mar. 13, 1961, p. 14.

FRIDDELL TERMED THEM "PROGRESSIVE" . . . DARDEN HIMSELF SAID THEY WERE "MIDDLE-GROUNDERS": Darden, *Conversations*, 181.

p. 170 THE BOARD LISTED AMONG ITS CONCERNS THE "ACHIEVEMENT OF MAXIMUM CONTINUITY": The entire regulation is quoted in *Bradley v. School Board of the City of Richmond*, 338 F. Supp. 67, 140 (E.D. Va. 1972).

THIS PRACTICE WAS CONTINUED UNTIL 1965: *Id.*, 147.

POWELL AND WILLETT HAD DESEGREGATED THE ANNUAL CONVOCATION OF TEACHERS BACK IN THE EARLY 1950s: LFP, "Richmond School Board," Jan. 13, 1989.

NO ONE IN THE STATE DEPARTMENT OF EDUCATION WAS ASSIGNED TO WORK ON DESEGREGATION: *Bradley v. School Board of the City of Richmond*, 338 F. Supp. 67, 146 (E.D. Va. 1972).

ALTHOUGH THE STATE BOARD HAD GENERAL SUPERVISION OF VIRGINIA'S SCHOOLS, LOCAL CONTROL PREDOMINATED: The legal framework as it then was is described in *Griffin v. Board of Supervisors of Prince Edward County*, 322 F.2d 332, 340–41 (4th Cir. 1963).

SO-CALLED FREEDOM OF CHOICE PLANS: For discussion of the operation of pupil placement laws and freedom of choice plans, see Wilkinson, *From Brown to Bakke*, 108–14. For criticism of the concept of freedom of choice, as well as its operation, see Gewirtz, "Choice in the Transition," *Columbia Law Review* 86:728–98.

p. 171 DESEGREGATION AT A SNAIL'S PACE: The figures reported in this paragraph are taken from the *Statistical Summary of School Segregation-Desegregation in the Southern and Border States*, published annually by the Southern Education Reporting Service.

THE STATE BOARD OF EDUCATION ASSURED HEW THAT IT WOULD COMPLY WITH FEDERAL GUIDELINES: This agreement and the responsibilities thereafter undertaken by the state are detailed in *Bradley v. School Board of the City of Richmond*, 338 F. Supp. 67, 146-53 (E.D. Va. 1972).

HEW ISSUED GUIDELINES IN THE SPRING OF 1965 AND TOUGHENED THEM CONSIDERABLY THE FOLLOWING YEAR: The evolution and content of the HEW guidelines are discussed in Wilkinson, *From Brown to Bakke*, 102–108.

IN THE FALL OF 1965, ONE IN NINE OF VIRGINIA'S BLACK STUDENTS ATTENDED SCHOOL WITH WHITES: Again, these figures are taken from the *Statistical Summary of School Segregation-Desegregation in the Southern and Border States*, published annually by the Southern Education Reporting Service.

p. 172 GREEN V. COUNTY SCHOOL BOARD OF NEW KENT COUNTY: 391 U.S. 430 (1968).

"PROMISES REALISTICALLY TO WORK NOW": *Id.*, 439 (emphasis in original).

THE NEW WATCHWORD WAS "NOW!": See, e.g., *Alexander v. Holmes County Board of Education*, 396 U.S. 19 (1969); *Carter v. West Feliciana Parish School Board*, 396 U.S. 290 (1970); *Northcross v. Board of Education*, 397 U.S. 232 (1970). The common theme of these decisions was the Court's belated insistence on instant action.

WHATEVER IT TAKES TO ELIMINATE RACIALLY IDENTIFIABLE PUBLIC SCHOOLS: 391 U.S. 442 ("The Board must be required to formulate a new plan . . . and fashion steps which promise realistically to convert promptly to a system without a 'white' school and a 'Negro' school, but just schools").

IN THE FALL OF 1968, 42 PERCENT OF VIRGINIA'S BLACK STUDENTS ATTENDED SCHOOL WITH WHITES: *Bradley v. School Board of the City of Richmond,* 338 F. Supp. 67, 153 (E.D. Va. 1972).

p. 173 "FOUND IT DIPLOMATICALLY SOUND NOT TO DO ANY MORE THAN ABSOLUTELY REQUIRED": *Id.,* 153.

IN A STATEMENT DELIVERED TO THE STATE BOARD OF EDUCATION AT THE TIME OF HIS RETIREMENT: LFP, "Reflections on the State of Public Education," Feb. 4, 1969.

p. 174 WIDE VARIETY OF LOCAL ACTS THAT AFFECTED DESEGREGATION IN VIRGINIA: An account of the details that underlie this generalization may be found in *Bradley v. School Board of the City of Richmond,* 338 F. Supp. 67, 116-27, 146-55 (E.D. Va. 1972).

FIGURES FROM THE END OF THE DECADE: *Id.,* 117. The numbers are taken from the 1969–70 school year.

THE OTHER CRITICISM OF POWELL'S YEARS ON THE STATE BOARD: See *id.,* 141–46.

POWELL'S VOTES APPROVING SUCH REGULATIONS WERE LATER CITED AS EVIDENCE: *Nomination Hearings,* 383 (statement of Rep. John Conyers, Jr., on behalf of the Congressional Black Caucus).

BARRING TUITION GRANTS FOR USE IN SEGREGATED ACADEMIES MAINTAINED PREDOMINANTLY BY SUCH GRANTS: *Griffin v. State Board of Education,* 239 F. Supp. 560 (E.D. Va. 1965).

THIS ALSO WAS CRITICIZED: *Nomination Hearings,* 384 (statement of Rep. John Conyers, Jr., on behalf of the Congressional Black Caucus).

CITED IN SUPPORT OF THE CHARGE THAT HE WAS IN FACT A "CHAMPION" OF SEGREGATION: *Id.,* 384, 387–89 (statements of Rep. John Conyers, Jr., on behalf of the Congressional Black Caucus, and of William A. Smith and Henry L. Marsh III of the Old Dominion Bar Association of Virginia).

p. 175 "A CLIMATE OF INTOLERANCE NOW EXISTS IN THE SOUTH": Quoted in Sperber, *Murrow,* 545–46.

"RURAL, REMOTE, AND RESOLUTE" PRINCE EDWARD COUNTY: Goodman, "Public Schools Died Here," *Saturday Evening Post,* Apr. 29, 1961, p. 86 (quoted in Wilkinson, *From* Brown *to* Bakke, 97).

EXTRAORDINARILY TANGLED HISTORY OF DESEGREGATION IN PRINCE EDWARD COUNTY: A good short account appears in Muse, *Ten Years of Prelude,* 187–91. A more comprehensive history is given in Sullivan, *Bound for Freedom.*

AN OFFER WAS MADE TO FUND SIMILAR FACILITIES FOR BLACKS: *Griffin v. School Board of Prince Edward County,* 377 U.S. 218, 223 (1964); Muse, *Virginia's Massive Resistance,* 152–53.

p. 176 DARDEN ORGANIZED A PRIVATE COMMITTEE: Darden, *Conversations,* 174–79.

UNDER ORDER OF THE UNITED STATES SUPREME COURT: *Griffin v. School Board of Prince Edward County,* 377 U.S. 218 (1964).

BY 1960–1961, THEY DEPENDED ON PUBLIC MONEY: *Id.,* 223.

ENJOINED STATE OFFICIALS FROM "RECEIVING, PROCESSING OR APPROVING APPLICATIONS": *Allen v. County School Board of Prince Edward County,* 198 F. Supp. 497, 504 (E.D. Va. 1961).

THE ATTORNEY GENERAL REPLIED: *Bradley v. School Board of the City of Richmond*, 338 F. Supp. 67, 143–44 (E.D. Va. 1972).

"TRANSPARENT EVASIONS" OF CONSTITUTIONAL DUTY: *Griffin v. Board of Supervisors of Prince Edward County*, 359 F.2d 486, 492 (4th Cir. 1964).

"PRINCE EDWARD IS INCREASINGLY BECOMING A SERIOUS REFLECTION": LFP to Albertis S. Harrison, Nov. 30, 1963.

DONATION OF $100 F.D.G. Ribble to LFP, Jan. 21, 1964.

p. 177 "ESTABLISH AND MAINTAIN AN EFFICIENT SYSTEM OF PUBLIC FREE SCHOOLS THROUGHOUT THE STATE": Section 129.

PROHIBITED THE STATE FROM CLOSING PUBLIC SCHOOLS TO AVOID INTEGRATION: *Harrison v. Day*, 200 Va. 439, 106 S.E.2d 636 (1959).

BUT DID NOT PREVENT LOCALITIES FROM DOING THE SAME THING: *Griffin v. Board of Supervisors*, 203 Va. 231, 124 S.E.2d 227 (1962).

p. 178 WHEN THE SUPREME COURT OF THE UNITED STATES RULED THAT THE CLOSED SCHOOLS VIOLATED THE FEDERAL CONSTITUTION: *Griffin v. County School Board of Prince Edward County*, 377 U.S. 218 (1964).

GENERAL ASSEMBLY "SHALL PROVIDE FOR A SYSTEM OF FREE PUBLIC ELEMENTARY AND SECONDARY SCHOOLS": Constitution of Virginia, art. VIII, sec. 1. The languaged quoted in this and subsequent references comes from the Constitution as approved by referendum in 1970. This version differs from the original proposal of the Commission on Constitutional Revision, which was modified by the General Assembly in various minor respects. For the language of the commission's original proposal, see the *Report of the Commission on Constitutional Revision.*

"EACH UNIT OF LOCAL GOVERNMENT *SHALL* PROVIDE ITS PORTION OF SUCH COST": Constitution of Virginia, art. VIII, sec. 2. This language is more direct than the commission's proposal, which required the state to step in and fund schools if a locality would not and which contemplated various state sanctions against a defaulting locality. For detailed discussion of the changes, see Howard, *Commentaries on the Constitution of Virginia* II:901–903.

"THAT FREE GOVERNMENT RESTS, AS DOES ALL PROGRESS, UPON THE BROADEST POSSIBLE DIFFUSION OF KNOWLEDGE": Constitution of Virginia, art. I, sec. 15. For an account of a minor change in phrasing made in the General Assembly, see Howard, *Commentaries on the Constitution of Virginia* I:285–87.

p. 181 HILL AND TUCKER HAD APPEARED AS COUNSEL IN MOST OF THE STATE'S DESEGREGATION CASES: E.g., *Davis v. County School Board of Prince Edward County*, 347 U.S. 483 (1954) (reported with *Brown*); *Griffin v. County School Board of Prince Edward County*, 377 U.S. 218 (1964).

THE STATE BAR HAD TREATED HILL AND TUCKER VERY SHABBILY: Some of the history of the state's attempt to restrict the NAACP lawyers is recounted in *N.A.A.C.P. v. Button*, 371 U.S. 415 (1963). See also Murphy, "The South Counterattacks: The Anti-NAACP Laws," *Western Political Quarterly* 12:371–90.

CHAPTER VII: NATIONAL CITIZEN

p. 183 PROSE WAS GEORGE GIBSON'S: Freeman, *The Style of a Law Firm*, 162. Gibson acknowledged indebtedness to the partnership agreement of Davis, Polk, & Wardwell for the "philosophical introduction." *Id.*, 266.

p. 184 $250,000 TWENTY YEARS LATER: Powell's share of the firm's profits from April 1, 1971, through January 2, 1972, when he withdrew, was $186,775. On an annualized basis, that comes to nearly $250,000, plus $25,000 to $30,000 a year in director's fees.

p. 185 GEORGE DANDRIDGE GIBSON: Freeman, *The Style of a Law Firm,* 170–90.

"IMPRESSED AND EXHILARATED BY THE BREEZY HAUTEUR": *Id.,* 174 (quoting Gibson).

DISLIKED ANDERSON, WHOM HE INSISTED ON CALLING "MR.": Mrs. George D. Gibson, interview.

WHICH GIBSON ARGUED TWICE BEFORE THE SUPREME COURT: *Reconstruction Finance Corp. v. Denver & Rio Grande Western Railroad Co.,* 328 U.S. 495 (1946); *Insurance Group Committee v. Denver & Rio Grande Western Railroad Co.,* 329 U.S. 607 (1947).

"A PERFECTIONIST—NEVER CONTENT WITH ANYTHING": Mrs. George D. Gibson, interview.

"HE DID NOT SUFFER FOOLS GLADLY": Freeman, *The Style of a Law Firm,* 183.

STOOD OUTSIDE HIS OFFICE POLISHING THE DOORKNOB: *Id.,* 183 (quoting John W. Riely).

p. 186 "IN THE FUTURE, GEORGE, WHEN YOU ARE PLANNING TO GO ON HOLIDAY": *Id.,* 273.

GIBSON'S BEST FRIEND: LFP, interview; LFP, "Introduction" to Freeman, *The Style of a Law Firm,* x (referring to Gibson as "my closest friend among the named partners, and a dear friend until his death").

"I WOULDN'T SAY THEY WERE GOOD FRIENDS": Mrs. George D. Gibson, interview.

CARRIED A CANE: Freeman, *The Style of a Law Firm,* 170.

"NOT INTIMATE WITH MEN": Mrs. George D. Gibson, interview.

p. 187 OPERATION OF THE FIRM'S EXECUTIVE COMMITTEE: See Freeman, *The Style of a Law Firm,* 163.

HUNTON HAD "A LOT OF COMMON SENSE": H. Merrill Pasco, interview with Anne Hobson Freeman.

"SOCIAL CHAIRMAN": LFP, interview.

"GEORGE WOULD DO ANYTHING THAT LEWIS SAID": John W. Riely, interview with Anne Hobson Freeman.

"POWELL HAD PLENTY OF FLEXIBILITY": Norman A. Scher, interview with Anne Hobson Freeman.

p. 188 "WARWICK," HE SAID, "WE HAVE DISCUSSED IT ENOUGH": *Id.*

ELECTED TO THE BOARD OF DIRECTORS: J. Harvie Wilkinson, Jr., to LFP, Oct. 8, 1959.

p. 189 ALBEMARLE PAPER COMPANY: For its history, see Robert, *Ethyl,* 4–90.

UNDERNEATH FLOYD DEWEY GOTTWALD'S STRAIGHTFORWARD, NO-NONSENSE DEMEANOR: *Id.,* 55; Lawrence E. Blanchard, Jr., interview.

"AN INTIMATE MEMBER OF THE BUSINESS FAMILY": Robert, *Ethyl,* 82.

"HARDLY A MONTH WENT BY": Blanchard, "The Albemarle-Ethyl Deal in 1962." This memorandum, written in 1974, was originally intended for inclusion in a Hunton, Williams firm history.

p. 190 PROFITS HAD DECLINED BY 39 PERCENT: Robert, *Ethyl,* 212–13.

"A GOOD FOUNDATION FOR TEN YEARS ANYWAY": *Id.,* 220.

GOTTWALD "HAD THE VISION, IMAGINATION, AND DETERMINATION": *Id.,* 220–21.

p. 191 LARGE ROPE TIED TO THE RADIATOR: Lawrence E. Blanchard, Jr., interview.

TRANSACTION HAD TO BE COMPLETED BY THE END OF NOVEMBER: Blanchard, "The Albemarle-Ethyl Deal." The full story was more complex. Albemarle had to close the transaction or demonstrate its immediate ability to close by the mid-November, in which case an extension would be given to the end of the month. If, as seemed unlikely, any further extension were given, it would result in a change in the purchase price to Albemarle's detriment.

SUITE 42-H OF THE WALDORF TOWERS: Robert, *Ethyl*, 233.

"NOT . . . A SINGLE LAWYER": LFP, Speech to Ethyl Corp. Anniversary Dinner, Nov. 30, 1977.

"WE WENT TO BED THAT NIGHT AT THE WALDORF": LFP, "The Albemarle/Ethyl Deal in 1962," July 3, 1975.

p. 192 "OH NO," ONE REPLIED, "WE ARE THE *SPENDERS*!": Blanchard, "The Albemarle-Ethyl Deal."

"STILL BEGATTING": Robert, *Ethyl*, 250.

JONAH HAD SWALLOWED THE WHALE: *Forbes*, Dec. 1, 1962, p. 15.

ALBEMARLE HAD LESS THAN $1.50: *Id.*

BY THE END OF 1971: Financial information is taken from the company's annual financial statements (form 10-K) filed with the Securities and Exchange Commission. During the next ten years, progress was even more dramatic. Profits rose to $90 million, the ratio of debt to capital fell to 19 percent, and the share of revenue derived from lead compounds shrank to only 17 percent.

p. 193 "I CAN WELL IMAGINE THE HOWL THAT WOULD GO UP": Frank W. Rogers to Thomas B. Gay, Mar. 9, 1953.

p. 194 "I HAVE ALWAYS FELT AND STILL FEEL": William L. Zimmer III to LFP, June 14, 1957.

CONTINUED PRESENCE IN THE HOUSE OF DELEGATES "IN ANOTHER CAPACITY": Ernest T. Gearheart, Jr., to J. D. Bond, Feb. 18, 1957.

"SOMEWHAT DISINGENUOUS": LFP to James S. Cremins, Mar. 1, 1957.

"THE DISTINCTION ATTAINED BY THIS SENIOR MEMBER OF LEWIS POWELL'S FIRM": J. D. Bond to Ernest T. Gearheart, Jr., Feb. 20, 1957.

POWELL FEARED THAT HE WAS "UNDERPLAYING" THE CAMPAIGN: LFP to J. D. Bond, Feb. 21, 1957.

POWELL HAD 683 VOTES TO ZIMMER'S 493: Ruth White to Flo R. Crumpacker, May 28, 1957.

p. 195 "ALMOST LIKE APOSTOLIC SUCCESSION": George C. Freeman, Jr., interview.

THE INCOMING PRESIDENT OUTLINED HIS PRIORITIES: LFP, "Areas of Emphasis for 1964/65," Aug. 14, 1964.

"SPIRIT OF MARKED LENIENCE": *Id.*

"THEY MUST LAY DOWN CLEAR, PEREMPTORY RULES": LFP, "Annual Address," *ABA Journal*, Sept. 1965, p. 825.

p. 196 "A CLIMATE OF DEEP CONCERN": Quoted in ABA *Standards for Criminal Justice*, 2d ed., xxi.

p. 197 LEGAL AID MOVEMENT BEGAN IN THE 1920S: Johnson, *Justice and Reform*, 1–19.

"IT HAS BEEN CORRECTLY SAID": LFP, "Areas of Emphasis for 1964/65," Aug. 14, 1964.

p. 198 "LEGAL AID DISCHARGES ITS RESPONSIBILITY": Johnson, *Justice and Reform*, 13.

LYNDON JOHNSON'S "ANTIPOVERTY WARSHIP": *Id.*, 39.

"THE EQUIVALENT OF CONSORTING WITH THE ENEMY": *Nomination Hearings*, 181 (statement of Jean Camper Cahn).

LAYMEN WOULD SERVE AS "LEGAL ADVOCATES FOR THE POOR": Johnson, *Justice and Reform*, 50.

"WHAT IS BIG BROTHER UP TO NOW?": *Nomination Hearings*, 282 (letter of Jean Camper Cahn quoting Orison Marden, ABA president in 1965–1966).

LETTERS POURED IN: Johnson, *Justice and Reform*, 50.

p. 199 "DISTANCE TO BE BRIDGED COULD HARDLY HAVE BEEN CAST MORE DRAMATICALLY": *Nomination Hearings*, 281 (letter of Jean Camper Cahn).

"NO PRESIDENT COULD HAVE WORKED ANY HARDER OR MORE ARTFULLY": Johnson, *Justice and Reform*, 64.

p. 200 THAT MANY OEO OFFICIALS BELIEVED AN "IMPOSSIBILITY": *Id.*, 60, 64.

OEO BECAME EMBROILED IN AN INTERNAL DISPUTE: *Id.*, 64–70.

"THERE WAS EVERY SIGN OF A MAJOR REVOLT": *Nomination Hearings*, 284 (letter of Jean Camper Cahn).

"SYMBOLIC PUBLIC HANDSHAKE": Johnson, *Justice and Reform*, 64.

OEO OFFICIALS VOICED A NEWFOUND FLEXIBILITY: *Washington Post*, June 26, 1965, p. A2.

APOLOGIZED FOR THE DELAY AND PROMISED EARLY ACTION: Johnson, *Justice and Reform*, 67.

"ONE PRACTICAL METHOD OF GUARANTEEING THE INDEPENDENCE": Shriver, "The Organized Bar and OEO Legal Services," *ABA Journal*, Mar. 1971, p. 224.

p. 201 RECOUNTED THESE EVENTS IN A LETTER OF SUPPORT: *Nomination Hearings*, 281–85 (reprinting Jean Camper Cahn to James O. Eastland, Nov. 3, 1971).

AMONG THEM: The other members were John Feerick, who would write the definitive history of these events; Jonathan Gibson, chairman of the ABA committee on law reform; author Richard Hansen; former counsel to the Senate subcommittee on constitutional amendments James C. Kirby, Jr.; former Deputy Attorney General Ross Malone; Dean Charges B. Nutting of the George Washington Law Center; Martin Taylor of New York; and ABA House of Delegates chairman Edward L. Wright. See Feerick, *Twenty-Fifth Amendment*, 60.

p. 202 "IT IS TRUE," POWELL EXPLAINED: *Hearings on Presidential Inability*, 93–94.

p. 203 ON MAY 27, 1965, THE CONFERENCE COLLAPSED: Bayh, *One Heartbeat Away*, 279–304. Bayh states that the conference reached deadlock on Thursday, June 10, 1965, that Powell was called that evening, and that he reached Washington the next day. Powell's correspondence, however, makes plain that he was called in San Juan on Thursday, May 27, and returned to Washington on May 28. See LFP to Herbert Brownell, May 28, 1965; LFP to Emanuel Celler, May 30, 1965. In all other respects, Powell's records confirm Bayh's account.

MET WITH EMANUEL CELLER AND ALL FIVE HOUSE MEMBERS: LFP to Emanuel Celler, May 30, 1965.

POWELL BROUGHT THE TWO LEGISLATORS TOGETHER: LFP, interview.

"NOT SO MUCH THE RESULT OF MY EFFORTS AT MEDIATION": LFP to Herbert Brownell, May 28, 1965.

MINNESOTA AND NEVADA BECAME THE THIRTY-SEVENTH AND THIRTY-EIGHTH: Bayh, *One Heartbeat Away*, 341.

p. 204 WEPT AS HIS FIRST-BORN LEFT HOME: Josephine Powell Smith to author, July 22, 1991.

THE CHILD WHO "CAME FIRST TO HIS MIND": Josephine R. Powell, interview.

DISCUSSES JO'S PLANS FOLLOWING GRADUATION: LFP to Josephine McR. Powell, Mar. 31, 1960.

p. 205 "IF MOLLY HAD BEEN THE FIRST": Josephine R. Powell, interview.

"JUST AWFUL GUYS": Molly Powell Sumner, interview.

"I WAS GOING TO DO WHAT MY PARENTS EXPECTED": Id.

"MOLLY'S HIGHEST PRIORITY AS A YOUNGSTER": Lewis F. Powell III, interview.

p. 206 "RULE FOR LFP III": LFP, Sept. 27, 1964.

AWAY FROM HOME FOR A QUARTER OF THE YEAR: Richmond News Leader, Aug. 16, 1965, p. 11.

THEY NEEDED TO BE INTRODUCED: Id.

"WE ARE NOT REALLY VERY PARTICULAR": Lord Denning to LFP, Mar. 26, 1965.

p. 207 LETTER WRITTEN TO LEWIS III: LFP to Lewis F. Powell III, Oct. 13, 1965. This letter, which Powell meant to update from time to time, was never finished.

p. 208 A SECOND LETTER SHOWS POWELL'S TASTE FOR DETAIL: LFP to Michael D. Brittin, Mar. 21, 1972.

ADMONITIONS AGAINST BORROWING MONEY: LFP to Lewis F. Powell III, Mar. 26, 1980.

PROPER ACCOUTREMENTS OF WHITE TIE AND TAILS: LFP to Lewis F. Powell III, Nov. 4, 1981.

p. 209 "IT IS BEST TO HAVE THIS DONE IN NUMERALS THAT REFLECT LIGHT": LFP to Lewis F. Powell III, July 7, 1986.

LESSONS TO "BREAK THE BAD SPEECH HABITS OF EVEN EDUCATED SOUTHERNERS": LFP to Lewis F. Powell III, Feb. 7, 1980.

THE SUMNERS BE ADMITTED TO PRACTICE LAW BEFORE THE SUPREME COURT: New York Times, Nov. 30, 1976, p. 77.

"GOING THROUGH LIFE WITH THE SAME NAME AS A FAMOUS FATHER": Molly Powell Sumner, interview.

"LEWIS DIDN'T TALK BACK": Id.

p. 210 "YOU SHOULD KNOW THAT HIS CONDUCT": Robert E. Scott to LFP, Apr. 16, 1982.

FIRST STATEMENT TO DRAW NATIONAL ATTENTION: LFP, "Crisis in Law Observance," delivered to Conference of National Organizations, Mar. 10, 1964.

"TO PROTECT CITIZENS IN THEIR PERSONS AND PROPERTY": LFP, "A Lawyer Looks at the Crime Problem," Dec. 9, 1964.

"VALID REASONS FOR CRIMINALS TO THINK THAT CRIME DOES PAY": Little Orphan Annie, May 2, 1965.

p. 211 "IT WAS SERIOUSLY ARGUED FOLLOWING BROWN": LFP, "Respect for Law," University of Florida L. Rev. 28:4–5.

"MANY CENTURIES OF HUMAN MISERY": Id.

"FIRST PRIORITY TODAY MUST BE A LIKE CONCERN": LFP, "The State of The Legal Profession," ABA Journal, Sept. 1965, p. 827.

DENOUNCED THE "SMALL AND DEFIANT MINORITY IN THE SOUTH": Id.

CONGRATULATED THE MISSISSIPPI STATE BAR: Clipping from Congressional Record, labeled Sept. 22, 1964.

SPECIAL AWARD TO RICHMOND LAWYER GEORGE E. ALLEN, SR.: Richmond Times-Dispatch, Aug. 10, 1965, p. 1.

POWELL LAID TOO MUCH STRESS ON THE FAULT OF CIVIL RIGHTS DEMONSTRATORS: Erwin Griswold to LFP, Aug. 31, 1965.

p. 212 MESSAGE TO CONGRESS ON MARCH 8, 1965: Reprinted in *New York Times*, Mar. 9, 1965, p. 20.

JOHNSON ASKED POWELL TO CHAIR THE COMMISSION, BUT POWELL REFUSED: Lyndon B. Johnson to LFP, July 7, 1965; LFP to Lyndon B. Johnson, July 9, 1965.

"THERE IS USUALLY A MARKED DIFFERENCE": LFP to Nicholas deB. Katzenbach, July 9, 1965.

p. 213 LEON JAWORSKI SAID HE WOULD DISSENT: *New York Times*, Jan. 20, 1967, pp. 1, 18.

"A MAJORITY OF THE MEMBERS OF THE COMMISSION BELIEVE": *The Challenge of Crime in a Free Society*, 473.

"WEAK AND INEFFECTIVE STANCE": LFP to Henry S. Ruth, Jan. 19, 1967.

LEGISLATION OF THE SORT HE SUPPORTED WAS ENACTED: The Omnibus Crime Control and Safe Streets Act of 1968, now codified at 18 U.S.C. secs. 2510-2520.

p. 214 "DEEPLY CONCERNED ABOUT THE COMMISSION'S REPORT": LFP to Robert G. Storey and Ross L. Malone, Jan. 16, 1967.

"WHICH . . . UNDULY LIMIT REASONABLE LAW ENFORCEMENT ACTIVITIES": LFP to James Vorenberg, Jan. 29, 1967.

MIRANDA V. ARIZONA: 384 U.S. 436 (1966).

"QUESTIONING SUSPECTS IS INDISPENSABLE": *Culombe v. Connecticut*, 367 U.S. 568, 578 (1961).

p. 215 "THE RECOGNITION BY ALL CITIZENS THAT THEY HAVE DUTIES": *Constitution of Virginia*, art. I, sec. 15; A. E. Dick Howard, interview.

UNLIKE IN NEW YORK AND MARYLAND: Howard, *Commentaries on the Constitution of Virginia* I:x.

"ANYTHING THAT WASN'T WALKING ON TWO FEET": Lewis F. Powell III, interview.

p. 216 MCNAMARA'S PACKAGE PROCUREMENT CONCEPT: *New York Times*, July 28, 1970, p. 1.

p. 217 "[I]F THESE OBSERVABLE TRENDS CONTINUE": LFP, "Supplemental Statement," v, xi.

p. 218 "REVIEW THE REPORT IN SOME DETAIL": Henry A. Kissinger to David Packard, Feb. 18, 1971.

"U.S. SUPERIORITY HAS ENDED": *U.S. News & World Report*, Apr. 5, 1971, pp. 49–55.

"MORE NORMAL EMPLOYMENT OF AIR POWER": LFP to Lyndon B. Johnson, June 21, 1966.

"LET US FIGHT THE WAR TO WIN IT": LFP, interview.

ON-AGAIN, OFF-AGAIN APPROACH TO BOMBING: See generally Karnow, *Vietnam*, 504, 565, 642–43; Sharp, *Strategy for Defeat*, 85, 102, 119, 164, 251–58.

p. 219 GEORGE S. BROWN TOLD POWELL: LFP, interview.

"I SAW ENOUGH OF THE WAR": *Id*.

"POLITICAL WARFARE": LFP, "Political Warfare," June 30, 1971; LFP to Gilbert W. Fitzhugh, June 21, 1970.

POWELL RECEIVED A POLITE LETTER: Alexander M. Haig to LFP, Sept. 9, 1970.

p. 220 A PLAINTIVE LETTER: LFP to Richard M. Nixon, June 21, 1971.

CONSIDERED IT "PROFOUNDLY PERCEPTIVE": Richard M. Nixon to author, Mar. 15, 1990.

NEXT TIME POWELL SAW THE PRESIDENT: *Richmond News Leader*, Dec. 23, 1971, p. 24.

CHAPTER VIII: APPOINTMENT

p. 222 "PERHAPS THE MOST PERFECT GENTLEMAN": Frank, *Clement Haynsworth*, xiv.

JOHNSON INVEIGLED ARTHUR GOLDBERG: See Kalman, *Abe Fortas*, 241; Murphy, *Fortas*, 169–70; Shogan, A *Question of Judgment*, 106–108.

EVERYTHING FROM CAMPAIGN FINANCE TO THE DETROIT RIOTS: Kalman, *Abe Fortas*, 306–10.

ADVISED THE PRESIDENT ON VIETNAM: *Id.*, 293–306; Shogan, A *Question of Judgment*, 138 (quoting Townsend Hoopes on Fortas's "curious role . . . as spokesman for those private thoughts of Lyndon Johnson that the President did not wish to express directly").

p. 223 PARTLY KNOWN, OTHERWISE SUSPECTED, AND WIDELY CRITICIZED: See Kalman, *Abe Fortas*, 311–12.

FORTAS RECEIVED $15,000: *Id.*, 351–53; Shogan, A *Question of Judgment*, 178–80.

"THE DECISION SHOULD BE MADE BY THE NEXT PRESIDENT": *Id.*, 154.

"NOTHING ABOUT LAME DUCKS IN THE CONSTITUTION": Quoted *id.*

LATE NOMINATIONS ARE PARTICULARLY VULNERABLE: Of sixteen Supreme Court nominations made during a President's last year in office, nine have been rejected. *Id.*, 151.

p. 224 "A TRIUMPH OF LAWYERLIKE CRAFTSMANSHIP": Graham, "Abe Fortas," in Friedman and Israel, *Justices* IV:3026. See Murphy, *Fortas*, 557–58.

IF WOLFSON'S MONEY WAS PAYMENT FOR FORTAS'S HELP: See Shogan, A *Question of Judgment*, 230–33.

MET PRIVATELY WITH CHIEF JUSTICE EARL WARREN: See Frank, *Clement Haynsworth*, 9–10; Kalman, *Abe Fortas*, 367–70; Shogan, A *Question of Judgment*, 248–49.

MITCHELL'S "BACKSTAIRS CALL": *Newsweek*, May 19, 1969, p. 29.

"CERTAIN INFORMATION KNOWN BY ME": Quoted in Shogan, A *Question of Judgment*, 252.

"FORTAS INDICATED THAT HE WAS SOMEWHAT RESPONSIBLE": Quoted in Frank, *Clement Haynsworth*, 10; cf. Murphy, *Fortas*, 568.

"FOR THE EYES ONLY OF THE CHIEF JUSTICE": Frank, *Clement Haynsworth*, 10.

p. 225 "STILL TOO STUNNED BY THE FORTAS DEBACLE": Shogan, A *Question of Judgment*, 270.

"NOBODY REALIZED": William H. Rehnquist, interview.

DETERMINED OPPOSITION OF ORGANIZED LABOR: See Steele, "Haynsworth *v. the U.S. Senate* (1969)," *Fortune*, Mar. 1970, pp. 92–93.

VOTED FOR MANAGEMENT IN SEVERAL IMPORTANT CASES: See Frank, *Clement Haynsworth*, 19–20 and cases cited therein.

"LAUNDERED SEGREGATIONIST": Steele, "Haynsworth *v. the U.S. Senate* (1969)," *Fortune*, Mar. 1970, 155 (quoting Joseph L. Rauh, Jr.).

FAILED TO APPRECIATE THE NEED FOR STRONG JUDICIAL RESPONSE: See *Griffin v. County School Board*, 323 F.2d 959 (4th Cir. 1963) (according to Joseph Rauh the "one thing that Judge Haynsworth did that more than anything else infuriates the civil rights movement," quoted in Frank, *Clement Haynsworth*, 20).

DECIDED A CASE IN FAVOR OF THE BRUNSWICK CORPORATION: See Frank, *Clement Haynsworth*, 43, 45, 53–55.

THEN-PREVAILING STANDARDS FOR JUDICIAL DISQUALIFICATION: See *Id.*, 40–43.

p. 226 CAROLINA VEND-A-MATIC: See *id.*, 21, 29, 32, 36–38.

"APPEARANCE OF IMPROPRIETY": *Senate Executive Report No. 91-12*, 91st Cong., 1st Sess., Nov. 12, 1969, pp. 25–26.

"THE AMOUNTS INVOLVED": LFP to Sen. William B. Spong, Jr., Nov. 4, 1969.

p. 227 SUPPORT FROM SIXTEEN PAST PRESIDENTS OF THE AMERICAN BAR ASSOCIATION: Telegram to Sen. James O. Eastland, Chairman of the Judiciary Committee, Oct. 23, 1969. (Two past presidents who had been appointed to the bench were not asked.)

VIRGINIA SENATOR WILLIAM B. SPONG, JR.: LFP to William B. Spong, Jr., Nov. 4, 1969.

FELT HE OWED HAYNSWORTH THE SAME HARSH JUDGMENT: Joseph D. Tydings to LFP, Oct. 10, 1969.

"IF IT RESULTED IN YOUR APPOINTMENT, I WOULD BE TREMENDOUSLY PLEASED": Clement F. Haynsworth, Jr., to LFP, Dec. 8, 1969.

POWELL'S NAME WAS BRUITED: *Richmond Times-Dispatch*, Nov. 22, 1969, p. A-10. The Virginia Bar Association passed a resolution endorsing the suggestion.

"HIGH ON A SMALL LIST": LFP, "LFP, Jr.—Nomination to the Supreme Court: Chronology of Nomination," Nov. 28, 1971.

"THERE IS, IN CANDOR, NOTHING IN THE QUALITY OF THE NOMINEE'S WORK": *Hearings on the Nomination of George Harrold Carswell*, 136.

"THERE ARE A LOT OF MEDIOCRE JUDGES": Quoted in Harris, *Decision*, 110.

p. 228 A RACIST: See *id.*, 41–57; Frank, *Clement Haynsworth*, 104–17.

"POLITICAL—IN THE LEAST CREDITABLE SENSE OF THAT WORD": LFP, *Washington and Lee L. Rev.* 39:304.

"SPECIAL KIND OF HERO": Remarks at the Dedication of the Clement F. Haynsworth, Jr., Federal Building, May 3, 1983.

"MINDLESS MISJOINDER": The phrase comes from Powell's foreword to Frank, *Clement Haynsworth*, x.

"A MAN NAMED CARSWELL": Moyers, "In Search of the Constitution," June 25, 1987.

p. 229 NOT MERELY CONGRATULATIONS BUT ADVICE: LFP, inteview. Powell's correspondence suggests that Haynsworth's message may (also?) have been forwarded to Powell through Eppa Hunton IV.

HIS COUSIN HARRY: Frank, *Clement Haynsworth*, 31, 94–95.

"YOU KNOW WHY ALL THOSE LIBERALS ARE FOR POWELL?": William H. Rehnquist, interview. A version of this remark, which may have been made more than once, is quoted in Woodward and Armstrong, *The Brethren*, 162.

"LIVED FOR THE AMERICA THAT WAS DREAMT TO BE": Statement of Nov. 10, 1971, included in letter of the same date.

p. 230 FREDERICK P. BAMBERGER: Frederick P. Bamberger to Whitney North Seymour, Nov. 1, 1971.

p. 231 WORRIED ABOUT THE ALL-WHITE COUNTRY CLUB OF VIRGINIA: Allen C. Goolsby III, interview.

A SCURRILOUS LETTER: *Richmond Afro-American*, Nov. 6, 1971.

"WHEN DO WE LEAVE FOR WASHINGTON?": LFP, interview.

p. 232 LAST-MINUTE CHANGE IN SCHEDULE: The change accommodated the desire of Senators Byrd and Spong to attend the funeral of former Senator Willis Robertson of Virginia. The record does not identify which of these persons did not arrive in time.

"IT IS NOT RECORDED WHETHER A CHOIR OF ANGELS": J. Harvie Wilkinson, Jr., remarks at a testimonial dinner, Dec. 1971. The comment originated with Marshall Jay, "The Right Time for the 'Wrong Kind' of Conservative, *The Alternative*, Jan. 1972, p. 10.

p. 233 THE AMERICAN CIVIL LIBERTIES UNION BROKE A LONG-STANDING TRADITION: Abraham, *Justices and Presidents*, 3d ed., 321.

LETTER EXPLAINING THE ERROR: LFP to Senator Birch E. Bayh, Nov. 12, 1971.

"LADIES": LFP, remarks at testimonial dinner, Dec. 1971; LFP, interview.

"ABSENCE OF ANY DOCUMENTED EVIDENCE OF HIS AFFIRMATIVE ACTION": *Nomination Hearings*, 433 (statement of Wilma Scott Heide).

THE ATTACK WAS LED BY: *Id.*, 366–97.

p. 234 FOLLOWED "HIS OWN SEGREGATIONIST POLICIES": *Id.*, 372, 384, 393.

"EXTENSIVE SCHEME TO DESTROY THE CONSTITUTIONAL RIGHTS": *Id.*, 372.

"A MAN WHO HAS FOR MUCH OF HIS LIFE WAGED WAR ON THE CONSTITUTION": *Id.*, 386, 387.

p. 235 ACTED IN "VERY TURBULENT AND CONFUSED TIMES": *Id.*, 89 (statement of William B. Spong, Jr.).

"I SERVED ON THE RICHMOND CITY SCHOOL BOARD": Statement of Booker T. Bradshaw in the *Richmond Afro-American*, Nov. 6, 1971.

"A MAN WHOSE HEART IS RIGHT": Statement of Oliver W. Hill before the Senate Committee on the Judiciary, undated.

DR. FERGUSON REID: Letter of Dr. Reid to Senators Byrd and Spong, quoted in *Richmond News Leader*, Oct. 27, 1971, p. 15.

"THANK THE GOOD LORD THEY WOULD HAVE HIM ON THE SUPREME COURT": Statement of Armistead L. Boothe to the Senate Judiciary Committee, undated.

p. 236 STATEMENT OF FORMER SCHOOL SUPERINTENDENT: H. I. Willett, "Selected Items Relating to the Service of Lewis F. Powell, Jr., as Chairman of the Richmond City School Board," undated.

AN EXTRAORDINARY LETTER: *Nomination Hearings*, 281–85.

p. 237 A RIGHT OF PRIVACY WOULD BE "A VERY FINE THING": *Id.*, 206.

"I HAVE NEVER BEEN BEFORE A GRAND JURY": *Id.*, 228.

p. 238 LONG EXCHANGE WITH SENATOR EDWARD KENNEDY: *Id.*, 271–74.

"A LAWYER LOOKS AT CIVIL DISOBEDIENCE": LFP, *Washington and Lee L. Rev.* 23:205–31.

REPUBLISHED THESE VIEWS IN LESS SCHOLARLY FORM: LFP, "Civil Disobedience: Prelude to Revolution?," *U.S. News & World Report*, Oct. 30, 1967, pp. 66–69.

p. 239 "CIVIL LIBERTIES REPRESSION: FACT OR FICTION?": *Richmond Times-Dispatch*, Aug. 1, 1971, p. F1, F3; reprinted in *Nomination Hearings*, 213–17.

p. 240 PATTERN OF LAW ENFORCEMENT DIRECTED AGAINST THE LEFT: *Id.*, 269 (remarks of Senator Edward M. Kennedy).

"NEVER SHOWN ANY DEEP FEELINGS FOR LITTLE PEOPLE": Quoted in Abraham, *Justices and Presidents*, 3d ed., 313.

p. 241 THIS PROBLEM WAS SOLVED BY JO'S FRIEND: Mrs. William Biggs, interview; Josephine R. Powell, interview.

"I NEVER THOUGHT I WOULD BE ASKED": *Id.*

WOULD HAVE PLEASED HUGO VERY MUCH: Memorandum from George C. Freeman, Jr., Oct. 22, 1971.

CHAPTER IX: THE SUPREME COURT

p. 245 GRANTED REVIEW IN TEN OF THE 150 CASES: In an additional ten cases, the Court vacated the judgment below and remanded the case to the lower court so that it could be considered further in light of recently announced Supreme Court decisions.

p. 246 "THREE LEVELS OF ELBOW ROOM": Rehnquist, *The Supreme Court*, 288.

p. 247 THE CONFERENCE WAS ANOTHER MATTER: The following discussion is based chiefly on interviews with Justices. Cf. Rehnquist, *The Supreme Court*, 288–303.

p. 248 "A WARM AND CONSIDERATE FRIEND": *Id.*, 256.
THE CASE OF THE STOLEN FOOTNOTES: *Tennessee Valley Authority v. Hill*, 437 U.S. 153 (1978).

p. 249 BOTH FOOTNOTES SHOWED UP: Modified versions of these appear in *Tennessee Valley Authority v. Hill*, 437 U.S. 153, 159 nn. 7 and 8 (1978).
"PISSING CONTEST WITH A SKUNK": Robert D. Comfort, interview.
"PRIVATE FLAG OF GENTLE PROTEST": LFP to Burger, June 13, 1978.

p. 251 REDECORATED THE SUPREME COURT CAFETERIA: Totenberg and Barbash, "Burger Loved the Law But Not the Hassle," *Washington Post*, June 22, 1986, p. C2.

p. 252 WELCOMED HIM TO THE NUMBER-THREE CLUB: *New York Times*, July 25, 1988, p. B6.
"THE REST OF US ARE SO STUPID": William J. Brennan, interview.

p. 253 "MOST OUTSTANDING LAW PROFESSOR IN THE NATION": Douglas, *Go East, Young Man*, 164; Simon, *Independent Journey*, 109.

p. 254 "DARED TO BE DIFFERENT": White, "The Anti-Judge," *Virginia L. Rev.* 74:18.
IN THE FOOTHILLS OF WASHINGTON'S CASCADE MOUNTAINS: Douglas, *Go East, Young Man*, 35.
DICTATE A DISSENT ON THE SAME DAY AS ORAL ARGUMENT: *Remembrances of William O. Douglas*, 4 (remarks of Justice Brennan).
DISAPPOINTED IF OTHERS AGREED WITH HIM: Rehnquist, *The Supreme Court*, 255.

p. 255 ONLY FOUR DAYS A WEEK: Douglas, *The Court Years*, 4.
TOLD POWELL THAT HE WOULD HAVE JOINED POWELL'S DISSENT: Rehnquist, *The Supreme Court*, 255.
"IF EVERY JUSTICE HAD DONE THAT": Simon, *Independent Journey*, 432–33.
RELAXED, LOQUACIOUS, AND CHARMING: *Remembrances of William O. Douglas*, 31 (remarks of William Handler).
NOTE FROM CHINA: The decisions referred to are *San Antonio Independent School District v. Rodriguez*, 411 U.S. 1 (1973), and *In re Griffiths*, 413 U.S. 717 (1973), in both of which Powell wrote the opinion of the Court.
CASHIERED BY TELEPHONE BEFORE HE HAD EVEN MET THE JUSTICE: *Remembrances of William O. Douglas*, 18 (remarks of Fay Deusterman).
FIFTY-TWO WEEKS OF BOOT CAMP: *Id.*, 34 (remarks of Richard L. Jacobson).
"ABSOLUTE TERROR": *Id.*
FEUDED WITH FELIX FRANKFURTER: See generally Urofsky, ed., *The Douglas Letters*.
BARELY SPOKE TO CHIEF JUSTICE WARREN: William J. Brennan, interview.
"SIMPLY BECAUSE HE WAS BLACK": Douglas, *The Court Years*, 251.

p. 256 "NEVER LIKED" MARSHALL: William J. Brennan, interview.

"A REAL SOB": LFP, interview.

"A HELLUVA LOT BETTER SCHOOL": Molly Powell Sumner, interview.

"MOST INFLUENTIAL JUSTICE": Hentoff, "The Constitutionalist," *New Yorker*, Mar. 12, 1990, p. 45 (quoting Professor Burt Neuborne).

"NO INDIVIDUAL IN THIS COUNTRY": Markman and Regnery, "The Mind of Justice Brennan," *National Review*, May 15, 1984, p. 30.

p. 257 OWED MUCH TO CHANCE: See Hentoff, "The Constitutionalist," *New Yorker*, Mar. 12, 1990, pp. 48–52.

p. 258 "NINE SCORPIONS IN A BOTTLE": See Posner, "Tribute," *Harvard L. Rev.* 104:14.

ARRANGED MARRIAGE: *Id.*

"DEBILITATING PERSONAL RIVALRIES": *Id.*

"NEVER HAD A CROSS WORD": Quoted in Hentoff, "The Constitutionalist," *New Yorker*, Mar. 12, 1990, p. 58.

FOUND IT DIFFICULT TO DINE IN PUBLIC: Williams, "The Triumph of Thurgood Marshall," *Washington Post Magazine*, Jan. 7, 1990, p. 16.

p. 259 TELEVISION MINI-SERIES: "Separate But Equal," broadcast by ABC on April 7 and 8, 1991.

"MOST IMPORTANT LAWYER OF THE 20TH CENTURY": Williams, "The Triumph of Thurgood Marshall," *Washington Post Magazine*, Jan. 7, 1990, p. 14 (quoting Professor Thomas G. Krattenmaker).

MASTERFUL TWENTY-YEAR LITIGATION CAMPAIGN: See generally Kluger, *Simple Justice*; Tushnet, *The NAACP's Legal Strategy*.

HE WON TWENTY-NINE: Mackenzie, "Thurgood Marshall," *Justices, 1789–1969*, 3069.

"LIKE MOSES BROUGHT HIS PEOPLE THE TEN COMMANDMENTS": Williams, "The Triumph of Thurgood Marshall," *Washington Post Magazine*, Jan. 7, 1990, p. 17 (quoting Juanita Jackson Mitchell).

VIETNAM WAS "AN EXCUSE": *Id.*, 28 (quoting Justice Marshall).

p. 260 ASTONISHING HEIGHTS: The *Harvard Law Review*'s annual review of voting alignments show that Brennan and Marshall agreed with each other in 100 percent of the cases in the 1984 term and in 98 percent of the cases in the 1986 term, though both figures are slightly inflated by the method of calculation. See *Harvard L. Rev.* 99:323 and *Harvard L. Rev.* 101:363.

"HARRY, HOW DID BRENNAN VOTE?": Harry A. Blackmun, interview.

STOPPED SHORT OF CALLING HIS COLLEAGUES RACIST: See, e.g., Williams, "The Triumph of Thurgood Marshall," *Washington Post Magazine*, Jan. 7, 1990, pp. 28–29.

p. 261 "WHAT DO THEY KNOW ABOUT NEGROES?": *Id.*, 29.

"THERE'S NOT A WHITE MAN IN THIS COUNTRY": *Id.*,

ALSO LEFT AN AFTERTASTE OF REBUKE: *Id.*, 28 (quoting unnamed Justices).

p. 262 "THE NEXT THING I KNEW": Thurgood Marshall, interview.

"MOST CONSISTENT PHILOSOPHY": Tribe, "Justice Stewart," *Yale L.J.* 95:1328.

p. 263 "I FELT PARTICULARLY FREE TO TALK": LFP, interview.

p. 264 "EXCELLED IN EVERYTHING": Quoted in Israel, "Byron R. White," *Justices 1789–1969*, p. 2951.

DESCRIBED AS EVERYTHING: A cluster of inconsistent labels are collected in Lincoln, "Justice Byron White," 14–15.

SPLIT FIVE–FOUR IN TWENTY-ONE DECISIONS: Consolidated cases decided under the same opinion are counted only once.

EIGHT TIMES HE VOTED WITH THE FOUR NIXON APPOINTEES: *Apodaca v. Oregon,* 406 U.S. 404 (1972); *Branzburg v. Hayes,* 408 U.S. 665 (1972); *Gravel v. United States,* 408 U.S. 606 (1972); *Jefferson v. Hackney,* 406 U.S. 535 (1972); *Johnson v. Louisiana,* 406 U.S. 356 (1972); *Laird v. Tatum,* 408 U.S. 1 (1972); *Lloyd Corp. v. Tanner,* 407 U.S. 551 (1972); *Milton v. Wainwright,* 407 U.S. 371 (1972).

SEVEN TIMES HE VOTED WITH THE HOLDOVERS: *Deepsouth Packing Co. v. Laitram,* 406 U.S. 518 (1972); *Furman v. Georgia,* 408 U.S. 238 (1972); *Loper v. Beto,* 405 U.S. 473 (1972); *NLRB v. Burns Security Services,* 406 U.S. 272 (1972); *Strait v. Laird,* 406 U.S. 341 (1972); *Wright v. City of Emporia,* 407 U.S. 451 (1972); *Gelbard v. United States,* 408 U.S. 41 (1972).

"LEADING FROM THE CENTER": O'Donnell, "Leading from the Center," *ABA Journal,* June 15, 1986, p. 24.

p. 265 "IT WOULD TAKE MORE THAN ONE LUNCH TO DO THAT": Jonathan Varat to author, Aug. 18, 1992.

p. 268 "WENT ON HIS QUIET WAY": Greenhouse, "Supremely Sheltered," *New York Times Magazine,* Mar. 7, 1993, p. 84.

p. 270 "WITHIN ARM'S REACH": James Zagami, interview.

p. 273 "DRIVEN NUTS": Nina Totenberg, interview.

TOTENBERG UPBRAIDED POWELL: LFP, interview; Nina Totenberg, interview.

"A LENGTH OF GOLD CARPET": "Burger's Court Is Like King Arthur's," *Washington Post,* July 3, 1971, p. D15.

UNUSUALLY BARE KNUCKLED ATTACK: Shapiro, "Mr. Justice Rehnquist," *Harvard L. Rev.* 90:293–357.

"BECAUSE HE IS SO NICE TO THEM": Josephine R. Powell, interview.

p. 274 "NO MATTER HOW STUPID THE QUESTION": James Latimer, interview.

FINANCIAL DISCLOSURE STATEMENTS: Disclosure was required as of January 1, 1979.

THE *REGISTER* RAN AN EDITORIAL: *Des Moines Register,* June 11, 1980, p. 10A.

FRUSTRATED BY DISTANCE AND THE LACK OF INFORMAL ACCESS: Gilbert Cranberg, interview.

HE ASKED TO SEE THE LIST: Gilbert Cranberg to LFP, July 31, 1980.

POWELL DECLINED: LFP to Gilbert Cranberg, Aug. 12, 1980.

p. 275 "SUPREME COURT SECRECY": *Des Moines Register,* Aug. 28, 1980, p. 14A.

"WE HAVE NOT HEARD THE END": LFP to Sally Smith, Aug. 13, 1980.

"IT IS APPALLING": *Des Moines Register,* Sept. 14, 1980, p. C1.

p. 276 "LAW VIOLATION BY JUSTICES": *Des Moines Register,* Oct. 3, 1980, p. 10A.

ARTICLES IN OTHER PUBLICATIONS: Cranberg, "The High Court's Conflict of Interest Problem," *Nation,* June 13, 1981, pp. 722–25; Cranberg, "A Court of Supreme Secrecy," *ABA Journal,* May 1983, pp. 622–23; Cranberg, "Why all the secrecy at the nation's highest court?" *Bulletin of the American Society of Newspaper Editors,* May–June 1981, pp. 36–37.

"I HAVE SIMPLY THOUGHT IT BEST NOT TO PUBLICLY ANNOUNCE": William H. Rehnquist to Gilbert Cranberg, Nov. 24, 1981.

"IF THESE QUESTIONS WERE ASKED ME": LFP, draft letter to Gilbert Cranberg, Nov. 12, 1981 (not sent).

p. 277 CBS EVENING NEWS: Apr. 29, 1981.

p. 278 A LETTER RECOUNTING THE RESULTS: LFP to Fred Graham, June 3, 1981.

p. 279 "PREPARED TO EAT SOME CROW": Broadcast of June 30, 1981.

CALLED POWELL WITH A PRIVATE APOLOGY: LFP to Burger and Stewart, June 12, 1981.

"BY REMAINING TOTALLY SILENT": *Id.*

"BACKGROUND MEMO" ON DISQUALIFICATIONS: LFP, memorandum of June 15, 1981.

p. 280 FOLLOW-UPS AND A FEW REBUTTALS: See MacKenzie, "Stonewalling at the Court?" *New York Times*, Nov. 6, 1980, p. A34; Yoder, "'Conflicts of Interest' At Court a False Issue," *Washington Star*, June 12, 1981, p. A10; *Wall Street Journal*, Sept. 17, 1980, p. 30.

"THE WEAKEST CONFLICT-OF-INTEREST CASE I'VE EVER HEARD OF": *Omaha World-Herald*, Oct. 2, 1980, p. 10.

SHERLOCK HOLMES STORY: "The Adventure of Silver Blaze."

CHAPTER X: RACE AND THE PUBLIC SCHOOL

p. 282 GREEN V. COUNTY SCHOOL BOARD: 391 U.S. 430 (1968). All points of view agree that *Green* was of enormous consequence. See, e.g., Bell, *Race, Racism and American Law*, 385 (*Green* was considered "as important a victory as was *Brown*"); Graglia, *Disaster by Decree*, 67 (*Green* "worked a revolution in the law of school segregation comparable to, indeed more drastic than, that effected by *Brown*").

p. 283 CHARLOTTE, NORTH CAROLINA: *Swann v. Charlotte-Mecklenburg Board of Education*, 402 U.S. 1 (1971).

MORE THAN HALF THE BLACK ELEMENTARY PUPILS: The Supreme Court's opinion, 402 U.S., 8, states that more than half the black students would have attended schools between 86 and 100 percent black. Another source cites the District Court record for the proposition that the nine elementary schools in question would have been from 83 to 100 percent black. Graglia, *Disaster by Decree*, 108.

BLACK ENROLLMENT AT INDIVIDUAL SCHOOLS WOULD RANGE FROM 9 TO 38 PERCENT: These are the figures given by the Supreme Court, 402 U.S. 9. The record, however, apparently reveals that one aberrational school would have had only 3 percent black enrollment. See Graglia, *Disaster by Decree*, 109 (citing the record).

THE SCHOOL BOARD APPEALED: *Swann v. Charlotte-Mecklenburg Board of Education*, 431 F.2d 138 (4th Cir. 1970).

p. 284 MORE THAN ONE FOURTH OF THE SYSTEM'S CHILDREN RODE BUSES TO SCHOOL: Total enrollment was about 84,000, some 23,600 of whom had been transported by bus in the year before McMillan ordered busing to achieve desegregation. *Swann v. Charlotte-Mecklenburg Board of Education*, 402 U.S. 1, 6, 30 (1971).

"THE ISSUE IS NOT THE BUS": Quoted in McGovern, "Busing: The Issue Is Us," *Integrateducation*, Mar.–Apr. 1976, p. 15.

POWELL WAS ALMOST ASKED TO ARGUE THE CASE: Gaillard, *The Dream Long Deferred*, 88.

p. 286 "TIPPING POINT"—VARIOUSLY ESTIMATED AT 25 TO 50 PERCENT BLACK: Gewirtz, "Remedies and Resistance," *Yale L.J.* 92:630.

POWELL ARGUED, BUSING WAS UNPRODUCTIVE: *Brief of the Commonwealth of Virginia*, 16.

p. 287 CONSIDERATION OF SWANN WAS CONFUSED AND EMBITTERED: These events are reconstructed in Schwartz, *Swann's Way*, 100–84.

CHIEF JUSTICE WARREN'S ASTOUNDING SUCCESS: See Kluger, *Simple Justice*, 683–89.

"DOES NOT MEAN THAT EVERY SCHOOL IN EVERY COMMUNITY MUST ALWAYS REFLECT": *Swann v. Charlotte-Mecklenburg Board of Education*, 402 U.S. 1, 24 (1971).

ONLY "A USEFUL STARTING POINT": *Id.*, 25.

p. 288 BURGER'S REFUSAL TO STAY A LOWER COURT ORDER: *Winston-Salem/Forsyth Board of Education v. Stott*, 404 U.S. 1221 (1971).

SENT COPIES OF HIS STATEMENT MARKED "TO THE PERSONAL ATTENTION": Graglia, *Disaster by Decree*, 140.

TO SHOW THAT POWELL WAS AT HEART A SEGREGATIONIST: *Nomination Hearings*, 384 (statement of Rep. John Conyers, Jr., on behalf of the Congressional Black Caucus); *id.*, 393 (testimony of Henry L. Marsh III).

OPPOSITION TO BUSING PREVAILED IN THE NORTH AND THE SOUTH: The figures are cited in Glazer, *Affirmative Discrimination*, 84. The regional breakdown is instructive. The least hostile region was the East, with 71 percent of respondents against busing, not very different from the 82 percent reported opposed in the South.

p. 289 SUCH QUESTIONS "WOULD HAVE TO BE RESOLVED ON THE FACTS AND IN LIGHT OF THE SUPREME COURT DECISIONS": *Nomination Hearings*, 279.

p. 290 IN 1971 THE DEPARTMENT OF HEALTH, EDUCATION, AND WELFARE REPORTED: Quoted in *Keyes v. School District No. 1*, 413 U.S. 189, 218 n. 3 (1972) (Powell, J., concurring and dissenting).

THE COURT'S OPINION DEFINED THE PROBLEM IN TERMS THAT WERE UNMISTAKABLY, IF NOT INEVITABLY, SOUTHERN: 402 U.S. 1, 5–6 (1971):

This case and those argued with it [cases from Georgia and Alabama] arose in States having a long history of maintaining two sets of schools in a single school system deliberately operated to carry out a governmental policy to separate pupils in schools solely on the basis of race. That was what *Brown v. Board of Education* was all about. These cases present us with the problem of defining in more precise terms than heretofore the scope of the duty of school authorities and district courts in implementing *Brown*. . . .

"NOT BUSING AT ALL": *New York Times*, Apr. 22, 1971, p. 40.

PERHAPS BUSING WOULD NOT BE REQUIRED ELSEWHERE: A regional reading of *Swann* was supported by the Supreme Court's refusal to review lower court decisions finding no duty to desegregate schools outside the South. See *Deal v. Cincinnati Board of Education*, 369 F.2d 55 (6th Cir. 1966), cert. denied, 389 U.S. 847 (1967); *Downs v. Board of Education of Kansas City*, 336 F.2d 988 (10th Cir. 1964), cert. denied, 380 U.S. 914 (1965); *Bell v. School City of Gary, Indiana*, 324 F.2d 209 (7th Cir. 1963), cert. denied, 377 U.S. 924 (1964).

THE FIRST CASE TO TEST THAT ASSUMPTION: *Keyes v. School District No. 1*, 413 U.S. 189 (1973).

EXPRESSLY PROHIBITED THE "CLASSIFICATION OF PUPILS . . . ON ACCOUNT OF RACE OR COLOR": Constitution of Colorado, art. IX, sec. 8.

ADDED UP TO STATE-IMPOSED SEGREGATION IN PARK HILL: These facts are summarized in the opinions of the District Court. See 303 F. Supp. 279, 289 (D. Colo. 1969); 313 F. Supp. 61 (D. Colo. 1970).

p. 291 UNDER GUIDELINES THAT MADE CITYWIDE BUSING ALL BUT INEVITABLE: This conclusion was buried in technicality. Specifically, the Court declared that proof of de jure segregation anywhere in the system created a presumption—technically, a "prima facie case"—of de jure segregation elsewhere in the system. This shifted to the school board the burden of disproving purposeful segregation. The authorities were then required to show not merely that there were other explanations for the segregation, such as housing patterns, but also that the decisions of the school board either did not contribute to the segregation that in fact existed or were not "to any degree" motivated by segregative intent. 413 U.S. 210–22. Predictably, this proof of a negative turned out to be nearly impossible.

DESEGREGATION IN THE NORTH AND WEST WAS FAR FROM UNIFORM: See Wilkinson, *From* Brown *to* Bakke, 199–200.

"AS A LAWYER, I HAVE A DEEP RESPECT FOR PRECEDENT": *Nomination Hearings,* 219.

p. 292 THE CASE WAS ENTITLED: *Keyes v. School District No. 1,* 413 U.S. 189 (1973).

p. 293 AFTER SEVERAL WEEKS OF SILENCE, HARRY BLACKMUN SAID: Harry A. Blackmun to William J. Brennan, Jan. 9, 1973.

PUBLISHED AN ADMIRING ARTICLE ON POWELL'S IDOL: Wilkinson, "Justice John M. Harlan and the Values of Federalism," *Virginia L. Rev.* 57:1185.

"POWELL WAS ALL OVER JAY": William C. Kelly, Jr., interview.

p. 294 WILKINSON RESPONDED WITH A PREARGUMENT MEMORANDUM: The memorandum is undated. Internal evidence suggests that it was written shortly before the case was argued on October 12, 1972.

p. 295 "THERE IS A VAGUE RUMOR FLOATING ABOUT": LFP to Hammond and Kelly, Mar. 13, 1973.

p. 296 "FOR EXAMPLE, BOUNDARIES OF NEIGHBORHOOD ATTENDANCE ZONES SHOULD BE DRAWN TO INTEGRATE": 413 U.S. 240–41 (citations omitted).

"PUBLIC SCHOOLS HAVE BEEN A TRADITIONAL SOURCE OF STRENGTH": 413 U.S. 246.

p. 297 AMERICANS WERE BEING "CUT ADRIFT FROM THE TYPE OF HUMANIZING AUTHORITY": LFP, "Prayer Breakfast Speech to the American Bar Association," Aug. 13, 1972.

TO MANY BLACKS, NEIGHBORHOOD SCHOOLS "MEANT CONFINEMENT": Wilkinson, *From* Brown *to* Bakke, 173.

"I PERSONALLY SUPPORTED BROWN WHEN IT WAS EXTREMELY UNPOPULAR IN VIRGINIA": LFP to J. Harvie Wilkinson III, Jan. 9, 1973.

"TO THE DISMAY OF MANY SOUTHERN CONSERVATIVES": LFP to Larry Hammond and William C. Kelly, Jr., Mar. 13, 1973.

p. 298 "NO ONE CAN ESTIMATE THE EXTENT TO WHICH DISMANTLING NEIGHBORHOOD EDUCATION WILL HASTEN AN EXODUS TO PRIVATE SCHOOLS": 413 U.S. 250.

THE COURTS SHOULD RETURN TO A "MORE BALANCED EVALUATION": *Id.,* 253.

p. 299 THIS, POWELL COMPLAINED, WAS "ACCEPTED COMPLACENTLY": *Id.,* 219 (footnote omitted).

"THE EVIL OF OPERATING SEPARATE SCHOOLS IS NOT LESS IN DENVER THAN IN ATLANTA": *Id.,* 219.

INFECTED BY "CONFEDERATE EMOTION": LFP to J. Harvie Wilkinson III, Sept. 28, 1972.

A "CONSTITUTIONAL PHONY": *Id.*

"BOGUS LEGAL MUMBO JUMBO": J. Harvie Wilkinson III, memorandum on "Denver School Case," undated.

p. 300 AS POWELL EXPLAINED: Quotations in this and the succeeding paragraph are taken from *Keyes v. School District No. 1*, 413 U.S. 189, 219-23 (1972) (Powell, J., concurring in part and dissenting in part).

p. 301 SEGREGATED HOUSING WAS SUPPORTED BY OTHER AGENCIES OF GOVERNMENT: See Taeuber and Taeuber, *Negroes in Cities*, 11–95; Goodman, "De Facto Segregation," *California L. Rev.* 60:275–437.

"LONGSTANDING WHITE FEARS OF BLACK-INVADED NEIGHBORHOODS WORKING THEIR WAY INTO PUBLIC LAW AND POLICY": Wilkinson, *From* Brown *to* Bakke, 142.

THIS ARGUMENT DID NOT OFTEN PREVAIL IN THE COURTS: See, e.g., *Bell v. School City of Gary, Indiana*, 324 F.2d 209 (7th Cir. 1963); *Deal v. Cincinnati Board of Education*, 369 F.2d 55 (6th Cir. 1966); *Downs v. Board of Education of Kansas City*, 336 F.2d 988 (10th Cir. 1964).

"I LOOK AT IT FROM A RATHER COLD STANDPOINT": *Congressional Record, House* 117:39309 (Nov. 4, 1971).

p. 302 "MONUMENTAL HYPOCRISY" OF CONDEMNING SEGREGATION ONLY IN THE SOUTH: *Congressional Record, Senate* 118:3579 (Feb. 24, 1972).

JUSTICE DOUGLAS CIRCULATED A STATEMENT APPROVING COURT-ORDERED DESEGREGATION FOR DE FACTO SCHOOLS: The theory was that the segregated schools in Denver's core city, for which de jure segregation had not been shown, supplied unequal educational opportunity and that court-ordered desegregation was a permissible remedy therefor. A copy of this memorandum appears in the papers of Justice Hugo Black, Box 436, Case Files Nos. 281 and 349, housed in the Library of Congress. The first public mention of this memorandum and a useful analysis of its implications appears in Klarman, "An Interpretive History of Modern Equal Protection," *Michigan L. Rev.* 90:213.

p. 303 HARRY BLACKMUN LATER SAID THAT HE TOO WAS PERSUADED: Harry A. Blackmun to William J. Brennan, May 30, 1973.

BRENNAN RESPONDED THE NEXT DAY: William J. Brennan, Memorandum to the Conference, Apr. 3, 1973.

p. 304 "VERY CONCERNED THAT HIS POSITION BE SEEN ON THE WHOLE AND IN THE ROUND": J. Harvie Wilkinson III, interview.

p. 305 "YOU HAVE TO BE WILLING TO GO IT ALONE": Wilkinson, *Serving Justice*, 76.

p. 306 THE CONSTITUTIONAL GUARANTEE AGAINST RACIAL DISCRIMINATION IS VIOLATED ONLY WHERE THERE IS DISCRIMINATORY PURPOSE: See *Village of Arlington Heights v. Metropolitan Housing Development Corp.*, 429 U.S. 252 (1977); *Washington v. Davis*, 426 U.S. 229 (1976).

THE JUSTICES SOMETIMES QUIBBLED: In 1976–1977, a series of Supreme Court orders required lower courts to reconsider findings of de jure segregation. See *Austin Independent School District v. United States*, 429 U.S. 990 (1976); *United States v. Board of School Commissioners of the City of Indianapolis*, 429 U.S. 1068 (1976); *Brennan v. Armstrong*, 433 U.S. 672 (1977); *School District of Omaha v. United States*, 433 U.S. 667 (1977). The Court wanted to make sure that the findings of de jure segregation were consistent with rulings that violation of the Equal Protection Clause required proof of *intentional* discrimination. See *Washington v. Davis*, 426 U.S. 229 (1976); *Village of Arlington Heights v. Metropolitan Housing Development Corp.*, 429 U.S. 252 (1977).

CASES FROM COLUMBUS AND DAYTON ILLUSTRATE THE APPROACH: *Dayton Board of Education v. Brinkman*, 433 U.S. 406 (1977); *Dayton Board of Education v. Brinkman*, 443 U.S. 526 (1979); *Columbus Board of Education v. Penick*, 443 U.S. 449 (1979).

OHIO HAD OUTLAWED SCHOOL SEGREGATION IN 1888: *Board of Education v. State*, 45 Ohio St. 555 (1888).

p. 307 "I WOULD PARTICULARLY LIKE TO EMPHASIZE": LFP, memorandum to Paul B. Stephan III on "Columbus and Dayton School Cases," June 7, 1979.

HIS PUBLISHED OPINION RESTATED THE POINT: *Columbus Board of Education v. Penick*, 443 U.S. 449, 479 (1979) (Powell, J., dissenting).

p. 308 EACH STAGE IN THE LONG HISTORY OF SCHOOL DESEGREGATION WAS RECAPITU-LATED IN RICHMOND: See generally Leedes and O'Fallon, "School Desegregation in Richmond," *U. Richmond L. Rev.* 10:1.

A TASTE IN CLOTHES THAT MADE HIM "LOOK LIKE A SHERBET FACTORY": Couric, "Judge Robert R. Merhige, Jr.," *National L.J.*, Aug. 4, 1986, p. 21.

WON A FAVORABLE SETTLEMENT: Robert R. Merhige, Jr., interview.

p. 309 POWELL AND OTHERS WENT TO SEE RAMSEY CLARK: *Id.*; LFP, interview.

IN 1971 MERHIGE ORDERED BUSING: *Bradley v. School Board of the City of Richmond*, 325 F. Supp. 828 (E.D. Va. 1971).

MERHIGE'S "APPALLING DECISION": *Richmond Times-Dispatch*, Apr. 7, 1971, p. 12A.

LETTERS TO THE EDITOR MADE THIS DIATRIBE SEEM MILD: *Richmond Times-Dispatch*, Apr. 11, 1971, p. F6, and Apr. 12, 1971, p. 14A.

"THE BUSING ORDERS ACCELERATED THE PERCEIVED AS WELL AS THE ACTUAL DETERIORATION": Leedes and O'Fallon, "School Desegregation in Richmond," *U. Richmond L. Rev.* 10:47.

p. 310 RICHMOND'S SCHOOLS WERE 70 PERCENT BLACK: Amicus Brief of the Commonwealth of Virginia in *Swann v. Charlotte-Mecklenburg Board of Education*, 14.

BLACK ENROLLMENT WAS PROJECTED AT 63 PERCENT: *Bradley v. School Board of the City of Richmond*, 338 F. Supp. 67, 231 (E.D. Va. 1971).

BY THE END OF THE FIRST MONTH OF SCHOOL: *Id.*

BOTH COUNTIES OPPOSED PUBLIC HOUSING: See Leedes and O'Fallon, "School Desegregation in Richmond," *U. Richmond L. Rev.* 10:50–52 and the sources cited therein.

p. 311 MERHIGE ISSUED HIS ORDER: *Bradley v. School Board of the City of Richmond*, 338 F. Supp. 67 (E.D. Va. 1972).

"TIPPING POINT" AT WHICH "WHITE STUDENTS TEND TO DISAPPEAR . . . ENTIRELY": *Id.*, 194.

IN 325 PRINTED PAGES, MERHIGE MADE HIS CASE: This refers to the individual "slip" opinion published by the District Court. See *Bradley v. School Board of the City of Richmond*, 402 F.2d 1058, 1064 (4th Cir. 1972) ("We have searched the 325-page opinion of the district court. . . ."). As reprinted in the double-columned, small-type format of the bound reports, the opinion and appendices occupy "only" 181 pages. *Bradley v. School Board of the City of Richmond*, 338 F. Supp. 67 (E.D. Va. 1971).

THE FOURTH CIRCUIT REVERSED: *Bradley v. School Board of the City of Richmond*, 462 F.2d 1058 (4th Cir. 1972) (en banc).

THERE WAS NO EVIDENCE THAT THEY HAD BEEN DESIGNED FOR THAT PURPOSE:

The Court of Appeals was explicit in this conclusion: "We have searched the 325-page opinion of the district court in vain for the slightest scintilla of evidence that the boundary lines of the three local governmental units have been maintained either long ago or recently for the purpose of perpetuating racial discrimination in the public schools." *Bradley v. School Board of the City of Richmond*, 462 F.2d 1058, 1064 (4th Cir. 1972). In fact, there were some statements in the lower court opinion suggesting interdistrict cooperation, but these were dismissed as so "broad brush" as to be uninformative.

p. 312 "THE JUDGMENT IS AFFIRMED BY AN EQUALLY DIVIDED COURT": *School Board of the City of Richmond v. State Board of Education of the Commonwealth of Virginia*, 412 U.S. 92 (1973).

"AN ALL BLACK SCHOOL SYSTEM SURROUNDED BY PRACTICALLY ALL WHITE SUBURBAN SCHOOL SYSTEMS": *Milliken v. Bradley*, 484 F.2d 215, 245 (6th Cir. 1973).

p. 313 POWELL WROTE THE CHIEF JUSTICE: LFP to Warren E. Burger, June 5, 1974.

BORK FIRST CAME TO NIXON'S ATTENTION AS AN OPPONENT OF BUSING: Caplan, *The Tenth Justice*, 37.

p. 314 THE COURT'S OPINION WAS NOT PERSUASIVE: See, e.g., Lawrence, "Segregation 'Misunderstood,'" *U. of San Francisco L. Rev.* 12:15–56; Gewirtz, "Remedies and Resistance," *Yale L.J.* 92:644–50.

"A GIANT STEP BACKWARDS": *Milliken v. Bradley*, 418 U.S. 717, 782 (1974) (Marshall, J., dissenting).

"THE SAD BUT INEVITABLE CULMINATION OF A NATIONAL ANTI-BLACK STRATEGY": Jones, "An Anti-Black Strategy," *J. of Law and Education* 4:203.

HAPLESS WHITE BOXER WHO FOUND THAT HE COULD RUN BUT COULD NOT HIDE: Bell, "Running and Busing," *id.*, 214.

"ABANDONED THE IDEALS OF *BROWN* AT THE SIGN READING 'CITY LIMITS'": Wright, "Are the Courts Abandoning the Cities?," *id.*, 221.

p. 315 "LEGITIMATED AND ACCELERATED THE NATIONAL TREND TOWARD RESIDENTIAL, POLITICAL, AND EDUCATIONAL APARTHEID": *Id.*, 218.

"WHAT WHITE AMERICANS HAVE NEVER FULLY UNDERSTOOD": National Advisory Commission on Civil Disorders, *Report* 1, quoted in Wilkinson, *From Brown to Bakke*, 224.

"AN ACT OF ABSOLUTION": *Id.*

p. 316 "TODAY'S HOLDING," HE FEARED, "IS MORE A REFLECTION OF A PERCEIVED PUBLIC MOOD": *Milliken v. Bradley*, 418 U.S. 717, 814 (1974) (Marshall, J., dissenting).

"I HAVE A LIFETIME APPOINTMENT": Williams, "The Triumph of Thurgood Marshall," *Washington Post Magazine*, Jan. 7, 1990.

THE TRIAL JUDGE WANTED TO BUS THE DETROIT SUBURBS PRECISELY BECAUSE HE KNEW: Quoted in *Milliken v. Bradley*, 484 F.2d 215, 244 (6th Cir. 1973).

EVEN "NEW AND ENLARGED BOUNDARIES WOULD NOT LONG CONTAIN": Amicus Brief of the Commonwealth of Virginia in *Swann v. Charlotte-Mecklenberg Board of Education*, 17.

A MILLION PUBLIC SCHOOL CHILDREN IN AN AREA THE SIZE OF DELAWARE: *Milliken v. Bradley*, 418 U.S. 717, 729 n. 10 (1974).

p. 317 "CAN CARRY ONLY A LIMITED AMOUNT OF BAGGAGE": *Bradley v. School Board of the City of Richmond*, 462 F.2d 1066 (4th Cir. 1972) (en banc).

WILMINGTON, DELAWARE, AND LOUISVILLE, KENTUCKY: See *Evans v. Buchanan*, 393 F. Supp. 428, 446 (D. Del. 1975); *Newburg Area Council v. Jefferson County Board of Education*, 510 F.2d 1358 (6th Cir. 1974).

EXPERIENCED SUDDEN AND SUBSTANTIAL WHITE FLIGHT: Raffel, *The Politics of Desegregation*, 174–75. See generally Wilkinson, *From* Brown *to* Bakke, 243–45.

p. 318 "A PERENNIALLY DIVISIVE DEBATE OVER WHO IS TO BE TRANSPORTED WHERE": *Keyes v. School District No. 1*, 413 U.S. 189, 250 (1972).

BESET WITH INTERNAL CONTRADICTION: For a contemporary exposition of the inconsistency and contradiction underlying these cases, see Fiss, "School Desegregation: The Uncertain Path of the Law," *Philosophy and Public Affairs* 4:19–31.

p. 319 "DISSENSUS, INCONCLUSIVENESS, INDETERMINACY AND SUBJECTIVITY": Yudof, "School Desegregation," *Law and Contemporary Problems* 42 (no. 4): 73.

MOST ASSESSMENTS WOULD SUPPORT THE FOLLOWING OBSERVATIONS: See Gewirtz, "Remedies and Resistance," *Yale L.J.* 92:628–65; Liebman, "Implementing *Brown*," *Virginia L. Rev.* 76:357–58; Ravitch, "The White Flight Controversy," *Public Interest* 51:137–49; Rossell, "Applied Social Science Research," *J. of Legal Studies* 12:80–94.

AS JAY WILKINSON PUT IT: Wilkinson, *From* Brown *to* Bakke, 213, 215.

p. 320 WHICH BECAME SEPARATE ENTITIES FOR TAX REASONS: See Tushnet, *The NAACP's Legal Strategy Against Segregated Education*, 100.

p. 321 "GREEN FOLLOWS WHITE": Jones, "Is *Brown* Obsolete? No!" *Integrateducation*, May–June 1976, p. 35.

"COURT ORDERS MANDATING RACIAL BALANCE MAY BE (DEPENDING ON THE CIR-CUMSTANCES) ADVANTAGEOUS, IRRELEVANT, OR EVEN *DISADVANTAGEOUS*": Bell, "Serving Two Masters," *Yale L.J.* 85:480 (emphasis in original). Bell's views were rebutted in a letter from Nathaniel R. Jones published in *Yale L.J.* 86:378–82.

NINE BLACK STUDENTS YELLED AT AND SPAT UPON: Wilkinson, *From* Brown *to* Bakke, 90.

135 BLACK STUDENTS TRAPPED BY THE ANGRY WHITE MOB: Buncher, *Facts on File*, 248.

DISCIPLINARY SUSPENSIONS OF BLACK STUDENTS SEEMED UNACCOUNTABLY HIGH: See *Hawkins v. Coleman*, 376 F. Supp. 1330 (N.D. Tex. 1974); Hillson, *The Battle of Boston*, 176, 181.

"AN EDUCATIONAL WASTELAND FOR BLACK CHILDREN": Bell, *Race, Racism and American Law*, 427.

p. 322 THIS PLAN HAD SOME ODD IMPLICATIONS: See *Bradley v. Milliken*, 402 F. Supp. 1096, 1112 (E.D. Mich. 1975). The opinion broke down the systemwide ratio into separate figures for elementary, junior high, and high school students.

MAYOR COLEMAN YOUNG PRAISED THE PLAN: Wentworth, "Detroit Blacks Divided," *Washington Post*, Sept. 2, 1975, p. 1.

"A VERY REASONABLE SOLUTION TO HOW YOU DESEGREGATE A SCHOOL SYSTEM THAT IS PREDOMINANTLY BLACK": *New York Times*, Aug. 17, 1975, p. 1.

NAACP GENERAL COUNSEL NATHANIEL JONES CALLED IT "AN ABOMINATION": *Id.*; additional remarks quoted in Bell, "Serving Two Masters," *Yale L.J.* 85:484.

p. 323 "VIRTUALLY ASSUM[ING] THE ROLE OF SCHOOL SUPERINTENDENT AND SCHOOL BOARD": *Milliken v. Bradley (II)*, 433 U.S. 267, 279 (1977) (Powell, J., concur-ring in the result).

THE COURT WAS UNANIMOUS IN APPROVING THE EDUCATIONAL COMPONENTS: *Milliken v. Bradley (II)*, 433 U.S. 267 (1977).

DISTRICT JUDGE WILLIAM M. TAYLOR, JR., ORDERED DESEGREGATION IN DALLAS: *Tasby v. Estes*, 342 F. Supp. 945 (N.D. Tex. 1971).

AND WAS EVENTUALLY DISAPPROVED BY THE FIFTH CIRCUIT: *Tasby v. Estes*, 517 F.2d 92 (5th Cir. 1975), cert. denied, 423 U.S. 939 (1975).

p. 324 FELL FROM 69 TO 41 PERCENT OF THE TOTAL: *Tasby v. Estes*, 412 F. Supp. 1192, 1197 (N.D. Tex. 1976). Unless otherwise indicated, factual description comes from this opinion.

HE "NEVER FELT WE HAD ANY POTENTIAL FOR VIOLENCE": Trombley, "Dallas," *Integrateducation*, Nov.–Dec. 1977, p. 23.

THE "HEIGHT OF SHORTSIGHTEDNESS": *Id.*, 21.

IN DALLAS THE CONFIGURATION WAS DIFFERENT: The demography and geography of Dallas are described in *Tasby v. Wright*, 520 F. Supp. 683, 690–701 (N.D. Tex. 1981).

p. 325 THE EDUCATIONAL TASK FORCE AGREED ON THE FOLLOWING: See *Tasby v. Estes*, 412 F. Supp. 1192, 1202-1208 (N.D. Tex. 1976).

DALLAS ALREADY HAD ONE HIGHLY SUCCESSFUL MAGNET: The Skyline Career Development Center was thought to be a "model for the nation." Its enrollment in 1975 was substantially integrated. *Id.*, 1205 n. 49

THESE WOULD OFFER SPECIALIZED TRAINING IN: *Id.*, 1192, 1202–1203 nn. 44, 45; Trombley, "Dallas," *Integrateducation*, Nov.–Dec. 1977, p. 23.

p. 326 A TRAINING CENTER DESIGNED TO IMPROVE TEACHERS' "ABILITY TO PERFORM IN A MULTI-CULTURAL SETTING": *Tasby v. Estes*, 412 F. Supp. 1192, 1203 (N.D. Tex. 1976).

A COMMUNITY CAMPAIGN TO DEFUSE OPPOSITION TO BUSING: The facts in this paragraph are taken from Trombley, "Dallas," *Integrateducation*, Nov.–Dec. 1977, pp. 22–23.

p. 327 "[I]F THE KIDS GET THE SKILLS AND THE KNOWLEDGE THEY NEED, THEY WILL DESEGREGATE THE SOCIETY": *Id.*

POWELL'S FIRST REACTION: His handwritten comment on the cert pool memo reads in part: "Dallas school case in which CA5 [the Court of Appeals for the Fifth Circuit]—as usual—reversed a DC's [District Court's] desegregation order as not going far enough. CA5's remand for further findings, especially w/ respect to one race schools makes this case a marginal one to review."

THE 31 PERCENT DROP IN WHITE ENROLLMENT IN LOS ANGELES: Gustaitis, "Riding L.A.'s Troubled School Buses," *Washington Post*, June 10, 1979, p. D2. Powell's files also contained an article from the *Washington Star*, Sept. 21, 1980, on past and future white flight in Los Angeles.

THE 40 PERCENT DECLINE IN WHITE ENROLLMENT: *Washington Post*, Dec. 17, 1978, p. A29.

THE "UNHAPPY PARENTS NATIONWIDE" WHO WERE TURNING TO PRIVATE SCHOOL: *Washington Post*, May 28, 1979, p. A14.

"IT IS NOT THE CASE THAT SCHOOL DESEGREGATION": Coleman, "School Desegregation and City-Suburban Relations," (unpublished speech); Coleman, "Beneficial Desegregation *v.* Destructive Desegregation," *Washington Post*, Dec. 8, 1978, p. A19.

"THIS ISN'T INTEGRATION—IT LOOKS LIKE OUTEGRATION TO ME": *Washington Post*, Dec. 26, 1979, p. A3.

p. 328 "A SERIOUS AND COMPREHENSIVE EFFORT TO DEAL FAIRLY, EFFECTIVELY, AND CON-

STRUCTIVELY": Draft opinion dissenting from the denial of the petition for a writ of certiorari in *Estes v. Dallas* (2d draft, Jan. 1979).

ONLY HE, BURGER, AND REHNQUIST VOTED TO HEAR THE CASE: The petition for certiorari first came up for consideration at the conference of November 10, 1978, but was relisted without a vote being taken. The first vote was recorded at the conference of November 22, 1978.

p. 329 "SINCE LEWIS HAS A STRONG DESIRE TO WRITE HIS VIEWS," HE WROTE, "I WILL CHANGE MY VOTE": Warren E. Burger, Memorandum to the Conference, Nov. 2, 1979.

ANGLO ENROLLMENT, WHICH HAD BEEN 41 PERCENT IN 1975, HAD DROPPED: *Tasby v. Wright*, 520 F. Supp. 683, 693, 695 (N.D. Tex. 1981).

THE BLACK COALITION TO MAXIMIZE EDUCATION: This umbrella organization included such groups as the Dallas Black Chamber of Commercial, the Dallas Council of Black Parents and Citizens, the Dallas Ministerial Alliance, and the Dallas Urban League. The composition and role of this organization are described in detail in *Tasby v. Wright*, 520 F. Supp. 683, 689–90 (N.D. Tex. 1981).

"ADDITIONAL SYSTEMWIDE TRANSPORTATION IS NOT A FEASIBLE REMEDY": *Id.*, 686.

p. 330 "THE PEOPLE WHO WANTED BUSING IN 1976 NO LONGER WANT IT TODAY": E. Brice Cunningham, interview.

SOME SAY THAT THE TOLERANCE OF DELAY WAS A MISTAKE FROM THE OUTSET: Carter, "The Warren Court and Desegregation," *Michigan L. Rev.* 67:243–45; Black, "The Unfinished Business of the Warren Court," *Washington and Lee L. Rev.* 46:22.

IN 1958 AND AGAIN IN 1964, THE COURT FACED DOWN OUTRIGHT DEFIANCE: *Cooper v. Aaron*, 358 U.S.1 (1958) (rejecting the claim by Arkansas officials that they were not "bound" by the decision in *Brown*); *Griffin v. County School Board of Prince Edward County*, 377 U.S. 218 (1964) (rejecting the county's "massive resistance" strategy of closing its schools).

p. 331 IN SOME CITIES BUSING WORKED: The best account of busing's success is Liebman, "Desegregating Politics" *Columbia L. Rev.* 90:1466–67.

CHAPTER XI: ABORTION

p. 332 A PAIR OF CASES INVOLVING ABORTION: *Roe v. Wade*, 410 U.S. 113 (1973), and *Doe v. Bolton*, 410 U.S. 179 (1973). The personal background of the plaintiffs is taken from Tribe, *Abortion*, 4–6. See also Weddington, A *Question of Choice*.

ANTIABORTION LITIGATION SPRANG UP AROUND THE NATION: On the pre-*Roe* history of this litigation, see Garrow, *Liberty and Sexuality*.

p. 333 THE SUPREME COURT HAD REJECTED A CONSTITUTIONAL ATTACK ON THE WASHINGTON, D.C., ABORTION STATUTE: *United States v. Vuitch*, 402 U.S. 62 (1971).

THEN SOMETHING HAPPENED: These events are reported in Woodward and Armstrong, *The Brethren*, 165–75, and in Schwartz, *Unpublished Opinions*, 83–93.

MAY HAVE BEEN FAIRLY LIMITED: The possibility is suggested by Douglas's Conference notes (Douglas Papers, Box 1589, Case File O.T. 1972, Folder 5), which concluded: "In summary—WOD, WJB, PS & TM agreed that a state abortion law could require all abortions to be performed by a licensed physician, that a woman's psychological problems as well as her health problems must be considered, and that some period must be proscribed [?] protecting fetal life."

"WHICH, I MIGHT ADD, ARE QUITE PROBABLE CANDIDATES FOR REARGUMENT": Warren E. Burger to William O. Douglas, Dec. 20, 1971.

CONSPIRACY THEORIES ABOUNDED: These suspicions are retailed in Woodward and Armstrong, *The Brethren*, 172.

p. 334 HIS FIRST ASSIGNMENT FOR THE COURT WAS A CORPORATE TAX OPINION: *Commissioner of Internal Revenue v. First Security Bank*, 405 U.S. 394 (1972).

WHETHER ILLEGITIMATE CHILDREN COULD BE EXCLUDED FROM THEIR FATHER'S DEATH BENEFITS: *Weber v. Aetna Casualty and Surety Co.*, 406 U.S. 164 (1972).

WHETHER JURY VERDICTS HAD TO BE UNANIMOUS: *Johnson v. Louisiana*, 406 U.S. 356, 366 (1972) (Powell, J., concurring); *Apodoca v. Oregon*, 406 U.S. 404, 414 (1972) (Powell, J., concurring in the result).

WHETHER THE ORDINARY RULES FOR SEARCH AND SEIZURE APPLIED IN DOMESTIC SECURITY CASES: *United States v. United States District Court*, 407 U.S. 297 (1972).

WHETHER THE RIGHT OF FREE SPEECH APPLIED IN A PRIVATELY OWNED SHOPPING CENTER: *Lloyd Corp. v. Tanner*, 407 U.S. 551 (1972); cf. *Central Hardware Co. v. National Labor Relations Board*, 407 U.S. 539 (1972).

WHETHER A STATE COLLEGE COULD DENY OFFICIAL RECOGNITION TO THE LOCAL CHAPTER OF THE RADICAL SDS: *Healy v. James*, 408 U.S. 169 (1972).

WHETHER REPORTERS HAVE A CONSTITUTIONAL RIGHT TO REFUSE TO ANSWER: *Branzburg v. Hayes*, 408 U.S. 665, 709 (1972) (Powell, J., concurring).

HE ALSO WROTE IN CASES INVOLVING: *International Union v. Flair Builders, Inc.*, 406 U.S. 487, 492 (1972) (Powell, J., dissenting) (labor arbitration); *Lake Carriers' Association v. MacMullan*, 406 U.S. 498, 513 (1972) (Powell, J., dissenting) (exercise of federal jurisdiction); *First National City Bank v. Banco Nacional de Cuba*, 406 U.S. 759, 773 (1972) (Powell, J., concurring in the result) (Powell, J., international law); *Argersinger v. Hamlin*, 407 U.S. 25, 44 (1972) (Powell, J., concurring in the result); *James v. Strange*, 407 U.S. 128 (1972) (equal protection); *Barker v. Wingo*, 407 U.S. 514 (1972) (speedy trial); *United States v. Byrum*, 408 U.S. 125 (1972) (estate tax).

WHETHER CONVICTED MURDERERS COULD BE PUT TO DEATH: *Furman v. Georgia*, 408 U.S. 238, 375 (1972) (Powell, J., dissenting).

p. 335 THAT SPRING POWELL CALLED FORMER ABA PRESIDENT CHARLES RHYNE: LFP, interview.

p. 336 BLACKMUN CIRCULATED A DRAFT OPINION: Reprinted in Schwartz, *Unpublished Opinions*, 103–19.

A DRAFT OPINION IN THE GEORGIA CASE: See *id.*, 120–40.

p. 337 THEY URGED HIM TO CONDEMN ALL REGULATION OF ABORTION: William J. Brennan to Harry A. Blackmun, May 18, 1972; William O. Douglas to Harry A. Blackmun, May 19, 1972. The phrase quoted in the text appears in both letters.

"BE HELD INVALID IN FULL": A copy of this undated letter, with the notation in Douglas's hand "WJB's memo to Blackmun in May, 1972," appears in the Douglas papers in the Library of Congress, Box 1589, Case File O.T. 1972, Folder 6.

"THIS IS AS SENSITIVE AND DIFFICULT AN ISSUE": Warren E. Burger, Memorandum to the Conference, May 31, 1972.

"I WILL BE GOD-DAMNED!": Douglas Papers, Box 1589, Case File O.T. 1972, Folder 5.

BLACKMUN HIMSELF NOW ASKED: Harry A. Blackmun, Memorandum to the Conference, May 31, 1972.

"I WILL FILE A STATEMENT TELLING WHAT IS HAPPENING TO US": William O. Douglas to Warren E. Burger, June 1, 1972.

p. 338 TRULY SHOCKING: The version quoted in text is the first draft, which was circulated to Justice Brennan on June 2. See Douglas papers, Box 1588, Case File O.T. 1972, Folder 2. It differs in several respects from the sixth draft, circulated to all Justices on June 13. The most curious change is the introduction into the later version of the inexplicable and plainly false statement that the senior member of the majority "in this case was not myself."

"I HAVE BEEN ON THE COURT FOR MORE THAN HALF A TERM": LFP, Memorandum to the Conference, June 1, 1972.

p. 339 FIRST BRENNAN AND THEN BLACKMUN: See Woodward and Armstrong, *The Brethren*, 188–89.

WHAT BLACKMUN PRODUCED: The opinion, labeled "2nd draft" was circulated on Nov. 21, 1972, with a cover memo indicating that this was the first version seen by other chambers.

"WE WOULD NOT NORMALLY EXPECT THE COURT TO CONSIDER THE TEACHINGS OF CHRISTIANITY AND PAGANISM": "Abortion and the Court," *Christianity Today*, Feb. 16, 1973, p. 32.

DID NOT SHOW A TRADITION IN FAVOR OF ABORTION: Cf. Epstein, "Substantive Due Process by Any Other Name," *Supreme Court Rev.* 1973: 182 ("His exhaustive history of the abortion question indicates quite clearly that there is no consensus on the question. . . .").

p. 340 SPOUSAL RAPE OR THE USE OF OPIATES: On the historic legality of rape by a husband of his wife, see Estrich, *Real Rape*, 72–79. In most states, the so-called spousal exemption continued into the 1970s. On the history of the prohibition of opiates (which began in this country early in this century), see Pellens and Terry, *The Opium Problem*, 745; Teff, *Drugs, Society and the Law*, 60.

TO RECHARACTERIZE ROE: *Akron v. Akron Center for Reproductive Health, Inc.*, 462 U.S. 416, 419 (1983).

FETUSES WERE NOT PERSONS: Woodward and Armstrong, *The Brethren*, 233, state incorrectly that this point was introduced at Stewart's insistence later in the process, but the discussion appears, fully developed, in Blackmun's circulation of Nov. 22.

p. 341 "I HAVE CONCLUDED THAT THE END OF THE FIRST TRIMESTER IS CRITICAL": Harry A. Blackmun, Memorandum to the Conference, Nov. 21, 1972.

p. 342 POWELL QUOTED JUDGE JON O. NEWMAN: *Abele v. Markel*, 351 F. Supp. 224, 232 (D. Conn. 1972) (three-judge court).

BLACKMUN RESPONDED PRIVATELY TO POWELL AND SHORTLY THEREAFTER PUT THE ISSUE TO THEIR COLLEAGUES: Harry A. Blackmun to LFP, Dec. 4, 1972; Harry A. Blackmun, Memorandum to the Conference, Dec. 11, 1972. In Schwartz, *Unpublished Opinions*, 149, it is reported that this issue was first raised by Marshall in a letter dated Dec. 12, 1972. As neither Powell's letter of Nov. 29 nor Blackmun's response was circulated to the Conference, no copies appeared in the files to which Schwartz had access. The account in Woodward and Armstrong, *The Brethren*, 231, to the effect that Blackmun's original circulation focused on viability, is inaccurate.

p. 343 DOUGLAS AT ONCE ANSWERED: William O. Douglas to Harry A. Blackmun, Dec. 11, 1972.

MARSHALL HAD THE SAME THOUGHT: Thurgood Marshall to Harry A. Blackmun, Dec. 12, 972.

BLACKMUN AGREED: Harry A. Blackmun, Memorandum to the Conference, Dec. 15, 1972.

THE OPINION, MANY NOTED, READ LIKE A "MODEL STATUTE": This often-quoted remark is a simplication of Alexander Bickel's comment that *Roe* "may be a wise model statute," but that it lacked justification as a matter of constitutional law. Bickel, *The Morality of Consent*, 27.

"LAST WEEK TIME LEARNED": *Time*, Jan. 29, 1973, p. 46.

p. 344 BURGER, WHO WAS OUTRAGED: This story is based chiefly on interviews with Larry Hammond and Powell. A version from some other source appears in Woodward and Armstrong, *The Brethren*, 237–38.

THE CHIEF'S SENSIBILITIES HAD ALREADY BEEN RUBBED RAW: *Washington Post*, July 4, 1972.

DOUGLAS WROTE FROM GOOSE PRAIRIE: William O. Douglas to Warren E. Burger, July 4, 1972, Douglas Papers, Box 1588, Case File O.T. 1972, Folder 2.

p. 345 MORAL EQUIVALENT OF WIRETAPPING: Woodward and Armstrong, *The Brethren*, 238.

p. 346 "FELT HE WOULD JUST HAVE TO VOTE HIS 'GUT'": *Id.*, 230.

A WELL-EDUCATED, NON-CATHOLIC, UPPER-CLASS MALE: See Blake, "Abortion and Public Opinion," *Science*, Feb. 12, 1971, p. 548. ("Legalized abortion is supported most strongly by the non-Catholic, male, well-educated 'establishment.'")

p. 348 NOTHING IN THE USUAL SOURCES OF LEGAL REASONING TO SUGGEST THAT ABORTION WAS A CONSTITUTIONAL RIGHT: See Ely, "The Wages of Crying Wolf," *Yale L.J.* 82:920–49; Epstein, "Substantive Due Process by Any Other Name," *Supreme Court Rev.* 1973: 159–83.

1965 DECISION: *Griswold v. Connecticut*, 381 U.S. 479 (1965). See also *Eisenstadt v. Baird*, 405 U.S. 438 (1972) (strongly suggesting that the right to contraceptives also applied outside marriage).

RIGHTS . . . WITH NO CLEAR BASIS: See *Aptheker v. Secretary of State*, 378 U.S. 500 (1964) (declaring a right to travel); *Meyer v. Nebraska*, 262 U.S. 390 (1923) (striking down a law barring instruction in German); *Pierce v. Society of Sisters*, 268 U.S. 510 (1925) (striking down a law requiring children to attend public school).

p. 349 "I BELIEVE . . . IN THE IMPORTANCE OF JUDICIAL RESTRAINT": *Nomination Hearings*, 219.

"THE CONSTITUTION IS A DOCUMENT OF SPECIFIED WORDS AND CONSTRUCTION": *Blackmun Nomination Hearings*, 33.

TRADITION OF JOHN HARLAN: Among the best appreciations of Harlan are essays by J. Harvie Wilkinson III, who, when he became a judge, consciously placed himself in that tradition. See Wilkinson, "Justice John M. Harlan and the Values of Federalism," *Virginia L. Rev.* 57:1185–1221; Wilkinson, "The Role of Reason in the Rule of Law," *University of Chicago L. Rev.* 56:779–809.

p. 350 BICKEL IDENTIFIED THE SAME ASSUMPTION: Bickel, *The Supreme Court and the Idea of Progress*, 11, 13–14. The paraphrase is from Sir Lewis Namier.

p. 351 "AN UNCOMMONLY SILLY LAW": *Griswold v. Connecticut*, 381 U.S. 479, 527 (1965) (Stewart, J., dissenting). Stewart made this remark in a dissent arguing that an uncommonly silly "or even asinine" law was not for that reason unconstitutional.

"[T]HE CATHOLIC HIERARCHY MAY HAVE MADE ABORTION ITS LAST STAND: Alexander, "The Politics of Abortion," *Newsweek*, Oct. 2, 1972, p. 29.

p. 352 REQUIRING A MARRIED WOMAN TO HAVE THE CONSENT OF HER HUSBAND OR AN UNDERAGE GIRL TO HAVE THE CONSENT OF HER PARENTS: *Planned Parenthood v. Danforth*, 428 U.S. 52 (1976); *Bellotti v. Baird*, 443 U.S. 622 (1979). *Planned Parenthood v. Ashcroft*, 462 U.S. 476 (1983), approved a parental consent requirement, but only with the alternative of judicial approval despite parental opposition if the minor was sufficiently mature to understand the nature of the act.

REJECTING VARIOUS OTHER ATTEMPTS TO MAKE ABORTION DIFFICULT: See, e.g., *Planned Parenthood v. Danforth*, 428 U.S. 52 (1976); *Akron v. Akron Center for Reproductive Health*, 462 U.S. 416 (1983); *Planned Parenthood v. Ashcroft*, 462 U.S. 476 (1983); *Thornburgh v. American College of Obstretricians and Gynecologists*, 476 U.S. 747 (1986).

REQUIRING THAT AN UNMARRIED MINOR NOTIFY HER PARENTS: *H.L. v. Matheson*, 450 U.S. 398 (1981).

COMPEL GOVERNMENT FUNDING: *Beal v. Doe*, 432 U.S. 438 (1977); *Maher v. Roe*, 432 U.S. 464 (1977); *Poelker v. Doe*, 432 U.S. 519 (1977); *Harris v. McRae*, 448 U.S. 297 (1980); *Williams v. Zbaraz*, 448 U.S. 358 (1980).

p. 353 WEBSTER V. REPRODUCTIVE HEALTH SERVICES: 492 U.S. 490 (1989).

"PROFOUND AND UNNECESSARY DAMAGE TO THE COURT'S LEGITIMACY": 112 S. Ct. 2791, (1992).

ABOUT 1.6 MILLION A YEAR: "America's New Civil War," *U.S. News & World Report*, Oct. 3, 1988, p. 24.

p. 354 THE GALLUP POLL REPORTED: Gallup and Newport, "Americans Shift Toward Pro-Choice Position," *The Gallup Poll Monthly*, Apr. 1990, pp. 2–4.

THE CELEBRATE LIFE COMMITTEE OF LONG ISLAND: *Nomination Hearings*, 473–82. Other groups included the L.I.F.E. Committee of New York, and the Right to Life Committees from Brooklyn, Long Island, and Westchester County.

MOST NON-CATHOLIC ACTIVISTS DATE THEIR INVOLVEMENT: See, e.g., Ginsburg, *Contested Lives*, 43–57; Luker, *Abortion and the Politics of Motherhood*, 126–57.

p. 355 "THE EMBRYO WAS A HUMAN LIFE AS VALUABLE AS ANY": *Id.*, 140–41.

"MANY MISTOOK A CENTURY OF SILENCE": *Id.*, 140.

NO CLEARLY DEFINED POSITION AGAINST ABORTION: *Id.*, 99–101.

LEANED TOWARD FREEDOM OF CHOICE: See Spitzer and Saylor, *Birth Control and the Christian*, xxiii–xxxi.

p. 356 SHOWED THE SAME DIVIDED VIEWS: Fowler, *Abortion: Toward an Evangelical Consensus*, 70–71. See generally Stafford, "The Abortion Wars," *Christianity Today*, Oct. 6, 1989, pp. 16–20.

SCHOLARS RECANTED: Compare the views expressed by Dr. Bruce Waltke in 1969, see Spitzer and Saylor, *Birth Control and the Christian*, 10–11, with the quite different opinions voiced in Waltke, "Reflections from the Old Testament on Abortion," *Journal of the Evangelical Theological Society* 19:3–13. Also compare Geisler, *Ethics*, 218–27, published in 1971, with Geisler, "The Bible, Abortion, and Common Sense," *Fundamentalist Journal*, May 1985, p. 25.

C. EVERETT KOOP: See Koop, *The Right to Live*, 13–15. Koop collaborated with Francis A. Schaeffer on a film series, later reprised in a book of the same title, *Whatever Happened to the Human Race?*

FIFTY-NINE OF NINETY-NINE DENOMINATIONS: Fowler, *Abortion: Toward an Evangelical Consensus*, 75 n. 24.

THE RETREAT FROM CHOICE HAS CONTINUED: In 1988 the American Baptist Churches (formerly the American Baptist Convention), abandoned its long-standing pro-choice position in favor of neutrality. The United Methodist Church similarly moderated its pro-choice position. See *Time*, July 4, 1988, p. 44. See generally Ellingsen, "The Church and Abortion: Signs of Consensus," *Christian Century*, Jan. 3–10, 1990, pp. 12–15.

THE 1968 PRESIDENTIAL CAMPAIGN: See, e.g., "How the Candidates Differ on Issues," *Newsweek*, Nov. 4, 1968, p. 37; "Campaign Fighting Starts—and the Issues Sharpen," *U.S. News & World Report*, Sept. 23, 1968, pp. 36–37. Even an essay entitled "Those Little-Discussed Campaign Issues," *Time*, Oct. 25, 1968, pp. 38–39, did not mention abortion.

INFLATION, VIETNAM, DRUGS, CRIME, POVERTY, AND BUSING: See "The Big Campaign Issues—As Voters Rank Them," *U.S. News & World Report*, Sept. 4, 1972, pp. 24–26.

NOT MENTIONED IN INTERVIEWS WITH THE DEMOCRATIC NOMINEE: See, e.g., "How McGovern Sees the Issues," *U.S. News & World Report*, Aug. 7, 1972, pp. 18–22.

"HOW MR. NIXON WOOS THE DEMOCRATS": *Newsweek*, Oct. 2, 1972, pp. 15–17.

ONLY GLORIA STEINEM . . . SPOKE OF ABORTION: "The Real Issues of '72," *Newsweek*, July 10, 1972, pp. 21–37.

RELEGATED TO A LIST OF SUCH "OFF-BEAT" QUESTIONS: "The Yeas and Nays on Off-Beat Issues," *U.S. News & World Report*, Nov. 20, 1972, p. 50.

p. 357 "SET OF UNMISTAKABLY CONSERVATIVE SEXUAL VALUES": Petchesky, *Abortion and Woman's Choice*, 263.

"GOD DID NOT ORDAIN SEX FOR FUN AND GAMES": Quoted *id.*, 263.

"THE NEW ACTIVISTS WERE PEOPLE WHO HAD DIRECT EXPERIENCES WITH PREGNANCY": Luker, *Abortion and the Politics of Motherhood*, 145.

p. 358 EMPIRICAL RESEARCH: Sabato, *The 1988 Elections in America*, 33–34; *Christianity Today*, Jan. 18, 1985, p. 41.

"AMERICA'S NEW CIVIL WAR": *U.S. News & World Report*, Oct. 3, 1988, cover and pp. 23–31.

p. 359 OWEN J. ROBERTS: See, e.g., Wright, *The Growth of American Constitutional Law*, 202. The phrase concerns Roberts's apparent change of direction in *West Coast Hotel v. Parrish*, 300 U.S. 379 (1937), but internal documents show that his vote was cast before the Court-packing plan was announced.

"THE CONSTITUTION IS THE SUPREME LAW OF THE LAND": *United States v. Butler*, 297 U.S. 1, 62 (1936).

p. 361 "SIMPLY SAYS NOTHING, CLEAR OR FUZZY, ABOUT ABORTION": Ely, "The Wages of Crying Wolf," *Yale L.J.* 82:97.

p. 362 RENEWED ATTENTION TO THE MORAL REQUIREMENTS OF A JUST SOCIETY: See, e.g., Grey, "Do We Have an Unwritten Constitution?," *Stanford L. Rev.* 27:703–18. Grey originated the now-common distinction between "interpretivists" and "non-interpretivists" among constitutional law scholars, but has since suggested that the issue is more accurately described as a split between "textualists" and "supplementers." Grey, "The Constitution as Scripture," *Stanford L. Rev.* 37:1–25. See also Perry, *The Constitution, the Courts, and Human Rights,* and the substantial commentary thereon published in "Judiciary Review and the Constitution—The Text and Beyond," *University of Dayton L. Rev.,* and Wiseman, "The New Supreme Court Commentators," *Hastings Constitutional L.Q.* 10:315–431.

p. 363 DECISIONS STRIKING DOWN GOVERNMENT REGULATION OF THE ECONOMY: The most famous, which gave its name to the entire era, was *Lochner v. New York,* 198 U.S. 45 (1905).

885 LAW PROFESSORS WHO ASSERTED: *Brief for a Group of American Law Professors as Amicus Curiae* in *Webster v. Reproductive Health Services,* 492 U.S. 490 (1989).

AT FIRST HE ARGUED: Tribe, "Foreword," *Harvard L. Rev.* 87:1–53.

THE SURPRISING CLAIM: Tribe, "Structural Due Process," *Harvard Civil Rights–Civil Liberties L. Rev.* 10:269–321; Tribe, "Childhood, Suspect Classifications, and Conclusive Presumptions," *Law and Contemporary Problems* 39:8–37.

IN AN INFLUENTIAL TREATISE, HE ARGUES: Tribe, *American Constitutional Law,* 2d ed., 1353–56. See also Tribe, *Constitutional Choices,* 243–45.

p. 364 GENDER-EQUALITY ARGUMENT IS PLAINLY DOMINANT: *North Carolina L. Rev.* 63:375–86; Law, "Rethinking Sex and the Constitution," *University of Pennsylvania L. Rev.* 132:1020, 1028.

MADE CONCILIATORY NOISES ABOUT THE NEED FOR POLITICAL COMPROMISE: Tribe, *Abortion,* 197–228. Critics suggested that the search was neither serious nor sincere. See McConnell, "How Not To Promote Serious Deliberation About Abortion," *University of Chicago L. Rev.* 58:1181–1202.

PREOCCUPATION OF MODERN CONSTITUTIONAL SCHOLARSHIP WITH THE JUSTIFICATION OF ROE: In addition to the articles already cited, see Henkin, "Privacy and Autonomy," *Columbia L. Rev.* 74:1410–33; Heymann and Barzelay, "The Forest and the Trees," *Boston University L. Rev.* 53:765–84; Regan, "Rewriting *Roe v. Wade,*" *Michigan L. Rev.* 77:1569–1646.

OFTEN BEEN REMARKED: See especially Note, "The Changing Social Vision of Justice Blackmun," *Harvard L. Rev.* 96:717.

p. 365 BLACKMUN DISAGREED WITH BURGER IN ONLY ONE CASE IN TEN: This and other figures of aggregate annual disagreement among Justices come from the statistical abstracts published annually by the *Harvard Law Review* as part of its survey of the past year's work of the Supreme Court. Figures showing the rates of disagreement for two or more years are simple averages of the annual percentages reported by the *Review.*

"SEEMS TO KNOW THE RIGHT WAY TO GO": Transcript of Blackmun's Remarks to the Eighth Circuit Judicial Conference, *New York Times,* July 25, 1986.

p. 366 "HE TOLD HIM TO GIVE UP CAKE": Velvel, "Zeus Didn't Nod," *National L.J.,* Oct. 6, 1986, p. 13.

THE ABORTION FUNDING CASES: *Beal v. Doe,* 432 U.S. 438 (1977); *Maher v. Roe,* 432 U.S. 464 (1977); *Poelker v. Doe,* 432 U.S. 519 (1977).

IN SUPPORT OF THE DWINDLING LIBERAL MINORITY ON AN INCREASINGLY CONSERV-
ATIVE COURT: Examples include the school desegregation cases, where
Blackmun voted with Burger through the early 1970s, including *Millken v.
Bradley*, 418 U.S. 717 (1974), which struck down interdistrict busing. By the
late 1970s, Blackmun was changing direction. See *Dayton Board of Education
v. Brinkman*, 443 U.S. 526 (1979); *Washington v. Seattle School District*, 458
U.S. 457 (1982); *United States v. Spallone*, 493 U.S. 265, 281 (1990); *Missouri
v. Jenkins*, 495 U.S. 33, 36 (1990).

There was also a shift in Blackmun's willingness to protect vulgar or
extreme expression under the First Amendment, though this generalization
comprehends too many cases to be strictly true or false and does not take
account of the important area of obscenity, where Blackmun remained largely
consistent. Nonetheless, there are decisions from Blackmun's later years that
have a distinctly more liberal flavor than his early votes in free speech cases.
See, e.g., *Arcara v. Cloud Books, Inc.*, 478 U.S. 697, 708 (1986) (Blackmun, J.,
dissenting from a decision allowing adult bookstore to be closed because used
as a place for prostitution); *Rankin v. McPherson*, 483 U.S. 378 (1987) (disapproving the charge of a city worker for endorsing the attempted assassination
of President Reagan); *Texas v. Johnson*, 491 U.S. 397 (1989) (protecting flag
burning).

A final example is capital punishment. Blackmun voted to sustain the
death penalty in cases heard during the early 1970s, but then began to move
away from that position. After 1982 he voted with Brennan and Marshall in
approximately two thirds of the capital cases and with Rehnquist in fewer than
half.

BLACKMUN'S "FLEXIBILITY" AND "OPEN-MINDEDNESS": See, e.g., Neuborne,
"Blackmun: Intellectual Openness Elicits Needed Respect for the Judicial
Process," *National L.J.*, Feb. 18, 1990, p. 18; Dorsen, "A Change in Judicial
Philosophy?" *id.*, 13.

p. 367 "FAMOUS AS A HUMANE CHARTER OF LIBERTY FOR WOMEN": *Id.*

"AS A MATTER OF SIMPLE CRAFT, JUSTICE BLACKMUN'S OPINION FOR THE COURT
WAS DREADFUL": Tushnet, "Following the Rules Laid Down," *Harvard L. Rev.*
96:820. See also Powe, "The Court Between Hegemonies," *Washington and
Lee L. Rev.* 49:39 ("probably the weakest of any major decision in American
history").

FOUR WAYS TO KILL A BABY: See Sanders, "Enemies of Abortion," *Harper's*, Mar.
1974, pp. 26–30.

p. 368 AGAINST LAWS REQUIRING A HUSBAND'S OR PARENT'S CONSENT: *Planned
Parenthood v. Danforth*, 428 U.S. 52 (1976).

AGAINST A BAN ON ADVERTISING FOR ABORTION: *Bigelow v. Virginia*, 421 U.S. 809
(1975).

THAT THE DOCTOR DETERMINE WHETHER THE FETUS WAS VIABLE: *Colautti v.
Franklin*, 349 U.S. 379 (1979).

GET THE CONSENT IF NOT OF A PARENT, AT LEAST OF A JUDGE: *Bellotti v. Baird*,
443 U.S. 662 (1979).

THAT THE PARENTS OF AN UNDERAGE FEMALE BE NOTIFIED: *H.L. v. Matheson*, 450
U.S. 398 (1981).

ABORTION-FUNDING CASES: *Beal v. Doe*, 432 U.S. 438 (1977); *Maher v. Roe*, 432
U.S. 464 (1977); *Poelker v. Doe*, 432 U.S. 519 (1977).

WEBSTER V. REPRODUCTIVE HEALTH SERVICES: 492 U.S. 490, 537 (1989).

p. 369 TURNED BACK THE ATTACK ON ROE: *Planned Parenthood of Southeastern Pennsylvania v. Casey,* 112 S. Ct. 2791 (1992).

"THERE IS NO SECRET AS TO HOW I WOULD HAVE VOTED IN WEBSTER": Greenhouse, "Powell to Court: A Caution With Love," *New York Times,* Oct. 18, 1989. If taken literally, Powell's remark is confusing. The precise issue before the Court in *Webster* was abortion funding, and presumably Powell would have voted with the majority on that point. The more important aspect of *Webster,* however, was the majority's announcement of its willingness to overrule *Roe.* Powell's remark addressed that larger issue.

TOOK EVERY OPPORTUNITY TO SAY THAT HE STOOD BY ROE: See, e.g. Sanders, "The Marble Palace's Southern Gentleman," *Time,* July 9, 1990, p. 12; DeBenedictis, "The Reasonable Man," *ABA Journal,* Oct. 1990, p. 74.

CHAPTER XII: THE NIXON TAPES CASE

p. 371 THE STORY OF THE NIXON TAPES CASE: For detailed chronological accounts, see *The Watergate Hearings,* edited by *The New York Times,* the three volumes of *Watergate and the White House,* published by Facts on File, and Bernstein and Woodward, *All the President's Men.*

COX SOUGHT A COURT ORDER: So did the Senate committee, chaired by Sam J. Ervin, Jr., of North Carolina, but that suit was dismissed. *Senate Select Committee on Presidential Campaign Activities v. Nixon,* 366 F. Supp. 51 (D.D.C. 1973).

p. 372 APPROVED SIRICA'S RULING BY A VOTE OF FIVE TO TWO: *Nixon v. Sirica,* 487 F2d 700 (D.C. Cir. 1973).

p. 373 THREATENING THE DESTRUCTION OF THE STATE OF ISRAEL: *Time,* Nov. 5, 1973, p. 15.

NIXON ORDERED AMERICAN FORCES WORLDWIDE: The technical name for this alert is Def Con Three (for Defense Condition Three). See *Newsweek,* Nov. 5, 1973, p. 41.

"THE MOST DIFFICULT CRISES WE'VE HAD SINCE THE CUBAN [MISSILE] CONFRONTATION": *New York Times,* Oct. 27, 1973, p. 14.

BOTH TIME AND NEWSWEEK REPORTED "WIDESPREAD MUTTERINGS": The quote is from *Newsweek,* Nov. 5, 1973, p. 20. *Time's* issue of the same date contained an article entitled "Was the Alert Scare Necessary?"

KISSINGER HAD TO DENY REPEATEDLY THAT THE ALERT WAS CALLED FOR POLITICAL REASONS: See *New York Times,* Oct. 26, 1973, p. 14.

"THERE HAD TO BE A MINIMUM OF CONFIDENCE": Quoted in *New Republic,* Nov. 10, 1973, p. 14.

FOR MANY, THAT CONFIDENCE WAS PLAINLY LACKING: The judgment of history is similarly mixed. Some think that Nixon's action was at least partly political. See *The Yom Kippur War* (by The Insight Team of the London *Sunday Times*), 419. Others disagree. See Allen, *The Yom Kippur War,* 299 ("Certainly, Nixon was criticized soon after what many saw as an action designed to distract people from the latest Watergate scandals; but perhaps the were being unfair, for had he not acted, they conceivably would have had something even more devastating to worry about.").

"I WAS INFLUENCED": LFP to Gerald Gunther, Apr. 19, 1975.

p. 374 THIS PROMPTED SENATE MAJORITY LEADER MIKE MANSFIELD: The letter is reprinted in the *Congressional Record, 93d Cong., 2d Sess.* 120:17168 (May 13, 1974). The quotation comes from Mansfield's accompanying remarks to the Senate. Mansfield's repeated reference to the Court's "four-month recess" was by any reckoning incorrect. The Court remains in session through June, finishing opinions on cases argued earlier that term, and resumes sitting at the beginning of October. The Court is not in session during July, August, and September.

RESENTED THE IDEA THAT THE COURT'S ANNUAL SUMMER RECESS WAS A VACATION: See, e.g., Kohlmeir, "Justices and their Courtly Vacations," *Chicago Tribune,* Aug. 23, 1973, p. 18, and the response thereto, "The 'Vacation' and 'Workload' Facts," *ABA Journal* 60:106.

HAD NOT TAKEN A FULL WEEK'S VACATION IN HIS FIRST FOUR YEARS: LFP to Joseph L. Allbritton, Jan. 12, 1976.

p. 375 UNITED STATES V. UNITED STATES DISTRICT COURT: *United States v. United States District Court for the Southern District of Michigan,* 407 U.S. 297 (1972). The decision is often called the *Keith* case, in honor of District Judge Damon J. Keith.

MADE THE FBI'S MOST WANTED LIST: *New York Times,* Nov. 26, 1970, p. 13.

WHEN THE POLICE FINALLY CAUGHT UP WITH HIM, THEY FOUND: *New York Times,* Mar. 17, 1971, p. 51.

"NECESSARY TO PROTECT THE NATION": This language is taken from the affidavit of Attorney General John N. Mitchell, quoted in 407 U.S. 300 n. 2.

NOT ONLY IN HOMES, BUT ALSO IN TELEPHONE CONVERSATIONS: *Katz v. United States,* 389 U.S. 347 (1967).

p. 376 CONGRESS PASSED A LAW TO THAT EFFECT: Title III of the Omnibus Crime Control and Safe Streets Act of 1968, now codified at 18 U.S.C. secs. 2510–2520.

"AS HE DEEMS NECESSARY TO PROTECT THE UNITED STATES": 18 U.S.C. sec. 2511(3).

p. 377 "SO THAT CRITICISM PER SE IN ESSENCE BECOMES SUBVERSIVENESS": *Nomination Hearings,* 209.

p. 379 DOUGLAS INTERVENED: William O. Douglas to Warren E. Burger, Mar. 6, 1972.

BURGER REFUSED TO WITHDRAW THE ASSIGNMENT: Warren E. Burger to William O. Douglas, Mar. 6, 1972.

DOUGLAS SEIZED THE OPENING AND MADE HIS OWN ASSIGNMENT: William O. Douglas to LFP, Mar. 8, 1972.

BRENNAN THOUGHT THE DRAFT "SQUINT[ED] TOWARD" ACCEPTANCE OF WARRANTLESS WIRETAPS: Curiously, Brennan's objection is stated in a letter from Douglas, dated May 4, 1972. The published version merely cites the ABA Standards, as well as certain judicial pronouncements, as illustrations of that view. See 407 U.S. 297, 322 n. 20.

p. 381 THE SUPREME COURT ANNOUNCED ITS DECISION: *United States v. Nixon,* 418 U.S. 683 (1974).

NIXON SAID HE WOULD: *New York Times,* July 25, 1974, p. 20 ("I have instructed Mr. St. Clair to take whatever measures are necessary to comply with that decision in all respects").

p. 382 "THE PICTURE THAT EMERGES IS DISGUSTING": *Washington Star-Times,* Aug. 6, 1974.

p. 384 MEMO HE USED AS THE BASIS FOR HIS REMARKS: This memo is entitled "NIXON CASE: Notes for Conference" and was typed before Conference on July 9. Most likely, Powell dictated it the night before. (Douglas's papers in the Library of Congress usually contain conference notes, but the notes for *United States v. Nixon* are missing from the files.)

p. 387 *MILLIKEN V. BRADLEY*: 418 U.S. 717 (1974).

POWELL'S MEMO BEGAN: These quotations are taken from the original memo circulated to the Conference on July 6, 1974. The full text appears in Schwartz, *Unpublished Opinions*, 190–201, along with circulations from other Justices.

p. 389 BOB WOODWARD AND SCOTT ARMSTRONG'S BEST-SELLING EXPOSÉ: This account of the origins and methodology of *The Brethren* is based on interviews with Bob Woodward and Scott Armstrong and with some of those they interviewed. Stewart's role is confirmed in Lukas, "Playboy Interview: Bob Woodward," *Playboy*, Feb. 1987, p. 51.

p. 390 WOODWARD "STATED, WHEN REQUESTING THE INTERVIEW": LFP to former clerks, Jan. 16, 1980.

BRENNAN CASE HISTORIES: This description is based on the account of Brennan's official biographer, Stephen Wermeil, and on the recollections of others who have seen one or more of them. See also Lewis, *Make No Law*, 164–65. Lewis had access to the Brennan case history of *New York Times Co. v. Sullivan*.

p. 391 "HYPED-UP STUNT FOR POLITICAL VOYEURS": *Chicago Tribune*, Dec. 16, 1979, sec. 2, p. 14.

"A KEYHOLD COMPENDIUM OF SNIDE GOSSIP": Kilpatrick, "Nothing of Honor," *National Review*, Feb. 8, 1980, p. 162.

"DOUBTS NOT ONLY ABOUT THE AUTHORS' UNDERSTANDING": Lewis, "The Brethren: Inside the Supreme Court—A Review," *New York St. Bar J.* 152:205.

SOME CRITICS FOCUSED CHIEFLY ON THE LAW CLERKS: See Higgins, "The Brethren's Clerks," *Harpers*, Apr. 1980, p. 96; Lewin, "Supreme Court Touchable in a Free Society," *Legal Times of Washington*, Jan. 7, 1980, pp. 7–8; Stephan, "The Breach of Trust Behind 'The Brethren,'" *Norfolk Virginian-Pilot*, Dec. 9, 1979, p. C6.

"A SORRY EXAMPLE OF THE GUTTER LEVEL OF WHAT IS CALLED INVESTIGATIVE REPORTING": LFP to family members, Dec. 4, 1979.

"PERSONAL CRITICISM OF THE CHIEF JUSTICE ATTRIBUTED TO ME": LFP to former clerks, Jan. 16, 1980.

IN A SPEECH PUBLISHED IN THE ABA JOURNAL: LFP, "What Really Goes on at the Supreme Court," *ABA Journal* 66:721–23.

p. 392 THIS HAD BEEN DONE ONCE BEFORE: *Cooper v. Aaron*, 358 U.S. 1 (1958).

p. 393 AS DESCRIBED BY WOODWARD AND ARMSTRONG: Woodward and Armstrong, *The Brethren*, 315–16.

p. 394 "[H]AD WE BEEN IN THE MIDDLE OF THE TERM": Warren E. Burger to LFP, July 30, 1974.

p. 395 THE RANKING REPUBLICAN USED PRECISELY THIS ARGUMENT: *Watergate and the White House* III:207, 209.

"POWELL'S POSITION WAS MORE DANGEROUS THAN THE WHITE HOUSE'S, BRENNAN BELIEVED": Woodward and Armstrong, *The Brethren*, 299.

p. 396 A DECISION THAT CAST A VERY SMALL SHADOW: For the Court's subsequent effort to prevent encroachment on presidential powers, see *Nixon v. Fitzgerald*, 457 U.S. 731 (1982); see generally Carter, "Political Aspects of Judicial Power," *University of Pennsylvania L. Rev.* 131:1341–1401.

"MR. NIXON LOSES BUT THE PRESIDENCY LARGELY PREVAILS": Henkin, "Executive Privilege," *University of California at Los Angeles L. Rev.* 22:40–46.

p. 397 "CONSTITUTIONAL CRISIS BEYOND IMAGINATION": The quotation comes from Powell's interview with Bill Moyers on "In Search of the Constitution," broadcast on PBS, June 25, 1987.

THERE WAS ANY "AIR" IN THE COURT'S DECISION: See Osborne, *The Last Nixon Watch*, 31; cf. Nixon, *RN*, 195.

ASKED HOW COULD HE BE DESERTED BY THE MEN HE APPOINTED TO THE BENCH: Woodward and Bernstein, *The Final Days*, 264.

CHAPTER XIII: CRIME AND DEATH

p. 398 MIRANDA: *Miranda v. Arizona*, 384 U.S. 436 (1966). The phrasing quoted in text is that used by the FBI.

p. 399 CRIMINAL GOES FREE BECAUSE THE CONSTABLE BLUNDERED: *People v. Defore*, 242 N.Y. 13, 21, 150 N.E. 585, 587 (1926).

EDWIN MEESE, WHO CAMPAIGNED TIRELESSLY TO OVERRULE: *Washington Post*, Aug. 30, 1985, p. A6, and Oct. 11, 1985, p. A6; *New York Times*, Jan. 22, 1987, pp. A1 and B16; *Wall Street Journal*, June 13, 1986, p. 22.

POLICE LEARNED TO LIVE WITH THE NEW PROCEDURE: See Baker, *Miranda*, 403–406; Schulhofer, "Reconsidering *Miranda*," *U. Chicago L. Rev.* 54:435, 456; "Fighting Crime by the Rules: Why cops like Miranda," *Newsweek*, July 18, 1988, p. 53.

"DOES NOT PRESENT SERIOUS PROBLEMS FOR LAW ENFORCEMENT": ABA, *Criminal Justice in Crisis*, 28.

USE SUCH STATEMENTS TO CROSS-EXAMINE: *Harris v. New York*, 401 U.S. 222 (1971); *Oregon v. Hass*, 420 U.S. 714 (1975).

WHEN GIVING THE WARNINGS WOULD ENDANGER PUBLIC SAFETY: *New York v. Quarles*, 467 U.S. 649 (1984).

p. 400 THE FACTS OF AN EARLIER CASE: *Escobedo v. Illinois*, 378 U.S. 478 (1964).

THAT OF ROBERT WILLIAMS: *Brewer v. Williams*, 430 U.S. 387 (1977), was not technically a *Miranda* case but was decided under the authority of an earlier decision, *Massiah v. United States*, 377 U.S. 201 (1964). For an account of *Brewer*, see Kamisar, "The Warren Court," *Georgetown L.J.* 66:209–43.

p. 402 "FASTIDIOUS TO THE POINT OF FANATICISM": Will, *Washington Post*, Mar. 27, 1977, p. C7.

IN SOME AREAS, THE CASES MARKED A CLEAR RETREAT: Examples are the *Aguilar-Spinelli* rules on informants tips, see *Illinois v. Gates*, 462 U.S. 213 (1983), and certain requirements for the availability of habeas corpus. See *Wainwright v. Sykes*, 433 U.S. 72 (1977), overruling *Fay v. Noia*, 372 U.S. 391 (1963).

BURGER COURT ACTUALLY EXPANDED CONSTITUTIONAL PROTECTIONS FOR CRIMINAL DEFENDANTS: *Argersinger v. Hamlin*, 407 U.S. 25 (1972); *In re Winship*, 397 U.S. 358 (1970). The capital cases are described later in this chapter.

REFUSED TO EXTEND THE PRECEDENTS OF THE WARREN COURT: See, e.g., *Kirby v. Illinois*, 406 U.S. 682 (1971).

RECAST THEIR REASONING IN WAYS THAT IMPLIED LIMITATION: See, e.g., *United States v. Calandra*, 414 U.S. 338, 348 (1974).

THE WARREN COURT HAD RULED: *Mapp v. Ohio*, 367 U.S. 643 (1961).

BURGER RAILED AGAINST THIS RESULT: See, e.g., *Bivens v. Six Unknown Named Agents*, 403 U.S. 388, 411-24 (1971) (Burger, C.J., dissenting); *Stone v. Powell*, 428 U.S. 465, 496-502 (1976) (Burger, C.J., concurring).

MADE VARIOUS EXCEPTIONS DESIGNED TO MINIMIZE ITS COSTS: See, e.g., *United States v. Leon*, 468 U.S. 897 (1984); *Illinois v. Gates*, 462 U.S. 213 (1983); *Stone v. Powell*, 428 U.S. 465 (1976).

p. 403 "THE DIFFICULT AND PERPLEXING PROBLEMS": President's Commission on Law Enforcement and the Administration of Justice, *Supplemental Statement on Constitutional Limitations*.

p. 404 WHICH THE COURT SAID APPLIED TO ALL DEFENDANTS *TRIED* AFTER THE DATE OF THE DECISION: *Johnson v. New Jersey*, 384 U.S. 719 (1966).

p. 405 *McGAUTHA V. CALIFORNIA*: 402 U.S. 183 (1971).

p. 406 THIS TIME WAS SENTENCED TO DIE: *People v. Aikens*, 70 Cal.2d 369, 450 P.2d 258 (1969).

CALIFORNIA SUPREME COURT STRUCK DOWN THE DEATH PENALTY: *People v. Anderson*, 6 Cal.3d 288, 493 P.2d 880 (1972).

DISMISSED HIS CASE: *Aikens v. California*, 406 U.S. 813 (1972).

FURMAN V. GEORGIA: 408 U.S. 238 (1972).

ALMOST ALONE AMONG WESTERN INDUSTRIALIZED NATIONS: In Europe, only France and Spain still authorized execution. See "Death Penalty: A World Survey," *U.S. News & World Report*, May 31, 1971, pp. 37–40.

DR. GALLUP REPORTED: "Public Opinion and Capital Punishment," *Gallup Opinion Index*, Sept. 1978, p. 22.

ONLY TEN PERSONS HAD BEEN EXECUTED SINCE 1965: "Death to Capital Punishment," *New Republic*, Feb. 20, 1971, p. 12.

p. 407 "MYSTIFYING CLOUD OF WORDS": Cardozo, *Law and Literature*, 100.

IN THE YEARS 1930–1965: These figures are taken from the American Law Institute, *Model Penal Code and Commentaries*, Part II, I:119 n. 34. For analysis of these figures, see Wolfgang and Reidel, "Race, Judicial Discretion, and the Death Penalty," *Annals* 47:119–33.

APPEARANCE ALSO SEEMED TO MATTER: Defendants seemed to receive more lenient treatment if they were physically attractive and harsher treatment if their victims were physically attractive. See *McCleskey v. Kemp*, 481 U.S. 279, 317–18 nn. 43,44 (1987), and the sources cited therein.

USED "AGAINST SUCH ABJECT . . . SPECIMENS OF THE HUMAN RACE": *Nation*, May 17, 1971, p. 610.

p. 408 "THE SHORT OF THE MATTER": Quoted in *Time*, Jan. 24, 1972, pp. 54–55.

"I CANNOT BELIEVE THAT IT IS FAIRLY METED OUT": The remark is reconstructed from Douglas's Conference notes. See Douglas Papers, Box 1541, Case File O.T. 1971, Argued Cases.

"DO YOU HAVE YOUR CAPITAL PUNISHMENT OPINION WRITTEN YET?": Woodward and Armstrong, *The Brethren*, 204–205.

POWELL REJECTED THE STAFF'S DESIRE TO COME OUT AGAINST CAPITAL PUNISHMENT: LFP memorandum, June 25, 1966, written in anticipation of a Commission meeting two days later.

p. 410 "EVOLVING STANDARDS OF DECENCY": This phrase was first used by Chief

Justice Warren in a plurality opinion in *Trop v. Dulles*, 356 U.S. 86, 101 (1958), and has since been repeated in the Court's opinions.

"WE MUST NEVER FORGET THAT IT IS A *CONSTITUTION* WE ARE EXPOUNDING": *McCulloch v. Maryland*, 17 U.S. (4 Wheat.) 316, 407 (1819).

p. 411 THE OPINION POWELL PRODUCED OVER THE NEXT SEVERAL MONTHS: The quotations in this paragraph are taken from the first circulated draft of Powell's opinion.

CAPITAL PUNISHMENT WAS PLAINLY CONTEMPLATED BY THE CONSTITUTION: Powell quoted the Fifth Amendment: "No person shall be held to answer for a capital, or otherwise infamous offense, unless on a presentment or indictment by a Grand Jury . . . ; nor shall any person be subject for the same offense to be twice put in jeopardy of life or limb; . . . nor be deprived of life, liberty or property without due process of law. . . ."

TRIED NOT TO GET HIS HOPES UP: Larry A. Hammond, interview; Woodward and Armstrong, *The Brethren*, 212–15.

p. 412 "MORALLY UNACCEPTABLE TO THE PEOPLE OF THE UNITED STATES": All quotations in this paragraph are taken from *Furman v. Georgia*, 408 U.S. 238, 314, 360–70 (1972) (opinion of Marshall, J., concurring).

p. 413 THIS LINEUP LED THE *NEW REPUBLIC*: July 15, 1972, p. 8.

"SOMEDAY THE COURT WILL HOLD DEATH SENTENCES UNCONSTITUTIONAL": These remarks are reconstructed from Douglas's Conference notes. Douglas Papers, Box 1541, Case File O.T. 1971, Argued Cases.

p. 414 POPULAR SUPPORT FOR CAPITAL PUNISHMENT: "Public Opinion and Capital Punishment," *Gallup Opinion Index*, no. 158, pp. 20–25 (Sept. 1978).

HAD SIXTY-FOUR OCCUPANTS: *U.S. News & World Report*, Mar. 4, 1974, p. 46.

p. 415 LOUISIANA, FOR EXAMPLE, PASSED A LAW REQUIRING A DEATH SENTENCE: The full text of the statute appears in *Roberts v. Louisiana*, 428 U.S. 325, 329 n. 3 (1976) (opinion of Stewart, Powell, and Stevens, JJ.).

p. 416 STILL MORE EXTREME WAS NORTH CAROLINA: See *Woodson v. North Carolina*, 428 U.S. 280, 285–86 n. 4 (1976) (opinion of Stewart, Powell, and Stevens, JJ.).

BY LATE 1975 THERE WERE NEARLY 400 PERSONS SENTENCED TO EXECUTION: Specifically, there were 376 persons under sentence of death as of November 5, 1975. See James B. Ginty, Memorandum to the Conference, Capital Cases, Jan. 8, 1976.

NEARLY EIGHTY: James B. Ginty, Memorandum for the Chief Justice, Subject: Status of Capital Cases Docket, June 23, 1976.

p. 417 SADDEST CHAPTER IN THE LIFE OF A PROUD MAN: See Woodward and Armstrong, *The Brethren*, 356–62, 367–69, 384–94.

EARLIER CASES WHERE A COMMITTEE OF JUSTICES HAD VISITED A FAILING COLLEAGUE: See, e.g., Hughes, *The Supreme Court of the United States*, 75–76 (citing the first Justice Harlan's approach to Justice Stephen J. Field, then ninety years old, as later recounted by Harlan to Justice Charles Evans Hughes). In a later time, Justice Black and the second Justice Harlan reportedly decided to put over for reargument any case in which Justice Whittaker cast the deciding vote, but Whittaker resigned before any action was taken. George C. Freeman, Jr., to author, Feb. 26, 1992.

WHITE POINTED OUT THAT THE CONSTITUTION "NOWHERE PROVIDES": Byron White to Warren E. Burger, Oct. 20, 1975.

p. 418 HE ANNOUNCED HIS PLAN TO PARTICIPATE AT CONFERENCE: William O. Douglas to Warren E. Burger, Dec. 20, 1975.

FORMAL LETTER SIGNED BY ALL EIGHT JUSTICES: Warren E. Burger et al. to William O. Douglas, Dec. 22, 1975.

p. 419 THE CHOICE OF STEVENS CAME AS CLOSE TO THE CIVICS-BOOK IDEAL OF NONPO-LITICAL SELECTION: See Abraham, *Justices and Presidents*, 321–25, 201–205; O'Brien, *Yearbook 1989 of the Supreme Court Historical Society*, 20–39.

"FIND ME ANOTHER LEWIS POWELL": Edward H. Levi to author, Aug. 27, 1990; John J. Buckley, Jr., interview.

"FRIGHTENED TO DEATH THAT THE ATTORNEY GENERAL OF THE UNITED STATES WAS GOING TO BRING SUIT": LFP, interview.

"PROVIDE STRONG REINFORCEMENT TO THE COURT'S MOST CONSERVATIVE WING": Quoted in O'Brien, *Yearbook 1989 of the Supreme Court Historical Society*, 30.

p. 420 RAISED SEVERAL POSSIBILITIES BUT FOCUSED ON TWO: "Memorandum for the President," Nov. 10, 1975, in the Cheney Papers, Box, 11, Gerald R. Ford Presidential Library, portions of which are quoted in O'Brien, *Yearbook 1989 of the Supreme Court Historical Society*, 30–32.

FORD PONDERED THE MATTER: Ford, *A Time to Heal*, 335.

WHO TOOK "ABOUT TWO SECONDS" TO ACCEPT THE NOMINATION: Quoted in O'Brien, *Yearbook 1989 of the Supreme Court Historical Society*, 34.

p. 421 "WELL WRITTEN, HIGHLY ANALYTICAL, CLOSELY RESEARCHED AND METICULOUSLY PREPARED": *Hearings Before the Judiciary Committee on the Nomination of John Paul Stevens*, 19.

STEVENS WROTE SEVENTEEN SEPARATE CONCURRENCES AND TWENTY-SEVEN DIS-SENTS: Orland, *The Justices of the Supreme Court* V:151.

p. 422 "WHAT IT'S LIKE TO HEAR JESUS CHRIST": Christina Whitman, interview.

p. 423 THERE WERE FIRM MAJORITIES TO UPHOLD TWO STATUTES: Powell's conference notes reveal seven votes to uphold the statutes from Georgia and Florida, five or six votes (including his) to uphold the Texas and Louisiana statutes, but only three firm votes to sustain the North Carolina law. After originally voting to uphold all five statutes, Blackmun asked to be recorded as a "pass" on North Carolina. Powell then did the same thing, although his own notes added that he would "probably reverse." See Woodward and Armstrong, *The Brethren*, 435.

p. 426 WHICH STEVENS CALLED A MONSTER: *Id.*, 434.

STEWART AND STEVENS WERE QUEASY ABOUT THE TEXAS STATUTE: Powell's notes state that Stewart was "not at rest" on the Texas statute, while Stevens voted to affirm its validity. Apparently, others thought Stevens voted against. See *id.*, 435.

SOMEONE HAD TO TELL WHITE: LFP, interview; Christina Whitman, interview; Woodward and Armstrong, *The Brethren*, 436–41.

p. 427 THE LEAD CASE UPHOLDING THE DEATH PENALTY: *Gregg v. Georgia*, 428 U.S. 153 (1976). Powell drafted parts I, II, and III of the plurality opinion; Stewart wrote part IV.

STEVENS UNDERTOOK TO WRITE THE FACTS OF THE OTHER FOUR CASES: *Proffitt v. Florida*, 428 U.S. 242 (1976); *Jurek v. Texas*, 428 U.S. 262 (1976); *Woodson v. North Carolina*, 428 U.S. 280 (1976); *Roberts v. Louisiana*, 428 U.S. 325 (1976). In each of these cases, Stevens wrote part I of the plurality opinion.

TO STEWART FELL THE GREATEST CHALLENGE: Stewart wrote part IV of the opinion in *Gregg* and part III in the other four cases.

p. 428 POWELL WROTE STEWART: LFP to Potter Stewart, May 1, 1976.

p. 429 STAYING THE CAPITAL CASES WOULD INEVITABLY "AROUSE A CERTAIN AMOUNT OF SPECULATION": Warren E. Burger, Memorandum to the Conference, Re: Capital Cases, July 20, 1976.

HURRIED TELEPHONE CONSULTATIONS ELICITED: The Chief Justice's memorandum of July 20, 1976, recounts Powell's report of support from Stewart and Stevens. The backbone comment comes from Woodward and Armstrong, *The Brethren*, 441.

p. 430 SCORCHING DISSENTS FROM BRENNAN: *Stone v. Powell*, 428 U.S. 465 (1976); *United States v. Martinez-Fuerte*, 428 U.S. 543 (1976).

"YOU DON'T GO AROUND CHASING RABBITS": *Washington Star*, June 20, 1976, p.1.

"I DON'T KNOW IF BILL BRENNAN IS READY": Woodward and Armstrong, *The Brethren*, 443.

p. 431 PROPOSED A MAJOR CHANGE IN SEARCH AND SEIZURE CASES: *Schneckloth v. Bustamonte*, 412 U.S. 418, 250 (1973) (Powell, J., concurring).

p. 432 STONE V. POWELL: 428 U.S. 465 (1976).

p. 433 "'BLACK IS BEAUTIFUL'": *Washington Post*, July 6, 1976, p. 3.

"YOU HAVE GIVEN US A BIRTHDAY PRESENT BEYOND PRICE": *Charlottesville Daily Progress*, July 6, 1976, p. 1.

p. 434 COULD DEATH BE MADE MANDATORY FOR MURDER OF A POLICE OFFICER: *Roberts v. Louisiana*, 431 U.S. 633 (1977).

MURDER BY A PERSON ALREADY UNDER A SENTENCE OF LIFE IN PRISON: *Sumner v. Shuman*, 483 U.S. 66 (1987).

p. 435 BARRED FROM CONSIDERING CERTAIN FACTORS AS POSSIBLE MITIGATIONS: *Lockett v. Ohio*, 438 U.S. 586 (1978).

PUT TO DEATH FOR HELPING ANOTHER TO COMMIT ROBBERY AND MURDER: *Enmund v. Florida*, 458 U.S. 782 (1982); but see *Tison v. Arizona*, 481 U.S. 137 (1987).

SIXTEEN-YEAR-OLD BOY BE SENTENCED TO DIE WITHOUT CONSIDERATION OF HIS HISTORY OF FAMILY VIOLENCE: *Eddings v. Oklahoma*, 455 U.S. 104 (1982).

COULD A DEATH SENTENCE BE BASED IN PART ON A PSYCHIATRIST'S TESTIMONY: *Barefoot v. Estelle*, 463 U.S 880 (1983).

COULD FLORIDA AUTHORIZE A JUDGE TO IMPOSE CAPITAL PUNISHMENT: *Spaziano v. Florida*, 468 U.S. 447 (1984).

STRIKE FROM THE JURY PROSPECTIVE JURORS WHO OPPOSED CAPITAL PUNISHMENT: *Darden v. Wainwright*, 477 U.S. 168 (1986); *Wainwright v. Witt*, 469 U.S. 412 (1985); *Adams v. Texas*, 448 U.S. 38 (1980).

COULD THE STATE EXECUTE A KILLER WHO HAD GONE INSANE: *Ford v. Wainwright*, 477 U.S. 399 (1986).

IN MOST OF THESE CASES: The only exception among those listed was *Enmunds v. Florida*, 458 U.S. 782 (1982).

"QUITE IMPOSSIBLE" TO DECLARE THE DEATH PENALTY UNCONSTITUTIONAL FOR RAPE: *Furman v. Georgia*, 408 U.S. 238, 458 (1972) (Powell, J., dissenting).

THE CASE OF EHRLICH ANTHONY COKER: *Coker v. Georgia*, 433 U.S. 584 (1977). The facts are taken from that opinion and from *Coker v. State*, 234 Ga. 555, 216 S.E.2d 782 (1975). See also *Time*, Apr. 11, 1977, p. 80.

p. 436 "GROSSLY DISPROPORTIONATE AND EXCESSIVE PUNISHMENT FOR THE CRIME OF RAPE": The quotation comes from the plurality opinion, *Coker v. Georgia*, 433 U.S. 584, 592 (1977).

POWELL ANSWERED: The quotations come from a dictated draft opinion of May 13, 1977.

p. 437 THE CASE OF WARREN McCLESKEY: *McCleskey v. Kemp,* 481 U.S. 279 (1987).

AND WAS KILLED BY A BULLET TO THE HEAD: The evidence supporting McCleskey's guilt was summarized by the appeals court in *McCleskey v. Kemp,* 753 F.2d 877, 882 (11th Cir. 1985):

> McCleskey was identified by two of the store personnel as the robber who came in the front door. Shortly after his arrest, McCleskey confessed to participating in the robbery but maintained that he was not the triggerman. McCleskey confirmed the eyewitness' accounts that it was he who entered through the front door. One of his accomplices, Ben Wright, testified that McCleskey admitted to shooting the officer. A jail inmate housed near McCleskey testified that McCleskey made a "jail house confession" in which he claimed he was the triggerman. The police officer was killed by a bullet fired from a .38 caliber Rossi handgun. McCleskey had stolen a .38 caliber Rossi in a previous hold-up.

Subsequent proceedings revealed that the inmate who testified to the "jail house confession" was a police informant.

p. 438 AN ELABORATE STATISTICAL STUDY: The authors of the study (actually two related studies) were Baldus, George Woodworth, and Charles Pulaski. Their results were published in *Equal Justice and the Death Penalty.* For a similar study with generally compatible conclusions, see Gross and Mauro, "Patterns of Death," *Stanford L. Rev.* 27:27–153.

THE DIFFERENCE DISAPPEARED: According to one way of stating the results, the figures showed that black defendants were 1.1 times as likely as white defendants to be sentenced to death.

p. 439 AN EARLY MEMORANDUM URGING HIS COLLEAGUES NOT TO HEAR McCLESKEY'S CASE: LFP, Memorandum to the Conference, June 27, 1986.

"[M]Y UNDERSTANDING OF STATISTICAL ANALYSIS: LFP, "Memo to Leslie," Sept. 16, 1986.

ANTHONY LEWIS: "Bowing to Racism," *New York Times,* Apr. 28, 1987, p. A31. See also the thoughtful criticism in Kennedy, "*McClesky v. Kemp,*" *Harvard L. Rev.* 101:1388–1443.

"NO PERFECT PROCEDURE": The quotations in this and the next paragraph come from Powell's published opinion, *McCleskey v. Kemp,* 481 U.S. 279, 309–13 (1987).

p. 440 IN AN OPINION BY POWELL: *Batson v. Kentucky,* 476 U.S. 79 (1986).

p. 441 PREVENTING THE PROSECUTION FROM PRESENTING THIS KIND OF EVIDENCE: *Booth v. Maryland,* 482 U.S. 496, 506 (1987).

p. 443 "THE INCENTIVES IN THESE CASES": LFP, "Reform of Capital Habeas Corpus Procedures," Statement before the Senate Committee on the Judiciary, Nov. 8, 1989, p. 4.

THE CASE OF WARREN McCLESKEY: The litigation history is recounted in *McCleskey v. Kemp,* 481 U.S. 279, 283–91 (1987), and *McCleskey v. Zant,* 499 U.S. ___, ___ (1991).

p. 445 REQUIRED ONLY THREE VOTES: See *Watson v. Butler,* 483 U.S. 1037, 1038 (1987) (Brennan, J., dissenting).

POWELL WOULD PROVIDE A FIFTH VOTE TO STAY THE EXECUTION: See *Darden v. Wainright,* 473 U.S. 927, 928 (1985) (Powell, J., concurring).

p. 446 "THE WAR OF THE STAY MEMOS GOT VERY HEATED": Andrew Leipold, interview.

THE CASE OF RONALD STRAIGHT: *Straight v. Wainwright*, 476 U.S. 1132 (1986). For criticism of Powell's vote in *Straight*, see Revesz and Karlan, "Nonmajority Rules and the Supreme Court," *U. of Pennsylvania L. Rev.* 136:1112–17.

WITH HIM WERE: The committee members were Charles Clark, Chief Judge of the Fifth Circuit; Paul H. Roney, Chief Judge of the Eleventh Circuit; Terrell Hodges, Chief Judge of the Middle District of Florida; and Barefoot Sanders, Acting Chief Judge of the Northern District of Texas. They were assisted by Albert M. Pearson, a University of Georgia law professor with experience representing defendants in capital cases; William R. Burchill, Jr., General Counsel of the Administrative Office of the U.S. Clerks; and Powell's law clerk, R. Hewitt Pate.

"[T]HE HARD FACT IS": LFP, "Reform of Capital Habeas Corpus Procedures," Statement Before the United States Senate Committee on the Judiciary, Nov. 8, 1989.

"ATTORNEYS APPEAR TO HAVE INTENTIONALLY DELAYED": Report of the Ad Hoc Committee on Federal Habeas Corpus, 5. The report is reprinted at *Criminal Law Reporter* 45:3239–41 (Sept. 27, 1989).

p. 447 "CAPITAL CASES SHOULD BE SUBJECT TO ONE COMPLETE AND FAIR COURSE: Report of the Ad Hoc Committee on Federal Habeas Corpus in Capital Cases, 6.

POWELL WANTED A SOLUTION "THAT WOULD BE PERCEIVED AS A FAIR COMPROMISE": R. Hewitt Pate, interview.

p. 448 A PROVISION WAS ADDED TO A PENDING BILL: Anti-Drug Abuse Act of 1988, § 7323 of P.L. 100-690, 102 Stat. 4467.

THEY THOUGHT THE POWELL COMMITTEE TOO SOUTHERN: See, e.g., Berger, "Justice Delayed or Justice Denied?" *Columbia L. Rev.* 90:1675 and n. 65; Goldstein, "Expediting the Federal Habeas Corpus Review Process in Capital Cases," *Capital U. L. Rev.* 19:602. For an example of the alarm triggered in some quarters by the appointment of the Powell committee, see Coyle, *National L.J.*, Nov. 28, 1988, p. 1.

ITS REPORT, RELEASED IN NOVEMBER 1989: American Bar Association, Criminal Justice Section, Report of the Task Force on Death Penalty Habeas Corpus. This was approved as modified by the ABA's House of Delegates in February 1990 as Report 115E.

"DID NOT THINK IT UNREASONABLE": William H. Rehnquist, interview.

p. 449 FOURTEEN JUDGES WROTE THE HOUSE AND SENATE COMMITTEES: *New York Times*, Oct. 6, 1989, p. A1.

"THE MOST RADICAL CURTAILMENT OF THE WRIT OF HABEAS CORPUS": *Los Angeles Times*, Nov. 7, 1989, p. B7.

"THE EXECUTION EXPRESS": *New York Times*, Oct. 3, 1989, p. A22.

"DEATH PENALTY FUMBLE": *Boston Globe*, 10 Oct. 1989, p. 10.

IN AN ACTION WIDELY REPORTED AS A REBUFF TO THE CHIEF JUSTICE: See, e.g., Greenhouse, *New York Times*, Mar. 15, 1990, p. A16.

p. 450 COLUMNIST EDWIN YODER DECRIED "THE REHNQUIST ASCENDANCY": *Washington Post*, June 30, 1991, p. C1.

RARELY VOTED AGAINST CAPITAL PUNISHMENT: Critics frequently remarked that Rehnquist had never voted to invalidate a death sentence except in the obvious cases indicated by a unanimous Court. See Berger, "Justice Delayed or Justice Denied?" *Columbia L. Rev.* 90:1675 n. 66.

"WHAT TROUBLES ME": *Coleman v. Balkcum*, 452 U.S. 949, 959 (1981) (Rehnquist, J., dissenting from denial of certiorari).

"LITERALLY YEARS AND YEARS AND YEARS": Remarks to the ABA, Feb. 1989, quoted in Berger, "Justice Delayed or Justice Denied?" *Columbia L. Rev.* 90:1669.

UPHELD THE EXECUTION OF PERSONS WHO WERE ONLY SIXTEEN: *Stanford v. Kentucky*, 492 U.S. 361 (1989). Apparently, those under sixteen at the time of the crime are still protected from the death penalty by *Thompson v. Oklahoma*, 487 U.S. 815 (1988).

REAFFIRMED JURY DISCRETION IN FINDING AGGRAVATING CIRCUMSTANCES: *Walton v. Arizona*, 497 U.S. 639 (1990); *Lewis v. Jeffers*, 497 U.S. 764 (1990).

BEAR THE BURDEN OF PROOF ON THE EXISTENCE OF MITIGATION: *Walton v. Arizona*, 497 U.S. 639 (1990). But see *Mills v. Maryland*, 486 U.S. 387 (1988).

"DECIDED BY THE NARROWEST OF MARGINS AND OVER SPIRITED DISSENTS": *Payne v. Tennessee*, ___ U.S. ___, ___ , 111 S.Ct. 2597, 2611 (1991), overruling *Booth v. Maryland*, 482 U.S. 496 (1987).

p. 451 A PREEXISTING RULE AGAINST "ABUSE OF THE WRIT": *McCleskey v. Zant*, 499 U.S. ___ (1991).

SURVEYED THE PROBLEMS OF "EXCESSIVELY REPETITIOUS LITIGATION": LFP, "Commentary," *Harvard L. Rev.* 102:1035–46.

"[I]F I WERE IN THE STATE LEGISLATURE, I WOULD VOTE": DeBenedictis, "The Reasonable Man," *ABA Journal*, Oct. 1990, p. 69.

p. 453 "I DON'T THINK THERE IS ANY POSSIBLE ARGUMENT TO THE CONTRARY": *Id.*

CHAPTER XIV: *BAKKE* AND BEYOND

p. 455 HE STOOD JUST UNDER SIX FEET TALL: The description of Bakke's appearance and background is taken from Lindsey, "White/Caucasian—and Rejected," *New York Times Magazine*, Apr. 3, 1977, p. 42. The "Teutonic" characterization comes from an interviewer quoted in that article.

"A STORYBOOK LIFE OF MIDDLE-CLASS VIRTUE": Wilkinson, *From Brown to Bakke*, 254.

p. 456 "APPLICANTS CHOSEN TO BE OUR DOCTORS": Lindsey, "White/Caucasian—and Rejected," *New York Times Magazine*, Apr. 3, 1977, p. 44.

HIS AVERAGE ON THE FOUR MCAT CATEGORIES: The figures are recounted in *Regents of the University of California v. Bakke*, 438 U.S. 265, 277–78 n. 7 (1978) (opinion of Powell, J.), as follows:

MCAT PERCENTILES

	Verbal	Quantitative	Science	Gen. Info.
Bakke	96	94	97	72
1972 Special Admittees	46	24	35	33
1973 Special Admittees	34	30	37	18

THE CALIFORNIA SUPREME COURT SIDED WITH BAKKE: *Bakke v. Regents of the University of California*, 132 Cal. Rptr. 680, 553 P.2d 1152 (1976).

p. 457 THREE CIVIL RIGHTS WORKERS WERE KILLED IN MISSISSIPPI: See Williams, *Eyes on the Prize*, 230–40; Kornbluth, "The '64 Civil Rights Murders: The Struggle

Continues," *New York Times Magazine,* July 23, 1989, p. 16. A fictionalized version of these events was presented in the 1988 film *Mississippi Burning.*

GOVERNOR ROSS BARNETT PHYSICALLY BARRED THE DOOR: See Branch, *Parting the Waters,* 647–53, 656–72.

THE SUPREME COURT'S "ROOT AND BRANCH" ATTACK ON THE SEGREGATION OF SOUTHERN SCHOOLS: *Green v. County School Board,* 391 U.S. 430, 438 (1968).

BUSING HAD BARELY BEGUN: In the South, widespread busing began after *Swann v. Charlotte-Mecklenburg Board of Education,* 402 U.S. 1 (1971). The extension of that remedy to the rest of the country gained speed after *Keyes v. School District No. 1,* 413 U.S. 189 (1973).

"WHERE ARE THE BLACK STUDENTS?": Brief of Respondents, *DeFunis v. Odegaard,* 416 U.S. 312 (1974).

p. 458 THIRTY HAD NUMERICAL QUALIFICATIONS LOWER THAN DEFUNIS: The chief criterion was the applicant's Projected First Year Average, a formula combining grades from the last two years of undergraduate study and the average score on the Law School Admissions Test. If the PFYA was above 77, admission was almost automatic. If the PFYA fell below 74.5, rejection was routine. DeFunis scored 76.23 on this index, placing him in the middle group of persons with a realistic but uncertain prospect of admission. See *DeFunis v. Odegaard,* 507 P.2d 1168, 1173 (Wash. Sup. Ct. 1976).

ALLOWED HIM TO STAY IN SCHOOL WHILE THE CASE WAS PENDING: In his capacity as Circuit Justice for the Ninth Circuit, Justice Douglas preserved the trial court's order pending review by the Supreme Court. *DeFunis v. Odegaard,* 416 U.S. 312, 315 (1974).

THE CASE WAS THEREFORE DISMISSED AS MOOT: *DeFunis v. Odegaard,* 416 U.S. 312 (1974).

SEVERAL JUSTICES THOUGHT THE COURT SHOULD ADDRESS THE MERITS: *DeFunis v. Odegaard,* 416 U.S. 312, 348 (1974) (Brennan, J., dissenting). Justices Douglas, White, and Marshall joined Brennan's dissent.

p. 459 IT DID NOT WORK FOR THE "STRONG-MINDED, NONCONFORMIST, UNUSUAL, ORIGINAL, OR CREATIVE" INDIVIDUAL: *Id.,* 328 (quoting Hoffman, *The Tyranny of Testing,* 91–92).

HE HAD ALREADY CONTACTED A LAWYER: Schwartz, *Behind* Bakke, 9.

RULED IN BAKKE'S FAVOR: *Bakke v. Regents of the University of California,* 553 P.2d 1152 (Cal. 1976). The original ruling declared that minority preferences were unlawful and that Bakke had to be admitted unless the University could prove that he would have been rejected anyway. In a petition for rehearing, the University conceded that it could not make such a showing. This cleared the way for immediate Supreme Court review without the necessity of further hearings in the trial court. For a detailed account of these matters, see Schwartz, *Behind* Bakke, 22–25.

IN SAN FRANSISCO, TWO THOUSAND PEOPLE MARCHED IN PROTEST: Arons, "Friends of the Court . . . and the Man Who Started It All," *Saturday Review,* Oct. 15, 1977, p. 12.

p. 460 MISTRUSTFUL SECOND-GUESSING OF THE UNIVERSITY'S LITIGATION STRATEGY: These arguments are detailed in the amicus brief filed in the Supreme Court by the National Conference of Black Lawyers. See also Smith, "Reflections on a Landmark," *Howard L.J.* 21:77–79.

"ARROGANCE" AND "SELF-RIGHTEOUSNESS" IN IGNORING MINORITY CONCERNS: Bell, *Race, Racism and American Law,* 446–47 n. 8.

p. 461 THURGOOD MARSHALL PREDICTED: Schwartz, *Behind* Bakke, 42–43.

INCLINED TO THINK RACE A "FACTOR THAT CAN LAWFULLY [BE] CONSIDERED": Douglas Papers, Box 1654, Case Files O.T. 1973.

p. 462 MOST CONTROVERSIAL BY FAR WAS THE BRIEF OF THE UNITED STATES: See Caplan, *The Tenth Justice,* 39–48; Osborne, "White House Watch: Carter's Brief," *New Republic,* Oct. 15, 1977, pp. 13–16.

WROTE PRESIDENT CARTER THAT THE DRAFT BRIEF WAS "BAD LAW, AND PERNICIOUS SOCIAL POLICY": Califano, *Governing America,* 238–39.

THE CONGRESSIONAL BLACK CAUCUS WARNED CARTER THAT HE WOULD "DISCREDIT HIS PRESIDENCY IN THE EYES OF HISTORY": *Washington Post,* Sept. 13, 1977, p. A1.

MOST OF THESE PRESSURES REPORTEDLY NEVER REACHED McCREE: Caplan, *The Tenth Justice,* 45–46.

p. 463 THE MOST INFLUENTIAL VOICE CAME FROM OUTSIDE THE ADMINISTRATION: Frank Easterbrook, interview.

THE FINAL PRODUCT BORE "ALL THE SCARS OF ITS TORTURED CREATION": Lewin, "The Bakke Brief," *New Republic,* Oct. 1, 1977, p. 17.

DISMISSED THE GOVERNMENT'S ARGUMENT AS "SIMPLY OUT IN LEFT FIELD": Robert D. Comfort, interview.

"OUR CONSTITUTION IS COLOR-BLIND": *Plessy v. Ferguson,* 163 U.S. 537, 559 (1896) (Harlan, J., dissenting).

p. 464 MARTIN LUTHER KING, JR., DREAMED THAT "MY FOUR LITTLE CHILDREN": King, *A Testament of Hope,* 219. King's statement was later used by Shelby Steele as the title to his attack on affirmative action, *The Content of Their Character.*

THE NAACP HAD CONDEMNED RACE CONSCIOUSNESS: Graham, *The Civil Rights Era,* 110.

"THERE IS NO UNDERSTANDABLE FACTUAL BASIS FOR CLASSIFICATION BY RACE": Kluger, *Simple Justice,* 264.

"LAWS WHICH GIVE EQUAL PROTECTION ARE THOSE WHICH MAKE NO *DISCRIMINATION* BECAUSE OF RACE IN THE SENSE THAT THEY MAKE NO *DISTINCTION* BECAUSE OF RACE": Brief of the Committee of Law Teachers Against Segregation in Legal Education in *Sweatt v. Painter,* 339 U.S. 629 (1950), p. 8. The principal author was Thomas I. Emerson of Yale.

SO SAID ALEXANDER BICKEL: Bickel, *The Morality of Consent,* 132–33.

"[T]HERE CAN BE NO BLINKING THE ENORMOUS AND UNIQUE SET OF HANDICAPS": Bundy, "The Issue Before the Court," *Atlantic,* Nov. 1977, p. 42.

p. 466 "DISCRETE AND INSULAR MINORITIES": The phrase comes from *United States v. Carolene Products Co.,* 304 U.S. 144, 152 n. 4 (1938).

THE ARGUMENT THAT ANIMATES MUCH OF CONSTITUTIONAL LAW: See generally Ely, *Democracy and Distrust.*

HIGHER INFANT MORTALITY, HIGHER MATERNAL MORTALITY, LOWER LIFE EXPECTANCY: U.S. Bureau of the Census, *Current Population Reports: The Social and Economic Status of the Black Population in the U.S.,* Tables 82 and 84 (1974). See generally Seham, *Blacks and American Medical Care.*

IN 1970 THERE WAS ONE PHYSICIAN FOR EVERY 649 PERSONS: Brief for Petitioner, *Regents of the University of California v. Bakke,* 23 (citing sources).

p. 467 "THE OBSTACLES AND SCARS OF HUNDREDS OF YEARS OF RACISM": King, in "More About the Bakke Case," *Atlantic*, Dec. 1977, p. 76.

"IF PARENTS OF FIVE CHILDREN RECOGNIZE THAT TWO OF THEM ARE SERIOUSLY ILL": Lowery, in "More About the Bakke Case," *Atlantic*, Dec. 1977, p. 76.

p. 469 "TOO LATE IN THE DAY": Robert C. Comfort, interview.

p. 470 "THE OUTCOME OF THIS CONTROVERSY": Brief for Petitioner, 13.

LAW SHOULD SERVE THE CAUSE OF SOCIAL STABILITY: See Wilkinson, *From Brown to Bakke*, 301.

p. 472 IN THE FIRST FIVE YEARS, DAVIS HAD TAKEN SEVENTY STUDENTS FROM MINORITY ADMISSIONS: Brief for Petitioner, 3.

p. 473 THUS IT WAS THAT COMFORT RECEIVED THE INSTRUCTION: Robert D. Comfort, interview.

HE EMERGED SOME WEEKS LATER WITH A BENCH MEMO: Robert D. Comfort, "Memorandum for Mr. Justice Powell," Aug. 29, 1977.

JUSTIFICATIONS OF THIS MAGNITUDE ARE EXCEEDINGLY RARE: Indeed, for a long time, one might have supposed that the only clear case of a *compelling* reason for restricting constitutional rights was the Second World War. See *Hirabayashi v. United States*, 320 U.S. 81 (1943), and *Korematsu v. United States*, 323 U.S. 214 (1944), which upheld otherwise unconstitutional restrictions on Japanese-Americans because of the "pressing social necessity" of war with the Japanese Empire.

"'STRICT' IN THEORY AND FATAL IN FACT": Gunther, "Foreword," *Harvard L. Rev.* 86:8.

p. 475 A STATEMENT FROM HARVARD COLLEGE: "Harvard College Admissions Program," an appendix to the Brief of Columbia University et al. as Amicus Curiae, *Regents of the University of California v. Bakke*, 2.

p. 477 THE STATE'S INTEREST WAS NOT, HIS OPINION LATER STATED, IN "SIMPLE ETHNIC DIVERSITY": All quotations in this paragraph come from Powell's published opinion in *Regents of the University of California v. Bakke*, 438 U.S. 265, 315–19 (1978).

p. 478 FIRST LIGHT ON WEDNESDAY, OCTOBER 12, REVEALED MORE THAN ONE HUNDRED PERSONS: *Time*, Oct. 24, 1977, p. 95; *Washington Post*, Oct. 13, 1977, p. A1.

PUSHING, SHOVING, AND BREAKING IN LINE: *Washington Post*, Oct. 24, 1977, p. A18 (letters to the editor).

"FELT HE COULDN'T MAINTAIN HIS SECLUSION FROM THE PRESS": *Los Angeles Times*, Oct. 13, 1977, p. 17.

p. 479 JUSTICES ARE MOST SUSCEPTIBLE TO PERSUASION IN OUT-OF-THE-WAY AREAS WHERE THEY HAVE NO FIRM VIEWS: Chief Justice Rehnquist has said that oral argument has to some degree changed his views in "a significant minority of the cases," but that the effect is "most likely to occur in cases involving areas of law with which I am least familiar." Rehnquist, *The Supreme Court*, 276.

p. 480 "THIS IS UNBELIEVABLE": Schwartz, *Behind* Bakke, 53. Schwartz's source is an unidentified Justice, who internal evidence suggests was probably Justice Blackmun.

COLVIN WAS SIMPLY "IN OVER HIS HEAD": *Id.*

WHO URGED THAT HE TURN THE ARGUMENT OVER TO AN EXPERT: *Id.* The specific suggestion was Philip B. Kurland, an eminent scholar and experienced Supreme Court advocate who had written an amicus brief supporting Bakke's position.

p. 481 SOME TALKED OF "TOO LITTLE, TOO LATE": Lawrence, "The Bakke Case," *Saturday Review*, Oct. 15, 1977, pp. 14, 15.

"STEADFASTLY REFUSED TO GO THROUGH A DRY RUN": Archibald Cox, interview.

p. 482 RESTED THERE NO MORE COMFORTABLY THAN A LIVE FOX: *Washington Star*, Oct. 14, 1977. See Avery (ed.), *The New Century Classical Handbook*, 1026. ("A well-known story of Spartan self-control and self-discipline is of the Spartan boy who stole a fox, hid it under his cloak, and stood motionless and silent while the fox gnawed at his vitals.")

p. 483 STATUTE BANNED RACIAL DISCRIMINATION IN ANY PROGRAM RECEIVING FEDERAL FUNDS: Specifically, sec. 601 of the Civil Rights Act of 1964, now codified at 42 U.S.C. sec. 2000d, provides: "No person in the United States shall, on the ground of race, color, or national origin, be excluded from participation in, be denied the benefits of, or be subjected to discrimination under any program or activity receiving Federal financial assistance."

POWELL RESPONDED THE NEXT DAY WITH AN OPPOSING MEMORANDUM: LFP, Memorandum to the Conference, Oct. 14, 1977.

MAJORITY AGREED TO CALL FOR ADDITIONAL BRIEFS: Specifically, the Court gave thirty days for each party to submit a supplemental brief "discussing Title VI of the Civil Rights Act of 1964 as it applies to this case." 434 U.S. 900 (1977). On this issue, White was joined by Burger, Blackmun, Rehnquist, and Stevens. Powell, Brennan, Stewart, and Marshall voted against.

BOTH BURGER AND REHNQUIST WANTED TO HOLD THE DAVIS PROGRAM UNCONSTITUTIONAL: They said so in memoranda to the Conference dated, respectively, Oct. 21 and Nov. 10, 1977. Some years later, these memoranda were published in Schwartz, *Behind* Bakke, pp. 167 et seq.

p. 485 "SO LONG AS NOTHING IS DONE IN AN UN-HARVARD-LIKE MANNER": Maguire, "The Triumph of Unequal Justice," *Christian Century*, Sept. 27, 1978, p. 882. This was what Maquire feared "at first cynical blush." His article goes on to make exceptionally perceptive and thoughtful criticisms of Powell's position.

p. 486 "THE CONSTITUTIONAL PRINCIPLE I THINK TO BE SUPPORTED BY OUR CASES": Brennan, Memorandum to the Conference, Nov. 23, 1977.

HE SAID HE HAD "CHANGED HIS MIND SEVERAL TIMES": LFP's notes, Dec. 9, 1977.

p. 487 BRENNAN MADE A BRILLIANT INTERVENTION: See Schwartz, *Behind* Bakke, 96–97.

LATER DESCRIBED POWELL'S ACQUIESCENCE AS "A CRUCIAL CONCESSION": *Id.*

"THUS, AT THE END OF MY OPINION, THE BOTTOM LINE WOULD BE": LFP to Warren E. Burger, Apr. 12, 1978.

"THAT THE PRINCIPLE OF AFFIRMATIVE ACTION WAS BEING UPHELD": Schwartz, *Behind* Bakke, 97.

p. 488 ONE INSIDE SOURCE REPORTED THAT MARSHALL WAS "LIVID" OVER POWELL'S OPINION: This comes from a draft of Brennan's "case history" of *Bakke*. See Brennan Papers, Box 464, Case File No. 78-811, Library of Congress.

"I CAN SWING INTO PLACE ONE WAY OR THE OTHER AFTER MY RETURN": Blackmun, Memorandum to the Conference, Dec. 5, 1977.

A FLURRY OF MEMORANDA: The details are recounted in Schwartz, *Behind* Bakke, 99–119.

GREW IRRITABLE WHENEVER *BAKKE* WAS MENTIONED: *Id.*, 122.

BAKKE WAS ADDED TO THE AGENDA OF A CONFERENCE IN EARLY MARCH: *Id.*

BURGER TRIED A DIFFERENT TACK: The account of this conversation is based on Powell's written response, dated two days later.

p. 489 "HOWEVER HIS VOTE MAY GO, THE COUNTRY WILL THEN HAVE AN ANSWER": LFP to Warren E. Burger, Apr. 12, 1978.

WHETHER MONTANA COULD CHARGE OUTSIDERS A HIGHER FEE: *Baldwin v. Montana Fish and Game Commission,* 436 U.S. 371 (1978).

BRENNAN DECIDED TO WITHHOLD HIS VOTE UNTIL ARGUMENT OF A RELATED CASE: *Hicklin v. Orbeck,* 437 U.S. 518 (1978).

BLACKMUN WAS OUTRAGED: The details of this story come from Schwartz, *Behind* Bakke, 125–27.

p. 490 BRENNAN MUST HAVE BEEN TEMPTED TO DO SOMETHING, ANYTHING, TO SATISFY BLACKMUN: *Id.,* 126. Schwartz reports that Brennan at first told his clerk to rearrange things in order to accelerate Blackmun's case, but then "decided that it would be wrong to give in to that kind of pressure" and so countermanded the order.

WHEN THE COURT PREPARED TO ANNOUNCE A BLACKMUN ANTITRUST DECISION: *National Broiler Marketing Association v. United States,* 436 U.S. 816 (1978). This story is taken from a fragment of the Brennan's "case history" of *Bakke.* See Brennan Papers, Box 464, Case File No. 76-811, Library of Congress.

FRANK LYON COMPANY V. UNITED STATES: 435 U.S. 561 (1978).

p. 491 POWELL'S REMARKS AT THE REHEARSAL DINNER: Characteristically, he had prepared a speech, dated June 1, 1978, for the occasion.

POWELL RESPONDED AS FOLLOWS: This portion of the response appears at 438 U.S. 294–95 n. 34.

p. 492 THE ORIGINAL VERSION THEN CONTINUED: The footnote first appeared in the fifth draft of Powell's opinion, circulated in late June.

AS POWELL RECORDED IN A MEMORANDUM TO THE FILE: LFP, Memo to the File, June 29, 1979.

p. 493 MOST ELOQUENT OF ALL WAS THE OPINION BY JUSTICE MARSHALL: 438 U.S. 265, 387 (1978) (Marshall, J., dissenting).

p. 494 "A CHIEF WITH NO INDIANS": LFP, Memorandum to the Conference, June 27, 1978.

THE OTHER TWO CASES WERE "PIPSQUEAKS": *Allied Structural Steel Co. v. Spannaus,* 438 U.S. 234 (1978), and *Swisher v. Brady,* 438 U.S. 204 (1978).

POWELL BEGAN WITH THE BAD NEWS: These excerpts are taken from the actual text of Powell's statement from the bench, which had been edited before delivery. Schwartz, *Behind* Bakke, 143–46, quotes from the first draft of Powell's statement. The earlier version is wordier but not substantially different.

p. 495 "I HAVE SEEN GREAT MOMENTS THERE": Lewis, "The Solomonic Decision," *New York Times,* June 29, 1978, p. A25.

"PACK UP AND FADE AWAY LIKE DRACULA BEFORE A CROSS": *Los Angeles Times,* June 2, 1978, p. 8.

p. 496 TOP BILLING AND LARGER TYPE USUALLY GIVEN TO THE PAPER'S EDITORIAL PREFERENCE: All headlines are from June 29, 1978. Capital letters denote larger type.

CONGRESSMAN RONALD V. DELLUMS FUMED THAT HE WAS "APPALLED": Washington Star, June 29, 1978.

"WE MUST REBEL": *Newsweek,* July 10, 1978, p. 20; *Time,* July 10, 1978, p. 15; *U.S. News & World Report,* July 10, 1978, p. 15.

"WE HAVE NOT WON TOTAL VICTORY, BUT THIS IS NOT DEFEAT": Abernathy, "Affirmative Action," ABA *Journal* 64:1234.

BENJAMIN HOOKS . . . AND VERNON JORDAN: See "The Reaction: A Ruling With Something for Every Group," *Washington Post*, June 29, 1978, pp. A1, A23.

MEG GREENFIELD OF THE *WASHINGTON POST* HAD HOPED THE COURT WOULD "FIND A WAY TO BLUR THE EDGES": Greenfield, "How to Resolve the Bakke Case," *Washington Post*, Oct. 19, 1977, p. A13.

p. 497 AS THE *POST* SAW IT, "EVERYONE WON": "The Bakke Decision," *Washington Post*, June 29, 1978, p. A26.

CHARLES ALAN WRIGHT . . . CALLED IT "A VERY CIVILIZED RULING": All three quotations are taken from *Newsweek*, July 10, 1978, p. 25.

THE "PEACE-MAKING AND CALMING EFFECT OF THE POWELL POSITION": Mishkin, "The Uses of Ambivalence," *University of Pennsylvania L. Rev.* 131:907.

"I THINK THE WHOLE COUNTRY OUGHT TO BE PLEASED": "The Reaction: A Ruling With Something for Every Group," *Washington Post*, June 29, 1978, p. A1.

GUIDO CALABRESI, FUTURE DEAN OF THE YALE LAW SCHOOL, BEMOANED THE "LOST CANDOR" IN POWELL'S EQUIVOCATION: Calabresi, "Bakke: Lost Candor," *New York Times*, July 6, 1978, p. A19. See also Calabresi, "*Bakke* as Pseudo-Tragedy," *Catholic University L. Rev.* 28:427–44.

"THE 14TH AMENDMENT ALLOWS SOME, BUT NOT TOO MUCH, REVERSE DISCRIMINATION": Bork, "The Unpersuasive Bakke Decision," *Wall Street Journal*, July 21, 1978, p.8.

RONALD DWORKIN CALLED THE OPINION "WEAK": Dworkin, "The Bakke Decision: Did It Decide Anything?" *New York Review of Books*, Aug. 17, 1978, p. 22.

COLUMNIST WILLIAM RASPBERRY: *Washington Post*, July 3, 1978, p. A23.

p. 498 "CLEARLY, A MAJORITY OF WHITES ARE WILLING TO ENDORSE 'SPECIAL CONSIDERATION'": Lipset and Schneider, "The Bakke Case," *Public Opinion*, Mar.-Apr. 1978, p. 43.

SUPREME COURT'S VIEW . . . WAS "AS DIVIDED AND CONFUSED AS THE AMERICAN PEOPLE IN GENERAL": *Baltimore Sun*, June 29, 1978. p. A16.

"IT REMINDS ONE OF MARK TWAIN'S REMARK THAT GOD PROTECTS": Henry J. Friendly, Jr., to LFP, July 1, 1978.

"I THINK YOUR STANCE WAS EXACTLY RIGHT": Gerald Gunther to LFP, June 29, 1978.

"JOHN MARSHALL AT HIS BEST": Colgate Darden to LFP, June 28, 1978.

"THERE'S MUCH TO BE SAID FOR THE BRITISH PRACTICE OF REWARDING MILITARY VICTORS": Gen. Maxwell D. Taylor (Ret.) to LFP, June 30, 1978.

p. 499 "IT IS A LONG WAY BACK TO OUR ARGUMENTS ABOUT *CHARLOTTE-MECKLENBURG*": John W. Riely to LFP, July 2, 1978.

WARREN WEAVER, SUPREME COURT REPORTER FOR *THE NEW YORK TIMES*, REMARKED ON THIS TENDENCY: Weaver, "Powell Either (a) Leads, or (b) Follows Very Well," *New York Times*, July 9, 1978, p.E4.

p. 500 SIX MAJOR AFFIRMATIVE ACTION CASES: *Fullilove v. Klutznick*, 448 U.S. 448 (1980); *Firefighters Local Union No. 1784 v. Stotts*, 467 U.S. 561 (1984); *Wygant v. Jackson Board of Education*, 476 U.S. 267 (1986); *International Association Sheet Metal Workers v. Equal Employment Opportunity Commission*, 478 U.S. 421 (1986); *Local No. 93, International Association of Firefighters v. Cleveland*, 478 U.S. 501 (1986); and *United States v. Paradise*, 480 U.S. 149 (1987). Three other cases were decided without squarely reaching the merits. See *Minnick v. California Department of Corrections*, 452 U.S.

105 (1981); *Johnson v. Board of Education of the City of Chicago,* 457 U.S. 52 (1982); *Schmidt v. Oakland Unified School District,* 457 U.S. 594 (1982). Finally, Powell did not participate in one important case, *United Steelworkers of America, AFL-CIO-CLC v. Weber,* 443 U.S. 193 (1979).

THE COURT'S ODD COUPLE WERE WHITE AND STEVENS, WHO SEEMED TO SWITCH PLACES: White's votes in the six cases listed in the preceding footnote were yes, no, no, no, no, no. Stevens' votes in the same cases were no, no, yes, yes, yes, yes.

BOTH OF THE AFFIRMATIVE ACTION PLANS THAT WERE STRUCK DOWN: *Firefighters Local Union No. 1784 v. Stotts,* 467 U.S. 561 (1984); *Wygant v. Jackson Board of Education,* 476 U.S. 267 (1986).

CHAPTER XV: CHANGING TIMES

p. 502 TO RECORD HIS HOPES FOR A DAUGHTER: LFP to Josephine McR. Powell, Oct. 22, 1942.

p. 503 MOLLY COVERED THE NAME ON HER LSAT SCORE: Josephine R. Powell, interview; Molly Powell Sumner, interview.

"FORGIVE US OUR DEBTS AS WE FORGIVE OUR DADDIES": Josephine R. Powell, interview.

"THE KIND OF GIRL": Penny Clark, interview.

"AN UNCONSCIOUS UNDERESTIMATION OF WOMEN'S ABILITIES": Mary Becker, interview. The remaining quotes in this paragraph are drawn from interviews with several female clerks.

p. 504 TOLD HIS FRIEND VICE PRESIDENT GEORGE BUSH: *Washington Post,* July 8, 1981, p. A1. See generally Abraham, *Justices and Presidents,* 330–39.

THE JUSTICES CHANGED THEIR STYLE: LFP, interview.

"UNTIL A WOMAN IS ON THE COURT AND HER PARTICULAR DESIRES ARE MADE KNOWN": Harry A. Blackmun to Warren E. Burger, Nov. 17, 1980.

p. 505 CALLED THE WHITE HOUSE WITH A GLOWING RECOMMENDATION: *Newsweek,* July 20, 1981, p. 17.

"KICK FALWELL RIGHT IN THE ASS": *Newsweek,* July 27, 1981, p. 24.

"WE'VE BEEN CHALLENGED": *Time,* July 20, 1981, p. 10.

"WE WERE IN A BAD STATE": Sandra Day O'Connor, interview.

POWELL CAME TO HER RESCUE: LFP, interview; Sandra Day O'Connor, interview; Linda Blandford, interview.

p. 506 "SAID, BY FRIEND AND FOE ALIKE, TO BE NOTABLY BRIGHT": *New York Times,* July 8, 1991, p. A1.

STRIVING FOR PERFECTION: *Time,* July 20, 1981, p. 18.

"IRON LADY" *Congressional Quarterly Weekly Report,* July 11, 1981, p. 1235.

"SHE DOES NOT TOLERATE NONSENSE": *Washington Post,* July 8, 1981, p. A6.

p. 507 "JUST WASN'T DONE": Sandra Day O'Connor, interview.

HE ASKED A FEMALE CLERKSHIP CANDIDATE: Christina B. Whitman, interview.

p. 508 STRUCK DOWN AN ARBITRARY PREFERENCE FOR MEN OVER WOMEN: *Reed v. Reed,* 404 U.S. 71 (1971).

THE NEXT CASE: *Frontiero v. Richardson,* 411 U.S. 677 (1973).

HE DID SO, HE SAID, AT THE REQUEST OF DOUGLAS AND WHITE: William J. Brennan, Memorandum to the Conference, Feb. 28, 1973.

p. 509 AFTER SOME STRUGGLE": Harry A. Blackmun to William J. Brennan, Mar. 5, 1973.

p. 510 PAID WOMEN LESS IN SURVIVOR'S BENEFITS AND OTHER DEFERRED COMPENSATION: See, e.g., *Weinberger v. Wiesenfeld*, 420 U.S. 636 (1975) (survivor's benefits); *Califano v. Goldfarb*, 430 U.S. 199 (1977) (same); *Wengler v. Druggists Mutual Ins. Co.*, 446 U.S. 142 (1980) (death benefits).

INVALIDATED A LAW EXCUSING WOMEN FROM JURY DUTY: *Taylor v. Louisiana*, 419 U.S. 522 (1975).

REJECTED A DISTINCTION IN THE DURATION OF CHILD SUPPORT: *Stanton v. Stanton*, 421 U.S. 7 (1975).

STRUCK DOWN A LAW ALLOWING HUSBANDS TO DISPOSE OF JOINTLY HELD PROPERTY: *Kirchberg v. Feenstra*, 450 U.S. 455 (1981).

"INSULATE SCHOOLCHILDREN FROM THE SIGHT OF CONSPICUOUSLY PREGNANT WOMEN": *Cleveland Board of Education v. LaFleur*, 414 U.S. 632, 641 n. 9, 654 (1974) (Powell, J., concurring in the result).

REFUSING TO RULE THAT THE LAW REQUIRED PRIVATE DISABILITY BENEFITS: *Geduldig v. Aiello*, 417 U.S. 484 (1974); *General Electric Corp. v. Gilbert*, 429 U.S. 125 (1976).

p. 511 GIVING WIDOWS BUT NOT WIDOWERS A PARTIAL EXEMPTION FROM PROPERTY TAXES: *Kahn v. Shevin*, 416 U.S. 351 (1974).

AN UP-OR-OUT RULE OF THIRTEEN YEARS FOR WOMEN NAVAL OFFICERS: *Schlesinger v. Ballard*, 419 U.S. 498 (1975).

TO PUNISH MEN BUT NOT WOMEN FOR CONSENSUAL SEXUAL INTERCOURSE: *Michael M. v. Superior Court of Sonoma County*, 450 U.S. 464 (1981).

REQUIRING MEN BUT NOT WOMEN TO REGISTER FOR THE DRAFT: *Rostker v. Goldberg*, 453 U.S. 57 (1981).

AN ALL-FEMALE NURSING SCHOOL: *Mississippi University for Women v. Hogan*, 458 U.S. 718 (1982).

CONSTITUTIONAL RIGHT TO USE CONTRACEPTIVES: *Griswold v. Connecticut*, 381 U.S. 503 (1965).

EXTENDED THAT RIGHT TO UNMARRIED PERSONS: *Eisenstadt v. Baird*, 405 U.S. 438 (1972).

p. 512 DOE V. COMMONWEALTH'S ATTORNEY: 425 U.S. 901 (1975).

A "MATURE INDIVIDUAL'S CHOICE OF AN ADULT SEXUAL PARTNER": *Doe v. Commonwealth's Attorney*, 403 F. Supp. 1199, 1203 (E.D. Va. 1975) (Merhige, J., dissenting) (footnote omitted).

p. 513 THE COURT WAS LATER CHASTISED FOR BACKHANDING A QUESTION OF SUCH IMPORTANCE: The controversy over the summary disposition of *Doe* sprang from a technicality in the Court's jurisdiction. Most cases come to the Supreme Court by a petition for a writ of certiorari. The Justices can refuse to hear such cases simply by denying the petition, and that action expresses no conclusion on the merits. Unusually, *Doe v. Commonwealth's Attorney* came to the Court as an appeal, which requires resolution on the merits. Technically, therefore, the Court's one-line summary affirmance was a decision rejecting the claim on the merits. In practice, however, the Justices often treated certiorari petitions and appeals more or less alike. Functionally, therefore, the affirmance in *Doe* represented little more than the Justices' decision not to schedule the case for full briefing and oral argument. For a later explanation of the meaning of such actions, see *Carey v. Population Services International*, 431 U.S. 678 (1988).

THE CASE THAT FINALLY FORCED THE ISSUE: See Irons, *The Courage of Their Convictions*, 381–403.

PROSECUTOR ABHORRED "THAT TYPE OF CONDUCT": *Id.*

"GOD BLESS THE POLICE OFFICER": *Id.*

p. 514 THE APPEALS COURT RULED: *Hardwick v. Bowers*, 760 F.2d 1202 (11th Cir. 1985).

ANOTHER APPEALS COURT REACHED EXACTLY THE OPPOSITE CONCLUSION: *Baker v. Wade*, 769 F.2d 289 (5th Cir. 1985). See also *Dronenburg v. Zech*, 741 F.2d 1388 (D.C. Cir. 1984).

p. 515 TRIBE'S INNOCUOUS ARGUMENT SET HIM OFF: The quotations in this and the succeeding paragraph come from a memorandum dated March 31, 1986.

p. 516 ARGUED POWERFULLY FOR LIMITING THE CONSTITUTIONAL RIGHT OF PRIVACY: All quotations in this and the succeeding three paragraphs come from a memorandum from Mike Mosman dated March 29, 1986.

p. 517 THE GHOST OF JOHN HARLAN: *Griswold v. Connecticut*, 381 U.S. 479, 499 (1965) (Harlan, J., concurring in the judgment).

MOORE V. CITY OF EAST CLEVELAND: 431 U.S. 494 (1977).

p. 518 "POLICE HAVE MORE IMPORTANT RESPONSIBILITIES THAN SNOOPING AROUND": LFP, Memorandum to Mike Mosman, Mar. 31, 1986.

p. 519 NOT CREATE A NEW CONSTITUTIONAL RIGHT OF CONSENSUAL SODOMY: The discussion in text is a slight simplication of the actual legal doctrine. Technically, the question before the Court in *Bowers v. Hardwick* was whether private sodomy between consenting adults was a "fundamental right." Although laws touching a fundamental right are almost always struck down, they may occasionally be upheld if the government can show a "compelling" interest for the regulation. This standard is rarely met. Therefore, although declaring a "fundamental right" to engage in homosexual sodomy would have been tantamount to striking down the laws against that activity, it is conceivable that some legal restraints might nevertheless have survived if the government could show a "compelling" reason for them. Given the outcome of the case, this possibility has not been tested.

p. 520 *ROBINSON V. CALIFORNIA*: 370 U.S. 660 (1962).

OTHERS THOUGHT THE *ROBINSON* ARGUMENT SIMPLY "CRAZY": Pamela Karlan, interview.

p. 521 ONE OF HIS CLERKS WAS GAY: This situation was imagined in Sedgwick, *Epistemology of the Closet*, 74–75.

p. 522 BURGER LED OFF WITH A TIRADE: The remarks of the Justices were reconstructed from Powell's Conference notes.

p. 523 "PRETTY MUCH ALL LAW CONSISTS IN FORBIDDING MEN TO DO SOME THINGS THAT THEY WANT TO DO": The quotation comes from *Adkins v. Children's Hospital*, 261 U.S. 525, 568 (1923).

p. 524 MOSSMAN WEIGHED IN WITH A MEMO URGING POWELL TO CHANGE HIS VOTE: This memorandum is not in Powell's files and has been reconstructed from interviews. The omission conceivably could have been advertent but likely was accidental.

p. 525 A REMARKABLY COMPLETE AND ACCURATE ACCOUNT OF THE SWITCH: *Washington Post*, July 13, 1986, p. A1.

"SUPERFICIAL, PEREMPTORY AND INSENSITIVE": Gewirtz, "The Court was 'Superficial' in the Homosexuality Case," *New York Times*, July 8, 1986, p. A21.

"FAILURE TO ACKNOWLEDGE IN ANY WAY THE HUMAN DIMENSION OF THIS ISSUE": *Id.*

p. 526 REJECTED LIFE SENTENCES FOR MINOR CRIMES: See *Solem v. Helm,* 463 U.S. 277 (1983).

p. 529 "THE MOST PREPOSTEROUS AND CONTRADICTORY RULING": *Boston Globe,* July 1, 1986, p. 18.

"A GRATUITOUS AND PETTY RULING": *New York Times,* July 2, 1986, p. A30.

INCLUDING ONE BY ALAN DERSHOWITZ: *New York Times,* Aug. 12, 1988, p. A20.

p. 530 "SOME EXCITED GRADUATES MUST SIT A ROW OR TWO AWAY FROM THEIR RAPISTS": *Yale Law Report* 36:12.

"I PROBABLY MADE A MISTAKE IN THAT ONE": Anand Agneshwar, "Ex-Justice Says He May Have Been Wrong," *National L.J.,* Nov. 5, 1990, p. 3. This publication gave the story national circulation, but it first appeared a few days earlier in an article by the same author for the *New York Law Journal.*

"I THINK IT'S AN ADMIRABLE THING": Quoted in the *National L.J.,* Nov. 5, 1990, p. 3.

TRIBE ALSO WROTE POWELL A PERSONAL LETTER: Laurence H. Tribe to LFP, Oct. 26, 1990.

"I HAD FORGOTTEN THAT YOU ARGUED *BOWERS*": LFP to Laurence H. Tribe, Nov. 2, 1990.

CHAPTER XVI: A SENSE OF DUTY

p. 531 THE MEDIAN AGE: The average age of the Justices had been slightly higher immediately before the retirement of Justice Van Devanter in 1937.

p. 532 REHNQUIST'S "DRUG PROBLEM": See *New York Times,* Aug. 13, 1986, p. A19, and Aug. 14, 1986, p. D22.

"STILL BEING PROCESSED": See Totenberg and Barbash, "Burger Loved the Law But Not the Hassle," *Washington Post,* June 22, 1986, p. C1.

HE BACKDATED THE DOCUMENT: Sally Smith, interview.

HE DENIED THAT LAW CLERKS WROTE HIS OPINIONS: LFP, interview.

"BORE NO RELATION TO REALITY": Totenberg and Barbash, "Burger Loved the Law But Not the Hassle," *Washington Post,* June 22, 1986, p. C1.

p. 533 BURGER WOULD "DRIVE US ALL CRAZY": William J. Brennan, interview.

THE POWELL COURT: Schwartz, *Packing the Courts,* 122.

HE THOUGHT POWELL TOO GIVEN TO DECIDING CASES "ON THESE PARTICULAR FACTS": William H. Rehnquist, interview.

p. 534 "THOSE TWO WOULDN'T AGREE": R. Hewitt Pate, interview.

p. 535 "TEN YEARS OF LEWIS POWELL": *New York Times,* Oct. 22, 1971, p.A25.

p. 536 LETTER LEWIS WROTE SHORTLY AFTER THEIR CONVERSATION: The letter is dated April 9, 1983, but two internal references to "Saturday morning" would seem slightly awkward if the letter were in fact written that same afternoon. Perhaps it was written the next day, Sunday, April 10.

LEWIS AGAIN WROTE TO OPPOSE: Lewis F. Powell III to LFP, April 30, 1983.

"ENRICH THE REMAINING INCHES": J. Harvie Wilkinson, Jr., to LFP, Mar. 21, 1979.

p. 537 THE "BRINK" OF RETIRING: LFP to Lewis F. Powell III, Aug. 14, 1985.

p. 539 TOLD HIS STARTLED CLERKS: *The Powell Chambers, 1972–1987,* p. 59.

THE EVENT ALMOST PROVED HIM RIGHT: This account is on medical records and on interviews with Dr. David C. Utz, Powell's surgeon, and with Dr. Jay Y. Gillenwater, head of urology at the University of Virginia.

"NOT ENOUGH FINGERS": Dr. David C. Utz, interview.

CHEMICALLY BLOCKED THE ABILITY OF THE BLOOD TO CLOT NORMALLY: To be more specific, the cancer elaborates an enzyme that interferes with the conversion of fibrinogen to fribin and thus inhibits coagulation. This hemolysis or fribrinolysis syndrome is well described in patients with prostatic cancer.

"THAT EXPERIENCE WAS HORRIFIC": Dr. David C. Utz, interview.

p. 540 THREE WERE REARGUED IN APRIL: *Pattern Makers' League of North America v. NLRB*, 473 U.S. 95 (1985); *Massachusetts Mutual Life Ins. Co. v. Russell*, 473 U.S. 134 (1985); *City of Cleburne v. Cleburne Living Center*, 473 U.S. 432 (1985). Additionally, *Jensen v. Quaring*, 472 U.S. 478 (1985), was affirmed by an equally divided Court.

BARELY CONSIDERED IT: The only evidence of attention to the issue at that time is a letter to Lewis III on August 14, 1985, stating that until he had the report of his doctors, "I am not *sure* that I should remain on the Court" (his emphasis) but adding, "I am assuming that I will, and already have read most of the briefs for the October Term."

p. 541 "PHYSICAL STRENGTH AND ENERGY TO PARTICIPATE FULLY AND EFFECTIVELY": LFP to Lewis F. Powell III, Aug. 14, 1985 (referring to the "final months of last Term").

p. 542 "PERSONAL AND CONFIDENTIAL" MEMORANDUM: Author to LFP, June 21, 1987.

"I THINK YOU'LL BE HAPPIER IF YOU KEEP GOING": Josephine Powell Smith to LFP, June 21, 1987.

"NO FUN TO PLAY IN THE MINORS AFTER A CAREER IN THE MAJOR LEAGUES": LFP, interview.

p. 543 "NOT JUST FOR SOMEONE HIS AGE": Andrew D. Leipold, interview.

p. 544 AT LEAST TWO OF HIS CLERKS THOUGHT HE SHOULD STEP DOWN: William J. Stuntz, memorandum to author, April 1, 1992.

POWELL SUFFERED FROM "CHRONIC FATIGUE": J. R. Reitemeier, M.D., to Walter W. Karney, M.D., June 11, 1987.

ON WEDNESDAY, JUNE 24, 1987: LFP, interview; William H. Rehnquist, interview. At a press conference held the day of his retirement, Powell said he had spoken with Rehnquist on Monday or Tuesday of that week, so it may be that some preliminary conversation occurred then, but it is clear that the main discussion took place later that week.

REHNQUIST BROKE HIS WORD: Bronner, *Battle for Justice*, 18.

HEATEDLY DENIES THIS ACCOUNT: William H. Rehnquist, interview. See *New York Times*, Sept. 17, 1987, p. 47.

HE FIRST SPOKE WITH REHNQUIST "ONLY MINUTES" BEFORE: Howard H. Baker, Jr., to author, Jan. 28, 1992.

p. 545 A FEW SAVVY REPORTERS ALERTED: Bronner, *Battle for Justice*, 16 (describing reactions of Richard Carelli of the Associated Press and Stephen Wermiel of the *Wall Street Journal*).

TOLD HIS CLERKS THE DAY BEFORE: Andrew D. Leipold, interview.

"JUST LIKE CHRISTMAS MORNING": *Id.*

"I'M STILL CRYING A BIT": Josephine Powell Smith to LFP, June 28, 1987.

p. 546 SERVED HALF AGAIN AS LONG AS THE TEN YEARS HE HAD PLANNED: This goal explains why Powell remembered that he first considered retiring in 1982, when he completed ten years on the bench. In fact, as his correspondence clearly shows, the date was 1983.

HAD GONE ONTO THE SUPREME COURT WHEN HE DID NOT WANT TO: This sentence is taken from a remark by William J. Stuntz.

p. 547 TELEPHONE TIPS: See *Washington Post*, June 22, 1992, pp. B1, B9.

p. 548 THE "MOST IMPORTANT PUBLIC SERVICE": Erwin N. Griswold to LFP, July 4, 1987.

p. 549 "NOTHING HAS SADDENED SO MUCH SINCE THE SECOND GREAT WAR": Woodrow Seals to LFP, Aug. 14, 1987.

"YOU WILL BE SORELY MISSED": Paul A. Freund to LFP, June 29, 1987.

"MODEL CONSERVATIVE": *New York Times*, June 27, 1987, p. A26.

"FORCE FOR MODERATION": Lewis, "Strength at the Center," *Harvard Law Bulletin*, Aug. 1987, p. 7.

p. 550 "DISTINGUISHED THE SUPREME COURT BY HIS PRESENCE": *Norfolk Virginian-Pilot*, June 27, 1987, p. A14.

"GENTLE, STUBBORN, INDEPENDENT REASONABLENESS": McDowell, "Verdict on Powell: Call It Affectionate Respect," *Richmond Times-Dispatch*, June 28, 1987, p. 1.

"AT HIS EXQUISITE BEST": Friddell, "Reluctant Justice Serves Well," *Norfolk Virginian-Pilot*, June 28, 1987, p. B5.

"THE MOST POWERFUL MAN IN AMERICA": Quoted in Bronner, *Battle for Justice*, 17. The original speaker was apparently Burt Neuborne. See *Washington Post*, June 27, 1987, p.A10.

ONLY WHEN JO WENT SHOPPING: Quoted in Bronner, *Battle for Justice*, 17.

TWENTY CIVIL LIBERTIES CASES: *Washington Post*, June 27, 1987, p. A10.

"WATCHING CAREFULLY . . . TO ENSURE THAT PRESIDENT REAGAN DOES THE RIGHT THING": Quoted in Bronner, *Battle for Justice*, 21–22.

"HE HAS BEEN A TRUE CONSERVATIVE, NOT A RIGHT-WING ZEALOT": *New York Times*, June 27, 1987, p.32.

p. 551 LIKE AN OLD TESTAMENT PROPHET: Powe, "From Bork to Souter," *Williamette L. Rev.* 27:782.

"ROBERT BORK'S AMERICA": Quoted in Bronner, *Battle for Justice*, 98–99.

"RECKLESS AND INTEMPERATE": Pertschuk and Schaetzel, *The People Rising*, 34.

"CHARACTER ASSASSINATION BY CALCULATED LIE": Powe, "From Bork to Souter," *Williamette L. Rev.* 27:785.

KENNEDY'S STATEMENT "FROZE THE SENATE": Pertschuk and Schaetzel, *The People Rising*, 101–2.

SENATOR HOWELL HEFLIN LED THE WAY: Bronner, *Battle for Justice*, 180, 294–95.

p. 552 "HIS PASSIONATE, RELENTLESS, ASSAULT": Pertschuk and Schaetzel, *The People Rising*, 15.

"REACTIONARY MONSTER": Carter, "Bork Redux," *Texas L. Rev.* 69:760.

"I KNOW HOW YOU'RE GOING TO VOTE": Bronner, *Battle for Justice*, 186.

ONLY SIX OF THE TWENTY-TWO SENATORS: *New York Times*, Oct. 24, 1987, p. A10.

FOURTEEN SOUTHERN SENATORS VOTED FOR [CLARENCE THOMAS]: *New York Times*, Oct. 16, 1991, p. A19.

TRIED EVERY MEANS TO PERSUADE POWELL TO ENDORSE BORK: LFP, Confidential Memorandum on the Nomination of Judge Robert Bork, Oct. 14, 1987, from which the quotations in the next two paragraphs are taken.

ON SEPTEMBER 25 THE WHITE HOUSE ADMITTED: *The New York Times*, Sept. 26, 1987, p. A1.

p. 553 WITH WHOM HE AND BORK PLAYED POKER: Bronner, *Battle for Justice*, 315.

"BILL SAYS HE SEES NO PROBLEM": Leonard Garment to LFP, Oct. 10, 1987.

"MADE IT EXPLICITLY CLEAR": LFP, Confidential Memorandum on the Nomination of Judge Robert Bork, Oct. 14, 1987.

HE SEEMED "ASTONISHINGLY OUT OF HIS DEPTH": Bronner, *Battle for Justice*, 301–303.

p. 554 "INAPPROPRIATE FOR A NEWLY RETIRED JUSTICE": LFP, Confidential Memorandum on the Nomination of Judge Robert Bork, Oct. 14, 1987.

"I AM CONCERNED": LFP to author, Oct. 16, 1987.

"TERRIBLE DAMAGE TO THE UNDERLYING VALUES OF THIS DEMOCRACY": Broder, "When Judges Are Lynched to Appease the Public," *Washington Post*, Oct. 6, 1987, p. A21.

"A CRUCIAL PRINCIPLE IS AT STAKE": Quoted in Bronner, *Battle for Justice*, 320.

p. 556 "EITHER A MARKEDLY MORE MODERATE": *Id.*, 337.

CONFIRMED HIM WITHOUT DISSENT: *New York Times*, Feb. 4, 1988, p. A18.

"THERE'S NO WAY I COULD HAVE KNOWN": *Cleveland Plain Dealer*, Oct. 15, 1987, p. 8-A.

THEY COUNTED THIRTY-TWO: Justice White, interview. The list apparently included *Lorance v. AT&T Technologies, Inc.*, 490 U.S. 900 (1989), which was decided by a vote of five–three with O'Connor not participating.

WEBSTER V. REPRODUCTIVE HEALTH SERVICES: 492 U.S. 490 (1989).

RULINGS IN A PAIR OF CAPITAL CASES: *Penry v. Lynaugh*, 492 U.S. 302 (1989); *Stanford v. Kentucky*, 492 U.S. 361 (1989).

p. 557 MORE DIFFICULT FOR CIVIL RIGHTS PLAINTIFFS: *Wards Cove Packing Co., Inc. v. Atonio*, 490 U.S. 642 (1989).

RESTRICTED THE RANGE OF FEDERAL REMEDIES FOR RACIAL HARASSMENT: *Patterson v. McLean Credit Union*, 491 U.S. 164 (1989).

LAW AGAINST DESECRATION OF THE AMERICAN FLAG: *Texas v. Johnson*, 491 U.S. 397 (1989). Cf. *United States v. Eichman*, 496 U.S. 310 (1990).

p. 558 COULD NOT CONSTITUTIONALLY BE PUNISHED WHEN USED AGAINST A POLICE OFFI-CER: *Lewis v. New Orleans*, 408 U.S. 913 (1972) (Powell, J., concurring in the result).

"LANGUAGE OF THE CHARACTER CHARGED MIGHT WELL HAVE BEEN ANTICIPATED": *Brown v. Oklahoma*, 408 U.S. 914 (1972) (Powell, J., concurring in the result); cf. *Papish v. Board of Curators of the University of Missouri*, 410 U.S. 667 (1973).

"GROSS ABUSE OF THE RESPECTED PRIVILEGE": *Rosenfeld v. New Jersey*, 408 U.S. 901, 904 (1972) (Powell, J., dissenting); cf. *Plummer v. Columbus*, 414 U.S. 2 (1973).

STRUGGLING TO COME TO GRIPS: See Kaplan, *A Worthy Tradition*, 112–15 (Powell's opinions showed that he was "serious about trying to find a basis for principled distinctions in this area").

"CONSCIENCE OF THE COURT": Gunther, "Law and the `Burger-Nixon' Court," *The New York Times*, Aug. 9, 1972, p. A37; Gunther, "In Search of Judicial Quality on a Changing Court," *Stanford L. Rev.* 24:1029–35.

"I CANNOT REMEMBER": Gunther, "Tribute," *Harvard L. Rev.* 101:411.

A SENSITIVE AND ALERT PROTECTOR OF FREE SPEECH: For notable cases from the early years, see *Healy v. James*, 408 U.S. 169 (1972) (a state-supported college could not deny official recognition to the local chapter of the SDS without clear justification); *Branzburg v. Hayes*, 408 U.S. 665, 709 (1972) (Powell, J., concurring) (emphasizing the "limited nature" of the holding that reporters have no constitutional right to refuse to cooperate with a grand jury); *Saxbe v. Washington Post Co.*, 417 U.S. 843, 850 (1974) (Powell, J., dissenting) (voting to strike down a U.S. Bureau of Prisons ban against press interviews of individual inmates); *Gertz v. Robert Welch, Inc.*, 418 U.S. 323 (1974) (reaching a middle position in a long-running dispute about whether and when the Constitution prohibits the award of money damages for libel and slander); *Erznoznik v. Jacksonville*, 422 U.S. 205 (1975) (striking down an ordinance barring all nudity from drive-in theaters).

"DEVOID OF SIMPLISTIC RULES AND CATEGORICAL ANSWERS": Gunther, "In Search of Judicial Quality," *Stanford L. Rev.* 24:1014.

POWELL RULED IN FAVOR OF FREE SPEECH DESPITE HIS REVULSION: *Street v. New York*, 394 U.S. 576 (1969). Compare *Spence v. Washington*, 418 U.S. 405 (1974) (per curiam written by LFP); *Smith v. Goguen*, 415 U.S. 566 (1974).

AS POWELL SAID THEN AND LATER: R. Hewitt Pate, interview; LFP, interview.

AT LEAST FIVE "LOST COURTS": William J. Brennan, interview.

p. 559 "SUPREMELY SURLY": *New York Times*, July 9, 1989, p. E26.

"INCLUDED LANGUAGE THAT IN TIME THE AUTHORS MAY REGRET": LFP, "Stare Decisis and Judicial Restraint," Remarks before the Association of the Bar of the City of New York, Oct. 17, 1989, p. 3.

"THE LOVING BUT CONCERNED VOICE OF A NONCOMBATANT": *New York Times*, Oct. 18, 1989, p. A14.

"I AM RATHER GLAD": LFP to Lewis F. Powell III, July 18, 1989.

"HUMANIZING INFLUENCE": O'Connor, "Tribute," *Harvard L. Rev.* 101:395.

"NO APPARENT PREDISPOSING CAUSE": Alexander C. Chester, M.D., to R.C.J. Krasner, M.D., July 3, 1989.

p. 560 TRIBUTES AND APPRECIATIONS: See, e.g., Freeman, "Justice Powell's Constitutional Opinions," *Washington and Lee L. Rev.* 45:411–65, and the collected tributes in *Harvard L. Rev.* 101:395–420 and *Baylor L. Rev.* 39:i–xxiii.

SIMPLY SHOWED THAT HE HAD "LITTE TO SAY": Kahn, "The Court, the Community and the Judicial Balance," *Yale L.J.* 97:60.

p. 561 MODERATION DID NOT MEAN "LUKEWARMNESS": Freund, "Foreword: Justice Powell," *Virginia L. Rev.* 68:170.

p. 562 "HE WILL HAVE HIS CRITICS": Wilkinson, "Tribute," *Harvard L. Rev.* 101:420.

BIBLIOGRAPHY

Abernathy, Charles F. "Affirmative Action and the Rule of Bakke." *American Bar Association Journal*, vol. 64, pp. 1233–37 (1978).

"Abortion and the Court." *Christianity Today*, vol. 17, Feb. 16, 1973, pp. 32–33.

Abraham, Henry J. *Freedom and the Court: Civil Rights and Liberties in the United States.* 4th ed. New York: Oxford University Press, 1972.

———. *Justices and Presidents: A Political History of Appointments to the Supreme Court.* 3rd ed. New York: Oxford University Press, 1992.

———. *Justices and Presidents: A Political History of Appointments to the Supreme Court.* 2d ed. New York: Oxford University Press, 1985.

Ad Hoc Committee on Federal Habeas Corpus in Capital Cases. *Committee Report and Proposal.* Washington: Ad Hoc Committee, 1989.

Ambrose, Stephen E. *Eisenhower,* vol. 1. New York: Simon and Schuster, 1983.

———. *Ike's Spies: Eisenhower and the Espionage Establishment.* Garden City, N.Y.: Doubleday, 1981.

———. *Nixon: The Triumph of a Politician, 1962–1972.* New York: Simon and Schuster, 1987.

American Bar Association. *Criminal Justice in Crisis.* Washington: American Bar Assocation, Criminal Justice Section, 1988.

American Law Institute. *Model Penal Code and Commentaries, Part II.* Philadelphia: American Law Institute, 1980.

Arons, Stephen. "Friends of the Court . . . and the Man Who Started It All." *Saturday Review,* Oct. 15, 1977.

Baker, Leonard. *Brandeis and Franfurter: A Dual Biography.* New York: Harper and Row, 1984.

Baker, Liva. *Felix Frankfurter.* New York: Coward-McCann, 1969.

———. *Miranda: Crime, Law and Politics.* New York: Atheneum, 1983.

Baldus, David C., George Woodworth, and Charles A. Pulaski, Jr. *Equal Justice and the Death Penalty: A Legal and Empirical Analysis.* Boston: Northeastern University Press, 1990.

Baring-Gould, William S., ed. *The Annotated Sherlock Holmes.* 2 vols. New York: Clarkson and Potter, 1967.

Bartley, Numan V. *The Rise of Massive Resistance: Race and Politics in the South during the 1950's.* Baton Rouge: Louisiana State University Press, 1969.

Bayh, Birch. *One Heartbeat Away: Presidential Disability and Succession.* Indianapolis: Bobbs-Merrill, 1968.

Beckman, Aldo. "How Nixon Chose Two for the Court." *Chicago Tribune,* Oct. 24, 1971, p. 16.

Bell, Derrick A., Jr. *Race, Racism, and American Law.* 2d ed. Boston: Little, Brown, 1980.

———. "Running and Busing in Twentieth-Century America." *Journal of Law and Education,* vol. 4, pp. 214–17 (1975).

———. "Waiting on the Promise of *Brown*." *Law and Contemporary Problems*, vol. 39, no. 1, pp. 341–73 (Winter 1975).

Bennett, Ralph. *Ultra in the West: The Normandy Campaign 1944–46*. New York: Charles Scribner's Sons, 1979.

Berger, Raoul. "The President, the Congress, and the Court." *Yale Law Journal*, vol. 83, pp. 1111–55 (1974).

———. *Executive Privilege: A Constitutional Myth*. Cambridge: Harvard University Press, 1974.

Berger, Vivian. "Justice Delayed or Justice Denied?—A Comment on Recent Proposals to Reform Death Penalty Habeas Corpus." *Columbia Law Review*, vol. 90, pp. 1665–1714 (1990).

Bertrand, Gustave. *Enigma ou la plus grande énigme de la guerre 1939–45* (Enigma: The Greatest Enigma of the War 1939–45). Paris: Plon, 1973.

BeVier, Lillian R. "Justice Powell and the First Amendment's 'Societal Function': A Preliminary Analysis." *Virginia Law Review*, vol. 68, pp. 177–201 (1982).

Bickel, Alexander M. *The Supreme Court and the Idea of Progress*. New York: Harper and Row, 1970.

Black, Charles L., Jr. "The Unfinished Business of the Warren Court." *Washington and Lee Law Review*, vol. 46, pp. 3–45 (1970).

Blackmun Nomination Hearings. See *Nomination of Harry A. Blackmun*.

Blake, Judith. "Abortion and Public Opinion: The Decade of 1960–1970." *Science*, Feb. 12, 1971, pp. 540–49.

Blasi, Vincent, ed. *The Burger Court: The Counter-Revolution That Wasn't*. New Haven: Yale University Press, 1983.

Bliss, Edward, Jr., ed. *In Search of Light: The Broadcasts of Edward R. Murrow, 1938–61*. New York: Alfred A. Knopf, 1967.

Blue Ribbon Defense Panel. *Report to the President and the Secretary of Defense on the Department of Defense*. Washington: Government Printing Office, 1970.

"Bombs on the Target: 319th Bomb Group Operational History." Pamphlet published by the 319th Bomb Group.

Bork, Robert H. "The Unpersuasive Bakke Decision." *Wall Street Journal*, July 21, 1978, p. 8.

———. *The Tempting of America: The Political Seduction of the Law*. New York: Free Press, 1990.

Branch, Taylor. *Parting the Waters: America in the King Years, 1954–1963*. New York: Simon and Schuster, 1988.

Broder, Davis S. "When Judges Are Lynched to Appease the Public." *Washington Post*, Oct. 6, 1987, p. A21.

Bronner, Ethan. *Battle for Justice: How the Bork Nomination Shook America*. New York: W. W. Norton, 1989.

Brown, Anthony Cave. *Bodyguard of Lies*. New York: Harper and Row, 1975.

———. *"C": The Secret Life of Sir Stewart Menzies, Spymaster to Winston Churchill*. New York: Macmillan, 1987.

Bryson, W. Hamilton. *Legal Education in Virginia, 1779–1979: A Biographical Approach*. Charlottesville: University Press of Virginia, 1982.

Buncher, Judith F., ed. *The School Busing Controversy, 1970–75*. New York: Facts on File, 1975.

Bundy, McGeorge. "The Issue Before the Court: Who Gets Ahead in America?" *Atlantic*, Nov. 1977, pp. 41–54.

Bunzel, John H. "Bakke v. University of California." *Commentary*, Mar. 1977, pp. 59–64.

Burger, Warren. "Potter Stewart." *Yale Law Journal*, vol. 95, pp. 1321–22 (1986).

Bush, George. "Potter Stewart." *Yale Law Journal*, vol. 95, pp. 1323–24 (1986).

Calabresi, Guido, "*Bakke* as Pseudo-Tragedy." *Catholic University Law Review*, vol. 28, pp. 427–44 (1979).

———. "Bakke: Lost Candor." *New York Times*, July 6, 1978, p. A19.

Califano, Joseph A., Jr. *Governing America: An Insider's Report from the White House and the Cabinet*. New York: Simon and Schuster, 1981.

Calvocoressi, Peter. *Top Secret Ultra*. New York: Pantheon Books, 1980.

Caplan, Lincoln. *The Tenth Justice: The Solicitor General and the Rule of Law*. New York: Vintage Books, 1987.

Cardozo, Benjamin. *Law and Literature*. New York: Harcourt, Brace, 1931.

Carter, Robert L. "The Warren Court and Desegregation." *Michigan Law Review*, vol. 67, pp. 237–48 (1968).

Carter, Stephen L. "Bork Redux, or How the Tempting of America Led the People to Rise and Battle for Justice." *Texas Law Review*, vol. 69, pp. 759–93 (1991).

———. "The Political Aspects of Judicial Power: Some Notes on the Presidential Immunity Decision." *University of Pennsylvania Law Review*, vol. 131, pp. 1341–1401 (1983).

Catton, Bruce. *Never Call Retreat*. Garden City, N.Y.: Doubleday, 1965.

The Challenge of Crime in a Free Society: A Report by the President's Commission on Law Enforcement and the Administration of Justice. Washington: Government Printing Office, 1967.

Choper, Jesse H. "Continued Uncertainty as to the Constitutionality of Remedial Racial Classifications: Identifying the Pieces of the Puzzle." *Iowa Law Review*, vol. 72, pp. 255–74 (1987).

Clarke, Carter W. "Statement for the Record of Participation of Brig. Gen. Carter W. Clarke, GSC, in the Transmittal of Letters from Gen. George C. Marshall to Gov. Thomas E. Dewey." SRH–043, RG 457, National Archives.

Commission on Constitutional Revision. *The Constitution of Virginia*. Charlottesville: Michie, 1969.

Committee for Courts of Justice, Senate of Virginia. *The Doctrine of Interposition: Its History and Application*. Richmond: Commonwealth of Virginia, Division of Purchase and Printing, 1957.

Cope, Richard. "The Frustration of Harry Byrd." *The Reporter*, Nov. 21, 1950.

Court–Ordered School Busing: Hearings Before the Subcommittee on Separation of Powers of the Committee on the Judiciary, United States Senate, 97th Congress, 1st Session. Washington: Government Printing Office: 1982.

Cox, Archibald. "Executive Privilege." *University of Pennsylvania Law Review*, vol. 122, pp. 1383–1438 (1974).

Coyle, Marcia. "Use of Habeas Writ Imperiled by Study: Death Row Bar Worried." *National Law Journal*, Nov. 28, 1988, p. 1.

Cranberg, Gilbert. "A Court of Supreme Secrecy." *American Bar Association Journal*, vol. 69, pp. 622–23 (May 1983).

———. "The High Court's Conflict of Interest Problem." *Nation*, June 13, 1981, pp. 722–25.

———. "Why all the secrecy at the nation's highest court?" *Bulletin of the American Society of Newspaper Editors*, May–June 1981, pp. 36–37.

Craven, Wesley Frank, and James Lea Cate. *The Army Air Forces in World War II,* vols. 1–3. Chicago: University of Chicago Press, 1948-51.

Crenshaw, Ollinger. *General Lee's College: The Rise and Growth of Washington and Lee University.* New York: Random House, 1969.

Dabney, Virginius. *Mr. Jefferson's University.* Charlottesville: University Press of Virginia, 1981.

———. *Richmond: The Story of a City.* Rev. ed. Charlottesville: University of Virginia Press, 1990.

———. *Virginia: The New Dominion.* Garden City, N.Y.: Doubleday, 1971.

Darden, Colgate, Jr. *Colgate Darden: Conversations with Guy Friddell.* Charlottesville: University Press of Virginia, 1978.

Davis, William C. *The Battle of New Market.* Baton Rouge: Louisiana State University Press, 1975.

DeBenedictis, Don J. "The Reasonable Man: A Conversation with Justice Lewis F. Powell, Jr." *American Bar Association Journal,* Oct. 1990, pp. 68–75.

"Dedication, Justice Lewis F. Powell, Jr." *Baylor Law Review,* vol. 39, pp. i–xxiii (1988). (Includes tributes by Byron White, John Paul Stevens, J. Skelly Wright, John R. Brown, Charles Allen Wright, George C. Freeman, Jr., and F. William McCalpin.)

Dorsen, Norman. "A Change in Judicial Philosophy?" *National Law Journal,* Feb. 18, 1985, p. 13.

———. "A Tribute to Justice William J. Brennan, Jr." *Harvard Law Review,* vol. 104, pp. 15–22 (1990).

Douglas, William O. *Go East, Young Man, the Early Years: The Autobiography of William O. Douglas.* New York: Random House, 1974.

———. *The Court Years, 1939–1975: The Autobiography of William O. Douglas.* New York: Random House, 1974.

Duke, Maurice, and Daniel P. Jordan. *A Richmond Reader: 1733–1983.* Chapel Hill: University of North Carolina Press, 1983.

Dworkin, Ronald. "The Bakke Decision: Did It Decide Anything?" *New York Review of Books,* Aug. 17, 1978, pp. 20–25.

———. "The Future of Abortion." *New York Review of Books,* Sept. 28, 1989, pp.47–51.

Ellingsen, Mark. "The Church and Abortion: Signs of Consensus." *Christian Century,* Jan. 3–10, 1990, pp. 12–15.

Ely, John Hart. "The Wages of Crying Wolf: A Comment on *Roe v. Wade.*" *Yale Law Journal,* vol. 82, pp. 920–49 (1973).

Epstein, Richard. "Substantive Due Process By Any Other Name: The Abortion Cases." *Supreme Court Review,* pp. 159–85 (1973).

Estrich, Susan. *Real Rape.* Cambridge: Harvard University Press, 1987.

Evans, Rowland, and Robert Novak. "Nixon and Material for the Court." *Washington Post,* Oct. 18, 1971, p. A23.

Faulkner, William. *Requiem for a Nun.* New York: Random House, 1950.

Feerick, John D. *The Twenty-fifth Amendment: Its Complete History and Earliest Applications.* New York: Fordham University Press, 1976.

Fiss, Owen M. "School Desegregation: The Uncertain Path of the Law." *Philosophy and Public Affairs,* vol. 4, pp. 3–39 (1974).

Fitzgerald, Penelope. *The Knox Brothers.* London: Macmillan, 1977.

Ford, Gerald R. *A Time to Heal.* New York: Harper and Row, 1979.

Fowler, Paul B. *Abortion: Toward an Evangelical Consensus.* Portland, Ore.: Multnomah Press, 1987.

Frank, John P. *Clement Haynsworth, the Senate, and the Supreme Court.* Charlottesville: University Press of Virginia, 1991.

Freeman, Alan David. "Legitimizing Racial Discrimination Through Antidiscrimination Law: A Critical Review of Supreme Court Doctrine." *Minnesota Law Review,* vol. 62, pp. 1049–1119 (1978).

Freeman, Anne Hobson. *The Style of a Law Firm: Eight Gentlemen from Virginia.* Chapel Hill: Algonquin Books, 1989.

Freeman, Douglas Southall. *Lee's Lieutenants.* New York: Charles Scribner's Sons, 1944.

Freeman, George Clemon, Jr. "Justice Powell's Constitutional Opinions." *Washington and Lee Law Review,* vol. 45, pp. 411–65 (1988).

Freund, Paul A. "Foreword: On Presidential Privilege." *Harvard Law Review,* vol. 88, pp. 13–39 (1974).

———. "Foreword: Justice Powell—The Meaning of Moderation." *Virginia Law Review,* vol. 68, pp. 169–73 (1982).

Friddell, Guy. "Reluctant Justice Served Well." *Norfolk Virginian-Pilot, Ledger-Star,* June 28, 1987, p. B1.

Friedman, Leon. "Byron R. White." In Leon Friedman, ed., *Justices of the United States Supreme Court: Their Lives and Major Opinions, 1789–1979,* vol. 5, pp. 3–21. New York: Chelsea House, 1978.

Gaillard, Frye. *The Dream Long Deferred.* Chapel Hill: University of North Carolina Press, 1988.

Galbraith, John Kenneth. *A Life in Our Times: Memoirs.* Boston: Houghton Mifflin, 1981.

Garlinski, Jozef. *The Enigma War.* New York: Charles Scribner's Sons, 1979.

Garrow, David. *Liberty and Sexuality: The Right to Privacy and the Making of Roe v. Wade, 1923–1973.* New York: Macmillan, 1993.

Gates, Robin L. *The Making of Massive Resistance: Virginia's Politics of Public School Desegregation, 1954–1956.* Chapel Hill: University of North Carolina Press, 1962.

Geisler, Norman L. "The Bible, Abortion, and Common Sense." *Fundamentalist Journal,* May 1985, pp. 24–27.

———. *Ethics: Alternatives and Issues.* Grand Rapids, Mich.: Zondervan, 1971.

Gewirtz, Paul. "Choice in the Transition: School Desegregation and the Corrective Ideal." *Columbia Law Review,* vol. 86, pp. 728–98 (1986).

———. "Remedies and Resistance." *Yale Law Journal,* vol. 92, pp. 585–681 (1983).

Gilbert, Martin. *Winston S. Churchill: Road to Victory, 1941–1945.* Boston: Houghton Mifflin, 1986.

———. *Winston S. Churchill: Finest Hour, 1939–1941.* Boston: Houghton Mifflin, 1983.

Ginsburg, Faye D. *Contested Lives: The Abortion Debate in an American Community.* Berkeley: University of California Press, 1989.

Ginsburg, Ruth Bader. "Some Thoughts on Autonomy and Equality in Relation to Roe v. Wade." *North Carolina Law Review,* vol. 63, pp. 375–86 (1985).

Glasgow, Ellen. *The Woman Within.* New York: Harcourt, Brace, 1954.

Glazer, Nathan. *Affirmative Discrimination: Ethnic Inequality and Public Policy.* New York: Basic Books, 1975.

Godbold, E. Stanly, Jr.. *Ellen Glasgow and the Woman Within.* Baton Rouge: Louisiana State University Press, 1972.

Gold, Gerald, ed., *The Watergate Hearings: Break-In and Cover-Up*. New York: Viking Press, 1973.

Goldstein, Steven M. "Expediting the Federal Habeas Corpus Review Process in Capital Cases: An Examination of Recent Proposals." *Capital University Law Review*, vol. 19, pp. 599–647 (1990).

Goodman, Frank I. "De Facto School Segregation: A Constitutional and Empirical Analysis," *California Law Review*, vol. 60, pp. 275–437 (1972).

Gordon, Linda. *Woman's Body, Woman's Right: A Social History of Birth Control in America*. New York: Penguin Books, 1977.

Graglia, Lino A. *Disaster by Decree: The Supreme Court Decisions on Race and the Schools*. Ithaca: Cornell University Press, 1976.

Graham, Hugh Davis. *The Civil Rights Era: Origins and Development of National Policy, 1960–1972*. New York: Oxford University Press, 1990.

Greenfield, Meg. "How to Resolve the Bakke Case." *Washington Post*, Oct. 19, 1977, p. A13.

Greenhouse, Linda. "Powell To Court: A Caution With Love." *New York Times*, Oct. 18, 1989, p. A14.

———. "Vote is a Rebuff For Chief Justice On Appeal Limits. *New York Times*, Mar. 15, 1990, p. A16.

Grey, Thomas C. "The Constitution as Scripture." *Stanford Law Review*, vol. 37, pp. 1–25 (1984).

———. "Do We Have an Unwritten Constitution?" *Stanford Law Review*, vol. 27, pp. 703–18 (1975).

Griswold, Erwin N. *Ould Fields, New Corne: The Personal Memoirs of a Twentieth Century Lawyer*. St. Paul, Minn.: West Publishing, 1992.

Gross, Samuel R., and Robert Mauro. "Patterns of Death: An Analysis of Racial Disparities in Capital Sentencing and Homicide Victimization." *Stanford Law Review*, vol. 37, pp. 27–153 (1984).

Gunther, Gerald. "Law and the 'Burger-Nixon' Court." *New York Times*, Aug. 9, 1972, p. 37.

———. "Foreword: In Search of Evolving Doctrine on a Changing Court: A Model for a Newer Equal Protection." *Harvard Law Review*, vol. 86, pp. 1–48 (1972).

———. "In Search of Judicial Quality on a Changing Court: The Case of Justice Powell." *Stanford Law Review*, vol. 24, pp. 1001–35 (1972).

———. "Judicial Hegemony and Legislative Autonomy: The Nixon Case and the Impeachment Process." *University of California at Los Angeles Law Review*, vol. 22, pp. 30–39 (1974).

Haines, William Wistar. "Ultra History of U.S. Strategic Air Force Europe vs. German Air Force." SRH–013, RG 457, National Archives. Published as U.S. Army Air Force, *Ultra and the History of the United States Strategic Air Force in Europe vs. the German Air Force*. Frederick, Md.: University Publications of America, 1980. (Cited as *Haines Report*.)

Harbaugh, William H. *Lawyer's Lawyer: The Life of John W. Davis*. New York: Oxford University Press, 1973.

Harris, Richard. *Decision*. New York: E. P. Dutton, 1971.

Hearings on Presidential Inability and Vacancies in the Office of Vice President Before the Subcommittee on Constitutional Amendments of the Senate Committee on the Judiciary, 88th Congress, 2d Session. Washington: Government Printing Office, 1964.

Heineman, Ben W., Jr."A Balance Wheel on the Court." *Yale Law Journal*, vol. 95, pp. 1325–27 (1986).

Henkin, Louis "Executive Privilege: Mr. Nixon Loses But the Presidency Largely Prevails." *University of California at Los Angeles Law Review*, vol. 22, pp. 40–46 (1974).

———. "Privacy and Autonomy." *Columbia Law Review*, vol. 74, pp. 1410–33 (1974).

Henry, Carl F. H. "Lost Momentum." *Christianity Today*, Sept. 4, 1987, pp. 30–32.

Hentoff, Nat. "Profile: The Constitutionalist." *New Yorker*, Mar. 12, 1990, pp. 45–70.

Heymann, Philip B., and Douglas E. Barzelay. "The Forest and the Trees: *Roe v. Wade* and Its Critics." *Boston University Law Review*, vol. 53, pp. 765–84 (1973).

Hill, Oliver. "A Tribute to Justice Lewis F. Powell, Jr." *Harvard Law Review*, vol. 101, pp. 414–16 (1987).

———. "A Tribute to Lewis F. Powell, Jr." *Washington and Lee Law Review*, vol. 49, pp. 11–13 (1992).

Hinsley, F. H. *British Intelligence in the Second World War: Its Influence Upon Strategy and Operations*, vol. 1-3. London: H.M.S.O., 1979–88.

Hirsch, H. N. *The Enigma of Felix Frankfurter.* New York: Basic Books, 1981.

Hodges, Andrew. *Alan Turing: The Enigma.* New York: Simon and Schuster, 1983.

Hoffman, Banesh. *The Tyranny of Testing.* New York: Crowell-Collier, 1962.

Howard, A. E. Dick. *Commentaries on the Constitution of Virginia*, vols. I and II. Charlottesville: University Press of Virginia, 1974.

———. "Mr. Justice Powell and the Emerging Nixon Majority." *Michigan Law Review*, vol. 70, pp. 445–68 (1972).

Hoyt, Edwin. *William O. Douglas: A Biography.* Middlebury, Vt.: P. S. Erikson, 1979.

Hoyt, William D. *Valley Views: Lexington and Rockbridge County, Virginia, 1924–40.* Captioned photographs printed by Martin J. Horgan, Jr., 1989.

Hutcheson, J. Morrison. "The Visceral Legions of Scleroderma." *Virginia Medical Monthly*, vol. 78, pp. 459–64 (1951).

Interposition: Editorials and Editorial Page Presentations, Richmond News Leader, 1955–56. (Pamphlet published by the *News Leader* and distributed upon request.)

Irons, Peter. *The Courage of Their Convictions.* New York: Free Press, 1988.

Irving, David. *The Destruction of Dresden.* London: William Kimber, 1963.

Israel, Fred L. "Bryon R. White." In Fred L. Israel and Leon Friedman, eds., *Justices of the United States Supreme Court: Their Lives and Major Opinions, 1789–1969,* vol. 4, pp. 2951–61. New York: Chelsea House, 1969.

Israel, Fred L., and Leon Friedman. *Justices of the United States Supreme Court.* New York: Chelsea House, 1969.

Jenkins, John S. *The Life of John Caldwell Calhoun.* Auburn, N.Y.: John M. Alden, 1850.

"John Peyton McGuire, '94." *University of Virginia Alumni News*, Jan. 1949.

Jones, Nathaniel R. "An Anti-Black Strategy and the Supreme Court." *Journal of Law and Education*, vol. 4, pp. 203–208 (1975).

Kahn, David, *The Codebreakers.* New York: Macmillan, 1974.

Kahn, Paul W. "The Court, the Community and the Judicial Balance: The Jurisprudence of Justice Powell." *Yale Law Journal*, vol. 97, pp. 1–60 (1987).

Kalman, Laura. *Abe Fortas: A Biography.* New Haven: Yale University Press, 1990.

Kalven, Harry, Jr. *A Worthy Tradition: Freedom of Speech in America.* Edited by Jamie Kalven. New York: Harper and Row, 1988.

Kamisar, Yale, "The Warren Court (Was It Really So Defense-Minded?), The Burger

Court (Is It Really So Prosecution-Oriented?), and Police Investigatory Practices." In Vincent Blasi, ed., *The Burger Court: The Counter-Revolution That Wasn't,* pp. 62–91. New Haven: Yale University Press, 1983.

Kannard, Douglas. *The War Managers.* Hanover, Vt.: University Press of New England, 1977.

Karnow, Stanley. *Vietnam: A History.* New York: Viking, 1983.

Karst, Kenneth L. "Foreword: Equal Citizenship Under the Fourteenth Amendment." *Harvard Law Review,* vol. 91, pp. 1–68 (1977).

———. "The Freedom of Intimate Association." *Yale Law Journal,* vol. 89, pp. 624–92 (1980).

Keegan, John. *The Face of Battle.* New York: Viking Press, 1976.

———. *The Second World War.* New York: Penguin Books, 1990.

Kendrick, Alexander. *Prime Time: The Life of Edward R. Murrow.* Boston: Little, Brown, 1969.

Kennedy, Randall L. "*McCleskey v. Kemp:* Race, Capital Punishment, and the Supreme Court." *Harvard Law Review,* vol. 101, pp. 1388–1443 (1988).

Key, V. O., Jr. *Southern Politics in State and Nation.* New York: Alfred A. Knopf, 1949.

Kilpatrick, James Jackson. "Nothing of Honor." *National Review,* Feb. 8, 1980, pp. 162–63.

———. *The Southern Case for School Segregation.* New York: Crowell-Collier Press, 1962.

———. *The Sovereign States: Notes of a Citizen of Virginia.* Chicago: Henry Regnery, 1957.

Kirby, James C., Jr. "A Breakthrough on Presidential Inability: The ABA Conference Consensus." *Vanderbilt Law Review,* vol. 17, pp. 463–78 (1964).

Klarman, Michael. "An Interpretive History of Modern Equal Protection." *Michigan Law Review,* vol. 90, pp. 213–318 (1991).

Kluger, Richard. *Simple Justice: The History of* Brown v. Board of Education *and Black America's Struggle for Equality.* New York: Vintage Books, 1977.

Knappman, Edward W., and Evan Drossman, eds. *Watergate and the White House,* vols. 1–3. New York: Facts on File, 1973–74.

Koop, C. Everett. *The Right to Live: The Right to Die.* Wheaton, Ill.: Tyndale House, 1976.

Kornbluth, Jesse. "The '64 Civil Rights Murders: The Struggle Continues." *New York Times Magazine,* July 23, 1989, p. 16.

Kozaczuk, Wladyslaw. *Enigma: How the German Machine Cipher was Broken, and How It Was Read by the Allies in World War Two.* Translated by Christopher Kasparek. Frederick, Md.: University Publications of America, 1984.

Krason, Stephen M. *Abortion: Politics, Morality, and the Constitution.* Lanham, Md.: University Press of America, 1984.

Kurland, Philip B. "The Brethren: a hyped–up stunt for political voyeurs." *Chicago Tribune,* Dec. 16, 1979, sec. 2, p. 14.

———. "*United States v. Nixon:* Who Killed Cock Robin?" *University of California at Los Angeles Law Review,* vol. 22, pp. 68–75 (1974).

Lader, Lawrence. *Abortion.* Indianapolis: Bobbs-Merrill, 1986.

———. *Abortion II: Making the Revolution.* Boston: Beacon Press, 1973.

Landynski, Jacob W. "Justice Lewis F. Powell, Jr.: Balance Wheel of the Court." In Charles M. Lamb and Stephen C. Halpern, eds., *The Burger Court: Political and Judicial Profiles.* Urbana: University of Illinois Press, 1991.

Lash, Joseph P. *From the Diaries of Felix Frankfurter*. New York: W. W. Norton, 1975.

Law, Sylvia. "Rethinking Sex and the Constitution." *University of Pennsylvania Law Review*, vol. 132, pp. 955–1040 (1984).

Lawrence, Charles, III. "The Bakke Case: Are Racial Quotas Defensible?" *Saturday Review*, Oct. 15, 1977, pp. 11–16.

Leedes, Gary, and James M. O'Fallon. "School Desegregation in Richmond: A Case History." *University of Richmond Law Review*, vol. 10, pp. 1–61 (1975).

Leeds, Jeffrey T. "A Life on the Court." *New York Times Magazine*, Oct. 5, 1986, pp. 24–72.

Lehman, Warren. "Crime, the Public, and the Crime Commission: A Critical Review of *The Challenge of Crime in a Free Society*." *Michigan Law Review*, vol. 66, pp. 1487–1540 (1968).

Letcher, John Seymour. *Only Yesterday in Lexington, Virginia*. Verona, Va.: McClure Press, 1974.

Lewin, Nathan. "The Bakke Brief: A Shoddy Political Document." *New Republic*, Oct. 1, 1977, pp. 17–18.

Lewin, Ronald. *Ultra Goes to War*. New York: McGraw-Hill, 1978.

Lewis, Anthony. "Bowing to Racism." *New York Times*, April 28, 1987, p. A31.

———. "The Brethren: Inside the Supreme Court—A Review." *New York State Bar Journal*, vol. 52, pp. 205–13 (Apr. 1980).

———. "Justice Lewis Franklin Powell '32: Strength at the Center." *Harvard Law Bulletin*, p. 6 (Aug. 1987).

———. *Make No Law*. New York: Random House, 1991.

Liebman, James S. "Desegregating Politics: 'All-Out' School Desegregation Explained." *Columbia Law Review*, vol. 90, pp. 1463–1664 (1990).

———. "Implementing *Brown* in the Nineties: Political Reconstruction, Liberal Recollection, and Litigatively Enforced Legislative Reform." *Virginia Law Review*, vol. 76, pp. 349–435 (1990).

Liebman, Lance. "Swing Man on the Supreme Court." *New York Times Magazine*, Oct. 8, 1972, pp. 16–100.

Lincoln, Michael R. "Justice Byron White: The Myth of an Ideological Transformation." Unpublished paper on file with author.

Lindsey, Robert. "White/Caucasian—and Rejected." *New York Times Magazine*, April 3, 1977, pp. 41–47, 95.

Lipset, Seymour Martin, and William Schneider. "The Bakke Case: How Would It Be Decided at the Bar of Public Opinion?" *Public Opinion*, Mar.–April 1978, pp. 38–44.

Lucas, Emmet S. *The Powell Families of Virginia and the South; Being an Encyclopedia of the Eight Major Powell Families*. Vidalia, Ga.: Georgia Geneological Reprints, 1969.

Lukas, J. Anthony. "Playboy Interview: Bob Woodward." *Playboy*, Feb. 1989, p. 51.

Luker, Kristin. *Abortion and the Politics of Motherhood*. Berkeley: University of California Press, 1984.

MacIsaac, David. *Strategic Bombing in World War Two: The Story of the United States Strategic Bombing Survey*. New York: Garland Publishing, 1976.

MacKinnon, Catharine A. "Commencement Address." *Yale Law Record*, vol. 39, pp. 11–13 (1989).

Maguire, Daniel C. "The Triumph of Unequal Justice." *Christian Century*, Sept. 27, 1978, pp. 882–86.

Maltz, Earl M. "Portrait of a Man in the Middle—Mr. Justice Powell, Equal Protection, and the Pure Classification Problem." *Ohio State Law Journal,* vol. 40, pp. 941–64 (1979).

Manarin, Louis H., and Clifford Dowdey. *The History of Henrico County.* Charlottesville: University Press of Virginia, 1984.

Mann, Jim. "Prepping for the Justices." *American Lawyer,* Nov. 1982, pp. 97–98.

Markman, Stephen J., and Alfred S. Regnery. "The Mind of Justice Brennan: A 25-Year Tribute." *National Review,* May 15, 1984, pp. 30–38.

Marshall, Thurgood. "A Tribute to Justice William J. Brennan, Jr." *Harvard Law Review,* vol. 104, pp. 1–8 (1990).

McConnell, Michael. "How Not to Promote Serious Deliberation About Abortion." *University of Chicago Law Review,* vol. 58, pp. 1181–1202 (1991).

McDowell, Charles. "Verdict on Powell: Call It Affectionate Respect." *Richmond Times-Dispatch,* June 28, 1987, p. 1.

McKee, Alexander. *Dresden 1945: The Devil's Tinderbox.* New York: E. P. Dutton, 1984.

Meese, Edwin. "Square *Miranda* Rights With Reason." *Wall Street Journal,* June 13, 1986, p. 22.

Merrill, Richard A. "Lewis F. Powell, Jr., and the University of Virginia Law School." *Virginia Law Review,* vol. 68, pp. 175–76 (1982).

Mets, David R. *Master of Airpower: General Carl A. Spaatz.* Novato, Calif.: Presidio, 1988.

Meyer, Virginia M., and John Frederick Doran, eds. *Adventures of Purse and Person.* Richmond: Order of First Families of Virginia, 1987.

Michelman, Frank J. "A Tribute to Justice William J. Brennan, Jr." *Harvard Law Review,* vol. 104, pp. 22–33 (1990).

Mikva, Abner J. "A Tribute to Justice William J. Brennan, Jr." *Harvard Law Review,* vol. 104, pp. 9–13 (1990).

Milbauer, Barbara. *The Law Giveth: Legal Aspects of the Abortion Controversy.* New York: Atheneum, 1983.

Mishkin, Paul J. "The Uses of Ambivalence: Reflections on the Supreme Court and the Constitutionality of Affirmative Action." *University of Pennsylvania Law Review,* vol. 131, pp. 907–31 (1983).

Motley, Constance Baker. "Race Discrimination Cases: The Legacy of Justice Lewis F. Powell." *Suffolk University Law Review,* vol. 21, pp. 971–87 (1987).

Moyers, Bill. "In Search of the Constitution: Justice Lewis F. Powell, Jr." Public Broadcasting Service, 25 June 1987.

Murphy, Bruce. *Fortas: The Rise and Ruin of a Supreme Court Justice.* New York: William Morrow, 1988.

Murphy, Walter F. "The South Counterattacks: The Anti-NAACP Laws." *Western Political Quarterly,* vol. 12, 371–90 (1959).

Muse, Benjamin. *Ten Years of Prelude: The Story of Integration Since the Supreme Court's 1954 Decision.* New York: Viking Press, 1964.

———. *Virginia's Massive Resistance.* Gloucester, Mass.: Peter Smith, 1969.

National Advisory Commission on Civil Disorders. *Report.* New York: Bantam Books, 1968.

National Student Federation of the United States of America. *Year Book for 1930.* New York: N.S.F. Central Office, 1930.

Neuborne, Burt. "Blackmun: Intellectual Openness Elicits Needed Respect for the Judicial Process." *National Law Journal,* Feb. 18, 1980, p. 8.

Nixon, Richard. *RN: The Memoirs of Richard Nixon*. New York: Grosset and Dunlap, 1978.

Nomination Hearings. See *Nominations of William H. Rehnquist and Lewis F. Powell, Jr.*

Nomination of George Harrold Carswell to the United States Supreme Court, 91st Congress, 2d Session. Washington: Government Printing Office, 1970.

Nomination of Harry A. Blackmun, of Minnesota, to be Associate Justice of the Supreme Court of the United States Before the Senate Committee on the Judiciary, 91st Congress, 2d Session. Washington: Government Printing Office, 1970. Cited as *Blackmun Nomination Hearings*.

Nomination of John Paul Stevens to be a Justice of the Supreme Court: Hearings Before the Senate Committee on the Judiciary, 94th Congress, 1st Session. Washington: Government Printing Office, 1975. Cited as *Stevens Nomination Hearings*.

Nominations of William H. Rehnquist and Lewis F. Powell, Jr.: Hearings Before the Committee on the Judiciary, United States Senate, 92d Congress, 1st Session. Washington: Government Printing Office, 1971. Cited as *Nomination Hearings*.

Note. "The Changing Social Vision of Justice Blackmun." *Harvard Law Review*, vol. 96, pp. 717–36 (1983).

O'Brien, David M. "Filling Justice William O. Douglas's Seat: President Gerald R. Ford's Appointment of Justice John Paul Stevens." *Yearbook 1989 of the Supreme Court Historical Society*, pp. 20–39.

————. *Storm Center: The Supreme Court in American Politics*. New York: W. W. Norton, 1986.

O'Donnell, Pierce. "Justice Byron R. White: Leading from the Center." *American Bar Association Journal*, vol. 72, pp. 24–27 (June 15, 1986).

Oaks, Dallin H. "Tribute to Lewis F. Powell, Jr." *Virginia Law Review*, vol. 68, pp. 161–67 (1982).

Orfield, Gary. *Must We Bus? Segregated Schools and National Policy*. Washington: Brookings Institution, 1978.

Orland, Leonard. "John Paul Stevens," in *The Justices of the Supreme Court, 1789–1978: Their Lives and Major Opinions: The Burger Court, 1969–1978* (Leon Friedman, ed.), vol. 5. New York: Chelsea House, 1980.

Osborne, John. *The Last Nixon Watch*. Washington: New Republic Book Co., 1975.

Paige, Connie. *The Right to Lifers*. New York: Summit Books, 1983.

Paillole, Paul. *Services Spéciaux (1935–45)*. Paris: R. Laffont, 1975.

Parramore, Thomas C. *Southampton County, Virginia*. Charlottesville: University Press of Virginia, 1978.

Parrish, Thomas. *The Ultra Americans: The U.S. Role in Breaking the Nazi Codes*. New York: Stein and Day, 1986.

Pellens, Mildred, and Charles E. Terry. *The Opium Problem*. Montclair, N.J.: Patterson Smith, 1970.

Perry, Michael J. *The Constitution, the Courts, and Human Rights*. New Haven.: Yale University Press, 1982.

Persico, Joseph E. *Edward R. Murrow: An American Original*. New York: McGraw-Hill, 1988.

Pertschuk, Michael, and Wendy Schaetzel. *The People Rising: The Campaign Against the Bork Nomination*. New York: Thunder's Mouth Press, 1989.

Petchesky, Rosalind Pollack. *Abortion and Woman's Choice: The State, Sexuality, and Reproductive Freedom*. New York: Longman, 1984.

Pogue, Forrest C. *George C. Marshall: Organizer of Victory, 1943–45.* New York: The Viking Press, 1973.

Posner, Richard A. "A Tribute to Justice William J. Brennan, Jr." *Harvard Law Review,* vol. 104, pp. 13–15 (1990).

Powe, L. A., Jr. "The Court Between Hegemonies." *Washington and Lee Law Review,* vol. 49, pp. 31–52 (1992).

———. "From Bork to Souter." *Williamette Law Review,* vol. 27, pp. 781–801 (1991).

Powell, Lewis F., Jr. "Civil Disobedience: Prelude to Revolution?" *U.S. News and World Report,* Oct. 30, 1967, pp. 66–69.

———. "Clement F. Haynsworth, Jr.—A Personal Tribute." *Washington and Lee Law Review,* vol. 39, pp. 303–306 (1982).

———. "Commentary: Capital Punishment." *Harvard Law Review,* vol. 102, pp. 1035–46 (1989).

———. "A Lawyer Looks at Civil Disobedience." *Washington and Lee Law Review,* vol. 23, pp. 205–31 (1966).

———. "Reflections." *Virginia Magazine of History and Biography,* vol. 96, pp. 315–32 (1988).

———. "Respect for Law and Due Process—The Foundation of a Free Society." *University of Florida Law Review,* vol. 18, pp. 1–8 (1965).

———. "What Really Goes on at the Supreme Court." *American Bar Association Journal,* vol. 66, pp. 721–23 (June 1980).

Powell, Lewis F., Jr., et al. "Supplemental Statement to Report of the Blue Ribbon Defense Panel on The Shifting Balance of Military Power." Washington: Government Printing Office, 1971.

Powell, Louis F. *Recollections and Observations.* Richmond: privately printed, 1958.

Pratt, Robert. "Richmond's Passive Resistance: The Controversy over School Desegregation." Master's thesis, University of Virginia, 1981.

Price, Janet R., and Jane R. Stern. "Magnet Schools as a Strategy for Integration and School Reform." *Yale Journal of Law and Policy,* vol. 5, pp. 291–321 (1987).

Price, Monroe E. "White: A Justice of Studied Unpredictability," *National Law Journal,* Feb. 18, 1980, pp. 24–25.

Price, Raymond K., Jr. *With Nixon.* New York: The Viking Press, 1977.

Putney, Diane, ed. *Ultra and the Army Air Forces in World War II: An Interview with Associate Justice of the U.S. Supreme Court Lewis F. Powell, Jr.* Washington: Government Printing Office, 1987.

Raffel, Jeffrey. *The Politics of School Desegregation: The Metropolitan Remedy in Delaware.* Philadelphia: Temple University Press, 1980.

Raspberry, William. "Welcome Ambiguity in the *Bakke* Decision." *Washington Post,* July 3, 1978, p. A23.

Read, Frank T. "Judicial Evolution of the Law of School Integration Since *Brown v. Board of Education.*" *Law and Contemporary Problems,* vol. 39, no. 1, pp. 7–49 (winter 1975).

Regan, Donald H. "Rewriting *Roe v. Wade,*" *Michigan Law Review,* vol. 77, pp. 1569–1646 (1979).

Rehnquist, William H. *The Supreme Court: How It Was, How It Is.* New York: William Morrow, 1987.

Reinhardt, Stephen. "Must We Rush the Executioner?" *Los Angeles Times,* Nov. 7, 1989, p. B7.

Remembrances of William O. Douglas by His Friends and Associates. (A collection of reminiscences compiled in 1989 on the fiftieth anniversary of Douglas's appointment.)

Report of the Commission on Constitutional Revision to His Excellency, Mills E. Godwin, Jr., Governor of Virginia, the General Assembly of Virginia, and the People of Virginia. Charlottesville: The Michie Company, 1969.

Revesz, Richard L., and Pamela S. Karlan. "Nonmajority Rules and the Supreme Court." *University of Pennsylvania Law Review,* vol. 136, pp. 1067–1133 (1988).

Rickover, Hyman G. *American Education—A National Failure.* New York: E. P. Dutton, 1963.

———. *Education and Freedom.* New York: E. P. Dutton, 1959.

Riley, Franklin L. *General Robert E. Lee After Appomattox.* New York: Macmillan, 1922.

Robert, Joseph C. *Ethyl: A History of the Corporation and the People Who Made It.* Charlottesville: University Press of Virginia, 1983

Rodman, Hyman, Betty Sarvis, and Joy Walker Bonar. *The Abortion Question.* New York: Columbia University Press, 1987.

Roney, Paul H. "Comments in Support of the Powell Committee Recommendations." *Capital University Law Review,* vol. 19, pp. 649–58 (1990).

Rosengarten, Adolph G., Jr. "With Ultra From Omaha Beach to Weimar, Germany— A Personal View." *Military Affairs,* vol. 42, pp. 127–32 (Oct. 1978).

Rossell, Christine H. "Applied Social Science Research: What Does It Say About the Effectiveness of School Desegregation Plans?" *Journal of Legal Studies,* vol. 12, p. 69 (1983).

Rucker, Marvin Pierce. "Acrosclerosis." *Virginia Medical Monthly,* vol. 76, p. 493 (1949).

———. *The Selected Writings of Marvin Pierce Rucker and Complete Bibliography of His Works.* Richmond: Whittet and Shepperson, 1958.

Ruth, Henry S., Jr. "To Dust Shall Ye Return?" *Notre Dame Lawyer,* vol. 43, pp. 811–33 (1968).

Ryan, Milo. *History in Sound: A Descriptive Listing of the KIRO–CBS Collection of Broadcasts of the World War II Years and After, in the Phonoarchive of the University of Washington.* Seattle: University of Washington Press, 1963.

Sabato, Larry J. *The 1988 Elections in America: The Change that Masks Continuity.* Glenview, Ill.: Scott, Foresman, 1989.

Salisbury, Harrison E. *A Journey for Our Times.* New York: Harper and Row, 1983.

Sanders, Alain L. "The Marble Palace's Southern Gentleman." *Time,* July 9, 1990, pp. 12–13.

Sanders, Marion K. "Enemies of Abortion." *Harper's,* Mar. 1974, pp. 26–30.

Schaeffer, Francis A. and C. Everett Koop. *Whatever Happened to the Human Race?* Old Tappan, N.J.: Fleming H. Revell, 1979.

School Desegregation: Hearings before the Subcommittee on Civil and Constitutional Rights of the Committee on the Judiciary, House of Representatives, 97th Congress, 1st Session. Washington: Government Printing Office, 1982.

Schulhofer, Stephen J. "Reconsidering *Miranda.*" *University of Chicago Law Review,* vol. 54, pp. 435–61 (1987).

Schwartz, Bernard. *Behind Bakke: Affirmative Action and the Supreme Court.* New York: New York University Press, 1988.

Schwartz, Bernard. *Inside the Warren Court.* Garden City, N.Y.: Doubleday, 1983.

———. *Swann's Way: The School Busing Case and the Supreme Court.* New York: Oxford University Press, 1986.

————. *The Unpublished Opinions of the Burger Court.* New York: Oxford University Press, 1988.

Schwartz, Herman. *Packing the Courts: The Conservative Campaign to Rewrite the Constitution.* New York: Charles Scribner's Sons, 1988.

Sedgwick, Eve K. *Epistemology of the Closet.* Berkeley: University of California Press, 1990.

Seham, Max. *Blacks and American Medical Care.* Minneapolis: University of Minnesota Press, 1973.

Seligman, Joel. *The High Citadel: The Influence of Harvard Law School.* Boston: Houghton Mifflin, 1978.

Shapiro, David L. "Mr. Justice Rehnquist: A Preliminary View." *Harvard Law Review*, vol. 90, pp. 293–357 (1976).

Sharp, U. S. Grant. *Strategy for Defeat.* San Rafael, Calif.: Presidio Press, 1978.

Shaw, Russell. *Abortion on Trial.* Dayton, Ohio: Pflaum Press, 1968.

Shogan, Robert. *A Question of Judgment: The Fortas Case and the Struggle for the Supreme Court.* Indianapolis: Bobbs-Merrill, 1972.

Shriver, R. Sargent. "The Organized Bar and OEO Legal Services." *American Bar Association Journal*, Mar. 1971, pp. 223–27.

Simon, James F. *Independent Journey: The Life of William O. Douglas.* New York: Harper and Row, 1980.

Smith, Melden E., Jr. "Dresden Revisited: New Perspectives on a Lingering Controversy." Powell Papers, USAF Historical Research Center, Maxwell Air Force Base, Alabama.

Smith, Ralph R. "Reflections on a Landmark: Some Preliminary Observations on the Development and Significance of Regents of the University of California v. Allan Bakke." *Howard Law Journal*, vol. 21, pp. 72–127 (1978).

Songer, Donald R. "The Relevance of Policy Values for the Confirmation of Supreme Court Nominees." *Law and Society Review*, vol. 13, pp. 927–48 (1979).

Sperber, A. M. *Murrow: His Life and Times.* New York: Freundlich Books, 1986.

Spitzer, Walter O. and Carlyle Saylor, eds. *Birth Control and the Christian.* Wheaton, Ill.: Tyndale House, 1969.

Stafford, Tim. "The Abortion Wars." *Christianity Today*, vol. 33, Oct. 6, 1989, pp. 16–20.

Statistical Summary of School Segregation-Desegregation in the Southern and Border States. (Pamphlets published annually from 1957 to 1966, with slight variations in titles, by the Southern Educational Testing Service.)

Steele, John L. "Haynsworth v. U.S. Senate (1969)." *Fortune*, Mar. 1970, 90–93, 155–61.

Steele, Shelby. *The Content of Our Character: A New Vision of Race in America.* New York: St. Martin's Press, 1990.

Stevens, John Paul. "The Life Span of a Judge-Made Rule." *New York University Law Review*, vol. 58, pp. 1–21 (1983).

Stevens, Leonard A. *Trespass!* New York: Coward, McCann and Geoghegan, 1977.

Stevens, Robert. *Law School: Legal Education in American from the 1850s to the 1980s.* Chapel Hill: University of North Carolina Press, 1983.

Stewart, Potter. "The Road to *Mapp v. Ohio* and Beyond: The Origins, Development and Future of the Exclusionary Rule in Search-and-Seizure Cases," *Columbia Law Review*, vol. 83, pp. 1365–1404 (1983).

Sullivan, Neil V. *Bound for Freedom: An Educator's Adventures in Prince Edward County, Virginia.* Boston: Little, Brown, 1965.

Taeuber, Karl E., and Alma F. Taeuber. *Negroes in Cities: Residential Segregation and Neighborhood Change.* Chicago: Aldine Publishing, 1965.

Taylor, Stuart, Jr. "The Last Moderate." *The American Lawyer*, June 1990, pp. 48–54.

Teff, Harvey. *Drugs, Society and the Law.* Lexington, Mass.: Lexington Books, 1975.

Thomson, Judith Jarvis. "A Defense of Abortion." *Philosophy and Public Affairs*, vol. 1, pp. 47–66 (1971).

"The 319th in Action." Records obtained from the Albert F. Simpson Historical Research Center, United States Air Force, Maxwell Air Force Base, Alabama. Edited by Harold E. Oyster and Ester M. Oyster.

Totenberg, Nina. "Intrigue and Agony: Nixon and the Court." *National Observer*, Nov. 6, 1971, pp. 1, 18.

———. "A Tribute to Justice William J. Brennan, Jr." *Harvard Law Review*, vol. 104, pp. 33–39 (1990).

Tribe, Laurence H. *Abortion: The Clash of Absolutes.* New York: W. W. Norton, 1990.

———. "The Abortion Funding Conundrum: Inalienable Rights, Affirmative Duties, and the Dilemma of Dependence." *Harvard Law Review*, vol. 99, pp. 330–43 (1985).

———. *American Constitutional Law*, 2d ed. Mineola, N.Y.: Foundation Press, 1988.

———. "Childhood, Suspect Classifications, and Conclusive Presumptions: Three Linked Riddles." *Law and Contemporary Problems*, vol. 39, pp. 8–37 (1975).

———. *Constitutional Choices.* Cambridge: Harvard University Press, 1985.

———. "Foreword: Toward a Model of Roles in the Due Process of Life and Law." *Harvard Law Review*, vol. 87, pp. 1–53 (1973).

———. "Justice Stewart: A Tale of Two Portraits." *Yale Law Journal*, vol. 95, pp. 1328–33 (1986).

———. "Structural Due Process." *Harvard Civil Rights-Civil Liberties Law Review*, vol. 10, pp. 269–321 (1975).

"A Tribute to Justice Lewis F. Powell, Jr." *Harvard Law Review*, vol. 101, pp. 395–420 (1987). (Tributes by Sandra Day O'Connor, Richard H. Fallon, Jr., George Clemon Freeman, Jr., Gerald Gunther, Oliver W. Hill, and J. Harvie Wilkinson III.)

Trombley, William. "School Desegregation in America: Experiences and Explorations—Dallas." *Integrateducation*, vol. 15, no. 6, pp. 20–23 (1977).

Turner, Charles W., ed. *Mrs. Ecker's Lexington (1918–1929).* Roanoke: Virginia Lithography and Graphics Co., 1974.

Tushnet, Mark V. "Following the Rules Laid Down: A Critique of Interpretivism and Neutral Principles." *Harvard Law Review*, vol. 96, pp. 781–827 (1983).

———. *The NAACP's Legal Strategy against Segregated Education, 1925–1950.* Chapel Hill: University of North Carolina Press, 1987.

United States Commission on Civil Rights. *Fulfilling the Letter and Spirit of the Law: Desegregation of the Nation's Public Schools.* Washington: Government Printing Office, 1976.

Urofsky, Melvin I. "Mr. Justice Powell and Education: The Balancing of Competing Values." *Journal of Law and Education*, vol. 13, pp. 581–627 (1984).

———, ed. *The Douglas Letters: Selections from the Private Letters of Justice William O. Douglas.* Bethesda, Md.: Adler and Adler, 1987.

Velvel, Lawrence. "Zeus Didn't Nod: There's Hope After All For Justice Blackmun." *National Law Journal*, Oct. 6, 1986, p. 13.

Waltke, Bruce K. "Reflections from the Old Testament on Abortion." *Journal of the Theological Society*, vol. 19, pp. 3–13 (winter 1976).

Wasby, Stephen L., and Joel B. Grossman, "Judge Clement F. Haynsworth, Jr.: New Perspective on his Nomination to the Supreme Court," *Duke Law Journal*, vol. 1990, pp. 74–80 (1990).

Watergate, Politics, and the Legal Process (AEI Round Table). Washington: American Enterprise Institute for Public Policy Research, 1974.

Weaver, Warren, Jr. "Powell Either (a) Leads, or (b) Follows Very Well" *New York Times*, July 9, 1978.

Webster, Charles, and Noble Frankland. *The Strategic Air Offensive Against Germany.* London: H.M.S.O., 1961.

Weddington, Sarah. *A Question of Choice.* New York: Grosset/Putnam, 1992.

Welchman, Gordon. *The Hut Six Story: Breaking the Enigma Codes.* New York: McGraw-Hill, 1982.

White, G. Edward. "The Anti-Judge: William O. Douglas and the Ambiguities of Individuality." *Virginia Law Review*, vol. 74, pp. 17–86 (1988).

Whitebread, Charles H., and Christopher Slobogin. *Criminal Procedure: An Analysis of Cases and Concepts*, 2d ed. Mineola, N.Y.: Foundation Press, 1986.

Whitman, Christina B. "Individual and Community: An Appreciation of Mr. Justice Powell." *Virginia Law Review*, vol. 68, pp. 303–32 (1982).

Wigdor, David. *Roscoe Pound: Philosopher of Law.* Westport, Conn.: Greenwood Press, 1974.

Wilkins, Roy (with Tom Mathews). *Standing Fast: The Autobiography of Roy Wilkins.* New York: The Viking Press, 1982.

Wilkinson, J. Harvie, III. *From Brown to Bakke—The Supreme Court and School Integration: 1954–1978.* New York: Oxford University Press, 1979.

———. *Harry Byrd and the Changing Face of Virginia Politics, 1945–1966.* Charlottesville: University Press of Virginia, 1968.

———. "Justice John M. Harlan and the Values of Federalism." *Virginia Law Review*, vol. 57, pp. 1185–1221 (1971).

———. "The Role of Reason in the Rule of Law." *University of Chicago Law Review*, vol. 56, pp. 779–809 (1989).

Will, George F. "A Distorted Sense of Justice." *Washington Post*, Mar. 27, 1977, p. C7.

Williams, Juan. *Eyes on the Prize.* New York: Viking/Penguin, 1987.

———. "The Triumph of Thurgood Marshall." *Washington Post Magazine*, Jan. 7, 1990, pp. 12–29.

Wilson, James Q. "A Reader's Guide to the Crime Commission Reports." *Public Interest*, Fall 1967, pp. 64–82.

Winter, Ralph K., Jr. *Watergate and the Law: Political Campaigns and Presidential Power.* Washington: American Enterprise Institute for Public Policy Research, 1974.

Winterbotham, F. W. *The Ultra Secret.* New York: Dell, 1974.

Wiseman, Laurence E. "The New Supreme Court Commentators: The Principled, the Political, and the Philosophical." *Hastings Constitutional Law Quarterly*, vol. 10, pp. 315–431 (1983).

Wohlstetter, Roberta. *Pearl Harbor: Warning and Decision.* Palo Alto: Stanford University Press, 1962.

Wolfgang, Marvin E., and Marc Riedel. "Race, Judicial Discretion, and the Death Penalty." *Annals*, vol. 401, pp. 119–33 (1973).

Woodward, Bob, and Scott Armstrong. *The Brethren.* New York: Simon and Schuster, 1979.

Woodward, Bob, and Carl Bernstein. *All the President's Men*. New York: Simon and Schuster, 1974.

———. *The Final Days*. New York: Simon and Schuster, 1976.

Woodward, Calvin. "The Limits of Legal Realism: An Historical Perspective." *Virginia Law Review*, vol. 54, pp. 689–739 (1968).

Wright, Benjamin. *The Growth of American Constitutional Law*. New York: Holt, 1942.

Wright, J. Skelly. "Are the Courts Abandoning the Cities?" *Journal of Law and Education*, vol. 4, pp. 218–26 (1975).

Yackle, Larry W. "Thoughts on *Rodriquez*: Mr. Justice Powell and the Demise of Equal Protection Analysis in the Supreme Court." *University of Richmond Law Review*, vol. 9, pp. 181–247 (1975).

Yarbrough, Tinsley E. *John Marshall Harlan: Great Dissenter of the Warren Court*. New York: Oxford University Press, 1992.

Yoder, Edwin M., Jr. "'Conflicts of Interest' at Court a False Issue." *Washington Star*, June 12, 1981.

Yudolf, Mark G. "School Desegregation: Legal Realism, Reasoned Elaboration, and Social Science Research in the Supreme Court." *Law and Contemporary Problems*, vol. 42, no. 4, pp. 57–110 (1978).

Zimmer, Kenneth, Howard Davis, and William Edwards. *A Study of the Effectiveness of a Citizens Association in Municipal Government with Specific Reference to the Richmond (Virginia) Citizens Association*. Richmond: Richmond Professional Institute of the College of William and Mary, 1960.

INDEX

Abortion, 332–70; constitutionality of, 347–52, 354, 357, 359, 368, 369; gender equality and, 363–64; government funding of, 352–53, 366, 368, 370; 1972 presidential election and, 338–56; O'Connor and, 505; reasons for Powell's position, 346–52; religion and, 338n, 339n, 347, 350, 351; right of privacy, 336, 340, 348, 512, 516, 517; right-to-life movement, 354–59; *Roe*, 340, 369–70; *Time* magazine article, 344–46; timing of, 340–43; transformation of constitutional theory, 359–64. *See also Doe v. Bolton; Roe v. Wade*
Abrams, Gen. Creighton, 218
Adams, Arlin M., 420
Affirmative action, 456; Asians and, 472–73; vs. color blindness, 463–64, 467–68, 487, 501; decisions after *Bakke*, 500; *DeFunis v. Odegaad*, 458–59; goal vs. quota in, 471–72, 477, 484, 485–87, 492, 501; judicial review and, 465–68; origins of, 457; Powell's position on, 469–70, 499–501
Agnew, Spiro, 203
Aikens, Ernest, 406
Ainsworth, Robert, Jr., 524n
Air Force Intelligence School, 61–62, 79–80
Albemarle Paper Co., 125, 126, 189–93
Alexander, Gen. Sir Harold, 73
Alexander, Shana, 351
Algeria, 66–73
Alibi Club, 547–48
Alleghany Box Company, 14, 16, 17
Allen, George E., Sr., 211
Allen, Lt. Col. Julian, 93, 94, 95, 96
Almond, J. Lindsay, Jr., 132, 134, 153, 154, 168, 175, 235
Alt, Jim, 477
Ambrose, Stephen, 112
American Bank and Trust Company, 45–46
American Bar Association, 123–24, 193–203; Canons of Professional Ethics, 195–96: Code of Judicial Conduct, 237; Code of Professional Responsibility, 196; committee rating judicial nominees, 3, 4, 9; House of Delegates, 193–94; Powell as president of, 1,

194–204, 207, 210–11; report on repetitive review, 448; on wiretapping, 376, 379
American Civil Liberties Union (ACLU), 233; *Hardwick* case and, 513; on Powell, 550
American College of Trial Lawyers, Powell as president of, 1
American Law Institute, Model Penal Code of, 414–16
Amsterdam, Anthony, 408, 422, 429
Anderson, Henry W., 47–50, 61, 126, 129, 130, 185
Anderson, Jack, 273
Anderson, Maj. Gen. Frederick L., Jr., 95, 99–101, 103, 104, 112
Anderson, Scott, 158
Antonov, Gen., 100
Armstrong, Scott, 346, 389. See also *Brethren, The*
Army Air Forces, 61–79; 319th Bombardment Group, 62–71
Arnold, Gen. "Hap," 104
Atomic bomb, 108
Avon Products, 275, 281

Bain, Baldwin, 52
Baker, Howard, 9, 552
Baker, Howard H., Jr., 544, 545
Bakke, Allan: personal characteristics of, 455; privacy and, 478
Bakke case. *See Regents of the U of C v. Bakke*
Baldus, David C. (Baldus study), 438–40, 444
Ballard, Bill, 73
Bamberger, Frederick P., 230
Bank of Virginia, 124, 128
Barnett, Ross, 457
Batten, Frank, 152
Battle of New Market, 29
Bayh, Birch, 202, 203, 226, 230, 233, 377
Bean, Gleason, 29
Bear Island, Virginia, 14–16, 21, 24, 35, 60, 76, 79, 115, 118, 119
Beckwith, Dave, 344–46
Bell, Derrick A., Jr., 314, 321
Bell, Griffin, 462–63, 497

677